TRANSFORMATIONAL-GENERATIVE GRAMMAR

NORTH-HOLLAND LINGUISTIC SERIES

17

Edited by S.C. DIK *and* J.G. KOOIJ

TRANSFORMATIONAL-GENERATIVE GRAMMAR

An introductory survey of its genesis and development

Second, revised edition

BENT JACOBSEN
|||

Department of English
The Aarhus School of Economics,
Business Administration and
Modern Languages

1978

NORTH-HOLLAND PUBLISHING COMPANY
AMSTERDAM · NEW YORK · OXFORD

North-Holland ISBN: 0 444 85240 9

Published by:
NORTH-HOLLAND PUBLISHING COMPANY
AMSTERDAM · NEW YORK · OXFORD

Distributors for the U.S.A. and Canada:
Elsevier North-Holland, Inc.
52 Vanderbilt Avenue
New York, N.Y. 10017

First edition 1977
Second, revised edition 1978

Library of Congress Cataloging in Publication Data

Jacobsen, Bent.
    Transformational-generative grammar.

    (North-Holland linguistic series ; 17)
    Includes bibliographical references.
    1. Generative grammar.   I.   Title.
P158.J3   415   77-8154
ISBN 0-7204-0761-3

PRINTED IN THE NETHERLANDS

... for all knowledge and wonder
(which is the seed of knowledge)
is an impression of pleasure in
itself.

.Sir Francis Bacon

v

PREFACE

The present introduction to the transformational-generative paradigm in linguistics is intended for students who have reached a fairly advanced stage in their study of a modern language - in particular English. It may, I hope, also be of some use to teachers who left the university at a time when the transformational revolution in the study of grammar had not yet made itself felt. The book does not presuppose any specialist knowledge, and the exposition, I would like to think, is reasonably elementary - as elementary, that is, as the complexity of the theory, in turn determined by the complexity of the data, allows it to be.

There is little in the book that is new. My main concern has been to select some central topics and try to give a coherent presentation of them. The number of topics dealt with must necessarily result in a certain measure of superficiality. It is my hope, however, that this will be remedied by the bibliographical notes: the reader should have no difficulty in embarking on a more detailed study of individual areas of the grammar.

The structure of the book is reflected in the title. Chapter I is a brief introduction to the main tenets of American structuralism - in particular immediate-constituent analysis, which is the most important link between the structuralist and transformational-generative paradigms. Chapter II deals with some fundamental theoretical assumptions. Chapter III illustrates some of the points of contact between traditional grammar and transformational-generative grammar. Chapter IV constitutes the main bulk of the book. It falls into seven subsections. Section A introduces the notion

'rule of grammar' - with minimum attention to formalism. Section
B provides a brief overview of developments from 1957 to the present day. Sections C, D, E, and F are devoted to a discussion of
the four major components of a grammar: the base component, the
semantic component, the transformational component, and the phonological component. Finally, in section G, some important transformational rules in a grammar of English are considered. Chapter V
is concerned with post-_Aspects_ developments. It is considerably
shorter than Chapter IV. This should not be taken to imply a value
judgment on my part. However, many of the general principles as
well as many of the individual syntactic rules discussed in Chapter
IV carry over to the more semantically orientated versions of the
theory. Hence there is no need to repeat them.

I owe a great debt of gratitude to those of my friends and
colleagues who read through earlier versions of the manuscript. I
must especially mention Professor Hans Hartvigson of Odense University and Mr John Dienhart, lecturer, Odense University. Their
detailed comments and criticisms have had a profound influence on
the book. I also wish to thank Dr. Maurice Chayen of the University
of Jerusalem, from whose advice and encouragement I greatly prof-
ited when we met at the University of Pisa in the summer of 1974.
Last, but not least, my thanks are due to my wife Bodil and to my
children Anne and Morten for their never failing support and as-
sistance.

Aarhus, December 1976\
Bent Jacobsen

PREFACE TO SECOND REVISED EDITION

In this second revised edition a number of errors have been corrected. First, I have made a determined effort to root out all typing errors (probably an unattainable goal); secondly, I have corrected some rather more substantial mistakes in the exposition; thirdly, I have attempted in a number of cases to make the argument rather less abstruse than it must have appeared in the first version. I hope that, by these endeavours, I have managed to improve the book in an overall way. I apologize to the reader for those errors which, no doubt, still remain.

Some additional references have been inserted on p. 508. Their number had to be limited by the space available there.

I should like to take this opportunity to thank the editors of the North-Holland Linguistic Series, Professors Simon C. Dik and Jan G. Kooij, for their encouragement during the period when the writing of the book was in progress. Without this, it would never have been completed. Also, I wish to place on record my gratitude to the staff of the North-Holland Publishing Company. In particular, I would rather not try to imagine what the first version might have looked like without the boundless patience and helpfulness of Ms. Anne Vickerson during the pre-production processing period in the spring of 1977.

Aarhus, August 1978
Bent Jacobsen

TABLE OF CONTENTS

CHAPTER I

AMERICAN STRUCTURALISM

I.1. The influence of behaviourism

An essential factor in the development of American structural linguistics was the influence of <u>behaviouristic psychology</u>. The central assumption of behaviourism is that every aspect of human behaviour can be explained by indicating a certain <u>stimulus</u> which calls forth a certain <u>response</u>:

$$S \longrightarrow R$$

All response-conditioning stimuli are held to be amenable to precise empirical investigation and thus ultimately reducible to observationally accessible data. It follows from this that behaviourism is in direct opposition to older dualistic approaches to psychology which had accepted introspection as a valid heuristic and had relied heavily on such impalpable data as 'mind', 'idea', 'image', etc. In other words, human behaviour receives an entirely physicalistic and antimentalistic interpretation (cf. below, section II.4).

Bloomfield, one of the prime movers of American structuralism, was the first linguist to appeal to behaviourism in order to explicate his conception of the central function of language. By way of illustration, he invented the following famous little story (1933, 22):

> Suppose that Jack and Jill are walking down a lane. Jill is hungry. She sees an apple in a tree. She makes a noise with her larynx, tongue and lips. Jack vaults the fence,

1

climbs the tree, takes the apple, brings it to Jill, and
places it in her hand. Jill eats the apple.

Now, if Jill had been alone, she would have performed the acts of
vaulting the fence and climbing the tree herself (unless, of
course, she had preferred to stifle her hunger). However, as it is,
a speech act mediates between the stimulus to one organism and the
response in another. The speech act is a linguistic substitute response, which in turn acts as a linguistic substitute stimulus on
the hearer and results in a response on his part. Schematically:

(1) $S \longrightarrow r \ldots s \longrightarrow R$

(where r = verbal response and s = verbal stimulus).

A speech act or utterance, then, is a special aspect of human behaviour, and the totality of utterances which can be made in
a speech-community constitutes the language of that speech-community (cf. Bloomfield, 1926, 155).

(1) is made up of three components: S, R, and r ... s. S and
R are closely interrelated and constitute the content side of an
utterance. By contrast, r ... s, a physically manifest stretch of
sound, constitute the expression side of an utterance.

In principle, it is the goal of linguistics to account for the
relationship between the content side and the expression side of
language. Bloomfield gave explicit recognition to this goal (1933,
27):

> To put it briefly, in human speech different sounds have
> different meanings. To study this co-ordination of certain
> sounds with certain meanings is to study language.

However, Bloomfield further argued that the precise definition of
the meaning of words presupposes the full 'scientific' description
of the objects or states to which they refer, i.e. the stimuli for
which they serve as substitute responses. Therefore, since anything in the world can act as the stimulus of an utterance, the
systematic statement of meaning, which, on this interpretation, is
a property of the extralinguistic world rather than of language,
must await the exhaustive description by other, nonlinguistic
sciences of every conceivable aspect of human experience. Clearly,
this view does not hold out high hopes for semantics as an integral
part of linguistics, and it is not surprising that Bloomfield
(ibid., 140) reached the somewhat pessimistic conclusion that

The statement of meanings is therefore the weak point in language-study, and will remain so until human knowledge advances very far beyond its present state.

One consequence of the influence of behaviourism, then, was the relegation of semantics from the purview of linguistics.

There remains the expression side. It was to this that Bloomfield and his followers - the so-called post-Bloomfieldians - directed their attention.

I.2. The analysis of the expression side - an overview

In the analysis of the expression side of language, the linguist has at his disposal a corpus of recorded utterances. An utterance is a stretch of speech before and after which there is silence (cf. Harris, 1960, 14). In approaching his corpus, the linguist makes the following assumptions:

(1) Utterances are tokens of an underlying system.

(2) Given a set of carefully defined procedures (formulated in terms of such notions as distribution, environment, equivalence, contrast, substitution, differential meaning, sameness or difference in meaning, etc.) the underlying system, i.e. the grammar of the language under analysis, can be discovered by processing the data.

(3) No constructs may appear in the grammar so established which are not directly warranted by the physical data.

It is clear, then, that a grammar of a language receives a physicalistic, antimentalistic interpretation: at no point of the analysis is any appeal made to the mental processes which might be operative in the mind of the speaker when he is actually producing the utterances which constitute the data of linguistic inquiry. It was precisely for this reason that the structuralists regarded their discipline as an objective, empirical science (cf. below, section II.4).

One of the most important concepts in a structural grammar is that of 'class of'. This being the case, structural linguistics is often referred to by transformational-generative grammarians as taxonomic linguistics.

The taxonomic model of linguistic description, as it developed over the years, may be represented diagrammatically in roughly the following way:

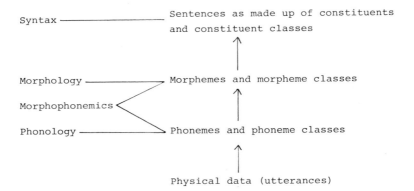

The grammar has four major components (or levels of analysis):
phonology, morphology, morphophonemics, and syntax. The upwards-
bound arrows indicate the important principle of analytical unidirectionality away from the primary data: phonological analysis should
precede and be independent of morphological analysis, morphological
analysis should precede and be independent of syntactic analysis.

The first step in the analysis of a language is to determine
the phonological system underlying the physical facts. To accomplish
this task, the linguist applies a set of procedures of the kind
mentioned in (2) to define the phonemes, i.e. the classes of sounds,
of the language.

The second step is the morphological analysis. The input to
this is sequences of phonemes. By applying to these the appropriate
set of procedures, the linguist defines the morphemes of the language, i.e. the classes of sequences of phonemes. Morphemes are
those units which make contact with the content side: they have
meaning.

The morphological and phonological levels of structure are
sometimes referred to as the first and second articulation of language respectively (cf. Martinet, 1960, sections 1.8 and 2.10).
What is meant by this is simply that all languages make use of a
very small set of phonemes to form a much larger set of morphemes
(for example, a language might have forty phonemes, but thousands
of morphemes). The phonemes, then, are continually recurring
units. In themselves they are meaningless, but they have differen-

tial meaning in the sense that they can distinguish pairs of morphemes of widely different meanings. For example, the English
morpheme 'pun' consists of three phonemes, each of which distinguishes this particular morpheme from other morphemes such as
'fun', 'pin', or 'puff'. In brief, the principle of double articulation ensures unity in variety.

The morphophonemic component of the grammar has as its domain
the explication of the compositional structure of morphemes in
terms of phonemes. In other words, it is concerned with relating
the first and second articulation of language in a systematic manner.

The input to the syntactic component is sequences of morphemes. By the application of the relevant set of procedures, the
linguist establishes the constituents, i.e. classes of sequences
of morphemes, of which sentences are made up.

It will be apparent that a structural grammar of a language
is essentially an inventory of units established at the various
levels of analysis and suitably classified with respect to a set
of procedurally defined classificational constructs.

I.3. Anthropological linguistics

During the first half of the twentieth century, American linguistics was closely linked with anthropology. The main task confronting anthropological linguists was that of recording and analysing the numerous Indian languages on the North American con-
tinent. We will not go into the details of this; for our purposes,
it is sufficient to emphasize two consequences of the intimate connection between the two disciplines:

(1) Anthropological linguistics reinforced the taxonomic conception of grammar sketched in the preceding section. It takes
little reflection to see why this was so. The field linguist, whose
job it is to provide a structural description of a language totally unknown to him, must necessarily begin by reducing mere noise -
his corpus of utterances - to organized noise. In other words, he
must break the code, as it were, to get on with his work. Hence
the overall insistence on the progression from sound to sentence
in linguistic analysis can be viewed as a practical expedient con-

verted into a theoretical principle.

(2) The Indian languages were found to display a large measure of structural diversity. This greatly confirmed structuralists
in their view that each language was a unique system of communication which should be studied in its own terms. Dissimilarities
rather than similarities were emphasized, and one linguist even
went so far as to claim that "languages can differ without limit
and in unpredictable ways" (Joos, 1957, 96).

I.4. The generative revolution

The advent of generative grammar with the publication of
Chomsky's monograph Syntactic Structures in 1957 was a scientific
revolution (in the sense of Kuhn, 1962). From the beginning, this
revolution was directed almost exclusively against the taxonomic
conception of syntax. In particular, the operational procedures
which had yielded such remarkable results at the lower levels of
analysis - especially in phonology - were shown to be inadequate
when it came to the analysis of sentence structure: there were a
number of syntactic problems to which the taxonomic model could
offer no satisfactory solutions.

Since the generative revolution was essentially a syntactic
revolution, our starting point must be syntax. We will devote the
rest of this chapter to a brief examination of taxonomic syntax,
indicating also some of the problems with respect to the solution
of which it is inadequate. We return to phonology, morphology, and
morphophonemics at a later stage.

I.5. The constituent structure of sentences

I.5.1. The word

We will take the word as the basic unit of syntactic structure. In doing this, we are making the assumption that there is a
set of procedures which, when applied to sequences of morphemes,
will define a class of constituents consisting of one or more morphemes which may suitably be named 'words'. In other words, the
word is not an intuitively given unit, but a procedurally defined classificational construct.

We will make the further assumption that there is a set of

procedures by means of which words can be classified into such
well-known classes as 'nouns', 'verbs', 'adjectives', 'adverbs',
'pronouns', 'conjunctions', etc. (cf. for example Fries, 1952).

I.5.2. Tree-diagrams

At this point, let us introduce some technical terms from the
generative theory of syntax. The terms are not used in taxonomic
grammars, but the notions underlying them are implicit in the analysis of constituent structure. Consider the following abstract
tree-diagram:

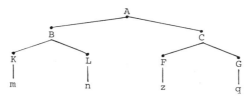

The dots in the diagram are called nodes. The capital letters are
node lables. The lower-case letters represent words. The relationship between the higher and lower nodes in the tree is one of
domination. One node immediately dominates another if there is no
intervening node between them. In the tree, A immediately dominates
B and C; it dominates all the other nodes (and the lower-case letters). C immediately dominates F and G; it dominates z and q. There
is no relation of domination between C and B, between K and G, etc.
Conversely, if we move up the tree, the relationship is one of
"is a". Thus m "is a" K, K + L "is a" B, etc. Besides these relations, the tree specifies relations of precedence. For example, B
precedes C, F precedes G, etc.

I.5.3. Immediate-constituent analysis

The concept of constituent structure is based on the observation that units which occur next to each other tend to belong together in the sense that they are structurally intimately related.
Let us refer to this observation as the principle of "togetherness-
by-ranks".

Consider now the following sentence:

(1) The nice scouts who were camping in the wood have gone home

It consists of twelve words. These form the ultimate constituents
of the sentence. As a first step in our analysis of the constituent
structure of (1), we attempt to group the words together in pairs.
Likely candidates are 'nice' and 'scouts', 'were' and 'camping',
'the' and 'wood', and 'have' and 'gone'. Once we have grouped these
words together, they are to be considered as functional units (i.e.
constituents). An operational test of the correctness of the analysis is substitution: if the groups are indeed constituents, it
should be possible to substitute single words for them without affecting the basic syntactic pattern of the sentence (though its
meaning may change quite radically). This is possible:

(2) The women (nice scouts) who worked (were camping) in there
    (the wood) went (have gone) home

We proceed like this through the sentence until all words have
been paired off with a constituent. Let us assume that the final
result of the analysis can be represented in terms of the following bracketed string:

(3) (((The (nice scouts)) (who ((were camping) (in (the wood)))))
    ((have gone) home)))

Observe that we might proceed the other way. The first step, then,
would be to segment (or cut) the sentence into two parts, the next
to segment each of these into two parts; and so on, until the rank
of the word. Again, the analysis would have to be controlled by
environmentally determined substitution tests, studies of the distributional range of the units established by segmentation, etc.
Assuming that this analysis would yield the same result as that
suggested in (3), we can illustrate the procedure in the following
way (0 indicating where the first cut was made, 1 where the second
cuts were made, etc.):

(4) The nice scouts who were camping in the wood have gone home
        2   3   1   2   4   3   4   5   0   2 . 1

Let us now proceed to convert (3) and (4) into a tree-diagram of
the kind illustrated in the preceding section (see next page).
There are eleven nodes in the tree. Each of these immediately dominates two constituents, and these two constituents are immediate
constituents (henceforth abbreviated IC(s)) of a construction

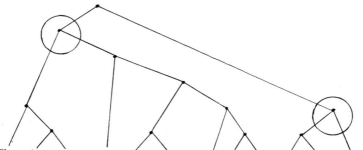

(5) The nice scouts who were camping in the wood have gone home

represented by the immediately dominating node. The tree shows
a _hierarchical layering_ of structures - the principle of together-
ness-by-ranks. In other words, syntactic structure is not solely
a matter of _linearity_, but also a matter of _depth_.

We said that substitution was one of the checks on the analysis. The two encircled nodes represent the last possibilities of
substitution. At those nodes we can substitute, say,

(6) Jack left

The sentence, then, can be viewed as successive _expansions_ of this
basic structure.

We may now try to omit some of the constituents to see what
happens in terms of _grammaticality_ (ungrammatical sentences are
marked by an asterisk):

(7) The scouts who were camping in the wood have gone home
(8) * The nice who were camping in the wood have gone home
(9) * The nice scouts were camping in the wood have gone home
(10) * The nice scouts who have gone home[1]
(11) The nice scouts have gone home
(12) * The nice scouts who were camping the wood have gone
    home
(13) * The nice scouts who were camping in have gone home

----

1. (10) is not a _favourite_ sentence. It may, of course, occur as
   a reply to a question like 'who are you talking about?'. For
   the distinction between favourite and nonfavourite sentences,
   see Bloomfield, 1933, 177ff.

(14) * The nice scouts who were camping in the wood home

(15) The nice scouts who were camping in the wood have gone

The omission of 'nice' in (7) does not make the sentence ungrammatical. In (8) 'scouts' has been omitted and this results in ungrammaticality. Consequently, 'scouts' must be syntactically more
important in the sentence than 'nice'. (9), (10), and (11) show
that 'who' and 'were camping in the wood' must either both be present in the sentence or both be omitted. (12) and (13) show that
'in' and 'the wood' are interdependent in the same way. Finally,
(14) and (15) reveal that 'have gone' is more important in the
structure of the sentence than 'home'.

The pattern of (un)grammaticality revealed by (7) through (15)
suggests that we have to do with two fundamentally different types
of construction. In one type, one of the ICs is the <u>head</u> (or centre)
of the construction. In the other type, neither of the ICs constitutes the head: both are equally important.

Constructions which have a head are referred to as <u>endocentric</u>,
whereas those which have no such head are termed <u>exocentric</u>. It
will be apparent that the defining criterion of endocentricity and
exocentricity is distribution: a construction is endocentric only
if one of its ICs has the same (or roughly the same) distribution
(i.e. potentiality of occurrence in certain environments) as the
whole construction, whereas, in an exocentric construction, neither
of the ICs has the same distribution as the whole construction.

Two kinds of endocentricity must be recognized: <u>subordinative</u>
and <u>coordinative</u>. In a coordinative endocentric structure, each
of the ICs (not only one) has the same distribution as the whole
structure[1]. An example is 'strong and courageous', in which both
'strong' and 'courageous' have the same distribution as 'strong and
courageous'. We can use graphic devices to illustrate the three
types of construction (in the way of Nida, 1966):

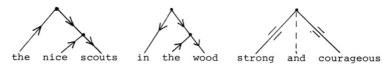

```
the  nice  scouts    in  the  wood    strong  and  courageous
```
----

1. This is true only with heavy modifications. For counterexamples,
   see Dik, 1968, 21f.

Each node is related to the two symbols on the branches immediately below. If one arrow points towards the node, the other away
from the node, the structure is endocentric. If both arrows point
away from the node, the structure is exocentric. The equation marks
indicate a coordinative endocentric structure.

So far the analysis has been purely procedural: no grammatical
categories of any kind have been invoked. The only tools have been
observation, substitution, omission of constituents, and judgments of grammaticality (based, we will assume, on responses elicit-
ed from informants rather than on introspection). If we were to
analyse hundreds of sentences in this way, we would need some kind
of labels to designate the classes of constituents and constructions, and - perhaps - the different <u>functions</u> which such classes
have, or else any ordered statement of the results of the analysis
would be impossible. Let us assume that the classificational and
functional constructs that have been gradually defined by operationally determined criteria in the process of analysis are such
that (5) can be labelled in the following way:

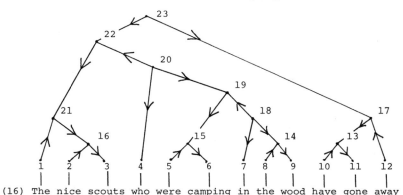

(16) The nice scouts who were camping in the wood have gone away

Each integer from 13 to 23 specifies a construction[1]. The two
lines branching from each node represent the functions of the ICs
of the construction. Each of the constructions of which the sen-

----

1. Observe that all constituents except the smallest (i.e. the
words) are also constructions and all constructions except the
largest (i.e. the entire sentence) are also constituents.

tence is made up, and - ultimately - each word, is a member of
a form class. If we adopt the following notational convention:
F_1 = function of left-branching constituent from a given node,
F_2 = function of right-branching constituent, and C = class/con-
struction, we can assign the following structural_description to
(16):

    23: F_1 = subject, F_2 = predicate, C = predication
    22: F_1 = nominal head, F_2 = postmodifier, C = noun phrase
    21: F_1 = premodifier, F_2 = nominal head, C = noun phrase
    20: F_1 = subject, F_2 = predicate, C = relative clause
    19: F_1 = predicate head, F_2 = adverbial modifier, C = predi-
        cate phrase
    18: F_1 = phrase governor, F_2 = prepositional object, C = prep-
        ositional phrase
    17: same as 19
    16: F_1 = premodifier, F_2 = nominal head, C = nominal group
    15: F_1 = verbal premodifier, F_2 = verbal head, C = verb phrase
    14: same as 21 and 22
    13: same as 15
    1-12: specification of word classes

A tree-diagram with labelled nodes is called a phrase-marker (abbreviated P-marker).

    Observe that by following the arrows in (16) consistently
downwards from 23, we will invariably arrive at the words 'scouts'
and 'gone'. These two words constitute the structural core of the
sentence (cf. (6)). Three constructions in (16) are exocentric,
namely 18, 20, and 23. Of these, 23 and 20 are subject-predicate
constructions, whereas 18 is a prepositional phrase[1].

    The reader will have observed, no doubt, that with respect to
grammatical functions we added a tentative qualification. Many
structural linguists eschew such functional notions as 'subject',
'object', 'indirect object', or 'modifier' altogether (e.g. Harris,
1960 and Gleason, 1961). The reason is not far to seek: such con-

----

1. No doubt all linguists would define these two constructions as
   exocentric. In other cases there is a good deal of disagreement.
   For example, not all linguists would agree that the relationship
   between 'have' and 'gone' and between 'were' and 'camping' is
   endocentric. We need not go into the details of this question.

cepts are too tainted by the semantic notions attributed to them
in traditional grammar. Other linguists, who do make use of functional concepts, are always careful to insist that they should be
defined in purely formal terms without any appeal to meaning. The
following statement made by Fries (1952, 175) is typical, in this
respect:

> It is necessary to insist that such terms as "subject",
> "indirect object", "direct object" have no relation to the
> actual facts of a situation in the real world. As grammati-
> cal terms they are simply names for particular formal struc-
> tures within an utterance.

The definition of grammatical functions, then, is incidental
to distributional analysis.

In conclusion we can say that in the taxonomic conception of
syntax, a sentence, provided it is of reasonable length, is a
pyramidal structure of class-exponents (i.e. constituents). Furthermore, since words are composed of morphemes of certain classes,
and morphemes (allowing for morphophonemic statements) of phonemes,
which in turn are defined as classes of sounds, it follows that all
syntactic constructs are assumed to be directly reducible to the
physical facts by purely classificational procedures.

I.5.4. Some problems

IC-analysis encounters problems in a number of cases. In this
section we will briefly discuss a few of these problems.

Discontinuous constituents. IC-analysis cannot assign a
natural P-marker to sentences containing discontinuous constituents.
For example, in

(1) Is John coming

it is obvious that the ICs of the sentence are not 'is' and 'John
coming', but rather 'is - coming' and 'John'. There is no non-ad-
hoc way of representing this diagrammatically (for attempts, see
Hockett, 1958, 155 and Nida, 1966, Chapter 1). (1) is a very simple
example. However, sentences frequently show much more complex patterns of discontinuity. Consider for example

(2) Who was it actually that Jane said you had so generously
    promised to give the money to

It would be next to impossible to account for the IC-structure
of this in terms of operationally determined classificational statements.

Relationship between sentences. For any two sentences which
differ in structure, but which are obviously related, IC-analysis
can make explicit only the differences, but not the similarities.
This is true of declarative versus interrogative sentences, active
versus passive sentences, cleft versus noncleft sentences, etc.

Pairs of sentences which are syntactically identical, but
'logically' different. Examples are sentences like (cf. Chomsky,
1964a, 34):

    (3) John is difficult to leave
    (4) John is reluctant to leave

Taxonomic analysis would assign identical P-markers to (3) and (4)
and thus fail to make it explicit that in (3) 'John' is the 'logical' object of 'leave', whereas in (4) it is the 'logical' subject
of 'leave'. A similar problem arises with such sentences as (cf.
Chomsky, 1965, 22ff.):

    (5) John expected the doctor to examine Helen
    (6) John expected Helen to be examined by the doctor
    (7) John compelled the doctor to examine Helen
    (8) John compelled Helen to be examined by the doctor

IC-analysis of these would pair off (5) with (7), and (6) with (8).
But this would be misleading. Why? Observe first of all that all
four sentences consist of two sentences, one of which is embedded
in the other. That this is so is revealed quite clearly by the
active-passive relationship: in both cases it is the subject noun
phrase and the object noun phrase of the embedded sentence which
have been permuted, whereas the subject noun phrase (and the verb)
of the governing or matrix sentence are unaffected. Next, consider
the meaning of the sentences: (5) and (6) have the same meaning,
whereas (7) and (8) do not. The reason for this seems to be that
in (7) 'the doctor' has a double function: it is the subject of
'examine' and the object of 'compelled'. In (8) it is 'Helen' which
has this double function. In (5) and (6), however, the whole of
the embedded sentence is the object of 'expected', whereas the
noun phrase immediately following 'expected' ('the doctor' and

'Helen' respectively) bears no special (i.e. semantically significant) relation to the verb of the matrix sentence. It follows from this that (5) should be syntactically differentiated from (7) and that (5) and (6) are not related to each other in the same way as (7) and (8). Since IC-analysis could not possibly account for these facts, it is inadequate.

<u>Syntactic ambiguity</u>. Syntactic ambiguity may be defined as follows: a sentence is syntactically ambiguous if it has two (or more) meanings which cannot be ascribed to the semantic structure of the words of which it is made up[1]. Consequently, syntactic ambiguity must involve the assignment of two (or more) P-markers to the same sentence. Consider the following example:

(9) John washed the car in the garage

(9) is ambiguous. It may mean (a) that the car was washed by John in the garage, or (b) that the car in the garage was washed by John. The two meanings can be syntactically differentiated in terms of the following bracketed strings:

(10) (John ((washed (the car)) (in (the garage)))) (a)
(11) (John (washed ((the car) (in (the garage))))) (b)

The labels of the nodes in the corresponding trees would make the structural difference more explicit; in particular, 'in the garage' would be an adverbial modifier in (10) and a nominal postmodifier in (11).

Let us next turn to a rather more complex example (adapted from Chomsky, 1967a (in Lenneberg, 1967) 416ff.):

(12) What disturbed John was being disregarded by his friends

(12) has two possible interpretations which may be paraphrased roughly as

(12a) John's friends disregarded him, which disturbed him
(12b) John's friends were disregarding what disturbed him

The paraphrases reveal the essential syntactic facts which determine the two meanings of (12). Thus in the interpretation corresponding to (12a), 'John' is the object of 'disturb' as well as

----

1. Syntactic ambiguity is sometimes referred to in the literature as <u>constructional homonymy</u>. Cf. Wells, 1947, 97. For a general discussion, consult Kooij, 1971, Chapter 3.

the 'logical' object of 'disregard'; 'was' is the main verb,
and 'being' is the gerund form of the passive auxiliary. By contrast, in the interpretation of (12) paraphrased by (12b), the
'logical' object of 'disregard' is the clause 'what disturbed
John', whereas the noun 'John' bears no special relation to 'disregard'; 'was being disregarded' is a past/progressive/passive
verb phrase. IC-analysis could assign two different structures to
(12). In terms of bracketed strings, they might look something like
this:

(13) ((What (disturbed John)) (was ((being disregarded) (by
     (his friends))))) (12a)

(14) ((What (disturbed John)) ((was (being disregarded)) (by
     (his friends)))) (12b)

However, it is an open question whether (13) and (14) are adequate
representations of the different structures involved in the ambiguity. Observe in particular that the corresponding P-markers
would fail to make it explicit that in the interpretation corresponding to (12a), 'John' has a double function, whereas in the
other interpretation, this is not the case.

     There are a number of instances in which IC-analysis cannot
account for syntactic ambiguity at all. Consider the following sentence:

(15) The children are ready to eat

In one interpretation of this, 'the children' is the subject of
'ready' as well as the 'logical' subject of 'eat'. In the other
(cannibalistic) interpretation, 'the children' is the subject of
'ready', but the 'logical' object of 'eat' (the subject being unspecified ('someone')). No amount of data-processing could make
these syntactic relationships explicit.

     It was recalcitrant cases such as those discussed in this sec-
tion which determined the generative revolution in syntax. Observe
that all the examples adduced are characterized by the same common denominator: the observationally accessible data (i.e. linguistic behaviour) fail to provide direct access to the 'deeper'
syntactic facts underlying the data (cf. section II.4).

Notes and some further references

General. There are a number of excellent introductions to general
linguistics. Among the best are Robins, 1964, Bolinger, 1968, and
Lyons, 1968. The different schools of modern linguistics - American
as well as European - are surveyed in Dinneen, 1967.

American structuralism. Bloomfield, 1933 is the basic work. Harris,
1960 (first published in 1951) represents Bloomfield's thought carried to its logical terminus. In particular, much emphasis is placed
on developing a set of adequate procedures for linguistic analysis.
It is not an easy work to read. More manageable introductions to the
main tenets of structuralism are such works as Hockett, 1958, Hall,
1960, and Gleason, 1961. A particularly clear illustration of the
sound-to-sentence sequence is provided by Hill, 1958.

I.5. Most modern syntactic theories recognize the notion of constituent structure in some form or other. In this connection, we
need to qualify the statement concerning grammatical functions
made in the text somewhat: there is one taxonomic model of syntax
in which functional notions play an integral part in providing
sentences with a structural description, namely the tagmemic approach developed by Pike and his followers. We will not go into
that. The interested reader is referred to Cook, 1969. Gleason,
1965, 151ff. provides an excellent survey of IC-analysis. The
most thorough examination of the procedures involved is Wells,
1947, whereas Nida, 1966 is - in principle - a full-scale IC-gram-
mar of English. Perhaps the best overall introduction to taxonomic
syntax is Fries, 1952.

CHAPTER II

FROM TAXONOMIC TO GENERATIVE GRAMMAR -
NEW ASSUMPTIONS

II.1. The creative use of language

In any representative corpus of utterances, no matter how
large, the vast majority of sentences occur only once. Furthermore, it is likely that most - if not all - of the sentences which
do occur more than once can be characterized as 'ritualistic':
they are closely tied up with the many rituals which constitute
an integral part of human behaviour. From this observation we can
draw the following conclusions:

(1) On the assumption that the end of the world is not im-
minent, the largest class of sentences in L (where L = 'any natural
language') is constituted by those which have not yet been (and
perhaps never will be) uttered; the second largest class of sentences in L is constituted by those which have been uttered, but
not recorded. Consequently, any corpus of recorded utterances can
only be a very imperfect representation of the vast potentialities
of L.

(2) The primary meaning of the sentence 'X speaks L' is that
X has the ability to produce and understand novel sentences all
the time without reflecting at all about what he is doing. In
other words, X can use his language creatively.

In taxonomic linguistics the principle of creativity received
little explicit recognition. In the theory of generative grammar
it is of vital importance. In particular, it determines the form
a grammar of L must take and the way in which this grammar is in-

terpreted with respect to the speakers of L.

II.2. An infinite set of sentences

It is clear from what was said in the preceding section that
the number of possible sentences in a language is huge. The question arises whether it is finite or whether a language is an infinite set of sentences. At first blush, this question seems to
be impossible to answer: since the largest class of sentences in L
is constituted by those which never have been, and probably never
will be, uttered, there is obviously no direct empirical evidence
which can settle the issue. Consequently, the claim that a language is an infinite set of senences - if it is to be upheld -
must be justified by theoretical considerations. To illustrate
this, let us turn to the following sentence:

(1) I know the man who owns the car that lost a wheel which
    killed the dog that harassed the cat that chased the
    rats that ate the corn

We can make two points about (1) which are relevant to the problem
under discussion. First, it is immediately obvious that length and
structural diversity are not synonymous terms. In particular, we
observe that there is a main clause ('I know the man') and a
number of successively embedded relative clauses; both the main
clause and the relative clauses have the same basic pattern:
subject-verb-object. The 'formation' of (1) involves the recursive
application of this pattern (cf. Latin 'recurrere' = 'run back').
Secondly, in theory, there is no limit to the number of relative
clauses which can be embedded in (1). In practice, of course,
there are limits, but these are dictated by such grammatically
irrelevant factors as restrictions on the capacity of the human
memory, facts about the length of life, etc.[1].

Now, a grammar of English is a theory of (the sentences in)
English. The grammar must account for a sentence like (1). In order to do this, it must - in some way or other - incorporate
the principle of recursion. Furthermore, since an indefinitely
large number of relative clauses can be embedded in (1), there can

----

1. Cf. the distinction between 'competence' and 'performance' discussed in section II.5.

be no limits to the recursive power of the grammar. In other words, the grammar specifies (1) (and, more generally, each sentence in the langauge) as being <u>potentially</u> infinite. This being the case, the grammar necessarily defines an infinite set of sentences.

II.3. <u>The term 'generative'</u>

A <u>generative</u> grammar is a special kind of grammar. A <u>trans-formational</u>-generative grammar is a special kind of generative grammar. It follows from this that a generative grammar need not necessarily incorporate the notion of 'transformation'.

The word 'generative' has been borrowed from mathematics. As applied in linguistic theory it means 'predict' and 'define explicitly'.

A generative grammar of L consists of a <u>finite set of symbols</u> and a <u>finite set of rules</u>, which, by manipulating the symbols, generate (in the sense defined) <u>all and only</u> the sentences in L (the number of which, as we have seen, is infinite).

Let us proceed to give a brief explanation of these notions (assuming, wherever this is relevant, that we are discussing a grammar of English).

<u>All and only</u>. It is not sufficient to require of a grammar of English that it generates <u>all</u> the sentences in the langauge. In that case, we could formulate the grammar in such a way that it would generate all possible combinations of the set of English words. Obviously, part of the output of this grammar would be the set of English sentences. However, in addition, there would be a much larger number of word-combinations which would not be English sentences. The qualification 'and only', then, implies that the output of the grammar must be the set of <u>syntactically well-formed</u>, i.e. <u>grammatical</u>, English sentences (cf. below, p. 30, note).

<u>The grammar predicts</u>. To say that the grammar has predictive power implies that its output includes the set of English sentences which have never been observed or recorded. This does not mean, of course, that the linguist, in constructing the grammar, does not take into account the empirical evidence provided by what is observationally given (for example a corpus of recorded utterances). What it does mean is that the primary goal the linguist sets him-

self is to move beyond the set of recorded utterances. Only thus
can the grammar be said to account for the creative principle of
language.

It will be apparent that this constitutes an important difference between taxonomic and generative grammars. A taxonomic
grammar, as we have seen, is essentially a data-cataloguing device.
In particular, there is little or no insistence on grammars as
rule-systems. Hence the "leap" from the finite set of observed sentences to the potentially infinite set of unobserved sentences
is not made explicit (though it is often implied).

The grammar is explicit. Essentially this means that each
step in the generative process must be incorporated in a precisely
formulated causal chain. Nothing must be left to the imagination
or intelligence of the user of the grammar.

The grammar defines. The grammar does not merely enumerate
sequences of words (properly combined). It automatically assigns
to each sequence, i.e. each sentence, a structural description
which specifies all relevant information about the sentence. For
the momement we will leave this notion undefined.

The grammar is a finite system. A generative grammar is assumed to reflect the mental capacities of the speaker. We shall
discuss this assumption in greater detail in subsequent sections.
Meanwhile, we may point out that since the storage capacity of the
human memory is limited (though quite large) a grammar could not
possibly take the form of a list of grammatical sentences, each
with its own structural description. It must necessarily be a finite system. As we have seen, it is the principle of recursion
which makes it possible for this finite system to generate an infinite set of sentences.

'Generate' and 'produce' are not synonymous terms: the speaker produces sentences, the grammar generates sentences. This distinction is crucial. It has been succinctly stated by Gleason in
the following terms (1965, 247):

> "Generation" does not ... mean the physical production of
> sentences. The latter is accomplished by some other instru-
> mentality - a man or a machine - operating with a generative
> grammar. ... A generative grammar does not generate one sen-
> tence now, and another at another time. Rather, it generates
> all the sentences it is capable of at all times. The mere
> fact that the grammar exists is sufficient for it to generate.

A generative grammar - and this in part follows from what has
just been said - is _neutral_ with respect to speaker or hearer (cf.
below, section II.5).

It was pointed out at the beginning of this section that the
term 'generative' has been borrowed from mathematics. This being
the case, it will be appropriate to conclude our discussion of the
term by a simple mathematical analogy. Consider the multiplication table, which we had to learn by heart during our first couple
of years at school. Once we had learnt the table up to 9 x 9 = 81,
we were taught a few rules for the recursive application of this
fundamental knowledge (such as carrying numbers, shifting multiplication answers, and applying the rules of addition). For example,
we do not need to store in our memory the fact that 546 x 741 =
404586. Instead, we make use of the recursive principle in the following manner:

(1)   546 x 741
         546
        2184   2 2
        3822   4 3
       404586

Suppose now that we view the multiplication table and the rules
for its recursive application as a generative 'grammar'. We can
then say that 404586 is a sentence generated by the grammar. Furthermore, (1), which is a perfectly explicit operation, constitutes
one possible structural description of the sentence 404586. Why
one possible structural description? Because 404586 is defined by
the grammar as being n-ways ambiguous (where n = the number of possible values for p x q in p x q = 404586).

II.4. Mentalism

We have emphasized that the predominant characteristic of
structural linguistics in America was antimentalism and physicalism, and that this was largely ascribable to the influence of be-
haviouristic psychology. In contrast, the theory of generative
grammar is mentalistic and antibehaviouristic, but not necessarily
antiphysicalistic. There are two distinct, but interrelated sides
to the mentalist-physicalist issue: a philosophical and a methodolo-

gical side.

The philosophical side. In his discussion of the general implications of the story about Jack and Jill (cf. section I.1)
Bloomfield made the following comment on two possible theories
about human behaviour (1933, 32f.):

> The mentalistic theory, which is by far the older, and
> still prevails both in the popular view and among men of
> science, supposes that the variability of human conduct is
> due to the interference of some non-physical factor, a spirit
> or will or mind ... that is present in every human being.
> This spirit, according to the mentalistic view, is entirely
> different from material things and accordingly follows some
> other kind of causation or perhaps none at all. Whether Jill
> will speak or what words she will use, depends, then, upon
> some act of her mind or will, and, as this mind or will does
> not follow the patterns of succession (cause-and-effect se-
> quences) of the material world, we cannot foretell her actions.
>   The materialistic (or, better, mechanistic) theory supposes
> that the variability of human conduct, including speech, is
> due only to the fact that the human body is a very complex
> system. Human actions, according to the mechanistic view, are
> part of cause-and-effect sequences exactly like those which
> we observe, say in the study of physics or chemistry.

Observe that Bloomfield's critique of mentalism is directed exclusively against the traditional, dualistic approach to psychology which involves data that cannot be subjected to objective, empirical investigation. Since few modern linguists, generative or
otherwise, would disagree with this critique, Bloomfieldian antimentalism is not at issue. What is at issue is Bloomfield's conception of causation. Every human action is viewed as the effect
of some physically demonstrable cause and hence is explicable in
purely mechanistic terms. As far as language is concerned, this
means that each utterance is the effect of some extralinguistic
cause and therefore - in principle at least - completely predictable from this cause. In other words, behaviourism results in a
deterministic philosophy of language. In this philosophy there is
no room for the independent contribution of the speaker in the
process of communicating by language.

Now, as the reader will readily appreciate, determinism is
fundamentally incompatible with creativity. Hence, as was pointed
out at the end of section II.1, focus on the creative aspect of
language inevitably leads to a new conception of the relationship
between a grammar of L and the speaker of L. The keyword to this

new conception is knowledge: a grammar (in particular a generative grammar) is viewed as a device which reflects or duplicates the internalized, unconscious linguistic knowledge of which the speaker must be assumed to be in possession in order to be able to produce and understand an indefinitely large number of novel sentences. Furthermore, the implementation of this knowledge in the actual use of language is held to be independent (in principle at least) of any external stimuli in the speech-situation. In this sense, the theory developed by Chomsky and his followers is a mentalistic theory. However, unlike the "species of spiritualism or soul psychology" (Katz, 1971a, 119) inveighed against by Bloomfield in the statement quoted above, Chomskyan mentalism is not, in principle, incompatible with physicalism: the linguist assumes that his grammar constitutes a viable hypothesis about the neurophysiological mechanisms which are operative in the speaker's brain when he is actually putting his knowledge to use. In other words, behind the causal chain of the theory - and a generative grammar is pre-eminently a causal chain - there is assumed to be - ultimately - a physical reality: the theoretical constructs of the grammar are symbols, not fictions.

On the philosophical side, therefore, the new mentalism is a showdown with determinism rather than with physicalism.

The methodological side. A grammar of L, as we have said before, is a theory of (the sentences in) L. In the taxonomic conception of grammar, it was assumed that, given a set of 'discovery procedures' (for this term, see Chomsky, 1957, 51) the theoretical - in particular classificational - constructs relevant to the description of L could be established by inductive data-processing (the data being a corpus of recorded utterances). As we have already dealt with this conception of grammar in some detail, we only need to point out here that the preoccupation with the physically manifest features of language, i.e. the empiricist methodology, can be seen as a natural corollary of the general philosophical orientation of structural linguistics.

A generative grammar, as will be apparent by now, is something entirely different. It aims at providing a symbolic representation of the speaker's unconscious linguistic knowledge. This representation takes the form of a deductive calculus: there is

an <u>axiom</u> from which an infinite set of <u>theorems</u> (i.e. sentences)
are derived by symbol-manipulating rules (some of which are recursive). The formulation of a grammar of L depends on the linguist's hypotheses about the structure of (the sentences in) L;
these hypotheses need not be the outcome of a meticulous analysis
of a corpus of utterances; they may just as well be the result of
sudden flashes of insight. However, the validity of the theorems
derived by the rules in terms of which the hypotheses are formulated must be put to the empirical test: in particular, the theorems must predict what native speakers of L <u>might</u> say. In other
words, the heuristic procedures employed by the linguist in arriving at a set of interrelated hypotheses are quite distinct from
and independent of the subsequent empirical validation of the
hypotheses.

Since the goal of the grammar is to provide an explicit account of the speaker's internalized linguistic knowledge, the
most important heuristic available to the linguist in the process
of constructing the grammar is the judgments made by the native
speaker (often the linguist himself) about such issues as relations
between sentences, grammatical versus ungrammatical sentences, ambiguity, etc. In other words, the question the linguist asks is
this: what precisely is it that the speaker knows about his language?

By way of illustration, let us consider briefly the following
three sets of examples (restricting our attention to syntax):

I   (1) John owns the house
     (2) John owns the house, doesn't he
     (3) John does not own the house
     (4) John doesn't own the house, does he
     (5) Does John own the house
     (6) The house is owned by John
     (7) Is the house owned by John
     (8) Who owns the house
     (9) What does John own
    (10) What John owns is the house
    (11) It is John who owns the house

II (12) He said (that) Jane would send the letter

(13) What did he say (that) Jane would send
(14) Who did he say (* that) would send the letter

IIIa (15) Peter seems to be certain to be there
     (16) That Peter is there seems to be certain
     (17) It seems to be certain that Peter is there
     (18) It seems that it is certain that Peter is there
     (19) It seems that Peter is certain to be there
     (20) What seems to be certain is that Peter is there

IIIb (21) Peter seems to be content to be there
     (22) * That Peter is there seems to be content
     (23) * It seems to be content that Peter is there
     (24) * It seems that it is content that Peter is there
     (25) It seems that Peter is content to be there
     (26) * What seems to be content is that Peter is there

The speaker knows that the sentences in I are systematically interrelated. Thus, if he were asked to form a similar set for a sentence like, say, 'the old man with the grey beard admires the
warm coat in the display window', he would be able to do this
quite unreflectingly. In order to explicate this knowledge, the
linguist must invoke notions like 'interrogative', 'tag-question',
'negative', 'passive', 'clefting', 'pseudo-clefting', etc. (12),
(13), and (14) illustrate what the speaker knows about the interrelationship between the formation of wh-questions and the behaviour of the complementizer 'that'. In (12) 'that' is optional. The
optionality of 'that' is unaffected when the object of the embedded sentence is questioned and appears at the front of the sentence,
whereas 'that' is ungrammatical if the subject of the embedded sentence is questioned and fronted. As regards the sentences in III,
(15) and (21) seem to have quite identical structures (IC-analysis
would assign the same P-markers to the two sentences (cf. sentences (3)-(8) of section I.5.4)). (15)-(20) are identical in cognitive meaning (perhaps with the exception of (20)): they provide
a set of syntactic options available to the speaker who wishes to
express a certain fact about the world (the six sentences are not
equally felicitous from a stylistic point of view, but they are
all grammatical). Evidently, the speaker who wishes to express
the fact about the world conveyed by (21) does not have at his dis-

posal the same set of options. Why not? It is the task of an adequate generative grammar of English to provide the answer to this
question. At this point, we may suggest that the similarity between (15) and (21) is a superficial phenomenon ('superficial' to
be taken in a technical sense).

Let us conclude this section by returning to our critique of
IC-analysis in section I.5.4. In the light of what we now know,
it is clear that this was based on the notion of linguistic knowledge. What we were concerned to point out was that procedural
analysis of the observationally accessible data fails in many cases
to provide access to that knowledge (which at that point we referred to as 'deeper' syntactic facts). Furthermore, in order to prove
this, we appealed quite unblushingly to introspective judgments
about the 'logical' structure of the sentences we were considering.
In particular, we made use of such traditional notions as 'logical'
subject', 'understood subject', 'double function', etc. In doing
this, we failed to meet the structuralist on his own ground, whereas we were well within the confines of the theory of generative
grammar: just as the empiricist methodology was a natural consequence of the general structuralist philosophy of language, so
introspectionism is a logical methodological consequence of the
new mentalism. In the words of Chomsky, 1965, 194: "To maintain,
on grounds of methodological purity, that introspective judgments
of the informant (often, the linguist himself) should be disregarded is, for the present, to condemn the study of language to utter
sterility".

II.5. Competence and performance

In the theory of generative grammar competence is defined as
"the speaker-hearer's knowledge of his language" and performance
as "the actual use of language in concrete situations" (Chomsky,
1965, 4). The term 'speaker-hearer' implies that the speaker can
put to use his knowledge in two different ways: he can use it to
produce utterances, or he can use it to recognize (or perceive)
utterances. The investigation of the relationship between competence and performance, therefore, requires a model of speech production and a model of speech recognition. We can illustrate the
different concepts involved in the following way:

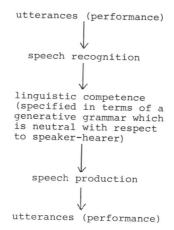

utterances (performance)

speech recognition

linguistic competence
(specified in terms of a
generative grammar which
is neutral with respect
to speaker-hearer)

speech production

utterances (performance)

Theoretical linguistics is concerned primarily with developing an adequate theory of linguistic competence. It is assumed that such a theory forms a necessary prerequisite for the construction of models of speech recognition and speech production by psychologists or psycholinguists (the latter term bears evidence to the close interrelationship between linguistics and psychology[1]).

Now, in ideal circumstances, there would be no extralinguistic factors to interfere with the functioning of the psychological mechanisms which underlie the production and recognition of speech, and utterances as produced or perceived by the speaker would always be direct reflections of sentences as generated by the grammar. However, as it is, this ideal state is far from obtaining: there is a large measure of 'skewness' between sentences and utterances. Since the linguist is always under the obligation to provide empirical evidence for his hypotheses, he cannot avoid taking this skewness into consideration, although, in principle, he is not (or need not be) concerned with matters pertaining to performance.

Let us consider a few examples.

In recent years tape recordings of informal speech have shown effectively just how great the distance between the utterances produced by the speaker and the sentences defined by the grammarian

----

1. There is also a sociolinguistic side to the distinction between competence and performance. We return to this in section III.9.

(traditional, taxonomic, generative, or otherwise) can be. The
following utterance transcribed by Quirk, 1955, 182 (quoted in
Strang, 1962, 18) is probably not exceptional in any way (the
dashes indicate pauses of varying length):

> (1) he - seemed of course he had that kind of n er I I'm
>   er I I er I I er I I er er are you northern by any chance I was
>   going to say that kind of northern -- er -- scepticism
>   or at least questioning mind -- which er - but of course
>   he would mislead you with that he er he gave you the im-
>   pression that he only er you know he gave you the impres-
>   sion that he was - sceptical and at times sceptical and
>   nothing else --- but I think he er -- I think he appre-
>   ciated the course there you know - from one or two things
>   he said when I bumped into him

The utterance is characterized by such factors as false starts,
repetitions, memory lapses, shifts in attention, etc. Now, we can
say that these factors represent a certain malfunctioning of the
mechanisms involved in speech production. However, it would seem
that this malfunctioning does not reach the point where it presents
serious difficulties to the hearer in terms of speech recognition:
it is a fair bet that the hearer had no trouble in understanding
the message conveyed by (1). What this means, we assume, is that
the speech recognition apparatus of the hearer, whatever its precise structure may be, is such that it can easily recover the
underlying grammatical structure of (1).

We must now introduce the distinction between grammaticality
and acceptability (cf. Chomsky, 1965, 10ff.) The former belongs
to the level of competence, the latter to the level of performance.
We will define a grammatical sentence as an abstract object which
is specified by the grammar as being syntactically well-formed[1].

----

1. Henceforth, we will take the term 'grammatical' to mean syntactically well-formed. This is the original meaning of 'grammatical' in transformational-generative grammar: from the beginning, semantics was not incorporated in the theory. Once semantics becomes an integral part of the theory, the domain of
   the concept of well-formedness must be extended accordingly.
   It should be noted, however, that the borderline between syntax and semantics, and hence between grammaticality and semantic well-formedness, is by no means clear-cut. For example,
   as we shall see later (below, pp. 92, 117ff.), a sentence like

In contrast, we will define an <u>acceptable utterance</u> as a sequence
of words which, though it <u>may</u> be ungrammatical - it need not be of
course - provides (relatively) easy access to the underlying grammatical structure. Both grammaticality and acceptability are
gradable concepts: a sentence may be more or less grammatical,
and an utterance may be more or less acceptable.

Returning now to (1), we can say - provided our conjecture
about the hearer's reaction to it is correct - that it is high on
the scale of acceptability, but low on the scale of grammaticality.

Next, consider the following sentences:

(2) The boy's sister's friend's father's family's property
    was sold
(3) I watched the bird on the roof of the house on the top
    of the hill through my binoculars
(4) This is the dog that worried the cat that killed the rat
    that liked the malt

All of these show repeated recursion in the sense that certain syntactic structures are successively embedded in structures of the
same type (e.g. prepositional phrases in prepositional phrases).
(2) is an example of <u>left-branching</u> structures (left recursion),
whereas (3) and (4) are examples of <u>right-branching</u> structures
(right recursion). The two types of structures can be illustrated
in terms of the following abstract P-markers:

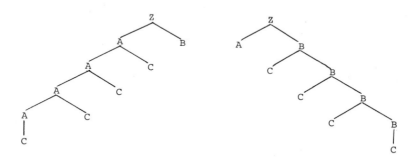

'colorless green ideas sleep furiously' can be characterized
either as ungrammatical or as grammatical but semantically
ill-formed - depending on the overall structure of the grammar.

Compare now (5) and (6):

    (5) This is the dog that worried the cat

    (6) This is the cat (that) the dog worried

The difference between these two sentences is that in (5) the
speaker directs his attention to the dog, whereas in (6) it is
the cat which is in focus. A grammatical consequence of this shift
in focus is that in (5) the relative pronoun 'that' is the subject
of the embedded clause, whereas in (6) 'that' is the object of the
clause (and hence optional). Apart from these differences, which
are conditioned by the external world (either the dog or the cat
is in the vicinity of the speaker), the two sentences express the
same reality. In particular, the relationship between the dog and
the cat is the same.

    Suppose now that in expressing the reality conveyed by (4),
the speaker wished to focus his attention on the malt rather than
the dog. The result would then be this:

    (7) This is the malt (that) the rat (that) the cat (that)
        the dog worried killed liked

(7) is an example of <u>self-embedding</u>: one structure - in this case
a sentence in the form of a relative clause - is completely embedded in (i.e. embedded in the centre of) another structure of the
same type. The following abstract P-marker defines self-embedding:

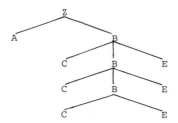

The question we can now ask is this: how do (2), (3), (4), and
(7) compare in terms of grammaticality and acceptability? As far
as (2), (3), and (4) are concerned, the answer seems to be straightforward: they are both grammatical and acceptable (they present
no 'processing' problems at all). In contrast, (7) is quite unacceptable and would clearly never be uttered. Is it ungrammatical
then? The answer to this question cannot be given off-hand. It is

theoretically determined. In particular, it depends on whether some other explanation of the unacceptability of (7) is available. Observe now that if we remove the deepmost embedded relative clause from (7), the result is a reasonably acceptable sentence:

> (8) This is the malt (that) the rat (that) the cat killed liked

By contrast, the embedding of additional elements to the left and right of (2) and (4) respectively does not have any appreciable effect on the degree of acceptability. On the basis of such evidence, it would be natural to hypothesize that the difficulties caused by (7) should be ascribed to the severely limited capacity of the short-term memory. In particular, the processing of (7) (we take the term 'processing' to be neutral between speech production and speech perception) is interrupted after 'rat'; consequently, 'liked' must be stored temporarily in the memory. After 'cat' the processing is again interrupted; this time 'killed' must be stored, but not for so long as 'liked'. No doubt, this is an essential factor, but it is not the whole explanation. Consider the following sentence:

> (9) The senators who think that if this step proves insufficient more drastic measures should be taken are likely to be right

(9) is structurally similar to (7) in that two elements have been successively centre-embedded. Consequently, in the processing of (9) the short-term memory is taxed to the same degree as in (7). Nevertheless, (9) is much higher on the scale of acceptability than (7). Why? It has been argued (cf. Chomsky, 1965, 10ff., 195ff. and references cited there) that the unacceptability of sentences with excessive self-embedding[1] is due to a special kind of limitation inherent in the mechanisms underlying speech production and perception: difficulties arise if these mechanisms are called upon to perform a certain operation at a point when they are still engaged in performing an operation of precisely the same kind. If this

----

1. Self-embedding is a special case of centre-embedding. Note that (3) is also an example of centre-embedding: a right-branching structure is embedded in the centre of the verb phrase (cf. the tree on p. 71). Observe that the sentence is slightly more acceptable if the object noun phrase and the adverbial are permuted: 'I watched through my binoculars the ...'.

hypothesis is valid - and it seems quite plausible - we are in a
position to explain the relative degree of acceptability manifested
by (7), (8), and (9).

(7), then, is a grammatical sentence in the sense defined -
irrespective of the fact that it would probably never be uttered.
This being the case, we do not have to complicate the grammar in
such a way that it would generate (8), but not (7).

As a further example of the bearing of the distinction between
grammaticality/competence and acceptability/performance on the construction of a grammar, consider the following two sentences:

(10) The firm which that I did not pay my bills did not worry
     has gone broke

(11) The firm which (↑) did not worry (that I did not pay
                      it
     my bills) has gone broke

(10) is low on the scale of acceptability. The trouble is that the
embedded relative clause has a clause as its subject. Observe now
that (10) forms the input to a rule which, by shifting the clausal
subject to the right and substituting 'it' for the removed clause,
can render the sentence quite acceptable. We might want to say
that the application of the rule in such cases is <u>obligatory</u> and
so define (10) as an ungrammatical sentence: an obligatory rule
has failed to apply. On the other hand, it turns out that the rule
which moves clausal subjects in this way is <u>optional</u> in the vast
majority of cases. Since, furthermore, it is quite likely that (10)
is yet another example of processing difficulties caused by centre-
embedding, it is no doubt preferable to avoid complicating the grammar by imposing a fairly arbitrary condition of obligatoriness on
the rule in restricted contexts (cf. also below, p. 358). In other
words, (10) is a grammatical sentence[1].

We will conclude this section by reiterating the point that
the generative grammarian is concerned with the construction of a
viable theory of linguistic competence. Since the actual realization of this competence in acts of performance involves so many
<u>grammatically</u> irrelevant variables, the linguist is forced to
stipulate that (Chomsky, 1965, 3):

----

1. The points made here about such sentences as (7), (10), and (11)
   should be compared with the discussion in sections IV.E.4 and
   IV.E.9 below.

Linguistic theory is concerned primarily with an ideal speaker-listener, in a completely homogeneous speech-community, who knows its language perfectly and is unaffected by such grammatically irrelevant conditions as memory limitations, distractions, shifts of attention and interest, and errors (random or characteristic) in applying his knowledge in actual performance.

II.6. Levels of adequacy

A grammar of a given language can attain two different levels of adequacy: it can be observationally adequate and it can be descriptively adequate. A grammar meets the requirement of observational adequacy if it provides a description of the observed set of sentences[1]. In contrast, a descriptively adequate grammar is one which makes correct predictions about the set of unobserved sentences. In other words, it must explicate the speaker's internalized linguistic knowledge, in particular his ability to use his language creatively.

It follows from these definitions that in the view of generative linguists, taxonomic grammars were mainly concerned with attaining the level of observational adequacy (cf. for example Chomsky, 1964a, 29ff.).

II.7. Weak and strong

A grammar weakly generates a set of sentences and strongly generates a set of structural descriptions to characterize the sentences. The set of sentences generated by a grammar constitutes its weak generative capacity, the set of structural descriptions its strong generative capacity. Two grammars which generate the same set of sentences are weakly equivalent. Two weakly equivalent grammars which assign the same set of structural descriptions to the sentences they generate are strongly equivalent.

Suppose now that the linguist, in constructing a descriptively adequate grammar of L, is confronted with two formal systems (i.e. two grammars) which are weakly but not strongly equivalent. He must then evaluate the structural descriptions assigned by the two grammars and on the basis of this evaluation select one of the two grammars as being more descriptively (or, equivalently,

----

1. Strictly speaking, the sentences underlying the observed set of utterances.

strongly) adequate. We shall provide some examples of this later. Meanwhile, we must consider the nature of the general linguistic theory which determines the notion 'generative grammar of L'.

II.8. Language acquisition and general linguistic theory

The axiomatization of grammars (i.e. the formulation of grammars as deductive calculi) has aligned linguistics with the natural sciences. Thus the grammar (i.e. the theory) of L is analogous to, say, a theory of physics: in both theories theorems are derived from axioms by rules and in both theories the theorems must be tested against the observable facts.

There is, however, an important difference between linguistics and physics (or any other natural science). This difference is ascribable to the nature of the data. The data which are explained by, say, the kinetic molecular theory, are unaffected by place and time. In contrast, the data of linguistics show great diversity according to place (there are perhaps three thousand widely different natural languages) and according to time (linguistic competence is not something with which human beings are born, but something which they acquire). Consequently, since a grammar of L is a theory of the linguistic competence of the mature speaker of L, a general linguistic theory is a theory about theories (i.e. a metatheory) which purports to explain the way in which the speaker of L acquires this competence, given the primary data to which he is exposed.

It is a well-known fact that a child learns to speak remarkably quickly. By the age of five or six, he has mastered the grammatical system of his language. In view of the enormous complexity of the grammatical systems of natural languages, this is a truly amazing achievement. How can it be explained? Three possible hypotheses present themselves:

(1) The grammar of a particular language is something which is transmitted genetically from generation to generation.

(2) The child is born with a special capacity for language.

(3) The child is born as a linguistic tabula rasa - he 'discovers' the grammar of the language to which he is exposed.

(1) is falsified by the fact that the child learns whatever language to which he is exposed during the first few years of his

life. Thus, if a child of, say, Italian parents is transplanted
to a new speech-community immediately after his birth, he will
learn the language of that speech-community as easily as he would
have learnt Italian.

It is the second hypothesis which is adopted by Chomsky and
other generative linguists. The special capacity for language
learning can be conceived of as a general linguistic framework
capable of processing input material and formulating a set of hypotheses about the structure of the language which is being fed
into it. Following Chomsky (e.g. 1964a, 26 and 1965, 30) we may
refer to this innate capacity as an <u>acquisition device</u>. The process of grammar-construction can be illustrated in terms of the
following diagram:

What a child has to learn, then, is not a total grammar of L,
but rather those structural peculiarities which differentiate L
from all other languages; the features common to all languages –
<u>linguistic universals</u> (see next section) – are specified in the
acquisition device. This view of language acquisition is now generally referred to as the <u>rationalist view</u>[1].

There is a good deal of evidence in favour of the rationalist
view. In the first place, language acquisition, unlike learning
in general, would not seem to be dependent on intelligence: even
children with a relatively high degree of intellectual deficiency
learn to speak, whereas they have a very poor capacity to learn
in general. Secondly, language is species-specific: only human
beings learn to speak. In contrast, animals like chimpanzees,
which are anatomically quite similar to human beings and which
can learn to perform a number of human activities, make very poor,
in fact hardly any, progress towards learning a language (in particular, they seem to fail to acquire the syntactic patterns,
whereas they can learn to handle a considerable repertoire of
signs). Thirdly, as has already been pointed out, human language

----

1. The use of the term 'rationalism' in this connection is historically determined. See further below, section III.6.

is enormously complex, and nothing like a total grammar of any
one language has ever been written (and probably never will be);
yet the child knows more at the age of six than many generations
of scholars. It seems unbelievable that he should be able to learn
all this in such a short time without the support of a genetically
transmitted device which tells him how to set about the task.

The detailed study of language acquisition falls within the
purview of psycholinguistics. We will not be concerned further
with this issue, but simply assume that the rationalist theory is
essentially correct and proceed to examine its bearing on the
formulation of a general linguistic theory.

The first point to be made is that the terms 'grammar of L'
and 'general linguistic theory' are used in a systematically ambiguous way (cf. Chomsky, 1965, 25). 'Grammar of L' means (a) the
mature speaker's internalized "theory" of L, and (b) the linguist's
representation of this theory. In contrast, 'general linguistic
theory' means (a) the child's innate "theory" of language, and (b)
the linguist's representation of this theory. Consequently, in
discussing the nature of a general linguistic theory, we are also,
by implication, discussing the nature of the psychological mecha-
nism which is assumed to determine the acquisition of language.

The structure of a general linguistic theory can be subsumed
under the following five points:

(a) Since the input signals are 'sounds in the air', the
theory must provide a way of assigning a phonetic representation
to these signals. In other words, it must contain a general phonetic theory which delimits the class of possible sentences in
natural languages.

(b) The theory must define the notion 'structural description'. The precise nature of this concept will become clearer as
we go along. Suffice it to say at this point that the structural
description of a sentence is a device which spells out explicitly
the way in which sounds and meanings are related (see, however,
above, p. 30, note and below, section IV.B.2).

(c) The theory must define the concept 'generative grammar'
and impose restrictions on the class of possible generative grammars available to the largest possible degree compatible with the
diversity of natural languages. In particular, the theory meets

the requirement of descriptive adequacy, if, for any natural language, it defines a grammar which is descriptively adequate in
the sense of section II.6. For example, a general linguistic theory which did not define a grammar that could make explicit the
intuitively apprehended relation between the following two English sentences:

(4) That you didn't get yourself killed was sheer luck
(5) It was sheer luck that you didn't get yourself killed

would be descriptively inadequate and hence defective.

(d) The theory must provide for the automatic assignment of
a structural description to each sentence generated by any grammar.

(e) It was pointed out in the preceding section that for any
given corpus of data the theory may define two (or more) grammars
(or subparts of grammars) which are weakly but not strongly equivalent and thus force the linguist to make a choice. This being the
case, the theory must define an <u>evaluation procedure</u> which provides
a principled basis for selecting one grammar over the other(s).
Schematically (cf. Chomsky, 1957, 51):

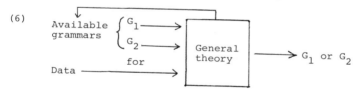

(6)   Available { $G_1 \longrightarrow$
       grammars { $G_2 \longrightarrow$ General
                          for   theory $\longrightarrow G_1$ or G_2
       Data $\longrightarrow$

A theory which provides such a principled basis for selection is
said to attain the level of <u>explanatory adequacy</u>.

There are, then, three levels of adequacy. The level of observational adequacy is of no special interest in itself because
it is restricted to a fixed corpus. Consequently, a grammar which
does not move beyond the level of observational adequacy fails to
'predict explicitly', and this, as we recall, is part of the
general definition of a generative grammar. The level of descriptive adequacy can be attained both by "local" theories (i.e. grammars of individual languages) and the general theory of language.
The level of explanatory adequacy, however, can only be attained
by the general theory.

Compare now with (6) (cf. Chomsky, <u>loc. cit.</u>):

(7)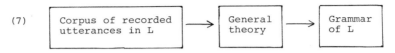

(7) defines the structuralist conception of linguistic theory. In
particular, the theory should be thought of as a set of discovery
procedures (in the sense of section I.2) which, when applied to
the raw data of L, automatically result in an optimal grammar of
L.

A linguist who adopts a theoretical framework of this kind
is committed to the third hypothesis concerning language acquisition mentioned above: the tabula rasa, or empiricist, hypothesis. On this view, the child is born without any special capacity
for language; at the most, he is equipped with an adequate set of
discovery procedures and thus must approach the task of acquiring
his language in much the same way as the field linguist approaches
an unknown language. From the tiny and incomplete fragment of data
to which he is exposed (tiny and incomplete, that is, with respect
to the vast potentialities of the language) the child must build
up gradually his knowledge of the complex networks of interrelated
systems which constitute the grammar of his language by inductive
generalization, association, analogy, etc.

The terms 'association' and 'analogy' lead us back to behaviourism: the speaker's ability to use his language creatively
can only be explained if it is assumed that he first learns to as-
sociate a certain number of linguistic forms with certain situations (stimuli) and then by some process called 'analogy' manages
to produce (and properly respond to) new sentences in the language
which contain the same linguistic forms.

Both as regards the child and the mature speaker, then, the
new paradigm in linguistics is a showdown with behaviourism.

II.9. <u>Linguistic universals</u>

Any general linguistic theory presupposes the existence of
<u>linguistic universals</u> of some kind.

As we have seen, structuralism was concerned exclusively

with the observationally accessible features of language. Consequently, great emphasis was placed on the structural diversities
manifested by languages in their superficial form (cf. section
I.3) and the assumptions made about the features shared by all
languages were correspondingly weak. In the typical instance, the
theory merely specified that a language would have a set of phonemes and a set of morphemes (and morpheme classes) interrelated
in accordance with the principle of double articulation. In addition to this, the theory defined a set of discovery procedures of
universal applicability. Since the procedures were assumed to
yield an optimal grammar of L quite automatically, the problem of
selecting one grammar over other(s) did - in principle - not arise
(but see Chomsky, 1957, 52, note 3).

        In the generative theory of language, the discovery proce-
dures of taxonomic linguistics have been replaced by evaluation
procedures. However, the development of such procedures is possible
(and indeed meaningful) only within the confines of a linguistic
theory which provides a much more detailed specification of the
structure of grammars and a much narrower delimitation of the class
of possible grammars than did the taxonomic theory. Since the
power of the theory is inversely proportional to the number of different grammars it allows for, it follows that a maximally powerful
theory involves the postulation of a rich and diversified set of
linguistic universals.

        So again we are confronted with a fundamental difference be-
tween the two paradigms: whereas the taxonomic linguists were
virtually hypnotized by the superficial dissimilarities between
languages, the generative grammarian is concerned to unravel the
deep-seated similarities between languages, his ultimate goal being the construction of a universal grammar which provides an adequate symbolic representation of the child's innate language acquisition device.

        A universal grammar can be conceived of as a structure made
up of three components: (1) a vocabulary, (2) a formal component,
and (3) an organizational component.

        The vocabulary provides the stock of symbols or units which
must enter into the construction of any grammar. For example, it
is likely that all (or at least the vast majority of) languages

have nouns. Therefore N (= noun) is a candidate for admission to
the universal vocabulary. Similarly, since all languages can express commands, make statements, and ask questions, such terms as
'imperative', 'declarative', and 'interrogative' are to be found
in the universal vocabulary. Members of the universal vocabulary
are generally referred to as <u>substantive universals</u> (cf. Chomsky,
1965, 28).

In the formal component the <u>operators</u> and <u>abbreviators</u> employed in the formulation of rules are defined. Thus such symbols
as $\longrightarrow$ (= 'rewrite as') and $\left\{ \begin{matrix} A \\ B \end{matrix} \right\}$ (= 'choose either A or B'
(where A and B are vocabulary symbols)) are <u>formal universals</u>.
Furthermore, the formal component specifies a number of <u>constraints</u>
which the rules of any grammar must obey. Thus in a theory of
generative grammar which incorporates transformational rules (and,
as we shall see later, a theory - if it is to be descriptively
adequate - does require the incorporation of such rules in the
grammar of L^1) a number of restrictions are imposed on the operations that may be carried out by such rules.

In the organizational component the overall structure of the
grammar is defined. Thus it seems a reasonable assumption that a
grammar of L must contain at least three components: one which
deals with syntax, one which deals with meaning, and one which
deals with sound. Furthermore, the components must be interrelated
in certain specific ways.

It should be pointed out in conclusion that linguistic universals cannot be arrived at by a process of inductive generalization
(cf. Bloomfield, 1933, 20). The task which the generative linguist sets himself is to define universals through the formal linguistic investigation of a wide range of languages. However, this
investigation is determined by the deductive nature of the theory:
universals are not necessarily observable in the data, but may
emerge from the formal systems which are set up to account for the
data.

<u>Notes and some further references</u>

<u>General</u>. For the reader who wishes to familiarize himself with
Chomsky's philosophy of language, a good starting point would be
the famous review of Skinner's <u>Verbal Behavior</u> (1959a). It is

----

1. This in itself is an extremely important formal universal.

significant that Skinner's work was published in the same year as
Syntactic Structures. A brief, but excellent, introduction to
Chomsky's thought, is Lyons, 1970a. For a general critique of the
generative paradigm, see Hockett, 1968 and Derwing, 1973.

II.1. For the notion of creativity, see especially Chomsky, 1964a,
16ff. and 1966a, 3ff.

II.2. On the infinitude of sentences, see Chomsky, 1957 (opening
paragraph) and Bach, 1974, 24ff. A critique of this notion may be
found in Ziff, 1974.

II.4. The most detailed analysis of the new mentalism is provided
by Katz, 1964a. Consult also Katz, 1971a, 117ff. On induction and
deduction, see for example Bach, 1965a.

II.5. Useful brief introductions to some of the problems relating
to the study of speech recognition and production may be found in
Fry, 1970 and Laver, 1970. The distinction between competence and
performance has caused a good deal of debate. See for example
Harman, 1967. For a discussion of Harman's criticism (and Chomsky's
reply to this criticism) see Katz, 1972, 24ff. The illustrative
examples discussed in the text are fairly clear-cut in that they
all involve excessive embedding (except (1), in which other factors
are involved). In recent research, efforts have been made to provide a principled account of (un)grammaticality/(un)acceptability
in rather more subtle cases. Thus Langendoen and Bever, 1973 consider such sentences as

    (1) A not happy person entered the room
    (2) A not unhappy person entered the room

Of these, (1) is clearly much lower on the scale of acceptability
than (2). The authors argue - convincingly - that both sentences
are defined by the grammar as being ungrammatical. The acceptability
of (2) is explained in terms of a general principle of processing
strategies. They further point out that it would lead to considerable complications of the grammar if it were to rule out (1) as
ungrammatical, while defining (2) as grammatical. The systematic
study of performance, then, can result in an overall simplifica-
tion of linguistic theory also in such cases.

II.6. On levels of adequacy, consult Chomsky, 1964a, Chapter 2
and Bach, 1974, Chapter 10.

II.7. For the concepts 'weak' and 'strong', see Chomsky, 1965,
60ff.

II.8. For a recent critical discussion of the alignment of linguistics with the natural sciences, see Itkonen, 1975. The rationalist
conception of language acquisition and its interdependence with
general linguistic theory was not apparent in Syntactic Structures.
However, it was not long before this psychological orientation of
the generative paradigm became predominant. For example, it underlies the whole battery of arguments mustered against behaviourism
in Chomsky, 1959a. The fullest statement of this is Chomsky, 1968.
On matters pertaining to language acquisition, consult also such
works as Lenneberg, 1967 and McNeill, 1970. For critical discussion,
see Derwing, 1973. On chimpanzees and language, consult Gardner and

Gardner, 1969. The structure of the general linguistic theory outlined in the text is an informal introduction to the notions discussed in Chomsky, 1965, 30ff. For a comparison between rationalism
and empiricism with respect to language acquisition, see Langacker,
1967, 233ff. and Katz, 1971a, Chapter 6.

II.9. The locus classicus for linguistic universals is Greenberg
(ed.), 1963. For discussion of universals in the context of the
generative theory of grammar, see for example, Chomsky, 1965,
27ff., Lakoff, 1970a, 4ff., Katz, 1972, 30ff., and Bach, 1965b,
1974, Chapter 11.

CHAPTER III

TRANSFORMATIONAL-GENERATIVE GRAMMAR
AND TRADITIONAL GRAMMAR

III.1. Introductory remarks

It is frequently said that transformational-generative[1] grammar is an outgrowth of taxonomic linguistics on the one hand and traditional grammar on the other. This is true on the interpretation that TG-grammar is <u>primarily</u> an outgrowth of (in particular a reaction against) taxonomic linguistics and <u>secondarily</u> a return to some of the main tenets of traditional grammar.

We shall not be concerned with the details of traditional grammar in this chapter, but only indicate some of the main points of contact between the two paradigms. For this purpose, some of the concepts introduced in Chapter II will stand us in good stead.

III.2. On the term 'traditional grammar'

The term 'traditional grammar' will be used in this book to refer to two distinct, but interrelated sets of data:

(1) The tradition of linguistic analysis which originated in ancient Greece and dominated the study of language until it was superseded by historical and comparative linguistics towards the end of the eighteenth century.

(2) The work of the twentieth-century "scholarly traditional"

----

1. Since the type of generative grammar with which we shall be concerned in this book incorporates transformational rules, the term 'transformational-generative' will be used to characterize it. Henceforth, 'transformational-generative' will be abbreviated TG.

45

grammarians (for this term, see Gleason, 1965, 76ff.).

III.3. The Greeks

In the Western world, needless to say, the study of language originated in ancient Greece. From the beginning, linguistics was inseparably intertwined with philosophy, i.e. the general inquiry into the nature of the universe, and logic.

The merging of the three disciplines is well illustrated in
the distinction made by Aristotle (and before him, Plato) between
subject and predicate as constituents of a proposition of logic
(of which the linguistic equivalent is a declarative sentence).
Aristotle conceived of the logico-semantic structure of the proposition in terms of the following ten categories of predication:
'substance', 'quality', 'quantity', 'relation', 'place', 'time',
'position', 'state', 'action', and 'affection'. Of these, 'substance' was fundamental. The other nine categories were secondary
or accidental in the sense that they represented the various types
of statements that could be made of a substance. The categories
should be viewed as semantic abstractions. It was assumed by
Aristotle that they reflected the general structure of the universe: the world consisted of 'things' (substances) characterized
by properties referable to the nine accidental categories.

In a proposition, according to Aristotle, an 'onoma' combines
with a 'rhēma' to form a predication. Examples are

    (1) Jane works
    (2) John is wise
    (3) The girl is a student

The defining characteristic of a 'rhēma' is that it has "time-ref-
erence" (i.e. it is inflected for tense). In the sample sentences
the tense morpheme is attached either to the lexical verb ('work')
or to the copula verb ('be'). The 'rhēma', then, can be either a
verb, and adjective, or a noun. By contrast, the subject of a proposition is always a noun. From this it will be apparent that of
the parts of speech (or word classes), as we now think of them,
the noun was that which was first isolated and defined as being
interdependent with the functional notion 'subject'. No distinction was made between verbs and adjectives functioning as 'rhēmata'.

We will not go into a detailed discussion of the many philosophical problems relating to the subject-predicate distinction.
For our purposes, it is sufficient to note here that the traditional definition of 'subject' and 'predicate' as, respectively, 'the
thing or person which or whom the sentence is about' and 'the
statement made about the subject' is rooted in the Aristotelian
categories of predication.

In ancient Greece (and Rome) the linguistic debate was dominated for centuries by the controversy between anomalists and
analogists. In the clearest case the relationship between the universe and language was at issue. The anomalists viewed the universe as chaotic and interpreted the numerous irregularities in
language as a natural reflection of this state. By contrast, the
analogists, chiefly the Alexandrian champions of Aristotelian
philosophy, were convinced that natural phenomena were subject
to laws and that similar laws and regularities could be detected
in language.

It was the analogists of Alexandria - above all Dyonysius
Thrax (second century B.C.) - who first codified the patterns of
Greek grammar. The word was the central unit in this codification.
The method adopted by the analogists was, in principle, simple.
It can be illustrated by the following pattern:

    (a) X : books
    (b) line : lines
    (c) sword : swords
    (d) wood : woods
    (e) table : Y

On the basis of the regularities with respect to the relationship
between singular and plural nouns displayed by (b), (c), and (d),
it can be deduced that the variable X in (a) must have the value
'book', and the variable Y in (e) the value 'tables'. By this method, then, the parts of speech of the Greek language were classified according to paradigms which showed the systematic interrelationship between morphological regularities and such grammatical
categories as 'case', 'number', 'person', 'gender', etc. Furthermore, forms which did not fit into the paradigms were viewed with
suspicion: they violated the 'laws' of the language and should be

corrected wherever this was possible. The analogist philosophy
of language, therefore, was strongly conducive to prescriptivism.
We return to this in section III.9.

    The study of syntax - i.e. the principles by which the members
of the different paradigms combined to form sentences - was
initiated by the Alexandrian scholar Apollonius Dyscolus (second
century A.D.). His work is especially important because it provided the main source of Priscian's monumental grammar of Latin
(see next section). It was Apollonius Dyscolus who first discussed
the notion of transitivity: a transitive verb[1] was defined as one
which signified that the object noun was being 'acted upon' by
the subject. In other words, we owe to the Greeks also the traditional definition of 'subject' and 'object' as 'agent' and 'patient' respectively (and the concomitant (though much later) distinction between 'grammatical' and 'logical' subject in passive
sentences).

III.4. Greek and Latin

    In nearly every field of thought the Romans imitated the
Greeks. Grammar is no exception to this general rule. The Greek
and Latin languages were structurally very much alike; hence the
Greek grammatical categories could be adapted to Latin without
too much difficulty. It is to the Roman translations and adaptations of Greek grammar that we owe much of the terminology still
current in grammatical descriptions - traditional and otherwise.

    The final codification of Latin grammar is found in the works
of Donatus (about A.D. 400) and Priscian (about A.D. 500). The
grammars of these two scholars - especially that of the latter -
became the main source of influence throughout the medieval period.

III.5. The Middle Ages

    In the medieval period the Latin language reigned supreme as
the vehicle of religion, philosophy, science, and cultural activities of every kind.

    The grammatical categories of Latin had been exhaustively de-
----

1. By this time the verb had been recognized as a separate part
   of speech. Adjectives were classified with the nouns (for
   morphological reasons). The distinction between nouns and adjectives was not made until the Middle Ages.

scribed by Donatus and Priscian. There was little substantially
new to be added in that field. Instead, the medieval grammarians,
in particular the scholastics of the thirteenth century, devoted
their efforts to explicating the ways in which the laws of language reflected the logically apprehended structure of the universe, and the role played by the human mind in the process of
communicating by language.

The newly-restored works of Aristotle played an important
part in this inquiry. It was assumed that the Aristotelian categories of predication were universally valid generalizations of
the way in which things existed: they expressed the 'modes of being' (modi essendi) of the external world. Associated with each
part of speech were certain 'modes of signifying' (modi significan-
di): nouns denoted substances, verbs activity, adjectives quali-
ties, etc.[1]. Furthermore, it was assumed that through its 'modes
of understanding' (modi intellegendi)[2] the human mind conformed to
the structure of the world on the one hand and the structure of
language on the other.

The details of scholastic linguistic theory are complex and
at times rather abstruse. However, the main objective is clear:
the grammatical categories of Latin such as they had been success-
fully described by Donatus and Priscian should be provided with
logical explanations. In this undertaking the scholastics were not
entirely unsuccessful. Their success, however, was conditioned
by their a priori approach to linguistic matters and by the fact
that the diversity of human languages had not yet become apparent:
Latin grammar and grammar could confidently be assumed to be
synonymous terms.

It was the "logicization" of grammar in the medieval period
which first gave impetus to the idea of universal grammar.

III.6. The Renaissance and the Age of Rationalism

The Renaissance saw the termination of the unique position oc-
----

1. It will be apparent that the traditional semantic definitions
   of the parts of speech are rooted in the Aristotelian categories
   and the further linguistic interpretation of these by the
   scholastics.
2. Because of their preoccupation with different 'modes of', the
   scholastic grammarians are usually referred to as the modistae.

cupied by Latin throughout the Middle Ages. The vernaculars came
into their own and were accepted as the vehicle even of philosophy
and science. Furthermore, the Renaissance was the age of explora-
tion: in the wake of the numerous conquests made overseas followed the discovery of many new and 'exotic' languages. All in all,
the range of data which could be subjected to linguistic analysis
was enormously widened in the transition from the Middle Ages to
the Renaissance.

The intellectual climate of the seventeenth and eighteenth
centuries was dominated by two opposed philosophical schools:
rationalism and empiricism. The most important proponent of rationalism was Descartes, whereas the empiricist philosophy found its
clearest expression in the works of John Locke.

According to Descartes, the acquisition of knowledge is determined by a richly structured system of innate ideas which process the data supplied by the senses. In other words, it is assumed that the human mind makes an active contribution to the
learning process. By contrast, the empiricist view is that the
acquisition of knowledge depends exclusively on the data as perceived by the senses. The mind of the child is a tabula rasa:
'nihil est in intellectu quod non prius fuerit in sensu'.

It is clear that these two views of the way in which knowledge is acquired are related to the two different conceptions of
language acquisition discussed in section II.8. It hardly needs
to be told that TG-linguists align themselves with the rationalists (for full discussion, see Chomsky, 1966a).

Now, innate ideas in the Cartesian sense are of course universal. Hence rationalism in its seventeenth century form was as
conducive to the idea of universal grammar (or, equivalently,
philosophical grammar) as the logical speculations of the medieval grammarians had been. There is, however, one important difference, which relates to the facts mentioned in the opening paragraph of this section. In the Middle Ages universal grammar and
Latin grammar had been inseparably bound up owing to the enormous
prestige enjoyed by Latin. With the advent of a wider range of
data, the theory of universal grammar came to imply a distinction
between the underlying logical or ideational structure of language and the different surface manifestations of this structure

in different languages, between conceptual similarity and formal
dissimilarity. It is significant that this view had been expressed as early as the thirteenth century by Roger Bacon, who, in
addition to Latin, had studied Greek and Hebrew: "Grammar is substantially the same in all languages, even though it may vary accidentally" (quoted in Lyons, 1968, 15f.).

One important point of contact between TG-theory and the
grammatical tradition, then, is the concept of universal grammar
as defined by the seventeenth and eighteenth-century rationalists.
The work most frequently cited in this connection is the Grammaire
générale et raisonnée (1660) by the scholars of Port Royal, a
Cistercian convent near Versailles.

III.7. Jespersen and universal grammar

Jespersen, one of the greatest of the scholarly traditional-
ists, gave a good deal of attention to the question of linguistic
universals. He vigorously denounced the kind of philosophical grammar which was based on a "confusion of logic and Latin grammar"
(1924, 47ff.). On that point, of course, no modern linguist, of
whatever orientation, would disagree with him: it is clearly fal-
lacious to impose the categories of a model language on all other
languages. However, where more abstract or covert categories are
concerned, Jespersen is on a par with TG-linguists rather than
with structuralists. In particular, he was convinced that there
are universal 'notional categories' which are "beside, or above,
or behind the syntactic categories which depend on the structure
of each language as it is actually found". They are "rarely expressed in a clear and unmistakable way", and the notion underlying a
specific grammatical phenomenon may be as "elusive as Kant's ding
an sich". Jespersen concludes his discussion of notional categories
by emphasizing that the systematic study of the interrelationship
between underlying notional categories and observationally accessible syntactic phenomena in different languages will result in
"the nearest approach to a [universal grammar] that modern linguistics will allow". Translated into the terminology of the transformational-generative paradigm, this means that the general theory must be so constructed as to allow for as few different gram-

mars and (hence) as rich a set of universals as is compatible with
the observable diversity of human languages.

Unlike TG-grammarians, Jespersen saw no connection between
linguistic universals and language acquisition. His views here
are clearly in the empiricist tradition (see for example, 1922,
Book II and 1964, 29). Nevertheless, one may wonder whether he
would not have had strong leanings towards the rationalists in the
current debate. Certainly, there are a number of details in his
general conception of linguistic structure which might have supported such leanings.

III.8. Traditional grammar and descriptive adequacy

TG-linguists have often emphasized that traditional grammarians, unlike structuralists, attain the level of descriptive adequacy in the sense of section II.6: they provide explanations of
the speaker's intuitive knowledge of his language. Let us consider a few examples.

In his discussion of the grammar of the Port Royal scholars,
Chomsky has frequently commented on their analysis of the (French
equivalent of) the following sentence (e.g. 1964a, 15f., 1966a,
31ff., and 1968, 14ff.):

(1) Invisible God created the visible world

The essence of their analysis is that the underlying conceptual
structure of the sentence can be expressed in terms of the following three propositions (i.e. subject-predicate structures): (a)
'God is invisible', (b) 'God created the world', and (c) 'the
world is visible'. Of these, (b) is the principal proposition,
whereas (a) and (c) are incidental or accessory. In (1) the incidental propositions are not overtly expressed as propositions.
In (2), however, they are:

(2) God who is invisible created the world which is visible

Since (1) and (2) have the same meaning, the sentences are formally
different reflections of the same underlying conceptual structure.

Jespersen would have analysed (1) along the same lines as
the Port Royal grammarians. Relevant here is the notion of rank:
Jespersen classified words as primaries, secondaries, and ter-

tiaries. To a large extent (though by no means exclusively) there is a one-to-one correspondence between primaries and nouns on the one hand, and between secondaries and verbs and adjectives on the other (we leave tertiaries out of account). Secondaries combine with primaries to form nexus-structures (i.e. subject-predicate structures) and junctions (i.e. adjective-nominal head structures). In such structures, the secondary modifies the primary. Basically, therefore, the relationship between the underlined words in the following nexus-structures and junctions is the same[1]:

 (3) God is invisible
 (4) Invisible God
 (5) God created the world
 (6) The world is visible
 (7) The visible world

Jespersen further distinguished between restrictive and nonrestrictive adjuncts (i.e. secondaries in a junction) and related this distinction to that between restrictive and nonrestrictive relative clauses. He would have equated 'invisible' and 'visible' in (1) with relative clauses in the following manner:

 (8) God, who is invisible, created the world (,) which is
   visible

That is, 'invisible' is unambiguously nonrestrictive, whereas 'visible' may be either restrictive or nonrestrictive (in the former case there are many worlds, only one of which is visible and was created by God; in the latter case there is only one world, which is visible)[2].

 Clearly, apart from some terminological differences,

----

1. For the ideas discussed here, see Jespersen, 1924, Chapters VII-X and 1933, Chapters VIII-IX. Jespersen attempted to distinguish junctions from nexus-structures in somewhat idiosyncratic semantic terms: "Whereas the junction is more stiff and rigid, the nexus is more pliable; it is, as it were, animate or articulated ... A junction is like a picture, a nexus is like a process or drama" (1924, 116).

2. The Port Royal grammarians also made the distinction between restrictive and nonrestrictive relative clauses. For some discussion of this, see Chomsky, 1966a, 38. Note that since 'God' has unique reference, the first relative clause in (1) can only be nonrestrictive. See below, p. 343.

Jespersen's analysis is indistinguishable from that of the Port
Royal grammarians. Hence he may be said to provide a link between
philosophical grammar and TG-grammar, in this respect at least.

The next example to be taken up relates to <u>nominalization</u>.
In his discussion of the so-called <u>nexus-substantives</u>, Jespersen
considers such structures as (1933, Chapter XXX):

(9) The doctor's arrival

(10) The love of God

(11) The accidental discovery by Miss Knag of some correspondence

and points out that they reflect the structure subject-verb(-ob-
ject). In (9) 'arrival' is a nominalized form of the intransitive
verb 'arrive' (hence there is no object). (10) is ambiguous: 'God'
may be the subject of the transitive verb 'love', the object being unspecified ('someone'). Alternatively, 'God' may be the object, in which case the subject is unspecified. In (11) the underlying sentence is in the passive ('Miss Knag' being the logical
subject (agent), 'the correspondence' the object). Observe now
that in all three structures we have a genitive - either an "s-
genitive" or an "of-genitive"[1]. Jespersen's definition of nexus-
substantives as discussed so far is, in effect, a restatement -
in terms of his own conceptual framework - of the functions 'subjective' and 'objective' assigned to the genitive in traditional
case theory. Jespersen, however, goes further than this: he also
defines abstract (and agentive) nouns as nexus-substantives. In
other words, he postulates an underlying subject-predicate relation also for such nouns as 'pride' and 'driver' even though
there is no overt representation of the subject. Thus we may infer that he would have analysed a sentence like

(12) Poverty defeated me

along the following lines:

----

1. Note that we can resolve the ambiguity of (10) by substituting
   'God's' for 'of God': 'God's' can only be the subject. Similarly, (11) can be converted into the active by substituting
   'Miss Knag's' for 'by Miss Knag': 'Miss Knag's accidental discovery of some correspondence'. Finally, (9) is synonymous
   with 'the arrival of the doctor'.

(13) I be poor defeated me

'I' is the 'understood' subject (or, as Jespersen might have said, the 'inherent primary' (cf. 1924, 143)) of which the quality 'poor' is predicated. In this particular sentence the subject of the nexus underlying the abstract noun is identical with the object of the main verb and thus "recoverable" from the linguistic context. In other cases it may be unspecified:

(14) Poverty is a curse[1]

The last example we will consider concerns the notion 'understood subject' in general. Long (1961, 11) declares that "all predicators have subjects, expressed or implied". As examples of implied subjects he cites such sentences as (ibid. 77, 90f.):

(15) Just give me one more chance
(16) The children are ready to eat[2]
(17) Circumstances have forced us to postpone the exhibition[2]
(18) His desire has been to be frank without giving offense
(19) Taking courses is a silly way to get an education

Long comments on these sentences in the following way: (15) is an imperative sentence, and in imperative sentences the subject is "of course you, singular or plural". In (16) it is "the subject of the larger clause within which an infinitival clause is contained [which] suggests the subject" (Long does not comment on the ambiguity of (16)). The subject of the infinitival clause in (17) is identical with the complement (i.e. the object) of the larger clause (this was what we referred to as 'double function' in section I.5.4). In (18) the subject is supplied from the possessive determiner 'his'. Finally, in (19) the implied subject is "general" (i.e. 'someone').

We have now examined three areas of a grammar of English in which the accounts given by traditional scholars attain the level of descriptive adequacy. TG-linguists would say that the analyses suggested by the Port Royal grammarians, Jespersen, and Long are

----

1. Compare with this Chomsky's discussion of the noun 'sincerity' (1965, 186). For a detailed discussion of Jespersen's notion of nexus-substantives in the context of TG-theory, see Katz, 1971a, 60ff.

2. Compare (16) and (17) with (15) and (7) of section I.5.4.

essentially correct; only, they are not <u>formalized explicitly</u> within a coherent theory of linguistic structure. In particular, there must be rules which (a) specify the systematic interrelationship between attributive adjectives and relative clauses, (b) convert underlying sentences into nominal structures, and (c) account for the notion 'implied subject'.

III.9. The problem of correctness

The word 'grammar' derives from Greek 'gramma' = 'letter'. The title of the first grammar to be written in the Western world - Dionysius Thrax's short grammar of Greek (cf. above, p. 47) - was Technē Grammatikē, which may be translated roughly as 'the art of knowing one's letters'. This reveals a fundamental characteristic of traditional grammar: the assignment of priority to the written language - especially the language of the great and time-honoured masters of literature. This - the literary fallacy - persisted for some two thousand years: what the language of Homer had been to Dionysius Thrax, the language of the pre-Restoration writers was to Dr. Johnson. A consequence of the literary fallacy was that the nature of linguistic change was poorly understood: in particular, since the language <u>spoken</u> by the man in the street, whether in ancient Alexandria or eighteenth-century London, manifested a number of 'deviations' from the classical norm, it was viewed as 'corrupt' and 'degenerated'.

The codification of English grammar took its beginning in the eighteenth century. The overall goal was to establish an <u>absolute standard of correctness</u> based on the classical literary language and compatible with the canons of reason and logic (often synonymous with 'analogy'). The following often quoted statement by Robert Lowth sums up the goals of the prescriptive grammarian (1762, X):

> The Principal design of a Grammar of any Language is to teach us to express ourselves with propriety in that Language; and to enable us to judge of every phrase and form of construction, whether it is right or not. The plain way of doing this is to lay down rules and to illustrate them by examples. But, besides showing what is right, the matter may be further explained by pointing out what is wrong.

Structuralists have always taken strong exception to the literary and normative orientation of traditional grammar. To the structuralists, it is an article of faith that the primary medium of language is speech and that 'correctness' is not a valid linguistic concept: once the data are subjected to objective investigation, it becomes obvious that the literary language is in no way representative of what is going on in a speech-community; rather what the linguist is confronted with is a multifarious variety of regional and social dialects, professional jargons, stylistic registers, etc. All these varieties exist in their own right and can be appropriately used in specific social contexts. Of course, no linguist would deny that many languages have a standard form and that this is practical and advantageous inasmuch as it ensures unity in variety and makes a high degree of mutual comprehensibility possible. He would hasten to point out, however, that, viewed historically, a standard language is a dialect which has gained an ascendancy over other dialects for socio-economic rather than linguistic reasons. Thus, in England, the London dialect became prominent at the end of the Middle Ages owing to a variety of social, political, and economic factors, but not to any inherent 'purity' of the dialect itself.

We have said that one characteristic of structuralism is the inductive approach to the data. This being the case, the structuralist may treat the object of investigation in different ways. He may abstract from what he believes to be socially determined peculiarities of one kind or another in the utterances which make up his corpus and attempt to write a 'structural grammar' of the language. Alternatively, he may remain faithful to the utterances in his corpus with a view to writing a 'grammar of usage'. In the latter case, he may need the aid of sociologists and anthropologists to clarify the secondary values attached to such forms as 'he don't', 'I ain't got no money', etc. - forms which would have been dubbed 'incorrect' by traditional grammarians. In other words, the difference between linguistics 'proper' and sociolinguistics can be seen - essentially - as a difference in the degree of idealization imposed on the primary data[1,2].

----

1. The two different approaches are well illustrated in the works of Fries (1940 and 1952).

2. A certain measure of idealization will always be required, as witness (1) of section II.5. However, the peculiarities manifested by that utterance were psychologically rather than socially determined.

TG-theory has in common with the eighteenth-century tradition
the conception of language as a rule-determined phenomenon and the
deductive approach to grammar-construction. Does this mean, then,
that TG-theory is a revival of the conception of correctness characteristic of traditional grammar - as has sometimes been claimed?
By no means. In the first place, the TG-linguist is surely entitled
to idealize the data to the same degree as did the structuralist.
Secondly, as it turns out, TG-theory is - in many cases - in a position to explain socially determined variations, where structuralism
can only describe them. Consider the following sentences:

(1) There are a lot of books on the shelves
(2) There is a lot of books on the shelves

Let us agree (a) that both sentences are grammatical, and (b) that
the secondary value attached to (2) is 'sloppiness': the verb
'should be' in the plural. TG-theory can explain the difference
between the two sentences in terms of rule-ordering: in the minds
of 'sloppy' speakers, two rules - let us call them x and y - are
ordered in such a way that x applies before y, whereas, in the minds
of 'nonsloppy' speakers, y precedes x[1]. A competence model, then,
can, in principle, be made to accommodate sociolinguistic data.

Sociolinguistics is not limited to the study of the way in
which different speakers (or groups of speakers) utilize the linguistic system of language L. It is also concerned with the way in
which each individual speaker utilizes the linguistic system in
specific social contexts. Consider such sentences as

(3) Have a nice trip
(4) We wish you a pleasant flight

In a certain sense (3) and (4) are synonymous. Yet, as is immediately
obvious, they are appropriately uttered in widely different social
contexts. In particular, the air-hostess who utters (3) rather than
(4) after take-off knows that she is likely to get the sack. Since
TG-theory aims at making explicit the linguistic knowledge of the
ideal speaker-listener, it is arguable that it should explain this
knowledge. Since (3) and (4) would both be defined as syntactically
well-formed by the grammar, the explanation must be located in the

----

1. It would be premature to go into details at this point. The two
   rules involved are agreement and there insertion. See below,
   sections IV.G.2 and 8. Compare also notes to section IV.G.15.

semantic component. Now, it is possible that an adequate theory of
semantics - as an integral part of a TG-grammar - should incorporate
the notion of pragmatic presuppositions (as distinct from semantic
presuppositions (for these concepts, see further below, section
IV.D.16)). Assuming that this is the case, we can say that (3) and
(4) differ in their pragmatic presuppositions: the utterance of (3)
pragmatically presupposes a relation of 'solidarity' between speaker
and hearer, whereas the utterance of (4) pragmatically presupposes
a relation of 'power' between speaker and hearer.

In section II.5 we considered the psycholinguistic implications of the distinction between competence and performance. This
distinction, no doubt, is relevant from a sociolinguistic point
of view as well. In neither case is it entirely clear where the
boundary between competence and performance should be drawn. However, most TG-linguists would argue that a prerequisite for the
development of what we may call a general use theory of language
is an adequate theory of linguistic competence.

III.10. Historical and comparative linguistics

The end of the eighteenth century saw the beginning of a new
important and far-reaching development in the study of language.
In 1786 Sir William Jones made the following celebrated statement
(quoted in Jespersen, 1922, 33):

> The Sanscrit language, whatever be its antiquity, is a
> wonderful structure; more perfect than the Greek, more copi-
> ous than the Latin and more exquisitely refined than either;
> yet bearing to both of them a stronger affinity, both in the
> roots and verbs and in the forms of grammar, than could pos-
> sibly have been produced by accident; so strong, indeed,
> that no philologer could examine them all three without be-
> lieving them to have sprung from the same common source, which,
> perhaps, no longer exists.

Throughout the nineteenth century the reconstruction of the
Indoeuropean 'ancestor' language was pursued with great enthusiasm;
the various languages of Europe and India were subjected to comparative study and shown to be 'genetically' related in the sense
that they had all sprung from this common source.

One important consequence of the historical and comparative
study of language was the development of phonetics as an exact
science. The Indian scholars had been excellent phoneticians, and
the discovery of their treatises strongly influenced European lin-

guists. Moreover, it gradually became apparent that, in order to
explain linguistic change, attention should be focused on the
spoken rather than the written language, and towards the end of
the century linguists were primarily preoccupied with language as
a system of sounds undergoing predictable changes in specific
phonetic contexts.

It was in the nineteenth century that linguistics emerged as
an empirical science in the sense that observed facts came to provide the basis for generalizations and hypotheses.

Structuralism was an outgrowth of the nineteenth-century
tradition. At the beginning of this century, the methods which had
yielded such brilliant results in the historical (or diachronic)
study of language came to be applied to the synchronic description of language (i.e. the description of the language-system as
it exists at a fixed point in time[1]). Furthermore, structuralism -
in particular American structuralism - shared with the nineteenth-
century paradigm the preoccupation with language as sound - at
the expense of syntax. We have already commented on this and will
not go into further detail.

TG-theory is essentially concerned with the synchronic description of language (the notion of linguistic competence is obviously synchronic in nature: the speaker does not know the history of his language). However, recent research has shown that
the study of diachronic linguistics can supply important empirical
evidence for the construction of descriptively adequate synchronic
grammars.

Apart from these scanty remarks, we will not be further concerned with diachronic linguistics in this book'.

III.11. Conclusion

We have now considered four major paradigms in the development of linguistic science: traditional grammar, (American) structuralism, diachronic linguistics, and TG-grammar. At the risk of
oversimplifying the matter, we can illustrate the interrelationship between these four paradigms in terms of the following dia-
gram (where $\longrightarrow$ = 'a (partial) continuation of' and $\longleftrightarrow$ = 'an
outgrowth of and reaction against'):

----

1. For the distinction between 'diachronic' and 'synchronic', see
   de Saussure, 1916.

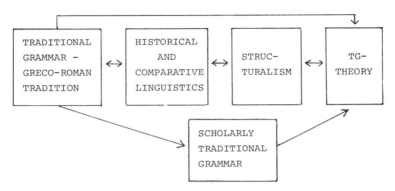

The relationship between traditional grammar and TG-grammar, which has been our main concern in this chapter, is summed up by Lees in the following statement (1962 (in Allen, H.B., 1964) 137):

> The goals of traditional grammatical studies were high, in the sense that the classical grammarian attempted sincerely to account for what kind of knowledge the mature user of a language must have in order to construct correctly formed sentences and to interpret new sentences which he hears. The traditional grammarian was, however, severely handicapped in achieving this goal by his ignorance of the fact that one can actually specify explicitly a finite characterization of a complex infinite set, such as he knew the set of well-formed sentences of a natural language to be, namely by the use of a productive system of ordered rules which recursively enumerate the members of the desired set. He therefore resorted to vague semantic notions in order to specify what could qualify as well-formed expressions.

We must now turn to an examination of the nature of the rules mentioned by Lees.

Notes and some further references

General. Fairly detailed accounts of the development of the study of language may be found in Arens, 1955 and Robins, 1967. Traditional grammar is given extensive treatment in Dinneen, 1967. Lyons, 1968 presents a thorough treatment of recent developments in linguistics and relates them systematically to the grammatical tradition. Shorter treatments are Dykema, 1961 and Hartung, 1962. For typical structuralist discussions of traditional grammar, see Bloomfield, 1933, 4ff., Hall, 1960, 9ff., and Levin, 1960. A succinct comparison of structuralism and traditional grammar may be found in Dinneen, 1967, 166ff.

III.2. The greatest scholarly traditional works are Sweet, 1891, Jespersen, 1909-49 (of which Essentials of English Grammar is a

shorter version) Poutsma, 1914-29, and Kruisinga, 1925. Shorter
works in the same tradition are Zandvoort, 1957, Long, 1961, and
Schibsbye, 1965.

III.3. From a linguistic point of view, the most important of
Aristotle's works is De Interpretatione. The genesis of the subject-predicate relation is dealt with at some length in Lyons,
1968 (especially, p. 334ff.). See also Jespersen, 1924 and Sandmann, 1954. At a later point we shall relate the discussion in
this section to the category of 'case'. For the analogy-anomaly
controversy, see Dinneen, 1967 and Robins, 1967. The controversy
was rooted in an even older dispute: that between naturalists and
conventionalists. The main issue of this dispute was the place oc-
cupied by language in relation to man-made social institutions and
conventions on the one hand and nature on the other. Was language
conventional or natural? The discussion centred on the relationship between the sound structure and meaning of individual words.
Conventionalists claimed that the sound-meaning relationship was
entirely arbitrary: the meaning of words was solely a matter of
agreement among the members of the speech-community. Naturalists,
on the other hand, held that there was a deep-seated connection between word form and word meaning: the sound structure of the word
was "an echo to the sense". They argued that onomatopoeia (i.e.
words whose sound structure (total or partial) reflect their
meaning) constituted the true and original core of the vocabulary.
They were well aware, of course, that the majority of the words
in their language were not directly onomatopoeic. However, they
claimed that it was the task of etymology to establish the connection between phonologically opaque words and their more transparent "roots". Nowadays most linguists, while recognizing the
existence of onomatopoeia, would agree that, in principle, the relationship between sound and meaning is conventional. Indeed,
viewed from the vantage point of the twentieth century, most of
the etymologies established by the ancients in support of the
naturalist hypothesis seem naive and are obviously wrong. However,
a certain measure of perspectivism is called for: in itself, the
naturalist hypothesis is perfectly legitimate, but, as we now
know, its confirmation (or disconfirmation) depends on a much
wider range of linguistic knowledge than that which was at the
disposal of the ancient scholars. We shall see in section IV.B.3
that TG-theory gives explicit recognition to the arbitrary relationship between sound and meaning.

III.5. For medieval linguistics, see Bursill-Hall, 1963, Robins,
1951, 1967 and Dinneen, 1967. The parts-of-speech tradition is
dealt with by Lyons, 1966a and Robins, 1966.

III.6,8. Chomsky has seen in the Grammaire générale et raisonnée
a precursor of his own distinction between deep and surface structure. This interpretation of the seventeenth-century tradition has
been subjected to a good deal of criticism. See for example Dik,
1968, 119ff. and (especially) Aarsleff, 1970.

III.7. For a general discussion of Jespersen in relation to structuralism and TG-theory, see Gefen, 1968.

III.9. Eighteenth-century normative grammar is dealt with in detail by Leonard, 1962. A brief, but excellent, overview of the
eighteenth-century grammatical tradition may be found in Baugh,

1959, Chapter 9. For some further discussion of the competence-
performance distinction, see Lyons, 1966b, Hymes, 1970, Halliday,
1970, 1973, and Derwing, 1973. A useful introductory article to
sociolinguistic problems is Pride, 1970.

III.10. Jespersen, 1922 and Pedersen, 1931 are excellent introductions to nineteenth-century scholarship. A brief survey of the
methods of historical and comparative linguistics may be found in
Lehmann, 1962 (contains a useful annotated bibliography). Many
textbooks contain brief introductory chapters; consult for example
Bloomfield, 1933, Hockett, 1958, Robins, 1964, Dinneen, 1967, and
Lyons, 1968. Kiparsky, 1970 provides examples of the interrelationship between diachronic and synchronic linguistics within the
framework of TG-theory. See in this connection also Halle's discussion of the role of paradigms in a generative grammar (1973).
More general treatments of diachronic linguistics within TG-theory
may be found in King, 1969 and McLaughlin, 1970.

III.11. It is essential to stress that the term 'structuralism'
has been restricted in this book to pre-generative American linguistics. European structuralism took a different course. We will
not go into the details of this, but merely note the following two
points (of which (b) is in part a consequence of (a)): (a) European
structuralism was always much more theoretically orientated than
American structuralism; (b) there has never been any insistence on
the sound-to-sentence sequence in European structuralism; consequently, the epithet 'inductive' is hardly applicable to the work
of the European scholars. Examples of abstract theories of language developed by European linguists are Halliday, 1961 (so-called
scale-and-category grammar) and Hjelmslev, 1953 (glossematic theory).
Hudson, 1972 is an attempt to reformulate scale-and-category grammar in generative terms. On the relationship between glossematics
and TG-theory, see Bierwisch, 1972. For generative grammar in
Europe, see Kiefer and Ruwet, 1971. Not all TG-linguists would go
so far as Lees in their praise of traditional grammar. For a dis-
claimer, see Rosenbaum, 1967, 109ff.

CHAPTER IV

TRANSFORMATIONAL-GENERATIVE GRAMMAR -
AUTONOMOUS SYNTAX

IV.A. PRELIMINARY DISCUSSION OF THE NATURE
AND FUNCTION OF SYNTACTIC RULES

IV.A.1. Introductory remarks

The fundamantal characteristic of a TG-grammar is that it is a
formal system of rules. This way of stating grammars took its in-
spiration in the study of the deductive systems of logic and mathematics. We will not go into the highly technical details of the
provenance of grammatical rules. The reader is referred to the
works cited in the bibliographical notes. The significance of the
term 'autonomous syntax' will become apparent in section IV.B.

IV.A.2. Context-free phrase structure rules

Let us begin by considering a simple artificial language. The
language has only three lexical items[1]: 'zip', 'zap', and 'zup'.
The following conventions govern the use of the language: each
sentence consists of a minimum of two lexical items, and if it
contains more than two, it is always an even number. Clearly, an
infinite number of sentences are generated by the grammar of this
language because there is no longest possible sentence. The question now is this: can we formalize this infinitude in terms of a
finite set of rules? Can we make the infinitude explicit? The

----

1. Henceforth, we will use the term 'lexical item' instead of
   'word'. For some discussion, see notes to IV.A.2.

65

following two rules would do the trick:

(1) 1. S $\longrightarrow$ X (S) X

   2. X $\longrightarrow$ $\left\{ \begin{array}{c} \text{zip} \\ \text{zap} \\ \text{zup} \end{array} \right\}$

The two rules constitute a theory of the language. S (= 'sentence')
is the <u>axiom</u> of the theory. $\longrightarrow$ (= 'rewrite as') is an <u>operator</u>;
() and $\{\ \}$ are <u>abbreviators</u>. Both operators and abbreviators are
formal universals and hence defined in the metatheory (cf. above,
p. 42). Observe that the two abbreviators have collapsed the following five rules into two:

(2) 1. S $\longrightarrow$ X + X
   2. S $\longrightarrow$ X + S + X
   3. X $\longrightarrow$ zip
   4. X $\longrightarrow$ zap
   5. X $\longrightarrow$ zup

The <u>plus</u> occurring in the first two rules of (2) is another formal universal. It defines the operation of <u>concatenation</u>, indicating that the symbols are 'chained together' in a <u>string</u>[1]. There
are five vocabulary symbols in the grammar: S, X, and the three
lexical items. All the symbols appearing to the left of the arrow are <u>nonterminal</u>. These may also occur to the right of the arrow, but they must all be rewritten, one at a time. By contrast,
<u>terminal symbols</u> can never occur to the left of the arrow. S and
X, then, are nonterminal symbols, whereas the three lexical items
are terminal symbols.

   Suppose now that we apply the first rule of (1) and obtain
the string X + S + X. The second rule now[2] applies twice and results in, say, zip + S + zap. The occurrence of S in this string
forces us back through rule 1 and we may now obtain zip + X + S +
X + zap. Exactly the same happens now: the second rule applies
twice, and we run back through rule 1 once more. This will go on
until the symbol S is no longer chosen in the first rule and can,
in principle, go on for ever. In other words, the grammar contains

----

1. Observe that in rule 1 of (1) there are no plus signs: concate-
   nation is defined by (). We could in fact dispense with + in the
   rules and instead insert it by convention in derived strings.
2. This is not quite correct: the rules are unordered; cf. below,
   p. 72.

a <u>recursive rule</u>.

    Consider now the following 'sentence':

    (3) zip + zap + zup + zip + zup + zap

It consists of a string of terminal symbols and is generated by
the grammar in the following way:

    (4)

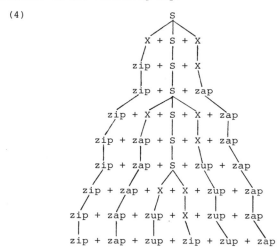

(4) is a <u>derivation</u>. The derivation consists of ten strings of
symbols: one <u>initial</u> string (the axiom of the theory), eight
<u>intermediate</u> (or <u>nonterminal</u>) <u>strings</u>, and one <u>terminal string</u>.
Note that each rule rewrites one and only one symbol from the
string it operates on. Rules whose power is restricted in this
way are known as <u>phrase structure rules</u> (henceforth abbreviated
<u>PS-rules</u>).

    Now, we have said that a grammar must automatically assign
a structural description to each sentence it generates. Let us
assume that the notion 'structural description' is defined in the
general theory as a P-marker (i.e. a constituent-structure diagram
specifying all the grammatical relations in the sentence in terms
of (a) domination, (b) 'is a (member of the category)', and (c)
precedence (cf. above, section I.5.2)). What we need, then, is a
set of operational procedures which can convert (4) into a P-marker.
Sets of operational procedures which, when applied to a given problem, automatically produce the correct result are known as <u>algo-</u>

<u>rithms</u>. Informally, the algorithm required can be stated as fol-
lows:

(5) 1. Given a derivation like (4), draw lines (or <u>branches</u>)
        linking the initial string with the terminal string
        such that each symbol in any given string is con-
        nected with its corresponding identity in the im-
        mediately following string or with the symbol(s)
        that has (have) replaced it by the operation of a
        rule[1].

     2. Reduce all branches of the form a - b - b - b ... c
        (where a is the initial string and c a terminal sym-
        bol) to branches of the form a - b - c.

Given (5), we can convert (4) into the following P-marker:

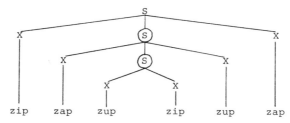

        zip   zap   zup   zip   zup   zap

        Observe that we have assumed that our artificial language
is self-embedding: the two encircled S nodes are completely embedded in a higher S of the same type. We might have constructed
the grammar in such a way that the structures assigned by the
rules would have been either left-branching or right-branching.
All we would have to do would be to alter the first two rules:

S ———⟶ (S) X + X   S ———⟶ X + X (S)

(By 5)

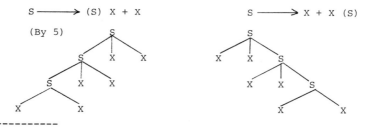

----

1. For convenience, we have already done that in (4). It should
   be emphasized, however, that these branches are not assigned
   by the rules of L, but by the general theory.

The following rule:

S ——————→ (S) X (S) X (S)

would provide for all three kinds of embedding.

We turn now to an example from English. We will try to formulate a set of PS-rules which will generate sentence (9) of section I.5.4 and sentence (3) of section II.5:

(6) John washed the car in the garage
(7) I watched the bird on the roof of the house on the top
    of the hill through my binoculars

We will hypothesize that every sentence consists of a noun phrase
functioning as subject and a verb phrase functioning as predicate[1].
The rule rewriting the axiomatic symbol S must make this explicit.
Given the correctness of this hypothesis, the rules we need look
something like this:

(8)   1. S ——————→ NP + VP
      2. VP ——————→ V + NP (PP)
      3. NP ——————→ (Det) N (PP)
      4. PP ——————→ Prep + NP
      5. V ——————→ {washed, watched}
      6. N ——————→ {John, I, car, garage, bird, roof, house,
                    top, hill, binoculars}
      7. Det ——————→ {the, my}
      8. Prep ——————→ {in, on, of, through}

where NP = noun phrase, VP = verb phrase, N = noun, V = verb,
PP = prepositional phrase, Prep = preposition, and Det = determiner.
These rules would assign two different structures to (6) (which,
as we have seen, is ambiguous):

(6a)

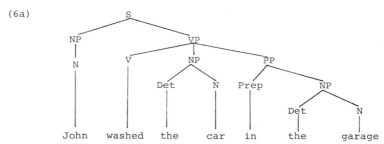

----

1. For grammatical functions, see section IV.A.7.

(6b)

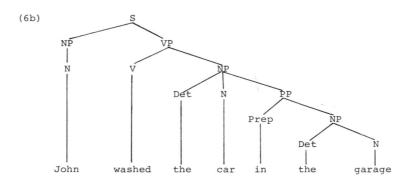

Note that in (6a) the PP is immediately dominated by VP. It is a
locative adverbial. In (6b) the PP is immediately dominated by
NP. It is a postmodifier of N.

    Another way of representing the information specified in
P-markers is by way of <u>labelled bracketed strings</u>:

```
(6a)   (   (  ( John )  )   (  ( washed )  (   ( the )   ( car )  )  )
       S  NP  N          N  NP  VP  V          V  NP Det    Det N     N  NP
       (   (  in  )   (   ( the )   ( garage )  )  )  )  )
       PP Prep     Prep  NP Det    Det N          N  NP PP VP S

(6b)   (   (  ( John )  )   (  ( washed )  (   ( the )   ( car )
       S  NP  N          N  NP  VP  V          V  NP Det    Det N      N
       (   (  in  )   (   ( the )  ( garage )  )  )  )  )  )  )
       PP Prep     Prep  NP Det   Det N          N  NP PP NP VP S
```

where in each pair of brackets labelled ( ) X dominates every-
                                   X X

thing included in the brackets. In a TG-grammar P-markers or
labelled bracketed strings form the input to transformational
rules. Frequently, such rules operate on symbols high up in the
tree, affecting everything which is dominated by the symbol. Consequently, it is not always necessary to state all the structural
details in the labelled bracketed strings or their associated
trees.

    The rules (or, more precisely, the structure assignment algo-
rithm) would assign the following P-marker to (7):

(7a)

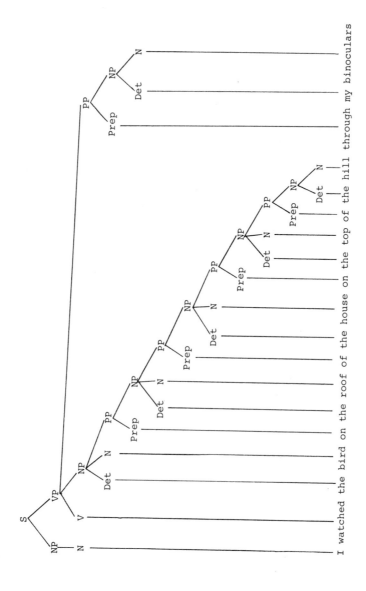

(7a) shows very clearly that our grammar is recursive: the symbols NP and PP may recur (interdependently of each other) an infinite number of times.

We may conclude this introductory treatment of PS-rules by making the following three points:

(a) PS-rules are a formalization of IC-analysis. Observe that, given the rules, node-labelling follows automatically.

(b) The two sets of rules we have considered in this section ((1) and (8)) are underlined. That is to say, we need not impose any ordering on them. Note, however, that they impose their own ordering, as it were. Thus the rule rewriting NP cannot operate before the rule which introduces NP into the string has operated; and so on. This kind of ordering is known as intrinsic ordering (as opposed to extrinsic ordering (for which, see below, sections IV.A.4 and IV.E.6)).

(c) The rules are context-free. This means that the symbols occurring to the right of the arrow are not restricted by any contexts (or environments).

IV.A.3. Context-sensitive rules

Context-free rules have the following general form:

A $\longrightarrow$ B

We can also have rules of the form

A $\longrightarrow$ B/X __ Y

meaning 'rewrite A as B after X and before Y'. Rules of this kind are known as context-sensitive[1].

Consider now the relation of concord between subject and verb in English[2]. Roughly, this can be stated as follows:

singular: noun + $\emptyset$ + verb + s
plural: noun + s + verb + $\emptyset$
(where $\emptyset$ = 'zero-element').

The relationship can be formalized in terms of the following set

----

1. X and Y are variables. If we stipulate that the values of X and Y are unrestricted and hence may be null, context-free grammars will be seen to form a subset of context-sensitive grammars: the set of languages generated by context-free grammars is properly included in the set of languages generated by context-sensitive grammars.

2. For a more detailed discussion of the example presented in this section, see Lyons, 1968, 242ff.

of context-<u>free</u> PS-rules:

1. $S \longrightarrow \left\{ \begin{array}{l} NP_{sing} + VP_{sing} \\ NP_{plur} + VP_{plur} \end{array} \right\}$

2. $VP_{sing} \longrightarrow V_{sing} \left(\left\{ \begin{array}{l} NP_{sing} \\ NP_{plur} \end{array} \right\} \right)$

3. $VP_{plur} \longrightarrow V_{plur} \left(\left\{ \begin{array}{l} NP_{sing} \\ NP_{plur} \end{array} \right\} \right)$

4. $NP_{sing} \longrightarrow Det + N + \emptyset$

5. $NP_{plur} \longrightarrow Det + N + s$

6. $V_{sing} \longrightarrow V + s$

7. $V_{plur} \longrightarrow V + \emptyset$

Given three sets of lexical items, these rules would assign the
following structure to a sentence like

(1) The cats chase the rats

(1a)

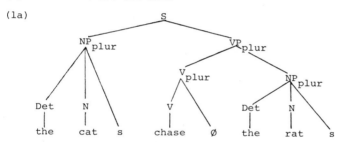

The concord relation could also be stated in terms of the following set of context-<u>sensitive</u> rules:

1. $S \longrightarrow NP + VP$

2. $VP \longrightarrow Verb \ (NP)$

3. $NP \longrightarrow \left\{ \begin{array}{l} NP_{sing} \\ NP_{plur} \end{array} \right\}$

4. $Verb \longrightarrow \left\{ \begin{array}{l} V + s/NP_{sing} \underline{\quad} \\ V + \emptyset/NP_{plur} \underline{\quad} \end{array} \right\}$

5. $NP_{sing} \longrightarrow Det + N + \emptyset$

6. $NP_{plur} \longrightarrow Det + N + s$

The rules would assign the following structure to (1):

(1b)

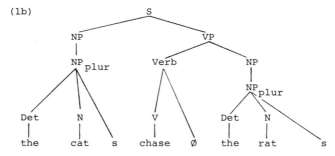

Now, it is obvious that, given identical sets of lexical
items to replace N, V, and Det, the two concord-grammars generate
the same set of sentences. In other words, they are weakly equivalent (cf. section II.7). However, a comparison of (1a) and
(1b) reveals that the two grammars assign different structural
descriptions to the sentences they generate: they do not have the
same strong generative capacity and are therefore not strongly
equivalent. Hence we must choose between them. The choice is determined by the evaluation measure, and this in turn is bound up with
the requirement of descriptive adequacy. The context-free grammar
predicts that the speaker distinguishes between singular and plural <u>sentences</u> (rule 1) <u>as well as</u> between singular and plural (nonsubject) noun phrases (rules 2 and 3). This is obviously a counterintuitive and (hence) incorrect claim. By contrast, in the context-
sensitive grammar, 'number' is not introduced until rule 3. Rule 4
shows that concord is dependent on the choice of number made in the
subject noun phrase in rule 3. The context-sensitive grammar, then,
defines the category 'number' as being solely an attribute of noun
phrases which is unrelated to S. There can be little doubt that
this correctly explicates our intuitions about 'number'. Therefore,
the context-sensitive grammar is the descriptively more adequate,
and hence preferable, grammar.

IV.A.4. <u>The inadequacy of PS-grammars and the notion of transfor-
         mations</u>

The question arises whether it would be possible to construct

a grammar of a natural language in terms of PS-rules. The first
point to be made is that context-sensitive grammars are more
powerful than context-free grammars and that it has actually been
shown that natural languages are beyond the scope of context-free
grammars; hence, if we were to countenance the task, we would
have to use context-sensitive rules. Secondly, given the general
theory of generative grammar, we would have to require of the
grammar that it attain the level of descriptive adequacy (i.e. it
must be strongly, not just weakly, adequate). Thus, if it is the
case that the speaker's intuitions about his language tell him
that (1) and (2) are interrelated (as seems a reasonable assumption):

   (1) Peter is there
   (2) Is Peter there

then the grammar must predict that this is so.
   The following context-<u>free</u> rules generate (1):

   1. S ⎯⎯⎯⟶ NP + VP
   2. VP ⎯⎯⟶ V + Adv
   3. NP ⎯⎯⟶ N
   4. N ⎯⎯⟶ Peter
   5. V ⎯⎯⟶ is
   6. Adv ⎯⟶ there

(where Adv = adverb) and assign the following structural description to the sentence:

   (1a)

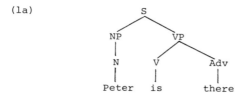

This is reasonable. However, if we want both (1) and (2) to be
generated by the <u>same</u> set of rules, we shall need the following
set of context-<u>sensitive</u> rules:

   (see overleaf)

The rules, furthermore, must be <u>extrinsically</u> ordered[1] in the fol-
----
1. It is the linguist who orders the rules (cf. above, p. 72).

1. S $\longrightarrow$ NP + VP
2. VP $\longrightarrow$ V + Adv
3. NP $\longrightarrow$ V/ __ V
4. V $\longrightarrow$ NP/V __
5. NP $\longrightarrow$ N
6. N $\longrightarrow$ Peter
7. V $\longrightarrow$ is
8. Adv $\longrightarrow$ there

lowing way: The rules apply in strict order from 1 to 8, but rule 3 may optionally be passed over. If it <u>is</u> passed over, rule 4 is inapplicable and the grammar generates (1) with the structural description (1a). If it is not passed over, all the rules apply, generating (2) with the following structural description[1]:

(2a)

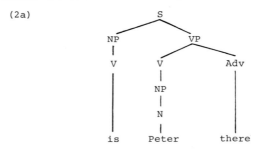

Clearly, (2a) is incorrect. In particular, it cannot be the case that 'NP is a V' and 'V is an NP'. In other words, there is something wrong with the strong generative capacity of the grammar. The structural descriptions it assigns are highly counter-intuitive and hence do not satisfy the requirement of descriptive adequacy.

----

1. Note that, contrary to what I assumed earlier, the rules must be extrinsically ordered, even if rule 3 is optional. If they were unordered, i.e. intrinsically ordered, they could apply in the order 1,2,3,7,7,8, generating the terminal string 'is is there' with the following structural description:

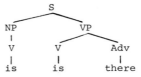

This is obviously empirically incorrect.

The only way of preventing context-sensitive rules from assigning incorrect structures like (2a) is to constrain them in
such a way that they cannot <u>permute</u> (i.e. switch around) elements.
However, once we do that, PS-grammars can no longer capture the
relationship between sentences like (1) and (2) and hence are descriptively inadequate. What we need is a rule which can relate
the P-markers of (1) and (2) without absurd consequences for the
labelling.

Another serious inadequacy of PS-rules is that they can only assign <u>one</u> P-marker to a sentence. Consider again sentences
(3) and (4) of section I.5.4:

(3) John was difficult to leave
(4) John was reluctant to leave

It would be fairly easy to construct a set of PS-rules which would
generate (3) and (4). However, they would assign the same structural description to the two sentences. Compare now with (3) and
(4)

(5) It was difficult to leave John
(6) John left reluctantly

It is part of the speaker's knowledge that (5) is a paraphrase of
(3) and that (6) is a paraphrase of (4)[1]. Observe that in (3)
'John' is the subject of the sentence, whereas in (5) 'John'
is the object of the sentence. A comparison of (4) and (6) reveals that 'John' is the subject of 'be reluctant' as well as of
'leave' in (4). PS-rules cannot account for these relationships.
The only way of making them explicit is to have two P-markers related by rules. As far as (3) is concerned, one P-marker (whose
terminal string might look roughly like (5)) would specify that
'John' is the object. The rule deriving (3) from (5)[2] would (perhaps) replace 'it' in (5) by 'John': the object "becomes" the subject. In the case of (4), one P-marker would contain two occurrences
of 'John'. A rule would <u>delete</u> the subject of 'leave' to derive

----

1. There is one difference between (4) and (6): in (4) it is uncertain whether John actually left, whereas this is not the
   case in (6). Strictly speaking, therefore, (6) is not quite a
   paraphrase of (4).

2. For the moment we are begging the question of which sentence
   should be derived from the other.

(4). Rules which can relate pairs of sentences like (1) and (2)
in the proper way and account for the grammatical relations in
(3) and (4) by relating them to (5) and (6) are <u>transformational
rules</u> (henceforth abbreviated <u>T-rules</u>).

It would seem, then, that a grammar which aims at descriptive adequacy must contain T-rules over and above PS-rules.

IV.A.5. <u>Deep and surface structure</u>

A T-rule has the following general form (we follow the convention of using a double arrow where a T-rule is concerned):

$$A \Longrightarrow B$$

A and B are P-markers. A T-rule, then, converts a P-marker into
a new, <u>derived P-marker</u>.

The PS-rules generate an infinite set of <u>base P-markers</u>[1]. A
base P-marker constitutes the <u>deep structure</u> of a sentence. This
is converted into a <u>final P-marker</u> by the operation of one or
more T-rules. The final P-marker constitutes the <u>surface structure</u>
of the sentence. If it takes more than one T-rule to derive the
surface structure of a sentence from its deep structure, there will
be a set of <u>intermediate P-markers</u>. Schematically, the derivation
of the surface structure of such a sentence can be represented as
follows:

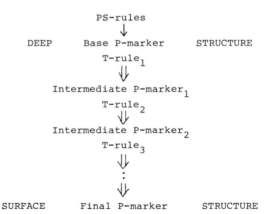

```
                        PS-rules
                           ↓
        DEEP        Base P-marker        STRUCTURE
                        T-rule₁
                          ⇓
                Intermediate P-marker₁
                        T-rule₂
                          ⇓
                Intermediate P-marker₂
                        T-rule₃
                          ⇓
                          ⋮
                          ⇓
        SURFACE      Final P-marker       STRUCTURE
```

----

1. Because some of the rules are recursive. See, however, below,
   section IV.B.2.

No sentence can be generated without the operation of at
least one T-rule (in fact, there are probably no cases in which
one rule would suffice). We must revise the definition of the
notion 'structural description' accordingly: the structural description will always specify a set of P-markers: P_1 ... P_n (where P_1 =
base P-marker (deep structure) and P_n = final P-marker (surface
structure)).

IV.A.6. Grammatical categories and grammatical functions

Consider the following P-marker (which we assume is (part
of) a base P-marker):

(1)

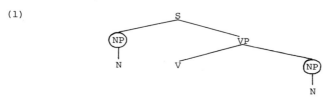

The symbols are grammatical categories. N and V, furthermore, are
lexical category symbols (to which we return in section IV.C.2).
The encircled NP nodes are the subject and object of the sentence.
Grammatical functions are defined in terms of the deep-structure
configurational representation of grammatical categories. Thus the
deep-structure subject is that NP which is immediately dominated
by S, and the deep-structure object that NP which is immediately
dominated by VP. The relations can be represented as follows:

(2)   [NP,S] : subject

      [NP,VP,S] : object

By the same token, such functional notions as 'predicate', 'main
verb', and 'indirect object' can be defined in terms of such structural relations as

(3)   [VP,S] : predicate

      [V,VP,S] : main verb

      [NP,PP,VP,S] : indirect object

In (2) and (3) each category symbol is the only one of its type
generated by the PS-rule rewriting the next category symbol to
the right.

Concentrating now on the notions 'subject' and 'object',
we might consider incorporating them in the PS-rules in the following way:

    1. S ⟶ Subject + VP
    2. VP ⟶ V + Object
    3. Subject ⟶ NP
    4. Object ⟶ NP

These rules would assign the following structure to (1):

    (4)

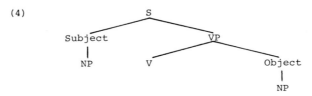

It is argued by TG-linguists that (4) (a) confuses categorial
and functional notions (by defining functions in the same way
as categories (i.e. in terms of the 'is a' relation) and thus
failing to underscore the purely relational character of the
former) and (b) results in needless redundancy (cf. for example
Chomsky, 1965, 68f. and Postal, 1964a, 33ff., 104f.).

    The definition of 'subject' and 'object' formulated in (2)
has occasioned a good deal of discussion, the details of which
we will not go into at this point. We will assume that, given the
distinction between deep and surface structure, (2) is a valid
definition of the two functions[1].

    Before we leave this subject, two further points should be
made: (a) to all intents and purposes, the deep-structure subject of a sentence corresponds to the 'logical subject' of traditional grammar, and (b) the terms 'subject' and 'object' do not
have any independent status in the grammar. They are really only
useful abbreviations for (2) (but see below, p. 508).

IV.A.7. What T-rules do

    In this section we will illustrate the operation of T-rules
by considering some simple (and simplified) examples.
    Let us assume that our grammar contains the following PS-rules:

----

1. Cf. above, p. 11f. The definition of grammatical functions we
   gave in our analysis of (the surface structure of) (16) were
   clearly relational in nature.

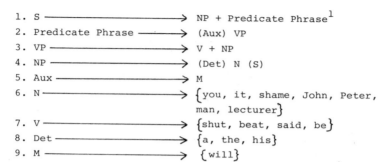

1. S ─────────────────────→ NP + Predicate Phrase[1]
2. Predicate Phrase ──────→ (Aux) VP
3. VP ────────────────────→ V + NP
4. NP ────────────────────→ (Det) N (S)
5. Aux ───────────────────→ M
6. N ─────────────────────→ {you, it, shame, John, Peter, man, lecturer}
7. V ─────────────────────→ {shut, beat, said, be}
8. Det ───────────────────→ {a, the, his}
9. M ─────────────────────→ {will}

where Aux = <u>auxiliary</u> and M = <u>modal verb</u>.

   There is some evidence that the deep structure of an imperative sentence contains the personal pronoun 'you' as subject and
the modal verb 'will'[2]. This being the case, we will assume that
the deep structure of a sentence like

   (1) Shut the door

is as follows:

(1a)

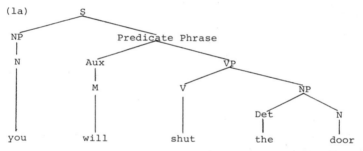

This P-marker may <u>optionally</u> undergo the <u>imperative transforma-</u>
<u>tion</u>. The rule operates in two steps. First 'will' is removed
or <u>deleted</u>. This step results in the following derived P-marker:

----

1. For this symbol, see below, section IV.C.1.
2. One of the arguments supporting this assumption is the fact
   that 'you' and 'will' appear in the <u>tag-questions</u> appended to
   imperative sentences: 'Shut the door, will you'. In later sections the transformations used here for illustrative purposes
   will be dealt with in greater detail.

(1b)

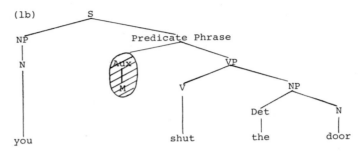

The encircled nodes (which are now nonterminal symbols not dominating a terminal symbol) are eliminated from the tree by a general
<u>tree-pruning convention</u>. The derived P-marker of 'you shut the
door' qualifies as a surface structure. However, it may optionally undergo the second step of the imperative T-rule; this deletes
'you' and results in the following P-marker:

(1c)

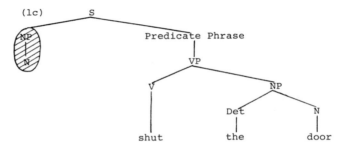

The encircled nodes are pruned from the tree. After this operation
'Predicate Phrase' is the only node under the immediate domination
of S. (1c) is the surface structure of (1).

The imperative T-rule, then, is an example of a <u>deletion
transformation</u>.

T-rules may also <u>insert</u> elements into a deep structure. Only
elements which are relatively empty in meaning may be inserted.
Consider the following sentences:

    (2) John's beating Peter is a shame
    (3) For John to beat Peter is a shame
    (4) That John beats Peter is a shame

The three sentences are identical in cognitive meaning and have the following rough deep structure[1]:

(5)

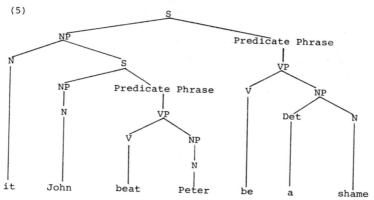

For this deep structure to be converted into a surface structure,
two <u>obligatory</u> T-rules must apply: (a) a <u>complementizer</u> must be
inserted, and (b) 'it' must be deleted[2]. In the present case there
are three possible complementizers: <u>Poss - ing</u>[3] (as in (2)),
<u>for - to</u> (as in (3)), or <u>that</u> (as in (4)). Suppose that we choose
'that'; the surface structure then looks as follows (after the application of it deletion)[4]:

(4a)

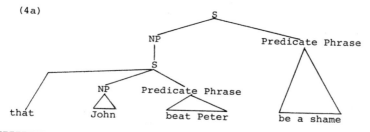

----

1. The PS-rules we have formulated in this section are, of course,
   not detailed enough. For example, rule 3 expands the VP into
   a verb followed by a noun phrase. Thus the grammar does not distinguish between the construction consisting of the verb 'be'
   and a predicative complement and a transitive verb followed by
   an object. In the same way, tense has been disregarded. However,
   in this section we are concerned with general principles, not
   with details.

2. For the presence of 'it' in the deep structure, see next section.

3. That is, a possessive morpheme is affixed to the subject NP and
   'ing' to the verb.

4. Triangles are used as abbreviatory devices: they substitute for
   nodes which are immaterial to the point under discussion.

Further, T-rules may <u>move constituents</u>. To illustrate this,
we return to the derivation of (4a). After the insertion of the
complementizer 'that', but before the deletion of 'it', the rule
of <u>extraposition</u> may optionally apply, moving the embedded sentence to the end of the sentence. The result of this operation
appears from the following P-marker:

(4b)

'It' is left behind, and instead of being deleted, it "takes
over" the role of subject in the sentence.

Finally, T-rules may <u>substitute</u> one element for another. As
an example of this, consider the following sentence:

(6) The man said that he was a lecturer

(6) has the following rough deep structure:

(6a)

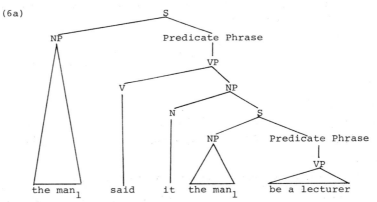

The numerical subscripts assigned to the two noun phrases are <u>ref-
erential indices</u>. They indicate that the two occurrences of the
lexical item 'man' are <u>coreferential</u> in the sense that they refer
to the same entity in the external world (see further below, section IV.D.15). Since they <u>are</u> coreferential (which they need not
have been) the <u>pronominalization rule</u> must obligatorily apply, sub-

stituting 'he' for 'the man' in the embedded sentence. By the
further application of the complementizer insertion rule and it
deletion, (6) is derived.

Observe the distinction between 'optional' and 'obligatory':
in the derivation of a sentence some rules _must_, others _may_ apply. We shall see later that the borderline between 'optional'
and 'obligatory' is theoretically determined.

IV.A.8. On the relationship between PS-rules and T-rules

It should be emphasized that in the process of constructing
a grammar it is by no means <u>a priori</u> given which phenomena should
be handled by the PS-rules and which by the T-rules. To illustrate
this point, let us turn to the rule of extraposition.

Since T-rules have the power to substitute one element for
another, we may ask why the 'it' in sentence (4b) of the preceding
section should be generated by a PS-rule rather than be transformationally substituted for the embedded sentence just in case this
is moved by the extraposition rule (cf. also above, p. 34):

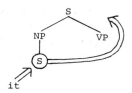

Either solution would seem to be workable. The choice is a purely
empirical issue, and to test the correctness of the assumption
that 'it' is generated by a PS-rule, it is necessary to examine
a wide range of facts. Consider the following sets of sentences:

   (1a) The theory that 'it' should be generated by a PS-rule
        is due to Rosenbaum
   (1b) The theory is due to Rosenbaum that 'it' should be
        generated by a PS-rule
   (2a) The thought that he had let his friend down kept
        bothering him
   (2b) The thought kept bothering him that he had let his
        friend down
   (3a) * It that John gave up the business came as a surprise

(3b) It came as a surprise that John gave up the business

(3c) That John gave up the business came as a surprise

The (b)-sentences suggest that if 'it' is generated in the deep structure, the extraposition rule can be generalized to cover sentences in which the constituent immediately preceding the sentence undergoing extraposition is a lexical noun:

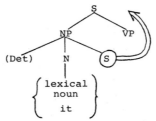

Furthermore, (1) and (2) show that the rule is optional. (3c), then, must be derived by it deletion. This rule is obligatory, as shown by the ungrammaticality of (3a).

It is often the case that evidence from other languages may (dis)confirm a proposed analysis of a given problem (indeed, given the theory of generative grammar, this ought to be the general rule). Consider the following pairs of English and Danish sentences (the (a) and (b) sentences are exact translational equivalents):

(4a) It is nice

(4b) Det er dejligt

(5a) ✲ It to be home again is nice

(5b) (Det) at[1] være hjemme igen er dejligt

(6a) It is nice to be home again

(6b) Det er dejligt at være hjemme igen

(7a) ✲ It that John gave up the business came as a surprise

(7b) (Det) at[1] John opgav forretningen kom som en overraskelse

(8a) It came as a surprise that John gave up the business

(8b) Det kom som en overraskelse at John opgav forretningen

In (5b) and (7b) 'det' (which corresponds to English 'it' (as shown by (6b) and (8b), in which the embedded sentences have been extraposed) may optionally precede the complementizers in surface

----

1. Observe that in Danish there is phonological identity between the complementizers 'that' and 'to': 'at'.

structure. This suggests that in writing a grammar of Danish it
would be natural to opt for the deep structure analysis of 'det'
with a corresponding optional det deletion rule. On the basis of
such evidence, it is perhaps not unreasonable to conclude that the
absence of 'it' from the surface structure of English sentences of
the type considered here is an accidental 'freak' of the language
(but see notes to section IV.G.16).

So far, we have considered extraposition only in relation to
sentences embedded in the subject noun phrase. However, our analysis must also accommodate the facts which appear from the following sentences:

(9a) I take it that you have understood the message
(9b) ✱ I take that you have understood the message
(10a) I hate it that you always contradict me
(10b) ? I hate that you always contradict me
(11) I expect (✱ it) that he will be here soon

Now, the rule which obligatorily deletes 'it' requires as its input the following subpart of a P-marker:

(12)

Given that this is so, how can we account for (9a) and (9b) (and
for (10a) and (10b) (many English speakers find (10b) ungrammatical without 'it'))? By assuming that extraposition applies <u>vacuous-
ly</u> to the deep structure of (9a) (and, perhaps, (10a)). It effects
the following change in the P-markers (we disregard the node
'Predicate Phrase'):

(9c)

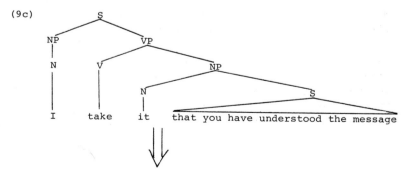

(9d)

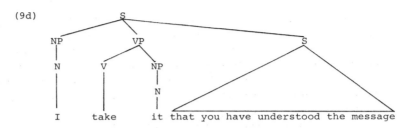

I   take   it that you have understood the message

'It' cannot be deleted from (9d) because there is no longer a subpart of the P-marker corresponding to (12). By contrast, extraposition has not applied to (11). Hence 'it' must be deleted. What
this means is that we would have to make vacuous extraposition
of an object sentence (more precisely a sentence embedded in the
object NP) sensitive to a feature of the verb in the matrix sentence (for such features, see below, section IV.C.2.4). Thus 'take'
would have a feature like, say, (+ Extraposition from object),
whereas 'expect' would have the feature (- Extraposition from object). In other words, whereas exptraposition from a subject NP
is (generally) optional, this is not the case with extraposition
from object: the latter is a governed rule.

    The transformational analysis of 'it' would also have to
tackle sentences like (9a)-(11). One way of doing this would be
to claim that vacuous extraposition from object always applies.
After the application of the rule, 'it' is inserted, but then deleted again after the majority of verbs: the deletion transformation must be made dependent on a feature of the governing verb.

    Vacuous extraposition from object seems to be required by
both approaches in order to account for the facts. It is a somewhat dubious rule in that it does not move the embedded sentence
across any other constituent, but merely changes the constituent
structure of the P-marker to which it applies (cf. Ross, 1967,
99f. and below pp. 382f., 392, note 2).

    We will say no more about extraposition and 'it' now. The
main objective has been to demonstrate that the construction of
grammars must be based on arguments. The arguments in turn must
be based on the observationally accessible facts. The choice which
must be made between the two solutions is - as always - determined
by the evaluation measure. In this case, however, the construction

of such a measure is rather more complicated than in the case considered in section IV.A.3: it involves the examination of a wide
range of data from different languages, and the ascertainment of
what possible consequences the two solutions might have for other
areas of the grammar (for example pronominalization and semantic
interpretation).

Henceforth, we will assume that 'it' is introduced by a PS-
rule.

Notes and some further references

General. PS-grammars are subject to certain formal constraints
which distinguish them from unrestricted rewriting systems. For example, in the rule A ——> B, B must be a nonnull string which is
distinct from, and at least as long as, A. Such constraints are
necessary for two reasons: (1) unrestricted rewriting systems define far too large a class of possible natural languages, and (2)
unrestricted rewriting systems do not provide a natural way of associating a structural description (i.e. a P-marker) with the sentences enumerated by the grammar. For more technical discussions
of the formal properties of grammatical rules, see such works as
Chomsky, 1956, 1959b, 1961a, 1962, and 1963, Postal, 1964a (especially the first three chapters), Gross, 1972, Wall, 1972, and
Bach, 1974. Koutsoudas, 1966 is an excellent introduction to grammar-construction; it contains an instructive set of problems from
a wide range of languages.

IV.A.2. We shall use the term 'lexical item' to refer to the 'abstract' entities underlying words as they are manifested in their
grammatical forms and the phonological realizations of these forms.
In other words, we shall make a threefold distinction between lexical items, grammatical words, and phonological words (cf. Lyons,
1963, 11, 1968, 197, and 1970b, 21f.). This distinction is made
necessary by the fact that in many cases there is no one-to-one
correspondence between lexical items, grammatical words, and phonological words. Consider the following example (we assume that the
past tense and past participle forms of verbs are two grammatical
words even though they are not phonologically distinct; lexical
items are distinguished from grammatical words by the use of capitals):

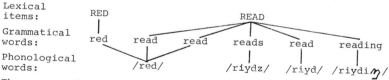

Lexical items:	RED			READ		
Grammatical words:	red	read	read	reads	read	reading
Phonological words:		/red/		/riydz/	/riyd/	/riydiŋ/

There are, then, two lexical items, six grammatical words, and
four phonological words. As a further example of such skewness,
consider the case of idioms. An idiom may be defined as an expression or phrase which is composed of two or more words, but whose

meaning is not the sum of the meanings of the words of which it is
made up. Consider the following sentence:

(1) Linguists had recourse to semantic criteria

In this, 'have recourse to' is an idiom. In terms of our threefold
distinction, it is one lexical item: HAVE RECOURSE TO[1] which consists of three independent grammatical (and phonological) words.
That this is so is proved by the fact that the words of which the
item consists may be separated from each other by certain transformational rules (in particular the passive rule and the interrogative rule):

(2) Recourse was had to semantic criteria by linguists
(3) To what did linguists have recourse

Furthermore, as is evident from the examples, 'have' undergoes inflection in the normal way[2,3]. See also notes to IV.D.4.

IV.A.4. Postal, 1964a is a discussion of the limitations of PS-grammars. In particular, it is shown that taxonomic grammars, had they
been formalized, would, in the majority of cases, be equivalent
to context-free PS-grammars. See also in this connection Postal,
1964b.

IV.A.6. For some discussion of grammatical functions in TG-theory,
see Chomsky, 1965, 68ff., 124ff., Matthews, 1967, Dik, 1968, 147ff.,
Seuren, 1969, Lyons, 1970c, Katz, 1972, 108ff., and Bach, 1974,
259ff. We return to the question of grammatical functions in Chapter V.

IV.B. THE DEVELOPMENT OF TRANSFORMATIONAL-GENERATIVE THEORY -
      AN OVERVIEW

IV.B.1. Introductory remarks

      Since its inception in 1957 with the publication of Syntactic
Structures, TG-theory has undergone major revisions. Some of these
revisions have been so far-reaching as to result in competing theories within the overall goal of generativity. In this section we
will briefly sketch the line of development from 1957 to the present day. Let us take the year 1965 - which saw the publication
of Chomsky's Aspects of the Theory of Syntax - as our point of de-
----

1. Note that RECOURSE does not exist as an independent lexical item
   at all. As against this, consider the words 'kick' and 'bucket'
   of which the idiom KICK THE BUCKET is made up: they both exist
   as independent lexical items. Such independent lexical status
   may, but need not, result in ambiguity. Compare 'he kicked the
   bucket' with 'he took offense'.

2. This is not always the case. Consider the idiom HAD BETTER.

3. In many cases the words by which idioms are realized cannot be

parture and distinguish three phases relative to that year: (1)
before 1965, (2) 1965, and (3) after 1965.

IV.B.2. Before 1965

In this period <u>Syntactic Structures</u> is, of course, the most
important work. We will refer to the theory of TG-grammar embodied
in that work as the <u>SS-model</u> and discuss it briefly under four
headings.

<u>Kernel sentences</u>. Ordered context-sensitive PS-rules generate
a set of terminal strings (with their associated P-markers) underlying simple kernel sentences. Examples of such sentences are[1]:

(1) John is a linguist
(2) John laughs
(3) John read the book
(4) John went away
(5) Beer tastes good

<u>Transformations</u>. The SS-model contains obligatory and optional
T-rules. Each underlying string must undergo a few obligatory T-
rules[2]. If it undergoes no optional rules, it will be converted
into a kernel sentence. There are two kinds of optional T-rules:
<u>singulary</u> and <u>generalized</u>[3]. Singulary T-rules have as their input
the P-marker associated with the underlying string of a <u>single</u>
sentence. Examples are (stated informally):

(6) John is here $\Longrightarrow$ is John here
(7) John is here $\Longrightarrow$ John is not here
(8) John read the book $\Longrightarrow$ the book was read by John

Observe that T-rules may be <u>meaning-changing</u>. This is the case in
(6) and (7). Generalized T-rules operate on <u>two</u> P-markers. They
form <u>conjunctions</u> of sentences (i.e. compound sentences) or <u>embed</u>
one sentence into another. An (informally stated) example of an
embedding transformation is (cf. sentence (3) of section IV.A.4):

----

separated by transformations. Thus 'he kicked the bucket' can
only be passivized and questioned in its nonidiomatic sense.

1. A good elementary introduction to the notion of kernel sentences
is Roberts, 1962.

2. Such as <u>agreement</u> and <u>affix hopping</u> (for these, see below,
sections IV.C.1 and IV.G.2,3).

3. Generalized T-rules are also referred to as <u>double-base</u> T-rules.

(8) Something was difficult $\Big\}$ $\Longrightarrow$
(9) I left John

(10) To leave John was difficult $\Longrightarrow$

(11) $\left\{\begin{array}{l}\text{It was difficult to leave John} \\ \text{John was difficult to leave}^1\end{array}\right\}$

One very essential difference between the SS-model and later versions concerns the recursive power of the grammar: in the SS-model there are no recursive PS-rules. The set of kernel sentences generated by the PS-rules and the obligatory T-rules is finite. The recursive power of the grammar resides exclusively in the transformational component - in particular in the generalized transformations.

Mention should be made of the concept of <u>transformation-markers</u>[2]. They form part of the structural description of a sentence and keep track of the transformational history of the sentence, as it were: they specify what T-rules have applied in the derivation, and in what order.

<u>Semantics</u>. Semantics is not an integrated part of the SS-model. Rather, this is a formalized continuation of the IC-approach typical of American structuralism. However, the organization of a grammar in a PS-component and a transformational component and the concomitant distinction between deep and surface structure (the terms used in <u>Syntactic Structures</u> are 'underlying' and 'derived') makes the model capable of handling phenomena which IC-analysis of surface structures cannot account for - e.g. many kinds of syntactic ambiguity.

<u>Grammaticality</u>. Since semantics is not an integrated part of the theory, "the notion "grammatical" cannot be identified with "meaningful" or "significant" in any semantic sense" (Chomsky, 1957, 15). Consequently, the now famous sentence

(12) Colourless green ideas sleep furiously

is to be regarded as a grammatical sentence. By contrast,

(13) ✹ Furiously sleep ideas green colourless

is ungrammatical (for obvious reasons). Elsewhere in <u>Syntactic</u>

----

1. For further examples, see Lees, 1962.
2. For a detailed example of a transformation-marker, see Chomsky, 1965, 130ff.

<u>Structures</u> Chomsky introduces the notion of "degree of grammati-
calness"[1]. For example, he discusses the relative grammaticality
of such sentences as (14) and (15):

    (14) John admires sincerity

    (15) Sincerity admires John

thus foreshadowing the further development of the theory embodied
in <u>Aspects of the Theory of Syntax</u>[2].

    1963 and 1964 are important years in the history of TG-theory.
In 1963 Katz and Fodor published their famous paper "The Structure of a Semantic Theory". One of the subparts of the paper is
entitled "Linguistic Description Minus Grammar Equals Semantics"
(where 'grammar' = syntax and phonology). This formula is significant in that it (a) recognizes semantics as an integral part of
linguistic description, and (b) underscores the idea that syntax
and semantics, though both part of a grammar, are separate: syntax
is still <u>autonomous</u> (we shall see more precisely how in the next
section). The semantic theory developed in the 1963-paper was designed to meet the requirements of the SS-model of syntax. In 1964
Katz and Postal published <u>An Integrated Theory of Linguistic De-
scriptions</u>. In this work the ideas embodied in the 1963-paper
are further developed. Two points are especially important to take
note of: (1) All optional singulary transformations are removed
from the grammar (e.g. the rules of interrogation, imperativization,
and negation). The application of these rules is made contingent on
the presence in deep structure of such formatives as <u>Q</u>, <u>Imp</u>, and
<u>Neg</u>. These formatives, furthermore, determine the semantic interpre-
tation of the sentences in which they occur. Consequently, all singulary transformations are <u>meaning-preserving</u>. (2) In a few remarks
on p. 67f. the authors align their semantic theory with the new model of syntax which was then being developed by Chomsky and others
(see next section). This model would make it possible to hypothesize
that <u>all</u> transformations are meaning-preserving and that, accord-

----

1. Pp. 42f., 78. See also in this connection Chomsky, 1961b
   (in Allen, H.B., 1964) 186ff.

2. Two important studies within the framework of the SS-model are
   Lees, 1960a and Fillmore, 1963. For an overview of pre-1965
   developments, see Dingwall, 1963.

ingly, <u>semantic interpretation is determined exclusively by deep
structures</u>. Henceforth, we will refer to this hypothesis as the
KP-hypothesis after the names of the authors.

IV.B.3. <u>1965 - the standard theory</u>

In 1965 <u>Aspects</u> was published. In this Chomsky summarizes
the development of TG-theory from its beginning to 1965 and for-
malizes the version of the theory which is now generally referred
to as the <u>standard theory</u> (for this term, see Chomsky, 1972, 66).

The most conspicuous changes are:

(1) The recursive property of the grammar is accounted for
in the PS-rules (in the way we have indicated in section IV.A.2).
In particular, the symbol S can occur on the right side of the arrow in a PS-rule.

(2) As a consequence of (1), there are no generalized T-rules.
T-rules operate <u>cyclically</u> on <u>generalized P-markers</u> (cf. below, section IV.E.7). The epithet 'generalized', then, is shifted from the
T-rules to the PS-rules. The concept 'transformation-marker' is removed from the theory[1].

(3) Kernel sentences have no independent status in the grammar.

(4) The KP-hypothesis is adopted.

We can now illustrate the structure of the standard theory
in terms of the following diagram (see next page):

I is referred to as the <u>base component</u>, III as the <u>transfor-
mational component</u>. I + III constitute the <u>syntactic component</u>.
II is the <u>semantic component</u>, and IV the <u>phonological component</u>.
II and IV are <u>interpretive components</u>: they process the output of
I and III respectively.

It is especially to be noted that there is an <u>autonomous
level of deep syntactic structure</u> which forms the input to the semantic component and which specifies all the grammatical relations
which are necessary for semantic interpretation.

One last point should be made: the postulation of two interpretive components (semantics and phonology) makes explicit - and
provides a theoretical basis for - the arbitrary relation between

----

1. There are, of course, compelling reasons for making these
   changes. For discussion, see Chomsky, 1965, 135ff.

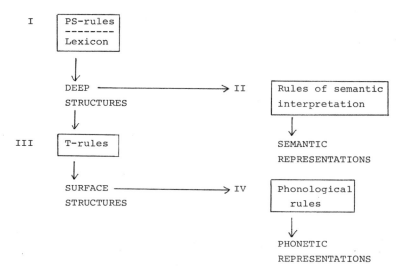

I   PS-rules

      Lexicon

DEEP ————————————→ II   Rules of semantic
STRUCTURES   interpretation

III   T-rules   SEMANTIC
                             REPRESENTATIONS

SURFACE ————————————→ IV   Phonological
STRUCTURES   rules

                             PHONETIC
                             REPRESENTATIONS

sound and meaning discussed in the notes to section III.3 (cf.
Katz and Postal, 1964, 2, 161f.)[1].

The separation of sound from meaning in this sense is common
to all versions of TG-theory.

IV.B.4. After 1965 - generative semantics - the extended standard theory - case grammar

It has been said about the standard theory that it is "self-
destructive" (Seuren, 1972, 247). The reason for this is to be
sought in the KP-hypothesis: if the grammatical relations specified in the deep structure of sentences uniquely determine semantic interpretation, it is necessary in a number of cases to set
up much deeper deep structures than envisaged in the standard theory. Such deep deep structures strongly resemble abstract representations of the meaning of sentences. If this line of argument is
pursued to its logical terminus, the result is generative semantics. This means, essentially, that underlying structures and
semantic representations are identical. The structure of a gram-
----

1. Consult also McNeill, 1970, 120 for some comments on the possible connection between the arbitrary sound-meaning relation
   and the relatively slow course of lexical development in language acquisition.

mar, according to the generative semanticist position, is roughly
as follows:

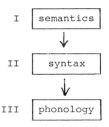

Proponents of generative semantics are scholars like Lakoff,
McCawley, and Postal[1].

A different version of TG-theory is the extended standard
theory (for the term, see Chomsky, 1972, 134). If we return for
a moment to the diagram of the preceding section, we can illustrate the main tenets of the extended standard theory by adding a
line between SURFACE STRUCTURES and 'rules of semantic interpretation'. That is, semantic interpretation is determined by the pair
$P_1 \ldots P_n$, not by deep structure alone. This is the position held
by Chomsky until recently[2]. The fullest account of the extended
standard theory (or the interpretivist position[3]) is Jackendoff,
1972.

Finally, mention must be made of the theory of case grammar
developed by Fillmore and others. Case grammar has much in common
with generative semantics: it too results in more abstract deep
structures than those postulated in the (extended) standard theory.

The rest of Chapter IV will, in all essentials, be an exposition of the standard theory. The extended standard theory, case
grammar, and generative semantics will be taken up in Chapter V.

----

1. Observe that Postal no longer adheres to the semantic theory
   outlined in Katz and Postal, 1964. By contrast, the standard
   theory is still advocated by Katz (see especially Katz, 1972).

2. See the papers "Deep Structure, Surface Structure and Semantic
   Interpretation" and "Some Empirical Issues in the Theory of
   Transformational Grammar" in the 1972-volume. Recently, Chomsky
   has proposed that semantic interpretation is determined entirely
   by surface structure. Cf. below, p. 488.

3. As against the deep structure interpretivist position of the
   standard theory.

IV.C. THE BASE COMPONENT

IV.C.1. A set of PS-rules for English

We must now try to set up some of the PS-rules necessary for the generation of infinite set of base P-markers for T-rules to operate on. It should be apparent from what has been said so far that as long as such rules meet certain formal requirements specified in the general theory of language, there is no absolute yardstick against which the "correctness" of the rules can be measured. They must always be considered in relation to the other components of the grammar (in particular the transformational and semantic components) and their validation is an entirely empirical issue.

Let us first state the rules and then proceed to discuss them in some detail.

1. $S \longrightarrow \left\{ \begin{matrix} and \\ or \end{matrix} \right\} S^n, \; n \geq 2^1$

2. $S \longrightarrow$ (Presentence) Nucleus

3. Presentence $\longrightarrow \left(\left\{ \begin{matrix} Q \\ Imp \end{matrix} \right\} \right)$ (Neg) (Emp)

4. Nucleus $\longrightarrow$ (Sentence Adv) NP + Predicate Phrase

5. Predicate Phrase $\longrightarrow$ Aux + VP (Adv_{place}) (Adv_{time})

6. $VP \longrightarrow \left\{ \begin{matrix} be \left\{ \begin{matrix} NP \\ AP \\ Adv_{place} \\ Adv_{time} \end{matrix} \right\} \\ V \; (NP) \; (PP) \; (Adv_{place}) \; (Adv_{direction}) \\ \quad (Adv_{duration}) \; (Adv_{frequency}) \; (Adv_{manner}) \; (S) \end{matrix} \right\}$

7. $Adv_x^2 \longrightarrow \left\{ \begin{matrix} PP \\ NP \\ S \\ \triangle \end{matrix} \right\}$

8. $AP \longrightarrow (Adv_{degree}) \; Adj \; \left(\left\{ \begin{matrix} PP \\ S \end{matrix} \right\} \right)$

----

1. ≥ 2 = 'no less than two'.
2. Where x is an ad-hoc abbreviation for different types of adverbs.

9. $\text{Adv}_{\text{degree}} \longrightarrow \left\{ \begin{array}{l} \left\{ \begin{array}{l} \text{less-than} \\ \text{more-than} \\ \text{as-as} \end{array} \right\} \text{S} \\ \\ \triangle \end{array} \right\}$

10. PP $\longrightarrow$ Prep + NP

11. NP $\longrightarrow \left\{ \begin{array}{l} \text{and} + \text{NP}^n, \ n \geqslant 2 \\ \text{NP} + \text{S} \\ \text{(Det) N} + \text{No} \ \left(\left\{ \begin{array}{l} \text{PP} \\ \text{S} \end{array} \right\} \right) \end{array} \right\}$

12. Aux $\longrightarrow$ T (M) (have + en) (be + ing)

13. T $\longrightarrow \left\{ \begin{array}{l} \text{Present} \\ \text{Past} \end{array} \right\}$

14. Det $\longrightarrow \left\{ \begin{array}{l} \text{Definite} \\ \text{Indefinite} \end{array} \right\}$

15. No $\longrightarrow \left\{ \begin{array}{l} \text{Sing} \\ \text{Plur} \end{array} \right\}$

16. L $\longrightarrow \triangle$

(where L = V, N, M, Adj, Prep, Definite, and Indefinite)

The rules are all <u>context-free</u> and <u>unordered</u> (i.e. they are not extrinsically ordered).

Rule 1 is a <u>rule schema</u>. It asserts that S can be expanded into any number of S's (minimally two). <u>Mutatis mutandis</u>, the same applies to the first option in rule 11. We return to rule schemata in the section on coordination (IV.G.13.1).

Rule 2 expands S into two constituents (the first of which is optional). 'Presentence', as defined in rule 3, is needed to account for interrogative, imperative, negative, and emphatic sentences. Rule 3 should be interpreted as follows: Q and Imp are mutually exclusive (as is always the case with symbols included in braces). The three parentheses specify that all three, any pair, or any one of the symbols may be chosen.

Rule 4 expands the sentence nucleus. We will assume that sentence adverbs are the kind of adverbs which occur in the following sentences (for a corrective, see below, section IV.G.9.3):

(1) $\left\{ \begin{array}{l} \text{Evidently} \\ \text{Fortunately} \\ \text{From my point of view} \end{array} \right\}$, it was a success

Rule 5 introduces locative and temporal adverbs. An example would be:

(2) They played football <u>in the garden</u> <u>yesterday</u>

Note that rule 7 defines Adv as a prepositional phrase, a noun phrase, a sentence (i.e. an adverbial clause), or a lexical item ($\triangle$ being a dummy symbol for lexical items - we return to that in section IV.C.2). An example of an adverbial noun phrase is

(3) I saw him <u>this morning</u>

Further, rule 5 introduces <u>the auxiliary</u>. This category in turn is expanded by rule 12. The rule asserts that the only obligatory element is Tense (Present or Past (as shown by rule 13)). The reason why T precedes all the other elements is that it must invariably be attached to whatever is chosen first (if none of the optional elements is chosen, it must be attached to the main verb (V or 'be' in rule (6))). 'en' is a cover symbol for the <u>past participle</u> morpheme, whether this is ultimately realized as /id/ (as in 'wanted'), /n/ (as in 'driven'), /t/ (as in 'wished'), Ø (as in 'cut'), etc. 'en' is included in the same parenthesis as 'have' because 'have' conditions it; in the same way 'ing' is conditioned by 'be'. Thus the surface structure string 'has been driving' is derived from 'Present + have + en + be + ing + drive' by <u>affix hopping</u> (cf. section IV.G.3) in roughly the following way:

This derivation makes it explicit that 'have' and 'en', and 'be' and 'ing' are discontinuous constituents in surface structure. Rule 12 is one of the most celebrated formulae in TG-theory. It was first introduced by Chomsky (1957, 38ff.). With the further development of TG-theory, the formula has been subjected to a good deal of criticism. In particular, a number of arguments have been presented in support of the hypothesis that auxiliaries (including Tense) should be analysed as main verbs. We will not go into the details of these arguments here, but merely note that such an analysis would eliminate categories like Aux and M from the grammar. This in turn would simplify deep structures and make them look more 'universal'.

We turn now to rule 6. Observe first of all that the rule distinguishes the verb 'be' from all other verbs (V). The reason for this is that 'be' may behave in the same way as auxiliary verbs under transformations. We can illustrate this by such sentences as

(4) John is my friend
(5) John is not my friend
(6) Is John my friend
(7) John has read the book
(8) John has not read the book
(9) Has John read the book
(10) John is reading
(11) John is not reading
(12) Is John reading
(13) John can do this
(14) John cannot do this
(15) Can John do this
(16) John smokes
(17) John does not smoke
(18) * John smokes not
(19) Does John smoke
(20) * Smokes John

We are interested in the principles governing the formation of negative and interrogative sentences. It is clear from the examples, and in particular the ungrammaticality of (18) and (20), that we must split up the relevant rules in two subparts: one in which the main verb either is 'be' preceded by no auxiliary verb(s) or any verb (including 'be'[1]) preceded by one (or more) auxiliary verb(s), and one in which the main verb (any verb except 'be') is preceded by no auxiliary verb(s). Informally, the principles involved can be illustrated in the following way (cf. below, section IV.G.4):

(21a) Negative: NP + Tense $\left\{\begin{array}{l} M \\ have \\ be \end{array}\right\}$ ⇑ + Y
                                                    not

(21b) Interrogative: ⇑ NP + Tense $\left\{\begin{array}{l} M \\ have \\ be \end{array}\right\}$ + Y

----

1. As appears from such sentences as 'John is being fair'/'John is

(22a) Negative: NP + Tense + V + Y
                           do / not inserted

(22b) Interrogative: do — NP + Tense + V + Y

(21a) through (22b) are nonterminal strings (the nonterminal symbols dominate terminal symbols). In (21a) 'not' is inserted <u>after</u>
Tense + one of the relevant verbs. In (21b) Tense + one of the
relevant verbs are moved to the left of the subject (the NP in the
strings being that NP which is immediately dominated by S in the
P-marker). In (22a), however, 'not' is inserted <u>between</u> Tense and
V. Consequently, Tense is left "floating" in the string and must
be supported by the dummy 'do'. Finally, in (22b) Tense is moved
to the left of the subject, leaving V behind. In its new position
Tense is "floating" again and must receive do support.

There is ample reason, then, for distinguishing between 'be'
and V (thus aligning 'be' with the auxiliaries as much as with
the 'ordinary' verbs). But this is not the whole story: our grammar generates 'be' as a deep-structure element and it is highly
debatable whether this is reasonable (i.e., more precisely, descriptively adequate). It could be argued that 'be' in a sentence
like

(23) Jane is a widow

has been transformationally inserted to support the "floating"
tense morpheme in the string NP + Present + NP. 'Be', then, would
have much the same function as 'do' in (22a) and (22b). This argument receives substantial empirical support from the fact that
there are many languages in which there is no element at all between the two NPs in a sentence like (23). In other words, it is
an idiosyncratic property of some languages that they require
the overt expression of Present in such cases[1].

The last point to be made about 'be' is that it has several

----

not being fair'/'Is John being fair'/'John can be there'/'John
cannot be there'/'Can John be there'

1. Note that this is true only of Present, not Past: Present is
<u>unmarked</u> in this respect (for the term 'unmarked', see next
page). 'Be' is frequently analysed as being transformationally
inserted. See for example Jacobs and Rosenbaum, 1968. For general discussion, consult Lyons, 1968, 322ff.

different semantic functions (in the sense that it 'signals' different semantic relations between the subject and the complement).
This appears quite clearly from the following examples:

(24) John is foolish

(25) John is a lecturer

(26) Charles Dickens is the author of Hard Times

(27) The result was a failure[1]

(28) Some people were still at table

(29) Tea will be in an hour

(30) The tendency to suppress the freedom of the press is
     more dangerous

(31) More dangerous is the tendency to suppress the freedom
     of the press

In (24) and (25) the constituent following 'be' (AP and NP respectively) characterizes the subject. This is the attributive function of 'be'. In (26) 'be' has an identificatory or equative
function. Semantically, it has much the same value as an equation
mark in mathematics. Observe that equative 'be' can be diagnosed
by the reversibility of the two NPs[2]:

(32) The author of Hard Times is Charles Dickens

(27) is clearly ambiguous between the attributive and equative functions of 'be'. (28) and (29) illustrate the existential function
of 'be'. In English, existential 'be' must usually be followed by
a locative or temporal adverbial complement[3] (cf. below, section
IV.G.8). (31), which is not defined by the PS-rules, is derived
transformationally from (30) by thematic fronting of the attributive
predicative AP. Of the two sentences, (31) is marked, (30) unmarked
(for the concept of markedness, see notes to this section).

     The second part of rule 6 defines a number of possible struc-
tures of the verb phrase. The optional NP immediately following V
distinguishes transitive and intransitive verbs. Note that the
rule does not provide for two successive NPs after V. In other words,

----

1. The verb 'be' is discussed in detail in Halliday, 1967 a and b.
   Example (27) is borrowed from Halliday. See also Lyons, 1968,
   388ff.

2. For discussion of this point, see Huddleston, 1971, 134ff.

3. There is at least one well-known exception to this, namely the
   sentence 'God is'. Observe that this sentence is not generated
   by our rules: all constituents following 'be' are obligatory.

a sentence like

    (33) I gave John a book

in which 'John' is the indirect object, must be derived by a T-rule
from

    (34) I gave a book to John

The structure underlying (34) _is_ defined by the rule (the PP) (cf.
section IV.G.5). The optional S provides a possibility of embedding
a sentence under the immediate domination of VP.

    The many different types of adverbs specified in the rules call
for special comment. First it should be emphasized that adverbs constitute one of the most complex areas of English syntax. In a TG-
grammar, there are, in principle, two ways of dealing with adverbs:
(a) they can be generated in deep structure, or (b) they can be
generated by T-rules. Both approaches are legitimate and the choice
between them is an empirical issue. Obviously, we have opted for
(a), thus following in the main the standard theory[1]. It is clear,
however, that our rules are largely ad-hoc. In particular, a symbol
like, say, $Adv_{duration}$ ascribes categorial status to what is essentially a functional notion. Furthermore, optionally converting the
various adverbs into PPs (which are 'true' categories) is a makeshift
device for providing each PP with a functional definition. The reason
why this is necessary is that the different kinds of adverbs (unlike
such notions as 'subject of' and 'object of', etc.) can simply not
be defined in relational terms: there may be more than one adverb
under the immediate domination of a node[2]. It should also be noted
that the proper generation of adverbial prepositional phrases causes
some difficulties. Consider the following configurations:

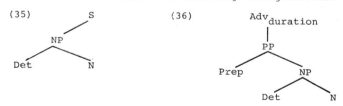

----

1. Perhaps some adverbs should be generated in deep structure, others
by T-rules. For some discussion, see Chomsky, 1965, 218f.

2. The only way to avoid this would be to set up as many different
nodes in deep-structure trees as there are types of adverbials.
Such nodes would be entirely arbitrary (cf. next page).

In (35) the categorial symbol NP imposes no constraints on the
strings of lexical items which it dominates. In (36), however,
the set of permitted prepositional phrases is strictly limited.
This limitation, of course, is due to the label 'duration'. Consequently, some formal way of stating this limitation must be de-
vised. We will not go into this problem (for some discussion, see
Chomsky, 1965, 89, 215 and Fillmore, 1966a (in Reibel and Schane,
1969) 362, and 1968 (in Bach and Harms, 1968) 16). Note that Adv_{time}
and Adv_{place} occur at different points in the rules. The temporal
and locative adverbs introduced by rule 5 occur freely with verbs -
that is, there are no restrictions of cooccurrence between the adverb and the verb (for an example, see sentence (2) above). The
existence of such freely occurring adverbs is one of the reasons
for setting up a separate - intuitively well motivated - node
Predicate Phrase, which makes it explicit that the adverb modifies
the whole VP independently of the verb (cf. Chomsky, 1965, 102)[1]:

(37)   Predicate Phrase

              Aux   VP   Adv

The locative adverb introduced by rule 6 will be discussed in the
section on passive sentences (IV.G.7.1). In general, the types of
adverbs defined by the second part of rule 6 are related to V by
a number of cooccurrence restrictions. We return to this point in
section IV.C.2.2. The following tree, then, defines the different
configurational possibilities with respect to adverbs:

(38)   S
                              |
                           Nucleus

          Adv   NP   Predicate Phrase

                          Aux   VP   Adv

                               V   Adv

T-rules may move adverbs. We shall discuss the <u>adverb preposing</u>
<u>rule</u> at various points.

    Rule 11 expands the noun phrase. Note especially that S may
be embedded in two different ways. The first of these defines rel-
----
1. In addition to this, (37) captures the cooccurrence restrictions
   holding between the aspectual form of the verb and certain ad-

ative clauses. Repeated recursion may result in two different
structures:

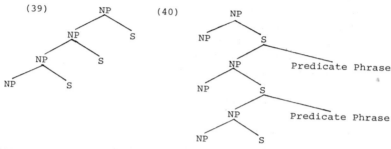

(39) provides for the <u>stacking up</u> of relative clauses, (40) for
self-embedded relative clauses (cf. below, section IV.G.14.5 and
above, section II.5). The second way of embedding S defined by
the rule results in such sentences as those discussed in section
IV.A.8. Here, too, repeated recursion results in self-embedding.
An example would be (cf. below, section IV.E.9):

> (41) That that my mother drinks so much doesn't worry my
>   father is beyond me

Rule 8 defines the <u>adjective phrase</u>. The S in the rule is
related to the S in rule 6 and the S optionally following No in
rule 11 (cf. section IV.G.16.3).

Rule 9, which expands the optional constituent Adv_{degree}
introduced by rule 8, contains yet another S. This is relevant to
the generation of <u>comparative sentences</u> (cf. below, section IV.G.12).

The category PP is introduced at various points. Observe that
a prepositional phrase is not necessarily defined as adverbial.
Thus the PP in rule 11 accounts for such structures as that illustrated by (7a) in section IV.A.2. As we go along, we shall have
more to say about prepositional phrases. In particular, we shall see
that various arguments can be adduced in support of the hypothesis
that they should be introduced by T-rules rather than by PS-rules.

A few remarks should be made about the lexical category symbols - in particular V and Adj. Consider the following sentences:

> (42) He rejoiced at my recovery

----

verbials. Cf. such sentences as 'I have not heard from her since
Easter'/'✱ I didn't hear from her since Easter'/'He has been
sleeping since yesterday'/'✱ He slept since yesterday'.

(43) He was happy about my recovery

(44) He feared the critics

(45) He was afraid of the critics

(46) John is handsome

(47) * John is being handsome

(48) John knows his grammar

(49) * John is knowing his grammar

(50) John mows the lawn

(51) John is mowing the lawn

(52) John is silly

(53) John is being silly

The sentences show that adjectives and verbs have many points of
similarity. Thus the only difference between 'rejoice' and 'happy' in (42) and (43) - the two sentences are identical in cognitive
meaning - is that 'happy' must obligatorily be preceded by the
tense-carrier 'be'. The same factor distinguishes (44) and (45).
However, in addition to this, 'fear' and 'afraid' are further
differentiated by the fact that the noun phrase following 'afraid'
must be preceded by a preposition, whereas this is not the case
with 'fear' (cf. 'rejoice'). (46) through (53) reveal another feature common to adjectives and verbs: they both fall into two sub-
classes: stative and nonstative (or dynamic). Stative verbs cannot
take the progressive aspect, as shown by the ungrammaticality of
(49). The ungrammaticality of (47) indicates that the same restriction applies to adjectives like 'handsome'. (50)-(53) show that
'silly' differs from 'handsome' in the same way as 'mow' differs
from 'know'[1]. On the basis of such syntactic evidence (and more
of the same kind) some scholars (notably Lakoff, 1970a, 115ff.,
but see also Lyons, 1966a) have argued that deep down verbs and
adjectives are the same category. To the extent that such an
analysis can be corroborated by empirical evidence from a wide
range of different languages, a category like, say, VERB would
become a likely candidate for admission to the vocabulary of the
universal grammar[2].

----

1. The stative/nonstative distinction is relevant also to nouns.
   Consider the following sentences: 'John is an engineer'/* John
   is being an engineer'/'John is a gentleman'/'John is being a
   gentleman'.

2. This would provide a formally motivated corroboration of the

In this exposition a somewhat more conservative approach is
adopted: adjectives and verbs are distinguished in terms of categorial symbols (compare in this connection for example Jacobs and
Rosenbaum, 1968 (especially, p. 63ff.)). However, for the purpose
of the discussion in section IV.D, it will be convenient to give
terminological recognition to the similarity between verbs and
adjectives (and between these two categories and nouns) at this
point. Consider the following sentences:

(54) John smokes
(55) The man read the book
(56) John is a professor
(57) John lent Peter his lawn-mower
(58) Pamela was virtuous
(59) The virtuous Pamela was finally rewarded

Henceforth, the term predicate will be used to refer to lexical
items which have the same syntactic functions as the items underscored in the sample sentences. Two points are particularly to be
noted about this terminology: (a) 'Predicate' is used less inclu-
sively than is frequently the case in traditional grammar; thus,
in (57), 'predicate' refers only to the verb, not to the direct
and indirect object. (b) The characterization of 'virtuous' in
(59) as a predicate reflects a hypothesis about a certain relationship between (58) and (59) (cf. below, section IV.G.14.4 and
above, section III.8).

Let us conclude this section by having the PS-rules generate
the following sentence:

(60) The journalist interviewed the author of the pamphlet

(the left-most numbers indicate the stages in the derivation, the
numbers in parenthesis the rule operating on the preceding string):

1.   S
2.   (3)   Nucleus
3.   (4)   NP + Predicate Phrase
4.   (5)   NP + Aux + VP
5.   (6)   NP + Aux + V + NP
6.   (11) Det + N + No + Aux + V + NP

----

logico-semantically based analyses of Jespersen, the Port-
Royal grammarians, and - ultimately - Aristotle.

7. (11) Det + N + No + Aux + V + Det + N + No + PP

8. (10) Det + N + No + Aux + V + Det + N + No + Prep + NP

9. (11) Det + N + No + Aux + V + Det + N + No + Prep +
Det + N + No

10. (12) Det + N + No + T + V + Det + N + No + Prep + Det +
N + No

11. (13) Det + N + No + Past + V + Det + N + No + Prep + Det +
N + No

12. (14) Definite + N + No + Past + V + Det + N + No + Prep +
+ Det + N + No

13. (14) Definite + N + No + Past + V + Definite + N + No +
Prep + Det + N + No

14. (14) Definite + N + No + Past + V + Definite + N + No +
Prep + Definite + N + No

15. (15) Definite + N + Sing + Past + V + Definite + N + No +
+ Prep + Definite + N + No

16. (15) Definite + N + Sing + Past + V + Definite + N +
Sing + Prep + Definite + N + No

17. (15) Definite + N + Sing + Past + V + Definite + N +
Sing + Prep + Definite + N + Sing

18. (16) △ + N + Sing + Past + V + Definite + N + Sing +
Prep + Definite + N + Sing

19. (16) △ + N + Sing + Past + V + △ + N + Sing + Prep +
Definite + N + Sing

20. (16) △ + N + Sing + Past + V + △ + N + Sing + Prep +
△ + N + Sing

21. (16) △ + △ + Sing + Past + V + △ + N + Sing + Prep +
△ + N + Sing

22. (16) △ + △ + Sing + Past + V + △ + △ + Sing + Prep +
△ + N + Sing

23. (16) △ + △ + Sing + Past + V + △ + △ + Sing + Prep +
△ + △ + Sing

24. (16) △ + △ + Sing + Past + △ + △ + △ + Sing + Prep +
△ + △ + Sing

25. (16) △ + △ + Sing + Past + △ + △ + △ + Sing + △ +
△ + △ + Sing

By applying to this derivation the algorithm defined in section
IV.A.2, we can assign the following P-marker to (60):

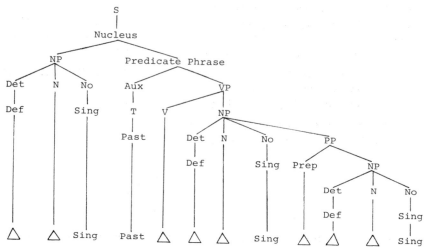

So far we have referred to the last string of a derivation
as the terminal string. We must now draw a distinction between <u>pre-
terminal strings</u> and <u>terminal strings</u> (cf. Chomsky, 1965, 84).
25 is a preterminal string. It consists of a number of <u>grammatical
formatives</u> plus dummy symbols. After the appropriate lexical items
have replaced the dummy symbols, the preterminal string becomes
a terminal string[1].

IV.C.2. The lexicon

IV.C.2.1. The lexicon in the SS-model

Let us begin by comparing the PS-grammar of section IV.A.7
with that of the preceding section. The main difference between
them (apart from the obvious difference in degree of detail) is
that the former introduces lexical items by PS-rules of the following nature:

    N ———⟶ {boy, girl, book, etc.}
    V ———⟶ {watch, drive, kill, etc.}

whereas the latter converts lexical category symbols into a dummy symbol.

Introduction of lexical items by PS-rules is characteristic
----
1. We shall see in section IV.G.17.2 that the derivation of (60)
   suggested here may well turn out to be incorrect.

of the SS-model. Now, a TG-grammar, like any other grammar, must
subclassify, or <u>subcategorize</u>, lexical items. How can this be accomplished? Let us restrict the attention to nouns. In traditional
grammar nouns are subclassified according to such notions as

(1) <u>Proper</u> versus <u>Common</u>, <u>Abstract</u> versus <u>Concrete</u>, <u>Countable</u>
versus <u>Mass</u>, <u>Animate</u> versus <u>Inanimate</u>, <u>Human</u> versus
<u>Nonhuman</u>, <u>Masculine</u>, <u>Feminine</u>, or <u>Neuter</u>, etc.

Consider now once again the nature of a P-marker like

(2)

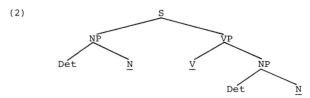

in which the underscored nodes are lexical category symbols. The P-
marker illustrates a principle of <u>hierarchical inclusion</u>. This
principle can, as we have seen, be stated in terms of the "is a"-
relation. Suppose now that we wanted to account for the subcategorizational notions of (1) in terms of PS-rules. We would then be assuming that the principle of hierarchichal inclusion could be continued below the lexical category symbols of a P-marker like (2).
To make this explicit, we would need rules of the following type:

(3) 1. N $\longrightarrow$ $\begin{Bmatrix} \text{N Proper} \\ \text{N Common} \end{Bmatrix}$

2. N Proper $\longrightarrow$ $\begin{Bmatrix} \text{N Proper, Animate} \\ \text{N Proper, Inanimate} \end{Bmatrix}$

3. N Common $\longrightarrow$ $\begin{Bmatrix} \text{N Common, Animate} \\ \text{N Common, Inanimate} \end{Bmatrix}$

4. N Proper, Animate $\longrightarrow$ $\begin{Bmatrix} \text{N Proper, Animate, Human} \\ \text{N Proper, Animate, Nonhuman} \end{Bmatrix}$

5. N Common, Animate $\longrightarrow$ $\begin{Bmatrix} \text{N Common, Animate, Human} \\ \text{N Common, Animate, Nonhuman} \end{Bmatrix}$

etc.

These rules would assign the following hierarchical <u>paths</u> to such
nouns as 'London', 'Fido', 'Peter', 'boy', 'lion', and 'stone'
(where P = Proper, C = Common, I = Inanimate, and A = Animate):

(4)

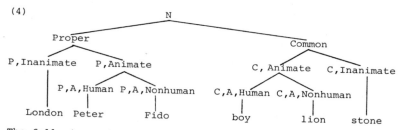

The following points can be made about this way of handling subcategorization:

(a) The five rules we have stated are obviously only a tiny fragment of the full set of rules which would be required to account for the complex network of relations into which even the relatively small set of subcategorizational notions listed in (1) enter. The total number of PS-rules will be enormous.

(b) The choice of the top of the hierarchy is arbitrary. We might equally well have chosen the following way of expanding N:

(5) 1. N $\longrightarrow$ $\begin{Bmatrix} \text{N Animate} \\ \text{N Inanimate} \end{Bmatrix}$

2. N Animate $\longrightarrow$ $\begin{Bmatrix} \text{N Animate, Human} \\ \text{N Animate, Nonhuman} \end{Bmatrix}$

3. N Animate, Human $\longrightarrow$ $\begin{Bmatrix} \text{N Animate, Human, Proper} \\ \text{N Animate, Human, Common} \end{Bmatrix}$

etc.

(c) Rules like 4 and 5 of (3) specify such subcategories as 'Proper, Animate, Human Noun' and 'Common, Animate, Human Noun'. It is immediately obvious that these subcategories have much in common. Yet the formalism of PS-grammars defines them as totally unrelated: they are introduced by two different rules and therefore, in principle, have as little in common as, say, N and V. This is counter-intuitive.

(d) Suppose that the application of a certain T-rule is contingent on the opposition between Human and Nonhuman nouns. Then, for this to be made explicit, the rule must be formulated in such a way that it refers also to the distinction between Animate and Inanimate nouns and between Proper and Common nouns (cf. (4)). A generalization is missing. The trouble here is that the PS-formalism provides no natural way of handling cross-cutting classifications.

For these reasons, subcategorization by way of PS-rules is
inadequate.

The dummy symbol which was introduced in section IV.C.1 and
referred to again at the beginning of this section forms an integral part of the major revisions which subcategorization underwent in Aspects of the Theory of Syntax. To these we now turn.

IV.C.2.2. Features

In Aspects lexical items are defined as bundles of phonological, syntactic, and semantic features. In this section we are
chiefly interested in syntactic features[1]. They can be subdivided
as follows:

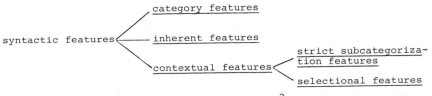

Examples of category features are $(+ V)$[2], $(+ N)$, and $(+ Adj)$.
It will be apparent that these features match the lexical category
symbols generated by the PS-rules.

Next we turn to inherent features (of which the category features form a subset). Let us concentrate on nouns. If we reconsider
the features listed in (1) of the preceding section, it is clear
that many of them are binary in the sense that they may be characterized in terms of + or - with respect to a certain feature. Thus
the opposition between Proper and Common can be stated as $(\pm Common)$,
i.e. any noun having the feature (- Common) is a proper noun. Further examples are $(\pm Abstract)$, $(\pm Animate)$, $(\pm Human)$, and
$(\pm Countable)$. Some of the features are hierarchically interrelated
in the sense that a feature X may logically imply a feature Y. For
example, in (1) and (2), a implies b and c:

----

1. Semantic and phonological features will be taken up in sections
   IV.D. and IV.F.

2. Strictly speaking, syntactic features should be included in
   brackets. For practical reasons, I shall use parentheses in
   many cases.

	a	b	c
(1)	(+ Human)	(+ Animate)	(- Abstract)
(2)	(+ Abstract)	(- Animate)	(- Human)

In other words, the lexicon must contain <u>redundancy rules</u> of the following kind[1]:

(3) (+ Human) $\longrightarrow$ $\begin{bmatrix} - \text{ Abstract} \\ + \text{ Animate} \\ + \text{ Human} \end{bmatrix}$

(4) (+ Abstract) $\longrightarrow$ $\begin{bmatrix} - \text{ Human} \\ - \text{ Animate} \\ + \text{ Abstract} \end{bmatrix}$

As a further example, consider the following matrix (redundant features are marked $\oplus$ and $\ominus$):

(5)	girl	Ann	dog	justice
N	+	+	+	+
Common	+	-	+	+
Countable	$\oplus$	$\ominus$	$\oplus$	-
Abstract	$\ominus$	$\ominus$	$\ominus$	+
Animate	$\oplus$	$\oplus$	$\oplus$	$\ominus$
Human	+	+	-	$\ominus$

Other features, however, are not hierarchically related. Consider for example the relationship between (± Human) and (± Masculine) as illustrated in

(6) (+ Human) (+ Masculine) ('boy','man', etc.)
(7) (+ Human) (- Masculine) ('girl', 'woman', etc.)
(8) (- Human) (+ Masculine) ('stallion', 'bull', etc.)
(9) (- Human) (- Masculine) ('mare', 'bitch', etc.)[2]

It is clear, then, that the specification of lexical items in terms of features provides a way of distinguishing between hierarchical and cross-classificational relations. In other words, it is now possible to refer to the class of Human nouns or the class of Nonhuman nouns without invoking other, irrelevant fea-

----

1. To the extent that such redundancy rules are of universal application (i.e. specify relations among features which may be assumed to be substantive universals) they should be stated in the universal grammar rather than in the grammar of L.

2. It should be noted, of course, that the two features under discussion are not sufficient to distinguish the lexical items given as examples.

tures.

The third type of features are strict subcategorization features. They are contextual in the sense that they specify the structural frames into which lexical items may be inserted. The sentence

(10) * He resembles

is ungrammatical because 'resemble' has the strict subcategorization feature (+ __ NP). The feature asserts that 'resemble' can only be inserted in a P-marker in which VP immediately dominates NP[1,2] (for lexical insertion, see next section). Consider next

(11) * He put the book
(12) * He put on the shelf
(13) He put the book on the shelf

The ungrammaticality of (11) and (12) shows that 'put' must be strictly subcategorized as follows (+ __ NP, Adv_{place}). This brings us back to the different types of adverbs immediately dominated by VP (cf. PS-rule 6). The cooccurrence restrictions holding between verbs and adverbs can be stated in terms of strict subcategorization features. Thus verbs like 'last' and 'word' might have the features (+ __ —— ($Adv_{duration}$)) and (+ __ NP, Adv_{manner}) respectively. These would account for the following sentences:

(14) Their friendship lasted
(15) The lecture lasted for three hours
(16) * The lecture lasted three times a day
(17) John worded the letter meticulously
(18) * John worded the letter
(19) * John worded
(20) * John worded the letter for five hours

In other words, 'last' can either occur without an adverb or else only with an adverb of duration, whereas 'word' is obligatorily followed by an object and an adverb of manner. Strict subcategorization features are <u>local</u> in the following sense: given a lexical category symbol X immediately dominated by the nonterminal symbol

----

1. The feature, then, defines a transitive verb. An intransitive verb might be defined in terms of the feature (+ __ ——).

2. In <u>Aspects</u>, strict subcategorization features are also considered to be binary. For reasons of simplicity, we shall not adopt this approach.

Y, X is strictly subcategorized with respect to other categories
immediately dominated by Y and none other. The features are especially important in the subclassification of verbs. However, they
are relevant to nouns as well. Consider the distinction between
proper nouns and common nouns. Common nouns may cooccur with a
determiner, which proper nouns may not. This can be stated in
terms of the following strict subcategorization features (+ Det __)
and (+ ——— __)[1]. Furthermore, certain abstract nouns may be followed by a sentence. Again, this can be expressed by a strict subcategorization feature: (+ Det __ (S))[2].

   There remain the selectional features. These are attributes
of predicates (as defined in section IV.C.1). Consider the following sentences, which are all (we assume) ungrammatical:

   (21) * The man is pregnant
   (22) * The stone stabbed the tree
   (23) * This man is a wolf

(21) is ungrammatical because 'pregnant' "selects" the feature
(- Masculine) in its subject. In the same way 'stab' requires a
(+ Human) subject and a (+ Animate) object. (23) is a contradic-
tion. In particular, the predicate 'wolf' requires a (+ Animate,
- Human) subject (cf. also below, p. 152, note 1)[3].

   Concentrating now on the verb 'stab', we can represent its
selectional feature in the following way: (+ (+ Human) Aux __ Det
(+ Animate)). The total lexical entry for 'stab' would have roughly the following form:

$$
\begin{bmatrix}
\underline{stab}\ \text{(i.e. a phonological specification)} \\
+\ V \\
+\ \_\!\_\ NP \\
-\ \text{object deletion}^{4} \\
+\ (+\ Human)\ Aux\ \_\!\_\ Det\ (+\ Animate) \\
+\ F_{n}\ \text{(i.e. a set of semantic features}
\end{bmatrix}
$$

----

1. This analysis is not without its difficulties. In the first
place, it does not account for the fact that plural common
nouns may occur without a determiner: 'houses are expensive
these days'. Secondly, proper nouns may be preceded by a determiner if they are followed by a relative clause: 'the Peter
I knew is dead'. Clearly, a complete grammar must account for
(notes to be continued on next page).

IV.C.2.3. <u>Lexical insertion</u>

We must now examine how preterminal strings are converted into terminal strings. In <u>Aspects</u> Chomsky considers two different
formulations of the rule which effects lexical insertion. The
first of these involves a reformulation of the base rules: in addition to category-expansion rules (or <u>branching rules</u>) of the
type discussed in section IV.C.1, there is a set of <u>subcategoriza-
tion rules</u>. Some of these are context-free, others are context-
sensitive. The structure of the base is as follows:

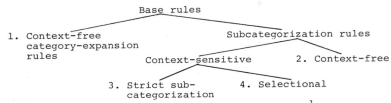

Base rules

1. Context-free   Subcategorization rules
   category-expansion
   rules   Context-sensitive   2. Context-free

      3. Strict sub-   4. Selectional
         categorization

We will discuss the operation of the rules informally[1]. Rules of
type 1 generate base P-markers of the nature illustrated in section IV.C.1. Rules of type 3 subcategorize nouns and verbs with
respect to other constituents under the immediate domination
of NP and VP respectively. For example, if N occurs in the structure

NP

Det   N   No

it will automatically be strictly subcategorized (+ Det __). This
feature forms the input to rules of type 2:

    (+ Det __) ————→ (± Countable)

----

such facts. See further below, sections IV.C.2.4 and IV.G.14.1.

2. Cf. sentences (1) and (2) of section IV.A.8. Observe that the
   category No has been disregarded. For further discussion of
   this, see section IV.C.2.4.

3. We disregard the possible metaphorical interpretation of (23).
   See further below, section IV.D.12.

4. This is a <u>rule feature</u>. We return to such features in section
   IV.C.2.4.

----

1. For details, the reader should consult the fragment of a grammar in Chomsky, 1965, 107.

The rule asserts that any noun preceded by a determiner is either a countable or a mass noun. A further rule asserts that a countable noun is either Animate or Nonanimate:

$$(+ \text{ Countable}) \longrightarrow (\pm \text{ Animate})$$

and so on. Finally, rules of type 4 spell out the selectional features of verbs and adjectives. In essence, this means that the inherent features of the surrounding nouns are copied under the nodes V and Adj. The output of rules of type 2, 3, and 4 is a set of <u>complex symbols</u>. The operation of the base rules can now be illustrated with respect to the sentence

(1) The man stabbed the woman

in terms of the following diagram (details with respect to the definite article are ignored):

(see overleaf)

Lexical insertion is a <u>context-free</u> substitution operation of the following nature: A member of the <u>unordered set of lexical entries</u> whose syntactic feature composition (after the operation of redundancy rules) matches the complex symbol generated by the base rules replaces this symbol. In particular, what is added to the base P-marker by lexical insertion is sets of phonological and semantic features.

There are two important points to note about this theory. The first is that selectional features are syntactic. This means that, unlike what was the case in the SS-model, the sentence

(2) ✱ Colourless green ideas sleep furiously

is ungrammatical (i.e. <u>syntactically</u> ill-formed). The second point is that the noun is <u>selectionally dominant</u>. We return to these points in sections IV.D.10 and 12.

The second proposal made by Chomsky is simpler (see especially <u>Aspects</u>, p. 120ff.). According to this, there are no subcategorization rules in the base. Consequently, no complex symbols are generated. Lexical items are inserted by a <u>substitution transformation</u>: they substitute for the dummy symbol $\triangle$. T-rules, as we have seen, operate on P-markers. In this case the rule would affect that part of the P-marker which is defined by the contextual features of the lexical items (if there are any - in some cases (such as M)

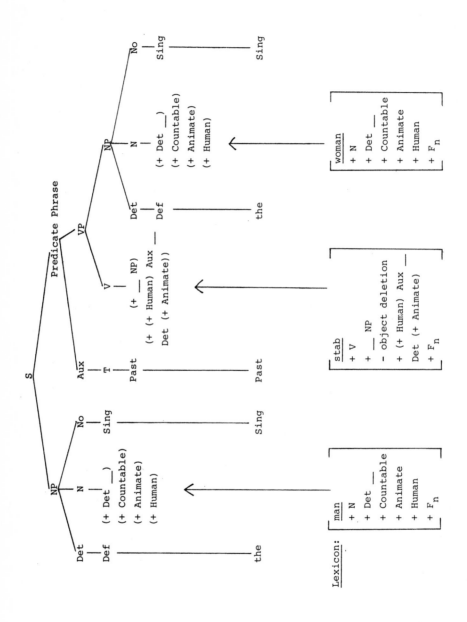

there would only be the category feature.

This second proposal would make it possible to claim that selectional features are entirely semantic in nature. We could say that lexical items are inserted freely under category symbols (obeying strict subcategorization features[1]), whereas selectional restrictions are handled by the rules of the semantic component. By this proposal, (2) would be defined once again as a syntactically well-formed sentence.

We conclude this section by redefining the notion 'structural description of a sentence' as follows: $P_1 \ldots P_i \ldots P_n$, where P_1 is the initial P-marker generated by the categorial subcomponent of the base (i.e. the branching rules), P_i the deep structure (i.e. P_1 <u>after</u> lexical insertion), and P_n the surface structure derived from P_i by (nonlexical (i.e. "properly" syntactic)) T-rules. P_i and P_n are interpreted by the semantic and phonological component respectively.

IV.C.2.4. <u>The further significance of syntactic features</u>

The conception of lexical items as bundles of features rather than as unanalysed entities has had great influence on the further development of TG-theory. Mention must be made here of <u>rule features</u>. Consider the following sentences:

(1) He was reading the book
(2) He was reading
(3) He stood watching the crowd
(4) He stood watching
(5) He went to fetch the car
(6) * He went to fetch
(7) He stabbed the woman
(8) * He stabbed

All four verbs are transitive and as such have the strict subcategorization feature (+ __ NP). However, whereas 'read' and 'watch' may occur in surface structure without an overtly expressed object, this is not the case with 'fetch' and 'stab'. This suggests that there is a T-rule which optionally deletes the object of transitive verbs. However, the rule is <u>governed</u> in the sense that it is contingent on a feature of the verb: 'read' and 'watch' are

----

1. Note that we would now no longer have to define strict subcategorization features as local. The separation of selectional and strict subcategorization features by this criterion is a consequence of the formalism of the subcategorization model.

specified (x object deletion)[1], 'fetch' and 'stab' (- object deletion).

     Syntactic features furthermore enable us to formulate a num-
ber of <u>segmentalization transformations</u>. Consider for example the
relationship between nouns and determiners. A descriptively adequate grammar must predict the <u>dependency relations</u> between a
noun and the set of determiners with which it can cooccur. Recall now the difficulty involved in distinguishing between proper
nouns and common nouns in terms of a strict subcategorization
feature (cf. above, p. 115, note 1). Suppose now that we add to
the grammar a set of <u>segment structure rules</u> which can modify
lexical entries for nouns, in particular add features to them. For
example, there might be a rule which specifies nouns as ($\pm$ Sing).
A further rule would define nouns as ($\pm$ Def). (+ Def) would be
specified ($\pm$ Demonstrative) by a third rule, (+ Demonstrative)
($\pm$ Proximity) by a fourth rule; and so on[2].

     After the operation of such rules, the lexical entry for
a noun like 'girl' might look something like (9a) (see next
page):

     Segmentalization transformations would operate on this entry
and (a) create two new segments: <u>Article</u> and <u>Affix</u>, and (b) copy
all relevant features of the noun in the article and affix segments[3]. The outcome of the rules would be roughly (9b) (see next
page):

     We are now in a position to account for the sentence cited
on p. 115, note 1:

     (10) Houses are expensive these days

in the following way: 'house' is specified by the segment struc-

----

1. We shall make the assumption that any lexical item marked x
   for the rule feature F_i in the lexicon is obligatorily specified
   either + F_i or - F_i when it is entered into a preterminal string.
   The application of the rule is contingent on this specification.
   For further discussion of rule features, see below, pp. 209,
   212.

2. For further discussion, see notes.

3. We return to segmentalization transformations in connection with
   pronominalization (section IV.G.18.2.). We shall see that it is
   possible to analyse pronouns as articles and that this analysis
   requires that all of the noun features are copied in the article segment. Here we have copied only those features which are
   relevant to the generation of 'ordinary' determiners.

(9a)

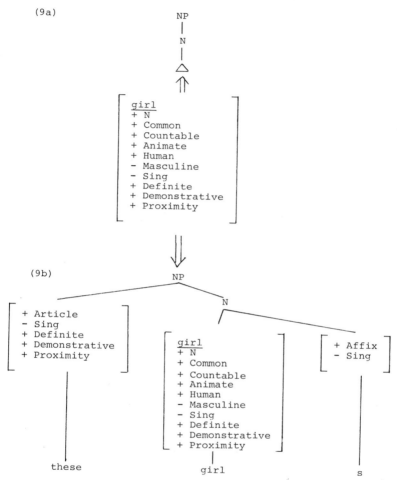

ture rules as (- Sing, - Def). The segmentalization rule copies these features in the article segment. However, lexical insertion cannot operate because the lexicon does not contain a plural non-definite article[1].

By adopting such an analysis of articles and number, we would

----

1. Alternatively, we could say that when the segmentalization rule scans the feature specification of 'house' it fails to apply because of the features (- Sing, - Def).

be able to remove the categories No and Det from the base. Rule
15 would disappear from the PS-rules. Base P-markers would look
slightly less language-specific (cf. the discussion of the status
of Aux in section IV.C.1).

It has further been suggested that prepositions might be
generated as features of nouns and be spelled out by a preposition segmentalization rule. We will not go into that at this point
(cf. below, section IV.G.14.6).

One last point should be made in this section. If the lexical
category symbols can profitably be analysed into distinctive syntactic features, the question arises whether this approach might
not be extended to cover other, prelexical (i.e. nonterminal), category symbols such as NP. We return to this point in section IV.G.17.3.

IV.C.2.5. The second lexical pass

It follows from the discussion in the preceding section that
not all lexical items are inserted into deep structures (i.e., more
precisely, prior to P_i): if we incoporate segmentalization transformations in the grammar, there must be a post-transformational
lexical insertion rule which can substitute lexical items for the
feature complexes generated by segmentation. Even if we do not incoporate segmentalization rules, post-transformational lexical insertion is still required. For example, (part of) the relativization rule may be defined as a feature attachment operation: the
features (+ Wh), (+ Rel), and (+ Pro) are attached to the NP
to be relativized. Consequently, there must be a rule which can
substitute the appropriate form of the relative pronoun for the
complex of features. Following Jacobs and Rosenbaum (1968, 84,
157), we may refer to post-transformational lexical insertion as
the second lexical pass.

Notes and some further references

IV.C.1. The rules formulated in this section should be compared
with the PS-rules suggested in other textbooks (e.g. Burt, 1971,
Fowler, 1971, Lester, 1971, and Liles, 1971). Such a comparison
would make it abundantly clear that there is no a priori given
set of PS-rules: the PS-rules suggested by any writer are determined by the way he or she proposes to work out the rest of
the grammar. As remarked in the text, the question of adverbs is
excessively complex. For a recent discussion of adverbs (within
the framework of the interpretivist version of TG-theory) see

Jackendoff, 1972. Jackendoff argues that the category Adv should
be generated at various points in the base and interpreted by
semantic rules. In other words, such labels as 'manner' and 'direction' are removed from base P-markers. The overall advantage
of generating adverbs directly in the base is that this approach
eliminates from the grammar a great proliferation of T-rules which
are otherwise required to derive -ly-adverbs from their corresponding adjectives (for discussion and examples, see Jackendoff, 1972,
52f.). On adverbs, see further Jacobson, 1964. Jacobson, 1971,
Chapter 6 is an interesting attempt to account for adverbs in terms
of segments generated by subcategorization rules and branching
from the constituents to which they belong (i.e. without segmentalization transformations). For discussion of some of the problems
caused by adverbs in such areas of the grammar as negation
and interrogation, see Lakoff, 1970a, Appendix F. We shall see
in section V.B that in case grammar a number of adverbial prepositional phrases can be redefined as noun phrases (arguments).
A detailed discussion of problems relating to Aux may be found in
Borkin et al., 1972. Consult further Bach, 1967, Ross, 1969a (and
Chomsky's reply, 1972, 122f.), McCawley, 1971a, and Huddleston,
1974. Ross, 1969b has pointed out that adjectives and nouns are
syntactically similar in a number of ways. Thus the traditional
three-ways distinction between verbs, adjectives, and nouns may
perhaps be eliminated from the base. See also in this connection
Bach, 1968. Bach proposes a (substantive universal) category 'Contentive', which underlies surface nouns, verbs, and adjectives.
For critical discussion of such proposals, see Chomsky, 1970 (in
Jacobs and Rosenbaum, 1970) 198f. and Schachter, 1973a.

<u>Syntagmatic and paradigmatic/marked and unmarked</u>. We must now make
a digression in order to introduce some concepts which are of fundamental importance to linguistic analysis. De Saussure (1916)
distinguished between two different kinds of linguistic relations:
<u>syntagmatic</u> and <u>paradigmatic</u> relations[1]. The former hold between
units cooccurring in the chain of speech, the latter between any
one unit in the chain and other, comparable units outside the chain.
We can illustrate the two-dimensionality of linguistic relations
in terms of the following abstract example:

(1) (a   ((b   c) (d   e)))
(2) (f   (g   (h   c)))

in which the brackets indicate syntagmatic relationships and ⟵⟶
paradigmatic relationships. We will leave it at that for the moment
except note that syntagmatic and paradimatic relations are relevant
at all levels of analysis[2]. Of a paradigmatically related set of
units or categories, one may be <u>marked</u>, the other(s) <u>unmarked</u>[3].
In the typical instance, the term 'marked' is used to characterize

----

1. De Saussure used the term 'associative'. 'Paradigmatic' was
   suggested by Hjelmslev and is now in general use.

2. The reader might try to substitute for (1) and (2) 'He has lost
   his mother' and 'She lost her father' respectively and work out
   the relevant syntagmatic and paradigmatic relations, say, at the
   syntactic level of analysis.

3. This distinction is originally due to the Prague linguists
   (see Vachek, 1966).

the <u>less typical</u> (or less natural) member of a set. Consider for
example the following pair of sentences:

    (3) If you had not failed, we should have overcome
    (4) Had you not failed, we should have overcome

Of these, (4) is marked because of the omission of the conjunction
'if' and the concomitant inversion of the (auxiliary) verb and
the subject. By the same token, sentence (31) in the text is
marked relative to (30) because it has undergone the thematization
transformation. The terms 'marked' and 'unmarked', however, are
also used in a somewhat more abstract way to refer to those cases
in which one member of a set of paradigmatically related units or
categories "includes" the other(s). Schematically, this relation
of inclusion can be illustrated in the following way (X being the
unmarked member of the set):

The following sentence is an example from the grammatical level:

    (5) They smeared paint $\left\{\begin{array}{l}\text{on}\\\text{under}\\\text{inside}\end{array}\right\}$ the box

In this, the three prepositional phrases can be defined as locative
adverbials. However, 'under' and 'inside' are more specific than
'on': 'on the box' may be anywhere, including 'under the box' and
'inside the box'. 'On', therefore, is the unmarked locative preposition with respect to the verb 'smear'. The same phenomenon
may be observed in the tense system. Thus the past tense may sometimes be used instead of the pluperfect, particularly after the
conjunctions 'when' and 'after':

    (6) $\left\{\begin{array}{l}\text{When}\\\text{After}\end{array}\right\}$ his mother $\left\{\begin{array}{l}\text{died}\\\text{had died}\end{array}\right\}$ he went to Belgium

Similarly, the so-called <u>historical present</u> ranges over the province of the past tense. The pattern, then, is this:

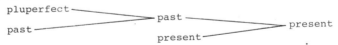

There are many examples of marked/unmarked relations in the lexicon. One is the relationship between <u>antonyms</u> like 'young' and
'old'. Of these, 'old' is the unmarked term: one does not ask
'how young' but 'how old is the baby in the pram?'. Nor yet does
one expect the answer 'he is three days young'. 'Old', therefore,
has a wider range than 'young'.

<u>IV.C.2.1.</u> For some discussion of the difficulties involved in the
subclassification of verbs by PS-rules, see Lees, 1960a (Preface
to the third printing, XLf.), Fowler, 1971, 51f., and Bach, 1974,
64ff. The difficulties are essentially the same as those relating
to the subclassification of nouns. The first scholar to propose
that subcategorization should be removed from the categorial component (i.e. the branching rules) was Matthews. See especially
Matthews, 1961 and 1965. Many of the proposals made there are quite
similar to the ideas developed in <u>Aspects</u>.

IV.C.2.2,3. An overall introduction to the Aspects-framework is
provided by Dingwall, 1966. For critical discussion, see also
Matthews, 1967. The discussion of lexical insertion in Aspects
is characterized by a high degree of formalism. A somewhat more
accessible account may be found in Chomsky, 1966b, 68ff.

IV.C.2.4. Rule features (and the general question of exceptions in
a transformational grammar) are discussed in Lakoff, 1970a. For
a detailed treatment of problems relating to object deletion, see
Lehrer, 1970. The notion of segmentalization transformations is
due to Postal, 1970a (first published in 1966). Segment structure
rules were first proposed by Rosenbaum. They play an integral part
in Jacobs and Rosenbaum, 1968. The tree presented in the text
(apart from the dummy symbol, which is presently to be discussed)
is taken from that work. The possible revision of the article rule
discussed in section IV.G.14.5 is also proposed by Jacobs and
Rosenbaum. Segment structure rules take the following form:

$$(1) \quad N \longrightarrow \begin{bmatrix} + \text{ N} \\ \pm \text{ Sing} \end{bmatrix}$$

It is clear that (1) is a subcategorization rule. It is the only
example given by the authors, but presumably features like ($\pm$ Def),
($\pm$ Demonstrative), and ($\pm$ Proximity) should be generated in the
noun segment by similar rules. In order to make this proposal work,
it is necessary to allow a general convention in the grammar that
nouns, when they are inserted from the lexicon, may 'take on'
certain features specified in the complex symbol. If such an assumption is not made, all the segment structure rules would have
to be duplicated in the lexicon, for lexical insertion by matching
to be possible. For example, (1) would have to be supplemented by

$$(2) \quad (+ \text{ N}) \longrightarrow (\pm \text{ Sing})$$

Since we have opted for the dummy-symbol approach, our grammar
cannot contain (1). The only rule which can operate on such category
symbols as N, V, or Adj is the one which converts them into a
dummy symbol. However, a set of rules matching the segment structure rules could be stated in the lexicon. Therefor the dummy-
symbol approach and the notion of segment structure rules (with
an associated set of segmentalization transformations) are not incompatible. In this book a more conventional analysis of determiners
has been adopted. As it stands, it is inadequate on two scores.
First, in a grammar containing syntactic features, Definite and
Indefinite should be defined as features, not categories. In other
words, Definite and Indefinite must be removed from PS-rule 16
(cf. above, p. 98). Secondly, we have defined Det as optional.
There can be little doubt that this is wrong. For example, it predicts that proper nouns have no determiner (which is true about
surface structure of course) and hence are unrelated to the feature (+ Def). But proper nouns are always definite, and clearly
the grammar should make this explicit. The generation of a separate determiner node under which feature complexes are inserted
from the lexicon does not preclude segmentalization transformations.
Indeed, such rules may well be the most natural way of stating the
dependency relations holding between certain noun features (such
as ($\pm$ Countable) and ($\pm$ Abstract)) and the determiner system.

We should note perhaps that the generation of determiners constitutes one of those areas in which a sentence grammar cannot attain
the level of descriptive adequacy. Consider such sentences as

   (3) Jane wants to buy <u>a new hat</u>
   (4) <u>A hat</u> must be smart

On the assumption that the underlined NPs in (3) and (4) are coreferential, (4) is ungrammatical: the article must be definite. This
fact is clearly part of the speaker's competence; consequently, a
grammar which cannot make explicit the relationship between (3)
and (4) is, by definition, descriptively inadequate. The study of
intersentence relations such as those manifested by (3) and (4)
falls within the province of <u>text grammar</u>[1]. We will not go into
further details over the question of determiners. Suffice it to
have indicated the complexity of the area and to have admitted
that the PS-rules we have formulated are probably inadequate in
this respect (even within the confines of a sentence grammar).
The different approaches to determiners from the beginning of TG-
theory up through 1968 are discussed in detail by Stockwell et al.,
1968, Vol. I, 85ff. This work is indispensable for the study of
the development of transformational syntax. It has now been repub-
lished by Holt, Rinehart and Winston under the title <u>The Major Syntactic Structures of English</u> (1973) (all references in this book
are to the first, mimeographed edition). Mention should be made
of Perlmutter, 1970a. Perlmutter presents an impressive array of
arguments in support of the hypothesis that the indefinite article
should be derived from the numeral 'one'. We may note in passing
that although diachronic considerations should play no role in the
construction of a grammar, this would be an interesting synchronic
reflection of the diachronic development of the indefinite article
in English. Fowler, 1971 sketches a transformational framework for
the derivation of determiners. Fowler includes 'number' directly
in the determiner system: all determiners are defined by the following rule (p. 64):

$$(5) \; \text{Det} \longrightarrow \begin{bmatrix} \text{Number} \\ \text{Universality} \end{bmatrix}$$

These two features form the input to a set of transformational
rules whose SIs[2] mention the feature composition of the following
noun. In this way, then, the dependency relation between determiners
and noun features is made explicit. For a critique of Fowler's analysis, see Noll, 1975. Different treatments of prepositions may be
found in Jacobs and Rosenbaum, 1968, Postal, 1971 (segmentalization
of features from nouns), Lakoff, 1970a (all verbs are assumed to
be followed by prepositions at some stage of the derivation),
Becker and Arms, 1969 (prepositions analysed as predicates),
Fillmore, 1966a, 1966b, 1968 (prepositions as case markers), and
Jackendoff, 1973 (transitive and intransitive prepositions).

----

1. Cf. the problems posed by pronouns which have anaphoric reference beyond the sentence (below, p. 420).

2. For this concept, see below, p. 187.

IV.D. THE SEMANTIC COMPONENT

IV.D.1. Introductory remarks

In IV.D we will attempt to trace - in broad and maximally informal outlines - the development of semantics as an integral part
of TG-theory from the beginning of the sixties to the present day.

As was pointed out in sections IV.B.3 and 4, one of the main
issues in the present-day debate concerns the interrelationship
between syntax and semantics. We return to this in Chapter V. For
the moment, we will take the standard theory as our point of departure. It may be safely assumed, however, that the majority of
the problems dealt with in this section are of general relevance,
irrespectively of what side one might eventually choose to take
in the battle of deep structure (for this term, see Langacker,
1967, VI).

IV.D.2. Syntax and semantics

We saw in section IV.B.2 that the semantic theory developed
by Katz, Fodor, and Postal in the early sixties was intended to
meet the requirements of the SS-model of syntax. We will not push
back the frontiers that far. Instead, we will assume (a) that the
PS-rules generate generalized P-markers in the now familiar way,
and (b) that the lexicon contains all relevant semantic information[1].

In order to illustrate the way in which syntax and semantics
are assumed to interact, we will analyse in more detail sentence
(12) of section I.5.4 and sentences (15) and (21) of section II.4:

(1) What disturbed John was being disregarded by his friends
(2) Peter seems to be certain to be there
(3) Peter seems to be content to be there

We noted that (1) is syntactically two-ways ambiguous and that the
two meanings can be paraphrased roughly as follows:

----

1. By making these assumptions, we avoid having to draw a distinction between two kinds of projection rules (for such rules, see
below, section IV.D.9). We further need not distinguish between
the dictionary and the lexicon. These distinctions are now mainly of historical interest. The interested reader is referred to
Katz and Fodor, 1963, Katz and Postal, 1964. On the relationship between dictionary and lexicon, see also Katz, 1972, 66f.

(1a) John's friends were disregarding what disturbed him

(1b) John's friends disregarded him, which disturbed him

Now, it follows from the KP-hypothesis, which, as we have seen, is associated with the standard theory, that a sentence which is n-ways syntactically ambiguous must have n deep structures. (1), then, must have two different deep structures which determine the interpretations paraphrased by (1a) and (1b). Let us tentatively assume that these deep structures can be represented in roughly the following way (see pp. 129-30)[1]:

It is clear that the two trees differ quite considerably. In particular, they assign quite different functions to the constituents. Thus in (1b) it is made explicit that 'John' is the object of 'disturb' as well as of 'disregard'. Furthermore, the relative clause is embedded in the subject NP of (1b), whereas in (1a) it is embedded in the object NP.

For (1) to be derived from (1a), the following T-rules must apply (among others): (a) relativization: 'the thing the thing' $\Longrightarrow$ 'the thing which' $\Longrightarrow$ 'what', (b) passivization, which permutes NP_1 and NP_2 (inserting also the passive auxiliary 'be + en' and the preposition 'by' in front of NP_1), and (c) pronominalization, which substitutes 'his' for 'John's'.

The following rules (among others) operate on (1b): (a) relativization, (b) passivization (this time, however, the rule applies to the embedded S_1, not to the whole sentence), (c) complementizer insertion, (d) it deletion, and (e) pronominalization.

----

1. The two P-markers call for several comments. (a) The form 'John's' dominated by Det should probably be derived from a sentence: 'John has friends'. Strictly speaking, therefore, (1a) and (1b) are intermediate rather than deep structures. However, this is immaterial to the present argument. (b) The trees have been somewhat simplified. Thus the category No is disregarded. (c) The numerical subscripts assigned to some of the nodes serve no other purpose than to facilitate reference to the trees in the discussion of the T-rules in the text. By contrast, the numerical subscripts assigned to the lexical items are referential indices in the sense discussed in connection with sentence (6) of section IV.A.7 (see further below, section IV.D.15). Co-referentiality, we assume, is a necessary condition for relativization and pronominalization. (d) It is far from certain that the derivation of 'what' suggested in the text is correct. (e) (1b) is a <u>pseudo-cleft</u> sentence. The deep structure suggested here is not indisputable. There are other possible ways of analysing such sentences. Cf. below, section, IV.G.15.2.

(1a)

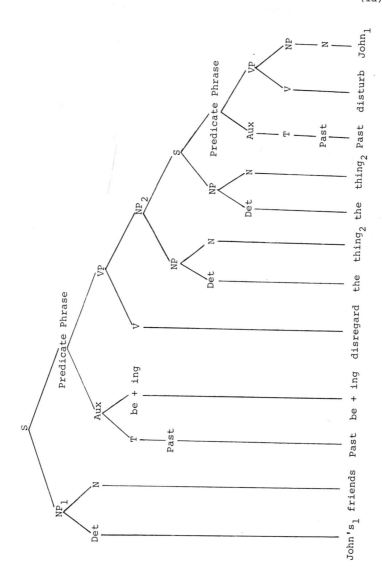

(1b)

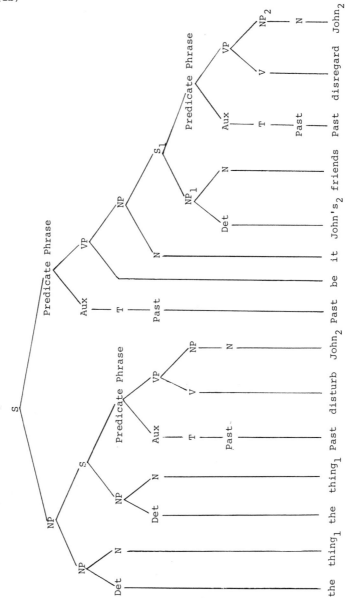

The complementizer insertion rule makes it possible to derive several versions from (1b)[1]:

    (4) What disturbed John was that he was disregarded by his
        friends

    (5) What disturbed John was for him to be disregarded by his
        friends

    (6) What disturbed John was his being disregarded by his friends

By a rule which optionally deletes the noun to which the first part of the complementizer 'Poss - ing' is attached provided this is identical to a noun in the matrix sentence - the rule of equi NP deletion (often referred to as just equi)[2] - (1) is derived from (6). Equi may also delete 'him' in (5); if it does, 'for' must obligatorily be deleted, the result being:

    (7) What disturbed John was to be disregarded by his friends

Observe that we have now provided explicit substantiation of the claim made in section I.5.4 concerning the structure of the string 'was being disregarded': In (1a) the string 'T + be + ing' is generated by the Aux-expansion rule. After passivization the suffix 'ing' is adjoined to the passive auxiliary by affix hopping. In (1b) 'being' is the gerund form of the passive auxiliary derived by complementizer insertion, whereas 'was' is the main verb.

Note finally that 'be' in (1b) is equative. Thus the two NPs may be reversed without any significant change in meaning[3]:

    (8) Being disregarded by his friends was what disturbed John

Let us now turn to (2) and (3). We noted in section II.4 that the two sentences are quite alike in surface structure but that they differ widely with respect to the structural paradigms of which they are members. It should be clear by now that this difference is due

----

1. It is possible to assume that 'ing' of the complementizer 'Poss - ing' and 'to' of the complementizer 'for - to' replace the T node of the embedded sentence (S_1). If the complementizer 'that' is inserted, tense is realized in the normal way. Cf. section IV.G.16.5.

2. All the rules mentioned in this section will be discussed in greater detail in section IV.G.

3. The situation is rather more complex if equative 'be' is both preceded and followed by a 'what'-clause. For examples and discussion, see Huddleston, 1971, 135f.

to the fact that they have undergone different T-rules. Since P_i
constitutes the input to the first T-rule in the derivation of
any sentence, we are led to suspect that (2) and (3) have different
deep structures (more precisely, different base P-markers). Intuitively, it would seem to be a reasonable guess that this difference
is bound up with the syntactic functions of the noun 'Peter' in the
two sentences. In particular, 'Peter' is the subject of both 'to be
content' and 'to be there' in (3), whereas in (2) 'Peter' is the
subject of 'to be there', but not of 'to be certain'. Let us proceed to formalize this intuitive guess in terms of tentative P-
markers (much simplified):

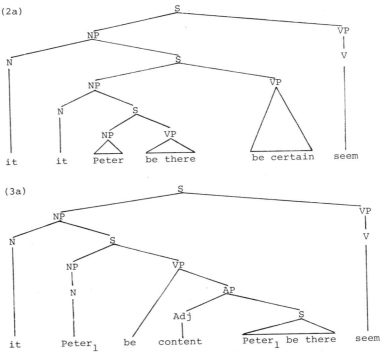

(2a)

(3a)

We will not go into the T-rules required to convert (2a) and (3a)
into surface structures at this point (see further below, section
IV.G.16.6). We can draw the following conclusions from the discussion in this section:

(a) The integration of syntax and semantics cannot possibly
be achieved on the basis of the surface structure of sentences.
Thus, although, as we suggested in section I.5.4, procedural analysis might assign two different structures to (1), it is nevertheless clear that the semantically relevant syntactic relations are
so intricate and subtle that they simply cannot be captured by ob-
serving the data[1]. In the same way, the embedding patterns illustrated by (2a) and (3a) (which - begging the question - we assume
to be correct) must be of vital importance to the semantic processing of (2) and (3).

(b) If we consider the different surface structures derivable
from (1b) and recall also the paradigm of which (2) is a member,
it becomes apparent that T-rules can distort deep structures quite
considerably without changing the meaning of sentences. Consequently,

(c) it seems to be a reasonable theoretical assumption that
T-rules are meaning-preserving (cf. above, p. 93 and below, p. 301).

IV.D.3. Semantic knowledge

Bloomfield, as we saw in section I.1, assumed that meaning was
determined exclusively by extralinguistic factors and that, hence,
semantics, if it were to be a scientific discipline, could not be
integrated in linguistics before the entire universe had been exhaustively described by the relevant sciences. Twenty years after
the publication of Language, the substance of Bloomfield's philosophy was repeated by Carroll in the following statment (1953, 12):

> The linguist limits his field of inquiry by refusing to be
> concerned except in a rather indirect way, with the content
> of the communication, that is "what is being talked about".
> The linguist is not interested in what is communicated; he is

----

1. It should be emphasized in this connection that structuralists
have never denied that syntax is relevant to semantics. In point
of fact, 'syntactic semantics' was the only area in which they
felt on relatively safe ground, where meaning was concerned.
Thus Fries (1952, 56) defined the grammar of a language as the
set of "devices that signal structural meanings". But Fries (and
the other structuralists) never doubted that these devices were
superficially manifested and hence open to observational inspection. Often the devices were illustrated by the analysis of nonsense sentences. The favourite example was the first stanza of
Jabberwocky in Alice in Wonderland (see for example Hockett,
1958, 262ff. and Strang, 1962, 78).

interested primarily in the vehicle of communication, that is,
the language system. If he became concerned with the content
of the communication, he would in effect be concerned with
the totality of human knowledge (my emphasis).

The fallacy of this position becomes apparent once it is
viewed in the light of the notion of linguistic competence: the
speaker of L clearly knows what he is talking about without knowing everything there is to know in the world. This being the case,
semantic inquiry is perfectly justified independently of what dis-
coveries might be made in other sciences.

TG-semanticists have argued from the beginning that the question 'what is meaning?' asked at one swoop is not likely to result
in an adequate semantic theory. Rather, this question must be
broken down into smaller, more modest ones of the following kind:
'What is sameness of meaning (i.e. synonymy)?', 'What is semantic
ambiguity?' - 'What is contradictoriness?' - 'What is analyticity?' -
'What is incompatibility?' - 'What is semantic redundancy?' - 'What
is semantic anomaly?' - 'What is presupposition?', etc. By implication, the 'What is' of these questions also means 'What explanation can be given for our knowledge of?'.

IV.D.4. The semantic structure of the lexical item

Consider the following sentences:

(1) A spinster is an adult, unmarried, human, female
(2) This tigress is a spinster
(3) My five-year-old sister is a spinster
(4) Peter's wife is a spinster
(5) Jane is an unmarried spinster

(1) is the definition of the meaning of the lexical item 'spinster'
(it might occur in a dictionary). Into this definition enter the
items 'adult', 'unmarried', 'human', and 'female'. This suggests
that the meaning of 'spinster' is not an unanalysable entity: it
can be stated in terms of smaller ingredients - semantic features[1]:
ADULT, UNMARRIED, HUMAN, FEMALE[2]. Assuming now that the meaning of
----

1. Also referred to in the literature as 'markers', or 'components',
   or 'sememes'. We opt for the term 'feature' in order to align
   semantics with syntax and phonology.
2. We will adopt the convention of writing semantic features in
   capitals (without brackets). An alternative way of stating the

the other lexical items in (2)-(5) can be stated in terms of similar sets of features, we are in a position to give a systematic
explanation of the oddity of the four sentences. In (2) the feature NONHUMAN in the subject is contradicted by the feature HUMAN
in the predicate. Mutatis mutandis, the same is true of (3) and
(4)[1]. (5) is an instance of semantic redundancy: the predicate
('unmarried') lexicalizes one of the defining features of 'spinster'.

In later sections, we shall deal in more detail with the different types of semantic relations manifested by our sample sentences. Meanwhile, let us pursue the notion of semantic features
a little further. Consider the following matrix (where x = 'has
the feature', 0 = 'unspecified for the feature', and +/- =
binariness with respect to a certain feature[2]):

	EQUINE	BOVINE	HUMAN	MALE	ADULT
stallion	x			+	+
mare	x			−	+
foal	x			0	−
filly	x			−	−
colt	x			+	−
bull		x		+	+
cow		x		−	+
calf		x		0	−
heifer		x		−	−
bull-calf		x		+	−
man			+	+	+
woman			+	−	+
child			+	0	−
girl			+	−	−
boy			+	+	−

----

four features is − MALE, + ADULT, − MARRIED, and + HUMAN. That
is, the four features can be interpreted as binary. We return
to this presently.

1. Note that (2) can be uttered in a zoo about a tigress who has
   no male partner in the cage. Likewise, (4) could be used to
   characterize the kind of woman Peter is married to. However,
   this would clearly be a nonnormal use of the lexical item
   'spinster'. Hence, if anything, it corroborates the analysis.

2. The blank spaces indicate redundant features (cf. below, p.
   137f.). For example, x EQUINE implies − HUMAN; and so on.

The matrix shows very clearly the principle of <u>economy</u> involved
in feature analysis: there are fifteen lexical items and five features; furthermore, three features are sufficient to distinguish
each lexical item from all the others. The matrix also reveals the
fact that feature analysis makes it possible to explicitly cross-
classify lexical items. For example, 'bull' is to 'cow' as 'stallion' is to 'mare' with respect to ± MALE.

It would perhaps not be unreasonable to assume that the fifteen lexical items listed in the matrix occur in the vast majority
of languages. Furthermore, if some are missing in some languages,
it is a likely guess that it is those specified 0[1]. Consider the
following relationship between Danish and English:

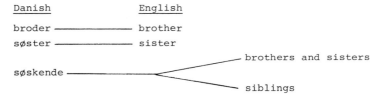

Danish	English
broder ——————— brother	
søster ——————— sister	
søskende ———————— brothers and sisters / siblings	

English does not have a lexical item corresponding to Danish
'søskende' (cf. German 'Geschwister'). This does not mean, of
course, that English cannot express the same thought (cf. below,
section IV.D.7). There are two possibilities: (a) 'grammaticaliza-
tion' (in this case by means of coordination), or (b) the invention of a new lexical item like 'sibling' which enters into the
lexical system by <u>neutralizing</u> the distinction between + MALE and
- MALE[2].

----

1. The items specified 0 with respect to a certain feature are
   those which are least specific in meaning. The guess made with
   respect to the lexical items under discussion here should not
   be taken to imply that the absence of the least specific item
   is necessarily to be expected as a general rule. For a number
   of examples of lexical 'skewness' between languages (i.e. lack
   of <u>lexical isomorphism</u>), see Whorf (in Carroll (ed.), 1956)
   207ff.

2. The term 'sibling' is historically (or dialectically) motivated
   (cf. Old English 'sibb' = 'akin to'). Such motivation is, of
   course, not necessary: any sequence of phonemes would do, provided it did not violate the phonological rules of the language (that is, the rules which specify the combinatorial possibilities of the phonemes). 'Sibling' is used in kinship semantics (see for example Lounsbury, 1964, 1082). It should be
   borne in mind in this connection that componential analysis
   was first fully developed in the analysis of the semantic structure of kinship terms in different languages.

As has already been suggested, semantic features can, to a large extent, be stated in terms of binary oppositions. Thus 'woman' is distinguished from 'man' solely in terms of the opposition between + MALE and - MALE. In some cases, however, binary oppositions cannot capture the facts. For example, semantic phenomena relating to dimensionality must obviously be accounted for in terms of (at least) three features (for further discussion and examples, see Langendoen, 1969, 40ff. and Leech, 1974, 114ff.). Furthermore, some features are <u>relational</u> in nature. Thus the semantic structure of, say, 'brother' cannot be made explicit unless, in addition to features like + ANIMATE (rather perhaps + HUMAN), + MALE, 0 ADULT, there is a further relational feature: X OFFSPRING OF PARENT OF Y (for further discussion, see Bierwisch, 1970a (in Lyons, 1970b) 172ff. and Leech, 1974, 110ff.).

Let us now assume that a semantic theory must contain the following features (cf. Katz, 1972, 39ff. for more detailed discussion): $\pm$ HUMAN, $\pm$ ADULT, $\pm$ PHYSICAL, $\pm$ OBJECT, and $\pm$ ARTIFACT (to distinguish such items as 'boy', 'girl', 'man', 'woman', 'animal', 'table', 'stone', 'dream', etc.). Now, as we have stated these features, they present an arbitrary, unordered list. However, it takes little reflection to see that some of the features logically imply some of the others. As was the case with syntactic features[1], this relation of logical implication can be stated in terms of <u>redundancy rules</u> of the following nature:

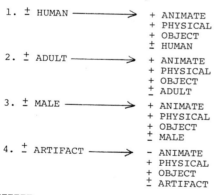

1. $\pm$ HUMAN ⟶ + ANIMATE
   + PHYSICAL
   + OBJECT
   $\pm$ HUMAN

2. $\pm$ ADULT ⟶ + ANIMATE
   + PHYSICAL
   + OBJECT
   $\pm$ ADULT

3. $\pm$ MALE ⟶ + ANIMATE
   + PHYSICAL
   + OBJECT
   $\pm$ MALE

4. $\pm$ ARTIFACT ⟶ - ANIMATE
   + PHYSICAL
   + OBJECT
   $\pm$ ARTIFACT

----

1. For the distinction between syntactic and semantic features, see below, section IV.D.14.

5. $\pm$ ANIMATE ────────⟶ + PHYSICAL
                              + OBJECT
                              $\pm$ ANIMATE

6. $\pm$ PHYSICAL ───────⟶ + OBJECT
                              $\pm$ PHYSICAL

We can translate what these rules assert into a diagram showing the
interrelationship of the features:

(6)

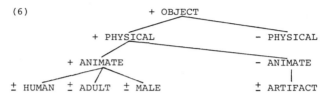

Observe that the features in the bottom row in this diagram never
occur on the right side of the arrow in a redundancy rule[1]: they
are purely cross-classificational and hence not predictable by
general rule. By contrast, + OBJECT never occurs on the left side
of the arrow: it is the most abstract feature of the set. All the
other features are hierarchically related to it. Features like
$\pm$ ANIMATE occupy a position in between: they are cross-classificational in that they define two subsets of the set of physical objects and they are hierarchical in that they are predictable by
general rule.

Semantic features are interrelated in a network of hierarchical
and cross-classificational patterns the complexity of which the
simple example discussed here does not even begin to unravel.

In TG-theory, as we have seen, it is assumed that lexical
items are stored in the mental lexicon without their redundant features. However, at the point of the derivation when lexical insertion takes place, the redundancy rules must operate, inserting the
redundant features. Consider the following two sentences:

(7) John was his best friend

(8) He carried John up the stairs; he was very heavy

'John' is sepcified + HUMAN in both (7) and (8). In (7) + HUMAN

----

1. Unless they form the input to the rule: the set of features on
   the right side of the arrows in the rules represent the full
   semantic specification of lexical items (in terms of the features we are considering).

is the most important feature (along with + MALE). In (8), however, this is not the case: all physical objects can be carried and all physical objects can be heavy. Consequently, in uttering (8), we think of John as a physical object as much as we think of him as a human being. The features + PHYSICAL and + OBJECT, then, are necessary for the proper semantic interpretation of (8), and these, as we have seen, are inserted by a redundancy rule[1].

Henceforth, we will assume that the semantic structure of the vocabulary of a language can be stated in terms of features. It should be stressed, however, that the examples adduced in this section are relatively simple. Thus the matrix discussed on p. 135 represents a clearly circumscribed subset of the lexical items of the language. A number of questions naturally present themselves: Precisely how many and precisely what features would be required to define the semantic structure of the whole vocabulary? Precisely where do we overstep the point of diminishing returns in constructing an inventory of features? What is the relationship between the features[2], which, to all intents and purposes, are lexical items spelt in capitals (by some), and the corresponding "real" lexical items?[3] And so on. We will not go into these questions here. The reader is referred to some of the critical discussions cited in the bibliographical notes.

IV.D.5. Cognitive and noncognitive meaning

A semantic theory concerned with making explicit the semantic competence of the ideal speaker-hearer must needs draw a distinction between cognitive and noncognitive meaning. Instead of defining these terms in the abstract, we turn immediately to an example. The Advanced Learner's Dictionary defines 'stallion' as follows: '(a) fully grown (b) male (c) horse (d) esp. one used for breeding'. It is clear that (a), (b), and (c) correspond to the features + ADULT, + MALE, and x EQUINE. We saw that these features were suf-

----

1. For a somewhat different explanation of the semantics of sentences like (7) and (8), see McCawley, 1968a (in Bach and Harms, 1968) 130ff.

2. It should be borne in mind that, in principle, the features are unanalysable theoretical primitives.

3. See in this connection the distinction drawn by Katz between primitive semantic markers and semantic markers (1971a, 101, 1972, 38).

ficient for distinctive purposes. Now, it is certainly true that
a stallion is used for breeding purposes. Yet, it may perhaps be
the case that 'used for breeding' is a personal, possibly profes-
sionally conditioned, association accompanying the primary meaning
of 'stallion'. It is by no means certain that this association is
uppermost in the minds of all speakers. For example, if X asserts
that 'a stallion is a <u>beautiful</u>, <u>proud</u> animal with a <u>wonderful</u>
<u>mane</u>', no one would be in a position to refute this. X would mere-
ly be defining his own private interpretation of a phenomenon in
the world. It would, however, be absurd to attempt to account for
this in terms of semantic features. If we did that, we should be
forced to take into consideration the personal associations of
each individual speaker, and then, in the last analysis, predict
that communication by language is impossible. But it is not: people
who talk about stallions understand each other despite whatever
personal associations they might have. The three defining features
which we have set up are those which provide the most natural explanation of this. They constitute the cognitive (i.e. the 'intellectual', or 'conceptual', or 'denotative') meaning of 'stallion',
dissociated from any personally or socially conditioned connota-
tions.

There are many kinds of noncognitive meaning. For example,
the synonymous lexical items 'steed', 'horse' and 'nag' can be
distinguished along a <u>stylistic</u> dimension of meaning ('poetic',
'neutral', 'slang'). Likewise, the synonyms 'freedom' and 'liber-
ty' may perhaps (as has often been suggested) be differentiated in
terms of <u>emotive</u> meaning; and so on.

The preoccupation with cognitive meaning characteristic of
the present semantic theory should not be taken to imply that noncognitive meaning is held to be of no linguistic interest. What
<u>is</u> being claimed is that priority must be assigned to cognitive
meaning, and that the incorporation of noncognitive aspects of
meaning in a semantic theory presupposes a thorough understanding
of problems relating to cognitive meaning.

----

1. For discussion of different types of meaning, see Leech, 1974,
   Chapter 2.

IV.D.6. <u>Semantic and pragmatic knowledge</u>

The semantic model associated with the standard theory is
a <u>compositional</u> model: it purports to explain in terms of explicitly formulated rules how we can combine lexical items (defined as
bundles of features) in accordance with the syntactic relations
specified in base P-markers to form <u>semantically well-formed</u> sentences. We shall have more to say about this as we go along. Meanwhile, one question which arises in the context of such a semantic
theory is where to draw the borderline between <u>semantic</u> and <u>prag-
matic</u> knowledge, i.e. between our knowledge of meaning and our knowledge of the world. Consider such sentences as

    (1) My horse is a linguist
    (2) The dog was chewing the cud

Both of these are internally contradictory. The difference between
them resides in the features involved in the contradiction. In (1)
- HUMAN in the subject is contradicted by + HUMAN in the predicate.
In (2) 'dog' is specified as, say, - RUMINANT, and this feature is
obviously contradicted by the predicate. We will argue at this point
that $\pm$ HUMAN are central to the linguistic system, whereas the
fact that mammals can be divided into ruminants and carnivores
is something which we learn in zoology.

    Consider now further

    (3) I dreamt that my horse is a linguist
    (4) I tried to imagine what Peter might possibly have meant
        by saying that his horse is a linguist

in which (1) has been embedded under the domination of the 'world-
creating' verbs 'dream' and 'imagine'. (3) and (4) are semantically perfectly well-formed. It would seem, then, that the combinatorial rules of the theory must somehow take into consideration
the fact that the semantic oddity of an embedded sentence may be
'cancelled out' by a 'world-creating' verb higher up in the P-
marker. In other words, in such cases at least, the semantic theory must provide for the notion 'true, or meaningful in a possible
world'. We return to the problem of semantic and pragmatic knowledge in section IV.D.11.

IV.D.7. Semantic universals

In this section we will consider briefly two opposing views
concerning the possible universality of semantic constructs. One
is the Sapir-Whorf hypothesis, the other is what has come to be
known as the hypothesis of effability (for this concept, see Katz,
1972, 18ff.).

The Sapir-Whorf hypothesis expounds the view that (Carroll
(ed.), 1956, 213f.):

> We dissect nature along the lines laid down by our native
> language ... the world is presented in a kaleidoscopic flux
> of impressions which has to be organized by our minds. We cut
> nature up, organize it into concepts, largely because we are
> parties to an agreement to organize it in this way - an agree-
> ment that holds throughout our speech community and is codi-
> fied in the patterns of our language ... We are thus intro-
> duced to a new principle of relativity, which holds that all
> observers are not led by the same physical evidence to the
> same picture of the universe, unless their linguistic back-
> grounds are similar, or can in some way be calibrated.

Semantic structure, then, is viewed as a kind of contrat social
by which the members of a speech-community are bound[1].

The principle of effability asserts that all possible human
thoughts can be expressed by sentences in any natural language.
If this is the case, then, by definition, all languages are inter-
translatable. It is unavoidable that this principle (or hypothesis)
should be tied up with a theory of semantic universals. In particular, if the translation process involves the invention of new
words in the target language (specified as possible words by the
phonological rules of the language) the speaker of that language
must have at his disposal a set of semantic features by means of
which he can process new words (just as the speaker of English
has at his disposal a set of features which define the word 'sibling'). In direct opposition to the relativistic theory of Sapir
and Whorf, then, is the hypothesis embraced by TG-linguists that
semantic features constitute a set of innate substantive universals.

The following statement by Bierwisch (1970a (in Lyons, 1970b)
181f.) illustrates the strongest possible version of the universalist hypothesis:

> It seems natural to assume that these components represent

----

1. Carroll has named this hypothesis linguistic Weltanschauung
   (1953, 43). For some examples, see Carroll (ed.), 1956, 207ff.

categories and principles according to which real and fictitious, perceived and imagined situations and objects are structured and classified. The semantic features do not represent, however, external physical properties, but rather the psychological conditions according to which human beings process their physical and social environment. Thus they are not symbols for physical properties and relations outside the human organism, but rather the internal mechanisms by means of which such phenomena are perceived and conceptualized. This, then leads to the extremely far-reaching, though plausible hypothesis that all semantic structures might finally be reduced to components representing the basic disposition of the cognitive and perceptual structure of the human organism. According to this hypothesis semantic features cannot be different from language to language, but are rather part of the general human capacity for language, forming a universal inventory used in particular ways by particular languages ... All these basic elements are not learned in any reasonable sense of the term, but rather are an innate predisposition for language acquisition. They have to be actualized and released by experience during the process of language acquisition, but as a possible structure they are already present in the learning organism. Hence what is learned during the process of language acquisition, is not the semantic components, but rather their particular combinations in special concepts.

IV.D.8. Some semantic relations and properties

Lexical items and the sentences in which they occur are interrelated in a number of different ways. Before we embark on a treatment of some of these relations, we need to introduce the notions of implication and truth value. We will use these concepts in the following way:

(a) X implies Y if it is the case that Y is necessarily true given the truth of X. This implicational relation is known as entailment. For example, (1) entails (2) (and (2) is entailed by (1)):

(1) I am a woman
(2) I am an adult[1]

(b) X and Y mutually imply each other if it is the case that Y is necessarily true or false if X is true or false and vice versa. In other words, X and Y always have the same truth value.

----

1. Note that the relation does not hold if (1) is negated: 'I am not a woman' does not entail 'I am an adult'. Compare this with the definition of 'semantic presupposition' quoted below, p. 164.

Synonymy. Items like 'buy' and 'purchase' are _synonyms_
because sentences like

   (3) This was a dearly bought victory
   (4) This was a dearly purchased victory

have the same truth value. Within a componential theory of semantics, this means that the meaning of 'buy' and 'purchase' in
(3) and (4) is defined by one set of semantic features. Before we
go on, let us agree to call the semantic interpretation of a lexical item associated with a specific set of semantic features a
reading. Consider now the following sentences:

   (5) This is a handsome sum of money
   (6) This is a considerable sum of money
   (7) This is a handsome woman

(5) and (6) have the same truth value. By contrast, they have nothing semantically in common with (7) (apart from 'this is a'):
'handsome' must have (at least) two readings. Returning now to (3)
and (4), it would seem to be a reasonable guess that the two verbs
are synonymous in all contexts (this is of course an empirical
question). If this is true, they have the same set of readings and
we can say that they are _full synonyms_. By contrast, 'handsome'
and 'considerable' are synonyms: they have different sets of readings, but they have _one_ reading in common. Finally, we may call
(3) and (4), and (5) and (6) _semantic paraphrases_ of each other.

   Hyponymy, incompatibility, and redundancy. Consider the following diagram:

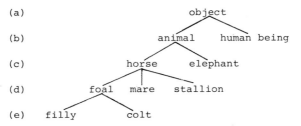

   (a)   object
   (b)   animal   human being
   (c)   horse   elephant
   (d)   foal   mare   stallion
   (e)   filly   colt

The relationship between the items in (e), (d), (c), (b), and (a)
is one of _hyponymy_[1]. Thus 'filly' and 'colt' are _hyponyms_ of

----

1. The term 'hyponymy' in this sense is due to Lyons, 1963, 68f.
   The relation is frequently discussed in terms of _meaning in-
   clusion_: the meaning of one lexical item is included in that
   of another.

(i.e. they imply) the <u>superordinate term</u> 'foal'; 'foal', 'mare', and 'stallion' are hyponyms of the superordinate term 'horse'; and so on. Furthermore, hyponymy is a <u>transitive</u> relation in the following sense: if the items in (e) are hyponyms of the superordinate term in (d), they are also hyponyms of the superordinate term in (c); and so on. For example, if 'colt' implies 'foal', and 'foal' implies 'horse', and 'horse' implies 'animal', then 'colt' also implies 'animal'. At the level of sentence semantics, the relation of hyponymy can be defined in terms of entailment. Thus in each of the following pairs (a) entails (b)[1] (9a and b show transitivity as defined):

    (8a) I saw some horses
    (8b) I saw some animals
    (9a) I saw some colts
    (9b) I saw some animals

The horizontal relationship between the items in each row is one of <u>incompatibility</u>. Thus, since 'colt' implies 'male' and 'filly' implies 'female' (or 'not male'), the following two sentences are contradictions[2]:

    (10) I saw a female colt
    (11) I saw a male filly

By the same token, (12) is an example of semantic <u>redundancy</u>:

    (12) I saw a male colt

It is immediately obvious that the semantic relations we have been considering here can be stated in terms of semantic features. Thus

----

1. Note that the object nouns in the four sentences all have 'specific' meaning. If nouns have 'general' (or 'universal') meaning, the superordinate term entails its hyponyms. For example, 'I like animals' entails 'I like horses, cats, elephants, etc.'. At all events, however, the implicational relation remains <u>unilateral</u> (or <u>asymmetrical</u>). In contrast to this, the implicational relation holding between synonyms is always <u>bilateral</u> (or <u>symmetrical</u>). For discussion of synonymy as a special case of hyponymy, see Lyons, 1968, 455f.

2. Technically, the implicational relations discussed here are known as <u>meaning postulates</u> (cf. Carnap, 1956). In the theory of meaning postulates, the meaning of a lexical item is defined as the sum of the meaning postulates in which it occurs. Thus part of the meaning of 'colt' can be expressed in terms of the postulates 'colt' $\longrightarrow$ 'foal', 'colt' $\longrightarrow$ 'male'.

X is a hyponym of Y if X contains all the features of Y, but Y
does not contain all the features of X. X and Y are incompatible
if they have opposite specifications for at least one feature;
and so on.

    Antonymy. Antonymy is a special kind of incompatibility. X
and Y are antonyms if they have opposite specifications for one
feature, but are otherwise identical in meaning. By this definition 'colt' and 'filly' are antonyms. Other examples would be
'man'/'woman'; 'boy'/'girl'; 'spinster'/'bachelor'; etc. In all
these cases the opposition between the two items is absolute in
the sense that there is no middle ground between them; that is,
X implies not Y, and not Y implies X (and vice versa). In many
cases, however, the relation between antonyms is graded. An example
is the pair 'big' and 'small'. Here the implicational relationship
is as follows: X implies not Y, but not Y does not imply X (and
vice versa) (for example, 'the house is big' implies 'the house
is not small', but 'the house is not small' does not imply 'the
house is big' (and vice versa)). Consider further the following
sentences:

    (13) I have a big house
    (14) I have a bigger house than John
    (15) John has a small house
    (16) John has a smaller house than me

Here (14) implies (16), and vice versa. However, (14) does not
imply (15). To see why this is so, we must examine the meaning of
(13). Relevant here is the lexical item 'medium-sized'. Clearly,
this is intermediate between 'big' and 'small' and can therefore
be said to neutralize the distinction between them. Another way
of saying this is that 'medium-sized' constitutes the norm on the
'big' - 'small' scale. It would follow from this that (13) (and
(15)) logically imply a sentence containing a comparative form:

    (13a) I have a bigger house than X
    (15a) John has a smaller house than X

where X is the norm. In contrast to this, (14) and (16) do not involve a norm: (14) may mean 'John has a very big house, but mine
is even bigger'/'John has a fair-sized house, but mine is bigger'/
'I have a small house, but John's is even smaller', etc. Mutatis

mutandis, the same applies to (16). In other words, the positive
forms of many adjectives involve comparison relative to a norm,
whereas comparative forms involve comparison relative to an arbitrary point on a scale between two poles. Just where that point
is depends on what is being talked about.

  Converses. Consider the following sentences:

  (17a) I sold the car to John
  (17b) John bought the car from me

(17a) and (17b) mutually imply each other and are therefore paraphrases of each other. Note that the only difference between the
two sentences (apart from the difference between 'buy' and 'sell')
is the order of occurrence of the three noun phrases (and the prepositions). A semantic theory must be able to specify explicitly the
paraphrase relation between the two sentences[1,2].

  Polysemy and homonymy. Normally, the semantic relations holding
between lexical items are completely independent of phonological
factors (this follows from the principle of arbitrariness discussed in the notes to section III.3). However, phonological considerations are relevant to two important semantic phenomena: homonymy and polysemy. Homonymy implies phonological identity between
different lexical items with different meanings (and, frequently,
different grammatical classifications). An example is (18) (see
overleaf):

  By contrast, polysemous items have one phonological shape,
one grammatical classification, but several meanings, or senses.
An example is (19) (see overleaf):

----

1. For possible lexical entries for 'buy' and 'sell', see Katz,
   1972, 342f.

2. Observe that there is much similarity between the relation
   holding between (17a) and (17b) and that holding between (14)
   and (16). Following Halliday (e.g. 1970) we may say that in unmarked declarative sentences (i.e. sentences in which the leftmost constituent is the subject) the subject constitutes the
   theme of the sentence. Thus, if the speaker chooses 'John' as
   the theme in the situation which determines the utterance of
   sentences like (14) and (16), he is committed to the point on
   the scale which defines the size of John's house. The choice
   of adjective follows automatically from the choice of theme.
   In (17a) and (17b) the relationship between 'I' and 'John' is
   one of direction (the car passes from 'I' to 'John'). In his
   choice of theme, then, the speaker may focus his attention on
   either the source or the goal of this process. For further discussion, see below, section V.B.3.

(18) Lexical item

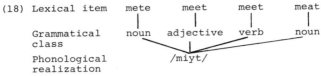

Grammatical
class

Phonological
realization

(19) Lexical item

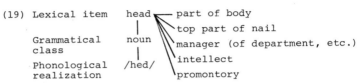

Grammatical
class

Phonological
realization

The two examples we have given seem to be fairly clear-cut. However, the distinction between polysemes and homynyms cause problems in some cases. We return to this in section IV.G.12.

Let us conclude this section by mentioning the distinction
between <u>synthetic</u>, <u>analytic</u>, and <u>contradictory</u> sentences. A synthetic sentence is one whose truth value depends on the world of
actuality. For example,

(20) My house was burnt down

is a synthetic sentence. An analytic sentence is one which is
true by virtue of meaning alone. An example is

(21) Women are females

in which the meaning of the predicate is contained in the meaning
of the subject (cf. also sentence (1) of section IV.D.4). Finally,
a contradictory sentence is one which is false by virtue of meaning
alone. Thus in

(22) Women are males

the meaning of the predicate is irreconcilable with that of the
subject (see also notes to this section)[1].

----

1. A distinction can be drawn between analyticity and contradictoriness on the one hand and redundancy and incompatibility
   on the other: the former are properties of sentence-semantics,
   the latter of constituency-semantics (in particular, the relationship between nominal heads and their modifiers). However,
   since in the present theory sentences like (10), (11), and
   (12) would be derived from deep structures containing contradictory and analytic sentences (in the form of relative
   clauses), this distinction does not seem to have much force
   (recall that deep structures form the input to the rules of
   semantic interpretation).

IV.D.9. <u>Semantic projection rules</u>

First of all, let us adopt the second proposal concerning
lexical insertion discussed in section IV.C.2.3: lexical items
are inserted into P_1 by a substitution transformation. We will
further assume that lexical items are inserted freely under category symbols and that hence selectional restrictions are semantic
in nature (for further discussion, see next section).

Katz, Fodor, and Postal (1963, 1964) proposed a set of <u>pro-</u>
<u>jection rules</u> to integrate the semantic structure of lexical
items and the syntactic structure of base P-markers. Let us illustrate the nature and function of such rules by way of the following abstract deep structure (a more specific example will be
given in the notes to this section):

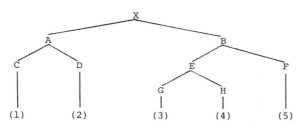

where the capitals should be interpreted as syntactic categories and
the bracketed integers as complexes of semantic features. It is assumed that (1-5) have been inserted in accordance with their syntactic feature specifications. The projection rules start from the
bottom of the tree and work upwards towards the highest node. First
the lexical readings immediately dominated by the category symbols C and D, and G and H are projected on to and <u>amalgamated</u> at
the nodes A and E respectively. The result is <u>derived readings</u> at
A and E. Then the derived reading of E is amalgamated with the
lexical reading of (5) at B; finally, the derived readings of A
and B are amalgamated at X to form the semantic reading of the
whole sentence. This constitutes the <u>semantic representation</u> of
the sentence. The process of forming the derived reading of a sentence blocks if at any given point selectional requirements are
not satisfied. Observe that although (2) and (3) are immediately
adjacent in the terminal string, they are not brought into semantic contact before the projection rules have amalgamated A and B

at X. Thus in the semantic interpretation of a sentence like

(1) The house was reading the paper thoroughly

the derived reading of 'the'[1] and 'house' at the subject NP and
the reading of VP derived from the readings of the constituents
of the verb phrase are both specified as being perfectly normal.
Violation of the selectional feature of 'read' (+ HUMAN in the
subject noun) does not take place until the derived readings of
the subject NP and the VP are amalgamated at S.

The reader should now reconsider (1a), (1b), (2a), and (3a)
of section IV.D.2 in the light of the theory of projection rules.

IV.D.10. The status of selectional features

We concluded our treatment of selectional features in section
IV.C.2.2 by pointing out that in a grammar whose base contains a
subcategorization component of the Aspects-type (a) such features
are defined as syntactic[2] (specifically, syntactic conditions on
lexical insertion), and (b) the noun is conceived of as being selectionally dominant. In this section we will discuss (a). We return to (b) in section IV.D.12.

Various objections - all of them quite weighty - have been
made to the proposal that selectional features are syntactic in
nature. Consider for example the following sentence (and compare
sentences (3) and (4) of section IV.D.6):

(1) I dreamt that my car kicked me

In (1) the embedded sentence is not (directly[3]) generated by the
subcategorization model at all. In particular, the rules spelling
out the structure of the complex symbol under the immediate domination of N in the subject NP may insert the feature (+ Animate).
Since 'car' is entered in the lexicon without this feature, it

----

1. In some formulations, as we have seen, 'the' would be a set of
   syntactic features dominated by N at the time of semantic interpretation.
2. Selectional features were first introduced in the 1963-paper
   by Katz and Fodor. From the beginning, they were defined as
   semantic features.
3. It is perhaps derivatively generated, provided the grammar is
   supplemented by a theory of 'semi-sentences'. See Katz, 1964b
   and Chomsky, 1965, 157ff., 227. For discussion of this point,
   consult also Weinreich, 1972, 39ff. and Haas, 1973, 82ff.

cannot be inserted by the lexical substitution rule. On the other
hand, if the complex symbol immediately dominated by N in the subject NP contains the feature (- Animate), this feature will automatically be copied as a selectional feature in the complex symbol generated under the immediate domination of V. Consequently,
the verb 'kick' cannot be inserted. This is a serious drawback
inasmuch as the 'world-creating' verb 'dream' makes (1) a perfectly well-formed sentence.

A different objection is that the subcategorization model
defines selectional restrictions as holding between <u>lexical items</u>
rather than between, say, a verb and an <u>NP</u>. However, as pointed
out by McCawley (1968a (in Bach and Harms, 1968) 133f.), there are
many cases in which the selectional restriction holds between the
predicate and the whole NP. Consider the following sentences:

   (2) * My sister is the father of two
   (3) The professor is the father of two
   (4) * The pretty professor is the father of two

In the subcategorization model (2) is defined as ungrammatical
(hence the asterisk). (3) is perfectly all right. Why, then, is
(4) ungrammatical? In TG-theory a sentence like (4) is derived
from

   (5) The professor who is pretty is the father of two

by the rules of <u>relative reduction</u> and <u>modifier-preposing</u> (for
which, see section IV.G.14.4). In other words, the deep structure
of (4) would look like this:

   (4a)

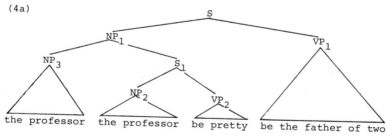

(4a) would be generated by the subcategorization model in roughly
the following way: the noun 'professor' dominated by NP_3 would be
assigned the feature (+ Male) (or perhaps rather (+ Masculine)).

Conversely, the noun 'professor' dominated by NP_2 would be specified (- Masculine). The items 'father' and 'pretty' can be inserted in VP_1 and VP_2 respectively without contradicting these
features[1]. But since (4) is clearly ungrammatical (or semantically
anomalous, as the case may be), the projection rules would need
to take account of selectional features in order to make it explicit that the anomaly arises when the derived reading of NP_1 is
amalgamated with the derived reading of VP_1 at S. In other words,
the statement of selectional restrictions must be duplicated in
the semantic component - even where the same features are involved.

A further objection is that it is only relatively few predicates whose selectional restrictions can be accounted for in terms
of such general concepts as Animateness, Abstractness, etc. Consider for example verbs like 'eat' and 'write'. 'Eat' would have
to be restricted with respect to its object by a feature like, say,
(+ Foodstuff) and 'write' by something like (+ Inscription). If
the context-free subcategorization rules were to generate such
subdistinctions, they would have to be enormously complex. Furthermore, given the distinction between syntax and semantics, it
seems counterintuitive to characterize such features as syntactic
rather than semantic.

Objections such as these suggest that selectional restrictions should be accounted for in the semantic component and that
lexical insertion should be a transformation inserting lexical
items freely under category symbols[2].

Even so, there are still problems. Compare with (1)

(6) I dreamt that my house walked out on me

(7) I dreamt that the rock was singing the national anthem

etc.

----

1. In Aspects the selectional rules are not formulated so as to
   cover the relationship between subject nouns and predicative
   nouns. We are assuming here with McCawley (cf. also Langendoen,
   1969, 50f.) that selectional restrictions hold between predicates (nouns, verbs, and adjectives) and the NPs with which
   they are in construction (cf. above, p. 115 and next section).

2. A further problem is that selectional features which hold across
   sentence boundaries cannot be generated by the rules (cf.
   below, p. 209). An example is: 'I ate the thing which I suddenly
   realized John had told me was $\left\{ \begin{array}{l} \text{* a copy of Hard Times} \\ \text{a piece of his mother's cake} \end{array} \right\}$'.

If the selectional feature of the predicate requires the <u>presence</u>
of some feature in another constituent, then the projection rules
cannot provide the embedded sentences in (6) and (7) with a semantic representation, simply because the required feature - + HUMAN -
is not present in the subject noun. Consequently, the interpretation of (1), (6) and (7) must be 'I dreamt + NONSENSE'. In other
words, the three sentences are defined as synonymous[1]. We return
to a possible solution to this problem in section IV.D.12.

Henceforth, we will assume that selectional restrictions are
implemented in the semantic component.

IV.D.11. Semantic anomaly

The question of <u>semantic anomaly</u> is bound up with the concept
of selectional features. It has been widely assumed that semantic
anomaly is something which pertains to linguistic rather than to
pragmatic knowledge. However, as suggested in section IV.D.6, the
borderline between the two kinds of knowledge is difficult - in the
last analysis perhaps impossible - to draw. Consider such sentences
as

(1) The horse owned the man
(2) The horse owned the house
(3) The dog was flying from one tree to another
(4) The dog was sharpening its beak
(5) The dog had lost one horn

(1) and (2) are discussed by Leech, 1974, 145. Leech concludes that
they are both anomalous because the verb 'own' requires the feature + HUMAN in the subject. It would, however, be erroneous to
say that (1) is more anomalous than (2): the verb 'own' does not
require the feature - HUMAN in its object; if we feel inclined to
think so, this is because we know that slavery is not an institu-
tion in our society; hence claiming that 'own' can only be combined with a - HUMAN object would be tantamount to "overstepping
the boundary of linguistic knowledge". It could, however, be argued that even the requirement that the subject of 'own' should
be specified + HUMAN is an instance of pragmatic rather than linguistic knowledge: ownership is determined by such extralinguistic
----

1. For this point, see McCawley, <u>op. cit</u>., 128f. Counterarguments
   are presented by Katz, 1972, 95ff.

phenomena as money, loans from a bank, bills of exchange, etc.
((2) would be perfectly all right in the world of the Houyhnhnms).
(3), (4), and (5) are absurd for obvious reasons. If we were to
explain this absurdity in terms of selectional violations, we
should have to include in the inventory of features x WINGS, x BEAK,
and x HORNS (they would hardly be binary). However, if we did that,
we would be well on the way to becoming involved with what Carroll
called "the totality of human knowledge". The question that can
be asked, of course, is this: is there any stopping point in feature analysis, that is, any point which precisely defines the
borderline between semantic competence and extralinguistic knowledge; and if there is, where is it and how can it be motivated
empirically?[1].

Let us conclude this section by making the following points:

(a) The borderline between semantic and pragmatic knowledge
seems to be extremely difficult to draw.

(b) If we accept the notion of a possible message in a possible world or possible situation, the problem of (a) seems to
be considerably reduced: putative semantic anomalies can be explained solely in terms of our assumptions concerning the nature
of the world. The consequence of this position is that there is
no difference in principle between such sentences as (1) and (2)
on the one hand, and (3), (4), and (5) on the other.

(c) Given the notion 'true or meaningful in a possible world',
many of the selectional restrictions which have been suggested in
the literature impose too heavy constraints on possible messages.
For example, 'own' is obviously too heavily constrained: the selectional feature posited is determined by one particular world - the
factual, nonbizarre, nonfictional world surrounding us. ·

(d) If many anomalies are factually rather than linguistically determined, the following question can be raised: is there a
way of defining the relationship between semantic and pragmatic
knowledge such that for any given sentence it is possible to say
that from one point of view it is semantically impeccable, whereas

----

1. Cf. Fillmore, 1971a (in Fillmore and Langendoen, 1971) 274.
   Compare in this connection also McCawley's famous sentence
   (1970a (in Jacobs and Rosenbaum, 1970) 167f.): 'My toothbrush
   is alive and is trying to kill me'. McCawley points out that
   "a person who utters" such a sentence "should be referred to
   a psychiatric clinic, not to a remedial English course".

from another point of view it is anomalous. We return to this
question in section IV.D.16.

IV.D.12. Transfer features

Selectional features, as we have seen, are properties of
predicates. The following sentences:

(1) The stones were friends
(2) Human beings are four-legged
(3) The horse laughed

are anomalous (with respect to our world) because (a) 'friends'
requires the feature + ANIMATE in the subject, (b) 'four-legged'
requires the feature - HUMAN in the subject, and (c) 'laughs' requires the feature + HUMAN in the subject.

Consider now

(4) We should be good to our four-legged friends

In this 'four-legged' is a predicate whose subject is 'friends'.
How should this sentence be interpreted? The noun 'friend' must
have among its features + ANIMATE, whereas it is unspecified with
respect to HUMAN. That this is so is evident from

(5) We have a cat and a canary who are great friends
(6) John and Eric are great friends

Now, 'friend' in (4) is obviously - HUMAN. Since the noun itself
is not specified for HUMAN, the presence of - HUMAN can only be
ascribed to 'four-legged'. It would seem, then, that to account
for (4), we must restate the theory of selectional features in the
following way: a predicate transfers into (or imposes on) the
reading(s) of the noun(s) with which it is construed its selectional features[1]. Thus in (4) the feature - HUMAN is transferred
from the predicate 'four-legged' into the reading of the subject
noun.

There is little doubt that in those cases where a noun is
unspecified for the selectional feature of the predicate, the restatement of selectional restrictions as a transfer of the selectional feature of the predicate into the reading of the noun is

----

1. This insight, above all, is due to Weinreich, 1972 (see especially sections 2.2.4 and 3.3). Compare also the discussion of
   pro-forms in Katz and Postal, 1964, 82f.

simply necessary. The question then arises whether this approach
to the problem of selection might not profitably be generalized
to all sentences.

It has often been pointed out that the meaning of predicates
completely "overflows" to the nouns with which they are construed[1].
To illustrate this, let us consider once again the sentence

(7) The man stabbed the woman

The meaning of (7) can be stated informally as follows (let X be
'the man' and Y 'the woman'): 'X performs an activity, X acts quickly, X has the purpose of killing or wounding Y, X uses a pointed
instrument, X causes Y to become penetrated and wounded (perhaps
dead)'. By contrast, the two nouns receive quite different interpretations in

(8) The man forgave the woman

As a further example, we consider the verb 'chase'[2]. Compare the
following sentences:

(9) The police were anxious to arrest the criminals

(10) The police were chasing the criminals through the streets

In (10) both the police and the criminals are engaged in rapid activity - obviously with different purposes. Furthermore, it is
implied that there is a certain distance between the two parties;
and so on. In (9), clearly, these semantic elements are not present.

Predicates, then, impose a number of features on the surrounding nouns. Since neither (7) nor (10) is in any way anomalous,
we may assume that the features transferred from the predicates
are _potentially_ present in the nouns and can be activated by the
relevant predicates. Hence the oddity of

(11) The snails were chasing each other down the lawn

and the absurdity of

(12) The cat was chasing the snail down the lawn

(in terms of the observationally accessible world).

----

1. See for example Langendoen, 1969, 44f. Langendoen discusses a
   number of interesting examples illustrating this principle.
2. For a formal discussion of the meaning of 'chase', see Katz,
   1972, 101ff, 165f.

Since so many features are transferred from predicates into the readings of nouns, it might seem reasonable to assume with
Weinreich that the feature normally singled out as selectional
is also transferred. Thus, in (7), + HUMAN is transferred from the
reading of 'stab' into the reading of 'man'. Since this feature
is already present in the reading of 'man', no anomaly ensues.

There are, then, two ways of treating selectional features:
(a) the collocational range of the predicate is dependent on the
presence of a feature in the reading of a noun, which means that
the noun is selectionally dominant, and (b) the predicate transfers a feature into the reading of a noun and thus is assigned a
more "active" role in the semantic process. These two approaches
make different empirical claims with respect to semantic anomaly.
Thus, according to (a), in

(13) The tiger stabbed the deer

the projection rules will search the reading of 'tiger', fail to
find the feature + HUMAN, and hence rule the sentence out as anomalous without explaining the anomaly. By contrast, according to
(b), the feature + HUMAN will be transferred at a certain point
into the reading of 'tiger'. It will clash with - HUMAN. However,
the notion of a clash is defined with respect to features competing,
as it were, within the confines of a single lexical item. In other
words, the anomaly receives a natural explanation. In this analysis, which makes explicit the notion of 'attempted interpretation',
sentences (3) and (4) of section IV.D.6 and sentences (6) and (7)
of section IV.D.10 would cause fewer theoretical problems (for
discussion of semantic anomaly, see Weinreich, 1972, 39ff., 96ff.).

Transfer features play an essential role in the explication
of metaphor. A metaphor involves three factors: (A) something
which is being talked about, (B) something with which (A) is being compared, and (C) the justification of the comparison. The
juxtaposition of (A) and (B) always involves a selectional violation. Consequently, (C) is some semantic feature of (B) (often
quite 'deep-seated'), which, when transferred into the reading of
(A), causes (A) to be reinterpreted in such a way that the selectional violation is overcome.

We will not go into the details of metaphor. Some works dealing with the phenomenon from a linguistic point of view will be
cited in the bibliographical notes.

IV.D.13. Semantic ambiguity

Consider the following sentence:

(1) John raised the child

(1) is ambiguous and the ambiguity can be ascribed to the two different senses of 'raise' (we take 'raise' to be a polysemous item)
which can be symbolized BREED and LIFT. Now, 'raise' in the sense
of BREED requires a + ANIMATE object, whereas in the second sense -
LIFT - it requires an object specified + PHYSICAL and + OBJECT.
The projection rule amalgamating the readings of 'raise' and 'the
child' at VP cannot filter out one of the two readings (i.e. cannot disambiguate the meaning of the VP) because the object noun
contains the features + ANIMATE, + PHYSICAL, and + OBJECT (all of
which have been inserted by redundancy rules). Compare now with
(1) sentences (5) and (7) of section IV.D.8:

(2) This is a handsome woman
(3) This is a handsome sum of money

'Handsome' has two readings. One spells out the sense BEAUTIFUL,
the other the sense MODERATELY LARGE. These readings have different
selectional features: the former requires in (alternatively imposes
on) its subject the feature + HUMAN, the latter the feature
+ AMOUNT[1]. These two features are totally unrelated. Hence the projection rules can discard the irrelevant readings of 'handsome'
in the interpretation of (2) and (3).

This, in essence, is the process of disambiguation within
the framework of the KP-hypothesis.

IV.D.14. The relationship between syntactic and semantic features

A distinction must be made between syntactic - in particular
inherent - features and semantic features. In some cases this distinction seems to be fairly clear-cut. For example, the syntactic
feature (± Countable) accounts for such syntactic facts as cooccur-
rence-restrictions between determiners and nouns: mass nouns cannot be construed with the indefinite article:

(1) * He gave a blood

----

1. For a suggested entry for 'handsome', see Katz, 1972, 44.
   We return to a discussion of this entry in section IV.G.12.

and so on.

The problem becomes more intricate in those cases where syntactic features resemble semantic features. Consider for example the grammatical category <u>gender</u>, which may be specified in terms of the features ($\pm$ Masculine) and (+ Neuter). What is the relationship between (+ Masculine) and + MALE in a noun like 'man'? One possible answer is that the former accounts for syntactic facts such as pronominalization. Against this it might be argued that one feature would be sufficient. As far as 'man' is concerned, this may well be true. However, there are cases in which such parsimony might perhaps lead to the wrong results. Consider the following sentences:

(2) Britain lost her independence

(3) John got married yesterday - a bachelor lost his independence

If we assume that 'Britain' has the feature (- Masculine) and 'bachelor' the feature (+ Masculine), the pronouns 'her' and 'his' can be readily explained. However, 'Britain' does not have the feature - MALE. If it did, (2) would entail

(2a) A female lost her independence

just as (3) entails

(3a) A male lost his independence

This is clearly not the case. Consequently, it is arguable that ($\pm$ Masculine) and $\pm$ MALE are separate features although this is not clear in every instance[1].

IV.D.15. <u>Reference and coreference</u>

When we speak, we generally use language about something which is not language, i.e. the extralinguistic world. This nexus between language and the world is established by what we will call the <u>referential property</u> of (some) lexical items.

One of the fundamental differences between the semantic theory we are considering here and the Bloomfieldian conception of meaning relates to the notion of reference. Bloomfield, as we have

----

1. For discussion of such examples, see Katz and Fodor, 1963 (in Fodor and Katz, 1964) 517f. and Katz, 1972, 80ff.

seen, felt on safe ground only when the <u>referent</u> of a given word
had been exhaustively described by the science under whose domain
it fell. Consequently, the semantic theory which he hoped would
emerge in due time (cf. the quotation on p. 3) would be based entirely on a referential conception of meaning. In other words, as
pointed out in section I.1, meaning would be something external
to language (cf. also section IV.D.3). Now, it is clear that a
theory of meaning which is based on the assumption that there exists a set of innate substantive semantic universals (cf. the quotation from Bierwisch on p. 142f.) cannot be a referential theory:
basically, meaning is conceived of as something internal to the language system. However, the fact that meaning and reference are not
identified does obviously not imply a denial of the referential
capacity of language.

The problem of reference has been one of the fundamental issues in the philosophical approach to the question of meaning. We
cannot go into the details of this (the interested reader is referred to the works cited in the notes). On the other hand, since
reference (and coreference, as we have already indicated in sections
IV.A.7 and IV.D.2) are notions of crucial importance to TG-theory,
particularly with respect to the formulation of certain T-rules,
it is necessary to outline briefly what is meant by reference and
coreference in this book.

Suppose first of all that we agree to make reference contingent on the notion of <u>ostensive definition</u>: for a lexical item
(but see p. 162, note) to have reference, it must be possible to
<u>point to</u> some observable object, process, activity, or quality in
the extralinguistic world. Consider now the following sentences:

(1) The dog is barking
(2) Peter is reliable

In (1) the subject is a <u>definite noun phrase</u>. It is clear that it
has a referent which can be identified at the moment of utterance.
In (2) the subject is a proper noun. Again, the referent of 'Peter'
can be ostensibly defined (though this time perhaps not at the
moment of utterance). We will assume that definite noun phrases
(with a (+ Common) head) and proper nouns are the most genuinely
referential expressions in (the) language. Next, consider the predicates 'bark' and 'reliable'. Do they have reference? The answer
to this question depends in part on what point of view one chooses

to adopt. In the case of 'bark', it would not be unreasonable to
say that it refers to an activity that can be ostensibly defined.
'Reliable' is more problematic. It would seem that its meaning cannot be defined in terms of reference, but only by examining its
place in the semantic network (or field) to which it belongs (in
particular, its meaning could be defined in terms of such relations
as synonymy, antonymy, incompatibility, and hyponymy)[1]. It could
also be argued that since, as we have seen, the meaning of a predicate seems to overflow completely to its subject, it really makes
no sense to invoke the notion of reference in this connection[2].
Consider the following examples:

> (3a) Both John and Peter laughed
>
> (3b) John laughed and Peter laughed
>
> (4) John and Mary danced all night

(3a) and (3b) mutually imply each other. In TG-theory, as we shall
see later, it is argued (by some) that (3a) is derived from (3b)
by the rules of conjunction reduction and identical conjunct collapsing. For these T-rules (in particular the latter) to operate in
this case, the two predicates must be weakly identical: they are
phonologically (or better perhaps lexically) identical, but not
coreferential. Now, saying that they are not coreferential seems
to be a flat contradiction of the remark just made about predicates
and reference. However, the contradiction disappears if we consider
what we really mean by calling the two occurrences of 'laughed' in
(3b) noncoreferential: they are associated with separate (or non-
joint) subjects. (4) is ambiguous. In one interpretation it means
that John and Mary danced all night, but not with each other. In
that case (4) entails

> (4a) John danced all night and Mary danced all night

----

1. This is true of 'bark' as well. Clearly, 'bark' is semantically
   closely related to such other lexical items as 'neigh', 'bleat',
   'crow', etc. We can make a distinction between relational meaning and referential meaning: all lexical items have relational
   meaning (i.e. are semantically related to other lexical items
   in certain specifiable ways), but not all lexical items have
   referential meaning in the sense that they satisfy the requirement of ostensive definition.

2. The reason why the question of predicates and reference, which is
   fraught with philosophical difficulties, is raised at all here is
   that the (non)coreference of predicates is invoked by some
   writers (see for example Jacobs and Rosenbaum, 1968, 258).

in which, clearly, the two predicates are not associated with the
the same subject. In the alternative interpretation of (4) John
and Mary danced with each other: the activity of dancing is associated with John and Mary as constituting a referential entity (this
might be made explicit by having 'John' and 'Mary' dominated by
one NP in the deep structure (which forms the input to the rules of
semantic interpretation (cf. below, p. 332f.)).

As far as predicates are concerned, therefore, the notion of
reference seems to be inseparably bound up with the subject (and
other noun phrases) with which they are construed.

Let us return now to nouns. Consider a sentence like

(5) John saw John in the mirror

(5) is a little odd at first sight. However, if we bring to bear
on it the notion of coreferentiality, the oddity is resolved: the
two occurrences of 'John' refer to different persons. If they had
been coreferential, the sentence would obligatorily have undergone
the rule of <u>reflexivization</u>:

(6) John saw himself in the mirror

The operation of this rule, then, is apparently contingent on
coreferentiality. Compare now with (6) the following sentence:

(7) A cat always cleans itself thoroughly

In this 'a cat' is an <u>indefinite noun phrase</u>. It is clearly not
referential: no specific cat is involved; the sentence makes a <u>ge-
neric statement</u>[1]. Now, (7) has undergone reflexivization in the
same way as (6). It would seem, then, that the statement of coreferentiality as a condition on reflexivization is insufficient since
the rule also operates in those cases where the noun phrases involved
do not have reference. And it <u>is</u> insufficient unless we are prepared
to extend the notion of (co)reference to cover cases of "hypothetical" (co)"reference" (cf. Partee, 1972 (in Davidson and Harman,
1972) 434 - and see in this connection also Lyons, 1968, 424ff.).
Hypothetical (co)reference in this sense, furthermore, would account for such cases as

----

1. In connection with (7) we can make a further important point
   (a modification, in fact, of what was said in the initial
   paragraph of this section): the notion of reference is not applicable to <u>individual</u> nouns, but only to nouns as they occur
   in sentences, that is, to noun phrases. Thus, although 'cat'
   in (7) is not referential, 'cat' in the following sentence is:
   'I hate that cat'.

(8) I am going to buy a new hat, and I hope you will like it

(9) The unicorn hurt itself

(10) It is a truth (which is) universally acknowledged, that a
single man ... must be in want of a wife

(8) has two readings. In one reading 'a new hat' is referential in
the sense that the speaker refers to a specific hat which he has
singled out. In the other reading 'a new hat' is not a referential
expression: no specific hat is referred to. In either case, however,
pronominalization, which is generally formulated as being dependent
on coreferentiality, has applied. In (9) 'the unicorn' obviously
only has hypothetical reference: unicorns are fictitious creatures.
In (10), in which relativization is assumed to be conditioned by
coreferentiality between the head noun phrase and the shared noun
phrase in the embedded clause, the notion of (co)reference is applicable only if it is extended to cover abstract noun phrases
('truth' does not satisfy the criterion of ostensive definition in
any straightforward sense).

Since many T-rules (notably relativization, pronominalization
(including reflexivization), conjunction, and equi NP deletion) are
dependent on coreferentiality, we will assume that each deep-structure noun phrase is arbitrarily assigned a referential index. For example, the deep structures of (5) and (9) would be, roughly (disregarding the constituent 'in the mirror' in (5)):

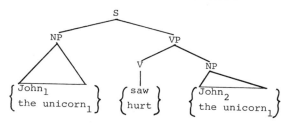

IV.D.16. Presuppositions

In recent years, the notion of presupposition has come to play
an increasingly important role in the semantic literature. The term
has been used in a variety of different senses by different writers.
Nevertheless, two main approaches can be distinguished. In the first
approach, 'presupposition' is a logical concept which is bound up
with truth-conditional semantics. In the second, presuppositions
express the conditions under which sentences (and lexical items) can

be appropriately used. We will refer to the former type as semantic,
and to the latter type as pragmatic presuppositions.

    Semantic presuppositions. There are two different approaches
to the concept 'semantic presupposition of a sentence'. The first
of these stems from the logician and philosopher Frege. According
to Frege and his followers (within the theory of TG-grammar notably
Katz), a presupposition is a referential condition under which the
proposition expressed by a nongeneric, declarative sentence can be
either true or false[1]. For example, (1) presupposes (1a):

    (1) John likes Mary
    (1a) John exists and Mary exists

By the same token, (2) presupposes (2a):

    (2) The present president of Britain is a woman
    (2a) There exists a person who is the president of Britain

Since (2a) is obviously empirically false, (2) does not succeed in
making a statement - it has no truth value[2].

    On the second approach, a presupposition is a sentence which
logically follows from the presupposing sentence and its negation.
Consider the following statement by Keenan (in Fillmore and
Langendoen, 1971, 45)[3]:

> A sentence logically presupposes a sentence S´ just in
> case S logically implies S´ and the negation of S, $\sim$S, also
> logically implies S´. In other words, the truth of S´ is a
> necessary condition for the truth or falsity of S.

In many cases, this conception of presupposition coincides with
the Fregean conception[4]. Thus (1) and (2) follow directly from
it (also if the presupposing sentences are negated). However, it
has a wider scope. For instance, one of the examples adduced by

----

1. Note that in this approach the concept of presupposition is
   closely bound up with the notion of reference. Since, as we
   have seen, the NPs of a generic sentence have no reference,
   the sentence has no presuppositions.
2. The truth conditions of a sentence are not coextensive with
   the presuppositions. Rather, a sentence is true if and only if
   what it refers to has the properties denoted by the predicate.
   For example, 'John is tall' can be true if and only if (a)
   John exists (the presupposition) and (b) John belongs to the set
   of tall men.
3. Cf. Van Fraassen, 1968 and Karttunen, 1973. Compare also the definition of entailment given above, p. 143 and note.
4. For a critical discussion of Keenan's definition, see Katz,
   1973a.

Keenan concerns selectional restrictions: (3) presupposes (3a):

(3) That arithmetic is incomplete (didn't) suprise(d) Magrid
(3a) Magrid is animate and intelligent

Since (3a) is not a referential condition for (3) to bear a truth
value, it is hardly encompassed by the Fregean conception of presupposition[1].

Pragmatic presuppositions. Pragmatic presuppositions, as the
name indicates, are conditions on the appropriate use of sentences
and lexical items. Consider the following example (cf. Kiparsky
and Kiparsky, 1970 (in Bierwisch and Heidolph, 1970) 149ff.):

(4) John cleaned the car

The speaker who utters (4) asserts (4a) and (4b):

(4a) John caused the car to become clean
(4b) The car became clean

and presupposes

(4c) The car was not clean prior to John's activity

(4c), then, constitutes a contextual condition on the appropriate
utterance of (4).

Consider next (5)[2]:

(5) His best friend is (not) a spinster

In uttering this, the speaker asserts

(5a) His best friend is (un)married

and presupposes

(5b) His best friend is human and female and adult

(5) relates to the semantic structure of the lexical item 'spinster'.
It will be apparent that we have restated its meaning as discussed
in section IV.D.4 in terms of an assertion feature (which defines

----

1. (3) sheds interesting light on the notion of selectional features. In particular, there would be no way of ruling out the
   following sentence by means of a selectional feature of the
   verb 'surprise': 'That arithmetic was incomplete (didn't) sur-
   prise(d) the unintelligent students'. In other words, (3) leads
   us back to McCawley's conception of selectional restrictions
   as presuppositions about intended referents (as do also sentences
   (5), (8), and (9) below (cf. notes to sections IV.D.10,11,12)).

2. For discussion of examples like (5), see Fillmore, 1969b (in
   Kiefer, 1969), 122f., Langendoen, 1971, Katz, 1972, 149f., and
   Wilson, 1975, 96ff.

the meaning 'proper' of the item) and a set of presupposition features (for this terminology, see Wilson, 1975, 95)[1].

Pragmatic assumptions play a crucial role in the concept of
relative well-formedness as discussed by Lakoff, 1971a. The argument goes like this: The grammar generates pairs: PR,S (where PR =
a set of presuppositions and S = sentence); well-formedness should
be defined on PR,S. Lakoff considers such sentences as

(6) John told Mary she was ugly and then she insulted him
(7) John told Mary she was beautiful and then she insulted him
(the underlined words are heavily stressed)

(6) and (7) presuppose (6a) and (7a) respectively:

(6a) That John told Mary she was ugly entails that John
insulted Mary
(7a) That John told Mary she was beautiful entails that
John insulted Mary

(6) and (7) are well-formed relative to (and only relative to)

----

1. Semantic (or logical) and pragmatic presuppositions are not
mutually exclusive. Rather, the former are properties of sentences, the latter properties of utterances. For example, (5)
satisfies Keenan's definition of semantic presupposition. From
a purely semantic point of view, (5b) has to do with the structure of the lexical item 'spinster'; from a pragmatic point of
view, it has to do with the appropriate use of this item in a
specific context. In the former case, it is the sentence, in
the latter, the speaker that has presuppositions. Similarly,
the speaker who sincerely utters (2) pragmatically presupposes
that (2a) is true and assumes that the hearer does the same.
Only, as it happens, the speaker is misinformed about the structure of the British constitution. This has a direct bearing on
the concept of relative well-formedness to be discussed presently. It has been argued by Stalnaker (1970) (for discussion, see
also Karttunen, 1973) that the following relationship holds
between semantic and pragmatic presuppositions: If a sentence
S semantically presupposes a sentence S´, then S´ is also a pragmatic presupposition of S, whereas the converse is not always
true. By this proposal, (1a), (2a), (3a), and (5b) are all both
semantic and pragmatic presuppositions. Whether (4c) is a semantic presupposition depends on the semantic structure of the
verb 'clean'. Suppose this could be shown to be 'cause to become
not dirty' (cf. below, p. 483ff.); in that case, 'dirty' would
be part of the assertion of (4) and hence not a semantic presupposition. If, on the other hand - as argued by the Kiparskys,
the semantic representation of 'clean' is 'cause to become clean',
then (4c) is a semantic presupposition. However this may be, it
is clearly a condition on any in-good-faith utterance of a sentence like 'clean the car, will you' that the speaker believes
(i.e. pragmatically presupposes) that the car is dirty and hence
needs cleaning.

(6a) and (7a). However, it is obvious that (7) is in conflict
with the general scale of values of our social world. Consequently,
an informant, if asked to give his opinion of (6) and (7), might
well say that (7) is semantically anomalous, whereas (6) is well-
formed. The reason for this judgment would be that in the former
case, there is a clash between the PR of S and the informant's
pragmatic assumptions, whereas, in the latter case, there is no
such clash. Lakoff would say that the _ability_ to spot this clash
is a matter of competence, whereas the clash itself is a matter of
performance. In other words, competence is defined as the ability
on the part of the speaker to pair off S with PR[1].

As a further example of this, we will consider the predicate
'feel sorry'. What would be the selectional feature of this with
respect to the subject NP? Suppose we decide on + HUMAN. In that
case, we define the following sentence as semantically anomalous:

(8) The dog feels sorry for having bitten you in the leg

On the other hand, if we adopt Lakoff's theory, (8), _paired with_

(8a) Dogs have a mental structure which makes them capable of
ruing their bad deeds in the same way as we humans

is well-formed (defined as such by the grammar). Now, it is probably
the case that many speakers, owing to their general assumptions
about dogs, would characterize (8) as ill-formed (or at least slightly odd). On the other hand, if the speaker is a passionate dog-lover,
his set of beliefs concerning the nature of dogs might well include
(8a). Furthermore, if this is so, it is not unlikely that he might
supplement (8) by, say,

(9) Can't you see he is apologizing

It is fairly certain that in a grammar incorporating selectional
features, the verb 'apologize' _would_ be assigned the feature '+ HU-
MAN subject' and that hence (9) would be ruled out as anomalous.
Under Lakoff's proposal, (9) is perfectly normal relative to its

----

1. Lakoff thus manages to retain the distinction between competence
and performance. It is clear that, in a general way, the notion
of pragmatic presupposition has a bearing on this distinction.
In particular, the question is precisely where the boundary
should be drawn (cf. also (10) below). For a recent discussion
of the relationship between semantic and pragmatic presupposition in the light of the competence-performance distinction,
see Katz and Langendoen, 1976.

presuppositions.

Different sets of beliefs concerning the nature of the world, then, may lead to different judgments about sentences which are defined by the grammar as being well-formed relative to their presuppositions.

The concept of relative well-formedness, so defined, provides a possible answer to the question which was raised at the end of section IV.D.11.

Consider finally the following example cited by Keenan, op. cit., 51: (10) presupposes (10a):

(10) Tu es dégoûtant
(10a) The addressee is an animal, child, socially inferior to the speaker, or personally intimate with the speaker

In other words, the linguistic competence of French speakers (and, more generally, of the speakers of all languages which have what has been referred to as "pronouns of power and solidarity" (cf. Brown and Gilman, 1960)) cannot be described independently of their social knowledge. The incorporation of such 'social' presuppositions in a semantic theory, therefore, would take an important step towards extending the notion 'well-formed sentence' to cover socially determined 'correctness' and the notion of linguistic competence to cover what is now generally referred to as 'communicative competence' (cf. above, p. 58f. and notes to section IV.D.17).

IV.D.17. Illocutionary force

We will begin our discussion of illocutionary force by introducing the concept of performative verbs. Examples of such verbs are 'authorize', 'beg', 'beseech', 'christen', 'command', 'enquire', 'entreat', 'name', 'offer', 'pronounce', 'request', 'sentence', 'say', 'state', 'warn', etc.

A distinction can be drawn between performative verbs and performative sentences. Rather than defining this distinction in the abstract, we will proceed immediately to some examples:

(1) I (hereby) name this ship the Explorer
(2) I (* hereby) named this ship the Explorer
(3) I (hereby) warn you not to come any nearer
(4) He (* hereby) warns you not to come any nearer
(5) I (hereby) pronounce you man and wife

(6) * Do I (hereby) pronounce you man and wife

(7) * I don't (hereby) pronounce you man and wife

From these we can extract the following definition of a performative sentence: (a) The subject of the sentence must be in the first person[1]; (b) the sentence must be affirmative and nonnegative; (c) the sentence normally (but see (1)) has a second-person indirect object[1]; (d) the adverb 'hereby' can occur in a performative sentence; (e) the aspect of the verb must be nonhabitual[2]. Note that although (2) and (4) contain performative verbs, they are not performative sentences. They are <u>constative</u> sentences. From a semantic point of view, a performative sentence is one in which the speaker <u>performs the illocutionary act</u> denoted by the verb at the moment of utterance. By contrast, a constative sentence makes an assertion about a certain state of affairs in the world. Constative sentences have a truth value, performative sentences do not.

Let us now turn to such sentences as

(8) John saw Stonehenge

(9) Did John see Stonehenge

(10) Who saw Stonehenge

(11) See Stonehenge

They illustrate the <u>mood system</u> of traditional grammar: declarative/interrogative/imperative (we leave out of account various other members (or terms) of the system (such as 'exclamatory')). Now, we can say that all four sentences have the same semantic presupposition:

(12) There exists some X (John)[3] and there exists some place named Stonehenge

Furthermore, we can abstract from (8), (10), and (11) the same underlying assertion (ignoring tense): 'X (or John) see Stonehenge'. As far as (9) is concerned, the underlying assertion is 'either John see Stonehenge or John not see Stonehenge'. Now, we have

----

1. Note that performative sentences can be converted into the passive, in which case the second person indirect object becomes the subject.

2. For example, the sentence 'I christen all the children in this parish' is not a performative sentence.

3. 'John' is obviously not part of the presupposition of (10) and (11): with respect to (10) X has the value 'someone'; with respect to (11) it has the value 'the addressee(s)'.

seen that in a declarative sentence, the fulfilment (i.e. the
truth) of the presupposition is a precondition for the sentence
to have a truth value. Hence, if (12) is true, (8) is true or false.
How about (9), (10), and (11)? They obviously have no truth value:
it is meaningless to talk about interrogative and imperative sentences in terms of truth and falsity. The question then arises
what role (12) plays relative to (9), (10), and (11). The answer to
this question is that the fulfilment of (12) is a necessary precondition for (9) and (10) to be answered and for (11) to be complied
with. In other words, the condition associated with the relationship between an assertion and its presupposition may be a truth
condition, an answerhood condition, or a compliance condition (for
more technical discussion, see Katz, 1972, 150ff., 201ff.). These
three types of condition are associated with the illocutionary
force of the sentence (i.e. the illocutionary act performed in the
utterance of the sentence) as this is determined by its syntactic
structure. In discussing the meaning of a sentence, then, we must
take into consideration (a) its place in the mood system, (b) the
illocutionary force as determined by the term in the mood system
represented by the sentence, and (c) the condition holding between
the underlying assertion and the presupposition as determined by
the illocutionary force.

The difference between sentences like (1), (3), and (5) on
the one hand, and (9), (10), and (11) (for the moment we restrict
the attention to nondeclarative sentences) on the other is that
the former set contain explicit performative verbs, whereas the
latter set do not. We might hypothesize, then, that the illocutionary force of (9), (10), and (11) is determined by the "understood" performative verb in a governing performative sentence:

(9a) I hereby ask you whether or not John saw Stonehenge
(10a) I hereby ask you who saw Stonehenge
(11a) I hereby advise you to see Stonehenge

Note that, apart from the performative verb and the first person
subject, (9a), (10a), and (11a) also contain the indirect object
'you'. In other words, it is made explicit that (9), (10), and
(11) involve a certain relationship between speaker and hearer.
This brings us to the question of the semantics of the illocutionary act itself. Generally, this is discussed in terms of felicity (or happiness) conditions (a special kind of pragmatic presup-

position). For example, for the utterance of (9) to be 'felicitous' or 'happy', the following conditions must be fulfilled:
(a) The speaker is ignorant about something, (b) believes that
the hearer can supply the missing information, and (c) believes
that he has a right to attempt to elicit information from the
hearer.

All sentences have an illocutionary force - including declarative sentences. Thus we might make the illocutionary force of
(8) explicit in the following way:

(8a) I hereby tell you that John saw Stonehenge

We shall see as we go along that illocutionary force plays
an important part in the development of TG-theory. The problem
is to what extent and in precisely what way this force should be
incorporated in a competence model.

Meanwhile, if we look at (4), (8), (9), (10), and (11) as
they appear on the surface, the difference between them is that
whereas (4) and (8) have certain statable truth conditions, this
is not the case with (9), (10), and (11). Consequently, we can
say that 'declarative' constitutes the unmarked term in the mood-
system (cf. also Huddleston, 1971, 8)[1]. This is the way in which
declarative sentences are generally treated in TG-theory after
1964 and prior to, say, 1970[2].

IV.D.18. Some concepts from symbolic logic

We will now very briefly, and as informally as possible, introduce some notions from symbolic logic. These will be necessary
when we come to discuss generative semantics in Chapter V, but
they will stand us in good stead at various points of the exposition.

The first point to be made is that a proposition of symbolic
logic - in particular the logic of the first order predicate
calculus - consists of a predicate and one or more arguments related to the predicate. A proposition may be symbolized in the
following way:

----

1. There is a problem here of course. In syntactic terms, a sentence like (1) is a declarative sentence. However, it differs
   from 'ordinary' declarative sentences in that it does not undergo the negative and interrogative rules.
2. The year when Ross's paper "On Declarative Sentences" was
   published.

(1) f(x)

(2) g(x,y)

For example, if f = 'smoke', g = 'love', x = 'John', and y = 'Mary',
(1) asserts that John has the property that he smokes and (2) that
John and Mary are related by love.

In natural language, predicates are, as we have seen, either
verbs, adjectives, or nouns. Consider the following sentences (in
which (b) are translations into logic-like formulae):

(3a) John is Mary's father

(3b) Father (x,y)

(4a) John swears

(4b) Swear (x)

(5a) John is handsome

(5b) Handsome (x)

(6a) John read the book

(6b) Read (x,y)

(7a) John gave Mary the book

(7b) Gave (x,z,y)

(8a) John sold the book to Mary for four pounds

(8a) Mary bought the book from John for four pounds

(8b) $\left\{ \begin{array}{l} \text{Sell} \\ \text{Buy} \end{array} \right\}$ (x,z,y,w)

(4) and (5) are examples of <u>one-place predicates</u> (i.e. predicates
with just one argument), (3) and (6) are <u>two-place predicates</u>,
(7) is an example of a <u>three-place predicate</u>, and (8) of a <u>four-
place predicate</u>. The variables in the parentheses stand for noun
phrases (plus, in some cases, the associated prepositions). Values
for the variables appear in the (a) sentences. The (b) structures
would suggest that the predicate is that constituent which comes
first in an English sentence. Obviously, this is not the case in
surface structure. Furthermore, we have assumed that it is not the
case in deep structure either. We shall see in Chapter V, however,
that syntactic arguments can be adduced in support of the hypothesis that the predicate is indeed the leftmost constituent in the
deep structure of an English sentence. For the moment, however,
we can look upon the (b) structures as a handy way of symbolizing
the relationship between predicates and arguments.

The next concepts to be introduced are the <u>propositional connectives</u>. They are (a) $\wedge$ = 'and', (b) $\vee$ = 'or', and (c) $\neg$ = 'not'. Thus, if a and b are propositions, a $\wedge$ b asserts that both a and b are true, a $\vee$ b that either a or b is true, etc. Presumably, all natural languages have lexical items corresponding to the propositional connectives.

Further important concepts are <u>quantifiers</u> and <u>set symbols</u>. There are two quantifiers: (a) the <u>universal</u> quantifier $\forall$ = 'for all', and (b) the <u>existential</u> quantifier $\exists$ = 'there exists at least one'. The set symbol is ϵ. Thus the following expressions:

(9) $\underset{x \,\epsilon\, M}{\forall} f(x)$

(10) $\underset{x \,\epsilon\, M}{\exists} f(x)$

can be read: (9) 'For all x, such that x are members of the set M, x have the quality denoted by the predicate f', and (10) 'there exists at least one x, such that x is the member of the set M and has the quality denoted by the predicate f'.

Let us proceed to examine what possible bearing such notions might have on the semantics of natural language. Consider the following sentences (cf. McCawley, 1967 (in Rosenberg and Travis, 1971) 521ff., Bach, 1968 (in Bach and Harms, 1968) 108ff., and Partee, 1972 (in Davidson and Harman, 1972) 430ff.):

(11) John likes John
(12) John likes himself
(13) Everybody likes everybody
(14) Everybody likes himself
(15) John wanted Peter to go
(16) John wanted to go
(17) Everybody wanted everybody to go
(18) Everybody wanted to go

(11) is, as we have seen in section IV.D.15, a perfectly normal sentence provided the two occurrences of 'John' are not coreferential. If they <u>are</u> coreferential, the sentence must undergo reflexivization (as in (12)). However, (13) and (14) cannot be so readily explained. In particular, the two occurrences of 'everybody' are coreferential in the ("hypothetical") sense that they

both refer to the set of all human beings. This being the case,
(13) should be ungrammatical unless it underwent reflexivization.
But it is not. The only way of explicating the semantics of such
sentences would seem to be by means of quantifiers and variables
in the following way:

(13a) $\underset{x \in H}{\forall} \underset{y \in H}{\forall} f(x,y)$

(14a) $\underset{x \in H}{\forall} f(x,x)$

  where H = 'human beings' and f = 'like'

Given (13a) and (14a), we can explain why reflexivization has
operated in (14), but not in (13). The difference between (15) and
(16) is that in (15) the predicates 'want' and 'go' have different
subjects, whereas in (16) the implied subject of 'go' is 'John'.
This is coreferential with the subject of the governing sentence.
Hence it has been deleted by the rule of equi NP deletion. The
problem relating to (17) and (18), then, is much the same as the
one we have just considered. The meaning of the two sentences can
be represented in terms of the following formulae:

(17a) $\underset{x \in H}{\forall} (f(x) \ (\underset{y \in H}{\forall} g(y)))$

(18a) $\underset{x \in H}{\forall} (f(x) \ (g(x)))$

  where f = 'want' and g = 'go'

(17a) explains why equi NP deletion has not applied in (17).

  Before we leave this subject for now, two points should be
made. The first is that symbolic logic, as it originated in the
nineteenth century and has since been developed, has as its goal
the creation of a system for the representation of the structure
of human thought which is freed from the ambiguities, irrationali-
ties, and vagueries of natural language. Consequently, the attempt made by some linguists to turn logic back on language, as
it were, has necessitated a good many adaptations in various areas.
The linguist is trying to construct a 'natural logic' which can
cope with language as it is. The second point is that linguists
are not agreed on the role that natural logic should play in linguistic description. Some would say that the role of logic should
be restricted to a set of rules of inference operating on semantic
representations, whereas others would claim that logical form
should be directly related to syntax (cf. below, section IV.D.20).

IV.D.19. <u>Scope and other matters</u>

We define the scope of X as the stretch of language over which
the meaning of X may range. Consider the following sentences:

(1) The stone didn't hit the boy

(2) John doesn't beat his wife because he loves her

In its most straightforward interpretation, (1) is a negation of

(3) The stone hit the boy

In this interpretation, then, the meaning of 'not' ranges over the
<u>whole</u> predication. To make this explicit, we will interpret 'not'
as a one-place predicate which takes a sentence as its argument
(predicates are written in capitals):

(4) (NOT (HIT (the stone, the boy)))

The interpretation of (1) discussed so far is marked by relatively
stronger stress on 'didn't hit' than on the other constituents.
It can be paraphrased by

(4a) It was not the case that the stone hit the boy

in which 'not' is relatively heavily stressed. Suppose now that
either 'stone' or 'boy' is strongly stressed in (1). We then obtain
two different interpretations, neither of which is related to (3)
in a straightforward manner. We can illustrate these interpretations in terms of the following paraphrases

(5) It was not the stone that hit the boy

(6) It was not the boy that the stone hit

in which it is clear that the meaning of 'not' ranges only
over the noun phrases immediately following the verb - not over
the 'that'-clauses. If we relate these interpretations to (4),
which is very similar to the deep structure of a negative sentence
in TG-theory, we see that the definition of 'scope' given above
still holds: 'stone' and 'boy' both fall within the scope of NOT.
However, the trouble with (4) is that it fails to <u>differentiate</u>
the three possible interpretations of (1). Let us leave it at that
for the moment. (2) - a chestnut in the literature - shows something
similar. The sentence is clearly ambiguous; provided we agree to
interpret 'because' as a two-place predicate which takes two clauses
as its arguments, we can illustrate the ambiguity in terms of the
following two formulae:

(7) (NOT (BECAUSE (LOVE (John, wife)) (BEAT (John, wife))))

(8) (BECAUSE (LOVE (John, wife)) (NOT (BEAT (John, wife))))

In (7), then, BECAUSE and its arguments fall within the scope of
NOT. By contrast, in (8), BECAUSE is outside the scope of NOT,
which now has its scope only the second argument of BECAUSE.
(7) and (8), too, have counterparts in natural language:

(7a) It is not because he loves her that John beats his wife

(8a) It is because he loves her that John doesn't beat his
     wife

We can bring to bear on our sample sentences the distinction
between new and given. Thus in the interpretation of (1) corresponding to (5), the speaker and the hearer share a certain amount
of information prior to the utterance of (1), namely

(9) Something hit the boy

(9), then, constitutes what is given in the speech situation. 'Something' is a variable. By 'substituting' 'the stone' for that, the
speaker supplies new information: 'the stone' constitutes the information focus and it is that which is being negated[1]. Mutatis
mutandis, the same relationship holds between (2) and (7a) and
(7b).

The question that can now be asked is how matters relating
to scope and focus should be worked into the semantic theory and,
in particular, what bearing they might have on the interpretation
of the interrelationship between syntax and semantics. We will not
go into this here[2]. In section IV.G.9.3, we shall see that the
analysis of sentences like (1) and (2) may well provide evidence
of Seuren's statement that the standard theory is 'self-destructive'
(cf. above, p. 95).

----

1. The terms 'new' and 'given' are used by many British linguists
   (e.g. Halliday, 1970). They correspond to the terms 'focus' and
   'presupposition' employed by Chomsky, 1972, 89ff. and Jackendoff,
   1972, Chapter 6. Observe that 'theme' (or, equivalently, topic)
   and 'focus' are not synonymous. Roughly, 'theme' may be defined
   as 'that about which a statement is being made'.

2. Chomsky and Jackendoff, writing within the framework of the extended standard theory, argue that the focus-presupposition
   dichotomy is determined by interpretive rules operating on surface structures. See also Katz, 1972, 424ff. For discussion of
   the notions 'focus' and 'topic' within the framework of generative semantics, see Lakoff, 1971b.

IV.D.20. Conclusion

Before we leave the topic of semantics, we must revise once again the notion 'structural description of a sentence':

(1) $P_1 \ldots P_i \ldots P_n$

$$SR$$

where SR = semantic representation

SR must contain information about the meaning of the sentence as derived (in the standard theory) by the operation of the projection rules. Furthermore, SR forms the input to a set of rules of inference by means of which (a) the sentence is defined as analytic or contradictory (or, if it is neither of these, as synthetic), and (b) the sentence is related to other sentences which are entailed by it, presupposed by it, synonymous with it, constitute its felicity conditions[1], etc.

It was pointed out in the introductory remarks to IV.D that the main issue in the present-day debate is the relationship between syntax and semantics. The difference between the standard theory and generative semantics can be illustrated preliminarily with respect to (1) in terms of the following modifications: (a) replace P_1 by SR, and (b) eliminate P_i.

Notes and some further references

General. The literature on semantics is vast. The reason for this is not far to seek: Semantics is the point where the interests of many different disciplines such as anthropology, linguistics, literary criticism, logic, philosophy, psychology, and sociology converge. Among the best introductory works to semantic concepts are Kronasser, 1952, Ullmann, 1957 and 1962 (of which the latter is more elementary than the former). The last part of Lyons, 1968 presents an all-round introductory survey and an up-dated version of the author's own theory of structural semantics as embodied in the 1963-volume. The first part of Leech, 1974 is devoted to a discussion of the semantic tradition. For the rest of the book, Leech is concerned to develop his own theory of semantics (for which, see also Leech, 1969a). Towards the end of the volume, Leech compares this theory to TG-interpretive semantics on the one hand and generative semantics on the other. There is a valuable annotated bibliography. A brief overview of semantic theories may be found in Ikegami, 1967. Ullmann, 1972 surveys the development of semantics in Western Europe and provides a full bibliography. The reader's attention is directed to the following major anthologies containing papers on semantics from the point of view of linguists,

----

1. Provided, that is, that felicity conditions, which are properties of utterances rather than sentences, are not assumed to fall outside the scope of a competence model.

philosophers, psychologists, and others: Kiefer (ed.), 1969,
Steinberg and Jakobovits (eds.), 1971, Rosenberg and Travis (eds.),
1971, Fillmore and Langendoen (eds.), 1971, and Davidson and
Harman (eds.), 1972.

IV.D.2. For a recent discussion of the interrelationship of syntax and semantics as conceived of in the standard theory, see Katz,
1972, 29ff.

IV.D.4. On componential analysis, see Goodenough, 1956, Lounsbury,
1964, and Bendix, 1966. Bendix analyses the semantic structure of
such English verbs as 'borrow', 'lend', 'give', 'get', etc. For discussion of Bendix's analysis, see Fillmore, 1969a. The theory of
semantic features has played a crucial role in the development
of semantics as an integral part of TG-theory. The reader interested in tracing this development should consult Katz and Fodor,
1963, Katz and Postal, 1964, Katz, 1966, 1971a, and 1972. The 1972-
volume is the fullest statement of the deep structure interpretivist
position which has been published to date. It is characterized
by a high degree of formalism. Bierwish, 1969 and 1970b are attempts to formalize semantic representations in terms of the predicate calculus. See also Bierwish, 1970a. For a brief comment on
this approach, see Katz, 1972, 166, note 21. A considerable amount
of criticsim of the componential theory has been generated. Consult for example Bolinger, 1965, Lyons, 1966c and 1968 (especially
p. 470ff.) and Macnamara, 1971. In addition to semantic features
(or markers) the original theory also contained the concept of
distinguishers. Essentially, these defined idiosyncratic properties of lexical items (i.e. properties not reducible to systematic
analysis in terms of semantic features). The famous example in
this connection is the analysis of the polysemous item 'bachelor'
(see Katz and Fodor, 1963 (in Fodor and Katz, 1964) 499f. and
Katz and Postal, 1964, 14). To a large extent Bolinger's criticism
in the paper referred to above is levelled against the concept
of distinguishers. Katz, 1972, 82ff. discusses the notion in the
light of the criticism to which it has been subjected. Idioms (cf.
above, p. 89f.) have often been invoked in support of the compositional conception of the meaning of phrases and sentences -
idioms are the exceptions which confirm the rule (see for example
Katz, 1971a, 104ff.). This does not, of course, exonerate the
theory from accounting for idioms. For some discussion of idioms
within the framework of a compositional theory of semantics, see
Katz, 1973b.

IV.D.7. One of the examples most frequently cited in support of
the theory of 'linguistic Weltanschauung' is the semantics of the
colour spectrum. The argument goes like this: In physical terms,
the colour spectrum is an unbroken continuum; however, it is
provable that different languages analyse the spectrum in different ways, as illustrated in the following diagram (where the
lower-case letters designate colour terms (see next page)):
In other words, language imposes an arbitrary structural grid
upon the flux (or the amorphous mass) of reality (see for example
Gleason, 1961, 4f. and Lyons, 1968, 56ff.). However, in 1969
Berlin and Kay published an important study which cast heavy
doubt on the validity of the relativist position. In particular,
the authors showed that there are certain implicational relations
holding among different colour terms, such that if L_1 has the term
X, it will predictably have the term Y, and so on. In other words,
relativism is replaced by 'conditional universality' (a brief

L_1	a	b	c
L_2	d	e	f
L_3	g	h	

summary of Berlin and Kay's results may be found in Leech, 1974,
234ff.; for a comparison with phonology, see also Bach, 1974,
254f.). As remarked in the text, Bierwisch's statement reflects
the strongest possible universalist position. It should be noted,
however, that any position intermediate between complete relativism and complete universalism is, in principle, possible. One
could hypothesize, for example, that there is a universal set of
semantic features from which each language selects a subset. This
would parallel the assumption made in phonological theory (cf.
below, p. 246). On semantic universals, see also Ullmann, 1963
and McCawley, 1968b.

IV.D.8. On semantic relations in general, see Öhman, 1953, Lyons,
1963 and 1968, Katz, 1972, and Leech, 1974. Ogden, 1932 gives an
excellent account of various kinds of oppositeness of meaning. The
relational meaning of adjectives is discussed by Sapir, 1949. A
number of entailment rules are formulated by Fillmore, 1971b. The
implications of the semantic theory developed by Katz, Fodor, and
Postal for the distinction between polysemy and homonymy are discussed by Weinreich, 1972. Analytic sentences have played an important role in the philosophical literature since they were first
discussed by Kant. Within the present theory, the properties of
analyticity have been studied in detail by Katz (1964c, 1972,
171ff., and 1971a, 148ff. (a less formal account)). The examples
given in the text all had the form NP + be + NP. With respect to
this simple copulative structure, analyticity arises if the subject NP includes all the features of the predicative NP. However,
analyticity goes beyond such structures. Consider the following
sentence cited by Katz, 1971a, 151, 1972, 172ff.:

(1) Kleptomaniacs steal out of a persistent neurotic impulse
without economic motive

(1) is analytic. It follows from this that the rule defining a sentence as analytic must be generalized to cover the subject-predicate relation in a wider sense (for a formal statement of the
rule, see Katz, 1972, 175). We need to qualify the definition of
an analytic sentence given in the text as one which is true by
virtue of meaning alone. Consider the following analytic sentence:

(2) The present King of Britain is a man

(2) semantically _presupposes_ (cf. section IV.D.16, sentence (2)):

(2a) There is a person who is King of Britain

(2a) is false. Hence (2) has no truth value. It can therefore not
be false. An analytic sentence can now be defined as one which is
protected from falsehood by its meaning. In other words, if the
presupposition of an analytic sentence is true, the sentence is

always true (in contradistinction to a synthetic sentence which
may be either true or false, given the truth of its presupposition);
if the presupposition is false, the sentence cannot be false. Contradictory sentences with the structure NP + be + NP can be defined in terms of selectional violation: predicative nouns require
in their subject nouns a set of features which match their own feature specification; if this condition is not met, a contradiction
results (cf. also Langendoen, 1969, 50f.). Also the definition of
contradictoriness must be extended to cover the subject-predicate
relation in a wider sense, as witness the sentence (cf. Katz,
1971a, 151 and 1972, 178):

(3) Kleptomaniacs steal only out of economic motives

For a formal definition of contradictoriness, see Katz, 1972, 180f.

IV.D.9. Let us illustrate in a little more detail the operation
of projection rules. Consider the following sentence:

(1) The man killed the woman

We will make the assumption that the meaning of this sentence can
be adequately represented in terms of the following formula:

(2) (CAUSE (the man (BECOME (DEAD (the woman)))))

Let us further assume that 'kill' is entered in the lexicon in
roughly the following way:

(3)

```
┌                                                          ┐
│  kill                                                    │
│  + V                                                     │
│  - object deletion                                       │
│                                                          │
│       [NP,S] _____ [NP,VP,Predicate Phrase,S]       │
│                                                          │
│  CAUSE (X (BECOME (DEAD (X))))                           │
│      + ANIMATE        + ANIMATE                          │
└                                                          ┘
```

The two Xs are subcategorized variables. In particular, the first
occurrence of X is subcategorized for the subject NP of the sentence, the second for the object NP (observe that we have not
taken strict subcategorization features to be local in the sense
defined on p. 114f. (cf. p. 119, note)). The deep structure of
(1) is, roughly

(4)

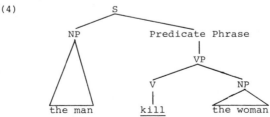

in which 'kill' should be identified with (3). The projection
rules now substitute 'the man' and 'the woman' for the two sub-

categorized variables (note that the two items satisfy the selectional features (now defined as semantic features and as properties of NPs rather than of Ns) specified in the entry). Given the
universal validity of the relational definitions of grammatical
functions illustrated in section IV.A.6, the projection rules,
(or more precisely, the projection rule) which substitutes the
readings of constituents for subcategorized variables, is a formal universal and hence should not be stated in the grammar of L.
For further discussion, see Katz, 1972, 104ff. Consult also
Bierwisch, 1970a.

IV.D.10,11,12. It would now probably be generally agreed that
selectional features are semantic in nature and that the complex-
symbol machinery developed in Aspects should not form part of a
grammar (it should be noted in this connection that Chomsky did
not feel strongly committed on this point but opted for the subcategorization model for certain formal reasons (1965, 120ff.,
153ff.); thus in Chomsky, 1966b no mention is made of subcategorization rules (p. 70ff.)). McCawley (1968a, 1968c, 1970a, and
1971b) and others have argued that selectional features should be
defined as presuppositions about intended referents (for discussion of this notion, see McCawley, 1968a (in Bach and Harms, 1968)
138ff.). One of the examples adduced by McCawley (op. cit., 140)
is

    (1) My neighbour hurt himself
    (2) My neighbour hurt herself

McCawley argues that the choice of reflexive pronouns is dependent on "whether the speaker's knowledge about the index of the
token of my neighbor in the sentence contains the information that
the individual is male or female". McCawley further argues that

    (3) My neighbour is tall

is predicted by the subcategorization model to be ambiguous: 'my
neighbour' is specified by the rules as being either (+ Masculine)
or (- Masculine). 'Neighbour' is entered in the lexicon with the
feature (0 Masculine) and must therefore obligatorily be specified
+ or - for that feature when it is entered into the preterminal
string. There is little doubt that McCawley's criticism of the
subcategorization model is justified with respect to (1), (2), and
(3). However, (3) could be accounted for in the dummy-symbol approach: 'neighbour' would be entered without any difficulty; since
the adjective 'tall' does not require in (alternatively impose
upon) its subject NP either of the features (± Masculine), the sentence would not contain information about the sex of the referent.
Relevant to the problem under discussion is also the distinction
between 'marked' and 'unmarked'. Consider the following sentence
(uttered by a speaker who lives in a semi-detached house):

    (4) I haven't seen my new neighbour yet, but last night
        there was such a terrible noise that I'm sure that
$$\begin{Bmatrix} \text{he} \\ \text{she} \end{Bmatrix} \text{ must have hurt } \begin{Bmatrix} \text{himself} \\ \text{herself} \end{Bmatrix}$$

If the speaker chooses 'she' (and 'herself'), he has obviously
heard about the sex of the intended referent. By contrast, if he
chooses 'he' (and 'himself'), he need not necessarily know whether
the neighbour is a male or a female: the masculine pronoun is unmarked in the sense that it may be substituted for a noun specified either (0 Masculine) or (+ Masculine). Now, if the noun 'neigh-

bour' is entered in the lexicon with the feature (0 Masculine),
the grammar can generate only the unmarked interpretation of the
masculine pronouns in (4). The point would seem to be that there
is no way of obtaining the specification (+ Masculine) or (- Masculine) for 'neighbour' unless the speech-situation is taken into
consideration. Therefore, although we may perhaps account for (3),
sentences like (1) (in which, presumably, 'himself' cannot be
unmarked), (2), and the relevant (marked) interpretations of (4)
strongly support McCawley's claim: selectional restrictions cannot be severed from the general semantic phenomenon of presuppositions (see also the discussion in section IV.D.16). McCawley's
proposals have caused a good deal of debate in the literature. For
critical discussion, see for example Katz, 1972, 149f., 1973c and
Antley, 1974. Kuroda, 1969 considers the problem with special
reference to French (in which the relationship between natural sex
and grammatical gender is quite intricate). On semantic theory and
metaphor, see Weinreich, 1972. A less formal discussion may be found
in Leech, 1969b. R.I. Matthews, 1971 discusses metaphor in terms of
the distinction between competence and performance. For a critique
of Matthews' views, see Price, 1974.

IV.D.13. On semantic ambiguity, see Kooij, 1971.

IV.D.14. In generative semantics, there would be no distinction
between syntactic and semantic features (in fact, there would
hardly be any features at all - except rule features and phonological features). See in this connection Lakoff's discussion of the
distribution of the relative pronouns 'who' and 'which' (1971a
(in Steinberg and Jakobovits, 1971) 330ff.) and compare Chomsky,
1965, 148ff. For some further comments on the relationship between
syntactic and semantic features, see McCawley, 1968a (in Bach and
Harms, 1968) 134f., Weinreich, 1972, 23ff., and Katz, 1972, 363ff.

IV.D.15. Many important philosophical discussions of reference
are reprinted in Steinberg and Jakobovits (eds.), 1971, Rosenberg
and Travis (eds.), 1971, and Davidson and Harman (eds.), 1972. The
theory of referential indices was first proposed by Chomsky, 1965,
145f. Chomsky is not very specific and merely notes that "of
course there are problems in specifying the notion "referential"
properly". The first large-scale discussion of the bearing of
reference and coreference on transformations is Postal, 1971
(written in 1968). Postal uses referential indices as a notational
device and only that (cf. p. 8, note 8). For critical discussion
of the notion of referential indices with respect to coordination,
see Dik, 1968, 82ff. Consult further such works as Lakoff, 1968a
and 1968b, Bach, 1968, McCawley, 1968a and 1970a, Sampson, 1969,
Partee, 1972, and Dik, 1973.

IV.D.16. For an overview of the concept of presupposition in philosophy and linguistics, see Garner, 1971. Katz, 1972, 127ff. is a
stringent discussion of the Fregean conception of presupposition.
Consult further Lakoff, 1971c, 1972a, and (for a discussion of the
applicability of the notions 'truth' and 'falsity' to natural language) 1972b. Wilson, 1975 is a strongly critical analysis of the
whole concept of presupposition (notably presuppositions of the
'assertion-assumption' type). Fillmore, 1969b and 1971a is especially concerned with presuppositions in relation to lexical items.
Special problems relate to presuppositions in compound sentences.
For discussion of such problems, see Langendoen and Savin, 1971
and Karttunen, 1973.

IV.D.17. The study of speech acts was initiated by Austin, 1962 and further developed by Searle, 1969. Ross, 1970a presents a number of arguments in support of the hypothesis that declarative sentences should contain a governing performative sentence in deep structure, which is deleted (in some cases) by a performative deletion rule. One of the arguments relates to reflexivization. Consider the following sentences (cf. below, p. 437, note 2):

(1) John says that guys like himself never make any headway
(2) * Guys like himself never make any headway
(3) Guys like myself never make any headway

The fact that (3) is grammatical, whereas (2) is not, can be explained if it is assumed that reflexivization (which requires an antecedent coreferential with the NP to be reflexivized) has operated prior to the deletion of a higher performative sentence 'I state to you'. A number of counterarguments are presented in Anderson, S., 1971 and Fraser, 1971. On illocutionary force, see further Lakoff, 1972a, section IV, Katz, 1972, Sadock, 1975, and Leech, 1974. Fraser, 1973 discusses the problems involved in determining the illocutionary force of sentences. Rosenberg and Travis (eds.), 1971 contains a number of papers on speech acts. A recent volume devoted to speech acts is Cole and Morgan (eds.), 1975. Brief mention should be made of what has come to be known as indirect speech acts. Research in this area was pioneered by Grice, 1975 (originally delivered as a lecture in 1967). Basically, the problem at issue is that we often use one sentence X to convey the meaning of another sentence Y. Consider such sentences as

(4) I want another beer
(5) Is this your coat lying on the floor

In uttering (4) the speaker may be making a statement. However, (4) may also be used to utter a command or request (i.e. 'go and get me another beer'). Furthermore, the felicitous utterance of (4) as a command presupposes a certain social relationship between speaker and hearer. For example, a father might utter (4) to his son and reasonably expect him to go to the fridge and get the beer. By contrast, (4) would be inappropriate, say, in a pub. Mutatis mutandis, the same applies to (5): it may be used to ask a question or issue a command (i.e. 'pick it up') depending on the social context. Several attempts have been made to deal with this kind of communicative competence - notably within the framework of generative semantics. Thus Gordon and Lakoff, 1975 (first published 1971) have formulated a special set of rules - so-called conversational postulates - which operate on semantic structures. For and alternative approach, see Sadock, 1975. Consult also Green, 1975. For a recent discussion of speech act theories and their status relative to the (extended) standard theory of transformational grammar, see Chomsky, 1975, Chapter 2 (the 'Chomsky-Searle controversy'). Consult further Katz, 1972, 442ff.

IV.D.18. A standard work on symbolic logic is Reichenbach, 1947. A shorter and more compressed introduction is Robbin, 1969. On linguistics and logic, see Lakoff, 1972a and McCawley, 1972.

IV.D.19. A relatively informal discussion of problems relating to scope and focus may be found in Quirk et al., 1972.

IV.E. THE TRANSFORMATIONAL COMPONENT

IV.E.1. Introductory remarks

    In this section we will examine some general properties of
the transformational component. We return to a more detailed discussion of some of the major transformational rules required in
a grammer of English in section IV.G.

IV.E.2. Elementary transformations

    First of all we must consider in some detail the elementary
operations which T-rules may perform on input P-markers. In section IV.A.7 we discussed four basic transformational processes:
deletion, insertion, movement of constituents, and substitution.
Let us illustrate these processes in terms of simple abstract P-
markers:

    Deletion

In (1b) a and B (which dominates no other constituent than a)
have been deleted. Thus, if a = 'you' and B = NP, the transformation illustrates the deletion of 'you' and the subsequent pruning
of the tree in imperative sentences[1].

    Insertion

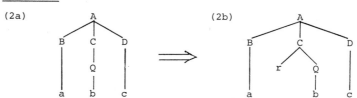

In (2a) B, C, and D are daughters of A because they are all immediately dominated by A. Specifically, B is the left daughter

----

1. Strictly speaking, we should say that 'you' may be deleted
   because it dominates itself. However, we need not go into this
   somewhat technical question.

of A, and D the <u>right daughter of</u> A (for any node to be the left
or right daughter of another node Z, it must be the leftmost or
rightmost node immediately dominated by Z). Furthermore, B is the
<u>left sister of</u> C, and D the <u>right sister of</u> C (for any node P im-
mediately dominated by a node Z to be the right or left sister of
another node Q also immediately dominated by Z, there must be no
other nodes intervening between P and Q). Given this metaphorical
terminology, we can say that in (2b) r has been <u>adjoined</u> as left
sister of Q (respectively left daughter of C). Insertion, therefore,
can be defined in terms of adjunction. For example, the passive
auxiliary string 'be + en' will have to be adjoined to some other
node in the tree (as will also the preposition 'by'). We return to
this in section IV.E.5 (see also note on the next page).

<u>Movement of constituents</u>

Movement of constituents can be stated in terms of a combination of adjunction and deletion:

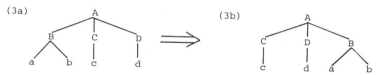

What has happened in (3b) is that a <u>copy of</u> B and everything dominated by B has been adjoined as right sister of D and that the
original B has been deleted (see note on the next page).

<u>Substitution</u>

Substitution can be defined in terms of the following trees:

In (4b) a copy of D has been substituted for B such that the substituted D is now immediately dominated by the same node as the
replaced B. An example of a transformation involving substitution
operations is the passive rule. Note that certain features may be
substituted for certain other features:

(5a)   (5b)

Chomsky-adjunction

A special kind of adjunction is known as Chomsky-adjunction
(so named by Ross, 1967, 143). This operation has structure-
building power and can be illustrated as follows:

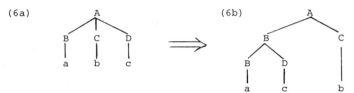

(6a)   (6b)

In (6b) D has been adjoined as right sister of B and has created a
new node B of which both D and the original B are daughters.

The four operations discussed in section IV.A.7 have now all
been restated in terms of (a) (various kinds of) adjunction, (b)
deletion, and (c) substitution[1].

IV.E.3. The formulation of T-rules

Consider now the following sentence:

(1) It did worry John that Peter failed Mary

which is derived by extraposition from

(2) That Peter failed Mary did worry John

The sentence has the following deep structure (see next page):
The vertical lines indicate how the terminal string has been analysed without residue into substrings:

(4) X - it - S - y
    1   2   3   4

X and Y are variables and may have the value null. In this case the

----

1. Note that 'insertion' and 'movement of constituents' can be
   stated in terms of substitution. Thus in (2b) Q with r adjoined
   as its left sister is substituted for Q. By the same token,
   in (3b) D with B adjoined as its right sister is substituted
   for D, the original B being deleted.

(3)

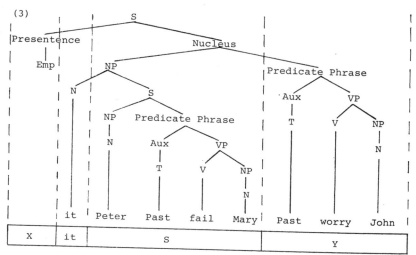

X	it	S	Y

value of X is Emp and the value of Y Predicate Phrase (and everything dominated by Predicate Phrase of course). (4) constitutes
the <u>structural index</u> (henceforth abbreviated SI) of the extraposition transformation[1,2]. It consists of four <u>terms</u> which have
been numbered successively from left to right. Any P-marker which
can be analysed in this way <u>meets</u> the SI of the extraposition rule.
We might wish to make it explicit that the sequence 'it - S' "is
an" NP. This would require the following revision of (4):

(5) X - [it - S] - Y
$\qquad$ NP $\qquad$ NP
$\quad$ 1 $\quad$ 2 $\quad$ 3 $\quad$ 4

Recall now the discussion in section IV.A.8. We saw there that the
head of the extraposed clause might be a lexical noun. Let us now -
just for the sake of the argument - assume that PS-rule 11 specifies an option between 'it' and N^3, where the latter will be
realized as a lexical noun. In that case we can formalize an SI

----

1. Also frequently referred to as the <u>structural analysis</u> (SA) or
   the <u>structural description</u> (SD).

2. We will not be concerned with the emphatic transformation here.
   Emp has been added in order to illustrate that the first variable
   in the SI need not be null (though it often would be in sentences
   of this type).

3. This would not be necessary: 'it' is entered in the lexicon with
   the features (+ N, + Pro), lexical nouns with the features (+ N,
   - Pro). I am twisting the facts a bit for pedagogical reasons.

which covers both types of extraposition in terms of the following
revised version of (5):

$$(6) \quad X - \left[\underset{NP}{\left\{ \begin{matrix} (Det) \ N \\ it \end{matrix} \right\}} - \underset{NP}{S} \right] - Y$$

$$1 \qquad\qquad 2 \qquad 3 \qquad 4$$

Recall further that we expressed some doubts about the validity
of 'vacuous extraposition from object'. Suppose now that we want
to exclude this operation from the grammar. How could we do that?
By adding a condition to (6) which says that 'Y must not be null'.

In section IV.D.18 we introduced some concepts from symbolic
logic. Among those were the propositional connectives 'and', 'or',
and 'not'. Consider now the statements made in (6): (a) The second
term is an N (optionally preceded by a determiner) or 'it'. (b)
2 and 3 consist of (Det) N and S (i.e. one of the options) and
this sequence is an NP. In addition to this, the condition specifies that Y is not null. In other words, we can describe the information contained in (6) (and the condition on the rule) exhaustively in terms of statements involving the three propositional
connectives. This being the case, (6) is said to satisfy a Boolean
condition on analysability[1].

Now, a T-rule performs one or more[2] elementary operations on
the P-marker which forms the input to the rule (and thus meets the
SI of the rule) and by so doing effects a structural change (henceforth abbreviated SC). The extraposition rule performs two such
operations: (a) It adjoins a copy of the third term as right sister
of the fourth term, and (b) it deletes the original third term
(alternatively, it replaces the fourth term by the fourth term
with the third term adjoined as its right sister and deletes the
third term). How can this be stated? There are various possibilities:

(a) The component structural change statement (cf. Stockwell
et al., 1968, Vol. I, 16). Essentially, this is a set of instructions. In the example under discussion, these instructions would
be: 'Adjoin a copy of 3 as right sister of 4 and delete 3'.

----

1. Named after the author of the first work on symbolic logic
   (Boole, The Laws of Thought, 1840). We shall see later that
   this condition may have to be abandoned in certain cases.

2. Unlike PS-rules, then, T-rules are not restricted in scope to
   one symbol.

(b) <u>Linear notation</u>:

$$\text{SI} \quad X - \left[\underset{\text{NP}}{\underbrace{\left\{ \begin{matrix} \text{(Det)} \ N \\ \text{it} \end{matrix} \right\}}} - S \underset{\text{NP}}{\underbrace{}} \right] - Y$$

$$\quad\quad\quad 1 \qquad\qquad 2 \qquad\quad 3 \qquad 4 \implies$$

$$\text{SC} \quad 1 \qquad\qquad 2 \qquad\quad \emptyset \qquad 4+3$$

in which $\emptyset$ means 'term deleted' and $+$ 'sister-adjoin'. We might supplement the SCs of linear-notation statements by various graphic devices to distinguish daughter-adjunction and Chomsky-adjunction from sister-adjunction. However, instead of that, we shall use the component structural change statement wherever it is necessary to make this distinction.

(c) <u>Tree-format</u>. Since the output of any T-rule, as we have seen, is a derived P-marker (intermediate or final) we can, of course, state the structural change effected by the rule by drawing up the derived P-marker (or <u>transform</u>) (it is not always so simple (cf. section IV.E.5)).

In conclusion: A T-rule consists of two parts:

(I) An SI satisfying a Boolean condition on analysability.
(II) An SC stating the elementary operations carried out by
     the rule.

IV.E.4. <u>The principle of variable reference</u>

Suppose that the SI of a T-rule mentions an NP. Then any elementary operation affecting this NP affects everything dominated by the NP. Since PS-rule 11 is recursive, it follows that the SI mentioning an NP characterizes not one, but an infinite set of P-markers[1]. The fact that in referring to a category like NP the SI refers to a potentially infinite set of substrings (and hence P-markers) is known as the principle of <u>variable reference</u>. By way of illustration, we will examine the relationship between active and passive sentences. Let us formulate the passive rule in the following way:

$$\text{SI} \quad X - NP_1 - \text{Aux} - V - NP_2 - Y$$

$$\quad\quad\quad 1 \quad\ 2 \qquad 3 \quad\ 4 \quad\ 5 \quad\ 6 \implies$$

$$\text{SC} \quad 1 \quad\ 5 \qquad 3 \ \text{be+en} \ 4 \quad \text{by} \ 2 \quad 6$$

----

1. In fact, the NP need not be mentioned in the SI: it may be under
   the domination of some other term mentioned (e.g. VP or S).

Three operations are carried out by the rule: (a) NP_1 and NP_2
are reordered in the string; (b) 'be+en' is inserted between the
third term and the fourth term; (c) 'by' is inserted between the
fourth term and NP_1. Note that we have not indicated how the reordered NP_1 and the inserted elements are adjoined to the other
constituents. We return to this question in the next section.

Let us now proceed to illustrate the effect of this rule on
the following two sentences (for (2), cf. section II.5):

(1) The man will kill the lion

(2) I will forget the malt that the rat that the cat that
    the dog worried killed liked

The deep structures of (1) and (2) are (omitting details under Aux):

(1a)

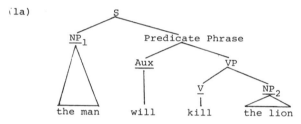

(for (2a), see next page).

In (1a) the underscored nodes are those mentioned in the SI of the
rule. Observe that the structure dominated by NP_2 in (1a) is quite
simple, whereas, in (2a), the structure under the domination of
the topmost NP_2 is extremely complex, ranging over three embedded
sentences (S_2, S_3, and S_4). Nevertheless, despite these differences,
both (1a) and S_1 in (2a) meet the SI of the rule.

By the operation of the passive rule, (1) is converted into

(3) The lion will be killed by the man

(2a) meets the SI of the rule no less than four times. As
formulated in this section, the passive rule is optional. This
means that the rule may apply to one or more of the four sentences
in (2a) (or not at all of course). Let us see what happens if it
applies to S_3 (relativization (which is obligatory) is assumed to
have operated immediately after the passive rule):

(4) I will forget the malt that the rat that was killed by
    the cat that the dog worried liked

(2a)

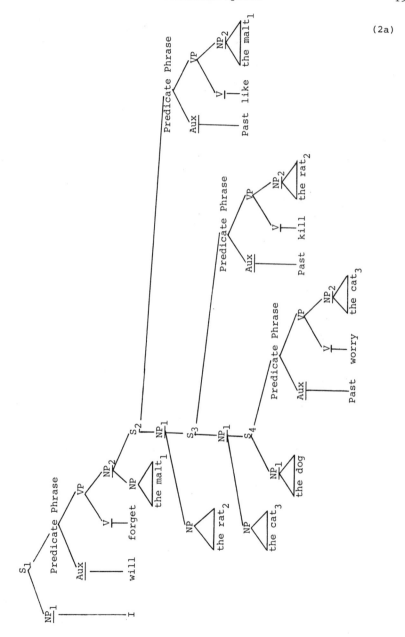

Note that everything dominated by NP_1 has been shifted by the
rule. The sentence is now considerably higher on the scale of
acceptability than (2). If the rule applies to, say, S_1 and S_4,
(5) is derived:

> (5) The malt that the rat that the cat that was worried by
> -   the dog killed liked will be forgotten by me

(5) is low on the scale of acceptability. If the rule applies to
S_2 and S_4, we obtain

> (6) I will forget the malt that was liked by the rat that
>   the cat that was worried by the dog killed

This is reasonably acceptable (though stylistically not very felicitous). Finally, if the rule applies to S_2, S_3, and S_4, (7) is
derived:

> (7) I will forget the malt that was liked by the rat that
>   was killed by the cat that was worried by the dog

Let us now consider again sentence (4) of section II.5:

> (8) This is the dog that worried the cat that killed the
>   rat that liked the malt

(8), too, meets the SI of the passive rule a number of times. The
relevant underlying structure can be represented in terms of the
following labelled bracketed string:

> (9) $($ This is the dog $($ $($ the dog $)$ worried $($ the cat
> $\quad S_1 \qquad\qquad\qquad\qquad S_2\ NP_1 \qquad\quad NP_1 \qquad\qquad NP_{2x}$
>
> $\quad ($ $($ the cat $)$ killed $($ the rat $($ $($ the rat $)$
> $\quad S_3\ NP_1 \qquad NP_1 \qquad\qquad NP_{2y} \qquad S_4\ NP_1 \qquad\quad NP_1$
>
> $\quad$ liked $\quad($ the malt $)$ $)$ $)$ $)$ $)$ $)$ $)$
> $\qquad\quad NP_{2z} \qquad\quad NP_{2z}\ S_4\ NP_{2y}\ S_3\ NP_{2x}\ S_2\ S_1$

Suppose the rule applies to S_2. NP_1 and NP_{2x} are interchanged;
after this the relative rule operates, moving NP_1 back to front
position in the sentence (with or without the preposition 'by'):

> (10) This is the dog by which the cat that killed the rat
>   that liked the malt was worried

If the rule applies to all three embedded sentences, the result
is

> (11) This is the dog by which the cat by which the rat by

which the malt was liked was killed was worried

or (if the preposition is left behind):

(12) This is the dog which the cat which the rat which the
malt was liked by was killed by was worried by

We conclude from this that the passive rule, owing to the
principle of variable reference, is a very powerful device. In
one case it unravels an incomprehensible sentence, in the other
it creates one. We return to this point in section IV.E.9.

IV.E.5. <u>The problem of derived constituent structure</u>

Consider the following sentence:

(1) The car killed the man

(1) has the following deep structure:

(1a)

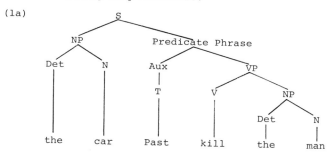

The passive rule as it was formulated in the preceding section would
convert (1a) into (1b) (we will make the assumption that it can be
proved that NP_1 should be dominated by VP):

(1b)

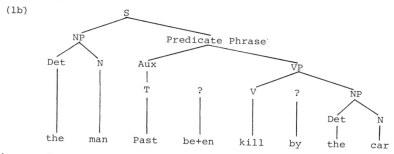

In other words, we do not know precisely what structure the derived

P-marker haṣ. Let us consider the question of 'by' first.

There is some evidence that the 'by + NP' in a passive sentence has the same syntactic status as an adverbial PP. Consider such noun phrases as

(2) The bed in which John slept
(3) The bed which John slept in
(4) The pistol by which John was killed
(5) The pistol which John was killed by

Now, our PS-rules would assign roughly the following underlying structure to (2) and (3):

(6)

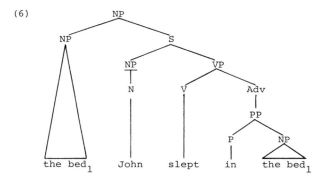

On this structure the relative rule would operate; in particular, the rightmost occurrence of 'the bed' would be converted into a relative pronoun and adjoined as the left sister of the underscored NP; the preposition 'in' would optionally be left behind. Consider now further such sentences as

(7) A sound beating may help, but by arguments he will never be convinced
(8) A sound beating may help, but by arguments you will never convince him

Since the second conjunct in (8) is an active sentence, 'by arguments' must be an adverb of manner (generated in the deep structure under the immediate domination of VP and fronted by the adverb preposing rule). By contrast, (7) is ambiguous: 'by arguments' may be an adverb of manner, in which case the underlying subject has been deleted by the rule of agent deletion (for which, see be-

low, section IV.G.7.2). (7), then, might be derived from something
like

> (9) A sound beating may help, but he will never be convinced
>   by arguments by anyone

Alternatively, 'by arguments' in (7) may be the deep-structure subject:

> (10) A sound beating may help, but arguments will never con-
>   vince him

from which is derived

> (11) A sound beating may help, but he will never be convinced
>   by arguments

By preposing 'by arguments' in (9) (assuming that agent deletion
also operates) and (11), (7) is derived.

   The reader will readily appreciate that if the grammar could
generate a derived structure for 'V + by + NP' matching that of
the VP in (6), we would be able to make some significant generalizations both with respect to the operations of the relative rule
(here it would be sufficient to 'know' that 'by + NP' is a prepositional phrase and that therefore 'by' behaves like all other
prepositions with respect to relativization (i.e. it may optionally be left behind when the NP is fronted)) and (perhaps) with respect to the adverb-preposing rule[1]. We shall see in the section

----

1. The argument from adverb-preposing is weak (in fact it has been
   invoked as a counterargument in this connection). Thus it is
   usually the case that the 'by + NP' of passive sentences does
   not undergo preposing, whereas other adverbial prepositional
   phrases (including manner adverbs) do:

   > (a) It rains a lot in England
   > (b) In England it rains a lot
   > (c) He counted his money with great enthusiasm
   > (d) With great enthusiasm he counted his money
   > (e) The dog has been run over by the car
   > (f) * By the car the dog has been run over

   However, it seems to be possible - in some cases at least - to
   prepose 'by + NP' in the second conjunct of two sentences coordinated by 'and' or 'but'. Thus (g) is a perfectly grammatical
   sentence:

   > (g) His close friends still refuse to believe that the
   >   charges can be true, but by everyone who doesn't know
   >   him he has already been stigmatized as a traitor

   Presumably, it is the polar opposition between the two conjuncts

on passive sentences (IV.G.7) that there is some further evidence
that 'by + NP' should be analysed as a manner adverbial.

   Meanwhile, we are confronted by another problem: in general,
transformations (with the exception of Chomsky-adjunction) reduce
syntactic structure. This is, of course, particularly obvious in
the case of deletion, but a rule like pronominalization has the
same effect; thus 'he' may be substituted for an NP consisting of
a single noun or for a complex NP. In view of this general tendency,
we would not wish the passive rule to have such enormous structure-
building power as would be required for the output VP to have the
same structure as the VP in (6). Since we are not yet prepared to
introduce the alternative analysis suggested above, we will consider other possibilities. Suppose for example that there is something wrong with our whole conception of adverbial prepositional
phrases. It might be that these are really noun phrases related
in certain semantically determined ways to their predicates, and
that hence prepositions are superficial categories introduced by
transformations, say, Chomsky-adjunction. We shall present some
evidence in section IV.G.14.6 that this may indeed be the best
way of analysing prepositional phrases. For the moment, let us
adopt this analysis without further ado. The structure of 'by + NP'
in a passive sentence would then be:

   (12)   NP
                            /   \
                        Prep   NP
                         |
                        by

Returning now to (1b), we still need to account for 'be + en'. We
will not go into great detail over this question. We have consistently referred to 'be + en' as the passive auxiliary and thus

----

which determines the (possible) thematic fronting of the noun
phrase governed by 'by'. Even so, there seem to be a number of
restrictions at work here. For example, it is difficult to
think of a context which might render (f) grammatical. Therefore the adverb preposing rule will have to be severely restricted with respect to 'by + NP'. It follows from these observations that if my judgment about (7) is wrong, the argument from adverb preposing presented in the text collapses.
Should this be the case, the example will nevertheless have
shown what would be required of the passive rule in terms of
structure-building power if it were to assign the correct derived structure to the VP.

verbalized our intuitions about it. Acting on these intuitions,
we will assume that 'be + en' should be adjoined as the daughter
of Aux. We may now proceed to reformulate the passive rule as follows:

(13) SI   X - NP_1 - Aux - V - NP_2 - Y
          1   2   3   4   5   6

     SC   Substitute 2 for 5 and 5 for 2; adjoin 'be + en'
          as the right daughter of 3; Chomsky-adjoin the pre-
          position 'by' to the left of 2.

The derived structure of the passive version of (1) would be, accordingly:

(1c)

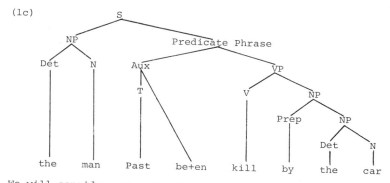

We will consider one more example. The sentence

(14) There is a man sitting in the chair

is derived from

(15) A man is sitting in the chair

by the rule of there insertion. The deep structure of (15) would be
something like this:

(15a)

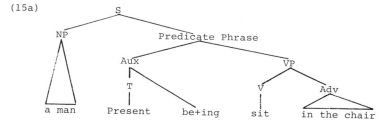

What might be the derived constituent structure of (14)? First
of all, we will assume that 'there' is inserted under the immediate
domination of the subject NP (i.e. that evidence can be provided
in support of the analysis of 'there' in (14) as a noun phrase).
Secondly, obviously, the subject NP of (15) must be moved. Where to?
Before we answer this question, we must consider the rule of affix
hopping. This operates at a late stage of the derivation - certainly after there insertion (for rule-ordering, see next section).
For the SI of affix hopping to be met, the relevant affixes and
verbs must remain immediately adjacent to each other. This means
that in (15a) 'ing' and 'sit' must not be separated. Consequently,
the only possible solution is to adjoin the original subject NP
as the right sister of 'be'. The output of the rule is, accordingly

(14a)

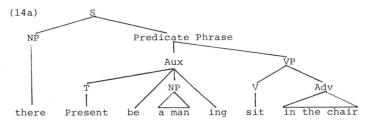

NP, then, is immediately dominated by Aux. This is highly counterintuitive, to say the least (more precisely, our grammar is strongly inadequate). Yet, there seems to be no help for it.

The reader may think that the arguments presented in this section are hair-splitting. However, he should bear in mind the fundamental requirement of a TG-grammar: the explicit generation of
all and only the sentences of the language, each provided with a
correct structural description, not only with respect to deep structure (given a set of PS-rules, that is not too difficult) but also
with respect to intermediate and surface structures.

The problems discussed in this section are examples of the
derived constituent structure problem. The assignment of correct
derived structures is difficult, and yet of paramount importance
for the following three reasons:

(a) The output of T-rule$_x$ frequently forms the input to T-
rule$_y$. Consequently, T-rule$_y$ requires a proper analysis of the
input-P-marker, or else the SI of the rule cannot be met.

(b) Surface structures form the input to the phonological
component. Since many phonological rules (such as the rules for
stress assignment) are directly dependent on grammatical categories,
it is necessary that the output of the transformational component
is a set of properly labelled bracketed strings.

(c) Any linguistic theory which cannot assign correct surface structures is clearly inadequate. However, for TG-theory, a
failure on that score would have disastrous consequences: if the
linguist cannot properly relate deep and surface structures, then
how can the child infer the rules which assign these structures?
After all, it _is_ surface structures which form the input to the
language acquisition device.

We pointed out in section I.5.4 that IC-analysis could not
assign a natural P-marker to a sentence like

(16) Who was it actually that Jane said you had so generously
     promised to give the money to

Within the context of the present theory, this might still not be
too easy.

IV.E.6. The ordering of T-rules

We will make the assumption in this book that T-rules are
extrinsically ordered. It should be stressed, however, that the
question of extrinsic order is currently the subject of much debate. In particular, it is being argued that the ordering strain
on rules (for this term, see Perlmutter, 1971, 130), which is
a (formal) universal restriction on the class of possible grammars, can be lessened if certain other types of constraints are
postulated. We return to this in section IV.E.8.

In the preceding sections we have considered the operation
of the passive rule in some detail. Let us now add the relative
rule to see how the two rules might interact in the derivation
of a sentence. The relative rule may be formulated as follows:

SI   X - [NP [Y - NP - Z]] - Q
         NP   S   S NP
     1   2   3   4   5   6

SC   Attach the features $\begin{bmatrix} + \text{Wh} \\ + \text{Pro} \\ + \text{Rel} \end{bmatrix}$ to 4; adjoin 4 as left sister
     of 3; delete the original 4.

Conditions: 2 = 4; obligatory[1].

The application of this rule to (la) would result in (lb):

(la)

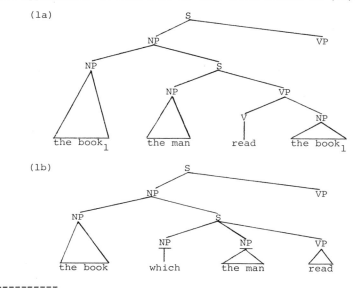

(lb)

----

1. The rule, as we have formulated it, asserts that the only ves-
   tige in surface structure of the relativized NP is the relative
   pronoun itself. There are exceptions to this. Consider such
   a sentence as

   (a) <u>Devon</u>, <u>which county</u> I have not yet visited, is said
       to be very beautiful

   In this the two underscored NPs are coreferential, whereas
   the two nouns are not lexically identical (cf. above, p. 161).
   Consequently, 'county' has not been deleted. It is possible
   that the underlying structure of 'which county' is 'the county
   of Devon', 'Devon' having been deleted under identity with the
   head noun. The relative clause in (a) is nonrestrictive, and the
   derivation of nonrestrictive clauses posits a number of problems. Even so, it is likely that at some stage of the derivation the structure underlying (a) will have to meet the SI of
   the relative rule (i.e. the rule should account for restrictive
   as well as nonrestrictive clauses). If this is the case, the
   rule, as it stands, is clearly inadequate. One possible reformulation would be to attach the features to the <u>Det</u> of the
   relativized NP and delete any noun(s) dominated by the relativized NP which is/are identical to the noun(s) dominated by
   the antecedent NP. However, this solution, even if it should
   turn out to be correct, is not available to us inasmuch as we
   have allowed Det to be an optional category. Suffice it, therefore, to have indicated the problem.

Observe now that (1b) does not meet the SI of the passive rule
(the relevant NPs (underscored in the P-marker) now being next to
each other). This means that the noun phrase 'the book which was
read by the man' cannot be derived. On the other hand, if the passive rule applies <u>prior</u> to the relative rule, it might derive
from (1a): 'the book$_1$ the book$_1$ was read by the man'. This structure would still meet the SI of the relative rule (in particular,
the third term would have the value null). We conclude, then, that
the passive rule precedes the relative rule[1].

Next let us examine the relationship between reflexivization
and passivization. The reflexive rule can be stated like this:

SI   X - NP - Y - NP - Z
     1   2   3   4   5

SC   Attach the features $\begin{bmatrix} + \text{ Pro} \\ + \text{ Reflexive} \end{bmatrix}$ to 4.

Conditions: 2 = 4; 2 and 4 occur in the same simplex
sentence[2].

If this rule applies before the passive rule, the latter will derive from a sentence like

(2) John likes himself

the ungrammatical

(3) * Himself is liked by John

By contrast, if we reorder the two rules, they derive (from 'John$_1$
likes John$_1$'):

(4) ? John is liked by himself

which is certainly better than (3)[3].

----

1. We are assuming in this example that T-rules apply to <u>total</u>
   P-markers - including those containing embedded sentences. For
   a corrective, see next section.

2. The second condition goes beyond the Boolean condition on analysability. We return to this point in section IV.E.8.

3. 'Himself' in (4) is weakly stressed. If it carries contrastive
   stress, the sentence is perfectly grammatical. For discussion,
   see Postal, 1971, 14ff. (and for stressed reflexive pronouns,
   230ff.). Postal examines in great detail the empirical consequences of positing a general <u>cross-over constraint</u>: roughly,
   if two coreferential NPs cross each other in a derivation, the
   result is an ungrammatical sentence. By this token, both (3)
   and (4) are ungrammatical. The argument then is that (3) is

Consider next the interaction of the imperative rule and the reflexive rule. We have noted that the imperative rule deletes 'you'. Now, if this happens prior to reflexivization, the SI of the latter cannot be met (one of the relevant NPs is no longer present in the P-marker). Consequently, given an underlying structure like 'you wash you', the output of the grammar will be the ungrammatical

(5) ✻ Wash you

whereas the perfectly grammatical (6) cannot be derived:

(6) Wash yourself

The reflexive rule, therefore, must precede the imperative rule.

Passivization must precede imperativization as well: it is quite possible (though often unnatural) to have passive imperatives as in[1]

(7) Study your failures and be instructed by them

Clearly, the SI of the imperative rule is not met by the second conjunct of (7) before the passive rule has applied. The derivation of 'be instructed by them' is 'your failures will instruct you' $\Longrightarrow$ 'you will be instructed by your failures' $\Longrightarrow$ 'be instructed by your failures' $\Longrightarrow$ 'be instructed by them' (by pronominalization, the ordering of which we are not considering here).

We will give no more examples of rule ordering here. For further details and discussion, the reader is referred to the works cited in the bibliographical notes.

IV.E.7. The cyclic principle

It will be convenient to start our discussion of the cyclic principle by illustrating it in the abstract. In order to do this, we will make the following assumptions:

(a) We are considering a sentence consisting of S_0, S_1, S_2, and S_3, such that S_3 is embedded in S_2, S_2 in S_1, and S_1 in S_0.

(b) Our grammar contains five T-rules which apply in linear order from T_1 to T_5.

----

much worse than (4) because it violates the cross-over constraint as well as the ordering constraint. We may note in passing that the cross-over constraint accounts for a number of interesting facts. Thus it predicts that a sentence like 'his hands were washed by Peter' is ungrammatical if 'his' (derived from 'Peter's') and 'Peter' are coreferential, but not otherwise.

1. Example from Schibsbye, 1965, 36.

Given these two assumptions, we can illustrate the cyclic principle in terms of the following abstract P-marker:

(1)

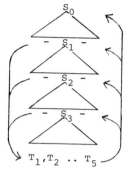

(1) should be interpreted as follows: T_1, T_2 .. T_5 all apply to S_3 first (provided, that is, that the SIs of the rules are met and that no rules are optionally passed over (they need not all be obligatory)). This completes the <u>first cycle</u>. The rules then apply to S_2 (which, be it noted, has S_3 under its domination). After this, the second cycle is completed; and so on, until the five rules have all applied on the last cycle (S_0 and everything dominated by S_0).

Since the publication of <u>Aspects</u>, it has generally been assumed that T-rules are extrinsically ordered and apply cyclically in the way illustrated in (1). A number of different paradigm cases are customarily invoked in support of this hypothesis. We will consider one such case[1]. It involves the interaction of the rules of reflexivization and <u>subject-to-object raising</u>. The following two sentences:

(2) I believe that John is honest
(3) I believe John to be honest

are <u>syntactic</u> paraphrases of each other. Consequently, we may assume that they have the same deep structure[2]. This may be represented

----

1. Cf. also Jacobs and Rosenbaum, 1968, Chapters 23 and 28.
2. It is essential to take note of the qualification 'syntactic'. In the standard theory two sentences which are <u>semantic</u> paraphrases of each other do not have the same deep structure - they contain different (synonymous) lexical items (cf. sentences (3) and (4) of section IV.D.8).

in terms of the following labelled bracketed string:

(4) (I believe it (John be honest))
    S_1 S_2 S_2 S_1

The complementizer insertion rule must insert a complementizer
in S_2. If 'that' is inserted, 'it' is deleted and (omitting details with respect to tense) (2) is derived. By contrast, if 'for -
to' is inserted, we obtain something like

(5) (I believe it (for John to be honest))
    S_1 S_2 S_2 S_1

To this structure the rule of subject-to-object raising applies
obligatorily, substituting the subject of S_2 for 'it' in the matrix
sentence[1]. The rule may be formulated roughly as follows:

(6) SI X - $\underset{NP}{[}$ it $\underset{S}{[}$ $\begin{Bmatrix} for \\ Poss \end{Bmatrix}$ - NP - Aux - VP $\underset{S}{]}$ $\underset{NP}{]}$ - Y
        1   2   3   4   5   6   7 $\Longrightarrow$

    SC 1   4 $\emptyset$ $\emptyset$ $\emptyset$ $\emptyset$ 7+3+5+6

Since 'for' is immediately adjacent to 'to' after the removal of
the subject of the embedded sentence, it is deleted. The outcome
of these operations is (3)[2].

    Consider now the following sentences:

(7) He_1 doesn't believe that John is capable of hurting him_1
(8) The $woman_1$ found a dog that obeyed her_1

In (7) and (8) the reflexive rule has not applied. This is correctly predicted by the constraint on the rule which requires that
the two coreferential NPs should be in the same simplex sentence.
With (3), (7), and (8), we may now compare

(9) John believes himself to be honest

derived by complementizer insertion, subject-to-object raising,
reflexivization, and for deletion from

----

1. The rule is also known as 'pronoun-replacement' (Rosenbaum,
   1967), or 'it-replacement' (Lakoff, 1968c), or just 'raising'
   (Kiparsky and Kiparsky, 1970, Postal 1974). It was Rosenbaum
   who first formulated the rule. More generally, it was he who
   pioneered the study of the complementation system in English.

2. We will not comment further on the formal properties of the
   rules involved at this point, but continue the discussion in
   simplified terms.

(10) (John$_1$ believes it (John be honest))
      S$_1$ S$_2$ S$_2$ S$_1$

Now, given the simplex-sentence constraint on reflexivization, it
is clear that the order of the two crucial rules must be

(11) 1. Subject-to-object raising
      2. Reflexivization

As against this, consider

(12) I believe Mary to have fooled herself

derived from

(13) (I believe it (Mary$_1$ have fooled Mary$_1$))
      S$_1$ S$_2$ S$_2$ S$_1$

Now, if the the two rules are applied to (13) in the order specified by (11), the subject ('Mary') will be removed from S$_2$ prior
to reflexivization. Consequently, this rule cannot apply (the two
occurrences of 'Mary' are no longer in the same simplex S - we are
assuming here that the S$_2$ node is unaffected by the raising rule;
as a matter of fact this is not certain - it depends on the total
analysis (cf. below, section IV.G.16.6)). However, if we reverse
the ordering of (11):

(14) 1. Reflexivization
      2. Subject-to-object raising

we can derive (12) from (13). (11) and (14) constitute an <u>ordering
paradox</u>.

We can resolve this paradox if we combine the ordering specified in (11) with the cyclic principle illustrated in (1). The
two relevant deep structures are (10) and (13). We start with
(10) and apply (11) to the deepmost embedded sentence (S$_2$): subject-to-object raising does not apply (it never does to the deepmost embedded sentence, of course). Reflexivization does not apply either. This completes the first cycle. On the second cycle
(S$_1$), subject-to-object raising does apply, and after this reflexivization applies (the coreferential NPs now being in the same
simplex S). The result is (9). In the case of (13), subject-to-object raising does not apply on the first cycle, reflexivization
does. On the second cycle, subject-to-object raising does apply,
reflexivization does not.

Observe that, if rules apply cyclically, the first ordering
problem considered in the preceding section does not arise: the
passive rule applies on the lowest cycle, that is, the cycle defined by the S node dominating the relative clause. The relative
rule applies on the top cycle. More generally, the relative rule
always requires two coreferential NPs which occur in different
simplex sentences.

Given the validity of the cyclic principle, we can consider
some further possibilities concerning the possible form of grammars defined by the theory:

(a) All rules apply cyclically in linear order.

(b) Some rules are cyclic, others are not.

It has been shown convincingly that (b) is correct.

Given (b), two further possibilities emerge:

(b1) There are two types of T-rules: rules of type 1 operate
precyclically on the entire base P-marker, whereas rules of type
2 operate cyclically.

(b2) There are three types of rules: rules of type 1 operate
precyclically, rules of type 2 operate cyclically, and rules of
type 3 operate last-cyclically (i.e. only on the last cycle).

There is some evidence that (b2) is correct.

Finally, a distinction can be made between last-cyclic and
post-cyclic rules. The former are ordered relative to the cyclic
rules operating on the last cycle (that is, a last-cyclic rule
may apply on the last cycle before a cyclic rule), the latter apply after the application of all cyclic rules (including last-
cyclic rules).

We will not explore the implications of these distinctions
at this point. We merely note that the general theory provides a
possibility of putting one of the following conditions on a T-rule:
(a) precyclic, (b) last-cyclic, and (c) post-cyclic. If it is not
so conditioned, the rule operates cyclically. We can say, then,
that the cyclic operation of rules is the unmarked case.

IV.E.8. On constraining the power of the grammar

The goal which the TG-linguist sets himself is, as we have
seen, to construct a device which generates all and only the sentences of language L (cf. section II.3). The reader will begin to

realize the formidable difficulties which the qualification 'and
only' entails.

The main source of trouble is that a TG-grammar is an enormously powerful device. Consequently, the linguist must seek to
limit its power: he must impose <u>constraints</u> on the operation of
rules. Furthermore, in principle, the constraints imposed on the
operation of the rules of individual languages should be motivated
to the highest possible degree by universal considerations. The
power of the general theory increases proportionally to the number of constraints that can be stated in the universal grammar.
The power of the grammar of L decreases correspondingly. By implication, the more universal constraints there are, the simpler
the task of language acquisition.

Base P-markers form the input to the transformational component and final P-markers form the output. It is therefore between these two poles that the constraints must be placed.

Consider first the base (i.e. the PS-rules[1] and the lexicon -
including the lexical insertion transformation). It takes little
reflection to see that the base generates ill-formed deep structures. An example is (1), which contains two successively embedded relative clauses:

(1)

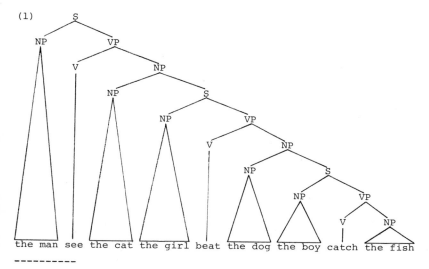

----
1. We have noted that PS-rules are themselves subject to certain
   formal constraints (cf. above, p. 89).

Observe that the lexical insertion transformation, which always operates within the confines of one simplex S, will insert the lexical
items in (1) without violating selectional restrictions (cf. above,
p. 152, note 2). Yet (1) cannot be brought to the surface because the
derivation is <u>blocked</u>: the relative rule cannot apply because the coreferentiality condition is not met. (1), then, underlies no well-
formed surface structure and hence does not qualify as a deep structure. This brings us to the first point to be made: the transformational component constitutes a <u>filter</u> through which base P-markers
must pass to become surface structures (and in turn qualify as deep
structures)[1]. This is known as <u>the filtering function of transforma-
tions</u> (cf. Chomsky, 1965, 138ff. and Perlmutter, 1971, 123ff.).

   Strict subcategorization features and (syntactic) selectional
features are constraints on possible deep structures. Furthermore,
the projection rules have a filtering function parallelling that of
the transformational component: they can disambiguate sentences by
discarding combinations of readings of lexical items (more generally,
constituents) which violate selectional restrictions. In addition
to this, they rule out semantically anomalous sentences (either all
of them, or, if the grammar contains syntactic selectional features,
some of them (cf. above, p. 151f.)).

   It has been argued by Perlmutter (1971, 1ff.) that a grammar of English must contain deep structure constraints of a kind
different from the feature constraints mentioned in the preceding
paragraph. Consider the following sentences:

   (2) I prefer for her to leave
   (3) I prefer her to leave
   (4) * I prefer for me to leave
   (5) * I prefer myself to leave
   (6) I prefer to leave
   (7) I shouted for John to leave
   (8) * I shouted for me to leave
   (9) * I shouted to leave

The difference between (2) and (3) is (we assume without arguing

----

1. More formally, if we assume that all embedded sentences are
   flanked by boundary symbols in base P-markers - $\#$ S $\#$ - any
   surface structure P-marker which contains internal sentence boundaries is ill-formed: the boundary symbols indicate that an obligatory T-rule has failed to apply because of a universal constrair
   on rule application (cf. below, p. 211, note). Conversely, if all
   obligatory rules have applied on each cycle, all internal boundary symbols are deleted, and the surface structure is well-formed
   (as is also the deep structure).

(cf. below, section IV.G.16.5)) that in (3) 'her' has been raised
into the matrix sentence by the rule of subject-to-object raising;
'for' has subsequently been deleted. The difference between (3)
and (4) involves the rule of equi NP deletion, which, as we have
seen before, deletes the subject of an embedded sentence, provided it is coreferential with an NP in the sentence next above.
Roughly, the rule may be stated as follows:

(10) SI   X - NP - Y - $\left[\begin{Bmatrix} for \\ Poss \end{Bmatrix} \right._S$ - NP - Aux - VP $\left._S \right]$ - Q

            1   2   3   4   5   6   7   8 $\Longrightarrow$

    SC   1   2   3   4 $\emptyset$ 6   7   8

          Conditions: 2 = 5; generally obligatory (cf. sentences
                         (5) and (6) of section IV.D.2).

Clearly, this rule must apply to (4), deleting 'me'. The result
is (6). Since 'me' must be deleted in (4), it follows that the
SI of the subject-to-object raising rule, which applies after
equi, cannot be met. Hence the ungrammatical (5) cannot be derived
at all. Next, we turn to (8) and (9). Why are they ungrammatical?
Might it be that a rule feature like (- equi) has been violated[1]?
The answer to this question is no; for if this were the case, (8)
would not be characterized as ungrammatical, which it clearly is.

     Consider now the following abstract base P-marker:

(11)

Now, in the <u>Aspects</u>-framework, lexical insertion would work independently in the two sentences. The fact that there are two coreferential NPs would have no influence on the verb substituted
for $\triangle$. Perlmutter's proposal is that some lexical items should
be allowed to impose constraints on base P-markers (across sentence boundaries). In particular, some verbs would require <u>non-</u>
<u>identity</u> between the subject of a complement sentence and the sub-
----
1. Rule features - as properties of the lexical items of L (in par-
    ticular verbs) - (a) constrain the power of the T-rules of L,
    (b) increase the power of the grammar of L, and, hence, (c)
    weaken the power of the general theory. On rule government, see
    Lakoff, 1970a. Consult also Stockwell et al., 1968, Vol. 2, 940ff.

ject of the matrix sentence. One such verb is 'shout', which, consequently, cannot be inserted in (11) (cf. (7)).

The argument in support of the constraint goes something like
this: Compare with (9)

(12) I shouted to be permitted to go there

which is a perfectly grammatical sentence. The underlying structure of (12) is (details aside):

(13) ($\underline{I}$ shout ($\underline{someone}$ permit me (I go there)))
     S_1 S_2 S_3 S_3 S_2 S_1

Clearly, 'shout' has been inserted here without violation of the
nonidentity constraint. On the second cycle (S_2), the subject of
S_3 will be deleted by equi NP deletion:

(14) (I shout (someone permit me to go there))[1]
     S_1 S_2 S_2 S_1

Passivization now applies on the second cycle, reordering the two
NPs:

(15) (I shout (I be permitted by someone to go there))
     S_1 S_2 S_2 S_1

Still on the second cycle, 'by someone' is deleted by the agent
deletion rule. On the last cycle (S_1), equi deletes the subject of
S_2, and (12) is derived. An elegant argument by all counts[2].

We turn now to the transformational component proper.

Let us first return to the notion of Boolean conditions
on analysability discussed in section IV.E.3. We noted in section
IV.E.6 that the simplex S constraint on reflexivization (first
noted by Lees and Klima, 1963) is a violation of these conditions.

----

1. Note that S_3 has disappeared. It is likely that it has been
   pruned from the P-marker. We return to this below and in section IV.G.16.6.

2. Lakoff, 1970a (note that this work was written in 1965) had
   tried to account for such sentences as (7), (8), and (9) in
   terms of his notion of absolute exceptions (cf. p. 49ff.).
   With regard to 'shout' this would mean specifying (a) that it
   must not meet the structural description of equi, and (b) that
   it must not undergo the rule (observe that (a) would be required
   to rule out (8)). The core of Perlmutter's argument, then,
   is that both (a) and (b) collapse on the first cycle in (15).
   In the preface to the published edition of his dissertation,
   Lakoff discusses and accepts Perlmutter's criticism. Perlmutter's
   constraint fits well with the generative semanticist view of
   lexical insertion (cf. below, p. 486).

The reason for this is that it is logically equivalent to a statement involving quantification: there is no node S such that S
dominates NP_2 (i.e. the noun phrase to be reflexivized), but not
NP_1 (i.e. the antecedent noun phrase), and there is no node S
such that S dominates NP_1, but not NP_2 (cf. Bach, 1974, 217 (observe
that Bach uses the term 'domination' in a different sense from the
one in which it is used in this book (cf. Bach, op. cit., 84 and
note)); consult also Ross, 1967, 32, 58, note 7). In other words,
although it would appear that a large number of rules can be stated
in Boolean terms, not all rules can be so restricted.

We have noted that an elementary operation is deletion. However, elements cannot be deleted wholesale from a P-marker. The
deletion operation is usually assumed to be subject to a general
condition of recoverability (for a formal statement of this condition, see for example Katz and Postal, 1964, 81; consult also
Chomsky, 1964a, section 2.2). Deletion may operate subject to
one of the following three constraints:

(a) The deleted element is mentioned in the SI of the rule.
This accounts for the deletion of 'you' (and 'will' - if it is
deleted (i.e. if it is there in the first place (cf. below,
section IV.G.10.4))) in imperative sentences.

(b) The deleted element is identical to some other element
in the string of terminal symbols. This constraint accounts for
the deleted NP in relative clauses (cf. above, p. 200, note)[1].
It is also relevant to deletion in comparative sentences (cf.
below, p. 328ff.) and to VP deletion (cf. below, p. 338).

(c) The deleted element is a pro-form. Thus a sentence like

(16) He was driving

is assumed to be derived from a structure like

(17) He was driving something

In particular, (17) forms the input to the semantic component.
This imposes the selectional feature of 'drive' on the pro-form
(whatever it may be (something like + ARTIFACT, + SELFMOBILE perhaps)) (for the formalism, see Katz and Postal, 83f. (cf. also
above, p. 155 and note)). After semantic interpretation, the pro-
form may be deleted. Conversely, if there had been no pro-form,

----

1. Observe that, fundamentally, it is this universal constraint
   on deletion which filters out (1). Cf Chomsky, 1965, 145.

the deleted NP-constituent could have been anything at all; consequently, the grammar would predict that (16) is infinitely ambiguous, which is clearly not the case[1].

We have seen how T-rules are formulated (though some of the
formulations we have presented are doubtless ad-hoc). For example,
it is evident that, given a T-rule whose SI mentions an NP, this
NP can be moved to some other place. There is virtually no limit
to such movement operations. Thus we might imagine a rule which,
given a P-marker with five cycles, detached an NP from a PP in S_2
and adjoined it as, say, right sister of the object NP in S_5. However, there seems to be no language whose rule-system would allow
such a quaint operation. The constraints on movement of constituents - in particular NPs - have been studied in great detail
by Ross, 1967. We shall illustrate some of Ross's constraints in
the sections on relative and interrogative sentences and will say
no more about them here.

Consider now the following configurations:

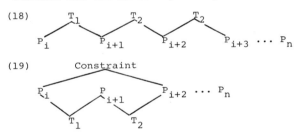

(18) illustrates that T-rules are _local_ constraints in the sense
that they relate (in particular specify well-formedness conditions
on) pairs of _adjacent_ P-markers in a derivation. T-rules defined
as local constraints is the hallmark of the standard theory. By
contrast, the constraint of (19) is a _global_ or _derivational_ constraint: it specifies a well-formedness condition on P_{i+2} based
on information contained in P_i although the two P-markers are nonadjacent in the derivation. Such constraints are typical of generative semantics (we shall give an example in Chapter V). They have
not, in general, formed a part of the (extended) standard theory

----

1. 'Drive' would presumably have to be marked by the feature
   (x object deletion). Note, however, that there are other
   senses of 'drive'. Thus one may drive a herd of cattle. This
   sense does not allow object deletion and must, accordingly,
   be specified (- object deletion). Consequently, 'he was driving
   to the market place' is not ambiguous.

(for critical discussion, see for example Chomsky, 1972, 133ff.).
On the other hand, such constraints are not, in principle, incompatible with the standard theory (or better, perhaps, with a
theory which postulates an autonomous level of syntactic deep structure). Thus Ross, 1969c (especially p. 276ff.) has argued that
some of his own constraints (referred to above) should be restated
as derivational constraints, and Koutsoudas, 1973 has shown that
the reformulation of one such constraint (the complex NP constraint)
as a constraint on derivations can lead to the abolition of language-specific extrinsic ordering of certain rules. It would, however, lead us far too far afield to become involved with the details of such arguments.

  Brief mention should be made of <u>transderivational constraints</u>
(see especially Lakoff, 1973). They are countenanced only within
the theory of generative semantics and have the power of constraining one derivation on the basis of some condition holding in another, related derivation[1].

  We turn finally to <u>surface structure constraints</u> (or <u>output
conditions</u>). We will consider here a paradigm case discussed by
Perlmutter, 1971, Chapter 4. Perlmutter examines a set of French
and English sentences. To these we add the German and Danish equivalents.

  Consider the following sets of sentences[2]:

(b)	Qui a-t-il dit que Pierre avait envie de voir
	Who did he say (that) Peter felt like seeing
	Hvem sagde han (at) Peter længtes efter at se
	* Wen hat er gesagt, dass Peter sehen wollte
(20) (a)	Il a dit que Pierre avait envie de voir son ami
	He said that Peter felt like seeing his friend
	Han sagde at Peter længtes efter at se sin ven
	Er sagte dass Peter seinen Freund sehen wollte

----

1. We will not go into this question. Langendoen and Bever, 1973,
   in discussing the sentences cited in the notes to section II.5,
   illustrate the way in which such sentences might be analysed
   in the standard theory, the extended standard theory, and generative semantics. The latter approach involves a transderivational
   constraint. Transderivational constraints also play an important
   part in the formulation of conversational postulates. See Gordon
   and Lakoff, 1975 (in Cole and Morgan, 1975) 104f.

2. The verb phrases in the embedded sentences are not quite translational equivalents, but this does not affect the argument.

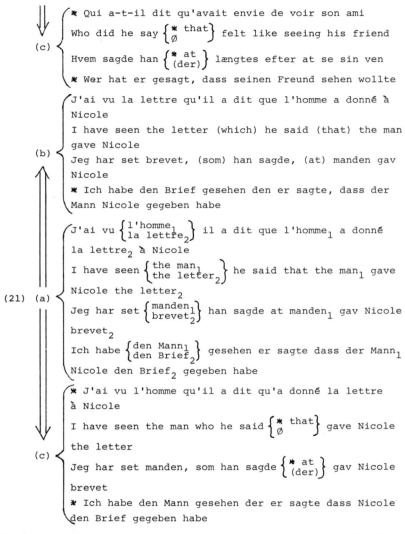

(21)

(c)
* Qui a-t-il dit qu'avait envie de voir son ami

Who did he say $\left\{\begin{matrix} \text{* that} \\ \emptyset \end{matrix}\right\}$ felt like seeing his friend

Hvem sagde han $\left\{\begin{matrix} \text{* at} \\ \text{(der)} \end{matrix}\right\}$ længtes efter at se sin ven

* Wer hat er gesagt, dass seinen Freund sehen wollte

(b)
J'ai vu la lettre qu'il a dit que l'homme a donné à Nicole

I have seen the letter (which) he said (that) the man gave Nicole

Jeg har set brevet, (som) han sagde, (at) manden gav Nicole

* Ich habe den Brief gesehen den er sagte, dass der Mann Nicole gegeben habe

(a)
J'ai vu $\left\{\begin{matrix} \text{l'homme}_1 \\ \text{la lettre}_2 \end{matrix}\right\}$ il a dit que l'homme$_1$ a donné la lettre$_2$ à Nicole

I have seen $\left\{\begin{matrix} \text{the man}_1 \\ \text{the letter}_2 \end{matrix}\right\}$ he said that the man$_1$ gave Nicole the letter$_2$

Jeg har set $\left\{\begin{matrix} \text{manden}_1 \\ \text{brevet}_2 \end{matrix}\right\}$ han sagde at manden$_1$ gav Nicole brevet$_2$

Ich habe $\left\{\begin{matrix} \text{den Mann}_1 \\ \text{den Brief}_2 \end{matrix}\right\}$ gesehen er sagte dass der Mann$_1$ Nicole den Brief$_2$ gegeben habe

(c)
* J'ai vu l'homme qu'il a dit qu'a donné la lettre à Nicole

I have seen the man who he said $\left\{\begin{matrix} \text{* that} \\ \emptyset \end{matrix}\right\}$ gave Nicole the letter

Jeg har set manden, som han sagde $\left\{\begin{matrix} \text{* at} \\ \text{(der)} \end{matrix}\right\}$ gav Nicole brevet

* Ich habe den Mann gesehen der er sagte dass Nicole den Brief gegeben habe

In all four languages the (a) structures are closest to the deep structure. Let us now examine what has happened in the transformations. In (20b) the <u>object</u> of the embedded sentence has been questioned and moved out of the sentence. In (20c) the same rule

has applied to the <u>subject</u> of the embedded sentence. In (21b) the
object of the embedded sentence has been relativized and 'raised'
into the sentence next above, whereas in (21c), these operations
have applied to the subject of the embedded sentence.

   It is clear that the grammar of French must be constrained
so as to rule out (20c) and (21c). One possible way of doing this
would be to place a constraint on the question rule and the relative
rule to the effect that the rules must not apply to the NP immediately dominated by S in a subordinate clause introduced by
'que'. Instead of this, Perlmutter proposes to filter out the ungrammatical French sentences by means of the following surface
structure constraint (<u>op. cit.</u>, 100):

> (22) Any sentence other than an Imperative in which there is
>   an S that does not contain a subject in surface struc-
>   ture is ungrammatical.

To illustrate: the deep structure of the French version of (21c)
(restricting the attention to the relevant NP) would look something like this:

> (23) (l'homme (il a dit (que <u>l'homme</u> a donné la lettre à
>   NP S_1 S_2
>
>   Nicole)))
> S_2 S_1 NP

The T-rule relativizes the underlined NP and adjoins it as left
sister of 'il' in S_1:

> (24) (l'homme (<u>qui</u> il a dit (que a donné la lettre à
>   NP S_1 S_2
>
>   Nicole)))
> S_2 S_1 NP

The crucial point, then, is that S_2 now no longer immediately dominates an NP. This being the case, it is filtered out by (22).

   Let us now turn to the English examples. It appears that
English permits the rules to apply to both object and subject in
the embedded sentence, with one important qualification: if the
operations apply to the subject of the embedded sentence, the <u>com-</u>
<u>plementizer 'that' must be deleted</u>. On the basis of a number of
related phenomena, Perlmutter argues convincingly that the surface
structure constraint is part of the grammar of English as well.

We cannot pursue the argument in detail, but the main point concerns the problems involved in formulating and ordering the T-rule
which may delete the complementizer 'that' in a sentence like

(25) I told you (that) he would come

but not in a sentence like

(26) The accused allowed $\left\{\begin{array}{l}\text{that}\\ \text{* } \emptyset\end{array}\right\}$ he knew the victim of the crime

in such a way that it will be predicted that

(27) Who did I tell you would come

is grammatical, whereas this is not the case with (28) and (29):

(28) * Who did the accused allow that knew the victim of the
     crime
(29) * Who did the accused allow knew the victim of the crime

   In order to make the constraint work for English, it is necessary to have recourse to the <u>S-pruning convention</u> (cf. Ross, 1967,
Chapter 3, 1969d). This states that any embedded S node which <u>does</u>
<u>not branch</u> (i.e. which immediately dominates <u>only one</u> constituent)
must be pruned from the P-marker. By way of illustrating this
principle, we may consider the derivation of (21c) from (21a).
(Part of) one intermediate P-marker looks like this:

(30)

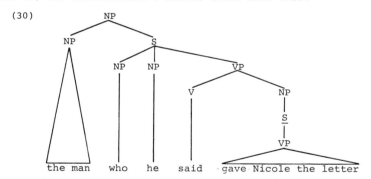

in which the underlined S no longer branches; consequently, S
(and presumably the NP immediately dominating it) must be pruned
from the tree. The result is (31) which constitutes the surface
structure of the NP:

(31)

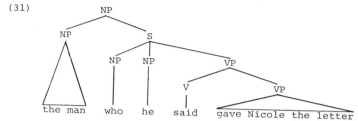

In sum, the English phrase 'gave Nicole the letter' <u>is not a sen-</u>
<u>tence</u>, which means that (31) is unaffected by (22). In French,
however, 'que a donné la lettre à Nicole' <u>is</u> a sentence in the
sense that the embedded S node branches into the ICs 'que' and
'a donné la lettre à Nicole'. Since 'que', unlike 'that'[1], cannot
be deleted, (22) filters the sentence out as ungrammatical. By the
same token, (29) is ungrammatical because 'allow' disallows the
deletion of 'that'. Consequently, the sentence cannot escape the
constraint.

The Danish versions show that Danish and English behave
exactly alike with respect to the two T-rules and the (un)gram-
maticality of the complementizer. Hence we may conclude that Danish
has (22) in its grammar[2].

Finally, the German versions of (20b and c) and (21b and c)
are all ungrammatical. Consequently, although German probably has
(22) in its grammar[3], the NP-movement rule must nevertheless be
constrained in such a way that the derivation of (20b) and (21b)
will be blocked.

Now, it is clear that the incorporation of surface structure
----

1. As noted by Perlmutter (pp. 113-114) the facts relating to
   pruning and that deletion may turn out to be rather more complex. However, this does not affect the argument as far as
   the sentences under consideration here are concerned.

2. We comment on the element 'der' in the Danish sentences in the
   notes to section IV.E.9.

3. The arguments presented in this section constitute only part
   of the evidence amassed by Perlmutter in support of (22).
   One further argument relates to the fact that languages which
   contain (22) in their grammar do not allow deletion of a subject pronoun although it would be uniquely recoverable on the
   basis of the morphological structure of the verb. Thus in the
   German sentence ' ✳ habe gestern gearbeitet' the subject can
   only be 'ich'. Nevertheless the sentence is ungrammatical.

constraints in the linguistic theory - all other things being
equal - greatly increases the power of individual grammars and
hence weakens the theory correspondingly. However, we have seen
that all other things are not equal. In particular, (22) makes it
possible to dispense with constraints on NP-movement in the grammars of all the four languages we have considered (though least so
in German). In the same way, it is no longer necessary to impose
a complex set of ordering constraints on the rule which deletes
'that' in English sentences. So, in this sense, the balance is being maintained at the same time as the facts are adequately accounted
for. We will say no more about this. The reader who is interested
in studying the rationale of constraints could wish for no better
starting point than the Epilogue to Perlmutter's 1971-monograph.

We will conclude this section by a brief mention of the distinction between root transformations and structure preserving
transformations proposed by Emonds, 1970. Root transformations apply on the last cycle and affect only the highest S (in contrast
to last-cyclic rules). A typical example of a root transformation
is the Aux inversion rule (illustrated informally in (21b) and (22b)
of section IV.C.1). Consider such sentences as

(32) Did he ask whether you would come

(33) * Did he ask whether would you come

(32) contains an embedded interrogative clause. The ungrammaticality of (33) shows that Aux inversion is restricted in application
to the highest S. Root transformations are those rules whose output structures are not defined independently by the PS-rules. Thus
the PS-rules do not generate a structure like Aux + NP + VP. By
contrast, the output structures of the structure preserving rules
are generated by the PS-rules. For example, our PS-rules would
generate a structure like NP + Aux + V + Prep + NP. But this is
precisely the structure that results from the application of the
passive rule. Emonds proposes, in essence, that all nonroot transformations should be structure preserving. His proposal, then,
amounts to a universal constraint of 'similarity' between deep
and surface structure[1]. We will not go into further details about
the implications of Emonds's theory at this point (for some discussion, see for example Chomsky, 1972, 116f., 124 and Bach, 1974,
213f., 259ff., 274ff.).

----

1. Rather shallow structure, defined as the level of structure which
   forms the input to root transformations (cf. Chomsky, op. cit.,
   124 and below, p. 487).

IV.E.9. On the justification of transformations

We saw in section IV.A.4 that a grammar which contains PS-rules must also contain T-rules. In particular, it became clear that context-sensitive rules, which, in terms of weak generative capacity, are quite powerful devices, must be constrained so as not to be able to permute elements. If they are not so constrained, the structures they assign are hopelessly inadequate. On the other hand, if they are so constrained, they cannot capture the interrelationship between sentences. Hence T-rules are required if the grammar is to be descriptively adequate.

It should be noted, however, that with the advent of syntactic features, it is theoretically possible to search for other solutions. Consider such sentences as

(1) Many scholars have studied semantics
(2) Semantics has been studied by many scholars

Within the framework of the subcategorization model, 'study' (in the relevant sense) would have the following selectional feature: (+ (+ Human) Aux __ Det (+ Abstract)). Clearly, this restriction is violated in (2), unless it is assumed either (a) that (2) is derived from (1) after lexical insertion and semantic interpretation, or (b) that the lexicon contains a redundancy rule of the following type[1]:

(3) (+ (+ Human) Aux __ Det (+ Abstract)) $\longrightarrow$
    (+ (+ Abstract) Aux __ by Det (+ Human))

If we posit (3), we do not need a T-rule to account for the relationship between (1) and (2): they can both be generated by the PS-rules and lexical insertion will work smoothly enough. This approach can be proved to be wrong if there are cases in which redundancy rules cannot account for the facts. Consider the following two sentences:

(4) At the staff meeting someone reported there to have been
    some disagreement among the students over this question
(5) At the staff meeting there was reported to have been
    some disagreement among the students over this question

Now, on the assumption that it can be proved that 'there' should be inserted transformationally rather than lexically, and, furthermore, that (5) should be derived from (4), the relation-

----

1. For some discussion of the theoretical implications of rules like (3), see Lakoff, 1970a, 148ff. and Bach, 1974, 174ff.

ship between (4) and (5) can only be explained in transformational
terms. Compare now with (4) and (5) (6) and (7):

(6) The constables reported the accident to headquarters
(7) The accident was reported to headquarters by the con-
     stables

We could easily explain (6) and (7) in terms of a redundancy rule.
However, this would mean that in order to account for the verb
'report' (and a great many other verbs) in passive sentences, we
would need redundancy rules as well as a T-rule. By contrast, the
transformational solution accounts for both (5) and (7). We may
conclude from this that a grammar of English which contains a passive rule and no redundancy rules like (3) is the preferable (i.e.
the more highly valued) grammar.

    We shall see in the section on nominalization that the use of
syntactic features can lead to important modifications of the theory (including a modification of the passive rule, but not its
elimination from the grammar).

    In recent years, some scholars (e.g. Langendoen, 1969, Chapter
8, Langendoen, 1970a, Bever, 1970, Langendoen and Bever, 1973, and
Langacker, 1974a) have considered transformations from a functional
point of view[1]. In particular, they have tried to establish a connection between the operations of transformations in the grammar
and the psychological mechanisms underlying speech production and
speech recognition. We will briefly consider the passive rule and
the extraposition rule in the light of this approach, relating also the two rules to traditional grammar.

    Jespersen defined the passive rule as follows (1933, 121ff.):

    The subject of a passive verb is what in the active would
    be an object ... The converted subject of a passive sentence,
    i.e. what would have been the subject if the idea had been
    expressed in an active form, is now regularly indicated by
    means of the preposition by.

Note that such terms as 'would have been' and 'converted subject'
clearly indicate that Jespersen conceived of the active as basic
and the passive as derived. It is also clear that Jespersen's
verbal definition is immediately convertible into a T-rule of the
type illustrated in section IV.E.4. The question we can ask is how

----

1. See in this connection also Chomsky and Miller, 1963, Part 2
   and Chomsky, 1965, 198.

Jespersen would have accounted for sentence (7) of section IV.E.4:

> (8) I will forget the malt that was liked by the rat that
>   was killed by the cat that was worried by the dog

In particular, if he had been asked to convert it into the active
in accordance with the principle laid down in his own rule, he
would have been forced to recognize self-embedding:

> (9) I will forget the malt that the rat that the cat that
>   the dog worried killed liked

Mutatis mutandis, the same applies to the relationship between
(8) and (11) (or (12)) of section IV.E.4.

The point that can be made, then, is that the existence of
the passive rule can be underlined in terms of its ability to make
deep structures which contain excessive self-embeddding intelligible.
Furthermore, since the rule is optional, it will not apply if it
increases self-embedding. In other words, the rule can unravel (9)
and is 'free' not to generate (11) (or (12)) of section IV.E.4. In
this sense, once again, TG-theory carries traditional grammar to
its logical terminus. In particular, with respect to the case under
consideration, TG-theory explores the power embodied in Jespersen's
rule and provides an explanation of it.

Observe that, given this property of the passive rule, it
might seem to be desirable to retain it as an optional rule. We return to this question in section IV.G.7.3.

Let us now turn to the extraposition rule. Again we will take
our point of departure in Jespersen's grammar. This is all the more
reasonable as it was he who coined the term 'extraposition' in the
first place. Jespersen defined extraposition as follows (1909-49,
Vol. III, 25):

> When for some reason or another it is not convenient to
> put a content-clause in the ordinary place of the subject,
> object, etc., the clause is placed at the end in extraposi-
> tion and is represented in the body of the sentence itself by
> it.

Again it is clear that this definition can be converted into the
rule which we have formulated in section IV.E.3. Jespersen, then,
would consider

> (10) That my son failed the exam grieves me

and

> (11) It grieves me that my son failed the exam

as interrelated by extraposition. This being the case, we may
wonder, once again, how he would have accounted for (12) (cf.
above, p. 105):

> (12) It is beyond me that it doesn't worry my father that my
> my mother drinks so much

To be consistent, he would have been forced to relate (12) to (13):

> (13) $($ $($ that $($ that my mother drinks so much$)$ doesn't
> S_1 S_2 S_3 S_3
>
>   worry my father $)$ is beyond me $)$
> S_2 S_1

Assuming that extraposition is a cyclic rule (and this is not at
all certain), it may apply on the second cycle, deriving (14)
(note that we have ignored 'it' in (13)):

> (15) That it doesn't worry my father that my mother drinks so
> much is beyond me

If the rule applies on the last cycle as well, (12) is derived.
   The rule, then, just like the passive rule, has the power
to unravel an unintelligible sentence. Perhaps this was what
Jespersen meant by his somewhat cryptic remark "for one reason
or another".
   Langendoen (1969, 140ff., 1970a (in Jacobs and Rosenbaum,
1970) 100f.) has shown that in those cases where extraposition applies to subject clauses of transitive verbs, it can both increase
and decrease intelligibility. Compare the following two sentences:

> (16) That my friend has told you that he has felt the energy
> crisis for years proves that it is likely that he thinks
> that he must try to make you believe that he is a witty
> fellow
> (17) It proves that it is likely that my friend thinks that
> he must try to make you believe that he is a witty fel-
> low that he has told you that he has felt the energy
> crisis for years

Clearly (17) is lower on the scale of acceptability than (16).
Langendoen concludes, convincingly it seems to me, that this offers
an explanation (in terms of speech recognition and production) of

the fact that the rule is optional in such cases.

We can conclude this discussion by emphasizing that functional explanations of the kind we have considered would seem to lend support to the correctness of the theory of transformational grammar. In Langendoen's terminology: T-rules provide 'access to' deep structures. It should finally be noted that functional explanations are valid in the standard theory as well as in generative semantics; that is, they are valid independently of the view one may choose to take of the nature of 'deep structure'.

Notes and some further references

IV.E.2,3. On elementary transformations and the formulation of T-rules, consult the works referred to in the notes to section IV.A.1. For a clear exposition, see further Ruwet, 1973, 210ff. Originally, the set of elementary transformations also contained permutations (defined as the interchange of two immediately adjacent elements). Permutations do not seem to be required: they can be stated in terms of deletion, substitution, and adjunction. This simplifies the assignment of derived constituent structure (cf. Chomsky, 1965, 144). For a discussion of some of the difficulties involved in permutations, see Bach, 1964, 78ff.

IV.E.5. Akmajian and Heny, 1975 discuss in great detail the problem of assigning a correct derived structure to passive sentences (p. 144ff.). For there insertion, see ibid., 174ff. (and references cited on p. 181f.). See also Borkin et al. (eds.), 1972, 1ff.

IV.E.6. Perhaps the most thorough-going introduction to TG-grammar based on the assumption that T-rules are extrinsically ordered is Burt, 1971. It should be studied in conjunction with Borkin et al. (eds.), 1972, 56ff. For some further discussion of this question, consult Koutsoudas, 1972 and 1973, Lehmann, 1972, Ringen, 1972, and Postal, 1974 (especially p. 280ff.). On the whole, it is fair to say that the case for extrinsic rule order seems to be growing weaker and weaker.

IV.E.7. On the cyclic principle, see for example Lakoff, 1968c. A clear illustration of the cyclic principle in action with respect to a specific area of the grammar of English is provided by the many derivations given in Rosenbaum, 1967. Grinder, 1972 is a critical examination of some of the arguments most frequently adduced in support of the cyclic hypothesis. Mention should be made of linear grammars. In a linear grammar, a rule T_1 applies to the P-marker from the bottom up before the application of the next rule, T_2, which then processes the P-marker from bottom up. On linear grammars, see Kimball, 1972. For discussion and examples, see also Bach, 1974, 112ff.

IV.E.8. The rule subject-to-object raising was first discussed extensively by Rosenbaum, 1967. The existence of the rule has been taken for granted by most TG-linguists since that time (al-

though in different forms and for somewhat different reasons).
Recently, the validity of the rule has been questioned by Chomsky
(1973). Chomsky proposes that sentences like

(1) John expected Mary to come
(2) Mary was expected by John to come
(3) .John expected (that) Mary would come
(4) * Mary was expected by John would come

should be explained in roughly the following way: Both (1) and (3)
meet the SI of the passive rule; the rule fails to apply to (3)
(or, more precisely, the (relevant) underlying structure of (3))
because of a general constraint which states that no elements may
be moved out of <u>tensed</u> clauses, i.e. clauses containing a finite
verb. Certainly, this constraint would block the derivation of
(4). On the other hand, it extends the power of the passive rule
to operate on constituents which are not 'clause mates' (for this
term, see Postal, 1971, 13). This is contrary to the assumption
which has generally been made that the passive rule is subject
to the same simplex S constraint as the reflexive rule. We shall
continue to impose this - relative to Chomsky's recent discussion -
conservative constraint on passivization. Consequently, to account
for the (un)grammaticality of (2) and (4), we need to postulate
the rule of subject-to-object raising: (in (2) it has applied
prior to passivization on the last cycle; in (4) it has not applied). For critical discussion of Chomsky's constraint, see Postal,
1974, 43ff. Mention should be made of the A-over-A principle formulated by Chomsky, 1964b (written in 1962 and later published in
a revised edition as Chomsky, 1964a) 930f. and discussed in detail
in Chomsky, 1968, 43ff. This principle asserts that, given a structure like (5):

(5)

a T-rule whose SI mentions A cannot perform any elementary operation on (5) which affects the dominated A, but not the dominating
A. Thus, if A is an NP, the principle predicts that no rule can
move the NP dominating 'my room' out of the phrase 'the bookshelves
in my room' if this is also an NP (which it need not be ('in my
room' might be a locative adverbial (as in 'I put the bookshelves
in my room'))); it must move the <u>whole</u> NP. The A-over-A principle
explains a number of phenomena, but is, as Chomsky himself points
out, too powerful (in the sense that it blocks the derivation of
well-formed sentences). It is examined in detail by Ross, 1967,
Chapter 2. Ross formulates a number of alternative constraints in
order to limit the power of the A-over-A principle. We return to
some of these constraints later. Ross's 1967-dissertation is one
of the most important documents in the history of transformational
grammar. Recent discussions of Ross's constraints may be found in
Kuno, 1973 and Cattell, 1976. On derivational constraints, see
Lakoff, 1970b, Baker and Brame, 1972 (a critique of Lakoff, 1970b),
Lakoff, 1972c (Lakoff's reply), Lakoff, 1971b, and Postal, 1972a.

<u>IV.E.9</u>. The first extensive discussion of the rule of extraposition
in TG-theory is Rosenbaum, 1967. Most linguists have accepted the

substance of Rosenbaum's analysis. The arguments which support
the rule of extraposition are summarized in Bach, 1974 (especially p. 152ff.). Emonds, 1970, Chapter III and 1972a rejects the
extraposition analysis, proposing instead an <u>intraposition rule</u>
(which is a root transformation as defined in the text). In other
words, given (1a) and (1b):

    (1a) It is clear to everyone that John has made a fool of
         himself
    (1b) That John has made a fool of himself is clear to every-
         one

Emonds would claim that (1a) underlies (1b), rather than (1b) (1a).
There are a number of weighty syntactic (and semantic) counterarguments to this proposal. For such arguments, consult Postal,
1974, 396ff. What interests us in this connection is that intraposition can never increase intelligibility. Therefore - all other
things being equal (which Postal has - convincingly it seems to
me - shown that they are not) - it would be preferable to retain
the extraposition analysis: in that way linguistic theory would
make contact with theories of speech recognition and production.
In other words, the competence model would provide a natural explanation of performance phenomena. Let us now turn again to
Perlmutter's surface structure constraint in the light of the functional explanations of transformations considered in this section.
Langendoen, 1970a offers the following explanation of the ungrammaticality of 'that' in (20c) and (21c) of section IV.E.8: 'that'
is phonologically identical to one form of the relative pronoun;
consequently, if it were retained in surface structure, the speaker's perceptual device would misinterpret it as the subject of the
truncated clause. Note that this raises the question why 'that'
is not erroneously interpreted as the object in (20b) and (21b)
(in case it is not deleted), and, by implication, why a misinterpretation of 'that' in (20c) and (21c) would render access to deep
structures more difficult than a potential misinterpretation of
'that' in (20b) and (21b). However, let us not quibble about that.
Langendoen's explanation is, it seems to me, of such a nature that
if it holds for language L_1, it must also hold for L_2, provided
the grammars of L_1 and L_2 allow the same transformational operations. It is evident from the examples that if L_1 is English, Danish
is a possible candidate for L_2. Now, in Danish the complementizer
'at' is not phonologically identical to anything that could con-
ceivably function as the subject of a sentence. Why is it, then,
that 'at' in the Danish versions of (20c) and (21c) is not optional?
Langendoen's hypothesis predicts that it should be. Nevertheless,
'at' is as ungrammatical in Danish as 'that' is in English. Consider next the second option specified in the Danish versions of
(20c) and (21c). For reasons of brevity, we will restrict the attention to relative clauses - that is, sentences of type (21c).
First, however, we must consider the syntactic status of the Danish
word 'der'. It can be defined as a grammatical operator which occurs with subject function in a number of different structures.
Thus it is the equivalent of English 'there' with respect to the
there insertion rule (all the b sentences are exact translational
equivalents of the English a sentences):

    (2a) Five men were in the room }
    (2b) Fem mænd var i værelset   } $\Longrightarrow$

    (3a) There were five men in the room
    (3b) Der var fem mænd i værelset

Furthermore, 'der' functions as a relative pronoun. Thus, corresponding to the option in the English sentence

(4a) A house $\left\{\begin{array}{l}\text{which}\\\text{that}\end{array}\right\}$ is too expensive is hard to sell

Danish has the following option:

(4b) Et hus $\left\{\begin{array}{l}\text{som}\\\text{der}\end{array}\right\}$ er for dyrt er svært at sælge

('som' - unlike 'der' - can have both subject and object function). Consider now the following sentences (modelled on (21c) of section IV.E.8):

(5a) The man (who) you thought $\left\{\begin{array}{ll}1 & \emptyset\\2 & * \text{ that}\end{array}\right\}$ would help you has failed you

(5b) Manden (som) du troede $\left\{\begin{array}{ll}1 & \emptyset\\2 & * \text{ at}\\3 & \text{der}\end{array}\right\}$ ville hjælpe dig har svigtet dig

In the Danish versions three possibilities are specified. The first two are straightforward: they match English perfectly. The third possibility is more interesting: in the ideolects of many Danish speakers (including my own) there is a very pronounced tendency to substitute 'der' for the raised subject - especially if this is deleted (which is possible in both languages). Clearly this is quite incompatible with Langendoen's explanation of the (un)grammaticality of 'that'. In fact we could now reverse the question: it is strange that English should disallow 'that' in a sentence like (5a) since, because of its phonological identity with one form of the relative pronoun, 'that' would provide a very suitable substitute for the removed subject. By contrast, the surface structure constraint formulated by Perlmutter accounts for the facts in both languages. Thus we can explain the facts of Danish in terms of the following option with respect to the constraint:

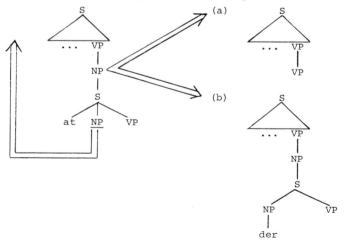

It is clear that both (a) and (b) escape the constraint: In (a)
the S node is pruned, in (b) there is a substitute subject. We
may conclude from this that not only does Danish have Perlmutter's
surface structure constraint in its grammar, but it provides strong
empirical evidence of its correctness.

IV.F.   THE PHONOLOGICAL COMPONENT

IV.F.1. Introductory remarks

In this section we will examine briefly the main principles
of generative phonology and how these are related to taxonomic
phonology. I shall make the assumption that the reader is familiar
with the basic categories of phonetic description, such as 'voice',
'alveolar', 'consonant', 'diphthong', 'glide', 'aspiration', and
'stop', to mention a few at random. It would be far too space-con-
suming to stop to define such concepts. The main objective is to
illustrate that a TG-grammar is a total commitment in the sense
that it does not, indeed cannot, 'stop' before the constructs of
the theory have been brought into direct contact with utterances
as physical events. We return to this point in the concluding remarks.

IV.F.2. Taxonomic phonology

IV.F.2.1. On defining the phoneme

First of all recall the overview of the taxonomic conception of a grammar given in section I.2. We saw there that the
starting point for the structuralist was the physical data - which
we may refer to as phonic substance. This substance was subjected
to inductive processing in accordance with a set of procedures defined in the general theory of language.

In the phonological analysis of a corpus of utterances, the
linguist must first of all segment the continuous flow of speech
into discrete units and represent each unit by a symbol. The units
established by segmentation are phones. The symbols by which they
are represented are defined in terms of the categories of articulatory phonetics.

When the linguist has completed the task of segmentation, he

must seek to discover the phonological pattern or system of which
the phones are the exponents.

Suppose now that we are engaged in an analysis of the phonological system of English. We have in our corpus the following
sequences of phones[1] (by convention, phones are included in brackets): $[p^hin]$ ('pin'), $[bin]$ ('bin'), and $[lit\pm]$ ('little'). We
are interested in ascertaining the status of $[p^h]$, $[b]$, $[l]$, and
$[\pm]$ in the sound system. In phonetic terms, $[p^h]$ is an <u>aspirated</u>,
<u>voiceless</u>, <u>bilabial</u> <u>stop</u>. $[b]$ is <u>voiced</u> and <u>unaspirated</u>. Otherwise
it is identical to $[p^h]$. Comparison of $[p^hin]$ and $[bin]$ reveals
that $[p^h]$ and $[b]$ stand in <u>contrast</u> to each other. What this means
is (a) that they occur in the same environment, and (b) that they
have <u>distinctive</u> (i.e. meaning-differentiating) value. Two words
which are differentiated by one sound contrast only are known as a
<u>minimal pair</u>. Phones which stand in contrast to each other in the
sense defined are <u>members of different phonemes</u>. Therefore $[p^h]$ and
$[b]$ belong to two different phonemes which may be symbolized /p/
and /b/ (phonemes are put in oblique strokes). Next we turn to $[l]$
and $[\pm]$ ('light' and 'dark' l). They are both <u>laterals</u>. The difference between the two phones is due to a difference in the shape
of the tongue during the articulation. Now, it is clear that on the
basis of the single word 'little' we can say nothing about the phonemic status of the two phones. We have to search through our corpus to see if we can find any environment in which they contrast. It
happens to be a contingent fact of English that there is no such environment. Two phones which never occur in the same environment are
said to be in <u>complementary distribution</u>. Complementary distribution
is a special case of <u>noncontrastive distribution</u>[2]. Noncontrastive
distribution is a necessary condition for two phones to be assigned
to the same phoneme. However, it is not a sufficient condition. It
must be supplemented by the condition of <u>phonetic similarity</u>. For
example, the English phones $[\eta]$ and $[h]$ are in noncontrastive (complementary) distribution; phonetically, however, they are so dis-
similar that it would be unnatural and counterintuitive (though logically possible) to regard them as members of the same phoneme. By
contrast, $[l]$ and $[\pm]$ are phonetically quite similar. In other

----

1. We can regard them as one-word utterances. Most words may occur as a whole utterance (for example as exclamations).
2. Noncontrastive distribution subsumes complementary distribution
   and <u>free variation</u>. For free variation, see below, p. 228.

words, they satisfy both requirements and hence can be classified
as members of the same phoneme.

The import of the term 'member of' will now be clear: a phoneme
may have two (or more) phonetically distinct members or <u>variants</u>.

Let us now turn to the initial <u>affricate</u> phones in words like
'chance' and 'John': [tʃ] and [dʒ] . Should they be analysed as
one phonemic unit (in contrast with, say, /d/ in 'dance' and 'don')
or as two-phoneme sequences? The answer to this question depends
on considerations of <u>pattern congruity</u>, the third important principle in phonemic analysis. To illustrate this, we may consider
the words 'church' and 'judge'. In those [tʃ] and [dʒ] occur both
in word-initial and word-final position. However, there are a number of similar two-phoneme sequences which cannot occur in both
positions. Thus /dz/ can occur finally, but not initially; the
same is true of /ts/ (except in such loanwords as 'tsetse' /tsetsi/
(a special kind of insect)). By contrast, /tr/ and /dr/ can occur
initially, but not finally. On the basis of such evidence (more
could be adduced) it is most natural to analyse [tʃ] and [dʒ] as
two phonemes: /tʃ/ and /dʒ/[1]. Otherwise the analysis would result
in pattern incongruity with respect to two-phoneme sequences (more
particularly, two-consonant <u>clusters</u> consisting of a stop and a
fricative).

A fourth principle relevant to phonemic analysis is the principle of <u>economy</u>. Consider for example the case of <u>diphthongs</u>. In
phonetic terms, a diphthong is a <u>vocalic glide</u>: during the articulation of the sound the tongue - and in some cases the lips - move
from one articulatory position into another. It is quite possible
to analyse a diphthong as one phoneme (as did for example Jones,
1950, 1964). On the other hand, diphthongs may equally well be
interpreted as two-phoneme sequences: a vowel + a <u>semivowel</u> (/y/
(alternatively /j/), /w/, and (in some analyses (e.g. Hill, 1958,
38ff. and Gleason, 1961, 33f.)) /h/). Much the same applies to
the so-called <u>long</u> vowels. Thus the vowel in a word like 'beat'
may be interpreted phonemically as /i:/ (that is, as a separate
phoneme) or, alternatively, as /i/ followed by a semivowel: /biyt/.
Clearly, the analysis of diphthongs and long vowels as sequences of

----

1. To make this explicit, we shall use the symbols /š/ (=/ʃ/),
   /ž/ (= /ʒ/), /č/ (= /tʃ/), and /ǰ/ (= /dʒ/) henceforth.

two separate phonemes, each of which is an independent member of
the phonemic inventory, reduces the total number of phonemes quite
considerably. We shall follow this analysis in the present exposition (for general discussion, see Gimson, 1962, 87ff.).

It should be noted that the principles of pattern congruity
and economy may well be in conflict. Thus the analysis of [tš] and
[dž] as separate phonemes (/č/ and /ǰ/) increases rather than reduces the number of phonemes.

Environmentally determined members of phonemes may show a considerable range of phonetic variation from speaker to speaker, or
from situation to situation. For example, there may be a varying
degree of aspiration in [pʰ] , but it will always be audible. In
the same way, the variant of /p/ which occurs in final position
in such words as 'map', 'gape', 'mishap', etc. may be accompanied
by a complete closure of the vocal cords - that is, glottal closure.
Such subvariation within a positionally defined variant is known
as free variation.

Collectively, the variants of a phoneme are known as allophones. Allophones are either in complementary distribution or in
free variation. Schematically, the allo and eme principle may be
illustrated in terms of the following diagram (the dots representing the free variants, the brackets the variants in complementary
distribution, and the slanting lines followed by capital letters
different environments):

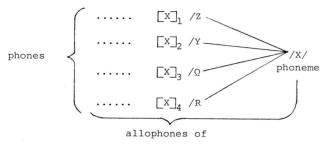

allophones of

We may conclude this brief and sketchy introduction to the
principles of taxonomic phonemic analysis by making the following
three points:

(a) Not all structuralists accepted the distinctive function
of the phoneme as a valid heuristic. Some maintained that the in-

ventory of phonemes could and should be established by distributional analysis without any consideration of meaning at all (cf.
for example Bloch, 1948 and Jones, 1950). Generally, however, differential meaning was recognized as a practical shortcut. Perhaps
the most famous statement to that effect is Hockett's (1955, 212):
"In the process of tabulation, minimal pairs are the analyst's de-
light".

(b) Although structuralists insisted on emphasizing the differences between languages rather than their similarities (cf.
above, sections I.3 and II.9), the categories employed in the analysis of the phonological structure of widely different languages
are nevertheless much the same. In other words, the existence of
some sort of universal system in terms of which the physical data
of any language can be given an adequate phonetic representation
has always been implicitly recognized (cf. for example the International Phonetic Alphabet).

(c) The principles of pattern congruity and economy both go
beyond the bounds of actual 'discovery'. They rest squarely on the
assumption that the linguist may have to choose between different
possible solutions to the same problem. Developing a set of criteria which define the application of these principles in practical
analysis is virtually equivalent to developing an evaluation procedure which ensures that the optimal description is arrived at.

IV.F.2.2. Phonotactic structure

In the preceding section we were concerned with paradigmatic
relations. In particular, we saw that if a relation of contrast
holds between two phones in the same environment, they are members
of different phonemes, and that if a relation of equivalence holds
between two phones in the same environment, they are allophones in
free variation.

In this section we will look briefly at the syntagmatic relations which English phonemes contract with one another. We restrict the attention to monosyllabic words (i.e. words consisting
of one syllable[1]).

----

1. The precise definition of a syllable is a complex matter. A distinction should be made between phonetic and phonological syllables. We are concerned here with phonological syllables. For
some discussion, see Gimson, 1962, 50ff.

The phonemic structure of a syllable (and hence of a monosyllabic word) is (C)V(C), where C = consonant(s), V = vowel (or
diphthong), and () = optional. A syllable, then, must contain a
vowel (or diphthong) which forms the <u>syllable nucleus</u>. It may contain consonants in <u>pre</u> and <u>post-nuclear</u> position (known as the <u>on-
set</u> and <u>coda</u> respectively). If there is more than one consonant,
the consonants form a <u>cluster</u>. There are two kinds of restrictions
on consonant clusters: (a) A limitation of number. In pre-nuclear
position a maximum of three consonants may occur, in post-nuclear
position a maximum of four[1]. (b) Combinatorial restrictions. For
example, in a pre-nuclear three-consonant cluster the first is always /s/, the second /p/, /t/, or /k/, and the third /l/, /r/, /y/,
or /w/. The three sets do not combine freely. The permitted sequences appear from the following diagram:

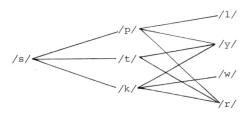

To some extent, combinatorial restrictions are determined by constraints on pronounceability. For example, it is unlikely that a
sequence like /pztg/ could occur in any language. Largely, however,
the restrictions are a product of the phonological rules of individual languages[2].

A full-scale investigation of the structure of pre and post-
nuclear consonant clusters would involve the <u>classification</u> of consonants according to their distributional range. For example, there
might be a class occurring before /X/ (where X is an arbitrary
phoneme), a class occurring before /Y/, a class occurring before
/Z/, a class occurring before /X/ and /Z/, but not before /Y/,
a class occurring before /X/, /Y/, and /Z/; and so on.

It should be emphasized that despite the heavy combinatorial
restrictions on consonant clusters, there is still room for a

----

1. If there are four, the last is always an inflectional suffix
   (e.g. 'prompts').

2. See for example Gleason's comparison of English and Serbo-
   Croatian pre-nuclear clusters (1961, 337f.).

great many new words in the language. Thus (to the best of my knowledge) the word 'sprut' does not exist in present-day English. But
it may turn up one day - perhaps as the name of a new product. It
would be a perfectly normal English word in the sense that it does
not violate the combinatorial rules of the language.

IV.F.2.3. Distinctive features

In most neo-Bloomfieldian accounts of phonology, phonetic considerations are restricted to the subphonemic level, i.e. to the
description of phones. In particular, phonetic criteria are employed
in the definition of allophones. The phonemes themselves are looked
upon as unanalysable entities. They are defined negatively: the
primary characteristic of any one phoneme is that it is not any
other phoneme. In other words, at the phonemic level the emphasis
is laid on difference rather than on similarity, whereas at the subphonemic level both similarity and difference count (allophones are
phonetically similar in some respects and phonetically different
in other respects).

The assumption that the phoneme is an unanalysable atomistic
entity was questioned some forty years ago by the scholars of the
Prague school of linguistics (notably Trubetzkoy and Jakobson). In
their view, the phoneme could and should be analysed into bundles
of distinctive features. Thus, if we assume (a) that distinctive
features are binary (in the now familiar sense)[1] and (b) that the
features have articulatory correlates, the English stop consonants
(among which we include the nasals) can be analysed in terms of the
following matrix:

	/p/	/t/	/k/	/b/	/d/	/g/	/m/	/n/	/ŋ/
bilabial	+	−	−	+	−	−	+	−	−
alveolar	−	+	−	−	+	−	−	+	−
velar	−	−	+	−	−	+	−	−	+
voice	−	−	−	+	+	+	+	+	+
nasal	−	−	−	−	−	−	+	+	+

The matrix is a kind of kinship chart of the nine phonemes. It is
quite clear that some of the phonemes are more closely related than

----

1. This assumption is, of course, not necessary for the analysis
   of phonemes into features. It is quite possible to posit multinary features (see for example Hill, 1958, 34ff.).

others. Those which are most closely related differ in just one
feature (such that one is specified + and the other - with respect
to that feature (e.g. /p/ and /b/)). The feature approach, then,
extends the statement of phonetic similarities and differences from
the subphonemic to the phonemic level.

IV.F.2.4. Redundancy

Recall the restrictions on pre-nuclear three-consonant clusters discussed in section IV.F.2.2. We saw that /s/ is the only
possible consonant in initial position. /s/ in a word like 'spray'
therefore carries much less underline{information} (in the sense 'choose this,
reject the others') and has a much higher degree of redundancy
than /s/ in a word like 'sill'. Within the phonemic framework, we
can only state this redundancy in quantitative terms. In particular, we can say that in the former case /s/ distinguishes 'spray'
from 'pray', whereas in the latter case it distinguishes 'sill'
from 'bill', 'dill', 'fill', 'gill', 'hill', 'ill', 'chill', 'Jill',
'kill', 'mill', 'nil', 'rill' and 'will'. If we adopt the theory
of distinctive features, however, the redundancy of /s/ in the environment /__ CCV/ can be made explicit in qualitative terms by
means of a redundancy rule of the same type as those which we have
seen at work in syntax and semantics:

$$(1) \quad \begin{bmatrix} + \text{ consonant} \end{bmatrix} \longrightarrow \begin{bmatrix} + \text{ consonant} \\ + \underline{\text{fricative}} \\ + \underline{\text{alveolar}} \\ - \underline{\text{voice}} \end{bmatrix} \ / \underline{\quad} \ CCV$$

(1) asserts that the three underscored features are redundant in
a consonant which precedes two consonants and a vowel. More particularly, if we assume that the four features mentioned in the
rule uniquely define /s/, (1) states that the only possible consonant in this environment is /s/.

Not all instances of redundancy are contextually determined.
To see that this is so, we return for a moment to the matrix of
the preceding section. It takes little reflection to see that some
of the specifications of that are redundant. For example, any stop
consonant which is [+ velar] is necessarily [- alveolar] and [- bi-
labial] . Furthermore, it is a contingent fact of English that all
nasal stops are voiced. Therefore [+ nasal] implies [+ voice] .
Taking cognizance of these redundancies, we can represent the dif-

ference between /p/, /b/, and /m/ as follows:

	/p/	/b/	/m/
bilabial	+	+	+
voice	−	+	⊕
nasal	−	−	+

A similar pattern defines the two other sets of stops.

Redundancy, then, is a very pervasive phenomenon in natural language (see notes to this section).

IV.F.2.5. Neutralization and the strong biuniqueness requirement

Consider a word like 'spill'. The second phone in this is an unaspirated, voiceless, bilabial stop which may be symbolized $[p]$. $[p]$ is in complementary distribution with both $[p^h]$ and $[b]$. Furthermore, it is phonetically similar to both of them. More particularly, $[p]$, $[p^h]$, and $[b]$ are similar in all phonetic properties except that where $[p^h]$ is aspirated, $[p]$ is unaspirated, and where $[p]$ is voiceless, $[b]$ is voiced. It follows from this that the combined criteria of complementary distribution and phonetic similarity cannot uniquely determine the phonemic status of $[p]$. Two solutions are available:

(a) We set up an archiphoneme /P/, in which the contrast between /p/ and /b/ is neutralized. The fact that /P/ is voiceless (or unaspirated (see (b))) is predictable from the context in which it occurs (in terms of features, this means that [- voice] is not part of the definition of /P/). Archiphonemes seemingly violate the principle of economy in that they increase the number of phonemic symbols. On the other hand, if phonemes are consistently analysed into features, this problem does obviously not arise.

(b) We insist that since $[p]$ is voiceless, it is an unaspirated member of /p/, or, alternatively, since $[p]$ is unaspirated, it is a voiceless member of /b/. Considerations of pattern congruity would support the former solution: since the distinction between voice and voicelessness is one which is pervasive in the entire consonant system - also where aspiration is not involved - it is most natural to analyse the contrast between /p/ and /b/ primarily in terms of voicelessness versus voice, and only secondarily in terms of aspiration versus lack of aspiration. Consequently, $[p]$ is a member

of /p/. The fact that /p/ and /b/ do not contrast in the environment /s ___ V/ is then accounted for in terms of defective distribution. The argument of (b) is an instance of biuniqueness in its
strong form (often expressed in the slogan 'once a phoneme, always
a phoneme'). What this means is that once two phonemes have been
shown to be in contrast in some environment(s), they remain phonemes (i.e. they retain their identity as it were) also in environ-
ment(s) in which the contrast between them is neutralized. We may
refer to this principle as BSF. In section IV.F.4 some further implications of BSF will be illustrated.

IV.F.2.6. Suprasegmental phonemes

The establishment of the segmental phonemes and the statement
of their distributional range do not bring us to the end of the
phonological analysis. We still have to account for those features
of sound which are attributes of a succession of segmental phonemes - the suprasegmental features.

It is a basic contention of American structuralism in the
Bloomfieldian tradition that everything which is phonologically
significant should be accounted for in terms of phonemes standing
in contrast. The only type of suprasegmental phonemes we will consider in this exposition is stress phonemes.

Four stress phonemes are set up: primary: /´/, secondary /ˆ/,
tertiary: /ˋ/, and weak: /ˇ/. The distinctive function of stress
can be shown in such pairs as 'abstract' (verb) - 'abstract' (noun
and adjective), 'import' (verb) - 'import' (noun), etc. The four
stress phonemes may be illustrated in a sentence like

What was the impact

IV.F.3. Morphology

IV.F.3.1. The morpheme

Let us begin by considering a word like 'decentralize'. It
is, of course, a verb, but it takes only a moment's reflection to
see that this verb has "nested" within it three other English
words, only one of which is itself a verb. The three words occur
independently in the following three sentences:

(1) It was in the centre of the town

(2) This problem is central

(3) The government tries to centralize the administration of
the coal mines

In passing from (1) to (2), the element 'al' is added to the noun
'centre' to form the adjective 'central'. 'Central' now constitutes
a new unit to which the element 'ize' may be added to form the verb
'centralize'. To this new unit the element 'de' may be added and
we obtain our original word. 'Decentralize', then, consists of four
elements. These elements are known as morphemes.

Morphemes can be classified by various criteria. The first
important distinction to be made is that between bound and free
morphemes. A free morpheme can occur independently as a word[1]. In
'decentralize' only {centre} is free, the others are all bound[2].
Morphemes may further be classified into prefixes and suffixes[3].
Prefixes are bound before, suffixes after a root, which, in turn,
is defined either as a free morpheme or as a bound morpheme which
is not an affix. An example of a bound root is {ceive} in a word
like 'deceive'.

The morpheme is generally defined as the minimal meaningful
grammatical unit. In other words, it is that unit on the expression side which makes contact with the content side (cf. above, p.
4)[4]. A distinction is frequently made between morph, allomorph, and

----

1. Bound morphemes may function as words when they are used meta-
linguistically. For example, a teacher of English as a foreign
language may correct a pupil who keeps saying 'unpossible' by
shouting "it is not un, it is im".

2. By convention, morphemes are included in braces.

3. A third type is infixes. Infixes are not normally considered
to be relevant to the description of English. See, however, section IV.F.4.

4. The meaning of morphemes is a troublesome question and one which
has received extensive treatment in the literature. Perhaps the
best way of approaching it is by way of the notion of a scale
between lexical meaning and formal meaning:

    lexical meaning   formal meaning

$$\longleftarrow \bullet \quad\quad \bullet \quad\quad\quad \bullet \quad\quad \longrightarrow$$

     roots   affixes   affixes   affixes   affixes

Thus, if we look at our sample word, it is clear that the lexically most meaningful morpheme is {centre}; {al} and {ize}

morpheme. A morph may be defined as the minimal meaningful, grammatically relevant <u>stretch of speech</u>. The criteria for classifying
physically distinct morphs as allomorphs of the same morpheme are
(a) sameness of meaning and (b) complementary distribution. To illustrate this, we turn to an examination of the present third person singular forms of verbs, the plural forms of regular nouns, and
the past and past participle forms of regular verbs. Consider the
following examples:

I leave /liyv/   leaves /liyv<u>z</u>/

$$\text{I}\left.\begin{array}{l}\text{leave /liyv/}\\\text{row /row/}\\\text{shout /shawt/}\\\text{wish /wiš/}\\\text{judge /j}\wedge\text{j/}\\\text{face /feys/}\\\text{disguise /disgayz/}\end{array}\right\} + \left\{\begin{array}{l}\text{Present}\\\text{third per-}\\\text{son sing.}\end{array}\right\} \text{ or } \{\text{Plural}\} = \left.\begin{array}{l}\text{leaves /liyv}\underline{z}\text{/}\\\text{rows /row}\underline{z}\text{/}\\\text{shouts /shaw}\underline{ts}\text{/}\\\text{wishes /wiš}\underline{iz}\text{/}\\\text{judges /j}\wedge\text{j}\underline{iz}\text{/}\\\text{faces /feys}\underline{iz}\text{/}\\\text{disguises /disgay}\underline{ziz}\text{/}\end{array}\right.$$

$$\text{II}\left.\begin{array}{l}\text{rake /reyk/}\\\text{cater /keytə/}\\\text{roll /rowl/}\\\text{bait /beyt/}\\\text{raid /reyd/}\end{array}\right\} + \left\{\begin{array}{l}\{\text{Past}\}\\\text{or}\\\left\{\begin{array}{l}\text{Past}\\\text{participle}\end{array}\right\}\end{array}\right. = \left.\begin{array}{l}\text{raked /reyk}\underline{t}\text{/}\\\text{catered /keytə}\underline{d}\text{/}\\\text{rolled /rowl}\underline{d}\text{/}\\\text{baited /beyt}\underline{id}\text{/}\\\text{raided /reyd}\underline{id}\text{/}\end{array}\right.$$

----

have formal meaning in the words 'central' and 'centralize' in
the sense that they "signal" the class-membership of the words.
Observe that we are suggesting that some affixes approach the
lexical pole more than others. For example, the meaning of {de}
in 'decentralize' may be paraphrased as "away from (the centre)".
By contrast, the meaning of {de} in 'deceive' is virtually impossible to define. It has little more than differential meaning
in the sense that it means something different from {per} and
{con} in 'perceive' and 'conceive'. By the same token, {tect} in
'detect' means something different from {ceive} in 'deceive'
(since it is impossible to define the lexical meaning of <u>any</u>
of the morphemes in 'deceive' and 'detect', we <u>could</u> argue that
they are both monomorphemic words). Suffixes usually operate
at the formal pole. But again, it is impossible to generalize.
Consider for example the relationship between the words 'profit'
and 'profiteer'. Clearly, {eer} does not merely turn 'profit'
into an agentive noun: 'profiteer' does not just mean "someone
who makes a profit" - it has an additional derogatory meaning.
On the other hand, this is not the case in a word like 'engineer'. Perhaps the following statement comes rather near to
the facts: Roots typically have lexical meaning; prefixes are
to be found somewhere on the scale between lexical meaning and
formal meaning; <u>inflectional</u> suffixes always have formal meaning
(they "signal" choices made from grammatical systems); <u>deriva-
tional</u> suffixes frequently have purely formal meaning (their
sole function often being to change the class-membership of the
unit to which they are added).

The underlined phonemes and sequences of phonemes in the right-most column are morphs; the morphs are allomorphs of the morphemes in the central column.

It would be easy to add a large number of words to the list given here. They would all exhibit the same regularity as that which the examples are intended to illustrate: /s/ is always preceded by a voiceless phoneme, /z/ by a voiced phoneme, /iz/ by a sibilant or affricate, /t/ by a voiceless phoneme, /d/ by a voiced phoneme, and /id/ by /t/ or /d/. In other words, the morphemes {Present third person singular} and {Plural} each have three allomorphs in complementary distribution. The allomorphs of the two morphemes are identical in terms of phonemic composition. In the same way, the morphemes {Past} and {Past participle} each have three allomorphs in complementary distribution. The allomorphs of these morpehemes, too, are identical in terms of the phonemes of which they are composed. Henceforth, let us agree to symbolize the four morphemes in the following way: Present third person singular: $\{-z_1\}$, Plural: $\{-z_2\}$, Past: $\{-D_1\}$, and Past participle: $\{-D_2\}$.

Morphemic analysis is not always so simple as may have appeared from the examples dealt with so far. Thus, as far as $\{-z_2\}$ is concerned, there are more possibilities than the regular realizations. Consider the forms 'sheep', 'oxen', and 'children'. In the case of 'sheep', the plural form is overtly identical with the singular form. Nevertheless, they are distinct (as is evident from the concord relation between verb and subject (cf. 'the sheep is/ are in the field')). To establish a parallel between a noun like 'sheep' and the regular nouns with respect to morphological structure, some linguists set up a zero allomorph of $\{-z_2\}$ (symbolized Ø). 'Oxen' may be segmented into two morphs: /ɔks/ and /ən/, of which the latter is yet another allomorph of $\{-z_2\}$. The analysis of 'children' presents a problem: If we segment the word after /r/, we obtain a morph which is identical to the second morph in 'oxen', but we are then left with a morph /čildr/ (an allomorph of the morpheme {child}) which violates the phonotactic structure of the language (/dr/ never occurs in word-final position). On the other hand, segmentation before /r/ results in an additional allomorph /rən/ of $\{-z_2\}$.

In the case of 'children', segmentation is still possible, and the analyst must choose between the alternatives (cf. below, p.

242, note 1). In some cases, segmentation is - seemingly (cf.
below, p. 242, note 2) - not possible. Consider a form like 'went'.
It has the same grammatical function as, say, 'looked': both can
occur in the environment 'I __ yesterday'. Both 'went' and 'looked',
then, contain the morpheme $\{-D_1\}$. We return to the theoretical
problems posed by such cases in section IV.F.4. Let us say for the
moment that the two morphemes $\{go\}$ and $\{-D_1\}$ are fused into the
phonological shape /went/.

Words, then, consist of morphemes. They may be monomorphemic,
bimorphemic, or polymorphemic. The morphemes may be realized as
(relatively) distinct segments (morphs) as in 'decentralize',
'polarization', 'children', 'bakes', 'householder', etc., or as
fusions as in 'worse', 'was', 'went', 'took', etc.

IV.F.3.2. Inflection and derivation

The morphological changes to which words are subject may be
divided into two main types: inflection and derivation. These may
both be defined as the modification of stems by the addition of
affixes, provided (a) that the term 'addition' is extended to
cover the phenomenon of fusion, and (b) that 'affix' is taken in
a rather abstract sense (for example, we can say that when the affix $\{-D_1\}$ is added to $\{go\}$, the result is /went/). A stem is a
form which permits the addition of affixes. Frequently, roots and
stems are identical. Thus the word 'rave' is both a root and a
stem. By contrast, the word 'raving' is not a root (because it contains the affix $\{ing\}$), but it is a stem (because it permits the
addition of a new affix (e.g. $\{ly\}$)).

In general, inflection can be distinguished from derivation
by the following three criteria: (a) Inflectional affixes typically occur either at the beginning or at the end of words - they
can neither be preceded nor followed by derivational affixes[1];
(b) an inflected form reflects one or more choices made from (a)
grammatical system(s); (c) inflection is general: the relationship
holding between 'boy' and 'boys' is one which recurs in a vast
number of nouns in the English language, whereas there is a considerable measure of variation from noun to noun with respect to
the possibilities of cooccurrence with particular derivational af-

----

1. In English, inflectional affixes are always suffixes (cf.
   German 'ge - arbeit - et').

fixes.

IV.F.3.3. Compounding

Two roots may combine to form a <u>compound word</u>. It is not a
condition that the two roots belong to the same class. Examples
are 'pickpocket' (verb + noun ⟶ noun), 'aircraft' (noun +
noun ⟶ noun), 'outstanding' (adverb + verb ⟶ adjective),
'spring-clean' (noun + verb ⟶ verb), etc. Note that bound roots,
too, may form compounds. For example, the word 'ethnobotany' consists of the two bound roots $\{$ethno$\}$ and $\{$botan$\}$ + the affix $\{$y$\}$[1].
Both compounding, inflection, and derivation may, of course, oc-
cur in one and the same word; 'maneaters' is an example.

IV.F.4. Morphophonemics

Every theory of language must link grammar (in the narrow
sense of the word) to phonic substance. A number of theoretical assumptions determine the way in which this task is accomplished.
Let us list some possible assumptions in the form of questions and
then proceed to examine some of the implications of the possible
answers:

(a) Should morphemes be described as <u>items</u> in a certain <u>ar-
rangement</u>, such that for each item there is a morph composed of
phonemes, or, alternatively, should morphological structure be described in terms of <u>processes</u>?

(b) Should morphemes always be described in terms of phonemes
(such as we have defined them so far), or, alternatively, should
more <u>abstract phonemes</u> be set up in certain circumstances?

(c) What are the implications of analytical unidirectionality
(or, equivalently, analytical autonomy)?

(a) The <u>item and arrangement</u> model was widely adopted in American structuralism. The English language lends itself reasonably
well to this approach in so far as, in many cases, segmentation
into morphs is possible. There are, however, a number of recalcitrant cases. Consider the relationship between 'take' and 'took',
which, grammatically, is like that between 'look' and 'looked'
Both 'took' and 'looked' consist of two morphemes. The question

----

1. Example from Robins, 1964, 211.

is how the two constituent morphemes of 'took' should be described.
A number of different proposals have been made[1]:

(1) 'took' consists of a discontinuous allomorph /t ... k/
of $\{\text{take}\}$ + an infixed allomorph /u/ of $\{-D_1\}$;

(2) 'took' is an allomorph /tuk/ of $\{\text{take}\}$ which occurs
before a zero allomorph of $\{-D_1\}$;

(3) 'took' consists of the morpheme $\{\text{take}\}$ and a _replacive_
allomorph /u ⟵— (ey)/ of $\{-D_1\}$.

All of these proposals manage - more or less artificially -
to preserve the notion of segmental physicality; morphemes are _rep-
resented by_ morphs, and morphs are _composed of_ phonemes (in the
limiting case they have zero phonemic representation)[2].

In the item and arrangement model, then, the allomorph is the
intervening variable par excellence between the two articulations
of language.

(3) very much resembles a process. This brings us to the
second part of (a). Suppose that we describe morphological structure in terms of items undergoing certain processes rather than in
terms of items and their arrangement. We can then state the relationship between 'look' - 'looked' and 'take' - 'took' in the fol-
lowing way: $\{\text{look}\} - \{\text{take}\} + \{-D_1\} \longrightarrow$ /lukt/ - /tuk/. In each
case the morpheme $\{-D_1\}$ coalesces with the stem and in so doing
leaves a mark on that. In one case the mark is a segment (/t/), in
the other it is a vowel change. This approach is known as the _item
and process_ model. It was viewed with some scepticism by many
structuralists. The reason for this is not far to seek: it implies
regarding 'look' and 'take' as the _underlying_ forms of 'looked'
and 'took', and this is not something which can be corroborated by
observation of the physically manifest data.

(b) and (c) In the light of what was said about neutralization

----

1. The fact that different solutions are possible suggests, once
   again, that linguistic description must be guided by some kind
   of evaluation procedure (cf. Chomsky, 1957, 52, note 3).

2. Note that, given such a methodological framework, we are in a
   position to provide an analysis of the form 'went' considered
   in section IV.F.3.1. In particular, we can say either (a) that
   /went/ is an allomorph of $\{\text{go}\}$ which occurs before a zero allomorph of $\{-D_1\}$, or (b) that /wen/ is an allomorph of $\{\text{go}\}$ which
   occurs before the allomorph /t/ of $\{-D_1\}$.

in section IV.F.2.5, let us examine once again the morphemes $\{-z_1\}$ and $\{-z_2\}$ and their complementarily distributed allomorphs /s/, /z/, and /iz/[1]. The question may be asked whether one of these is <u>basic</u> relative to the others. The answer that has sometimes been given to this question is that /z/ is the basic allomorph because its occurrence here is restricted to a degree higher than that otherwise specified by the phonological rules of the language: it is obligatory in environments where the feature [+ voice] is not dictated by any (grammatically independent) rule (e.g. after vowels and /n/ (cf. the minimal pairs 'rice' - 'rise' (/rays/ - /rayz/) and 'vans' - 'Vance' (/vænz/ - /væns/)). /s/ and /iz/, then, are phonologically determined alternants of the basic form [2,3]. In effect, what this description asserts is that the features [± voice] are always redundant in /z/ and /s/ when they are the exponents of $\{-z_1\}$ and $\{-z_2\}$. To make this explicit, we might postulate an abstract phoneme /Z/ in which the distinction between voice and voicelessness is neutralized.

    Consider next such forms as 'wolf' - 'wolves' (/wulf/ - /wulvz/) and 'shelf' - 'shelves' (/šelf/ - /šelvz/). Clearly there are two allomorphs of the stem in each case; the question is which of them is basic. The answer some (though not all[4]) have thought is that neither of them is basic. For the following reason: there are some corresponding pairs in which the phoneme /f/ is constant: 'muff' - 'muffs' (/mʌf/ - /mʌfs/), 'laugh' - 'laughs' (/lahf/ - /lahfs/); conversely, there are some in which /v/ is constant: 'hive' - 'hives' (/hayv/ - /hayvz/), 'cove' - 'coves' (/kowv/ - /kowvz/). The variation between /f/ and /v/, then, is a property of a few morphemes. To account for this fact, the concept of the <u>special morphophoneme</u> was introduced into linguistics. By this proposal, the morpheme $\{shelf\}$ would have the following morpho-

----

1. <u>Mutatis mutandis</u>, what is said here about $\{-D_1\}$ and $\{-z_2\}$ applies also to $\{-D_1\}$ and $\{-D_2\}$.
2. See for example Hockett, 1958, 282. Consult also Gleason, 1961, 214ff.
3. /z/ is phonemically impossible after voiceless consonants and must therefore be replaced by /s/. By the same token, any sibilant, voiced or voiceless, is impossible immediately after another sibilant (or affricate); hence /i/ must occur between them. Once /i/ has been 'inserted', the following sibilant obeys the same constraint as the plural morph in all other words ending in vowels: it is always voiced. Cf. below, p. 260.
4. See for example Hockett, 1958, 281f.

phonemic representation /šelF/. /F/ subsumes the variation between
/f/ and /v/ (in the same way as, say, /l/ subsumes the variation
between [l] and [ɫ]). To convert /F/ into a phonemic representation, we would need a statement, or rule, of the following nature:

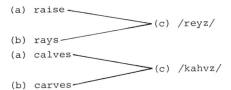

$$/F/ \longrightarrow \begin{bmatrix} /v/ \\ /f/ \end{bmatrix} \Bigg/ \underline{\quad} \begin{bmatrix} \{-z_2\} \\ \text{elsewhere} \end{bmatrix}^1$$

The rule asserts that /F/ is realized as /v/ when followed by
$\{-z_2\}$ and as /f/ in all other environments.

Let us now return to the BSF-principle discussed in IV.F.2.5.
By this, the phonemic representation of a word is uniquely determinable from the physical data. Consequently, two words with identical
pronunciation should have the same phonemic make-up. Thus, in the
following examples, (a) and (b) are both phonemically (c):

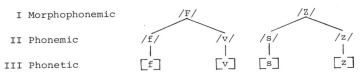

(a) raise
                      (c) /reyz/
(b) rays
(a) calves
                      (c) /kahvz/
(b) carves

Therefore, if we want to incorporate morphophonemes as well as the
BSF-principle in the theory, we must set up three levels of representation:

I Morphophonemic	/F/		/Z/	
II Phonemic	/f/	/v/	/s/	/z/
III Phonetic	[f]	[v]	[s]	[z]

The relationship between II and III is determined by BSF, which,
in turn, is inseparably bound up with the principle of analytical
autonymy. The admission of a morphophonemic level of representation is obviously incompatible with these two principles. In particular, it amounts to a concession that phonological analysis can-

----

1. The brackets should be interpreted as follows: The topmost
   item in the left bracket matches the topmost item in the right
   bracket; and so on.

not be undertaken independently of grammatical analysis ('grammatical' still to be taken in the narrow sense). Furthermore, once (and if) this concession is made, it becomes possible to question the psychological validity of the phonemic level of representation. For example, we can now ask whether the last segments in the words 'rice' and 'hats' have the same 'phonemic' status in any significant way.

(c) (and (b)) We will be concerned here mainly with British linguistics in the 'neo-Firthian' tradition. Two points are essential to note: (1) The phoneme plays a lesser role in this theory than in American structuralism, and (2) there is no insistence on analytical autonomy.

(1) In the phoneme theory the idea of a <u>segment</u> is fundamental. For example, the word 'mile' consists of four phonemes /mayl/. Phonetically, <u>each</u> of these is described as voiced. However, the vibration of the vocal cords continues uninterrupted throughout the articulation of the word. It might, therefore, be more in accordance with the phonetic facts to describe this particular word in terms of four <u>phonematic units</u> + one <u>suprasegmental prosody</u> of voice. The efforts of many British linguists have been directed towards establishing, for each language, a system of prosodies ranging over more than one phonematic unit. We will not go into the details of prosodic analysis[1]. What is relevant to the point under discussion is the feature 'voice' considered as a grammatically determined suprasegmental prosody.

(2) The fact that grammar is not considered to be an extension of phonology implies that grammatical analysis is theoretically independent of phonological analysis. Grammatical categories can, in principle, be related <u>directly</u> to their <u>phonetic</u> exponents. Within the framework of the prosodic approach to phonology, the phonetic exponents of the morphemes $\{-z_1\}$, $\{-z_2\}$, $\{-D_1\}$, and $\{-D_2\}$ can be stated in the following way: the exponent of $\{-z_1\}$ and $\{-z_2\}$ is <u>sibilance</u>, the exponent of $\{-D_1\}$ and $\{-D_2\}$ is <u>alveolar plosion</u>. $[\pm \text{ voice}]$ are suprasegmental prosodies ranging over these phonematic units. They are entirely predictable from the final sound of the word undergoing inflection (for the /i/ in /iz/, see p. 241,

----

1. The reader is referred to the works cited in the notes. For the point discussed here, see Firth, 1964, 23 and Palmer, 1964.

note 3). Observe that this analysis bypasses the phoneme entirely.

IV.F.5. The principles of generative phonology

IV.F.5.1. Preliminary overview

The main characteristics of generative phonology can be subsumed under the following points:

(1) The basic phonological construct is the distinctive feature. Phonemes, or rather morphophonemes, are conceived of as bundles of features.

(2) Redundancy plays an essential role.

(3) Morphophonemes are abstract entities set up in such a way
as to ensure maximum generalization in the statement of the phonological patterns of the language.

(4) Abstract phonemic representations are related to phonetic
representations by means of rules.

(5) The biuniquely determined phoneme of taxonomic phonology
plays no integral part in the grammar.

(6) The phonological component is interpretive. The input to
the rules is syntactic surface structures. Syntax and phonology
therefore interact. This interaction is particularly in evidence
in the stress assignment rules.

IV.F.5.2. The features

It is a basic assumption in generative phonology that there
is a universal inventory of binary distinctive features[1] from
which each language selects a subset. In other words, the features
constitute a set of substantive universals.

To isolate and define the appropriate set of features is obviously no easy task. The features must be based on the empirical
evidence supplied by a wide range of maximally different languages
(more paticularly, languages belonging to different 'families').

An inventory of features, once it has been set up, must meet
the following three requirements with respect to any arbitrary

----

1. In our discussion of distinctive features in section IV.F.2.3,
   we made the assumption that they are binary. We noted, however,
   that it is quite possible to posit multinary features. The
   binary analysis is due, above all, to Jakobson, Fant, and
   Halle (see bibliographical notes).

language: (a) It should provide a natural explanation of the
phonetic facts; (b) it should be capable of differentiating the
lexical items of the language; (c) it should define the natural
classes into which the morphophonemes fall[1].

   Chomsky and Halle, 1968[2], 302ff. discuss in great detail the
phonetic properties of a universal set of features. Of these,
English makes use of at least thirteen[3], which are defined as
follows:

$\begin{bmatrix} \pm \text{ vocalic} \end{bmatrix}$ Vocalic sounds are produced with an oral cavity
in which the most radical constriction does not
exceed that found in the high vowels $[i]$ and $[u]$
and with vocal cords that are positioned so as
to allow spontaneous voicing; in producing non-
vocalic sounds one or both of these conditions
are not met (p. 302)

$\begin{bmatrix} \pm \text{ consonantal} \end{bmatrix}$ Consonantal sounds are produced with a radical obstruction in the midsagittal region of the vocal
tract; nonconsonantal sounds are produced without such an obstruction (p. 302).

$\begin{bmatrix} \pm \text{ high} \end{bmatrix}$ High sounds are produced by raising the body of
the tongue above the level it occupies in the
neutral position; nonhigh sounds are produced
without such a raising of the tongue body (p. 304).

$\begin{bmatrix} \pm \text{ back} \end{bmatrix}$ Back sounds are produced by retracting the body
of the tongue from the neutral position; nonback
sounds are produced without such a retraction
from the neutral position (p. 305).

$\begin{bmatrix} \pm \text{ low} \end{bmatrix}$ Low sounds are produced by lowering the body of
the tongue below the level it occupies in the
neutral position; nonlow sounds are produced
without such a lowering of the body of the tongue
(p. 305).

$\begin{bmatrix} \pm \text{ anterior} \end{bmatrix}$ Anterior sounds are produced with an obstruction

----

1. Two morphophonemes which are members of the same natural class
   can be defined in terms of fewer features than those which are
   required to define each individual member of the class. Members of natural classes behave alike with respect to rules.

2. The Sound Pattern of English is by far and away the most important work in generative phonology. The following pages build
   mainly on the ideas developed by Chomsky and Halle and thus may
   be viewed as a brief introduction to their work.

3. We leave out of account a few features (such as $[\pm \text{ sonorant}]$
   and $[\pm \text{ delayed release}]$).

that is located in front of the palato-alveolar
region of the mouth; nonanterior sounds are produced without such an obstruction (p. 304).

$\begin{bmatrix} \pm & coronal \end{bmatrix}$ Coronal sounds are produced with the blade of the
tongue raised from its neutral position;
noncoronal sounds are produced with the blade
of the tongue in the neutral position (p. 304).

$\begin{bmatrix} \pm & round \end{bmatrix}$ Rounded sounds are produced with a narrowing of
the lip orifice; nonrounded sounds are produced
without such a narrowing (p. 309).

$\begin{bmatrix} \pm & tense \end{bmatrix}$ Tense sounds are produced with a deliberate,
accurate, maximally distinct gesture that involves
considerable muscular effort; nontense sounds are
produced rapidly and somewhat indistinctly (p. 324)

$\begin{bmatrix} \pm & voice \end{bmatrix}$ The distinction is well known. For a detailed
discussion, see Chomsky and Halle, op. cit.,
326ff.

$\begin{bmatrix} \pm & continuant \end{bmatrix}$ In the production of continuant sounds, the
primary constriction in the vocal tract is not
narrowed to the point where the air flow past
the constriction is blocked; in stops the air
flow through the mouth is effectively blocked
(p. 317).

$\begin{bmatrix} \pm & nasal \end{bmatrix}$ Nasal sounds are produced with a lowered velum
which allows the air to escape through the nose;
nonnasal sounds are produced with a raised velum
so that the air from the lungs can escape only
through the mouth (p. 316).

$\begin{bmatrix} \pm & strident \end{bmatrix}$ Strident sounds are marked acoustically by greater
noisiness than their nonstrident counterparts
(p. 329).

     Given this set of distinctive features, the morphophonemic
representation of 'stab' looks like this (see next page)[1]:

IV.F.5.3. <u>Morpheme structure rules</u>

     As was pointed out in section IV.F.2.4, some features auto-
matically imply other features, i.e. some features are redundant.
Furthermore, we saw that redundancy might be either intrasegmental-

----

1. Note that some of the spaces are blank. Blank spaces indicate
that the feature in question is <u>irrelevant</u> for that segment and
its classification.

	/s/	/t/	/æ/	/b/[1]
voc	–	–	+	–
cons	+	+	–	+
high	–	–	–	–
back	–	–	–	–
low	–	–	+	–
ant	+	+		+
coron	+	+		–
round	–	–	–	–
cont	+	–		–
nasal			–	–
strid	+			
voice	–	–	+	+
tense	+	+	–	–

ly or intersegmentally determined. Furthermore, redundancies may
be universal or language-specific. In the former case, they are
generally determined by limitations on pronounceability.

Given the features defined in the preceding section, redundancy can be stated with a much greater degree of precision than
we were capable of mustering in our initial discussion of the
phenomenon[2].

Examples of intrasegmental redundancy. If an English segment
has the features $\begin{bmatrix} + \text{ voc} \\ - \text{ cons} \end{bmatrix}$, it also has the features [– nasal,
+ voice] . The following features are irrelevant for all vowels:
[cont, strid, ant, coron] . They therefore need not be specified
at all. We are now in a position to set up the following redundancy rule:

$$\begin{bmatrix} + \text{ voc} \\ - \text{ cons} \end{bmatrix} \longrightarrow \begin{bmatrix} + \text{ voc} \\ - \text{ cons} \\ - \text{ nasal} \\ + \text{ voice} \end{bmatrix}$$

Obviously, this rule is not part of a grammar of French: French has
----

1. The phonemic (or rather morphophonemic) symbols are not part
   of the theory. However, they are still useful as abbreviatory
   devices.

2. The reader may think that we are merely repeating ourselves in
   this section. However, this is not the case: some structuralists
   (e.g. Hill, 1958, 44ff.) paid a good deal of attention to
   the interplay between features and qualitative redundancy.

nasal vowels[1]. Further examples of intrasegmental redundancy are
provided by such rules as

$$[+ \text{ high}] \longrightarrow \begin{bmatrix} + \text{ high} \\ - \text{ low} \end{bmatrix} \quad \text{(universal)}$$

$$[+ \text{ low}] \longrightarrow \begin{bmatrix} + \text{ low} \\ - \text{ high} \end{bmatrix} \quad \text{(universal)}$$

$$[+ \text{ nasal}] \longrightarrow \begin{bmatrix} - \text{ voc} \\ + \text{ cons} \\ + \text{ nasal} \\ - \text{ cont} \\ - \text{ low} \\ + \text{ voice} \\ - \text{ strid} \end{bmatrix} \quad \text{(English)}$$

An example of intersegmental redundancy. In section IV.F.2.2
we considered English pre-nuclear three-consonant clusters. We
saw there that the only possible phoneme in initial position is
/s/. Similar restrictions hold for pre-nuclear two-consonant clusters. In particular, if the first two consonants are 'true' consonants, the first must be /s/ and the second one of the following
five: /p, t, k, m, n/[2]. This fact can be stated in terms of the
following rule (where # in front of the brackets indicates that the
first segment occurs in word-initial position):

$$\# \begin{bmatrix} - \text{ voc} \\ + \text{ cons} \end{bmatrix} \begin{bmatrix} - \text{ voc} \\ + \text{ cons} \end{bmatrix} \rightarrow \# \begin{bmatrix} - \text{ voc} \\ + \text{ cons} \\ + \text{ ant} \\ + \text{ coron} \\ + \text{ strid} \\ - \text{ voice} \end{bmatrix} \begin{bmatrix} - \text{ voc} \\ + \text{ cons} \\ - \text{ cont} \end{bmatrix}$$

The first segment to the right of the arrow is unambiguously /s/.
The second segment specifies the features which /p/, /t/, /k/, /m/,

----

1. The part of the rule which inserts [+ voice] in [+ voc,
   - cons] segments is universal. In other words, the voice-voice-
   lessness opposition is never distinctive for 'true' vowels.
   Nevertheless, [+ voice] is relevant for vowels inasmuch as it
   defines them as members of the larger class of voiced segments.
   This class plays an important role in some phonological rules
   (cf. below, p. 260). Furthermore, in some languages (e.g. Japanese)
   [+ voice] forms the input to a rule which devoices vowels between voiceless consonants.

2. True consonants are those which have the features [- voc,
   + cons] . Other segments have the features [+ voc, + cons]
   or [- voc, - cons] . Examples are, respectively, /l/ (a liq-
   uid) and /w/ (a semivowel). In those cases the restriction does
   not hold (cf. the words 'lewd' (/ljuwd/) and 'twain' (/tweyn/)).

and /n/ have in common (in both segments further features are supplied by intrasegmental rules). A special rule prevents the occurrence of /ŋ/.

The formation of new English words must obey this rule. For example a word like '* ftut' is predictably impossible. By contrast,
the word 'sput' is well-formed, though probably nonexistent.

It has generally been assumed that lexical entries should be
specified in terms of matrices which directly reflect the redundancy patterns of (the) language (i.e. the matrices should not contain any redundant features[1]) (cf. for example Halle, 1962 (in
Fodor and Katz, 1964) 338ff. and Chomsky and Halle, 1968, 166).
This approach would provide a natural evaluation measure for lexical entries: the most highly valued grammar would be that which
provided the simplest entries (in terms of numbers of features
mentioned) by means of the least number of morpheme structure rules
(i.e. intra and intersegmental redundancy rules). However, further
research (see especially Stanley, 1967 and Schane, 1973, 44) has
shown that, in some cases, the two kinds of redundancy rules may
result in contradictions. To remedy this, it has been suggested
that lexical entries should be fully specified (except for irrelevant features). The evaluation measure, consequently, would be
the proportion between the number of lexical items X characterized
by the set of morpheme structure rules Y, such that the more X and
the fewer Y, the better the grammar.

In either approach, redundancy is defined as an essential factor in the speaker's knowledge of his language.

IV.F.5.4. Systematic phonemic, phonemic, and systematic phonetic representations

We saw in section IV.F.4 that the combined inclusion in the
theory of the BSF-requirement and abstract phonemes would necessarily result in three levels of representation. In generative
phonology there is no insistence on biuniqueness. This means that
the classic, relatively substantial[2], conception of the phoneme

----

1. For example, in accordance with the redundancy rules operating
   on pre-nuclear two-consonant clusters, the first segment in the
   entry for 'stab' would contain only two features (in fact, one -
   [+ cons] - would suffice). By the same token, the second segment would not contain the feature [- cont].

2. 'Substantial' to be taken in the sense 'closely related to
   phonic substance'.

can be dispensed with. In other words, there need only be two
levels of representation: the morphophonemic (or _systematic pho-_
nemic) level and the phonetic (or _systematic phonetic_) level. These
two levels are related by phonological rules.

The elimination of the phoneme from the grammar is motivated
by arguments relating to missing generalizations and descriptive
adequacy. To illustrate this, we turn to an example from German
(cf. Bach, 1964, 128). Any grammar of German must provide an explanation of the following facts[1]:

	I	II	
(a)	reissen	reisst	(= 'tear')
	/s/	/s/	
(b)	reisen	reist	(= 'travel')
	/z/	/s/	
(c)	kehren	antworten	(= 'turn'/'answer')
	/r/	/r/	
	[r]	[r̥]	

Ia and Ib are infinitives; the forms in IIa and IIb are present
third person singular (and present second person plural). Ia and
Ib illustrate the contrast between the phonemes /s/ and /z/.

In order to account for the relationship between Ib and IIb,
we need a morphophonemic statement of the following kind:

(1) $/z/ \longrightarrow /s// \underline{\quad} /t/$
where /t/ is a morph

Consider next the relationship between Ic and IIc. What we
have here is two allophones of /r/ in complementary distribution
([r] and [r̥] never contrast in German). We can state this as
follows:

(2) $/r/ \longrightarrow \left\{ \begin{matrix} [r̥] / \underline{\quad} /t/ \\ [r] / \underline{\quad} X \end{matrix} \right\}$
where X stands for all the environments in which /r/
is not devoiced

Clearly, (1) and (2) are rules of the same kind. A grammar which
----

1. Compare Halle's famous example from Russian phonology (1959)
   as discussed by Chomsky, 1964a, 88ff.

requires both misses a generalization and probably fails on the
score of descriptive adequacy. In order to generalize (1) and (2),
we would need to represent IIb morphophonemically as /reyzt/. The
rule could then be stated something like this:

$$(3) \quad \begin{bmatrix} /r/ \\ /z/ \end{bmatrix} \longrightarrow \begin{bmatrix} [\underset{\circ}{r}] \\ [s] \end{bmatrix} \Big/ \underline{\quad} /t/$$

BSF would preclude (3): 'reisst' and 'reist' are pronounced
in the same way and would therefore both have to be represented
phonemically as /reyst/.

In sum, if we abandon BSF, we can state the facts in terms of
two levels of representation related by one rule ((3)) (I is the
systematic phonemic, II the systematic phonetic level of representation):

	reissen	- reisst	- reisen	- reist	- kehren	- antworten
I	/s/	/s/	/z/	/z/ ↓	/r/	/r/ ↓
II	[s]	[s]	[z]	[s]	[r]	[$\underset{\circ}{r}$]

The example we have considered in this section is a good
illustration of the rationale of generative phonology: two rule-
related levels of representation - one abstract, the other concrete, and neither of them phonemic in the classical sense. In
this particular case we needed just one rule to move from the abstract to the concrete level. In the typical instance, however,
more rules are required. Furthermore, many of the rules must be
ordered. We return to this in section IV.F.5.6.

IV.F.5.5. Stress

When lexical items are inserted in base P-markers in the form
of complexes of phonological, syntactic, and semantic features,
they are, in general, unspecified for stress. This implies that
the stress pattern of a word is predictable by general rule.

Before we consider the stress rules in detail, it is necessary
to introduce some notational and terminological conventions. First
of all, the symbol C is used as a common denominator for all
morphophonemic units specified $\begin{bmatrix} - \text{ voc} \\ + \text{ cons} \end{bmatrix}$ and V for all those specified $\begin{bmatrix} + \text{ voc} \\ - \text{ cons} \end{bmatrix}$. Furthermore, an important factor is consonant-

clusters. We can simplify the statement of these by using such
notational devices as

$$V/ \_\_\_ \ C_2^3 \ = \ \text{V is followed by a minimum of two and a maximum of three consonants.}$$

$$V/ \_\_\_ \ C_2 \ = \ \text{V is followed by two or more consonants (i.e. no less than two).}$$

$$V/ \_\_\_ \ C_0 \ = \ \text{V is followed by any number of consonants, possibly none.}$$

$$V/ \_\_\_ \ CC \ = \ \text{V is followed by two consonants, neither more nor less.}$$

$$V/ \_\_\_ \ C_0^3 \ = \ \text{V is followed by a maximum of three consonants (i.e. either by none at all, one, two, or three).}$$

Finally, we will refer to the last syllable of a word as the ultimate, the last but one as the penultimate, and the last but two as
the antepenultimate syllable.

The most important feature relating to stress is [tense] .
Consider the following verbs (cf. Chomsky and Halle, 1968, 69):

1	2	3
admónish	sustáin	collápse
intérpret	debáte	abstráct
fínish	achíeve	evínce
prófit	surpríse	disrúpt

What principle determines the stress pattern in those words? Suppose that we adopt the following rule of thumb: Look for the last
vowel and check for tenseness. In the words in column 1 the last
vowel is [- tense] , and the primary stress consistently falls
on the penultimate syllable. In column 2 the last vowel is
[+ tense] , and the last syllable has primary stress. Seemingly,
the words in column 3 baffles the generalization which we may have
been tempted to make on the basis of 1 and 2: the ultimate syllables contain [- tense] vowels, yet they carry primary stress.
Observe, however, that the ultimate syllable consistenly ends in
two consonants. Apparently, this fact overrules the [± tense]
pattern.

We might now tentatively set up the following hypothesis
to account for the facts we have obsérved:

> Primary stress is assigned to the ultimaté syllable if it
> contains a [+ tense] vowel. If the ultimate syllable con-
> tains a [- tense] vowel, primary stress is assigned to the
> penultimate syllable, unless the ultimate vowel is followed
> by CC.

The same principle carries over quite nicely to a number of adjectives (cf. Chomsky and Halle, op. cit., 80):

1	2	3
mórbid	extréme	abrúpt
ecstátic	entíre	inténse
équal	matúre	robúst
émpty	ináne	distínct
sólar	devóut	augúst

It would seem, then, that we are well on the way to making a significant generalization. However, we still need to examine the third major lexical category, namely nouns. Consider the following examples (cf. Chomsky and Halle, op. cit., 71):

1	2	3
África	Veróna	Ugánda
gárrison	balaláika	ellípsis
sýllable	cathársis	intéstine
parálysis	coróna	uténsil
crysánthemum	Regína	surrénder

Apparently, these words do not fit the generalization. Observe, however, that they can be made to fit it if we add a further principle: the ultimate [- tense] vowel + the following consonants (if there are any) should be <u>disregarded</u> in nouns with respect to the stress assignment rule[1]. It is important to note that this principle applies only to [- tense] vowels: the ultimate vowels in nouns like 'police' and 'prestige' are [+ tense] and therefore receive primary stress in the normal way.

We are now in position to formulate a rule which defines the stress pattern in a large number of English words[2]:

$$\text{1. } V \rightarrow [1 \text{ stress}] \Big/ \underset{\downarrow}{\_\_} \left\{ \begin{array}{c} C_0 \begin{bmatrix} + \text{ voc} \\ - \text{ cons} \\ - \text{ tense} \end{bmatrix} C_0^1 \\ C_0 \end{array} \right\} \left\{ \begin{array}{c} \begin{bmatrix} + \text{ voc} \\ - \text{ cons} \\ - \text{ tense} \end{bmatrix} \\ {} \end{array} \quad C_0 \right\}_N$$

----

1. This also holds for a noun like 'promise': if the final syllable is disregarded, there is only one remaining syllable to carry the stress.

2. Cf. Chomsky and Halle, op. cit., 72. I have changed the rule

The rule assigns primary stress (1 stress) to the vowel which occupies the position indicated by the vertical arrow. Note that
the two sets of braces specify options which criss-cross in the following way:

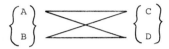

By convention, these four options must be 'tried out' in the following order: (1) A-C: If a lexical item is a noun whose final
syllable contains a $[-\text{tense}]$ vowel, that syllable is disregarded
and stress is assigned according to the specification of A, i.e.
if A is a syllable containing a $[-\text{tense}]$ vowel and not ending
in more than one consonant, stress is assigned to the preceding
syllable - the antepenultimate syllable of the whole word. (2)
B-C: If a lexical item is a noun whose final syllable contains a
$[-\text{tense}]$ vowel, that syllable is disregarded and stress is assigned according to the specification of B, i.e. if the word (or
what remains of it) ends in a $[+\text{tense}]$ vowel, or, alternatively,
two[1] or more consonants, stress is assigned to what is now the
ultimate syllable. (3) A-D: If the lexical item is not a noun whose
final syllable contains a $[-\text{tense}]$ vowel, the final syllable
of the word is relevant; the assignment of stress is conditioned
by A, i.e. if the syllable contains a $[-\text{tense}]$ vowel and ends
in no more than one consonant, stress is assigned to the penultimate syllable. Finally, if the conditions of (1), (2), or (3) are
not met, (4): B-D operates: stress is placed on the final syllable.

Rule 1, which is referred to as the <u>main stress rule</u>, is not
sufficient to account for the distribution of stress in lexical
items. It must be supplemented by an <u>alternating stress rule</u>. This
is a corrective to rule 1 and must, therefore, follow it. By the
operation of the alternating stress rule, the stress is moved from
the syllable on which it has been placed by rule 1 to the antepen-

----

slightly. It should be noted that the rule undergoes a good
deal of further revision in Chomsky and Halle so that it can
handle more cases than those considered here. The final statement is found on p. 240.

1. Observe that the sepcification in B, C_0, must necessarily mean
either no consonants or two or more consonants. This follows
automatically from C_0^1 in A.

ultimate syllable in a number of polysyllabic words. The rule can
be formulated as follows (cf. Chomsky and Halle, op. cit., 84):

2. $\text{V} \longrightarrow [\text{1 stress}] / \underline{\quad} \text{C}_0 \begin{bmatrix} + \text{voc} \\ - \text{cons} \end{bmatrix} \text{C}_0 \begin{bmatrix} + \text{voc} \\ - \text{cons} \\ 1 \text{ stress} \end{bmatrix} \text{C}_0 \Bigg]_{\substack{\text{N} \\ \text{V} \\ \text{Adj}}}$

Examples of the combined operation of rules 1 and 2 are provided
by such words as

	manifest	penetrate	anecdote
by rule 1	↓	↓	↓
	manifést	penetráte	anecdóte
by rule 2	↓	↓	↓
	mánifést	pénetráte	ánecdóte

The output of rule 2 contains two occurrences of primary stress.
By a general convention, the original primary stress is reduced by
one step:

$\qquad\qquad$ mánifêst $\qquad$ pénetrâte $\qquad$ ánecdôte

　　　Rules 1 and 2 specify stress in words, i.e. they operate on
brackets labelled by lexical category symbols such as N, V, and
Adj. They are both <u>cyclic rules</u>. In phonology the cycle is defined
by <u>innermost brackets</u>. Consequently, the lowest cycle is always
defined by lexical category labels. Thus rule 1 (rule 2 happens
not to apply in this case) would operate on such a structure as

$\qquad$ (1)　$\underset{\text{NP}}{(}$ $\underset{\text{Adj}}{(}$ sad $\underset{\text{Adj}}{)}$ $\underset{\text{N}}{(}$ plight $\underset{\text{N}}{)}$ $\underset{\text{NP}}{)}$

and assign primary stress to both lexical items. In so doing, it
would erase <u>innermost</u> brackets and the outcome would be

$\qquad$ (2) $\underset{\text{NP}}{(}$ sád plíght $\underset{\text{NP}}{)}$

Clearly, however, this is not the way in which it is pronounced:
the grammar must provide for stress contours ranging over larger
constituents. A third rule is needed for this task (cf. Chomsky and
Halle, op. cit., 90):

3. $\text{V} \longrightarrow [\text{1 stress}] / [_{\text{Q}} \text{X} \begin{bmatrix} \overline{\quad} \\ 1 \text{ stress} \end{bmatrix} \text{Y}]_{\text{Q}}$

　　　Conditions: Y contains no vowel with primary stress; the

bracketed structure Q is larger than a lexical
category.

3 - the <u>nuclear stress rule</u> - is also a cyclic rule. It asserts
that primary stress is assigned to the <u>last</u> syllable in a bracketed
string which already carries primary stress (assigned by 1 or 2).
This syllable therefore becomes <u>relatively</u> more heavily stressed
than all the other syllables in the structure. Consequently, these
are reduced by one step. In the case under consideration, 3 applies
to the NP (the structure which is larger than a lexical category).
The outcome of the rule is

(3)   (sâd plíght)
      NP   NP

Consider now a slightly more complicated case[1]:

(4) ((his (sad) (plight)) ((shocked) (the
    S NP   Adj   Adj N   N NP VP V   V NP
    (coroner))))
    N   N NP VP S

By repeated application of rule 1 (again rule 2 does not apply),
(5) is derived:

(5) ((his sád plight)   (shócked the córoner))
    S NP   NP VP   VP S

To (5) rule 3 applies twice, deriving:

(6) (his sâd plíght shócked the córoner)
     S   S

(6) forms the input to rule 3 on the top cycle. The final output
is

(7) his sàd plîght shòcked the córoner

This, then, is the regular derivation of the stress pattern of a
sentence. It is clear that the assignment of emphatic stress can
upset this pattern quite considerably, but we will not go into
that.

----

1. Determiners are always weakly stressed unless they are emphasized.
   Therefore they have been left unbracketed. The string has been
   simplified in other respects as well. For example, the subject
   NP should probably contain an additional NP node immediately
   dominating 'sad plight' (cf. below, section IV.G.14.5); however,
   it will do for illustrative purposes.

The principle of disregarding the last syllable in nouns if
it contains a [- tense] vowel enables us to account for the
stress pattern of lexical items which are derived from stems by
suffixation. Consider the following examples (cf. Chomsky and Halle,
op. cit., 81):

1	2	3
pérsonal	anecdótal	dialéctal
munícipal	adjectíval	incidéntal

which display the same distribution of stress as the nouns listed
on p. 255. Let us look at the derivation of the stress pattern of
'dialectal'. The word may enter into the following labelled bracketed string (where Y is a determiner and X a noun):

(8)   (Y ((dialect) al) X)
      NP Adj N   N Adj NP

On the innermost cycle (N), rule 1 assigns primary stress to the
first syllable in the noun (the final syllable, which contains a
[- tense] vowel, is disregarded; after this, the word ends in a syllable containing a [- tense] vowel and ending only in one consonant; stress therefore falls on the penultimate syllable in the
usual way). Rule 2 does not apply. Innermost brackets are erased;
this time, however, the consequence of this is a new lexical category symbol: Adj. Rule 1 must therefore reapply. Suppose now that
we disregard the syllable 'al'. We then predict, correctly, that
the stress must fall on 'ect', i.e. the penultimate syllable: the
vowel is [- tense] and is followed by two consonants. On the
next cycle (NP), rule 3 applies, reducing the stress of all syllables except one (the rightmost syllable in the NP with primary
stress) as in, say,

(9)   (ă dialêctal féature)
      NP   NP

The same principle would extend quite naturally to a noun
like 'municipality'. The reader is invited to try.

IV.F.5.6. Some examples of ordered phonological rules

Let us begin by returning to the discussion in section IV.F.4
(PP. 242f., 245ff.). Corresponding to the morphemes $\{-Z_1\}$, $\{-Z_2\}$,
$\{-D_1\}$, and $\{-D_2\}$, our grammar generates the grammatical formatives
Present, Plur, Past, and 'en'. We will assume, furthermore, that,

owing to the operation of a T-rule, Present dominates the features
(+ III Person, + Sing)[1]. We are now in a position to state the
facts discussed in section IV.F.4 in terms of the following three
ordered rules (the phonemic symbols should be interpreted as
morphophonemes, more particularly bundles of distinctive features,
/Z/ and /D/ as 'sibilant' and 'alveolar stop' respectively):

$$
1. \quad \begin{bmatrix} \begin{Bmatrix} \text{Plur} \\ \text{Present} \end{Bmatrix} \\[2ex] \begin{Bmatrix} \text{Past} \\ \text{en} \end{Bmatrix} \end{bmatrix} \longrightarrow \begin{bmatrix} /Z/ \\[2ex] /D/ \end{bmatrix}
$$

$$
2. \quad \emptyset \longrightarrow /i/ \;\Big/\; \begin{bmatrix} \begin{Bmatrix} /s/ \\ /\check{s}/ \\ /z/ \\ /\check{z}/ \\ /\check{c}/ \\ /\check{j}/ \end{Bmatrix} \\[1ex] \begin{Bmatrix} /d/ \\ /t/ \end{Bmatrix} \end{bmatrix} \underline{\quad} \begin{bmatrix} /Z/ \\[3ex] /D/ \end{bmatrix}^{2}
$$

$$
3. \quad /Z/,\ /D/ \longrightarrow \begin{bmatrix} + \text{ voice} \\ - \text{ voice} \end{bmatrix} \Big/ \begin{bmatrix} + \text{ voice} \\ - \text{ voice} \end{bmatrix} \underline{\quad}
$$

By rule 1 such forms as /kæt/ + Plur or /weyt/ + Past become /kætZ/
and /weytD/ respectively. Rule 1 is a <u>readjustment rule</u>: it converts a grammatical formative into a phonological representation.
Rule 2 inserts /i/ between any sibilant or affricate and /Z/ in
plural and present third person singular forms of nouns and verbs
respectively, and between /t/ or /d/ and /D/ in past and past
participle forms of verbs. Thus the rule converts /weytD/ into
/weytiD/; it does not apply to /kætZ/. Rule 3 deals with the distribution of voice. By this /weytiD/ becomes [weytid] and /kætZ/
becomes [kæts] [3].

----

1. Cf. below, section IV.G.2. Strictly speaking, there is an incon-
   sistency here: if the grammar contains the <u>features</u> (± Sing), it
   should not also contain the <u>formative</u> Plur. However, this does
   not affect the present argument.

2. The reader is invited to reformulate the somewhat clumsy rule 2 in
   terms of features. Note especially that the two sets of phonemes
   form natural classes with respect to the rule.

3. The brackets indicate that we have now reached the systematic pho-

Could we reverse the order of the rules - in particular rules
2 and 3? The answer to this question is no. For if we did, /weytD/
would be turned into /weytt/ by rule 3 (now rule 2) and rule 2
(now rule 3) would insert /i/, thus deriving the incorrect form
[weytit] . In the case of /kætZ/, the reordering would have no
effect since the /i/-insertion rule does not apply anyway. However,
the ordering given here predicts both correct results. Therefore
it must be upheld.

Recall now the rule operating on such special morphophonemes
as /F/ (cf. p. 244). Clearly, this must be ordered before the above
set of rules (in particular, for rule 3 to be able to apply, /F/
must receive the specification [+ voice] (i.e. it must be converted into /v/))[1].

It will be apparent that this analysis bears much resemblance
to prosodic phonology. More particularly, grammar (in the narrow
sense) and phonology are interrelated[2] and the phoneme is bypassed.
The difference rests solely in the notion of ordered phonological
rules.

Consider next such pairs as (cf. Chomsky and Halle, 1968,
50ff., 178ff.):

		I		II
(1)	(a)	expl<u>ai</u>n	-	expl<u>a</u>natory
	(b)	ser<u>e</u>ne	-	ser<u>e</u>nity
	(c)	div<u>i</u>ne	-	div<u>i</u>nity
	(d)	manag<u>e</u>r	-	manag<u>e</u>rial
	(e)	var<u>y</u>	-	var<u>ie</u>ty

The items in column II are derived by suffixation from the items
in column I. Observe that the quality of the underscored vowels in

----

netic level of representation. In fact we have been oversimplifying matters a good deal. In particular, the systematic phonemic representation of 'wait' would not be /weyt/. We return
to that presently.

1. For some discussion of this ordering (from the point of view of
   TG-theory as a mentalistic theory), see Katz, 1964a (in Rosenberg
   and Travis, 1971) 376f. For some critical remarks, see Dik, 1967,
   369ff.

2. Cf. Palmer, 1964, 339: " ... it is reasonable to demand a phonological statement of a kind that is appropriate to the requirements of grammar ... Phonology may thus be seen as providing a bridge between grammar and phonetics, and ought not,
   therefore to be undertaken without reference to the needs of
   grammar".

the two columns varies. We might try to account for this variation
by postulating a phoneme-change rule of the following kind:

$$
(2) \quad
\begin{bmatrix}
/ey/ \longrightarrow /æ/ \\
/iy/ \longrightarrow /e/ \\
/ay/ \longrightarrow /i/ \\
/ə/ \longrightarrow /ih/ \\
/i/ \longrightarrow /ay/
\end{bmatrix}
\Bigg/ \quad \underline{\quad} \ [\text{certain contexts}]
$$

If we were to state this rule in terms of features, we would find
(a) that it would be exceedingly complex, and (b) that it would
fail to bring out any generalization with respect to (1a)-(1e).

Let us examine (1a) in more detail. Clearly, 'explain' and
'explanatory' are the same word in some sense. It would be reasonable to assume that this would be reflected in the lexicon. We
might imagine an overall entry for the two forms along the following lines[1]:

$$
\text{by morphological rule X} \quad
\begin{bmatrix}
1. \ \underline{\text{explain}} \\
2. \ + \ V \ \lor \ + \ \text{Adj} \qquad \uparrow \\
\\
3. \ + \ \text{SynF}_n \\
4. \ + \ \text{SemF}_n
\end{bmatrix}
$$

where 1 = a matrix of distinctive features, 2 = category symbols,
3 = a set of syntactic features, and 4 = a set of semantic features.
The crucial question is this: what does 1 look like? There is no
a priori reason to believe that the diphthong /ey/ in 'explain' is
basic relative to /æ/ in 'explanatory'. It might equally well be
hypothesized that both /ey/ and /æ/ are the result of the operation of phonological rules on an abstract phoneme /Y/:

$$
/Y/ \left\langle
\begin{array}{l}
\longrightarrow /ey/ \ \Big| \ \underline{\quad} \ Q \\
\longrightarrow /æ/ \ \Big| \ \underline{\quad} \ P
\end{array}
\right.
$$

----

1. A third option would be (+ N) (to account for the noun 'explanation'). We return to some further theoretical implications of
   this entry in section IV.G.17. Meanwhile, we may note that it
   also has a bearing on our discussion of the similarities between verbs, adjectives, and nouns (cf. above, p. 105ff. and
   notes on p. 123).

The determination of the qualitative structure of /Y/ (in
terms of distinctive features) is an empirical issue. In particular, it depends on the possible generalizations to which the abstract segment may lead in conjunction with a set of phonological
rules. Let us tentatively assume that the systematic phonemic representation of 'explain'/'explanatory' is something like this
(we concentrate on the crucial vowel and omit a few features)[1]:

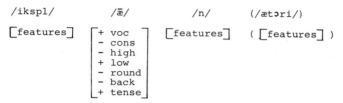

The segment /ǣ/ (where ⁻ indicates tenseness) will never be
realized in 'explain' or its derivatives, because on its way to
the level of systematic phonetic representation it will obligatorily undergo a number of phonological rules which modify its feature composition. The first rule to apply is a <u>laxing rule</u>. This
converts the feature [+ tense] into [- tense]. However, the
application of this rule is dependent on the context defined by
/ætɔri/ (more generally, it is dependent on the number of syllables following the tense vowel). Consequently, if the deverbal
adjectival suffix is not present in the word, the rule does not
apply. Instead, the <u>diphthongization rule</u> applies: all underlying
tense vowels (provided they have not become laxed of course)
diphthongize (i.e. become glides):

        /iksplǣn/ ⟶ /iksplǣyn/

The next rule to apply is the <u>vowel shift rule</u>. The effect of this
is that /ǣ/ moves to /ē/ (and - as illustrated by 'serene' and
'divine' in (1) - /ē/ to /ī/, and /ī/ to /ǣ/ (/ǣ/ being centralized
by a subsequent rule)):

----

1. One of the most important arguments supporting this representation derives from the stress rules: 'explanatory', to which
   the main stress rule (rule 1 of section IV.F.5.5) applies
   cyclically, (cf. the derivation of the stress pattern in
   'dialectal') requires a tense vowel on the innermost cycle -
   otherwise it would assign primary stress to /iks/. (On the
   next cycle, there are certain difficulties. The reader is invited to spot the source of these difficulties and then proceed to consult Chomsky and Halle, 1968, 132ff.).

/ikspl&æyn/ ——→ [iksplēyn]

To account for (d) and (e) of (1), we need a <u>tensing rule</u>
which converts [+ tense] into [- tense] in certain contexts.
When this rule has applied to the relevant vowels of the underlying
representations of 'managerial' and 'variety', these automatically
become subject to diphthongization and vowel shift.

We will not go into further detail. It should be apparent,
however, that the formulation of a few and simple rules operating
on the feature specifications of abstract underlying segments or
morphophonemes can capture significant generalizations with respect to the forms of (1). In terms of the conceptual apparatus
of TG-theory, this means that the rules we have just discussed attain the level of descriptive adequacy: they purport to explain
in maximally simple terms the speaker's knowledge of the phonological regularities of his language[1]. By contrast, the rules illustrated in (2) do not move beyond the level of observational
adequacy: they describe the data, but offer no explanation of the
facts[2].

The last example to be given relates to consonants (cf.
Chomsky, 1964a, 71ff.). Consider such forms as

	1		2		3
(3) (a)	opaque	-	opacity		
(b)	logic	-	logicism	-	logician
(c)	pirate	-	piracy		
(d)	delicate	-	delicacy	-	delicious
(e)	express				expression
(f)	erase				erasure
(g)	revise				revision
(h)	relate				relation
(i)	ignite				ignition
(j)	inflate				inflation

Let us look first at (a)-(d) in columns 1 and 2. It is immediately

----

1. Needless to say, there are irregularities as well. These can be
   defined by rule features in much the same way as in syntax.
   An example is the noun 'obesity'. In this the second vowel
   should have undergone the laxing rule, but it remains tense
   and therefore undergoes the diphthongization rule and vowel
   shift in the normal way (the underlying vowel being /ē/).

2. See in this connection Chomsky's distinction between <u>data</u> and
   <u>facts</u> (1961b (in Allen, 1964) 173).

obvious that the variations can be accounted for in terms of the following rule (the bracketed numbers will be explained presently):

$$(4) \quad \left\{ \begin{array}{c} /k/ \\ /t/ \end{array} \right\} \longrightarrow \text{ /s// } \underline{\quad} \text{ /i/ } \cdot \text{ [1]}$$

By the same token, the relationship between the two forms in (e), (f), and (g) can be expressed in terms of (5):

$$(5) \quad \left[\begin{array}{c} /s/ \\ /z/ \end{array} \right] + /i/ \longrightarrow \left[\begin{array}{c} /\check{s}/ \\ /\check{z}/ \end{array} \right] / \underline{\quad} v^1 \quad \text{[2]}$$

To account for the forms in column 3 (except of course (e), (f), and (g)), we need the following rule:

$$(6) \quad \left\{ \begin{array}{c} /k/ \\ /t/ \end{array} \right\} + /i/ \longrightarrow \text{ /}\check{s}\text{// } \underline{\quad} v$$

The three rules we have formulated here are, by and large, those which can be inferred from the classificatory approach to morphophonemics of the taxonomic linguists (e.g. Hill, 1958, 133f. and Harris, 1960, 221f.).

Suppose now that we order the first two rules in the way suggested by the bracketed numbers and permit rule 2 to apply to the output of rule 1. Then, clearly, (6) becomes superfluous. A consequence of this is that abstract underlying forms must be set up to supply the input to rule 1. In other words, we obtain stepwise derivations of the same kind as with the vowels[2]. Let us give a few examples (note the operation of the <u>vowel reduction rule</u> in weakly stressed syllables; + indicates morpheme boundaries (which are of course not part of the systematic phonetic representation)):

electricity	electrician	presidency	presidential
(a) ilektrik+iti	ilektrik+ian	prezident+i	prezident+ial
(b) ilektrisiti	ilektris+ian	prezidənsi	prezidens+ial
	ilektrišən		prezidenšəl

----

1. In other words, this rule predicts that the noun derived by suffixation from the verb 'express' is not pronounced [ikspresiən] , but [iksprešən] . Conversely, it predicts that the adjective 'expressive' is pronounced [ikspresiv] and not [iksprešiv] : /i/ is not followed by a vowel (so also, of course, forms like 'expressing' and 'erasing').

2. Stepwise derivations should not be confused with levels of representation. It is only the abstract phonemic and the concrete phonetic levels that count. Any step in between has no systematic status.

(a) constitutes the input to rule 1, and (b) the output of rule 1
and the input to rule 2.

Once again, what is achieved by the ordering of these two
rules is the uncovering of systematic relations in the language
which do not meet the eye, but which must form part of the speaker's
linguistic competence. A description which incorporates all three
rules with no ordering superimposed misses a possible generalization. For example, it will fail to make explicit that 'presidency'
and 'presidential' are systematically interrelated.

It will be apparent from the discussion so far that the
phonological component of a TG-grammar is an item and process
model (cf. above, p. 242).

The phonological rules which convert abstract phonemic representations into concrete phonetic ones not only have the power
to alter binary feature specifications (such as converting $[+ \text{tense}]$
into $[- \text{tense}]$); they can also assign integers to features, specifying the degree of intensity with which a feature should be
realized. For example, the vowel in the word 'mine' is nasalized
to some degree, owing to the surrounding nasal consonants. This
might be indicated by having a rule convert $[- \text{nasal}]$ into, say,
$[2 \text{ nasal}]$ in this environment. Likewise, the rules can add features which have no distinctive function in the language. Thus the
feature $[+ \text{aspiration}]$ must be added to the first segment in
such words as 'pill', 'kill', and 'till'.

In principle, then, the output of the phonological component
corresponds to the allophonic level of representation in taxonomic
phonology.

The phonetic representation constitutes the input to the or-
gans of speech on the one hand and to the sentence recognition device on the other (the grammar still being neutral with respect
to speaker and hearer).

IV.F.5.7. <u>Final revision of 'structural description'</u>

We are now in a position to give a final definition of the
notion 'structural description of a sentence' (where PH = phonetic
representation):

$$P_1 \ldots P_i \ldots P_n$$
$$\quad\quad | \quad\quad |$$
$$\quad\quad SR \quad\quad PH$$

On p. 177 we noted the changes which would have to be made in this

definition in order to move from the standard theory to generative
semantics. These changes would not affect the status of phonology
in the theory.

IV.F.5.8. Concluding remarks

We have said that the axiomatization of linguistic theory
aligns linguistics with the natural sciences (cf. above, p. 36).
This alignment is possible only because, in the last analysis,
language is sounds in the air. In other words, the natural sciences
and linguistics have in common the fact that they set up hypotheses to account for the relevant classes of physical events. This
is the reason, then, why TG-grammar cannot stop short of phonology:
it must proceed to the point where it makes contact with the
physical events it purports to explain (not only describe).

This argument works both ways. Since linguistics purports to
explain a class of physical events, the constructs of the theory
must be assumed to have the same ontological status as the events
they are set up to explain (cf. Katz, 1964a (in Rosenberg and
Travis, 1971) 377). We know precious little about how linguistic
knowledge is actually represented in the brain. Certainly, no linguist would dream of claiming for example (in the words of Lakoff,
1968c, 69) that "some nerve ends are marked NP". What is being
claimed is that there must be - in some way or other - a one-to-
one correspondence between the brain processes underlying linguistic
knowledge and the steps in the deductive chain that constitutes
the grammar. It is in this sense that the constructs of the theory
are "symbols, not fictions" (cf. above, p. 25). One day, perhaps,
the neurophysiological reality behind the symbols may be uncovered.
Until that day arrives, the linguist must be content to develop
his system of symbols in the maximally optimal way.

Notes and some further references

IV.F.1. Gimson, 1962 provides an excellent introduction to phonetics in general and to English phonology in particular. Briefer
introductions to phonetics and phonology may be found in such
textbooks as Hill, 1958, Hockett, 1958, Gleason, 1961, Strang,
1962, Robins, 1964, and Lyons, 1968.

IV.F.2.1. On different views of the nature of the phoneme, see
Fudge, 1970. Consult in this connection also Chomsky, 1964a, 76ff.
The discussion in the text rests on what may be called the (func-
tional-)physical view. By 'functional' is meant the meaning-dif-

ferentiating property of the phoneme. 'Functional' has been put
in parenthesis because, as we noted in the text, meaning was regarded by many as a shortcut to the physical description of the
phoneme (as 'a family of sounds'). (Note incidentally that Bloomfield himself took the opposite view: he considered the meaning-
differentiating property of the phoneme as its basic characteristic (1933, 136ff.)). The reader who wishes to familiarize himself
with the details of taxonomic phonology should consult such works
as Pike, 1947, Trager and Smith, 1951, Hockett, 1958, Hill, 1958,
Gleason, 1961, and Harris, 1960.

IV.F.2.2. The classificatory approach to phonotactics is well
illustrated in Hill, 1958, 68ff.

IV.F.2.3. As noted in the text, the theory of distinctive features
is due to the Prague linguists. See Trubetzkoy, 1939 (especially
p. 60ff.). For brief accounts of the origin and development of
the theory, see Ivić, 1965 and Vachek, 1966. The most important
works are Jakobson and Halle, 1956 and Jakobson, Fant, and Halle,
1963 (first published in 1952).

IV.F.2.4. The concept of redundancy stems from _information theory_.
We will not go into the details of that. The reader who wishes to
pursue this line should consult the relevant sections of such works
as Carroll, 1953 and Lyons 1968 and follow up the references cited
there. Gleason, 1961, Chapter 23 may also be consulted. As remarked
in the text, it is only with the advent of feature analysis that
redundancy can be stated succinctly in qualitative terms. In particular, in phonology, the qualitative approach to redundancy
makes it possible to study in much greater detail to what extent
sequential constraints are language-specific and to what extent
they are determined by limitations on pronounceability and hence
may be viewed as universal. For further discussion of redundancy,
see section IV.F.5.3.

IV.F.2.5. The concept of neutralization is due to the Prague scholars. It is closely interrelated with the 'marked'/'unmarked' distinction (which, as we have noted, stems from the same school).
With respect to the six stops /p/, /t/, /k/, /b/, /d/, and /g/,
cross-linguistic investigation reveals that it is often the voiceless member of the three pairs which occurs in positions of neutralization. Consequently, we may conclude that $[-\text{voice}]$ is unmarked in the stop consonants (we disregard the nasals - they are
not really stops anyway). Therefore we could represent the word
'spill' in the following way in terms of features (we concentrate

on the stop consonant): /s/ $\begin{bmatrix} + \text{bilabial} \\ \text{U voice} \\ - \text{nasal} \end{bmatrix}$ /i/ /l/. The feature

$[\text{U voice}]$ would automatically be interpreted as $[-\text{voice}]$.

IV.F.3. The concept of the morpheme has been the subject of much
discussion. Nida, 1949 is a major work on morphology. Shorter
papers dealing with morphemes and morphological analysis are Harris,
1942 and Hockett, 1947. Harris, 1955 attempts to formulate a set
of procedures which will yield a distributional definition of the
morphemes of a language (i.e. without recourse to semantic criteria). As noted in the text, the question of the meaning of the morpheme has been the subject of much debate. Consult for example

Bazell, 1962, Fowler, 1963, Coates, 1964, and Strang, 1964. An
overview of the problems relating to morphological analysis is
provided by Matthews, 1970. A classic work on word formation in
English is Marchand, 1969 (first published in 1960). A shorter
overview may be found in Quirk et al., 1972, Appendix I.

IV.F.4. Swadesh and Voegelin, 1939 first introduced the concept
of the special morphophoneme in American linguistics. It was
adopted by Harris, 1960. On the item and arrangement and item and
process models, see especially Hockett, 1954. Hockett, 1961 is an
important contribution to the discussion of the interrelationship
between the grammatical and phonological levels (the terms morph
and allomorph are due to Hockett). On the principles of prosodic
analysis, consult Robins 1957 and 1964, 157ff., Firth, 1964, and
Palmer (ed.), 1970.

IV.F.5. As is abundantly clear from the discussion in the text,
the standard work on generative phonology is Chomsky and Halle,
1968. In particular, the first fifty pages or so provide a lucid
overview of the main principles of English phonology. Brief introductions are Harms, 1968 and Schane, 1973. Consult further Halle,
1958, 1962, and Chomsky, 1967b. Generative phonology has been
the subject of intensive debate. Famous is the Chomsky-Halle -
Householder controversy. For this, see Householder, 1965, Chomsky
and Halle, 1965, Householder, 1966, and Matthews, 1968. Postal,
1968 is also a strongly polemic contribution to the discussion.
For critical discussion, see further Derwing, 1973. The 'marked'/
'unmarked' distinction plays an important role in generative phonology. Consult Chomsky and Halle, 1968, 404ff., Lakoff, 1970a,
137ff., and Schane, 1973, 112ff., 116ff. On redundancy rules, see
Stanley, 1967. Generative phonology and historical linguistics
is discussed by Kiparsky, 1968 and 1970.

IV.G. SOME TRANSFORMATIONS IN ENGLISH

IV.G.1. Introductory remarks

    We turn now to a more detailed examination of some of the
T-rules required in a descriptively adequate grammar of English.
The reader should be warned that the following sections do not in
any way constitute a complete grammar of English. Rather, they deal
only with a tiny fragment of the enormously complex network of
patterns and interrelationships which make up the grammatical
system of the language. It should be stressed, furthermore, that,
in many cases, the analysis of a given problem presented in the
text is only one of several possible solutions. Alternative approaches will be mentioned in the notes. The reader who consults
some of the references given will soon discover that transforma-

tional grammar has not by any means reached a state of finality.
The positive side of this, of course, is that the researcher who
wishes to investigate any individual area of the grammar will never
feel that the empirical facts do not offer sufficient challenges
to his ingenuity.

IV.G.2. <u>Agreement</u>

Our PS-rules would assign the following deep structure to a
sentence like 'the man throws the stone':

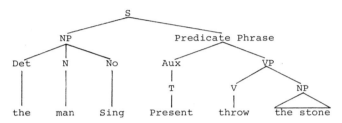

A T-rule is required to effect concord, or <u>agreement</u>, between the
subject NP and the verb. The rule could be stated as follows (cf.
Chomsky, 1957, 39):

$$(1) \quad \text{Present} \Longrightarrow \left\{ \begin{array}{l} \text{s/N + Sing} \underline{\quad} \\ \emptyset/\text{elsewhere} \end{array} \right\}$$

        Condition: N contains the feature (+ III Person).

The rule merely states that the formative Present is to be replaced by s if it follows a singular, third person noun, otherwise-
by ∅.

The reader will wonder, perhaps, why agreement is defined as
a transformational rule rather than as a context-sensitive PS-rule
(cf. above, section IV.A.3). However, it takes little reflection to
see that it must be a T-rule. Consider the following sentences:

    (2) The maids serve coffee
    (3) Coffee is served by the maids
    (4) The maid serves drinks
    (5) Drinks are served by the maid

In all of these sentences, the deep-structure subject is 'maid(s)'.

This follows from the fact that passive sentences must be accounted for by a T-rule (cf. above, section IV.E.9). Consequently, for (3) and (5) to be derived, agreement must be stated as a T-rule which follows the passive rule.

(1) presents some problems. Consider a sentence like

(6) The man may turn up

Working on the underlying structure of this, (1) (in conjunction with affix hopping (for which, see next section)) would convert Present + may into may + s. We would then need a special rule to ensure that may + s ends up as /mey/ and not as /✶ meyz/. It would be quite possible to incorporate such a rule in the grammar (as a phonological rule feature in the lexical entry for 'may')[1].

A worse problem arises with 'be' in such sentences as

(7) I am tired

(8) You are my best friend

(9) He is a fool

The condition on (1) distinguishes (9) from (7) and (8), but fails to distinguish (7) from (8). Clearly, however, an adequate grammar must account for all three sentences. Suppose now that we restate (1) in terms of features in roughly the following way[2]:

----

1. It is frequently the case that syntactic tense in verb phrases containing modal verbs does not correspond to their time reference. For example 'could' in 'you could come tomorrow' does obviously not refer to the past. This being the case, we might consider reformulating PS-rule 12 in the following way:

$$\text{Aux} \longrightarrow \begin{Bmatrix} T \\ M \end{Bmatrix} \text{ (have+en) (be+ing)}$$

and list all the forms of the modal verbs separately in the lexicon. If we did that, (1) would not apply to sentences containing modal verbs. On the other hand, as is well known, there are many cases in which syntactic tense in 'ordinary' verbs does not match their time reference. For example, syntactic present may refer to the future (as in 'the train leaves in an hour'), to the past (the so-called historical present), or to "no time at all" (as in 'it rains a lot in this country'). The motivation for the above revision of the rule therefore seems to be rather weak. The relationship between syntactic tense and time reference is exceedingly complex and far beyond the scope of this work. For discussion of the problem in a transformational framework, see for example Jacobson, 1971, Chapter 8 and McCawley, 1971a.

2. Cf. Akmajian and Heny, 1975, 198ff. and compare for example Burt, 1971, 207. α and β are variables standing for the values

(10) SI   NP   - $\left\{\begin{array}{l}\text{Present}\\\text{Past}\end{array}\right\}$

$\left[\begin{array}{l}\alpha\,\text{Person}\\\beta\,\text{Sing}\end{array}\right]$

          1   2 $\Longrightarrow$

   SC   1   2

$\left[\begin{array}{l}\alpha\,\text{Person}\\\beta\,\text{Sing}\end{array}\right]$

(10) makes it explicit that all three persons and both terms in
the number system are relevant to agreement. Obviously, we still
need special rules to account for the actual phonological shapes
of the different forms of 'be': the irregularities of the language cannot be eliminated from any grammar, transformational or
otherwise.

It is the output of (10) which (after the application of affix hopping) forms the input to the readjustment rule (cf. p. 260).

Henceforth, we consider the categories No, Sing, and Plur to
be eliminated from the PS-rules.

IV.G.3. Affix hopping

Consider a sentence like

(1) John has been working

After the application of the agreement rule, the P-marker looks
roughly like this:

(1a)

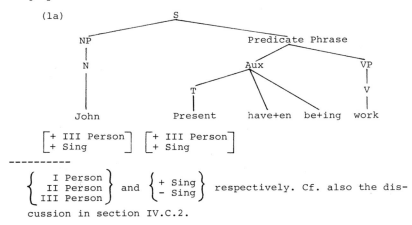

cussion in section IV.C.2.

A T-rule is needed to move the affixes into place[1]. There is evidence which indicates that the elementary transformation required here is one of Chomsky-adjunction[2]. This being the case, we are faced with the problem of providing a proper derived structure for (1). In particular, 'have' and 'be' are under the immediate domination of the same node: Aux. To remedy this defect, we might consider reformulating PS-rule 12 as follows:

$$\text{Aux} \longrightarrow \text{T (M) (Perf) (Prog)}$$

and have the lexical insertion rule insert 'have+en' and 'be+ing' under Perf and Prog respectively[3]. Given this reformulation (and the concomitant revision of (1a)), we can state the rule of affix hopping in the following way:

$$\text{SI} \quad X - \begin{Bmatrix} \text{T} \\ \text{en} \\ \text{ing} \end{Bmatrix} - \begin{Bmatrix} \text{M} \\ \text{Perf} \\ \text{Prog} \\ \text{Cop} \\ \text{V} \end{Bmatrix} - Y$$

$$\quad\quad 1 \quad\quad\quad 2 \quad\quad\quad\quad 3 \quad\quad\quad 4$$

SC Chomsky-adjoin 2 to the right of 3; delete the original 2.

The application of this rule to (the revised version of) (1a) would result in the following surface structure:

(1b)

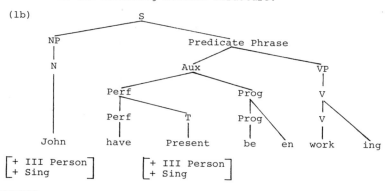

----

1. Note that the term 'affix' is really a makeshift device (a 'fudge'): 'affix' is not a category defined by any PS-rule.

2. The evidence stems from the stress rules. See Chomsky and Halle, 1968, 84ff.

3. Cf. for example Stockwell et al., 1968, Vol. I, 31, 312. There is also a problem relating to 'be' (as main verb). For discussion of this, see notes to this section.

The rule, which is obligatory, must be restricted by the following
two conditions: (1) Since it is frequently the case that the derived structure meets the SI of the rule once again (so (1b) for
example), the rule must apply only once to all affixes concerned.
If it kept reapplying to its own output, all the affixes would
end up on the main verb. (2) The rule is last-cyclic. To see that
this is so, consider the following sentence:

(2) John expected Peter to come

Suppose now that we want to argue that this is derived from something like

(3) (John expected it (Peter T come))
    S_1 S_2 S_2 S_1

by two ordered rules: subject-to-object raising and <u>to-replace-Aux</u>
(i.e. a rule which substitutes 'to' for T). Now, we know that the
former must apply on the S_1 cycle. Hence if affix hopping applies
on the S_2 cycle, to-replace-Aux cannot operate when subject-to-object raising has replaced 'it' by the subject NP of the embedded
sentence on the top cycle; consequently, the derivation is blocked.
Conversely, if affix hopping is last-cyclic, applying (after to-
replace-Aux) to all levels of the P-marker, it will simply fail
to operate on the truncated clause inasmuch as the SI of the rule
is not met ('to' is not mentioned in the second term).

One further point should be made. We have seen that one of
the complementizers is 'Poss - ing'. When this has been inserted
into the P-marker, the outcome may be a substring of the following kind:

Poss + N + ing + V

Obviously, Poss and ing must be moved to the right of N and V
respectively. We might propose to achieve this by extending the
affix hopping rule to cover these cases (cf. Rosenbaum, 1967).
The surface structure of, say, 'John's swearing' in a sentence
like 'I hate John's swearing' might then be, accordingly (see next
page):

On the other hand, it is arguable that by so extending the
scope of affix hopping, we force one rule to handle widely disparate areas of the grammar.

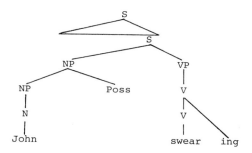

IV.G.4. Do support

Let us turn now to a more formal analysis of the rule of do support (cf. section IV.C.1 (items (22a) and (22b)). PS-rule 3 defines the category Presentence, specifying the following options: Neg, Q, Imp, and Emp.

(a) Neg. This occurs as the leftmost constituent in the deep structure of negative sentences[1]. To such sentences the Neg placement rule applies obligatorily. It can be formulated as follows:

$$(1) \quad SI \quad Neg - NP - \left\{ \begin{array}{l} T \qquad\qquad - VX \\ T \left\{ \begin{array}{l} M \\ have \\ be \end{array} \right\} - X \end{array} \right\}^2$$

$$\begin{array}{ccccc} & 1 & 2 & 3 & 4 \\ SC & \varnothing & 2 & 3+1 & 4 \end{array}^3 \implies$$

----

1. This is not quite true. Matters are complicated by sentence adverbs. We return to a discussion of this in section IV.G.9.3.

2. The braces collapse sets of mutually exclusive (i.e. disjunctive) rules. Thus the options specified by the inner braces make it explicit that Neg must always be adjoined to the first auxiliary verb which follows T. This does not mean, of course, that the input structure may not contain more than one auxiliary verb. What it does mean is that all auxiliaries, except the first, are covered by the variable X.

3. Given the reformulation of PS-rule 12 suggested in the preceding section, this rule would yield derived structures of the following kind (see overleaf):
   These structures do not block affix hopping (as would adjunction of Neg as the right sister of Perf or Prog). Note that the problem of derived constituent structure is always with us in the formulation of T-rules. It is not enough to state what happens to the constituents from a purely 'linear' point of view.

Now, if Neg (ultimately to be realized as 'not') is inserted immediately after T (in accordance with the SI defined by the topmost option in the outer braces), this becomes separated from the
main verb and affix hopping cannot apply. Consequently, the dummy
'do' must be inserted to ensure that the tense morpheme can be
realized phonologically. The rule of do support can be stated
formally as follows:

    (2) SI X - T - Y
           1   2   3

       SC Chomsky-adjoin 'do' to the left of 2.
             Conditions: $X \neq M$, Perf, Prog, Cop, V^1; obligatory.

An example of an output structure would be

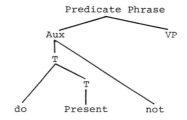

Predicate Phrase
Aux   VP
T
T
do   Present   not

    (b) Q. Q occurs in the deep structure of interrogative sen-
tences. We return to a more detailed discussion of this formative
in section IV.G.11. Meanwhile, we may examine the Aux inversion
rule, which precedes affix hopping and do support, but follows
Neg placement. The rule can be stated provisionally as follows
(we restrict the attention to yes-no questions) (see next page):
    The outcome of this rule would be such sentences as

    (4) May I come
    (5) Has he seen the film
    (6) Is he your friend
    (7) Did he find the book

Perf   Prog   Cop
have not en   be not ing   be . not

1. In conjunction with the ordering affix hopping - do support,
   this condition ensures that the two rules can never apply to
   the same sentence.

$$(3) \quad \text{SI} \quad Q - NP - \begin{Bmatrix} T & - (Neg) - VX \\ T \begin{Bmatrix} M \\ have \\ be \end{Bmatrix} - (Neg) - X \end{Bmatrix} \Longrightarrow$$

$$\begin{array}{cccccc} & 1 & 2 & 3 & 4 & 5 \\ \text{SC} & 1 & 3+2 & \emptyset & 4 & 5 \end{array}$$

Conditions: The rule is last-cyclic and applies only to the highest S^1; obligatory.

In the derivation of (7), T has been fronted alone; consequently, the output P-marker meets the SI of (2).

(c) _Imp_. Imp is present in the deep structure of imperative sentences. Do support is relevant also to the derivation of imperative sentences; however, it will be convenient to postpone the discussion of this to section IV.G.10.

(d) _Emp_. This formative occurs in the deep structure of emphatic sentences (cf. also above, p. 187). Consider the following examples (where the underscored words have emphatic stress):

(8) He has come

(9) He will come

(10) He was there

(11) He did come

(8)-(11) can be accounted for by the following obligatory rule:

$$(12) \quad \text{SI} \quad Emp - NP - \begin{Bmatrix} T\ (Neg) & - VX \\ T \begin{Bmatrix} M \\ have \\ be \end{Bmatrix} (Neg) & - X \end{Bmatrix} \Longrightarrow$$

$$\begin{array}{ccccc} & 1 & 2 & 3 & 4 \\ & \emptyset & 2 & 3+1 & 4 \end{array}$$

Ultimately, Emp is realized as emphatic stress on the immediately preceding word. Note that we have included Neg in the third term. In other words, we are assuming that a sentence like (13):

(13) John has not come

has the following surface structure:

----

1. In contradistinction to certain other last-cyclic rules (such as affix hopping and extraposition from NP (for which, see below, section IV.G.6)).

(13a)

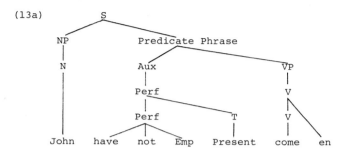

Before we go on, we must introduce the rule of <u>Neg contraction</u>.
Consider the following sentences:

    (14) ✻ Has not John come

    (15) Has John not come

    (16) Hasn't John come

    (17) ✻ Do not you smoke

    (18) Do you not smoke

    (19) Don't you smoke

    (20) ✻ Are not you married

    (21) Are you not married

    (22) Aren't you married

    (23) ✻ Can not you drive

    (24) Can you not drive

    (25) Can't you drive

From these we observe that 'not', if it is contracted to 'n't', is
fronted by rule (3) along with the third term; consequently, we
must formulate a Neg contraction rule which operates after rule
(1), but before rule (3), which must be revised accordingly. One
way of stating such a rule would be in terms of a feature attachment operation (cf. Stockwell et al., 1968, Vol. I, 314):

(26) SI X - T - $\left\{\begin{array}{c} \emptyset \\ M \\ have \\ be \end{array}\right\}$ - Neg - Y

         1   2   3   4 5 $\Longrightarrow$

     SC 1   2   3   4 5

                         (+ Ctrn)

The rule is optional.

    The revised version of (3) would look like this:

$$(3a)\ SI\quad Q - NP - \left\{ \begin{array}{l} T\qquad\qquad - (Neg) - VX \\[1em] T\left\{\begin{array}{l} M \\ have \\ be \end{array}\right\} - (Neg) - X \end{array}\right\}$$

$$1\quad 2\qquad\qquad 3\qquad\quad 4\qquad 5$$

SC　(a): If 4 dominates (+ Ctrn), adjoin 3 and 4 as
left sisters of 2.

(b): If 4 does not dominate (+ Ctrn), adjoin 3 as
left sister of 2.

The question now arises whether all the options defined by PS-rule
3 can be present in one and the same sentence (except, of course,
Q and Imp, which are defined as mutually exclusive). The answer
would seem to be that they can. Consider the following sentences
(in which the underscored words have emphatic stress):

(27) He did buy a car
(28) He did not buy a car
(29) He didn't buy a car
(30) Did he buy a car
(31) Didn't he buy a car
(32) Did he not buy a car

(27) is a straightforward example of the application of (12). In
(28) (1) and (12) have applied, in that order. In (29) the contraction rule has applied in addition to (1) and (12). How about (30)
and (31)? The derivation may be as follows: First Neg is inserted
(in (31)); then Emp is inserted; after this the contraction rule applies (in (31)) (these two rules do not need to be ordered relative
to each other); finally, (3a) applies ((2) must of course operate
in all the sentences). The reason for assuming such a derivation
would be that the realization of Emp as emphatic stress on the
preceding word must be implemented in the phonological component,
i.e. after the application of all syntactic rules; therefore Emp
must be fronted along with the third (and the contracted fourth)
term(s) of the rule. This requires the following revision of the
fourth term:

$$\left\{ \begin{array}{l} T\qquad\qquad - (Neg)\ (Emp) \\[1em] T\left\{\begin{array}{l} M \\ have \\ be \end{array}\right\} - (Neg)\ (Emp) \end{array}\right\}$$

$$3\qquad\qquad\quad 4$$

It should be noted that, no matter how we formulate the rules, we can, presumably, not avoid the generation of some rather odd surface structures. Thus the surface structure of

(33) Has John not been drinking

would be something like this[1]:

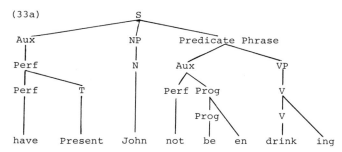

(33a)

To have 'not' dominated by Perf is perhaps not the paragon of naturalness (cf. above, p. 198).

Do support is a very pervasive phenomenon in the English language. We shall have occasion to note this as we go along. In this section we will present one further example (cf. Chomsky, 1957, 65f.). Consider the following sentences:

(34) My wife is a good driver, and so am I
(35) You will understand sometime, and so will he
(36) I have spent a lot of money recently, and so have you
(37) He failed to take these factors into consideration, and so did I

The relevant underlying structures of the underlined sentences are:

(38) I + Present + be + a + good + driver
(39) He + Present + will + understand + sometime
(40) You + Present + have+en + spend + a + lot ...
(41) I + Past + fail + to ...

To derive (34)-(37) from (38)-(41), we need a rule of the following kind:

----

1. Observe that we have assumed that the node Aux can be divided into two: the first part is fronted, the second part remains behind. It seems intuitively correct that 'has' in (33) should be defined as an auxiliary,

$$
(42) \text{ SI } \quad NP - \left\{ \begin{array}{ll} T & \cdot - VX \\ T \left\{ \begin{array}{l} M \\ have \\ be \end{array} \right\} & - X \end{array} \right\}
$$

$$
\begin{array}{cccc}
 & 1 & 2 & 3 \quad \Longrightarrow \\
SC \text{ so} & 2 & 1 &
\end{array}
$$

The rule asserts that the third term is substituted for the first
term and pronominalized, and that the first term is substituted
for the third term. When these operations apply to the topmost
option in the outer braces, T is left floating in the string (it
would now be followed by NP, not by V); consequently, affix hopping cannot apply, hence do support must apply. In (34) 'so' replaces a predicative NP ('a good driver'). In (37) 'so' replaces
a VP. (35) and (36) present us, once again, with the problem of
derived constituent structure. The point is that 'so' replaces a
VP and an Adv which are both under the immediate domination of the
node Predicate Phrase. Consequently, they do not form a constituent. The question then is precisely what kind of category 'so' is
in the surface structure of such sentences:

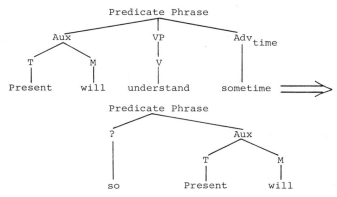

The difficulty arises from the analysis of adverbs which we have
adopted (cf. section IV.C.1). If we had not chosen the two-ways
differentiation between adverbs immediately dominated by Predicate
Phrase and VP, the matter would have been fairly straightforward:
'so' would have been a VP in surface structure. The generation of
adverbs under the immediate domination of different nodes, then,

may complicate the description in one area of the grammar, while
making it easier in other areas.

IV.G.5. Dative movement

The rule of dative movement accounts for the relationship between such sentences as (1) and (2):

(1) John gave some money to Mary

(2) John gave Mary some money

The first question that can be asked is which of the two sentences
should be derived from the other. In our grammar we have opted
for (1) as the basic structure (cf. section IV.C.1, items (33)
and (34)). There are at least two reasons for doing this: (a) If
we had PS-rule 6 generate a substring like V + NP + NP with the
structure:

(3)

then, obviously, the definition of 'object of' as 'that NP which
is immediately dominated by VP' would no longer stand up: 'object
of' would have to be defined in terms of the order of constituents
under the immediate domination of VP. Clearly, within the framework
of the standard theory, this is undesirable and should be avoided,
if possible[1]. (b) There are some verbs, such as 'explain' and 'describe', which cannot occur without a preposition:

(4) I explained the matter to John

(5) ✶ I explained John the matter

(6) I described the situation to my wife

(7) ✶ I described my wife the situation

This would suggest that the structure containing a prepositional
phrase is basic[2].

----

1. For some discussion, see Chomsky, 1965, 70f., 211f., 220f.,
   Matthews, 1967, 135, Dik, 1968, 151ff., Katz, 1972, 105, note
   35, and Postal, 1971, 125ff. and 1974, 134ff. (especially
   p. 145, note 49).

2. (a) is the most important argument. In fact, (b) is rather
   weak: there are also verbs which disallow the preposition.
   Examples are 'allow' and 'wish'. Note also such idiomatic expressions as 'they played us a number of tricks'; 'he kept me
   company' (cf. Jespersen, 1933, 115f.).

The preposition involved in dative movement is always either 'to' or 'for'. This being the case, we can formulate the rule as follows:

(8) SI X - V - NP - $\left\{ \begin{array}{c} \text{for} \\ \text{to} \end{array} \right\}$ - NP - Y

       1   2   3   4   5   6 $\Longrightarrow$

   SC 1   2   5+3 $\emptyset$ $\emptyset$ 6

The rule must be constrained in several ways. Note for example that, if the preposition is 'to' and the two NPs are personal pronouns, there is a tendency in British English for the second NP not to be moved around the first NP, whereas the preposition may still optionally be deleted:

(9) He gave it (to) me

(10) John showed them (to) me

However, (11) and (12) may also be heard:

(11) He gave me it

(12) John showed me them

In general, dative movement is optional. This is not the case, however, if the direct object NP dominates an S. Thus we can have

(13) I told my sister that I had been to England

but not

(14) * I told that I had been to England to my sister[1]

Consider now the following sentences:

(15) He sent the flowers to Helen $\left. \begin{array}{c} \\ \\ \end{array} \right\}$
(16) I have bought this house for you
(17) The flowers he sent to Helen
(18) To Helen he sent the flowers
(19) This house I have bought for you
(20) For you I have bought this house

(17)-(20) are derived from (15) and (16) by the rule of <u>topicaliza-tion</u> which may optionally front an NP for thematic reasons. Observe that the preposition in the input sentences is retained under top-

----

1. It is possible that (14) might be characterized as a grammatical but unacceptable sentence. Cf. above, p. 34 and below, section IV.G.14.6. For discussion of the concept 'complex NP', of which (14) is an example, see Ross, 1967, Chapter 3.

icalization[1]. It would seem, then, that dative movement and topicalization operate disjunctively (for further discussion, see
notes to this section).

The interrelationship between dative movement and the passive
rule should be noted. Recall that the passive rule operates on the
NP immediately following V. This being the case, the rule will
derive (22) from (21):

(21) The boy told a lie to the teacher
(22) A lie was told to the teacher by the boy

(22) may not be stylistically very felicitous, but let us concede
that it is grammatical. (23) would be better:

(23) The teacher was told a lie by the boy

However, (23) cannot be derived from (21) since 'the teacher' is
not the NP immediately following V. But if dative movement applies
first, 'the teacher' is moved into the proper position for the
passive rule. We may conclude from this, then, that if <u>both</u> rules
apply, dative movement must precede the passive rule.

Dative movement looks quite simple and is often adduced as
an elementary and clear-cut example of a syntactic transformation.
However, closer inspection soon reveals that it is just as difficult to constrain this rule properly as any other rule in the
grammar. Consider the following pairs of sentences ((25) is taken
from Borkin et al. (eds.), 1972, 18):

(24a) We restored the king to the throne
(24b) * We restored the throne the king
(25a) The storm brought much-needed rain to Michigan
(25b) The storm brought Michigan much-needed rain
(26a) I bought a house for Helen
(26b) I bought Helen a house
(27a) I told the story to my brother
(27b) I told my brother the story
(28a) She said some sweet words to me
(28b) * She said me some sweet words

(24a)-(28a) all meet the SI of the rule. If we look at (24) in
isolation, we might propose the following condition on the rule:

----

1. If the indirect object is fronted, the preposition is frequently,
   but not always, fronted along with the NP.

4 and 5 must not be dominated by Adv$_{direction}$. However, this assumption is immediately thwarted by (25). (26a) is ambiguous: it
may mean (a) 'meant for NP', or (b) 'by way of doing NP a favour'.
According to the general <u>rationale</u> of the standard theory, the two
readings should reflect different deep structures. Perhaps it could
be argued that in reading (a) 'for NP' is the remnants of a relative
clause (cf. below, section IV.G.14.4), whereas in reading (b) it
is generated by PS-rule 6. However, we would still have to explain why (26b) can only have reading (a). Furthermore, if reading
(a) of (26a) reflects an underlying relative clause[1], this would
also be true of

   (29) I bought some flowers for the table

But this does not undergo dative movement. The reason for all these
difficulties may well be that the application of the rule is dependent on the semantic relation holding between the predicate and
the PP undergoing dative movement, and that, ultimately, this relation cannot be defined in configurational terms. Rather, what
we seem to be in need of is the enrichment of syntactic theory by
a set of <u>semantic roles</u> which are played by NPs in relation to
their predicates. We return to a discussion of such roles in section
V.B. Finally, (28) shows that dative movement is a governed rule:
although, 'tell' and 'say' are semantically closely related, only
the former allows the rule to apply. In other words, 'tell' has the
feature (x dative movement), 'say' the feature (- dative movement).

IV.G.6. <u>Particle movement</u>

   There is in English a large number of "two-word verbs"; they
consist of a verb and a <u>particle</u>. Examples are 'give up', 'take off',
'put on', 'hand out', 'call up', etc. Note that the particles are
phonologically identical to prepositions, but for reasons to become
apparent later in this section they should be distinguished from
prepositions. Consider now such sentences as

   (1) He took off his coat
   (2) He took his coat off
   (3) He gave up the idea
   (4) He gave the idea up

It is obvious that the particle has been moved to the right of the

----

1. Note that this derivation would violate the A-over-A principle
   in its strongest form (cf. p. 224 and references cited there).

object NP (or rather to the right of the leftmost NP under the immediate domination of VP (cf. below, p. 288, note)). The rule can be stated as follows in tree-format:

(5)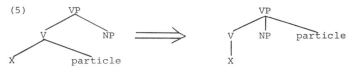

where X is any verb which can or must cooccur with a particle.

Note that the rule, which is generally optional, must be constrained so as to apply obligatorily if the NP is a personal pronoun:

(6) He looked up the words

(7) He looked the words up

(8) He looked them up

(9) * He looked up them

Before we go on, we need to make a slight digression. Consider the relationship between (10) and (11):

(10) The book which provides the final proof of the need for extrinsically ordered rules has yet to be written

(11) The book has yet to be written which provides the final proof of the need for extrinsically ordered rules

(11) is derived from (10) by the rule of <u>extraposition from NP</u>, which may be stated formally as follows:

(12) SI   X - $\begin{bmatrix} NP - S \end{bmatrix}$ - Y
 NP NP

 1   2   3   4 $\Longrightarrow$

 SC 1   2 $\emptyset$ $4+3^1$

Returning now to the main theme, we consider such sentences

----

1. Ross, who first formulated this rule, showed that all rules which move constituents to the right are <u>upwards-bounded</u> in the sense that the constituent which is moved must not be moved beyond the boundaries of the sentence within which the movement takes place (1967, Chapter 5). There is also evidence that the rule must be last-cyclic, but we will not go into that. Observe that the restriction of upwards-boundedness carries over to the 'normal' extraposition rule. This supports the extraposition analysis over the intraposition analysis: since not all rules which move constituents to the left are upwards-bounded, boundedness must be stated as a special restriction on intraposition (cf. Bach, 1974, 157f. and notes to section IV.E.9).

as

> (13) He picked up the paper which was covered with snow
> (14) He picked the paper up which was covered with snow
> (15) He picked the paper which was covered with snow up
> (16) He looked up the word which he had rubbed out
> (17) He looked the word up which he had rubbed out
> (18) He looked the word which he had rubbed out up

These sentences are - presumably[1] - all perfectly grammatical. Suppose now that we order the two rules concerned as follows[2]:

1. Particle movement
2. Extraposition from NP

Then (15) is derived from (13), and (14) from (15). By the same token, (18) is derived from (16), and (17) from (18). (18) is fairly low on the scale of acceptability. The reason for this is obvious: the relative clause ends in a particle; therefore the effect of particle movement is two successive particles in surface structure. However, the operation of extraposition from NP saves the situation. This being the case, we may speculate whether one reason for the existence of a rule like extraposition from NP is that it can prevent mind-bogglers from coming to the surface (cf. section IV.E.9)[3].

Different problems arise if we examine the relationship between particle movement and dative movement. Consider the following sentences:

----

1. There might not be general agreement on that. Cf. Ross, 1967, 28.

2. For some counterarguments to this ordering, see Lehmann, 1972.

3. In this connection it is interesting to compare English with Danish. In Danish particle movement is always obligatory. This appears from the following set of translational equivalents:

> (1a) He put on his coat
> (1b) ✻ Han tog på frakken
> (2a) He put his coat on
> (2b) Han tog frakken på
> (3a) He looked up the word
> (3b) ✻ Han slog op ordet
> (4a) He looked the word up
> (4b) Han slog ordet op

Now, if the Danish language had not had the rule of extraposition from NP, which it has, difficulties would arise with such sentences as (18) (see also notes to this section).

(19) The men were handing out propagandistic pamphlets to
     the passers-by
(20) The men were handing propagandistic pamphlets out to
     the passers-by

In (20) the particle movement rule works perfectly, but

(21) * The men were handing out the passers-by propagandistic
     pamphlets
(22) * The men were handing the passers-by out propagandistic
     pamphlets
(23) * The men were handing the passers-by propagandistic
     pamphlets out

are all ungrammatical. In (21) 'out' immediately precedes the indirect object. In (22) 'out' has been moved around the indirect
object. Seemingly, this is not possible. In (23) 'out' does follow the direct object, but an NP now intervenes between the object
and the verb. We can block the derivation of these three sentences
(or rather the derivation of (21) and consequently that of (22)
and (23)) by a constraint on dative movement, which, we assume,
precedes particle movement, to the effect that it is inapplicable
in case the verb is in construction with a particle[1].

It was emphasized at the outset of this section that particles and prepositions are different categories. This will be apparent from such sentences as

(24) John looked up the word
(25) John looked up the skyscraper

----

1. In fact, this constraint turns out to be too strong. Consider
   such sentences as

     (1) My wife picked out a new shirt for me
     (2) My wife picked a new shirt out for me
     (3) * My wife picked out me a new shirt
     (4) My wife picked me out a new shirt
     (5) My wife picked out a new shirt for my son
     (6) My wife picked a new shirt out for my son
     (7) (?) My wife picked my son out a new shirt

   In (4) dative movement has applied. After this particle movement applies obligatorily, moving the particle around the leftmost NP under the immediate domination of VP (cf. the ungrammatical (3) and above, p. 286). As a foreign speaker of English, I feel uncertain about (7) - but see Legum, 1968 (in
   Darden et al., 1968) 55; nevertheless, the sentence certainly
   seems better than (22). It would seem, then, that dative movement is inapplicable only if the preposition is 'to' (but see
   notes to this section).

(26) John looked the word up
(27) * John looked the skyscraper up
(28) He shot down the street (= 'hurried')
(29) He shot down the bird
(30) * He shot the street down
(31) He shot the bird down

The ungrammaticality of (27) and (30) shows that the relevant
items in (25) and (28) cannot be particles although they are phonologically identical to the corresponding items in (25) and (29).

The difference between particles and prepositions can become subtle. Consider the following sentences (cf. Langendoen,
1970b, 196):

(32) He called up his friend
(33) He called his friend up
(34) She was brushing the dust off something, but I forget what
     it was
(35) * She was brushing off something the dust, but I forget
     what it was
(36) She was brushing the dust off
(37) She was brushing off the dust

It is immediately obvious that 'up' in (32) and (33) is a particle: (33) has undergone particle movement. Now, if we were confronted with (36) and (37) in isolation, we might be tempted to
think that they parallel (33) and (32) respectively. However,
the matter is complicated by (34) and (35). In particular, (34)
shows that 'off' is a preposition: it is followed by a prepositional object; the ungrammaticality of (35) reveals that the prepositional phrase cannot intervene between the verb and the object. Since, as we know, underlying unspecified NPs may often be
deleted (cf. the object deletion rule), it is reasonable to assume
that this is what has happened in (36). After the deletion of the
unspecified NP, the preposition itself may be moved to a position
immediately following the verb.

If this analysis is correct, the grammar requires two different rules: (a) a particle movement rule operating left to
right, and (b) a preposition movement rule operating right to
left.

IV.G.7. <u>Passive</u>

IV.G.7.1. <u>A possible reformulation</u>

In section IV.E.5 it was suggested that there might be a connection between 'by + NP' of passive sentences and manner adverbs.
There is evidence supporting this analysis which is considerably
stronger than that considered in IV.E.5.

There is a class of verbs - so-called <u>middle verbs</u> (for this
term, see Lees, 1960a, 8) - which cannot cooccur with manner adverbs and which, although they take objects, do not undergo the
passive rule. Examples are

(1) The sister resembles the father (✱ thoroughly)

(2) ✱ The father is resembled by the sister

(3) John has a new car (✱ wisely)

(4) ✱ A new car is had by John[1]

(5) John married Mary (✱ enthusiastically)

(6) ✱ Mary was married by John

Conversely, it seems to be the case that verbs which can cooccur
freely with manner adverbs can also undergo the passive rule.
Such data suggest that the passive should perhaps be interpreted
as a particular realization of manner adverbs (see especially
Katz and Postal, 1964, 35f., 72f. and Chomsky, 1965, 103ff.).
To see how this proposal works, we consider the following two sentences:

(7) The problem has been analysed thoroughly

(8) The problem has been analysed thoroughly by the authorities

The deep structure of (7) and (8) would be something like (9)
(see next page (we disregard perfective aspect)):
The substring 'by + Passive' triggers the transformational processes: NP_2 takes the place of NP_1, NP_1 takes the place of 'Passive',
and 'be + en' is inserted in the normal way. Two points should be
noted about this tree: (a) 'by + Passive' must now be generated
optionally by the PS-rules. In a fully developed grammar, there would
have to be a rule like (10) defining Adv_{manner}:

(10) $Adv_{manner} \longrightarrow (Adv_{manner_1})$ (by + Passive)

----

1. Note that 'have' may occur in the passive in certain fixed
   phrases: 'a jolly good time was had by everybody'.

(9)

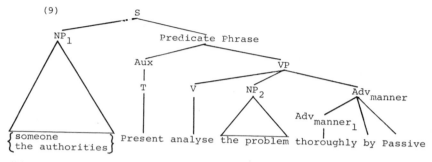

(b) The passive rule no longer lacks (nor, indeed, has) any structure-building power: the tree automatically provides us with the
information that 'by + NP' in a passive sentence is an adverbial[1,2].
The passive rule can now be reformulated as follows:

(11) SI   X - NP - Aux - V - Y - NP - Z - by - Passive - Q
          1   2   3   4   5   6   7   8   9   10

     SC   Sister-adjoin 6 to 2; substitute 2 for 9; delete
          the original 6 and 2; adjoin 'be + en' as right
          daughter of 3[3].

          Conditions: 5 must not contain an NP; obligatory.

The new formulation of the rule makes it possible to account
for the so-called <u>pseudo-passives</u>: 4 in the SI of the rule is no
longer restricted to the class of transitive verbs. In fact, the
analysis predicts that <u>any</u> verb which can cooccur with a manner
adverb may passivize. This is borne out by such sentences as

(12) John laughed heartily
(13) John laughed at me
(14) I was laughed at by John

The proper analysis of (13) meets the SI of the rule ('at' is
covered by the variable Y (5 in the SI of the rule)). Other examples of pseudopassives are

(15) This bed has been slept in

----

1. Note that the new formulation does not make it explicit that
   'by + NP' is a PP (cf. above, section IV.E.5). However, this
   information could easily be built into the rules, if necessary.
2. 'Someone' is eventually deleted by the rule of agent deletion
   (cf. (7)).
3. See notes to IV.G.3,4 (below, p. 438).

(16) The doctor was sent for

(17) He enjoys being looked up to

(18) This matter needs being looked into

(19) He doesn't like being talked about by his friends

(20) The job has been worked at for some time

(21) This house has not been lived in for some years

All these verbs may cooccur with adverbs of manner.

Observe that the rightmost NP worked upon by the rule (6 in the SI) must precede 'by + Passive'. The effects of this requirement may be illustrated by some examples adduced by Chomsky (1965, 105f.). Consider the following sentences:

(22) He decided on the boat

(23) He works at the job quite seriously

(24) The clerks work hard at the office from nine to five

(22) is ambiguous. It may mean either (22a) or (22b):

(22a) He made his decision on the boat

(22b) He chose the boat

The ambiguity stems from the fact that the PP 'on the boat' may have different syntactic functions. It may be a locative adverb immediately dominated by the node Predicate Phrase:

(22c)

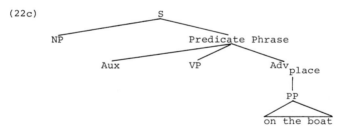

in which case the NP 'the boat' cannot be affected by the passive rule since it follows 'by + Passive' (which - as an adverb of manner - is always under the immediate domination of VP). (22c) underlies (22) in the sense of (22a). (22) in the sense of (22b) may undergo passivization:

(25) The boat was decided on by him

(25) has an entirely different deep structure:

(25a)
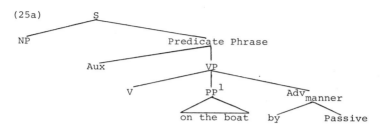

In (25a) the NP 'the boat' precedes 'by + Passive' and hence falls
within the scope of the passive rule. Note that (25) is not ambiguous. By the same token, (23) (cf. also (20)) may be converted
into

    (26) The job is worked at quite seriously by him

whereas (24) cannot be converted into

    (27) ✱ The office is worked hard at by the clerks from nine
        to five

    (22) through (27) can be said to constitute syntactic evi-
dence for the correctness of the hypothesis that adverbial prepositional phrases should be generated under the domination of different nodes: adverbial prepositional phrases under the immediate
domination of Predicate Phrase fall outside the scope of the passive T-rule. In many cases, however, the question of which node
dominates what can become rather complicated. Consider the following sentences:

    (28) He shopped in the town
    (29) A very poor family lived in the house
    (30) He put the books on the table
    (31) He drove the car in Germany
    (32) He remained in the hotel

All the underscored PPs seem to be locative adverbials. This being the case, we might expect them to be immediately dominated

----

1. The PP here is defined by our PS-rules. It is the same PP as
   the one we used to account for indirect objects. This is clearly ad-hoc. Furthermore, it is counterintuitive that 'on the
   boat' should have a totally different categorial status from
   ordinary objects. For some discussion of prepositions in this
   connection, see Lakoff, 1970a, 156ff. On the general question
   of prepositions, see references given on p. 126.

by the same node in deep structure, say, VP. However, if 'in the
town' in (28) were dominated by VP, the sentence should passivize
(since the verb 'shop' may cooccur with an adverb of manner (as
in 'she shopped quickly')). But

(33) * The town was shopped in by him

is ungrammatical; consequently, 'in the town' must be immediately
dominated by Predicate Phrase. A priori we might expect the same
to be true of 'in the house' in (29), but now note that (34) is
grammatical (cf. also (21)):

(34) The house was lived in by a very poor family

'in the house', then, must be dominated by VP. As far as (30) is
concerned, there is no problem: 'put' can never occur without a
locative adverb; consequently, this must be dominated by VP, and
since the object NP of 'put' can never be deleted, the NP of
a locative PP can never be affected by the passive rule. In (31)
it seems to matter little whether 'in Germany' is immediately
dominated by Predicate Phrase or VP. In the former case, it would
be unaffected by the passive rule, whereas, in the latter case, we
could prevent the generation of the ungrammatical

(35) * Germany was driven in by him

by ordering the passive rule before object deletion (cf. Lakoff,
1970a, 164). Finally, (32) presents a problem. Chomsky, 1965, 102
(and cf. Lakoff, loc. cit.) argues that 'remain' is so restricted
with respect to the types of adverb with which it can cooccur (the
only possible types seem to be Adv_{place} and $Adv_{duration}$) that it
must be strictly subcategorized accordingly. In other words, 'in
the hotel' in (32) is dominated by VP. However, since 'remain'
can take an adverb of manner (e.g. 'patiently'), this analysis predicts that (36) is grammatical:

(36) * The hotel was remained in by my wife

This is clearly not the case. From all this we may conclude that
there are many difficulties involved in providing an adequate configurational definition of a category like 'locative adverb'.

Let us end this section with a puzzle: if (21) and (34) are
grammatical sentences, why is it that

(37) * England is lived in by some fifty million people

is apparently not?[1]

IV.G.7.2. Agent deletion

In producing a sentence which contains a verb which allows
passivization, the speaker has a choice as to which noun he wants
to make the theme of the sentence (cf. our definition of 'theme'
above, p. 147, note 3). In the grammar this choice is implemented
either in the base component or in the transformational component,
depending on which analysis of the passive construction we opt for.
One reason for the existence of the passive rule (in addition to
the one considered in section IV.E.9) may be that it provides this
choice: if the deep-structure subject of a sentence is not semantically important, it is natural to choose the object as the theme
and get rid of the subject by the rule of agent deletion. In fact,
statistical surveys show that this happens in some seventy-five per
cent of English passive sentences. It is particularly characteristic
of certain stylistic registers, such as news bulletins, instruc-
tion manuals, scientific and technical language, etc. Examples are

(1) Recently, the government has been violently attacked
(2) His latest books have been widely read
(3) In a number of recent publications the category 'case'
has been postulated as a substantive universal

IV.G.7.3. Evaluation

The derivation of the passive construction by a manner adverb has much to recommend it. First, the (possible) need for the
passive rule to have structure-building power discussed in section IV.E.5 no longer arises. Secondly, some peculiarities which
the 'by + NP' of passive sentences has in common with adverbials
may now be explained. We have discussed adverb preposing in IV.E.5,
although, as we noted, this would have to be severely restricted
where passive is concerned. Similarly, like other adverbial PPs,
'by + NP' may be clefted (i.e. occur immediately to the right of

----

1. For an attempted explanation (within the framework of case grammar), see Langendoen, 1970b, 159f. The passive construction is
full of puzzles. Thus, as McCawley (1970b, 292) points out, no
analysis of the passive has yet managed to explain "why 'Hubert
loves God' is not funny in the same way as 'God is loved by
Hubert' is".

'be' in a cleft sentence)[1]:

(1a) The criminal was certainly not exposed by the police

(1b) It was certainly not by the police that the criminal
was exposed

(2a) You will not achieve your goals in that way

(2b) It is not in that way that you will achieve your goals

Thirdly, it is unquestionable that it provides a natural explanation of the fact that the vast majority of verbs which can cooccur
freely with manner adverbs may also undergo passivization. Finally, it provides for pseudo-passives, thus making the passive rule
independent of the notion of transitivity.

However, there are also a number of objections that can be
raised. Of these, we note three. First, it was pointed out by
Lakoff, 1970a that there are quite a few stative verbs, of which
the middle verbs form a subset, which, although they cannot cooccur
freely with manner adverbs, may nevertheless undergo the passive
rule. Examples are:

(3a) Everyone knew this (* cleverly)

(3b) This was known by everyone

(4a) Peter considered John a fool (* with great glee)

(4b) John was considered a fool by Peter

(4a) The workers believed (* naively) that everything their
leaders told them was true[2]

(4b) It was believed by the workers that everything their
leaders told them was true

Since these verbs cannot cooccur with an adverb of manner, the sentences in which they are contained can never meet the SI of (11).
To remedy this defect, we might consider having an additional
'by + Passive', dissociated from Adv_{manner}, generated elsewhere
in deep structures (for example under the immediate domination of

----

1. Again, this is not a very strong argument. Since NPs can of
course also be clefted (as in 'it was the man who did it'), we
could equally well use this as an argument that 'by + NP' is
an NP (cf. above, p. 196). On clefting, see section IV.G.15.1.

2. Note that if 'naively' occurs immediately in front of 'believe',
the sentence is grammatical. But then 'naively' is no longer
an adverb of manner, but rather what Jackendoff calls a subject-oriented adverb (1972, Chapter Three).

Predicate Phrase); this, however, would leave us with the middle
verbs: they should passivize under this analysis, but they do not.
Hence they must be marked in the lexicon by a rule feature like
(- passive). The adverb-of-manner analysis, then, cannot capture
all the facts. On the other hand, this is not an exceptional situation.

The second objection is semantic in nature. So far, we have
assumed that active and passive sentences have the same cognitive
meaning[1]. We have further assumed that deep structures contain all
and only the syntactic information which is relevant to semantic
interpretation. Given these two assumptions, it is clear that deep
structures which contain 'by + Passive' also contain semantically
irrelevant information. This being the case, it is arguable that
the reformulation of the passive rule we have been considering is
a makeshift device which is designed to account for some distributional regularities in the language, but which is, basically, incompatible with the semantic theory.

The third point has to do with functional explanations. Under
the manner-adverb proposal, the passive rule is obligatory (optionality now having been shifted to the base component). This
being the case, extraposition and the passive rule can no longer
be functionally aligned (cf. above, section IV.E.9).

IV.G.8. There insertion

Consider such sentences as

(1a) Five men were in the room
(1b) There were five men in the room
(2a) A cat was under the bed
(2b) There was a cat under the bed
(3a) * No taxi was
(3b) There was no taxi
(4a) Some people are outside
(4b) There are some people outside

The relationship between the (a) and (b) sentences can be stated in
terms of the following rule[2]:

----

1. We shall see in section V.C.1 that this may not always be the case.
2. The arguments which support the transformational rather than the
   lexical insertion of 'there' are summarized in Bach, 1974, 143ff.

```
(5) SI    NP - T - (M) - (have+en) - be - X
          1    2    3        4        5    6   =====>

    SC    There 2    3        4       5+1   6
          Conditions: 1 dominates (- Def); optional.
```

There are various comments that can be made on this rule.

(a) It was pointed out in section IV.C.1 that existential 'be' in English is nearly always construed with a temporal or a locative complement. In the typical instance, then, either of these two categories will be the value of the variable X (but see above, p. 198 and (b) below). However, the derivation of the perfectly grammatical (3b) spells trouble. In fact, it cannot be derived at all. The reason for this is obvious: the constituents following 'be' in PS-rule 6 are defined as obligatory; therefore the rules cannot produce a string like that underlying (3a). How to remedy this defect? One possibility would be to make the constituents following 'be', which are usually defined as obligatory, optional (cf. for example Burt, 1971, 243). But then, if we want to block the derivation of (3a), we can no longer allow the rule to be optional in every case; we must modify the second condition as follows: obligatory if X is null, otherwise optional. At first blush, this seems to be an acceptable solution. Thus it would have the advantage that the grammar would now generate the sentence 'God is' mentioned in note 3 on p. 102. This would not undergo the rule because 'God' is (+ Def). However, the grammar would now predict that such sentences as

(6) *❋ John is
(7) *❋ The man is

are grammatical: the subjects have the feature (+ Def). But they are not.

In summary, it would seem that there is no way of making PS-rule 6 and (5) interact in such a way that all and only the grammatical existential sentences of English are generated. The reason for this might well be that it takes a more semantically orientated grammar than the one we are considering here to harmonize the semantics and the syntax of existential sentences. This is further corroborated by (c) and (d) below.

(b) The SI predicts that the rule can apply to passive sentences (in which 'be' has been inserted transformationally). This is true. Consider such a sentence as

(8) There were 110 persons killed and 112 wounded in Palestine during January[1]

(c) The rule prevents there insertion from applying to sentences in which the deep-structure subject is specified (+ Def). This is not reasonable in every case. Thus

(9) There are still these two articles to be read
(10) There's always the car to be polished, you know

are perfectly grammatical. In such sentences the deep structure-subject seems to have the connotation 'among other things'.

(d) The rule requires that the input structure should always contain the verb 'be'. Again, this is not quite true, as appears from the following two sentences:

(11) From the body there burst a strange and appalling cry, a shriek so unearthly as to freeze the blood of all who heard him

(12) There limped into the room a self-conscious youth, with a handsome sulky head, fidgety movements, showy, ill-fitting clothes and a manner conspicuously lacking in the ease and naturalness usual in a man of his rank

in which 'there' has been inserted for stylistic reasons[2].

Finally, it should be noted that in a sentence with an initial 'there is', a relative pronoun may be deleted, even though it is the subject (cf. below, section IV.G.14.4):

(13) There's somebody wants to see you

IV.G.9. Aspects of negation

IV.G.9.1. Introductory remarks

Negation is one of the most complex areas of the grammar. In particular, in addition to 'not', there are a great many negative

----

1. Example from Schibsbye, 1965, 54.

2. It might be possible to isolate a semantic common denominator for verbs other than 'be' which allow there insertion. We will not go into this question.

words in the language; consequently, Neg need not always appear
in surface structure as 'not'. Thus (1) and (2) are synonymous:

   (1) He didn't say anything

   (2) He said nothing

and the Neg placement rule must therefore be supplemented by a
rule which optionally incorporates Neg into an indefinite pronoun
in certain circumstances. Consider further the following set of
sentences:

   (3) John is there, isn't he

   (4) John isn't there, is he

   (5) You doubt me $\left\{ \begin{array}{l} \text{* do you} \\ \text{don't you} \end{array} \right\}$

   (6) I have some money

   (7) * I have any money

   (8) I don't have (haven't got) any money

   (9) I said that he would make some remarks on that

  (10) * I said that he would make any remarks on that

  (11) I said that he would not make any remarks on that

  (12) I doubted that he would make any remarks on that

  (13) * I doubt any witnesses[1]

(3) and (4) show the very important principle of <u>polarity</u> between
a tag-question and the sentence to which it is appended: if the
sentence is positive (i.e. nonnegative), the tag-question is negative and vice versa. (5) obeys this principle beautifully[2]. (6),
(7), and (8) illustrate a well-known phenomenon: 'any' occurs in
negative sentences, but not in positive sentences. But consider
now (12): 'doubt' (in contradistinction to 'say' in (10)) can cooccur
with 'any' (but only when this occurs in a subordinate clause (cf.
(13)). We must conclude from all this that 'doubt' shares some of
the properties of Neg: both 'doubt' and Neg belong to the class
of <u>affectives</u>[3]. By the same token, a word like 'hardly' is a mem-

----

1. It is to be noted that the 'any' we discuss in this and subse-
   sequent sections is assumed to be weakly stressed.

2. 'do you' in (5) is grammatical with a rising intonation. It
   then has overtones of anger or perhaps threat. This is not the
   normal meaning of tags. Cf. below, sections IV.G.9.5 and
   IV.G.11.5.

3. For this term see Klima, 1964. Klima's study is a classic in
   this area of the grammar.

ber of the class of affectives. Furthermore, it is more of a
negative word than 'doubt' inasmuch as it satisfies both the tag-
question test and the 'any'-test:

(14) He hardly said anything

(15) He hardly spoke $\left\{ \begin{array}{l} \text{did he} \\ \text{✱ didn't he} \end{array} \right\}$

Enough has been said to indicate that the data relevant to
the study of negation present a number of different problems. By
implication, the Neg placement rule discussed in section IV.G.4
is only one of many interrelated rules that must be set up to account for those data. The following four subsections are devoted
to a brief discussion of those aspects of negation which are most
pertinent to the development of the theme of this book.

IV.G.9.2. Neg as a deep structure element

Recall the discussion of the SS-model of syntax above,
section IV.B.2. We saw there that negative sentences were derived
from their nonnegative counterparts by an optional, singulary,
meaning-changing transformation. We then proceeded to point out
that Katz and Postal, 1964 proposed that such rules should be replaced by obligatory meaning-preserving ones, whose operation was
made contingent on the presence of certain abstract triggering
elements in deep structures. These abstract elements, in turn,
determined the semantic interpretation of the sentences containing
them. In our formulation of the PS-rules in IV.C.1 and in our subsequent discussion of Neg placement, we tacitly assumed the correctness of this analysis.

Now, the claim that deep structures determine semantic interpretation, if it is to have any empirical content, must necessarily
be based on syntactic arguments, and in fact the most characteristic aspect of Katz and Postal's work is precisely the large array
of purely syntactic arguments they muster in support of their semantic theory.

In the field of negation, however, to which Katz and Postal
devoted relatively little attention, the syntactic arguments in
support of a single deep structure, sentence-initial negative element were provided by Klima, 1964[1]. Consider again (1) and (2) of

----

1. Cf. also Lees, 1960a, Chapter 1 and consult further Fillmore,
   1967.

the preceding section. The relationship between them can be captured quite naturally by positing the following common deep structure:

(1) Neg + he + T + say + something

and splitting up the Neg placement rule into two versions accordingly. A strong argument is also provided by such sentences as

(2) ✱ He lifted a finger to help me
(3) He didn't lift a finger to help me

In the SS-model, (3) would have to be derived from (2). This is
akward because (2) is ungrammatical. By contrast, if Neg occurs
in the deep structure, it becomes possible to state cooccurrence
constraints holding between Neg and certain idiomatic phrases[1].

It is syntactic evidence such as this (much more could be
adduced) that underlies the deep structure interpretivist position.

Once the hypothesis that deep structure determines semantic
interpretation is set up, further problems arise. Compare with
(1) and (2) of the preceding section, which, as we noted, are synonymous, (4) and (5):

(4) None of my students have read Aspects

(5) Some of my students have not read Aspects

According to Klima's analysis, (4) and (5) would both be derived
from the following rough underlying structure:

(6) Neg + some of my students have read Aspects

Neg would then either be placed after 'have', or else incorporated
into 'some', converting it into 'none'. The two rules would be
optional. This analysis is incompatible with the KP-hypothesis:
(4) and (5) are clearly not identical in meaning. We return to a
discussion of this in section IV.G.9.4.

IV.G.9.3. The scope of Neg

According to our PS-rules, sentence (1) of section IV.D.19:

(1) The stone didn't hit the boy

would have the following rough deep structure (we ignore the node
Presentence):

----

1. Cf. also sentences (1)-(3) of section IV.G.9.5, which can be accounted for in the same way.

(1a)

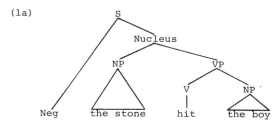

We must now introduce the notion <u>in construction with</u>[1]: 'a node
X is in construction with another node Y if the former is dominated
by the first branching node that dominates the latter'. Thus, in
(1a), everything dominated by the node Nucleus is in construction
with Neg. Nucleus forms the scope of the negation. We shall illustrate the significance of this scope principle with respect to a
specific syntactic phenomenon in the next section.

Meanwhile, we will briefly consider a semantic problem posed
by (1a). It was pointed out in section IV.D.19 that (1a) (or the
formula which was roughly equivalent to (1a)) cannot differentiate
the three possible interpretations of (1). Now, if we insist on the
KP-hypothesis, this defect should be remedied. There would seem to
be two possible solutions: (a) The grammar optionally generates a
focus-marker on one of the NPs. The projection rule then associates
the reading of Neg with the constituent bearing this marker. In
this way, the grammar would in effect provide for constituent-nega-
tion as well as for sentence-negation[2]. (b) We insist that the meaning of Neg always ranges over a whole sentence. In that case, we
must provide empirical evidence for deep structures deeper than (1a),
in particular deep structures which would define the two NPs as
predicates of embedded sentences (cf. section V.C.2). If we accept
neither (a) nor (b), we may retain (1a) and define the focus-'presupposition' dichotomy with which we are here concerned as a surface structure phenomenon.

----

1. Formulated by Klima, 1964 (in Fodor and Katz, 1964) 297. Compare
this with Langacker's notion of <u>command</u> to be introduced in section IV.G.18.3.

2. Recall our analysis of sentence (1) in section IV.C.1. We see
now that this will not stand up. It is true that the three adverbs are sentence adverbs, but they cannot be generated by PS-
rule (4) since this would predict that they fall within the scope
of Neg despite the fact that they are never affected by negation;
thus in (see overleaf):

As a further example, we consider again sentence (2) of section IV.D.19:

(2) John doesn't beat his wife because he loves her

We noted that the two readings of this could be paraphrased as (2a)
and (2b):

(2a) It is not because he loves her that John beats his wife
(2b) It is because he loves her that John doesn't beat his
     wife

It was Lakoff (1970a, Appendix F) who first pointed to the difficulties involved in the generation of such sentences. Clearly,
if we draw up the deep-structure tree in such a way that the whole
of the sentence (i.e. 'John beats his wife because he loves her')
is in construction with Neg, it will fail to predict the ambiguity.
In order to remedy this defect, Lakoff proposes to derive the
two readings of (2) from such structures as

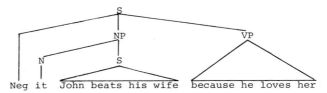

Neg it John beats his wife because he loves her

and (see next page):

Neg placement and extraposition will derive from these structures (2a) and (2b) respectively. Conversely, if extraposition
does not apply, the 'it' in both structures is deleted, and Neg
will be realized as 'not' in the Aux preceding 'beat' (the main

----

(1) Fortunately, Peter didn't come

'fortunately' is clearly not negated. To avoid this problem, we
would need to reformulate the PS-rules in such a way that they
would yield the following underlying structure for (1):

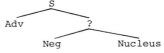

This shows, once again, the difficulties involved in bringing
to heel all the facts relating to adverbs. In this case, a transformational analysis of adverbs would presumably be preferable:
(1) could naturally be derived from

(1a) That Peter didn't come was fortunate

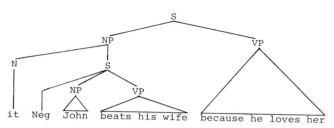

verb of a sentence being defined as the highest verb in the P-marker
which has a nonsentence NP as its subject). Consequently, the syntactically ambiguous (2) is derived. This approach, then, involves
the derivation of adverbs, including adverbial clauses, from higher
sentences[1].

We now begin to see the force of Seuren's claim that the standard theory is "self-destructive" (cf. above, pp. 95, 176). The
problem is the KP-hypothesis, which asserts that meaning should
be predictable from deep structure[2].

We return to problems of scope in section V.C.1. We shall see
that they are of vital importance in the current theoretical debate between generative semanticists and interpretivists (i.e. adherents of the extended standard theory).

IV.G.9.4. The relationship between 'some' and 'any'

A well-known problem to the foreign learner of English is
the relationship between 'some' and 'any'. In particular, 'any'
occurs only in negative sentences (or interrogative sentences (for
which, see below, section IV.G.11.1) or conditional clauses). We
noted in section IV.G.9.2 that, given the KP-hypothesis, the relationship between such sentences as 'none of my students have read
Aspects' and 'some of my students have not read Aspects' cannot be
accounted for in terms of optional rules because T-rules should
now be meaning-preserving. The same is true of (1) and (2):

(1) I didn't speak to some of my guests

(2) I didn't speak to any of my guests

----

1. 'Because' itself is a predicate which has a sentential object.
   From here there is not a far step to the interpretation of 'because' as a sentence-initial, two-place predicate (cf. IV.D.19.).
2. Recall that when Klima formulated his scope principle, the implications of the KP-hypothesis had not yet made themselves felt.

which are clearly not synonymous. A possible analysis of the relationship between (1) and (2) - one which has received much attention in the literature - has been proposed by Fillmore, 1967. In
this the operation of the <u>some any rule</u> is made contingent on a
feature (Specific) which may be specified + or - in the deep-structure occurrence of indefinite quantifiers, including 'some'. If
'some' is specified (- Specific) and occurs in a negative sentence,
the rule applies obligatorily, converting 'some' into 'any'. This
accounts nicely for the semantic difference between (1) and (2):
(1) means that there was a certain specifiable group of guests to
whom I did not speak; by contrast, (2) is synonymous with

     (3) I spoke to none of the guests

(in which 'not' + a (- Specific) 'some' has optionally been converted into 'none' rather than into 'not any').
This rule would also account for such sentences as

     (4) I sometimes read
     (5) I sometimes don't read
     (6) I don't ever read
     (7) I never read

where (6) and (7) are synonymous.
    It should be noted that the presence of Neg under the imme-
diate domination of the topmost S can trigger the application of
the some any rule as many times in a sentence (including subordinate clauses) as there are occurrences of a (- Specific) 'some'
in construction with Neg[1]. For example, we can have such sentences
as

     (8) No one wanted to say anything to any of those present
     (9) No one wanted to say anything to some of those present

    The some any rule has wide ramifications in the language, and
we cannot go into any detail[2]. However, mention should be made

----

1. Note that this constitutes a strong syntactic argument in favour
   of Klima's definition of scope.

2. Perhaps the most thoroughgoing investigation of the rule is
   that found in Stockwell et al., 1968, Vol. I, 253ff. They
   note a number of problems inherent in the analysis. One such
   problem should be mentioned: given that 'some' can be specified
   either (+ Specific) or (- Specific), one might expect all
   surface-structure occurrences of 'some' to be ambiguous. But
   this is not the case. Compare

of some interesting facts noted by Ross (1967, Chapters 5 and 6).
Consider the following sentences:

(10) I never read <u>the</u> book which $\left\{\begin{array}{l}\text{some} \\ \text{* any}\end{array}\right\}$ students
    recommended to me

(11) I wasn't <u>the</u> man who was looking for $\left\{\begin{array}{l}\text{some} \\ \text{* any}\end{array}\right\}$ girls

The grammatical versions of (10) and (11) are ambiguous: 'some'
in the relative clauses may be interpreted as either (+ Specific)
(= a certain group) or (- Specific) (= a certain number). Observe
now that in both sentences 'some' in the relative clause is in
construction with Neg in the matrix sentence and thus falls within
its scope. Why, then, has the some any rule failed to apply? It
seems to be the case that the operation of the rule in a relative
clause is contingent on the <u>determiner</u> in the head noun phrase.
Compare with (10) and (11) the following sentences:

(12) It was not <u>every</u> student who had $\left\{\begin{array}{l}\text{something} \\ \text{anything}\end{array}\right\}$ to say

(13) He disliked <u>every</u>one who $\left\{\begin{array}{l}\text{sometimes} \\ \text{ever}\end{array}\right\}$ dared object
    to what he said

Further, it appears that the determiner in the head noun phrase can
trigger the application of the rule even if there is no Neg in the
matrix sentence:

(14) He is interested in <u>every</u> woman who has $\left\{\begin{array}{l}\text{some} \\ \text{any}\end{array}\right\}$ money

(15) I want <u>all</u> those present who have $\left\{\begin{array}{l}\text{sometimes} \\ \text{ever}\end{array}\right\}$ had a
    similar experience to come forward

It should be noted that 'any' belongs to the class of determiners which allow the some any rule to apply in relative clauses.
Consider the following sentences:

(16) I cannot think of somebody who has presented some
    counterarguments
(17) * I cannot think of somebody who has presented any
    counterarguments

    (a) I am looking for some girls
with
    (b) She bought some apples
It is difficult to think of a context which would make a (+ Specific) interpretation of (b) natural.

(18) I cannot think of anybody who has presented some counter-
     arguments
(19) I cannot think of anybody who has presented any counter-
     arguments

In (16) the interpretation (+ Specific) is possible in both occurrences of 'some' (there was some particular person who had some
particular counterarguments, but I forget who it was). The ungrammaticality of (17) shows that 'some' does not belong to the class
of determiners which allow the some any rule in a relative clause.
In (18) the rule has operated in the matrix sentence ((18) means
something like this: there <u>are</u> some particular counterarguments
which I am now going to present, and, so far as I know, nobody
has come up with them before me). In (19) the 'any' of the matrix
sentence allows the application of the some any rule in the relative clause[1]. Among the determiners which have this property are
'no', 'all', 'any', and 'every'. These, then, belong to the class
of affectives.

Finally consider the following set of sentences:

(20) I don't like for any of my friends to be unhappy
(21) * I don't like the idea that any of my friends are
     unhappy
(22) * She didn't believe that there had been an explosion
     in the sewers and that any panes had been smashed

We comment on those in section IV.G.14.6.

IV.G.9.5. <u>Not transportation</u>

<u>Not transportation</u> is a rule which can lift a deep-structure
occurrence of 'not' in an embedded sentence into the sentence next
above in the tree. It is a governed rule: it affects such verbs as
'suppose', 'think', 'believe', etc., but not verbs like 'feel',
'realize', 'claim', etc. There is a good deal of syntactic evidence
for the existence of such a rule. Consider such sentences as

(1) John didn't leave until twelve o'clock
(2) * John left until twelve o'clock
(3) The guests kept arriving until twelve o'clock

----

1. The sentences discussed here involve certain theoretical problems with respect to the cycle. The reader is invited to try to
   spot these difficulties and then proceed to consult Ross, 1967,
   250 and Stockwell et al., 1968, Vol. I, 270f.

(2) is ungrammatical because 'until' must have a negative if it co-occurs with a punctual verb. Compare now with (1)-(3) (4)-(7):

(4) John claimed that he did not leave until twelve o'clock
(5) ✱ John did not claim that he left until twelve o'clock
(6) John thought that Mary had not left until twelve o'clock
(7) John didn't think that Mary had left until twelve o'clock

Given the existence of a governed rule of not transportation, the grammaticality of (7) as against the ungrammaticality of (5) receives a natural explanation: in (5) 'not' is generated in the matrix sentence, in which an ungrammatical sentence has been embedded. By contrast, in (7), 'not' is generated in the embedded sentence and subsequently removed by not transportation[1]. In other words, in (5) a cooccurrence restriction has been violated, whereas this is not the case in (7). Similar evidence is provided by certain idioms which must cooccur with a negative. An example is 'lift a finger':

(8) I realized you wouldn't lift a finger to help me
(9) ✱ I didn't realize you would lift a finger to help me
(10) Peter thinks Mary won't lift a finger to help him
(11) Peter doesn't think Mary will lift a finger to help him

Observe now that if tag-questions are appended to sentences like (10) and (11), they are formed on the topmost sentence. In this particular case, the tags are 'doesn't he' and 'does he' respectively. This is in perfect accordance with the principle of polarity noted in section IV.G.9.1. Apparently, then, the rule which forms tag-questions must operate _after_ not transportation. Compare now with (10) and (11)

(12) I don't suppose he will come

Here the tag-question is not 'do I' (as we would expect), but 'will he'. With a view to the principle of polarity, then, the tag must have been formed _prior_ to the operation of not transportation from

(13) I suppose he won't come

So we are saddled with an ordering paradox. How can this be resolved? In an elegantly conducted argument, R. Lakoff, 1969a proposes that the derivation of tag-questions should be made dependent on

----

1. We are assuming here that the rule is optional and meaning-pre-serving. That this may not be the case appears from the discussion in Lakoff, 1970c (in Jacobs and Rosenbaum, 1970) 158ff.

the presence of a higher 'understood' performative sentence containing the performative verb 'suppose' (for performative verbs,
see above, section IV.D.17). Compare with (13) the following two
sentences:

    (14) <u>I didn't suppose</u> he would come
    (15) <u>He doesn't suppose</u> John will come

In these, the two underlined sentences are not performative sentences; in particular, in (14) the verb is not in the present tense,
and in (15) the subject is not first person. Observe now that the
tag-questions here are 'did I' and 'does he' respectively. It follows from this that (13) behaves uniquely with respect to tag-
question formation. It may therefore safely be accorded a special
status in the grammar. Acting on this insight, R. Lakoff proposes
the following underlying structure for a sentence like (10):

    (10a) ($[$I suppose$]$ (Peter think (Neg - Mary will lift a
         S_1 S_2 S_3

        a finger to help him)))
                           S_3 S_2 S_1

On the lowest cycle (S_3) (we are skipping one which is irrelevant
to the argument), Neg placement operates. On the second cycle (S_2)
not transportation may optionally apply, lifting 'not' from S_3 into S_2. On the third cycle, the <u>abstract</u> verb 'suppose' (the abstractness of the performative sentence is indicated by the brackets) obligatorily triggers the formation of a tag-question. If not
transportation has applied on the second cycle, the tag - in accordance with the principle of polarity - will be 'does he'. By
contrast, if not transportation has not applied on the second cycle,
it will be 'doesn't he'. Not transportation cannot apply on the
top cycle because of the abstract character of the sentence. However, the abstract sentence may be "real" sometimes. This is precisely the case in (12), in which not transportation has moved
'not' into the sentence containing 'suppose' <u>after</u> the application
of the tag-question rule has been triggered by 'suppose'. By com-
bining the cyclic principle with the hypothesis of the abstract
underlying verb, then, it is possible to resolve the ordering
paradox. The order is

    1. Tag formation
    2. Not transportation

In addition to resolving the ordering paradox, however, R.
Lakoff's analysis also seems semantically well motivated. Tag-
questions, despite their formal similarities to yes-no questions,
are not real questions. Rather, they express the speaker's commitment with respect to the content of the sentence on which they
are formed. In particular, they can express anxiety, eagerness,
hope, etc. This being the case, they are naturally viewed as a
semantic reflex of an abstract verb 'suppose' (see further below,
section IV.G.11.5).

It should be noted that positing an abstract performative
sentence in such cases represents, once again, a step away from
the standard theory in the direction of generative semantics.

IV.G.10. Imperative sentences

IV.G.10.1. Introductory remarks

In section IV.A.7 we discussed the imperative transformation
provisionally. The approach adopted was the traditional one which
is summarized in the following statement by Thomas (1965, 196):

> The imperative transformation is quite simple. It operates
> only on strings that have (1) a second-person pronoun in the
> subject-position, (2) a present tense marker, (3) the
> auxiliary will, and (4) no other auxiliary.

As pointed out before (above, pp. 81, note 2, 202), the main argument in support of these assumptions is the behaviour of tag-
questions and reflexive pronouns in imperative sentences:

(1) You will wash
(2) Wash (yourself) (will you)
(3) Wash * himself/* myself/* itself/* herself
(4) Wash * will she/* will he/* will I

However, the facts turn out to be rather more complex than this
would suggest. Some of the points mentioned by Thomas are quite
problematic. This being the case, we will not attempt to formulate
the rule, but discuss the problems in informal terms.

IV.G.10.2. The deep structure of imperative sentences

If we define (the surface structure of) an imperative sentence

as 'one in which the understood subject is 'you' and in which the
verb is in the infinitive form without 'to'' (this is - more or
less - the definition that may be found in many traditional grammars), the following sentences would qualify:

(1) Close the door
(2) Wash yourself
(3) Behave now
(4) Sleep well
(5) Have a good time tonight
(6) Store in a cool place
(7) Add an ounce of salt
(8) Win a dish-washer to ease life for your husband

However, it takes little reflection to see that these eight sentences differ in terms of illocutionary force (cf. section IV.D.17).
They can all be associated with a performative *sentence*, but the
performative *verb* is not the same. In particular, (1)-(3) can be
associated with a performative verb like 'command' or 'request',
(4) and (5) with, say, 'hope', (6) and (7) maybe with 'advise', and
(8) with 'urge' (for (8), see also notes to this section). Suppose now that we postulate a deep-structure formative Imp which
is entered in the lexicon with a reading abstract enough to reflect what these performative verbs have in common (for a possible
reading of 'Imp', see Katz, 1972, 229). Assuming that 'Imp' occurs
in the deep structure of all imperative sentences, we can illustrate the deep structure of a sentence like 'drive carefully' in
the following way (accepting for the moment Thomas's definition
and ignoring the node Presentence (see next page[1])):

   Now, as was the case with Neg, Imp can (and must) also be
syntactically motivated. Consider such sentences as[2]

(10) Fortunately, you will help me
(11) * Fortunately help me
(12) You will want to finish your work soon
(13) * Want to finish your work soon

----

1. We could also, of course, posit a higer performative sentence
   such as 'I order you'. For discussion, see McCawley, 1968a (in
   Bach and Harms, 1968) 155ff. In actual fact, Katz and Postal,
   who first introduced the formative Imp into the theory of grammar, came very close to adopting the performative analysis (cf.
   Katz and Postal, 1964, 149, note 9).

2. Compare (10) and (12) with sentence (10) of section IV.G.10.4.

(9)

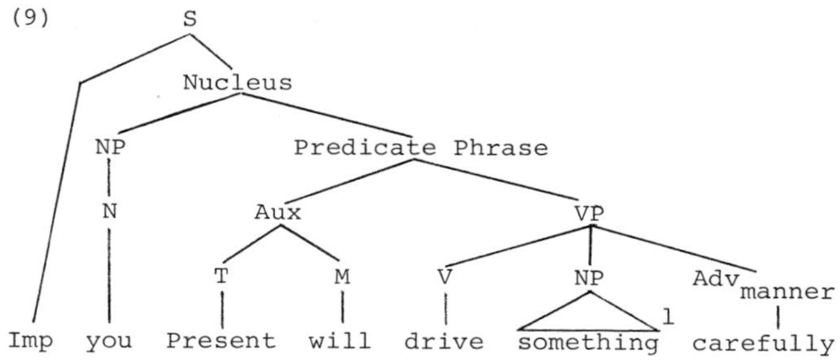

The ungrammaticality of (11) can be explained in terms of a violation of cooccurrence restrictions holding between Imp and certain sentence adverbs. (13) shows that Imp cannot cooccur with a verb whose meaning is such that it does not allow a free choice on the part of the subject of the imperative sentence (cf. Katz and Postal, op. cit., 76f.)[2]. By the same token, (14), in which the governing sentence is an overt representation of Imp, as it were, is anomalous:

(14) I request of you that you want to finish your work soon

We may conclude, then, that there is syntactic evidence in support of a deep-structure imperative formative which (a) accounts for the meaning of imperative sentences, and (b) obligatorily triggers the imperative transformation. By implication, the analysis presented in IV.A.7, in which we took the rule to be optional, should be abandoned (cf. below, p. 316, note).

IV.G.10.3. The subject of imperative sentences

There can be no doubt that the subject of imperative sentences is 'you' (or at least is given a second person interpretation). Furthermore, the subject of an imperative sentence is being addressed by the speaker (recall the second person indirect object typical of performative sentences). Consider such requests as

(1) Could your platoon please carry this stuff away

----

1. The pronominal object is deleted by the object deletion rule. The presence of the pronoun in deep structure is required by the recoverability condition on deletion (cf. p. 211f.).

2. 'Want' is a stative verb (cf. the ungrammaticality of a sentence like '* I am wanting to go to the cinema'). It is frequently the case that stative verbs cannot occur in imperative sentences (cf. also below, section V.B.4).

(2) Could the maid please brush my shoes by tomorrow morning

in which it is clear that there is not identity between the
subject of the sentence and the person addressed by the speaker.
Hence the ungrammaticality of the imperative versions of (1) and
(2):

(3) * Your platoon please carry this stuff away

(4) * The maid please brush my shoes by tomorrow morning

There are a number of cases in which imperative sentences
have (surface) third person subjects (notably indefinite pronouns):

(5) Everyone stand up

(6) Somebody clear the table

(7) All those who haven't got a clear conscience step
forward

(8) Everyone of you finish $\left\{ \begin{array}{l} \text{your} \\ \text{* his} \end{array} \right\}$ work now

(9) Everyone finish $\left\{ \begin{array}{l} \text{his/their} \\ \text{? your} \end{array} \right\}$ work now

In most of these sentences, however, the subject is interpreted
as second person. Thus in (5) the only possible partitive after
'everyone' is 'of you'. In (5) and (6), furthermore, the tag will
frequently be 'will you'[1]. The same is true of (7). In (9) 'your'
seems somewhat unnatural. Apparently, the syntactic third person
status of 'everyone' prevails over the logical second person interpretation, just in case there is no partitive specification (as in
(8)). In (9) there might even be a conflict between the anaphoric
possessive pronoun and a tag: (10) seems possible:

(10) Everyone finish their work now, will you

Note that if we change (9) in such a way that 'everyone' has a
purely vocative function, the pattern is reversed:

(11) Finish $\left\{ \begin{array}{l} \text{* his/their} \\ \text{your} \end{array} \right\}$ work now, everyone

We conclude, then, that the claim that imperative sentences
have a second person subject can be corroborated by facts of a
rather more subtle nature than those revealed by the pattern of
(un)grammaticality of sentences (1)-(4) of section IV.G.10.1.

----

1. There is a good deal of indeterminacy in such cases. For this,
   see Langendoen's "walrus and alligator" game (1970b).

IV.G.10.4. <u>The question of 'will'</u>

The presence of 'will' in the deep structure of every imperative sentence is harder to justify. First of all it should be noted
that the 'will'-hypothesis is based on the assumption that the formation of tags involves the <u>copying</u> in the tag of constituents in
the imperative sentence. But tags could equally well be derived
from two juxtaposed clauses, one of which undergoes imperativization, the other interrogation (cf. Huddleston, 1970a):

(1) You close the door, you will close the door
(2) You close the door, will you close the door
(3) Close the door, will you close the door
(4) Close the door, will you

In (4) constituents in the second conjunct have been deleted on
the top cycle under identity with constituents in the first conjunct by rules independently motivated in the grammar.

Under this approach, the fact that other modal verbs than
'will' can occur in imperative tags would not cause any problems:

(5) Close the door for me, can you
(6) Close the door, could you
(7) Be quiet, can't you

We still have to explain the obligatory presence of a modal
verb (usually 'will' to be sure) in an imperative tag. Presumably,
this can only be done in semantic terms. In particular, the meaning
of an imperative tag is typically an appeal to the addressee to
comply with the obligation created by the imperative sentence itself. The addressee is granted the right to refuse, as it were.
This notion is naturally expressed by means of a modal verb. It
could also be expressed by adding '(if you) please'. There seems
to be no difference in meaning between the following sentences:

(8) Leave the key, won't you[1]
(9) Leave the key, please

----

1. A further problem confronting the analyst is to explain why
   'won't you' is more <u>polite</u> than 'will you'. Compare for example

      (a) Have a drink, will you
      (b) Have a drink, won't you

   It should also be noted that it is not to every imperative sentence that a tag can be added. Thus 'sleep well, will you' is
   unnatural. No doubt, such constraints are bound up in intricate
   ways with the illocutionary force of the sentence.

The argument from tags in support of the hypothesis that 'will'
is present in the deep structure of every imperative sentence -
even if it were the case that 'will' was the only possible modal
verb in the tag - can be turned into a counterargument. Katz and
Postal, 1964, 75f. claim that a sentence like

(10) You will drive carefully

is ambiguous: it is either a peremptory declarative sentence, or
else an 'ordinary' declarative sentence. This being the case, it has
two different deep structures: one containing Imp, the other not[1].
Granted that this is the case, it would be reasonable to expect
that the imperative reading of (10) could be followed by an imperative tag. But now note what happens if a tag is appended to (10):

(11) You will drive carefully $\left\{ \begin{array}{l} \text{? will you} \\ \text{won't you} \end{array} \right\}$

'Won't you' disambiguates (10): it can now only be nonimperative.
'Will you' seems unnatural; and even if it is possible, it hardly
has the semantic force of an imperative tag. In other words, if
we insist that 'will' is present in the underlying structure of
every imperative sentence, and, furthermore, that tags are derived
by a copying process, we are faced with a very peculiar constraint:
if 'will' is overtly present in an imperative sentence (as in the
peremptory reading of (10)), no tag can be formed.

One further argument (advanced by Bolinger, 1967a, 337f.)
should be mentioned: with respect to such sentences as

(12) Do as I say
(13) Do as I say, will you

the natural reply to (12) - according to Bolinger - is 'yes' rather
than 'I will', whereas, as regards (13), these two replies are
more or less interchangeable. This would suggest that any reply
containing 'will' "responds to a structurally independent will you?,
not to the imperative". This would support the hypothesis that
imperative tags should be derived from a juxtaposed clause, rather
than from the imperative sentence itself.

----

1. In the analysis proposed by Katz and Postal, the only obligatory
   part of the imperative rule is the deletion of Imp. 'You' and
   'will' are optionally deleted. In that way, a sentence like (10)
   can come to the surface in its imperative reading. In the grammars proposed by other writers (e.g. Burt, 1971, 250), 'will'
   is obligatorily deleted (as is also 'you' (ironically, Imp is

We may conclude, then, that the syntactic evidence for an
underlying 'will' is rather thin and that it might be preferable,
from a semantic point of view, to explain the 'will' (more generally,
the modal verb) associated with imperative sentences as a constraint on the imperative tag question rule.

IV.G.10.5. The question of tense

The claim that the deep structure of imperative sentences
contains Present is motivated mainly by the fact that the PS-rules
cannot generate any sentence without a specification for Tense.
Therefore, Present is a better choice than Past. Even so, under
the assumption that imperative tags are derived by a copying process,
this claim would simply block the derivation of such a perfectly
well-formed sentence as

(1) Lay the table for me, would you

Yet, it seems to be necessary to assume that the deep structure
contains a tense element of some kind in order to account for a
number of characteristics which imperative sentences share with
other sentence types. Let us agree to use a makeshift device
(or a fudge) to explain some of these common properties: we will
assume that the rule which expands T should be reformulated as fo-
lows:

$$T \longrightarrow \left\{ \begin{array}{l} \text{Present} \\ \text{Past} \\ \emptyset \end{array} \right\}$$

$\emptyset$ is a phonologically empty realization of T.

The deep structure of a sentence like 'shut the door' would
now be (see overleaf and compare (9) of section IV.G.10.2):

What, then, are the characteristics shared by imperative sentences and other sentence types?

First, imperative sentences may be negated. Given a deep structure like that illustrated in (2), Neg would be adjoined as the
right sister of $\emptyset$; this would require do support, and we would get

(3) * You don't shut the door

----

the only constituent which remains in the string)). Under such
an analysis, the present argument would simply collapse. The ambiguity of (10) would then be semantic rather than syntactic in
nature ('will' has more than one reading). And why should this
not be the case? (Cf. also Lyons, 1966c, 120).

(2)

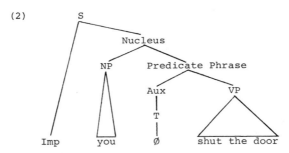

(3) is ungrammatical (as an imperative sentence): 'you' must obligatorily be deleted:

(4) Don't shut the door

Alternatively, an imperative version of Aux inversion may apply:

(5) Don't you shut the door

Secondly, the emphatic rule may apply to imperative sentences:
Emp is adjoined as the right sister of Ø; do support is again required (the underscored word carries emphatic stress):

(6) * You <u>do</u> shut the door

(6) is ungrammatical (as an imperative sentence); 'you' must again
obligatorily be deleted:

(7) <u>Do</u> shut the door

Aux inversion must be prevented from applying to (6), or else it
would derive the ungrammatical:

(8) * <u>Do</u> you shut the door

Note, furthermore, that Ø explains the behaviour of 'be' in
imperative sentences[1]:

(9) Be a good sport

but not

(10) * Are a good sport

----

1. Observe that T realized as Ø would also be needed to account for

   (1) I hereby order that these cars be removed

   (1) contains an embedded imperative sentence in which T is not
   phonologically materialized although the complementizer is 'that'.
   Note that in this discussion we have completely ignored the fact
   that, logically, imperative sentences always have future time
   reference (cf. above, p. 271, note 1).

Finally, we must simply take note of the fact that 'be' requires do support in imperative sentences:

   (11) Don't be a fool

   (12) <u>Do</u> be a sport

IV.G.11. Interrogative sentences

IV.G.11.1. Deep-structure elements

Consider the following set of sentences:

(1) He saw $\left\{\begin{array}{l}\text{some}\\ \text{* any}\end{array}\right\}$ girls around here

(2) Did you see $\left\{\begin{array}{l}\text{some}\\ \text{any}\end{array}\right\}$ girls around here

(3) He $\left\{\begin{array}{l}\text{sometimes}\\ \text{* ever}\end{array}\right\}$ reads

(4) Does he $\left\{\begin{array}{l}\text{sometimes}\\ \text{ever}\end{array}\right\}$ read

(5) He certainly came

(6) * Did he certainly come

(7) * I asked whether he would certainly come

(8) He said that he would certainly come

(9) Maybe I am not very helpful

(10) * Maybe am I not very helpful

(1)-(4) show that both 'some' and 'any' may occur in interrogative
sentences (just as was the case in negative sentences[1]). (5)-(10)
reveal that certain adverbials cannot occur in interrogative sentences. Syntactic facts such as these can be stated economically
and elegantly if it is assumed that the deep structure of interrogative sentences contains a special formative. Once such a deep-
structure formative is posited, it determines the semantic interpretation of interrogative sentences and triggers the application
of the transformational rules, which are now obligatory[2].

----

1. Though, as pointed out by Stockwell et al., 1968, Vol. I, 287f.,
   there is not always the same pronounced semantic difference
   between the two. See, however, below, section IV.G.11.5.

2. In the majority of cases; that is, we disregard intonation
   questions. Compare

      (1) What did you see

with

      (2) You saw what (note to be continued on next page)

The question of deep-structure elements in interrogative sentences has been the subject of much debate and many different proposals have been made[1]. In this exposition, we will follow, in all
essentials, the classic model[2] - that developed by Katz and Postal,
1964: each interrogative sentence contains (a) the unanalysed formative Q, which is entered in the lexicon with a reading something
like this: 'I (the speaker) request that you (the addressee) tell
me'[3], and (b) a focus-marker, Wh, indicating which constituent is
being questioned.

IV.G.11.2. Two kinds of questions

As is well known, there are two kinds of questions: yes-no
questions and wh-questions (or, in Jespersen's terminology, x-ques-
tions (1924, 303)). In the former case, the speaker seeks (dis)-
confirmation of the entire content of the questioned sentence,
whereas, in the latter case, he wants information about one or
more variables.

Let us now proceed to give the possible deep structures for
the following two sentences:

(1) Did the man come

(2) What did who see where

(1a)

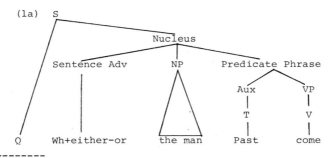

In (2) 'what' is pronounced with a rising intonation and has
therefore not been fronted (for the fronting rule, see next
section).

1. See in this connection Langacker, 1974b.

2. Classic, that is, within the confines of the standard theory.
   In the SS-model, questions were accounted for in terms of an
   optional, singulary, meaning-changing rule.

3. Note that this, too, is the equivalent of a performative sentence (cf. above, p. 312, note).

(2a)

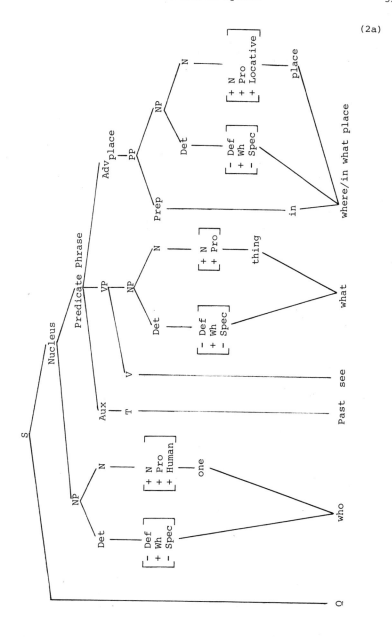

Observe now that in (1a) we have employed the Sentence Adv generated by PS-rule 4. 'Wh+either-or' is ultimately realized phonologically as 'whether' (in which form it occurs in embedded yes-no questions)[1]. In (2a) we have assumed that the appropriate determiners are defined in the lexicon in terms of complexes of features[2]. The determiners are transformationally attached to the following pro-forms. 'Who', 'what', 'where', and 'place' (if 'in what place' is chosen) are entered in the second lexical pass[3].

To convert (1a) and (2a) into surface structures, we need various T-rules. First of all, there must be a <u>Wh-fronting</u> rule (cf. the relative rule above, p. 199). It can be formulated provisionally in the following way (we restrict the attention to nonembedded interrogative sentences in this section):

(3) SI   Q - X - (Prep) - NP - Z
            1   2   3   4   5 ⟹
    SC (a) 1 4+2   3   ∅   5
    SC (b) 1 3+4+2   ∅   ∅   5
            Conditions: 4 dominates (+Wh); obligatory.

The division of SC into a and b is necessary for reasons to become apparent in the next section (cf. also below, p. 363). If the fourth term of the SI is immediately dominated by Nucleus (i.e. if it is the subject NP), then 3 will never be present, and, in a <u>simplex</u> sentence, X will always be null. This means that the rule ap-

----

1. The motivation for analysing 'Wh+either-or' as a sentence adverb is that the reply to a yes-no question may contain such an adverb:

        (1) Did he come ⟨ (1a) Yes/certainly he came
                          (1b) No/of course he didn't come

   As we have seen, such adverbs cannot cooccur with Q. Therefore, if what was said in note 2 on p. 303 is correct, the only function left for the Sentence Adv generated by PS-rule 4 is to define 'Wh+either-or'. See also notes to this section.

2. It would be reasonable to assume that the grammar should be constructed in such a way that relative pronouns were also aligned with determiners. Cf. above, p. 200, note. The structure of wh-words has received a good deal of attention in the literature. The reader is referred to the works cited in the notes.

3. Note that if the determiners of the three NPs had not contained the feature (+ Wh), the surface forms would have been 'someone', 'something', and 'somewhere'.

plies vacuously and has no effect on the structural description of
the sentence.

Wh-fronting must interact with Aux inversion (cf. above, p.
276ff.). We must reformulate this slightly so that it will apply
to the output of (3) (we leave out of account Neg and Emp)[1]:

$$
(4)\ \text{SI}\quad Q - X - (NP) - \left\{ \begin{array}{ll} T & VX \\ T \left\{ \begin{array}{l} M \\ \text{have} \\ \text{be} \end{array} \right\} - X \end{array} \right\}
$$

$$
\begin{array}{ccccc}
1 & 2 & 3 & 4 & 5 \quad \Longrightarrow \\
\text{SC}\quad 1 & 2 & 4+3 & \emptyset & 5
\end{array}
$$

Conditions: 2 dominates (+ Wh); otherwise as before.

Further rules, which we will not formulate, operate on the
output of (4), deleting Q and 'Wh+either-or', provided this occurs
in a nonembedded sentence.

The rules derive (1) from (1a). From (2a) three different sentences may be derived: (2), or

(5) Where did who see what

or

(6) Who saw what where

In (6) both Wh-fronting and Aux inversion have applied vacuously.
(2), (5), and (6) have the same cognitive meaning. The leftmost
constituent constitutes the theme of the sentence.

(2a) deserves closer examination. Thus note that the determiner is specified (- Def) and (- Spec(ific)). This can be justified
by the pattern revealed by such sentences as

(7) What books does he read

(8) Which books does he read

(9) Which of the books do you like best

In all of the sentences, the underlying determiner is (- Def)[2].

----

1. The two rules could also apply in the reverse order. For discussion of this, see Akmajian and Heny, 1975, 394f.

2. Katz and Postal, 1964, 129 analysed 'which' as a definite determiner. However, at that time, the full implications of feature
   analysis had not yet become apparent. Clearly, 'which' in (8)
   is not definite in the same way as 'those' in 'he reads those
   books'. For some discussion of this, see Stockwell et al., 1968,
   Vol. I, 151f.

In (7) it is (- Spec), whereas in (8) and (9), it is (+ Spec).
Thus 'which' in (8) and (9) indicates that the speaker expects
to receive information about a limited subset of books.

The pro-forms in the tree should also be noted. They are
bound up with the recoverability condition on deletions (cf.
above, 211f.). Thus in

(10) What does he read

the head noun (i.e. the underlying pro-form) has been deleted (or
at least has disappeared from the surface). However, in the deep
structure it was available to the semantic rules. In particular,
the noun which occurs in the reply must satisfy the selectional
restriction imposed by 'read' on its object NP.

In certain cases, the Wh-fronting rule seemingly applies recursively (i.e. to its own output). For example, we may have a sentence like:

(11) How, where, and when did you meet him

in which the three questioned constituents are coordinated adverbials. Identity with respect to categorial status is a condition,
as may be seen from the ungrammaticality of

(12) * What and why did you read

However, a sentence like (11) is probably derived from three underlying coordinated sentences, to each of which Wh-movement applies
once before the three sentences are collapsed by the rules of conjunction reduction and identical conjunct collapsing (cf. below,
section IV.G.13.2).

IV.G.11.3. Wh-fronting and the transformational cycle

Wh-fronting is an unbounded left movement rule (in interrogative as well as relative sentences). We have indicated this in the
formulation of the rule: the variable X (the second term in the SI)
may range over any set of embedded sentences. We have assumed, then,
that the SI of the rule is met on the last cycle (in a nonembedded
interrogative sentence, Q will always be generated under the immediate domination of the topmost S node). We could have formulated
the rule as a cyclic rule[1] (for example, we might have dispensed

----

1. In fact, it _is_ formulated as a cyclic rule. It is only because
   we are dealing exclusively with nonembedded interrogative sentences that it appears to be a last-cyclic rule.

with Q and made Wh-fronting contingent on the feature (+ Wh), such
that the questioned constituent would be fronted on the cycle in
which it occurs. The choice between these two formulations (ignoring here the semantic aspect of the matter) is an empirical
issue. The strongest argument in favour of the last-cyclic hypothesis is the so-called <u>preposition dangle argument</u> (cf. Postal,
1971, 74ff., 1972b). Consider the following sentence:

(1) What do you think Peter saw Jane sit on

The essentials of the deep structure of (1) can be represented in
terms of the following labelled bracketed string:

(1a) (you think it (Peter see it (Jane sit <u>on</u> Det   N)))
S_1 S_2 S_3 S_3 S_2 S_1
                                                          what

Observe now that an alternative version of (1) is

(2) On what do you think Peter saw Jane sit

in which the preposition governing the questioned NP has optionally
been fronted along with the NP (cf. the formulation of the rule on
p. 322). Suppose now that Wh-fronting were a cyclic (more precisely
a <u>successive cyclic</u>) rule. Then the questioned NP would first be
fronted in S_3; on the second cycle, it would be moved to the front
of S_2, and finally, on the third cycle, to the front of S_1. Since
the preposition may optionally be left behind each time the rule
applies, we predict that

(3) * What do you think Peter saw on Jane sit
(4) * What do you think on Peter saw Jane sit

are grammatical sentences, which is clearly not the case. In the
last-cyclic formulation of the rule, the preposition could not possibly be marooned in this way (in that formulation, Q would occur
under the immediate domination of S_1 in (1a) and trigger fronting
at one swoop).

Matters become more complicated in the case of embedded interrogative clauses. We discuss this question in the notes to this
section.

IV.G.11.4. <u>Some constraints</u>

The formation of interrogative sentences involves the movement of constituents, in particular NPs. This operation, as

we have suggested before, is subject to a number of constraints.
We return to a general discussion of these in section IV.G.14.6.
Meanwhile, the reader may speculate on what factors might determine the pattern of (un)grammaticality in the following set of
sentences:

(1) He said that Peter drove a Rolls
(2) What did he say that Peter drove
(3) The police have abandoned the theory that the murderer
     used a nylon stocking to strangle his victim
(4) * What have the police abandoned the theory that the
     murderer used to strangle his victim
(5) They said that the doctor arrived with his wife
(6) They said that the doctor and his wife arrived
(7) With whom did they say that the doctor arrived
     (alternatively: who(m) ... with)
(8) Who did they say arrived with his wife
(9) * Who did they say and his wife arrived

Recall that we said that performative sentences did not undergo interrogation (above p. 171, note 1). This seems to be discon-
firmed by (10)-(12):

(10) Do I warn you not to go
(11) Do I promise you never to let you down
(12) Do I request you to tell me whether you will remain
     faithful to me

However, these sentences are not real questions; rather they are
"echoic" questions in the sense that they are uttered as a hesi-
tant answer to yes-no questions not containing performative sentences (at least not overtly):

(13) Do you warn me not to go
(14) Do you promise me never to let me down
(15) Do you request me to tell you whether I will remain
     faithful to you

IV.G.11.5. A note on tag-questions

We said at the end of section IV.G.9.5. that tag-questions
appended to declarative sentences are not real questions. We must
now briefly try to substantiate that claim. Consider the following

sentences:

   (1) Have you got any money

   (2) Have you got some money

   (3) You have got $\left\{ \begin{matrix} \text{some} \\ \text{* any} \end{matrix} \right\}$ money, haven't you

   (4) You have got $\left\{ \begin{matrix} \text{some} \\ \text{* any} \end{matrix} \right\}$ money

The syntactic facts which appear from (1)-(4) are that 'some' and
'any' are interchangeable in interrogative sentences, whereas a
declarative sentence with a tag appended to it patterns with an
ordinary declarative sentence. In other words, syntactically, (3)
has more in common with (4) than with (1) and (2). This would suggest that tag-questions should not be derived by a rule whose SI
contains the Q-trigger under the immediate domination of the S
upon which the tag is formed: a contradiction would arise with respect to the statement of the cooccurrence restrictions holding between Q and the two quantifiers. This conclusion is confirmed by the
semantics of the sentences: (1) is an <u>open</u> question in the sense
that the speaker is uncommitted with respect to the truth or falsity
of the proposition '(have (you, money))'. In (2) the speaker is committed to the truth rather than the falsity of the proposition and
consequently expects the answer 'yes'. (3) is semantically similar
to (2); only, the speaker's commitment to the truth of the proposition is much stronger. The tag is an explicit invitation to the
hearer to confirm what the speaker believes to be true and has
little to do with a yes-no question. Q, therefore, would be a mere
syntactic trigger, devoid of its usual semantic content.

    On the whole, then, it seems reasonable to draw the borderline
between questions and declarative sentences between (2) and (3)
rather than between (3) and (4). This could be done by abandoning
Q and adopting the analysis of tags proposed by R. Lakoff.

IV.G.12. Comparative sentences

    We will assume that underlying a comparative sentence are
two sentences: (3) is derived from (1) and (2):

   (1) The man was surprised

   (2) The boy was surprised

   (3) The man was more surprised than the boy

What is the motivation for positing two underlying sentences?

Consider the anomalous

> (4) The man was more frightened than the house

We might try to account for the anomaly in terms of a selectional
violation. Something like this might do (a very ad-hoc statement):
the predicate 'frighten' requires a + ANIMATE object; consequently,
it cannot occur in a passive sentence in which the derived subject
is compared to a - ANIMATE noun phrase. A similar explanation might
be given for the anomalous

> (5) The alarm was called off sooner than the general

Observe now that

> (6) The alarm was called off sooner than the general expected

is perfectly normal. Why? The only difference between (5) and (6)
is the verb 'expected'. This suggests that the anomaly of (4) and
(5) cannot be explained merely in terms of <u>overtly present</u> elements
in the sentence. Rather, it is due to the violation of a selectional restriction obtaining between 'house' and 'general' and a
<u>deleted</u> predicate. The underlying structure of (4) and (5) would
be, accordingly:

> (7) The man was more frightened than the house was frightened
> (8) The alarm was called off sooner than the general was
>   called off

Consider next (9) and (10):

> (9) He was very happy
> (10) He was happier than Peter

In (9) 'happy' is modified by the intensifier 'very'. In (10)
'happy' is modified in the same way; only, this time the intensifier is a sentence. If we bring into action PS-rules 8 and 9, we
can set up the following deep structure for (10) (see next page[1]):

We will not go into the details of the transformational rules
required to convert (10a) into a surface structure. The most important rules are (a) a clause-movement rule which adjoins S_2 as
the right sister of the topmost Adj node, and (b) a rule which
deletes constituents in S_2 under identity with constituents in
S_1. The operation of the deletion rule may be illustrated by

----

1. For the node Cop, see the revision of PS-rule 6 discussed in
   the notes to IV.G.3,4. The degree adverb in the embedded sentence
   indicates the point on the 'happy' - 'unhappy' scale which forms
   the basis of the comparison. Cf. above, p. 146f.

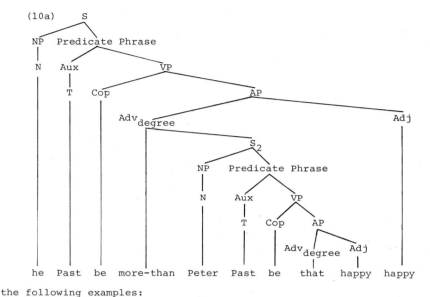

(10a)

he Past be more-than Peter Past be that happy happy

the following examples:

(11) ✹ You have always been more careful than I have been
     careful
(12) You have always been more careful than I have been
(13) You have always been more careful than I have
(14) You have always been more careful than I
(15) ✹ He understands English better than I understand English
     well
(16) He understands English better than I understand English
(17) He understands English better than I do
(18) He understands English better than I
(19) He understands English better than they say Jane does
(20) ✹ He understands English better than they say Jane
(21) He is rougher than you are gentle
(22) ✹ He is rougher than you gentle
(23) He likes me better than you
(24) He likes me better than he likes you
(25) He likes me better than you like me
(26) He understands English better than he understands French
(27) He understands English better than French
(28) The attacks come as frequently as once a day

(29) ✱ The attacks come as frequently as the attacks come
      once a day[1]

The ungrammaticality of (11) and (15)[2] would suggest that deletion of the identical adjective or adverb is obligatory. Furthermore, (11)-(14) indicate that deletion of identical constituents
proceeds from right to left. So do (16), (17), and (18). Note that,
whereas in (18) both the Aux (dominating Present) and the VP have
been deleted, in (17) only VP has been deleted. Consequently,
Present has been left floating in the string and must receive
do support. (19) and (20) reveal a remarkable constraint. The
sentence immediately dominated by Adv_{degree} contains an embedded
sentence, and it is in this that the identical constituents occur;
the grammaticality of (19) indicates that the VP may optionally
be deleted, whereas the ungrammatical (20) shows that Aux may not.
In (21) the rightmost constituents are not identical (though semantically closely related), hence deletion is impossible; the
ungrammaticality of (22), therefore, might be taken as a corroboration of the hypothesis that deletion must proceed from right
to left. But now note that (23) is ambiguous: it may be derived
either from (24) or (25). If it is derived from (25), the two
rightmost constituents (Aux and VP) have been deleted, whereas, if
it is derived from (24), the subject NP, the Aux, and the V have
optionally been deleted. This suggests that with transitive verbs
the deletion operation may skip a nonidentical object NP and then
delete all or none[3] of the constituents preceding the object. (26)
and (27) show the same phenomenon. In (28) and (29), however, deletion of all the constituents preceding nonidentical adverbs is
obligatory.

     All of this information will have to be worked into the de-
letion rule, which will be correspondingly complex. The main point
for us to note here is that deletion proceeds under identity with
some other element in the string. Hence no violation of the re-

----

1. (28) and (29) are taken from Lees, 1961, 180.

2. Strictly speaking, our grammar does not generate (15). For this
   sentence to be generated, we would have to add a rule allowing
   comparison to take place with adverbs. This would cause no problems.

3. It is in fact possible to retain the subject and the Aux:
   'he likes me better than he does you'.

coverability condition ensues (cf. above, p. 211).

Sentences like (21) are especially interesting in that they
pose a problem with respect to lexical identity (cf. Hale, 1970
(in Jacobs and Rosenbaum, 1970) 38ff.). In particular, the fact
that (21) is grammatical (which I take it to be) suggests that
'rough' and 'gentle' have semantic features in common which allow
comparison to take place. Since they are not phonologically identical, deletion cannot operate. Compare now with (21) the following sentences:

(30) My father is tall
(31) The cedar in the lawn is tall
(32) My mother is a handsome woman
(33) My mother received a handsome sum of money yesterday
(34) My father is taller than the cedar in the lawn
(35) * My mother is handsomer than the sum of money she re-
      ceived yesterday

(30) and (31) show that the lexical item 'tall' is not particularly
restricted with respect to the subject with which it can cooccur;
but it does impose on its subject the feature + VERTICAL (cf.
Langendoen, 1969, 45). Since both fathers and cedars can be tall,
the comparison in (34) works smoothly enough. By contrast, the
ungrammaticality of (35) (note that there are no violations of
selectional restrictions - cf. above, p. 158) suggests that the
two senses of 'handsome' involved here are more different than the
meanings of 'rough' and 'gentle'. Consequently, there is no reason
to assume that they should be stored in the lexicon as one polysemous entry. Rather, perhaps, they are homonyms, belonging to
two widely different semantic fields (for further discussion, see
Chomsky, 1965, 182ff., McCawley, 1968a (in Bach and Harms, 1968)
125ff., and Weinreich, 1972, 35f.).

IV.G.13. Conjunction

IV.G.13.1. Two kinds of conjunction

By conjunction we mean that two constituents are joined
together by one of the coordinators 'and, 'or', or 'but'. We will
limit our attention to conjunction with 'and'.

Consider the following sentence:

(1) John and Peter and Mary went to the cinema

(1) is four-ways ambiguous: it may mean

(1a) John went alone, and Peter and Mary went together
(1b) John and Peter went together, and Mary went alone
(1c) John, Peter, and Mary went together
(1d) John, Peter, and Mary went separately

Recall now PS-rule 11. The first option specified in the rule was

(2) NP $\longrightarrow$ and + NP^n, n $\geqslant$ 2

(2) would provide us with a structure like

(3)

('and' would be moved into its proper position by a T-rule). It is a reasonable assumption that (3) underlies (1) in sense (1c). Recursive application of (2) would yield

(4)

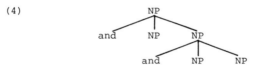

or

(5)

(4) and (5), we will assume for the moment, underly (1) in sense (1a) and (1b). This is as far as we can get by means of (2). In other words, (1) in sense (1d) is unaccounted for. However, we still have PS-rule 1 to resort to:

(6) S $\longrightarrow$ and + S^n, n $\geqslant$ 2

(6) would account naturally for (1) in sense (1d) (see next page):

On the basis of the evidence supplied by the ambiguity of (1) and such further examples as

(8) Helen and Tom are married

(7)

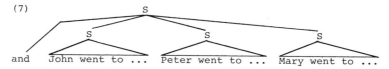

(9) Peter drank a lot of rum and cola last night
(10) George and Robin Lakoff have written a number of papers
     on generative semantics

and the ungrammaticality of a sentence like

(11) ✖ Helen and Peter both came together

we will assume that the grammar should provide for two kinds of
conjunction: (a) <u>conjunction reduction</u>, i.e. structures derived
by T-rules from conjoined sentences, and (b) <u>phrasal conjunction</u>
as defined by PS-rule 11. We will limit phrasal conjunction to
noun phrases[1].

     We now need to revise our assumption about (1a) and (1b):
rather than being generated by phrasal conjunction exclusively, they
are generated by a combination of phrasal conjunction and conjunction reduction.

     Suppose now that instead of (2) the grammar contained (12):

(12) NP $\longrightarrow$ NP + and + NP

In that case, it would generate structures like (4) and (5), but none
like (3). Consequently, the grammar would, in many cases, assign too
much structure to NPs having more than two NPs under their domination.
The difference between (2) and (12) is that (12) is <u>one</u> rule (which
may of course apply recursively), whereas (2) is a <u>rule schema</u>, i.e.
a rule-generating device which permits the generation of an infinite
set of structures consisting of conjoined NPs (each, in principle,
derived by a single rule defined by (2)) with any amount of internal
structure (including none at all). <u>Mutatis mutandis</u>, the same applies
to PS-rule 1.

     Rule schemata are also necessary in the transformational com-
ponent. More particularly, the rule which operates on (7), converting it into (1) by reduction, must contain in its SI the variable
n to ensure that it will apply to any number of conjoined sentences.

----

1. It would be quite possible to have the PS-rules generate, say,
   conjoined VPs (cf. for example Dougherty, 1970a, 1971). It should
   be noted here that there is by no means agreement on this issue.
   Some linguists would recognize only conjunction reduction, others
   only phrasal conjunction, and yet others both.

Having made these few remarks on the nature of rule schemata, which are required in an adequate account of coordination, we will continue the discussion in relatively informal terms.

IV.G.13.2. Conjunction reduction

The basic principle underlying conjunction reduction was first formulated by Chomsky, 1957, 36:

> If S_1 and S_2 are grammatical sentences, and S_1 differs from S_2 only in that X appears in S_1 where Y appears in S_2 (i.e $S_1 = .. X ..$ and $S_2 = .. Y ..$), and X and Y are constituents of the same type in S_1 and S_2, respectively, then S_3 is a sentence, where S_3 is the result of replacing X by X + <u>and</u> + Y in S_1 (i.e. $S_3 = .. X +$ <u>and</u> $+ Y ..$).

Schematically:

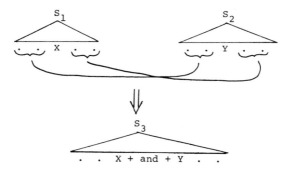

That is, given two conjoined sentences like

(1) John heard the crowd and John saw the crowd

we may derive by this schema:

(2) John heard the crowd and saw the crowd

or

(3) John heard and saw the crowd

Roughly, the derivation of (2) from (1) looks as follows in tree-format (see next page):

The two VPs have been conjoined under the domination of a common VP node and the two subject NPs under a common NP node. In both cases, 'and' is moved to a position between the two con-

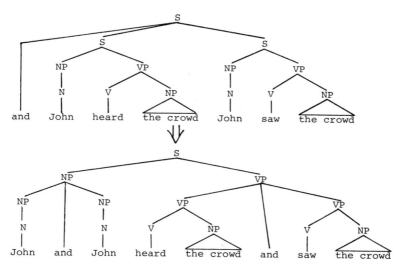

joined constituents. In this sentence the two subject NPs (we will
assume) are coreferential (cf. also above, section IV.D.15). Therefore they undergo the <u>identical conjunct collapsing rule</u>. The result of this is (2). In (3) the two Vs have been conjoined, and
here the object NPs as well as the subject NPs have undergone the
collapsing rule. The surface structure of (3) looks something like
this:

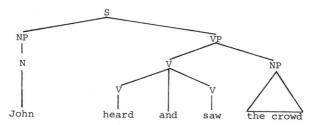

If the two object NPs in (2) had not been identical, we might
have obtained a sentence like

(4) John heard the concert and saw the film

If, instead of the two VPs, the two Vs and NPs are conjoined
separately (and so severed from each other) we obtain

(5) John heard and saw the concert and the film

As it stands, (5) is, presumably, ungrammatical. It requires
<u>respectively insertion</u>:

(6) John respectively heard and saw the concert and the film

or

(7) John heard and saw the concert and the film respectively

More generally, any sentence resulting from conjunction reduction
and having a derived structure meeting the schema

$$(8) \quad \underbrace{\left[Y_1 \text{ and } Y_2 \text{ and } \ldots Y_n \right]}_{Y} - \underbrace{\left[Z_1 \text{ and } Z_2 \text{ and } \ldots Z_n \right]}_{Z}$$

(i.e. having more than one set of conjoined nonidentical constituents) obligatorily requires respectively insertion. (6) and (7)
may not be very natural sentences. However, it is easy to construct
one which is worse. Thus

(9) John opened the door and John shot the girl

would result either in

(10) John opened the door and shot the girl

which is perfectly all right, or in

(11) John opened and shot the door and the girl respectively

which is a good deal more unnatural than (6) and (7). On the other
hand, it is also possible to come up with one which is better than
(6) and (7). For example,

(12) John likes coffee and John dislikes beer

would yield either

(13) John likes coffee and dislikes beer

or

(14) John likes and dislikes coffee and beer respectively

Respectively insertion seems to work most naturally when Y in (8)
applies to conjoined subject noun phrases:

(15) John and Bill respectively drove to Edinburgh and
     flew to London on Monday
(16) John and Bill went on Monday and Thursday respectively

In general, there seem to be a number of subtle and complex semantic factors which determine the scale of 'naturalness' in re-
spectively-constructions.

Next, consider the following sentence:

(17) Both Peter and John heard and saw the crowd

To account for this, it is necessary to assume four underlying
sentences which have undergone conjunction reduction:

(18) Peter heard the crowd and Peter saw the crowd and John
heard the crowd and John saw the crowd

In (17) 'both' has been inserted by the <u>both insertion</u> schema. Unlike respectively insertion, both insertion requires only one set
of nonidentical conjoined constituents:

(19) Both Peter and John saw the crowd
(20) John both heard and saw the crowd

The rule does not apply if the two conjoined constituents are sentences:

(21) Mary sang and Peter laughed
(22) * Both Mary sang and Peter laughed

If a sentence has two sets of conjoined constituents, respectively
insertion and both insertion cannot both apply:

$$
(23) \quad \begin{bmatrix} * \text{ Both} \\ \emptyset \\ \text{Both} \end{bmatrix} \text{ Peter and John heard and saw the crowd } \begin{bmatrix} * \text{ resp.} \\ \text{resp.} \\ \emptyset \end{bmatrix}
$$

Both insertion does not apply to sentences derived by phrasal conjunction; hence the ungrammaticality of sentence (11) of section
IV.G.13.1.

It should be noted that conjunction reduction does not necessarily apply to two conjoined deep structures: each of the conjuncts may have undergone T-rules separately before conjunction reduction applies. Consider such sentences as

(24) This argument is intricate and has been misunderstood by
many
(25) This argument has been misunderstood by many and is indeed
quite intricate
(26) In general his style is lucid and easy to read

In (25) and (24) the passive rule has operated in the first and
second conjunct respectively before conjunction reduction. In (26)
the deep structure object ('style') of the second conjunct has
undergone the rule of object-to-subject raising (for which, see
below, section IV.G.16.6). After this, it has been conjoined and
collapsed with the subject of the first conjunct.

Other rules than conjunction reduction may operate on two
conjoined sentences. Consider the following sentence:

> (27) John may want to buy a new house and Peter may want to
>   buy a new house

Conjunction reduction can convert (27) into

> (28) John and Peter may want to buy a new house[1]

Alternatively, the VP in the second conjunct may be deleted under
identity with that in the first:

> (29) John may want to buy a new house, and Peter may too

In that case, <u>too insertion</u> is obligatory. If the verb phrase in
(27) had been 'wants' instead of 'may want', VP deletion would result in a floating tense morpheme in the second conjunct and do
support would operate:

> (30) John wants to buy a new house, and Peter does too

(30) is synonymous with (31) (for the derivation of which, see
above, p. 280f.):

> (31) John wants to buy a new house, and so does Peter

The grammar, then, provides the speaker with a number of choices
in the encoding of his message:

> (32) Peter lives in London and Tom lives in London $\Longrightarrow$
>
> (33) $\left\{\begin{array}{l} \text{Peter and Tom live in London} \\ \text{Peter lives in London and} \left\{\begin{array}{l}\text{Tom does too}\\ \text{so does Tom}\\ \text{Tom lives there too}\end{array}\right\}\end{array}\right\}$
>
> (34) You have a car and I have a car $\Longrightarrow$

----

1. Observe that (28) is ambiguous in the same way as sentences
   (8)-(10) of the preceding section. The same is true of the
   first option in (35) on the next page.

$$(35) \left\{ \begin{array}{l} \text{You and I have a car} \\ \text{You have a car and} \left\{ \begin{array}{l} \text{I do too} \\ \text{have one too} \\ \text{so do I} \\ \text{so have I} \end{array} \right\} \end{array} \right\}$$

IV.G.13.3. Symmetric predicates

Consider the following sentences:

(1) The freighter and the tanker collided
(2) The tanker and the freighter collided
(3) The freighter collided with the tanker
(4) The tanker collided with the freighter

These four sentences, we will assume for the moment, are identical in cognitive meaning. More particularly, we can say that a verb like 'collide' is a two-place predicate: it must be construed with two noun phrases[1] which may show up on the surface in one of the following patterns (where P = predicate):

(a) NP_1 and NP_2 P
(b) NP_2 and NP_1 P
(c) NP_1 P Prep NP_2
(d) NP_2 P Prep NP_1

It seems clear that the conjoined NPs in a sentence like (1) cannot be derived by conjunction reduction inasmuch as the underlying sentence required is ungrammatical:

(5) * The freighter collided and the tanker collided

We must assume, then, that (1) and (2) are the result of phrasal conjunction. To derive (3) and (4) from respectively (1) and (2), two rules are required (for a formal statement of the rules, see Lakoff and Peters, 1969 (in Reibel and Schane, 1969) 127ff.). The first must substitute a preposition for 'and', and the second - the conjunct movement rule - must shift the PP so created to the right of the predicate. The former rule is optional, the latter obligatory.

Other examples of the operation of these two rules with symmetric predicates are provided by such sentences as

----

1. Alternatively, a plural NP, as in the sentence 'the ships collided in mid-ocean'. For discussion, see also McCawley, 1968a (in Bach and Harms, 1968) 148ff.

(6a) Tom and Peter are similar

(6b) Tom is similar to Peter

(7a) Kissinger and Nixon conferred

(7b) Kissinger conferred with Nixon

(8a) John and Mary are relatives

(8b) John is a relative of Mary

(9a) Peter and Helen differ in that ...

(9b) Peter differs from Helen in that ...

This account of symmetric predicates is not without its difficulties. Trouble arises with a sentence like

(10) The passenger liner collided with the Swedish rock

which cannot be derived from the ungrammatical

(11) * The passenger liner and the Swedish rock collided

(11) is ungrammatical (or anomalous) because the verb 'collide' imposes a selectional feature + MOTION on its subject. In (10) the passenger liner, as the only moving object, is responsible for the accident. This would suggest that sentences like (3) and (4) have two readings: one in which the subject is solely responsible (a reading which would match that of (10)), and one in which both NPs are responsible (because they are both moving). By contrast, two readings are not possible in (1) and (2): both vessels are moving. If this is correct, (3) and (4) should have two different deep structures, one of which cannot be derived by conjunct movement: only the responsible NP can occur in the deep-structure subject position, whereas, in accordance with our PS-rules, the PP must be some kind of adverbial.

The analysis can also lead to intricate problems in the form of ordering paradoxes. Lakoff and Peters (op. cit., 120) cite sentences like

(12) John and Bill killed a man (together)

(13) John killed a man with Bill

(14) John and Bill were killed (together)

(15) John was killed with Bill

in support of the conjunct movement hypothesis. Observe that (12) and (13) are cognitively synonymous, as are also (14) and (15). In both (13) and (15) the PP 'with Bill' belongs with the subject - in (13) with the deep-structure subject, and in (15) with the de-

rived subject (i.e. the deep-structure object). Two rules (apart
from preposition substitution) are involved: conjunct movement and
the passive rule. To ensure the correct derivation, the passive
rule must be ordered _before_ conjunct movement. As against this,
Dougherty, 1970a, 860 examines the sentences

(16) His understanding and his wisdom match
(17) His wisdom is matched by his understanding

How can (16) and (17) be related, as, clearly, they should be?
If conjunct movement applies to (16), we obtain (after the deletion
of the preposition):

(18) His understanding matches his wisdom

to which the passive rule may apply, deriving (17). In other words,
for (17) to be generated, the order of the two rules must be reversed: conjunct movement - passivization.

Under the analysis of the passive construction which we have
adopted in this book, there would seem to be no way of resolving
this paradox - but see notes to this section.

IV.G.14. Relative clauses

IV.G.14.1. Categories of relative clauses

Relative clauses may be divided into _dependent_ and _independent_
clauses. The defining criterion is the nature of the antecedent:
dependent clauses have an _overt_ antecedent, independent clauses do
not.

Traditional grammar recognizes two kinds of dependent relative
clauses: _nonrestrictive_ and _restrictive_. They are usually differentiated in semantic terms: a restrictive clause is semantically
"intimately" related to the noun phrase which it modifies, whereas
a nonrestrictive clause adds an extra comment, which might be dispensed with without affecting the content of the sentence. Furthermore, a nonrestrictive clause is marked by a separate intonation
contour. These differences are well illustrated by such sentences
as

(1) The girls, who were correspondents, had good jobs
(2) The girls who were correspondents had good jobs

It is clear that in (2) the relative clause cannot be left out
without affecting an essential part of the meaning of the sentence:

the implied polarity between those girls who were correspondents
and those who were not.

The crucial rules in the generation of restrictive clauses are
PS-rule 11 and the T-rule stated on p. 199. PS-rule 11 assigns the
following sub-P-marker to sentences containing a restrictive clause[1]:

(3)

In other words, S and its sister NP, i.e. the head noun phrase, are
immediately dominated by an NP node. There are various operational
tests which prove that the head NP and the clause "are an" NP.
(a) <u>Pronominalization</u>. In

(4) What impression has <u>the story I told you yesterday</u> made
    on your mind?/<u>It</u> has made a deep impression

'it' replaces the underlined structure, which must therefore be
an NP; (b) a noun phrase modified by a relative clause may occur
as the <u>reply to a questioned NP</u>:

(5) <u>Who</u> is coming tonight?/ <u>A fellow you have wanted to meet
    for a long time</u>

(c) a sentence containing a noun phrase modified by a relative
clause undergoes <u>passivization</u>:

(6) <u>The things that you told me yesterday</u> shocked me/I was
    shocked by <u>the things that you told me yesterday</u>

and (d) a noun phrase modified by a relative clause can be <u>pseudo-
clefted</u> (more precisely, perhaps, has a pseudo-cleft counterpart):

(7) <u>The semantic theory which McCawley and others have put
    forward</u> has caused a good deal of stir in linguistics
    recently/What has caused a good deal of stir in linguis-
    tics recently is <u>the semantic theory which ... put forward</u>

----

1. This is the way in which restrictive relative clauses are now
   normally generated. At the earlier stages of the theory, relative clauses were embedded in the Det node (cf. Smith, 1964,
   Katz and Postal, 1964, and Chomsky, 1965). Consult in this connection also Jackendoff, 1968 (cf. below, section IV.G.14.3).
   The different approaches are surveyed in Stockwell et al., 1968,
   Vol. I, 449ff. A more recent discussion is Bach, 1974, 265ff.
   Bach is especially concerned with the universal implications of
   the NP + S analysis. Schachter, 1973b proposes a radically different approach. So, too, Thompson, 1971.

In the next section we shall see that nonrestrictive clauses must be assumed to have a different source. Yet, at some stage of the derivation they probably have a structure like (3) (cf. also above, p. 200, note).

Smith, 1964 has established an interesting correlation between the classes of determiners and the distribution of restrictive and nonrestrictive clauses. The core of her argument is a 'scale of definiteness'. At the top of the scale is the unique determiner, which occurs with proper nouns and which, in English[1], always has zero realization (cf. above, pp. 115, note 1, 125). Proper nouns cannot occur with restrictive relative clauses[2]:

(8) Jane {, whom I like, / * whom I like} is his younger sister

At the other end of the scale are the unspecified determiners. They are quantifiers like 'each', 'any', 'all', and 'every' and generic 'a(n)'. These cannot occur with nonrestrictive clauses:

(9) Any car {*, which breaks down, / which breaks down} is a nuisance

In between these two extremes are the specified determiners ('the', 'a(n)', and Ø) which can occur with both restrictive and nonrestrictive clauses[2]:

(10) The Republicans, who fear the coming elections, want to get rid of Nixon

(11) The Republicans who fear the coming elections want to get rid of Nixon

(12) A cat, which had apparently broken its leg, was lying in the middle of the road

(13) I shall buy a book which I'm sure will interest you

(14) Milk, which is indispensable for children, has become far too expensive

(15) The problem is to find water which is drinkable

----

1. Cf. German: 'heute habe ich den Peter nicht gesehen'.

2. This distributional analysis does not stand up on all scores. Thus proper nouns can occur with 'the'; and when they do, they can only be followed by a restrictive clause, as witness the following sentence:

(a) The Peter {that I know / *, whom I know,} is a pleasant chap

IV.G.14.2. <u>Nonrestrictive relative clauses</u>

Generally, nonrestrictive clauses are assumed to be derived
from two conjoined sentences (see for example Lakoff, 1968c, 41ff.
Thompson, 1968, 1971, and Ross, 1967, 239ff.)[1]. Empirical evidence
supporting this hypothesis is the fact that a nonrestrictive clause
is frequently in free variation with a sentence containing two
conjuncts conjoined by 'and':

(1) Peter has travelled all over Europe, and Peter is
    still a student, mind you
(2) Peter - and Peter is still a student, mind you - has
    travelled all over Europe
(3) Peter, who is still a student, mind you, has travelled
    all over Europe

(3), then, is assumed to be derived from (1) and (2). The process
might be something like this (ignoring 'mind you'):

(3a)

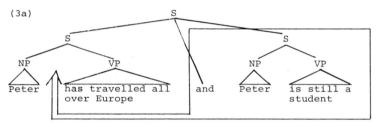

One of two things may now happen: (a) 'and' is dropped, after which
the second conjunct is Chomsky-adjoined to the right of the subject NP of the first conjunct. The structure now meets the SI of
the relative rule, which will derive (3)[2]. At a later stage, the

----

In other words, the definite article must be included in the
class of least definite determiners. Furthermore, 'a(n)', too,
must receive a double classification: specified (nongeneric)
and unspecified (generic). Also, it should be noted that there
are a number of constraints at work here. For example, a predicative noun phrase cannot be followed by a nonrestrictive relative clause (as witness the ungrammatical '✶ I have a friend,
who is a radical'). On the whole, however, Smith's points are
useful and well taken.

1. But see also Jackendoff, 1975a, 37f.

2. Lakoff, 1968c has provided a number of arguments that the rule
   which moves the second conjunct into place is last-cyclic.

clause is, presumably, moved out of the NP again; if this is the
case, the derived structure would be:

(3b)

This would account for the separate intonation contour assigned in
the phonological component (cf. also Jacobs and Rosenbaum, 1968,
262). (b) 'and' is retained, in which case the second conjunct
would not be Chomsky-adjoined to the subject NP of the first conjunct. The result would be (2).

A different type of nonrestrictive clauses are those which
are traditionally said 'to have a whole sentence as their antecedent'. They, too, are derived from conjoined sentences; only, the
second conjunct is not moved. Thus the source of a sentence like

(4) He is a thief, which is bad

is

(5) He is a thief, and his being a thief is bad

in (5) 'his being a thief' is an S embedded in an NP[1]. This NP
may be pronominalized:

(6) He is a thief, and <u>that</u> is bad

Alternatively, 'and' is dropped and relativization takes place,
as in (4). This is fairly straightforward. In some cases, however,
this type of clause raises some rather fundamental questions concerning the categorial status of constituents. Consider for example
the following sentences (cf. Ross, 1969b (in Reibel and Schane,
1969) 357):

(7) Tom is always foolish, which is too bad
(8) That Tom was so touchy, which he was, is not to be
    wondered at

In (8), unlike what is the case in (7), 'which' has not replaced
a nominalized version of the first conjunct (both the subject and
verb of that being present in the relative clause). What <u>has</u> been

----

1. Compare with (5)

(a) He is a thief, and it is bad that he is a thief

in which we know that the structure prior to extraposition is
(it (that ...)).
NP   S   S NP

replaced is the adjective phrase 'so touchy'. This shows that APs
and NPs are syntactically alike with respect to the operation of
this rule. More generally, it is facts such as these which have
led to the postulation of more abstract underlying categories
than those represented by the traditional parts of speech (cf.
section IV.C.1).

A different problem arises with such sentences as

(9) He stood on one arm, and I could never stand on one arm
(10) He stood on one arm, and stand on one arm I could never
     do
(11) He stood on one arm, and that I could never do
(12) He stood on one arm, which I could never do

In the second conjunct of (9) 'could never stand on one arm' is
clearly a VP (or, more precisely, a Predicate Phrase). In (10),
seemingly, this has been split up: 'stand on one arm' has been
fronted and 'do' has been inserted. The problem is to explain the
presence of 'do'. Thompson, 1971 argues that 'do' is inserted at
a late stage of the derivation in front of all activity verbs
(in this case 'stand'). Once inserted, it recategorizes the VP
as an NP: the NP is the object of 'do'. After this, relativization
may operate[1].

Consider finally

(13) He said that he had been sleeping, which he had

In this sentence 'which' has replaced 'been sleeping'; but this
is not even a constituent ('been' and 'had' being dominated by
Aux and 'sleep' by VP). The grammar we have constructed cannot
account for this (cf. also above, p. 281). It was evidence provided
by such sentences as (13) which first led to a reanalysis of the
celebrated Aux-formula of Syntactic Structures (cf. section IV.C.1
and references given in the notes on p. 123).

In summary, the analysis of the syntactic structure of nonrestrictive relative clauses is not without its problems.

----

1. If no T-rule moves the recategorized part of the VP, 'do' is
   deleted again. Thompson would analyse (8) along the same lines:
   'be' would be inserted and recategorize the AP as an NP. For
   a different approach to 'do', see Ross, 1972. Cf. also section
   IV.G.15.2.

IV.G.14.3. Coreferentiality

As we have seen, it is a condition on the relative rule that the two NPs involved are coreferential. This condition causes quite a few problems (we are now restricting our attention to restrictive clauses).

One problem relates to generic noun phrases. Consider the following sentence:

(1) A tiger which is met with at night is a very dangerous animal

In this sentence the relativized NP is not ("hypothetically") co-referential with the head NP inasmuch as (1) does not entail the generic sentence[1]:

(2) A tiger is met with at night

Observe now that there is a paraphrase relation between (1) and (3):

(3) A tiger is a very dangerous animal if it is met with at night

What happens in (3) is that a generic statement is qualified by a conditional clause in which a coreferential generic NP has been pronominalized. The semantic load of restricting the generic statement of the superordinate clause is carried by 'if'. It may be, then, that the source of (1) is something like (3)[2].

The determiners 'the', and 'a(n)' used generically are all-inclusive. This quality they share with such universal quantifiers as 'all', 'every', and 'no'. These, too, seem to yield reasonably well to an analysis involving a conditional clause. Thus the fol-

----

1. Compare with (1): 'A tiger which I met with last night nearly killed me'. This sentence, which entails 'I met with the tiger last night', is generated by the relative rule in a straight-forward manner (we ignore the question of the definiteness of, the relativized NP).

2. For this analysis, see Jackendoff, 1968. Observe that the postulation of (3) as the source of (1) makes it necessary to place a condition on the relative rule which prevents it from applying in case the shared NP of the relative clause has generic reference. In other words, the grammar must make it explicit that (1) is not the result of the 'ordinary' relative rule. For a more detailed discussion of all the problems involved, consult Stockwell et al., 1968, Vol. I, 454ff. See also notes to this section.

lowing (b) sentences may be derived from the (a) sentences:

(4a) No students fail the exam if they have a good profi-
ciency in English

(4b) No students who ... fail the exam

(5a) All cars are stopped by the police if they are more than
ten years old

(5b) All cars which ... are stopped by the police

(6a) Every student can learn this if he wants to

(6b) Every student who ... can learn this

(7a) All arguments are respected by teachers if they are well
presented

(7b) All arguments which ... are respected by teachers

However, some of these quantifiers, e.g. 'all', may also be
used nongenerically. This is the case in

(8) All the boys who left early are above suspicion

(8) cannot be analysed in the usual way: the sentence does not
entail

(9) All the boys left early

On the other hand, the relative clause cannot be derived from a
conditional clause because

(10) All the boys are above suspicion if they left early

is not a paraphrase of (8). It would seem that, in some cases, the
relationship between a head noun modified by a nongeneric quantifier and a relative pronoun is one of <u>set inclusion</u> in the sense
that the relative pronoun designates a set of which the head NP
is a subset. In (8) there is identity between the two sets[1]. A possible paraphrase of the sentence would be

(11) A set of boys all of whom left early are above suspicion

----

1. This is the usual state of affairs in relative clauses: (8) is
   not substantially different in cognitive meaning from 'the boys
   who left early are above suspicion'. As indicated by (11), the
   quantifier in (8) seems to be logically associated with the
   shared NP of the relative clause rather than with the head NP.
   For discussion of such sentences in terms of set inclusion, see
   Lee, 1971. It should be noted that Lee's analysis involves
   the postulation of deeper deep structures than those envisaged
   in the standard theory. In particular, the argument hinges on
   the semantic structure of the preposition 'of' (note that 'all
   the boys' in (8) is synonymous with 'all of the boys').

In (12), however, there is not identity between the two sets:

(12) Few of the boys who left early are above suspicion

The set designated by the head noun phrase 'few of the boys' is clearly included in the set designated by the shared NP of the relative clause.

Other nongeneric quantifiers like 'some', 'several', and 'many' seem to present less trouble. They can occur in embedded sentences and undergo relativization in the usual way. For example,

(13) Several students who had passed the first part of the examination failed in their finals

entails

(14) Several students had passed the first part of the examination

In general, the analysis of the syntactico-semantic status of quantifiers is extremely complex. We return to this question in section V.C.1 (cf. also above, section IV.D.18).

IV.G.14.4. Reduction of relative clauses

Relative clauses may be reduced by deletion of the relative pronoun and any form of 'be'. For example, (2) is derived from (1):

(1) The bird which is sitting on the roof is a sparrow
(2) The bird sitting on the roof is a sparrow

and (4) from (3):

(3) The car which is parked in front of the house belongs to my mother
(4) The car parked in front of the house belongs to my mother

The rule effecting this change may be stated as follows[1]:

$$(5)\ \text{SI}\quad Z - \underset{NP}{[}\ NP\ \underset{S}{[}\ NP - \text{Tense+be} - X - VP\ \underset{S}{]}\ \underset{NP}{]} - Y$$

	1	2	3	4	5	6	7
SC	1	2	$\emptyset$	$\emptyset$	5	6	7

Conditions: 3 dominates (+ Pro, + Rel); optional.

----

1. The variable X (the fifth term) is necessary to cover the remainder of the auxiliary (for example 'ing' in the example below).

The S node dominating the original relative clause is pruned
because it no longer branches. The operation may be illustrated
in tree-format with respect to (1) and (2) (we assume that affix
hopping has also applied to the derived structure):

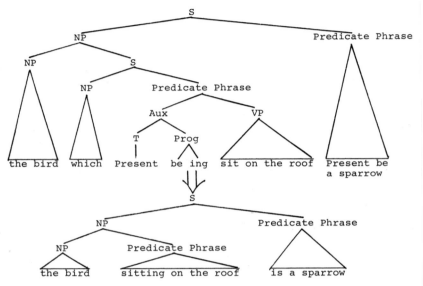

If the rightmost constituent dominated by 6 in the SI of the rule
is an adjective or a participle without a complement, a further
rule, the <u>modifier preposing rule</u> - must shift the adjective or
participle to front position. This rule can be formulated roughly
as follows (for a comment, see also below, p. 356, note):

> (6) SI   Z - $\begin{bmatrix} \text{NP - Predicate Phrase} \end{bmatrix}$ - Y
>   NP   NP
>   1   2   3   4
>
> SC   Chomsky-adjoin 3 to the left of 2; delete the original 3
>   Conditions: 2 does not take the form of an indefinite
>   pronoun ('someone' or 'something'); the
>   rightmost constituent dominated by 3 is
>   V or Adj[1]; obligatory.

----

1. This constraint may well turn out to be too strong. Thus
   Langendoen, 1970b, 200 cites the following ambiguous sentence:
   'my vegetarian aunt is coming'. The ambiguity can be accounted
   for, if it is assumed that 'vegetarian' is derived from a predicative NP in a (non)restrictive relative clause. For discussion
   of the rule, see also Lakoff, 1970a, 122ff.

Thus the derivation of

>(7) I have a new car

is: 'I have a car which is new' $\Longrightarrow$ '* I have a car new' $\Longrightarrow$
'I have a new car'. Intensifiers are shifted along with adjectives:

>(8) A conclusion which is totally wrong
>
>(9) * A conclusion totally wrong
>
>(10) A totally wrong conclusion

There are some adjectives that do not undergo the rule. Presumably,
they must be marked by a rule feature which blocks the application of (5). Examples are 'afraid' and 'glad'[1,2]:

>(11) * He is a glad fellow
>
>(12) * There is an afraid little bird

The first condition on the rule may be illustrated by the following
pair:

>(13) I want something exciting
>
>(14) * I want exciting something

and the second condition by (15) and (16):

>(15) Children behaving noisily
>
>(16) * Behaving noisily children

Relative reduction[3] is not limited to restrictive clauses.
Consider the following example:

>(17) Caesar, one of the greatest warriors of all times, was
>   cruelly assassinated

in which the appositional noun phrase is derived from a nonrestrictive clause. Note that the apposition, like the unreduced
relative clause, retains its independent intonation contour.

----

1. 'Glad' may be preposed in certain idiomatic phrases like 'the
   glad tidings'.

2. On adjectives, see especially Bolinger, 1967b. Consult also
   Quirk et al., 1972, 858ff.

3. Koutsoudas, 1973 discusses the interaction of relative reduction
   with such other rules as extraposition from NP, topicalization,
   and the S pruning convention in terms of extrinsic rule ordering
   versus the reformulation of Ross's complex NP constraint (for
   which, see below, p. 359) as a derivational constraint. See
   also above, p. 213.

It is also the case that some preposed adjectives are derived from
nonrestrictive clauses. Thus, since proper nouns can only occur
with nonrestrictive clauses, 'beautiful' in

    (18) Beautiful Evelyn Hope is dead

must be derived from a nonrestrictive clause (cf. Jespersen, 1933,
91 and above, p. 53, note 2).

    (19) The industrious lecturers are never criticized by the
          students

is ambiguous. In one reading, it means 'those lecturers who are
industrious', in which case the adjective is derived from a restrictive clause. In the other, nonrestrictive, reading, it means that
all lecturers are industrious (perhaps in contradistinction to less
industrious professors) (cf. also above, p. 53f.).

    At this point, the question arises whether the introduction
of attributive modifiers via reduced relative clauses is an over-
ingenious suggestion or whether it can be substantiated by other
facts in the language. Consider the case of prepositional phrases.
In a number of instances, these are undoubtedly related to relative
clauses. Thus (20) and (21)

    (20) I'm expecting a chap who is from London
    (21) I'm expecting a chap from London

are synonymous. Hence it is reasonable to assume that (21) is
derived from (20) by rule (5). After relative reduction, PPs
are not preposed; they take up a position immediately after the
noun. This constitutes evidence that the hypothesis concerning the
stepwise derivation of structures like (7) is correct, the pattern
being as follows with respect to rules (5) and (6):

$$\left.\begin{array}{l} \text{* Prepositional Phrase} \\ \text{Adjective} \end{array}\right\} \text{Noun} \left\{\begin{array}{l} \text{Prepositional Phrase} \\ \text{* Adjective} \end{array}\right.$$

Add to this the fact that there are adjectives which cannot be
preposed after relative reduction:

    (22) A devil incarnate
    (23) * An incarnate devil
    (24) Whisky galore
    (25) * Galore whisky

and that in rare cases prepositional phrases may be preposed[1,2,3]:

(26) An under-the-counter sale

Sentences may show great complexity in the patterning of embedded relative clauses. The reader is invited to provide a derivation for (27) (cf. also the discussion in the next section):

(27) The naughty boys over there stole the delicious apples hanging over the green hedge

Before we leave the subject of deletion in relative clauses, two further points should be made.

First, a relative pronoun which functions as the object in a restrictive clause may optionally be deleted (see also notes to this section):

(28) The girl $\left\{ \begin{array}{l} \text{whom} \\ \text{that} \\ \emptyset \end{array} \right\}$ I marry will have to be rich

(29) The film $\left\{ \begin{array}{l} \text{which} \\ \text{that} \\ \emptyset \end{array} \right\}$ I saw last night was no good

Secondly, the relative pronoun, if it is the subject, may not normally be deleted (unless Tense+be is deleted along with it). However, there are exceptions to this. Consider the following sentences (cf. also above, p. 299):

(30) There's a chap wants to see you

(31) It's your girlfriend wants to speak to you

In (30) and (31) deletion of the pronoun is conditioned by the presence of 'there's' and 'it's' respectively. This usage is colloquial. Consider next such sentences as

----

1. Cf. Bolinger, 1968, 201f.

2. We might also adduce evidence from other languages. Thus, as is well known, in French, the general principle is that adjectives are not preposed: 'une histoire intéressante'/'une femme danoise'; for discussion, see Ruwet, 1973, 269, note 14.

3. It has been pointed out that children learn to use structures containing attributive adjectives sooner than they learn to handle relative clauses. A possible explanation for this might be that relative reduction is obligatory in the early stages of language learning. Only later does it become an optional rule (cf. Langendoen, 1970b, 147). In functional terms, this seems a plausible hypothesis: reduction and preposing result in the pruning of an S node. Consequently, such sentences are easier to process.

(32) I dislike giggling students

(33) The girl working in the kitchen told me this

(34) In Denmark only people owning houses are safe from
     inflation

The most natural interpretation of (32) involves students who are
prone to giggling. In other words, the relative clause is reduced
from 'who giggle' rather than from 'who are giggling'. As against
this, (33) may be ambiguous. It may mean 'the girl who was engaged in some work in the kitchen when I - the speaker - passed
through', or, alternatively, it may mean 'the girl who has her work
in the kitchen' (in which case the speaker need not have been anywhere near the kitchen). In (34) there can be no doubt: 'own' is
a stative verb and hence cannot take the progressive aspect at
all. From this we conclude that there is an alternative version of
the relative reduction rule which deletes the subject of the relative clause and substitutes 'ing' for Tense. This 'ing' is totally unrelated to the 'ing' of the progressive aspect.

   IV.G.14.5. Stacking

   Stacking occurs when a relative clause modifies a head noun
phrase as already modified by another relative clause. (1), which
would probably be accepted by most speakers of English, is an example of stacking:

   (1) People that I know that[1] want to invest never
       seem to get the chance

It seems to be the case that one stacked relative clause constitutes
the limit of intelligibility on the performance level. This is not
the case, however, if stacked modifiers occur in prenominal position. A sentence like

   (2) He bought a (beautiful (old (yellow (English cottage))))

is probably interpreted as indicated by the brackets. Assuming that

----

1. Observe that the second 'that' can only be interpreted as a relative pronoun, not as a complementizer. If it were a complementizer introducing a sentential complement whose subject had
   been relativized and raised, the sentence would be ruled out
   as ungrammatical by Perlmutter's surface structure constraint
   (cf. above, p. 213ff.).

this is correct, the deep structure of (2) must be, roughly:

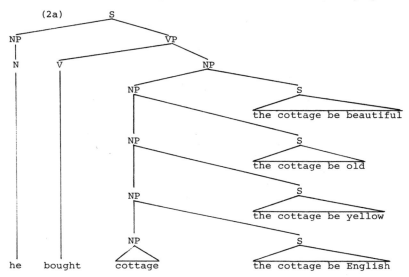

Relative reduction and modifier preposing would apply first to the deepmost embedded S, fronting 'English'. Next, 'yellow' is moved to the front of 'English', and so on. The surface structure of the object NP of (2) would look something like this:

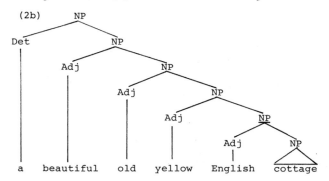

The details of the derivation of the underscored NP node are as follows:

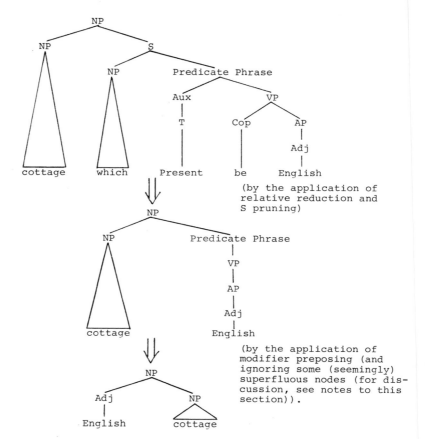

(by the application of
relative reduction and
S pruning)

(by the application of
modifier preposing (and
ignoring some (seemingly)
superfluous nodes (for discussion, see notes to this
section)).

Observe that the surface structure of the object NP contains a number of NP nodes. These are all required for pronominalization[1]:

----

1. In the light of the derivation considered here, we return to the
   formulation of the modifier preposing rule above, p. 350. In
   this, we have simply disregarded the fact that our PS-rules
   generate a determiner node and assumed that determiners are segmented from nouns and Chomsky-adjoined to the left of the
   dominating NP after preposing. Barring this assumption, it
   would seem to be impossible to provide a correct derived structure for NPs containing adjectival premodifiers. Thus sister-
   adjunction to the left of N (i.e. inserting the preposed modifier between a determiner and a noun under the immediate domination of the same NP) would make it difficult to account for
   the facts pertaining to pronominalization.

(3) He always wanted to buy NP_0, and finally he bought the
one out there[1]

(4) He was looking for NP_0, but found only a derelict one

(5) He bought NP_0, and I bought a beautiful new one

(6) He bought NP_0, and I bought a beautiful old green one

(7) He bought NP_0, and I bought a beautiful old yellow French
one

In each of these sentences, 'one' replaces an NP (see also notes
to section IV.G.18).

IV.G.14.6. Constraints on NP movement

Relativization involves the movement of an NP node and this
operation is subject to a number of constraints[2].

1. The sentential subject constraint. This applies to a structure like the following:

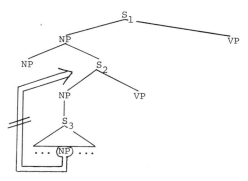

An example would be

(1) ✱ (the book (_which (it (that my mother didn't read
S_1 S_2 NP S_3
(NP))   ) annoyed me) was interesting)
S_3 NP S_2 S_1

in which the encircled NP has been relativized and moved out of an
S dominated by an NP (a subject sentence) which is itself immediately dominated by an S.

----

1. In each of the examples, NP_0 stands for 'a beautiful old yellow
English cottage'.

2. For the constraints discussed in this section, see Ross, 1967,
Chapter 4 and references cited on p. 224.

Observe now that (1) may undergo extraposition:

(2) The book which it annoyed me that my mother didn't read
was interesting

(2) is perfectly grammatical. For (2) to be derived, the constraint
must be overcome. This can be done (a) by means of the cyclic principle, or (b) by means of rule-ordering[1].

(a) Extraposition is a cyclic rule. On the S_2 cycle, it may or
may not apply. If it does apply, relativization can apply on the
top cycle. If it does not, the constraint blocks relativization.

(b) Extraposition is a last-cyclic rule (as is frequently assumed[2]). In that case, it must be ordered prior to relativization
(for this ordering, see Burt, 1971, 103ff.): S_3 must be moved out
of the NP to overcome the constraint[3].

Next, we consider again sentence (10) of section II.5. Relative to the constraint under discussion here, it has the following
bracketing:

(3) $(_{S_1}$ the firm $(_{S_2}$ which $($ it $($ that I didn't pay my bills $) _{S_3}$ $) _{S_3}$ NP

didn't worry (NP) $) _{S_2}$) has gone broke $) _{S_1}$

In other words, the derivation of the sentence is not blocked by the
constraint (the relativized NP is <u>not</u> moved out of S_3). Furthermore,
as we have seen, extraposition will derive from (3):

(4) The firm which it didn't worry that I didn't pay my bills
has gone broke

Ross proposes to block sentences like (3) by the following output
condition (<u>op. cit.</u>, 33):

Grammatical sentences containing an internal NP which exhaustively dominates S are unacceptable[4].

----

1. There might also be other possibilities. Thus the reader should
consult Ringen, 1972 and apply the proposals made there to the
problem at hand.

2. For some arguments, see Ross, 1967, Lakoff, 1968c, and McCawley,
1970b. It would be premature to discuss such arguments at this
point. See further below, section IV.G.18.4.

3. We are assuming here that relativization is also a last-cyclic
rule. Barring this assumption, the ordering argument would have
no force. This is especially clear if we embed (2) under a
governing sentence like 'I said that ...'.

4. Note that this output condition might also account for sentence
(14) of section IV.G.5. See also below, p. 370.

It is clear that (1) and (3) have much in common. Also, the relationship between (1) and (2), and between (3) and (4) shows us
once again the importance - in functional terms - of the extraposition rule.

    2. The complex NP constraint. According to this, no element
may be moved out of a sentence dominated by an NP with a lexical
head noun:

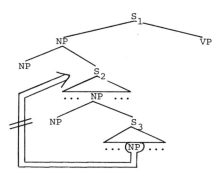

An example is (simplified to essentials):

    (5) ✳ (the car (which I hate ((the insinuation)   (that I
        S_1 S_2 NP NP   NP S_3
        have stolen (NP))   )) will remain in my garage)
                S_3 NP S_2 S_1

Note that if a nonlexical noun is substituted, the constraint does
not apply:

    (6) The car which I take it that people say that I have stolen
        will remain in my garage

    3. The coordinate structure constraint. This blocks relativiza-
tion on a single conjunct in a coordinate construction and applies
to a configuration like (see overleaf):
    The following example illustrates the constraint:

    (7) ✳ (I met the professor (whom I ((respect (NP)) and
        S_1 S_2 VP VP   VP
    (adore his wife))))
    VP   VP VP S_2 S_1

The constraints discussed briefly here apply to both relative

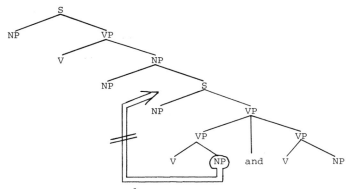

and interrogative clauses[1]. This is not surprising inasmuch as the derivation of the two kinds of clauses involves Wh-fronting. Indeed, the efforts of many scholars, not least Ross, have been directed to finding the common denominator of the two kinds of clauses[2].

Over and above the constraints, there is a general convention named by Ross **Pied Piping**, which concerns the movement of constituents in both interrogative and relative clauses. To illustrate the principle of this convention, we may look at the following rough deep structure configuration, which meets the SI of the relative rule (coreferentiality being indicated in the normal way by the referential indices):

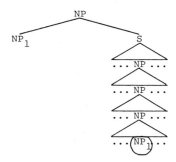

----

1. Reconsider now sentences (1)-(9) of section IV.G.11.4. The constraints might also account for sentences (20)-(22) of section IV.G.9.4.

2. See in this connection also such works as Chomsky, 1962, Kuroda, 1968a, and Postal, 1971, Chapter 10.

What the relative rule asserts is that the encircled NP should be
relativized and adjoined as the left daughter of the S node. The
Pied Piping convention states that one or more of the NPs dominating the encircled NP may be fronted along with the relativized
NP. For example, given a string like

> (8)   ((the house)   (I adore (the moss (on the straw
>   NP NP$_1$ NP$_1$ S   NP   NP
>
>   (of the roof   (of the house))))))
>   NP   NP$_1$ NP$_1$ NP NP NP S NP

which corresponds to the above tree, Pied Piping predicts the
following possibilities (the prepositions being for the moment
disregarded):

> (9) The house which I adore the moss on the straw of the
>   roof of ...
>
> (10) The house the roof of which I adore the moss on the
>   straw of ...
>
> (11) The house the straw of the roof of which I adore the
>   moss on ...
>
> (12) The house the moss on the straw of the roof of which
>   I adore ...

in which successively larger NPs have been moved. Piping is itself
subject to a number of constraints. Perhaps the most important
of these is the left branching constraint. Consider the following
interrogative sentences:

> (13) Whose mother's father's sister did you visit
>
> (14) * Whose did you visit mother's father's sister
>
> (15) * Whose mother's did you visit father's sister
>
> (16) * Whose mother's father's did you visit sister

Unconstrained, the piping convention would predict that (14)-(16)
are as grammatical as (13). This is obviously not the case. Piping
applies obligatorily to structures branching left. A very rough
underlying structure of (13) would be (see overleaf):
In this, the encircled NP is the one mentioned in the SI of the
WH-fronting rule. Nevertheless, the entire NP must be moved. This
was not the case in (8): in that the NPs branch to the right.

    Finally, we must touch briefly on the question of prepositions
in structures like (8). Let us choose a simpler set of examples:

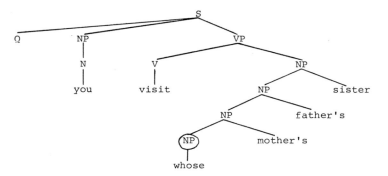

(17) The car which he arrived in was a wreck

(18) The car in which he arrived was a wreck

(19) The car which he had gone to sleep in the back seat of
was stolen

(20) The car the back seat of which he had gone to sleep in
was stolen

(21) The car in the back seat of which he had gone to sleep
was stolen

It is clear that Piping has applied to (20) and (21). The question
now is how to analyse the preposition 'in' in (18) and (21): if it
is dominated by a node PP:

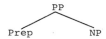

then the restriction of relativization in general and Piping in
particular to NPs does not stand up. Alternatively, it might be
argued that PP is a spurious category and that prepositional
phrases are indeed NPs. For example, as we suggested on p. 120,
prepositions might be generated by segmentalization transformations
from nouns and Chomsky-adjoined to the left of the dominating
NP[1]:

----

1. Cf. also the discussion of the status of 'by' in passive sentences in section IV.E.5.

The rule would apply to all NPs in deep structure. Some of the
prepositions would subsequently be deleted, notably those preceding
subject and object NPs. By this analysis, (18) would also be an
example of Piping[1].

   Returning now to the formulation of the Wh-fronting rule on
p. 322, we see that, given this analysis of PPs, we would no longer
have any need for including an optional Prep in the SI of the rule.
The NP in the fourth term would suffice. By the same token, we were
justified in not including a term Prep in the SI of the relative
rule (cf. above, p. 199).

   This approach, then, would simplify the statement of T-rules.
With respect to the _semantic_ explanation of prepositions, however,
it would not seem to be much of an improvement over the traditional
approach (cf. also below, section V.B.4).

IV.G.14.7. _Independent relative clauses_

   Let us begin by considering the pro-forms 'why', 'where',
'when', and 'how'.

   'Why' is unique in that, as a relative pronoun, it can have
only one antecedent, namely 'reason'[2]. Consider

   (1) Why he refused me was beyond me
   (2) * Why he refused was acceptable
   (3) The reason why he refused was acceptable
   (4) So this is why you dislike him so much

In (1) the clause is interrogative, not relative. (2), (3), and
(4) show that relative 'why' cannot occur in sentence-initial
position without its antecedent. Observe that in (3) a possible
variant for 'why' is 'for which'. The preposition 'for' is the
one which typically (perhaps the only one which) occurs with the
noun 'reason' - it is unmarked with respect to 'reason'. 'Why',
then, has the property of _incorporating_ an unmarked preposition
in itself[3] (cf. Huddleston, 1971 222ff.).

----

1. Cf. Jacobs and Rosenbaum, 1968, Chapter 18 and Postal, 1971,
   204ff. But compare also Jackendoff, 1973.

2. In 'the question why he did it still worries me', the 'why'-
   clause is not relative, but an embedded interrogative sentence.

3. Alternatively, we might say that 'why' obligatorily requires
   the deletion of an unmarked preposition. This would be in better
   harmony with the analysis of prepositions discussed in the preceding section.

'Where', 'when', and 'while' are less restricted with respect
to antecedent than 'why'. But they do require nouns having the features (+ Locality) ('where') and (+ Time) ('when' and 'while').
These three, too, have the property of incorporating an unmarked
preposition in themselves: 'in/at/on which' $\Longrightarrow$ 'where', 'at/in
which' $\Longrightarrow$ 'when', and 'during which' $\Longrightarrow$ 'while'. The interesting
point about these pro-forms is that they allow the deletion of the
antecedent with which they most frequently occur, namely the nouns
'place' and 'time'. Thus they can be said to provide a link between dependent and independent clauses. Furthermore, an unmarked
preposition governing the antecedent may be deleted along with its
object. Alternatively, the relative pronoun may be deleted. We can
thus obtain paradigms like

(5) I remember <u>the time</u> $\left\{ \begin{array}{l} \text{at which} \\ \text{when} \\ \emptyset \end{array} \right\}$ I was young and happy

(6) I remember when I was young and happy

(7) I told him (<u>at a time</u>) when it was too late

(8) I met him <u>in a place</u> $\left\{ \begin{array}{l} \text{in which} \\ \text{where} \\ \emptyset \end{array} \right\}$ neither of us had

been before

(9) I met him where neither of us had been before

(10) The robbery was committed <u>during the time</u> $\left\{ \begin{array}{l} \text{while} \\ \emptyset \end{array} \right\}$
the driver was changing wheels

(11) The robbery was committed while the driver was changing
wheels

In (6), (9), and (11), the pro-forms function as independent relatives.

It can sometimes be difficult to distinguish independent relative clauses from interrogative clauses. Thus the 'when'-clause
in the following sentence is ambiguous between the two underlying
structures indicated:

(12) He promised to tell me $\left\{ \begin{array}{l} \text{(a) at what time} \\ \text{(b) at the time at which} \end{array} \right. \hspace-1em \searrow \text{when} \right\}$
it happened

Note that only if 'when' is derived from (a) does (12) have a
pseudo-cleft counterpart:

(13) What he promised to tell me was when it happened

(13) is not ambiguous.

'How' is an independent relative proper in that it may never have an antecedent. It can occur in structures where it is unambiguously relative:

(14) How he manages to pass one examination after the other
     is simply marvellous

In (14) 'how' is the equivalent of 'the way in which'. In (15) the 'how'-clause is interrogative:

(15) How he manages to pass one examination after the other
     is the question everybody keeps asking themselves

Apart from the forms considered so far, the pronouns functioning as independent relatives are 'who', 'which' and 'what'. Of these, 'who' and 'which' are obligatorily[1], 'what' optionally accompanied by 'ever'.

Let us examine some of the arguments supporting the claim that these forms have antecedents, although they never show up on the surface. We concentrate on 'what'. Consider the following sentences:

(16) What I ate yesterday was delicious
(17) * What I wrote yesterday was delicious

Why is (17) ungrammatical (or at least somewhat odd)? Because selectional restrictions have been violated. The infringement is not against the restrictions holding between the predicative complement ('delicious') and the subject clause as a whole, but those holding between 'delicious' and 'what'. This suggests that underlying 'what' are two NPs: one is the subject of the matrix sentence, the other is the object of the embedded sentence. Since 'delicious' and 'write' have different selectional features, the ungrammaticality of (17) is due to the fact that relativization has taken place in spite of the coreferentiality condition - the subject of 'delicious' and the object of 'write' cannot be coreferential. Further evidence is provided by such sentences as

(18) What books Jane has <u>is</u> of no interest

----

1. There are a few exceptions to this such as 'you can marry who you like'. On the semantics of wh-ever forms, see Huddleston, 1971, 236ff.

(19) What books Jane has <u>are</u> of no interest

The 'what'-clause in (18) is interrogative. The singular form of
the verb indicates that the subject of the sentence is the whole
'what'-clause; this is corroborated by the fact that the clause
may be extraposed:

(20) It is of no interest what books Jane has

By contrast, the 'what'-clause' in (19) is relative. The plural
form of the verb indicates that the subject is 'books' modified
by a relative clause. Observe now that if we remove 'books' from
(18):

(21) What Jane has is of no interest

the sentence becomes ambiguous. It may mean that the speaker knows
what Jane has, but this is of no interest to him (relative - two
underlying NPs), or, alternatively, that the speaker is not interested in finding out about the nature of Jane's possessions (interrogative - one underlying NP, which is the object of 'have').

Although 'what' in (19) is relative, it is not necessarily
identical in meaning with 'the books which'. There is a tendency
for relative 'what' to carry overtones of depreciation whenever
it is followed by a lexical noun. This is perhaps most obvious in
a sentence like[1]:

(22) The squirrels are feasting on what walnuts the jays
        have left

This meaning is often overtly emphasized by an accompanying quantifier ('few' or 'little'):

(23) He spent what few shillings he had
(24) He spent what little money he had

IV.G.15. <u>Clefting</u>

IV.G.15.1. <u>'Ordinary' clefting</u>

By 'ordinary' clefting we mean sentences with the following
constituent structure:

A - B - C - D

----

1. Example borrowed from Schibsbye, 1965, 253.

in which A = 'it', B = a form of 'be', C = a constituent, and D =
a relative clause. An example is

    (1) It - was - John - who did it
        A - B - C -   D

    We might expect that a sentence like (1) should be derived
from

    (2) John did it

An immediate objection to this proposal would be that (1) and (2)
are not identical in meaning (provided (2) is uttered with a
neutral intonation). Therefore, according to the general rationale
of the standard theory, they should have different deep structures.
However, it would be possible to assume that 'John' in (2) may optionally be assigned a 'focus-marker' in deep structure, which, if
present, will obligatorily (a) result in the assignment of emphatic
stress to 'John', or (b) convert (2) into (1) (cf. also above, p.
303). By such an analysis, then

    (3) Mary gave the book to John

may be the source of such sentences as

    (4) It was Mary who gave the book to John
    (5) It was the book that Mary gave to John
    (6) It was to John that Mary gave the book

    However, aside from questions of meaning, there are strong syn-
tactic arguments against deriving (1) from (2). First of all, it
is obvious that the required T-rule would have to have considerable
structure-building power. In particular, it would have to insert
'it' and define it as an NP. That this is necessary is evidenced
by tags appended to such sentences as (1)[1]:

----

1. This counterargument would not be so strong today as it was
   prior to 1970: in his 1970-paper on nominalization (which was
   written a couple of years before it was published), Chomsky
   proposed that prelexical category symbols such as NP might
   profitably be analysed as feature complexes. Therefore, 'it'
   would be entered in the lexicon with the feature (+ NP); consequently, it could be inserted into a deep structure in the
   appropriate place without building structure arbitrarily.

(7) It was John who did it, wasn't _it_

No matter how we choose to analyse tags, the underscored 'it' in
(7) must be an NP on a par with 'he' in

(8) John did it, didn't _he_

or else generalization would be impossible[1]. Secondly, as pointed
out by Huddleston, 1971, 245f., (1) and (2) do not behave alike
syntactically. Consider the following two sentences:

(9) I watched John do it

(10) ✱ I watched it be John who did it

In (9), (2) has been embedded as the object of 'watch'. This is
possible because 'do' is a nonstative activity verb, and one can
watch an action being carried out. The ungrammaticality of (10),
then, in which (1) has been embedded in the same way, is due to
the fact that 'be' is not an activity verb. Rather, 'be' is _equative_
(cf. above, p. 102); it has idenficational function, and identification in this sense is not something that can be watched. This
would suggest that equative 'be' is too important semantically to
be introduced transformationally, as it would have to be if (1)
were to be derived from (2).

A possible deep structure of (1) would be, roughly:

(1a)

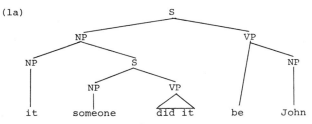

Assuming - with Huddleston, _loc. cit._ - that the predicative NP
imposes its selectional features on the head of the subject NP
('it'), the SI of the relative rule is met. After relativization,
the embedded sentence is adjoined as the right sister of VP by the
rule of _cleft extraposition_ (cf. Akmajian, 1970), and (1) is derived.

----

1. _Mutatis mutandis_, the same argument applies to 'there' in existential sentences: 'there's trouble brewing, isn't _there_':
   'there' must be an NP.

There are a number of structures closely akin to cleft sentences. Lees, 1963, 382 noted the difference between the following two sentences (in which the underlined words have emphatic stress):

(11) It's money that I <u>need</u>
(12) It's <u>money</u> that I need

In (11) 'it' has anaphoric function, i.e. it refers to some previous mention of money in the discourse (e.g. 'you certainly made good money on that bargain, didn't you'). 'Money' is the head noun of the relative clause. In (12) 'it' is not anaphoric[1]. The sentence may occur as a reply to a question like 'what is it that you need?' In (12), then, 'it' is the head noun of the relative clause and 'it ... that I need' is the subject of the sentence. In other words, it is only (12) that is a cleft sentence. (13) and (14) should also be carefully distinguished:

(13) It was a bad mistake that Peter left
(14) It was a scanty fortune that Peter left

There are two important differences between (13) and (14). First, 'that' in (13) is a complementizer, whereas in (14) it is a relative pronoun. Secondly, 'be' in (13) is attributive (cf. above, p. 102), whereas in (14) it is equative. In other words, (13) is derived by extraposition from

(15) That Peter left was a bad mistake

This rule is, as we know, optional. By contrast, cleft extraposition has applied obligatorily (but see notes) to the underlying structure of (14). It is not difficult to construct examples which are ambiguous because of these differences:

(16) It was $\left\{ \begin{array}{l} \text{a good job} \\ \text{a terrible mess} \end{array} \right\}$ that Peter left

We noted in section IV.G.14.4 that a relative subject could occasionally be deleted in a sentence beginning with 'it' and a form of 'be'. We can now be more precise: deletion of a relative subject can take place in cleft sentences in colloquial speech:

(17) It was John (who) did it

One of the most difficult things about cleft sentences is

----

1. Observe that only in (11) can 'that' be substituted for 'it'.

stating the restrictions on the clefted constituent in a non-ad-
hoc manner. A large variety of structures can be clefted, and
this in turn involves that relativization must be given a wider
scope in cleft sentences than in noncleft sentences. Certainly,
most NPs can be clefted, whatever their internal structure:

(18) It's the red-haired girl I met in London last year
     who is coming

(19) It's having been too gruff with him that worries me/that
     I regret

(20) ? It's for John never to be on time that irritates me[1]

To some extent, NPs governed by a preposition may be clefted out
of the prepositional phrase:

(21) It was $\left\{\begin{array}{l}\text{with a hammer} \\ \text{a hammer}\end{array}\right\}$ that the murderer had killed
     his victim (with)

(22) It was $\left\{\begin{array}{l}\text{on books} \\ \text{books}\end{array}\right\}$ that he spent most of his money (on)

But there are restrictions:

(23) It was $\left\{\begin{array}{l}\text{at dawn} \\ \text{✱ dawn}\end{array}\right\}$ that the wolf-pack launched their
     fiercest attack (✱ at)

(24) It is to a large extent $\left\{\begin{array}{l}\text{for fun} \\ \text{✱ fun}\end{array}\right\}$ that he studies
     archaeology (✱ for)

Of single-word adverbs, it would seem that those under the immediate domination of Predicate Phrase yield most readily to clefting:

(25) It was $\left\{\begin{array}{l}\text{yesterday} \\ \text{soon} \\ \text{there} \\ \text{here}\end{array}\right\}$ that I discovered it

Also adverbs of manner may frequently undergo clefting:

(26) The reason why I suspect him is that it was altogether
     too clumsily that he evaded my questions

Sentence adverbs cannot be clefted:

(27) ✱ It was $\left\{\begin{array}{l}\text{obviously} \\ \text{fortunately}\end{array}\right\}$ that he liked Mary

----

1. Stockwell et al., 1968, Vol. II, 806 point out that this sentence might be accounted for by Ross' output condition (quoted
   on. p. 358).

Some adverbial clauses may be clefted:

> (28) It was while she was shopping that someone pinched
> her purse
>
> (29) It is since she has quit drinking that Jane has become
> quite unapproachable

and some may not:

> (30) * It's although he wasn't there that he knows about it

Note

> (31) I began to worry $\left\{ \begin{array}{l} \text{as} \\ \text{because} \end{array} \right\}$ the child had not shown up
>
> (32) It was $\left\{ \begin{array}{l} \text{* as} \\ \text{because} \end{array} \right\}$ the child had not shown up that I
> began to worry

IV.G.15.2. Pseudo-clefting

In section IV.D.2 we examined a case of pseudo-clefting. As
we saw, the constituent structure of a pseudo-cleft sentence is

A - B - C

where A = a clause introduced by 'what', B = a form of equative
'be', and C = an NP.

Pseudo-cleft sentences should not be derived from the corresponding noncleft sentences for the same reasons as those discussed in the preceding section[1].

There are several difficulties about the analysis of pseudo-
cleft sentences. One of them concerns the source of the relative pronoun 'what'[2]. We suggested in section IV.D.2 that a
sentence like

> (1) What John bought at the auction was an old Ford car

----

1. We are treating clefting and pseudo-clefting as two unrelated
phenomena here. This is doubtless inadequate. Cleft and pseudo-
cleft sentences are often virtually synonymous:

> (a) What we need is political stability
> (b) It is political stability that we need

This being the case, it is reasonable to make the assumption
that there is a transformational relationship between them. For
arguments in support of the hypothesis that cleft sentences
should be derived from pseudo-cleft sentences, see Stockwell
et al., 1968, Vol. II, 839ff. and Akmajian, 1970.

2. Of course the source of 'what' in independent (nonpseudo-cleft)
relative clauses presents a similar problem.

might be derived from a structure of roughly the following kind:

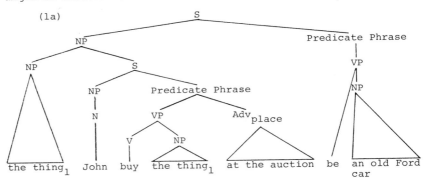

(1a)

'What', then, would be derived (optionally) from 'the thing which'.
However, this does not work too well in every case. Consider the
following sentences:

(2) $\left\{\begin{array}{l}\text{(a) The thing which}\\\text{(b) What}\end{array}\right\}$ John accidentally stumbled over

yesterday was the root of a tree

(3) $\left\{\begin{array}{l}\text{(a) } \ast \text{ The thing which}\\\text{(b) What}\end{array}\right\}$ they didn't consider at all

was an alternative theory which had been put forward

(4) $\left\{\begin{array}{l}\text{(a) The thing which}\\\text{(b) What}\end{array}\right\}$ the police found yesterday was

the conclusive piece of evidence

In (2) the predicative noun has the feature (- Abstract). This feature is also present in the head noun of the relative clause. The
ungrammaticality of (3a), then, is due to a selectional violation.
Seemingly (4) contradicts this. However, in (4a) 'be' is not
equative, but attributive: 'the thing' refers to some concrete
object of which 'the conclusive piece of evidence' is predicated.
(4b) is ambiguous between a pseudo-cleft and a nonpseudo-cleft
reading (the latter being synonymous with (4a)). This suggests that
the derivation of 'what' from 'the thing which' considered here
will not stand up unless the information be built into the grammar that the step from 'the thing which' to 'what' (alternatively
perhaps 'that which' (which is substitutable for 'what' and which
would also make (3a) grammatical)) is obligatory just in case the
predicative noun is (+ Abstract).

Another problem relates to reflexivization. Thus in

(5) What John saw in the mirror was himself

the reflexive pronoun is derived from a deep-structure occurrence
of 'John' which is coreferential with the subject of 'saw'. But
these two NPs do not occur in the same simplex sentence. Consequently, the most important constraint on reflexivization is violated
(cf. above, p. 201). However, as we shall see in section IV.G.18.6,
the simplex sentence constraint on reflexivization causes trouble
in a number of cases, and therefore the violation of it in a sentence like (5) may not be sufficient evidence to invalidate the
analysis of pseudo-cleft sentences illustrated in (1a).

The following sentence poses a more serious problem:

(6) What I shall do is warn him

The difficulty about (6) is determining the origin of 'do' and
defining the categorial status of 'warn him'. If all pseudo-clefted
constituents are NPs, then 'warn him' is an NP[1]. One solution that
immediately comes to mind is that which Thompson proposed in connection with relative clauses (cf. above, p. 346): 'do' has been
inserted preceding an activity verb. However, this will work only
if 'do' and 'warn him' are brought into immediate contact in the
deep structure. In other words, it will work only if 'warn him'
is generated in the embedded sentence to the left of 'be' (i.e.
the main verb). 'Do' would then be inserted immediately in front
of 'warn him', which in turn would be recategorized as an NP and
shifted to the right of 'be' (replacing, perhaps, a dummy symbol
under the domination of a node 'Predicate' (cf. Chomsky, 1970 (in
Jacobs and Rosenbaum, 1970) 209)). But this would not be enough.
There is no NP in the embedded sentence on which relativization
can operate. So the NP 'the thing' must be inserted as a new object of 'do'. Only then can (6) come to the surface.

That 'do' can only be inserted preceding nonstative activity
verbs is evidenced by such sentences as

(7) I didn't know the answer

(8) * What I didn't do was know the answer

----

1. This is obviously a circular argument. However, it seems reasonably clear that 'warn him' in (6) is indeed an NP functioning
   as the object of 'do'. Note for example that 'warn him' can occur as an independent reply to a questioned NP: 'What will you
   do about it?' - 'Warn him'.

(9) I cannot conceive how you could say such a thing
(10) * What I cannot do is conceive how you could say such
     a thing

Such evidence, then, would suggest that the analysis illustrated in (1a) may not stand up and that the pseudo-clefted constituent (i.e. C in the formula cited at the outset of this section) should be generated in the embedded sentence and extracted
by a T-rule. This approach, furthermore, would have the advantage
of resolving the problem relating to reflexivization noted above.

With these scanty remarks, we leave the subject. The analysis
of phenomena relating to clefting still constitutes a highly controversial and unsettled area of the grammar.

IV.G.16. Complementation

IV.G.16.1. Introductory remarks

We have already examined various kinds of sentence embedding:
embedded interrogative clauses, comparative clauses, and relative
clauses. In this section we shall direct the attention to sentences
embedded as complements of nouns[1] (by PS-rule 11):

(1)

as complements of verbs (by PS-rule 6):

(2)

and as complements of adjectives (by PS-rule 8):

(3)

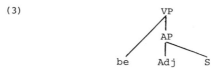

IV.G.16.2. The rules

It will be convenient to review briefly the array of T-rules

----

1. Embedded interrogative clauses form a subset of this type.

required for the adequate description of the complementation system in English. Most of the rules have been mentioned before:

(1) Complementizer insertion[1], which inserts one of the complementizers 'for - to', 'Poss - ing', or 'that' under certain
statable conditions.

(2) Extraposition.

(3) It deletion, which obligatorily deletes 'it' unless the
complement clause has been extraposed.

(4) Equi NP deletion, which was formulated above, p. 209[2].

(5) It replacement. So far, we have discussed this rule under
the name subject-to-object raising (formulated on p. 204). It replacement can also take the form of subject-to-subject raising, or
object-to-subject raising (cf. above, p. 338).

(6) Complementizer deletion, which may delete the first part
of the 'Poss - ing' complementizer or 'that'.

(7) The double-preposition deletion rule, which deletes 'for'
if this has been left behind in a position immediately before 'to',
i.e. in the ungrammatical string 'for - to'.

In addition to these seven rules, a number of further rules
are pertinent to the analysis, e.g. the passive rule, reflexivization, and there insertion.

IV.G.16.3. On the distinction between NP-complementation and
           VP-complementation

Recall sentences (5)-(8) of section I.5.4:

(1) John expected (for) the doctor to examine Helen
(2) John expected (for) Helen to be examined by the doctor
(3) John compelled (* for) the doctor to examine Helen
(4) John compelled (* for) Helen to be examined by the doctor

Note first of all that, whereas we may optionally have 'for' in
(1) and (2) (but see below, section IV.G.16.5), this is not pos-

----

1. In this exposition we have opted for the transformational insertion of complementizers (following Rosenbaum, 1967). For a
   different approach, see Bresnan, 1970. We return to complementizers in section IV.G.16.5 below.

2. In the formulation of the rule, we disregarded the control problem, i.e. the question of precisely with which NP in the matrix
   sentence the embedded subject NP is identical. We will not go
   into the details of that problem. The reader is referred to
   Rosenbaum, 1967, 17ff. and Postal, 1970b.

sible in (3) and (4). This is perhaps an indication that (1) and
(3) have different structures. The reason for the ungrammaticality of 'for' in (3) and (4) might be that the constituent break
between 'compelled' and the following NP is radically different
from that between 'expected' and the following NP. Observe further
that, whereas (1) has a pseudo-cleft counterpart:

(5) What John expected was for the doctor to examine Helen

(3) does not:

(6) * What John compelled was for the doctor to examine Helen

This suggests that, whereas 'for the doctor to examine Helen' in
(1) is an NP, this is not the case in (3) (indeed, in (3), it is
perhaps not even a constituent). Further evidence that this is a
correct conclusion is provided by passivization: (7)

(7) For the doctor to examine Helen was expected by John

is a grammatical (though stylistically not very felicitous) sentence, whereas (8)

(8) * For the doctor to examine Helen was compelled by John

is completely out. To this we may add the fact that, whereas (1)
and (2) are cognitively synonymous, (3) and (4) differ radically
in meaning. We might try to account for these facts by postulating
the following deep structures for (1) and (3) respectively (the
subscripts assigned to the nodes are for ease of reference with
respect to the transformations now to be discussed):

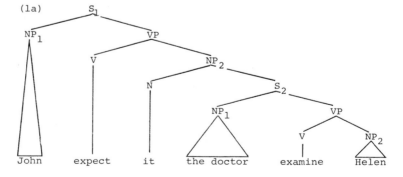

(3a)

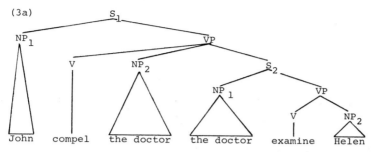

In other words, we claim (with Rosenbaum, 1967) that (1) is an instance of noun phrase complementation (S_2 is immediately dominated
by NP), whereas (3) shows verb phrase complementation (S_2 is immediately dominated by VP).

Let us now try to apply some of the rules discussed in the
preceding section to (1a) and (3a). First, we look at (1a). Let
us assume that we insert the complementizer 'that' as left daughter
of S_2:

(9) (John expect (it (that the doctor examine Helen)))
     S_1 NP S_2 S_2 NP S_1

From (9) it deletion may remove 'it', and the result is a grammatical sentence (provided, of course, that the auxiliary, which has
been ignored for reasons of simplicity, is materialized in some
form). Alternatively, the passive rule might apply on the S_2 cycle,
deriving

(10) (John expect (it (that Helen be examined by the
     S_1 NP S_2

     doctor)))
     S_2 NP S_1

Again, after the deletion of 'it', (10) is a fine sentence. But
the passive rule might also apply on the top cycle (S_1) (independently of whether or not the rule applies to S_2):

(11) ((it (that $\begin{Bmatrix} \text{the doctor examine Helen} \\ \text{Helen be examined by the doctor} \end{Bmatrix}$))
     S_1 NP_2 S_2 S_2 NP_2

     be expected (by John))
     NP_1 NP_1 S_1

From this, 'it' may be removed - or, alternatively, extraposition may derive

(12) (It be expected by John (that $\Big\{$ the doctor examine
    S_1 S_2 Helen be examined by

    Helen
    the doctor $\Big\}$)   )
                       S_2 S_1

Suppose now that, instead of 'that', we had inserted the complementizer 'for - to'[1]. The result might then be (1), (2), or (7).
However, it replacement (in the form subject-to-object raising)
might also apply, as roughly indicated in the following string:

(13) (John expect (it (for [the doctor] to examine
    S_1 NP S_2

    Helen)))
       S_2 NP S_1

or - after the application of the passive rule in S_2:

(14) (John expect (it (for [Helen] to be examined by
    S_1 NP S_2

    the doctor)))
         S_2 NP S_1

After this operation 'for' is deleted by the double-preposition
deletion rule. The subject NPs of the embedded sentences of (13)
and (14) (deep-structure subject NP and derived subject NP respectively) have now been lifted into object position in the sentence
next above. Since there are now two 'independent' NPs in the matrix
sentence, passivization may apply without affecting the infinitival
complement, deriving from (13):

(15) (The doctor be expected by John (to examine Helen $)^2$)
    S_1 S_2 S_2 S_1

and from (14):

(16) (Helen be expected by John (to be examined by the
    S_1 S_2

    doctor $)^2$)
        S_2 S_1

----

1. For the moment, we will assume that 'for - to' is inserted _en bloc_.
2. Presumably, S_2 is pruned. We return to this in section IV.G.16.6.

Let us now turn to (3a). The only possible complementizer is
'for - to'. For (3) to be derived from (3a), equi NP deletion must
apply. It removes the subject NP of the embedded sentence under
identity with (in this case) the object NP in the matrix sentence.
After this, 'for' is obligatorily deleted. Observe that there is
nothing to prevent the passive rule from applying to S_2:

(17) * (John compel the doctor (for Helen to be examined
      S_1 S_2

     by the doctor))
             S_2 S_1

But if this happens, equi NP deletion, which operates on the S_1
cycle, blocks the derivation: the <u>subject</u> of S_2 is no longer identical with any NP of the matrix sentence. At first sight, it might
seem that the reason for the ungrammaticality of (17) is that equi
NP deletion should operate on the <u>deep-structure</u> subject of the embedded sentence. But (4) constitutes evidence that this is not the
case. A possible deep structure for (4) is:

(4a)

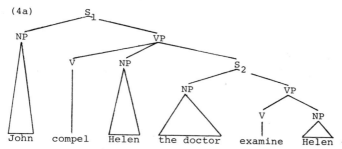

In (4a) equi NP deletion blocks the derivation on the S_1 cycle if
S_2 has <u>not</u> undergone the passive rule. In other words, equi deletes
the <u>derived</u> subject in S_2[1]. In (4), then, 'Helen' is the object of
'compel', whereas in (3) 'the doctor' is the object. The reason
(or perhaps rather one reason), therefore, why 'for' is ungrammatical in (3) and (4) - although seemingly inserted in the same
place as in (1) and (2) - is that it occurs between a transitive
verb and its (nonsentential) object. As a final piece of evidence

----

1. Recall that we have seen cases where <u>only</u> the derived subject
   can be deleted: '* I shouted to go'/'<u>I</u> shouted to be left in
   peace' (cf. above, p. 209f.).

for the viability of this analysis, consider the fact that the
object NP of both (3) and (4) may be shifted by the passive rule:

 (18) The doctor was compelled by John to examine Helen

 (19) Helen was compelled by John to be examined by the doctor

In summary, then, we may conclude that (1) and (2) have identical
deep structures, that (1) and (3) have different deep structures,
and that also (3) and (4) have different deep structures.

IV.G.16.4. Factivity

In an important article, "Fact", Kiparsky and Kiparsky argue
that the distinction between _factive_ and _nonfactive_ predicates is
an essential dimension of NP complementation.

Semantically, the distinction between the two kinds of predicates may be defined in terms of presuppositions. Factive predicates (verbs and adjectives) require that the speaker presupposes
that the semantic content of the embedded clause is true or factual, whereas with nonfactive predicates no such presupposition exists: the speaker merely asserts his _belief_ in the truth value of
the clause (op. cit., (in Bierwisch and Heidolph, 1970) 147f.).
The Kiparskys argue that this distinction should be represented in
the deep structures of sentences and would, accordingly, derive
sentences containing factive and nonfactive predicates from (a) and
(b) respectively:

(a)   NP   (b)   NP

fact   S   S

In this exposition we cannot follow this proposal inasmuch as we
have opted for the deep structure analysis of 'it' (cf. section
IV.A.8) - though for no strong reasons. What we _can_ say is that
a factive predicate may cooccur in deep structure with an NP whose
head noun is 'fact', whereas a nonfactive predicate may not. Consider now the following examples:

 (1) $\left\{ \begin{matrix} \text{The fact} \\ \emptyset \end{matrix} \right\}$ that a sentence consists of a subject and

   a predicate is well known

 (2) I have disregarded $\left\{ \begin{matrix} \text{the fact} \\ \emptyset \end{matrix} \right\}$ that he is your lawful

   heir

(3) $\left\{ \begin{array}{l} \text{\textasteriskcentered\ The fact} \\ \emptyset \end{array} \right\}$ that he was present was improbable

(4)   I doubt $\left\{ \begin{array}{l} \text{\textasteriskcentered\ the fact} \\ \emptyset \end{array} \right\}$ that he will go

They show 'well known' and 'disregard' to be factive, 'improbable'
and 'doubt' nonfactive predicates. A fairly reliable test of factivity, then, is the option between 'the fact that S' and 'that S'.
They are synonymous.

Further syntactic evidence of the relevance of the distinction to the complementation system is provided by the rules of
extraposition and it replacement (in the version subject-to-subject
raising). Consider the following sentences (of which the first contains a factive, the second a nonfactive predicate):

(5) $\left\{ \begin{array}{l} \text{The fact} \\ \emptyset \end{array} \right\}$ that the predicate is factive is relevant

(6) It seems that factivity is relevant

In (5) 'it' has been deleted ($\emptyset$). Alternatively, extraposition might
derive

(7) It is relevant that the predicate is factive

In (6) extraposition has applied obligatorily. It seems to be the
case that extraposition of a subject clause is obligatory if the
predicate is intransitive and nonfactive (other examples would be
'happen', 'appear', 'turn out', 'come to pass', etc.). Extraposition is also obligatory with nonfactive adjectival predicates:

(8) It is $\left\{ \begin{array}{l} \text{likely} \\ \text{sure} \\ \text{certain} \end{array} \right\}$ that factivity is relevant

In other words, obligatory extraposition of a subject clause is
predictable from nonfactivity.

(8) and (7) have identical surface structures. However, (8),
but not (7), may undergo subject-to-subject raising[1]:

(9) Factivity is $\left\{ \begin{array}{l} \text{likely} \\ \text{sure} \\ \text{certain} \end{array} \right\}$ to be relevant

(10) \textasteriskcentered\ The predicate is relevant to be factive

So, again, an important syntactic rule seems to be predictable
from nonfactivity.

----

1. We return to this rule in section IV.G.16.6.

Factivity is also closely interrelated with it replacement in
the version subject-to-object raising: it seems to be the case
that - with a few exceptions - the rule operates only with nonfactive predicates:

(11) I proved that John was wrong

(12) I proved John to be wrong

(13) I preferred for you to be there

(14) I preferred you to be there

(15) I wish for you to have all the best

(16) I wish you to have all the best

(17) He finally comprehended that his plan had failed

(18) * He finally comprehended his plan to have failed

(19) He regretted that this had taken place

(20) * He regretted this to have taken place

'Prove', 'prefer', and 'wish' are nonfactives and allow subject-to-
object raising, 'comprehend' and 'regret' are factives and disallow
the rule[1].

Finally, we will consider the rule of vacuous extraposition
from object. Suppose that we accept that this rule effects a structural change as described in section IV.A.8. In that case, it would
seem that the operation can be made contingent on the factive-nonfactive parameter in the following way (cf. Stockwell et al., 1968,
Vol. II, 563)[2]: the rule is generally optional with factive predicates; if it fails to apply, it deletion applies, and vice versa[3]:

(21) I $\left\{ \begin{array}{l} \text{deplore} \\ \text{resent} \\ \text{don't mind} \end{array} \right\}$ (it) that you object to my trying again

----

1. For subject-to-object raising, see also section IV.E.7 and notes
   on p. 224. It should be emphasized that not all linguists would
   be agreed that verbs like 'prefer' and 'wish' belong to the
   class of raising verbs. See for example the classification of
   verbs in Akmajian and Heny, 1975, 346ff. Postal, 1974, section
   4.16 presents a number of arguments that such verbs form a special subclass of raising verbs. I have followed Postal's analysis
   (cf. the discussion of the 'prefer' sentences on p. 208).

2. We are restricting the attention here to clauses introduced by
   the complementizer 'that'. We shall see in section IV.G.16.6
   that vacuous extraposition, which was first suggested by
   Rosenbaum, 1967, also plays an important part with respect to
   'for - to'-clauses.

3. For a different explanation of 'it' in sentences like (21), see
   Kiparsky and Kiparsky, op. cit., 166 and below, p. 445.

With nonfactive predicates, the rule does not apply; hence it deletion applies[1]:

(22) I $\left\{\begin{array}{l}\text{assume}\\\text{suppose}\\\text{claim}\\\text{conclude}\\\text{fancy}\end{array}\right\}$ (* it) that you are the only lawful heir

IV.G.16.5. The complementizers

In Rosenbaum's analysis of the complementation system, the complementizer insertion rule is the first rule to operate (on the cycle immediately above the embedded sentence). As regards the 'for - to' complementizer, he claims that 'for' is <u>always</u> present in deep structure. It may optionally be deleted by the complementizer deletion rule[2], unless the subject NP has been removed from the embedded sentence either by equi NP deletion or by it replacement, in which case the rule is obligatory:

(1) John persuaded Jane for Jane to go
(2) John persuaded Jane (* for) to go
(3) I expect for John to be present
(4) I expect John (* for) to be present

In this exposition, we will take a different approach, which, again, is inspired by the Kiparskys. In addition to the factive-nonfactive distinction, they incorporate in the grammar a feature (Emotive), for which predicates may be specified + or -. If a predicate has the feature (+ Emotive), it expresses "the subjective value of a proposition rather than knowledge about it or its truth value" (<u>op. cit</u>., 169). It is argued that this feature determines the occurrence of 'for': 'for' is inserted with (+ Emotive) predicates. If, once inserted, 'for' is left behind in front of 'to' because of the operation of equi NP deletion or it replacement, it is deleted by the double-preposition rule[2].

The analysis proposed by the Kiparskys has the unquestionable

----

1. There are exceptions. Thus the predicate in 'I take it that you will help me' is nonfactive. Nevertheless, extraposition is obligatory.

2. In Rosenbaum's rule system, complementizer deletion also accounts for the deletion of 'for' from the string 'for - to'. Since we have opted for a different analysis of 'for', we must refer this operation to the domain of the double-preposition deletion rule (for which, see also below, section IV.G.16.8).

advantage that it attempts to provide a semantic explanation of
the presence of 'for' in the surface structure of some sentences.
However, grammaticality judgments are sometimes difficult to make.
For example, the Kiparskys (unlike Rosenbaum, 1967, 69 (but cf.
Postal, 1974, 177)) would, presumably, characterize (5) as ungram-
matical:

(5) I expect for John to come

Postal, loc. cit also cites the following examples (in a different
context):

(6) ✱ I want for you to love me
(7) I wish for you to succeed

But, given the emotive nonemotive parameter, it is difficult to see
why 'want' should be less emotive than 'wish' (not all writers
would star (6) (cf. for example Lakoff, 1970a, 51)). Nevertheless,
even though judgments may vary in some cases, the features (± Emotive) seem to make the correct predictions in a number of cases.
Consequently, we will adopt this analysis.

The PS-rules cannot generate any sentence - embedded or otherwise - without an Aux node. Suppose now that we regard 'to' in

(8) I want to come

as a transformationally inserted Aux replacement morpheme. We can
say, then, that whenever a subject NP and a verb do not undergo the
agreement rule, 'to' replaces the Aux (cf. above, p. 274)[1]. This
happens (a) when 'for' is inserted in the environment of a (+ Emotive) predicate and governs the subject NP - a government relation
which is overtly marked only in personal pronouns in English:

(9) He wished for me to be happy
(10) He wished for his wife to be happy

(b) after it replacement:

(11) He wished me to be happy
(12) He is likely to fail

or (c) after equi NP deletion:

(13) He persuaded me to go

----

1. This is a somewhat ad-hoc statement. The problem here is the precise status of the agreement rule in the grammar. It is likely
   that, in the last analysis, it should be stated as a derivational
   constraint. See also below, p. 446.

If neither for insertion, it replacement, nor equi NP deletion has applied (for the moment, we disregard the 'Poss - ing' complementizer) to-replace-Aux cannot apply: the auxiliary, in particular Tense, must be phonologically realized, and the only possible complementizer is 'that'.

The statement that 'to' replaces Aux is not quite correct. Consider the following sentences:

(14) I expect to be hearing from you

(15) He wants to have done with it

It is evident from these that the progressive and perfective aspects may be present in embedded sentences. These, of course, are dominated by Aux in deep structure, but they are not replaced. As against this, the modal verbs never occur in nonfinite embedded sentences (i.e. they occur only with the complementizer 'that'). There are cases in which it seems to be fairly clear that 'to' must have replaced a modal as well. Rosenbaum, op. cit., 31 cites the following examples:

(16) I expect John to go

(17) Is it possible for John to leave early

and remarks that "the modal 'will' is, in some sense at least, an implicit aspect of the interpretation of" a sentence like (16), and that "similarly, the modal 'can' is an aspect of the interpretation of the complement sentence" in (17). "On the other hand, in the great majority of the predicate complement constructions there is no modal interpretation". Typically, then, 'to' replaces only Tense, as in[1]

(18) He continued to work

derived from[2]

----

1. In many cases (cf. (19)), Perf must be inserted if the embedded sentence contains Past. Thus from 'I expect it he Past say that' we obtain 'I expect him to have said that'. For some discussion of further tense constraints holding between the matrix sentence and the embedded clause, see Stockwell et al., 1968, Vol. II, 594ff.

2. This derivation is motivated by there insertion. That is, we can have a sentence like 'there continued to be some uneasiness among the students'. For details, see the derivation of sentence (24) of section IV.G.16.6 (below, p. 391f.).

(19) ((it (he Past work)) Past continue)
    S_1 NP S_2 S_2 NP S_1

In addition to to-replace-Aux, we need a rule to delete 'to'.
The operation of this rule is governed by a rule feature (+ to deletion) in a small subset of verbs, notably verbs of perception
and 'make' and 'let':

(20) I $\left\{\begin{array}{l} \text{saw} \\ \text{heard} \\ \text{watched} \\ \text{let} \\ \text{made} \end{array}\right\}$ him come

In other words, 'to' is claimed to be present at some stage of the
derivation of (20). This is not unreasonable, considering the fact
that 'to' shows up in the passive with many of these verbs:

(21) He was $\left[\begin{array}{l} \text{seen} \\ \text{made} \\ \text{observed} \\ \text{heard} \\ \text{* watched} \end{array}\right]$ to $\left[\begin{array}{l} \text{sneak into the garden} \\ \text{comply} \\ \text{behave strangely} \\ \text{sing in the bathroom}^1 \\ \text{dig a hole in the yard} \end{array}\right]$

Some verbs are specified (x to deletion). Examples are 'know' and
'help':

(22) I have never known him (to) tell a lie

(23) I helped her (to) wash the dishes

There remains the 'Poss - ing' complementizer. When this is
inserted, the possessive affix is adjoined to the subject of the
embedded sentence, and 'ing' replaces the Aux (except, again, progressive and perfective aspect). Consider such sentences as

(24) I hate to leave you

(25) I hate leaving you

(26) He continued to write

(27) He continued writing

(28) Undoubtedly, your having convinced him so easily is a
     surprise to most people

----

1. Postal, 1974, 316, note 16 draws attention to a curious constraint
   with 'hear': the verb in the embedded sentence must denote a
   verbal action:

       (a) Everyone heard John crack his joints
       (b) * John was heard by everyone to crack his joints
       (c) Everyone heard John burp
       (d) * John was heard by everyone to burp

(24) and (25) show an option between infinitivalization and gerundivization[1]. In (24) equi has applied; subsequently, 'for' has been
deleted. In (26) subject-to-subject raising has applied, but 'for'
has not been deleted (since 'continue' is (- Emotive) 'for' was
never there in the first place). In (25) equi has applied. In (27)
subject-to-subject raising has removed the subject NP of the embedded clause and 'Poss' has been deleted. (28) shows the presence
of perfective aspect. If the subject in the embedded clause is
not identical to an NP in the matrix sentence, the complementizer
deletion rule may delete 'Poss':

(29) I disliked $\left\{ \begin{array}{l} \text{John's} \\ \text{John} \end{array} \right\}$ deriding your efforts

Generally, the deletion of Poss in such cases is optional. However,
there are a number of complex constraints at work here. For example,
deletion often seems unnatural in an embedded subject clause. Compare with (29):

(30) $\left\{ \begin{array}{l} \text{John} \\ \text{John's} \end{array} \right\}$ deriding your efforts was a scandal

Gerundivization may apply to both factive and nonfactive
predicates, although only factive predicates allow the full range
of gerundial constructions (cf. Kiparsky and Kiparsky, op. cit.,
144ff.); this provides further syntactic evidence of the relevance
of the distinction to the complementation system.

Some nonfactive predicates allow only the gerund in the embedded sentence:

(31) He avoided seeing me
(32) I enjoy playing tennis
(33) He stopped smoking

They must be marked by a rule feature (+ gerund).

Mention should be made of the generic use of gerunds:

(33) Smoking is unhealthy
(34) Driving is dangerous

----

1. There are subtle semantic distinctions: (25) is a general statement, whereas (24) is more appropriate on a specific occasion.
Note further that with some verbs deletion of the subject may
lead to ambiguity: a sentence like 'I hate swearing' may mean
(a) 'I hate it when someone swears', or (b) 'I hate my own
swearing'. 'I hate to swear', again, would refer to a specific
occasion. It is arguable that, strictly speaking, such semantic facts make the transformational insertion of complementizers
incompatible with the KP-hypothesis: complementizer insertion
affects meaning, at least in some cases.

They have an understood generic subject which is obligatorily deleted by the <u>generic subject deletion rule</u>. The deleted subject
must have the feature (+ Human) as may be seen from[1]:

    (35) Eloping with a girl is not much in fashion these days
    (36) * Elapsing is a sad fact
    (37) Time's elapsing is a sad fact

IV.G.16.6. <u>It replacement, equi NP deletion, and S pruning</u>

It replacement, as we have seen, raises an NP from the embedded sentence into the sentence next above in the tree, in which
it replaces an 'it'. The most wide-spread version of this rule is
that which raises the subject NP of the embedded sentence to object position in the sentence next above. There are various arguments in support of the existence of this rule. One of them has
already been considered (cf. sentences (15) and (16) of section
IV.G.16.3), namely the so-called <u>second passive</u> (a term coined
by Lees). Let us consider one further example; given the sentence

    (1) Everybody present acknowledged that Jane was a beauty

the passive rule, which, we recall, requires two NPs in its SI, may
derive

    (2) That Jane was a beauty was acknowledged by everybody
        present

or

    (3) Jane was acknowledged by everybody present to be a beauty

(3) receives its most natural explanation if it is assumed that
'Jane' has been lifted out of the embedded sentence in (1) prior
to the application of the passive rule on the top cycle.

A second argument favouring this analysis is reflexivization.
Recall the constraint on this rule that it must apply to two co-
referential NPs in the same simplex sentence (cf. above, p. 201).
Consider now the following sentences:

    (4) John$_1$ bought a house which suited him$_1$

----

1. Adapted from Stockwell et al., 1968, Vol. II, 592. Observe that
   the ambiguity mentioned in the note on the preceding page stems
   from this: either a generic subject has been deleted, or the
   equi NP deletion rule has applied.

(5) She₁ believes that she₁ is a saint

    (5) She$_1$ believes that she$_1$ is a saint
    (6) She believes herself to be a saint
    (7) I don't want my children to despise me

The constraint on reflexivization predicts that (4) and (5) are
grammatical because the two coreferential NPs aré not in the same
simplex sentence. The constraint also accounts for (6) <u>if</u> it is assumed that the coreferential subject of the embedded sentence has
been raised prior to reflexivization. (7), however, presents a problem. Recall the S pruning convention which deletes a nonbranching
S node and the cyclic application of it replacement and reflexivization in that order (cf. section IV.E.7). If these principles are
maintained, the derivation of (7) will be roughly as follows:

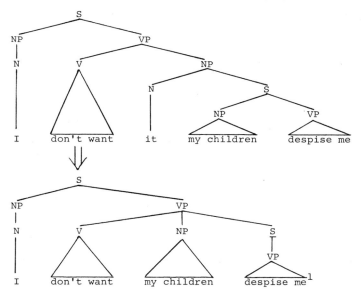

If the underscored S node is pruned at this stage, 'I' and 'me' are

----

1. The insertion of 'to' is immaterial to the argument. Since it is
   immediately dominated by Aux, it is not a daughter of S. S, therefore, does not branch even after the insertion of 'to'. However,
   in a different approach to complementizer insertion, the problem
   discussed here does not arise. Thus, if 'to' were immediately
   dominated by S, S would branch and consequently not be pruned
   (cf. the trees in Jacobs and Rosenbaum, 1968, 187ff.).

in the same simplex sentence, and reflexivization should apply on
the top cycle, but it does not. The derivation of (7), then, involves a paradox with respect to the interaction of it replacement,
reflexivization, and S pruning (we return to this point at the end
of this section).

Subject-to-object raising must be governed by a rule feature
(+ subject-to-object raising) in the matrix predicate. Only when
the predicate is inserted with this feature does the rule apply.
In this way we can derive both (5) and (6). Some predicates like
'consider' obligatorily require subject-to-object raising:

(8) * I considered that you were my friend

(9) I considered you to be my friend

Conversely, some disallow (or at least show restrictions with respect to) the rule:

(10) I alleged that he was the culprit

(11) * I alleged him to be the culprit

(12) I hope that you will be happy

(13) I hope for you to be happy

(14) * I hope you to be happy

If the subject of the embedded sentence is existential 'there'
(which has been transformationally inserted on the lower cycle) the
rule seems to work:

(15) The police alleged there to have been a murder

(16) ? I hope there to be a lot of people around tonight

Next, we turn to subject-to-subject raising. Let us consider
again the deep structure of sentence (2) of section IV.D.2. The
labelled bracketed string representing the structure of that sentence looks like this (cf. the tree on p. 132):

(17) ((it ((it (Peter be there)) be certain))
S_1 NP S_2 NP S_3 S_3 NP S_2 NP

seem)
S_1

The proper analysis of this sentence meets the SI of the raising
rule as it was formulated on p. 204. The rule is cyclic[1]. On the
S_2 cycle, 'Peter' replaces 'it' in S_2 and 'be there' is adjoined
----

1. On the cyclic nature of the rule, see Postal, 1974, 267ff. See,
   however, also Grinder, 1972.

as right sister of 'be certain' (i.e. right daughter of the VP of
S_2):

(18) ((it (Peter be certain be there)) seem)
     S_1 NP S_2 S_2 NP S_1

On the top cycle, the same operations apply, deriving

(19) Peter seems to be certain to be there

Note that (19) is synonymous with (20), in which the relevant subject-predicate relationships are more transparent (bearing in mind
the operation of extraposition)[1]:

(20) It seems that it is certain that Peter is there

Also a sentence like

(21) He began to sing madrigals

involves it replacement, the deep structure being something like
this[2]:

(21a)

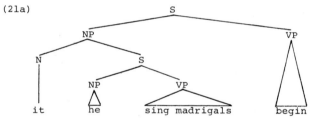

Is there any syntactic argument for this? Yes: there insertion.
Recall that in our discussion of that rule in section IV.G.8, we
pointed out that it applied almost exclusively with 'be'. Certainly,
(23) is ungrammatical:

(22) A riot began to break loose late in the evening

(23) * There began to break loose a riot late in the evening

But now observe that

(24) There began to be some understanding of the problem

----

1. (20) has the same deep structure as (19). Only, 'that' has been
   inserted instead of 'to'.

2. For detailed discussion of the verb 'begin', see Perlmutter,
   1970b. Consult also Huddleston, 1969, 258ff.

is perfectly all right: 'there' must be inserted (obligatorily) in
the embedded sentence as the subject of 'be', shifting 'some understanding of the problem' to the end of the sentence; the derivation is[1]:

$$(\quad (\text{ it } (\text{ some understanding of the problem be }) \quad) \quad \text{begin} \quad)$$
$$S_1 \text{ NP } \quad S_2 \qquad\qquad\qquad\qquad\qquad\qquad\qquad\quad S_2 \text{ NP} \qquad\quad S_1$$

                         ⇓   by there insertion

$$(\quad (\text{ it } (\text{ there be some understanding of the problem }) \quad)$$
$$S_1 \text{ NP } \quad S_2 \qquad\qquad\qquad\qquad\qquad\qquad\qquad\qquad\qquad S_2 \text{ NP}$$

begin)
         S_1 ⇓   by it replacement

$$(\text{ there begin to be some understanding of the problem })$$
$$S_1 \qquad\qquad\qquad\qquad\qquad\qquad\qquad\qquad\qquad\qquad\qquad S_1$$

By the same token, subject-to-subject raising has applied to (21a).
The rule would also derive from (21a):

     (25) He began singing madrigals

if, instead of 'to', the 'Poss - ing' complementizer were inserted[2].

----

1. The reader should now reconsider sentences (4) and (5) of section IV.E.9 and attempt to provide a derivation for them.

2. The rule which accounts for the two kinds of raising was stated
   in this form by Lakoff, 1968c, 28f. It has generally been assumed
   that subject-to-object raising and subject-to-subject raising
   should be viewed as a unitary phenomenon. Rosenbaum, who, as
   noted on p. 204, note 1, first formulated the rule, tried to
   achieve this by making all instances of raising dependent on
   the prior application of extraposition. To make this work, it
   was necessary to have extraposition apply vacuously in some
   cases. For example, 'John wants Jane to go' would have roughly
   the following derivation:

     (a) $(\text{ John want } (\text{ it } (\text{ Jane go }) \quad) \quad)$ ⟹
          $S_1 \qquad\qquad\quad \text{NP} \quad S_2 \qquad\quad S_2 \text{ NP } S_1$

by vacuous extraposition:

     (b) $(\text{ John want } (\text{ it }) \quad (\text{ Jane go }) \quad)$ ⟹
          $S_1 \qquad\qquad\quad \text{NP} \quad \text{NP } S_2 \qquad S_2 S_1$

by it replacement (subject-to-object raising):

     (c) John wants Jane to go

By contrast, the derivation of a sentence like 'John happened
to be there' would not involve vacuous extraposition, but extraposition proper:

Lastly, we will consider yet another version of it replacement: object-to-subject raising[1]. To illustrate this, we return to sentences (3) and (4) of section IV.A.4:

(26) John was reluctant to leave

(27) John was difficult to leave

They have the following deep structures:

(26a)

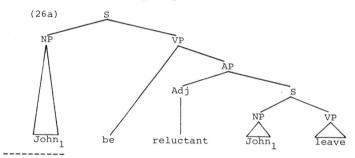

(a) ((it (John be there)) happen) $\Longrightarrow$
S_1 NP S_2 S_2 NP S_1

by extraposition:

(b) ((it) happen (John be there)) $\Longrightarrow$
S_1 NP NP S_2 S_2 S_1

by it replacement (subject-to-subject raising):

(c) John happened to be there

However, Rosenbaum insisted that extraposition was, in general, inapplicable to gerundial complement sentences (see also next section). Consequently, it was not possible to generalize the analysis to sentences like (25). This - in conjunction with a desire to get rid of the vacuous application of extraposition - led to the alternative formulation of the rule which was given on p. 204. An additional counterargument to the proposal that raising is contingent on the prior application of extraposition is given in Postal, 1971, Chapter 22. See also Postal, 1974, 11ff. When McCawley presented his hypothesis of English as a deep structure VSO-language (1970b), one of the most important arguments was that this would lead to a maximally simple statement of the raising rule (cf. below, p. 449). For an overview of the history of raising, see Postal, 1974, 1ff.

1. This operation is not accounted for by the raising rule. We will not attempt to formulate the rule of object-to-subject raising, but discuss the matter informally. Since the rule operates with a small subset of predicates which are (more or less) synonymous or antonymous with 'tough' (e.g. 'difficult', 'hard', 'easy', 'simple', etc.), it is often referred to in the literature as tough movement (a term coined by Postal, 1971, 27ff.). The rule might also be formulated in terms of equi rather than generic subject deletion. See Postal and Ross, 1971.

(27a)

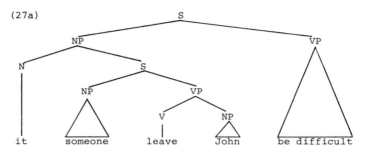

(26) is an ordinary case of verb phrase complementation (or perhaps rather adjective phrase complementation). 'John' in the embedded sentence is deleted by equi NP deletion (sentence (3) of
section IV.D.2 has the same derivation - except that subject-to-
subject raising must also apply (cf. the tree on p. 132)). As
against this, (27) is a case of noun phrase complementation. The
embedded S undergoes extraposition. After this, the object ('John')
replaces 'it'. If the subject of the embedded sentence is generic,
it is deleted by the generic subject deletion rule. If it is specific, it is retained after the emotive complementizer 'for'. An
example of this is

(28) John is difficult for his wife to please

Consider now such sentences as

(29) I expect John to scrape through
(30) * I expect myself to scrape through
(31) I expect to scrape through

In (29) 'John' has been raised to object position. Why is (30) ungrammatical? Because the coreferential subject of the embedded sentence has not been deleted. On the contrary, it has been raised
and consequently reflexivization must obligatorily apply. To rule
out (30), it is necessary to order equi NP deletion prior to
subject-to-object raising: if the former has applied, there is no
NP for the latter to raise (cf. also above, p. 209).

The interrelationship between reflexivization and equi NP
deletion also causes trouble with respect to the S pruning principle. Consider the structure

(32) (I persuade the psychiatrist (the psychiatrist give me
    S_1 S_2

LSD))
    S_2 S_1

On the first cycle (S_2), nothing of interest happens. On the second cycle, equi NP deletion applies, deleting 'the psychiatrist' in S_2. Suppose now that we order reflexivization after equi NP deletion: it will then apply on the S_1 cycle, S_2 having been pruned. The result of this will be

(33) * I persuaded the psychiatrist to give myself LSD

The ordering must be reversed to block (33). However, if (32) is embedded in a matrix sentence:

(34) (my mother think (I persuade the psychiatrist (the
      S_1 S_2 S_3
      psychiatrist give me LSD)))
                                S_3 S_2 S_1

there is nothing to prevent reflexivization from applying on the top cycle (S_1): since S_3 has been pruned, 'I' and 'me' are in the same simplex sentence when we reach S_1. The S pruning principle, therefore, is not so clear-cut as it might appear at first sight[1].

IV.G.16.7. A further note on extraposition

As remarked in note 2 on p. 392, Rosenbaum was at pains to stress that extraposition does not apply to gerundial complement sentences:

(1) John's smoking so many cigarettes bothered her
(2) She hated John's smoking so many cigarettes
(3) * It bothered her John's smoking so many cigarettes
(4) * She hated it (deeply) John's smoking so many cigarettes

There is, however, a different rule in the grammar which resembles extraposition very much. It is known as right dislocation[2] and may be seen at work in such sentences as

(5) The children behaved themselves last night ⟹
(6) They behaved themselves last night, the children

----

1. For discussion, see Postal, 1971, 74ff. and Perlmutter, 1971, 119, note 16. For a proposed solution to this problem in terms of the concept of 'quasi-clauses', see Postal, 1974, 231ff.

2. For right and left dislocation, see Ross, 1967, 232ff. Right dislocation is discussed by Huddleston, 1971, 142ff. under the name of pronoun replacement: a pronoun replaces the dislocated constituent.

The two sentences differ intonationally: in (6) there is a sharp
intonational break after 'night'. The same phenomenon may be seen
in (7) and (8) (where the underlined words are heavily stressed):

    (7) It was a pity that he <u>lost</u>
    (8) It was a <u>pity</u> that he lost

Only (7) is the result of extraposition: there is no intonational
break between 'pity' and 'lost'. By contrast, in (8), there <u>is</u>
a break between the two words: (8) is an instance of dislocation
(note that (8) is not a cleft sentence: 'be' is attributive, not
equative).

    Right dislocation may apply to gerundial complement sentences[1]:

    (9) It rather worried me(,) her having a temperature
    (10) It was a great pleasure(,) walking through the Queen's
         park with that sweet girl
    (11) It gives one a feeling of well-being(,) basking in the
         sun on the beach for hours and hours
    (12) It was a pleasant experience(,) listening to all that
         classical music during the festival week

    Note that exceptions to the principle that gerundial comple-
ment sentences do not undergo extraposition seem to be sentences
like[2]:

    (13) It's nice seeing you
    (14) It was nice hearing from you

IV.G.16.8. <u>Types of noun phrase and verb phrase</u>
<u>complementation</u>

    We have already seen that sentences may be embedded under the
immediate domination of the subject NP as well as the object NP.
There is no need to dwell on this again. However, noun phrase complement sentences may also occur in NPs under the immediate domination of PPs (if there is such a category in deep structures). Consider the verb 'decide' in such sentences as

    (1) I finally decided to go

----

1. If (3) and (4) are examples of right dislocation, they are grammatical.
2. Rosenbaum, 1967, 124 took note of such exceptions.

(2) I finally decided that I would go

(3) I finally decided on going

The problem now is this: are we to say that there are two different
lexical items: 'decide' and 'decide on' and complicate the grammar by stating restrictions on the distribution of complementizers
to the effect that only the 'Poss - ing' complementizer occurs
after prepositions? (cf. Rosenbaum, 1967, 81ff.). That this may
not be correct is suggested by the tests of pseudo-clefting and
passivization:

(4) What I finally decided (on) was to go

(5) That I should go was finally decided (on) by my parents

In (4) and (5), we note, the preposition may be present even if
the complementizer is 'to' or 'that'. This suggests that we should
set up one deep structure for (1)-(3):

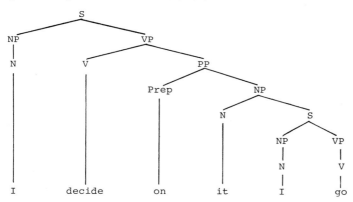

and extend the scope of the double-preposition deletion rule to
cover other cases than 'for - to':

SI   Prep - $\left\{\begin{array}{l}\text{that}\\\text{to}\end{array}\right\}$

         1   2 $\Longrightarrow$

SC   Ø   2

         Condition: obligatory.

This rule characterizes both 'for - to', 'on - to', and similar
strings as ungrammatical (exceptions are 'in that' and 'except that').

Similar paradigms occur with adjectival predicates:

(4) I was afraid of being wrong

(5) I was afraid that I was wrong

As regards verb phrase complementation, the most important distinction is that between transitive and intransitive complementation. Examples are respectively (6) and (7):

(6) He persuaded Jane to come

(7) He tended to underestimate the importance of the issue

IV.G.16.9. The progressive complementizer

We have mentioned at various points that the classic Aux-formula encounters difficulties in a number of fairly well-defined cases. In the notes to IV.C the reader was referred to some of the most important papers in which arguments are presented that the auxiliaries and the modal verbs should be analysed as main verbs and not occur in the grammar as disparate and totally unrelated elements. It is not my intention to repeat all those arguments here. When we reach the final section on generative semantics, we will merely make the assumption that they are main verbs. Meanwhile, we will cite just one argument relating to 'be' which has a bearing on the complementation system. Consider such sentences as

(1) John forced me to walk through the mud

(2) * John forced me to own a car

(3) John avoided reading the book

(4) * John avoided knowing the answer

(5) He regretted resembling his father

(6) He continued to resemble his father

(7) * He continued resembling his father

(8) He is watching the Olympic Games every evening

(9) * He is knowing the answer

(1) and (2) show that some verbs cannot take stative verbs in their complements. (3)-(7) reveal that such restrictions are also reflected in the complementizers: some verbs disallow the 'Poss - ing' complementizer if the embedded sentence contains a stative verb. Now, if we analyse 'be' in (8) and (9) as a main verb, we can make a generalization: the verb 'be' has in common with certain other verbs that it disallows 'ing' if the verb in the embedded sentence

is stative.

    Consider now (10) and (11):

(10) He saw them come

(11) He saw them coming

(10) we have accounted for in terms of to deletion. Assuming now
that 'be' is a main verb on a par with, say, 'avoid', we can set
up the following deep structure for (11) (in which 'ing' is the
progressive complementizer, not the gerund):

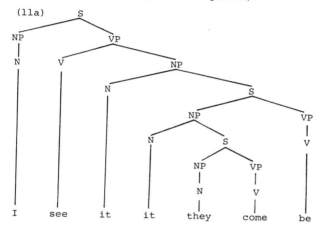

    The reader is invited to speculate what rules are required
for (11a) to surface (recall the cyclic principle and it-replacement).

    With this hint at more abstract deep structures than those
defined by our PS-rules, we leave the complementation system.

IV.G.17. Nominalization

IV.G.17.1. Introductory remarks

    Let us agree to call any S which at some stage of the deriva-
tion is immediately dominated by NP a <u>nominalized sentence</u>[1]. By this
----

1. The qualification 'at some stage of the derivation' is made
   necessary by the fact that both the S node and the immediately
   dominating NP node may be pruned after the operation of certain
   T-rules.

token, then, the following underlined sequences qualify as (the remnants of) nominalized sentences:

    (1) The cat <u>which was lying on the road</u>

    (2) The man <u>from London</u>

    (3) The <u>red</u> car

    (4) <u>What he was reading</u> was a novel

    (5) It was a novel <u>that he was reading</u>

    (6) <u>That he was wrong</u> was evident to everyone

    (7) I want John <u>to be there</u>

    (8) I preferred <u>to stay</u>

    (9) I avoided <u>seeing him</u>

  (10) I appreciate <u>your taking a firm stand</u>

Sentences like (1)-(10) have been dealt with in the preceding three
sections.

    In this section we will direct the attention to some further
aspects of nominalization. In particular, we shall be concerned (a)
with the question of how to account for the 'mirrored' syntactic
relationships in certain noun phrases, and (b) the "ing-form".

IV.G.17.2. <u>The transformational approach</u>

    Up to about 1967 (the year when Chomsky wrote "Remarks on
Nominalization"), it was uniformly assumed that nominalization
was a transformational process[1]. Let us turn immediately to the
following concrete example:

    (1) The teacher's criticism of the student was unjustified

In (1) the subject NP is 'the teacher's criticism of the student'.
It is intuitively obvious that this NP reflects the subject-verb-
object relationship in a sentence containing a transitive verb (cf.
also above, section III.8). It must, therefore, be derived from an
underlying structure containing this sentence. No attempt will be
made here to provide an exact deep structure for (1). However, it
is clear that within the standard theory it must take the form of
a generalized P-marker in which a nominalization trigger of some
kind appears in the sentence next above the one undergoing nominal-

----

1. Prior to 1965, that is, within the SS-model of syntax and before
   the advent of syntactic features, the transformational approach
   was the only possible one.

ization[1]:

(1a)

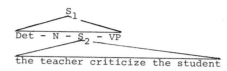

The nominalization transformation, which is obligatory, must perform a number of elementary operations: (a) it must move the subject of the embedded sentence under the Det node of the matrix sentence and possessivize it, (b) it must insert the affix which converts the verb 'criticize' into the noun 'criticism' (i.e. it must
perform a piece of derivational morphology), (c) it must adjoin
a preposition to the left of the object NP of the embedded sentence
(perhaps by Chomsky-adjunction), and (d) it must move the original
VP of the embedded sentence under the N node of the matrix sentence
and, in so doing, recategorize it[2].

----

1. For some discussion, see Lees, 1960a, 61ff. and Chomsky, 1964a,
   47ff. The discussion there is based on the SS-model of syntax.
   See further Chomsky, 1965, 184ff., Fraser, 1970, and Newmeyer,
   1970.

2. The informal discussion in the text glosses over a number of
   problems. One of these problems relates to the derived categorial status of 'criticism of the student'. Chomsky, 1964a, 47ff.
   argues that it is a noun. The argument is based on modifier
   preposing, which in turn is formulated as left-sister adjunction to N. However, we have seen that this formulation encounters
   difficulties with respect to pronominalization (cf. above, p.
   356, note). It would therefore seem that, if we want to be consistent, we must define 'criticism of the student' as an NP
   (cf. such a sentence as 'John's remarks about this were rather
   more to the point than the ones you made'). Even so, the derivation of an adjective like, say, 'severe' in the phrase 'severe
   criticism of the student' by relative reduction and modifier preposing is not without its difficulties. It would involve generating a relative clause on the host NP in S_1 (Det + N). In that
   case, clearly, nominalization would have to precede relativization on the S_1 cycle. However, we have argued that, in order
   to provide adequate derived structures for NPs containing premodifiers, it may turn out to be necessary to generate determiners by segmentalization and Chomsky-adjunction after modifier preposing. But if this is correct, the nominalization rule
   cannot move the subject NP of the embedded sentence anywhere:
   there is no Det node to receive it. On the other hand, it is
   by no means certain that 'severe' in our example should be derived by relative reduction and modifier preposing. It might
   equally well be derived from an adverbial in the sentence undergoing nominalization (e.g. 'criticize 'n a severe manner') (for
   some discussion of the source of adjectives in nominalized structures, see Fraser, op. cit., 93ff.)

Before we go on, we may pause to ask <u>why</u> a sentence like (1)
should be analysed as a transform. Why not have the PS-rules generate a structure like 'the teacher's criticism of the student' directly
We have already given one answer to this question: the grammar
should capture the intuitively apprehended relation between the NP
and the corresponding sentence. If it does not, it fails on the
score of descriptive adequacy. There is also a different (though
related), more technical reason. Consider such sentences as

    (2) The elephant criticised the stone severely

    (3) The elephant's criticism of the stone was severe

They are both anomalous. The anomaly of (2) is easily accounted for
in terms of a selectional violation. Now, if (3) were generated
directly, we would have to extend the machinery of selectional restrictions to nonpredicative nouns. This would lead to an unneces-
sary complication of the grammar: for each noun traditionally said
to be derived from a verb, the statement of selectional restrictions
would have to be duplicated[1]. Consequently, the evaluation measure
will select the transformational analysis of sentences like (1) as
the better solution (unless other solutions are available).

    The transformational approach to nominalization encounters prob-
lems in a number of cases. One problem relates to the interaction of
passivization and nominalization. Consider such sentences as

    (2) * The student's criticism by the teacher was unjustified

    (3) Germany's defeat by the Allies restored peace to Europe

    (4) The criticism of the student by the teacher was unjusti-
        fied

    (5) The defeat of Germany by the Allies restored peace to
        Europe

(2) and (3) are instances of the so-called 'objective genitive'.
This is fairly rare in modern English and easily results in ungrammatical sentences such as (2), which must, accordingly, be ruled
out although the correspondning passive sentence is perfectly well-
formed. The generation of (3) is fairly straightforward: the passive rule, which is cyclic, has applied on the cycle corresponding
to S_2 in (1a). On the next cycle, the derived subject has been
moved under the determiner and possessivized, and the embedded VP

----

1. This argument, then, parallels that given for the transformational derivation of attributive adjectives mentioned in the
   notes to section IV.G.14.

has been nominalized. (4) and (5) are more problematic: although
the prepositional phrases 'by the Allies' and 'by the teacher' are
intuitively felt as tokens of the 'by + NP' in passive sentences,
there is no way in which, under the formulation of the passive rule
which we have been assuming so far, the appropriate structure can
be derived on the S_2 cycle in (1a). To derive (4) and (5) we would
have to formulate a completely ad-hoc rule which obligatorily
moved the derived subject back into object-position in some cases[1].

Further difficulties relate to the numerous constraints which
must be placed on the nominalization rule with respect to the sentence which constitutes the source of the derived nominal. The
general nature of these constraints will appear from the following
ungrammatical NPs:

(6) The enemy's $\left(\left\{ \begin{array}{l} \text{✶ will} \\ \text{✶ has} \end{array} \right\} \right)$ destruction of the regiment

(7) The enemy's (✶ not) destruction of the regiment

(8) The enemy's (✶ certainly) destruction (✶ cruelly) of
    the regiment

which show that nominalization is blocked if the source sentence
contains a modal verb or aspect, if it is negated, or if it contains an -ly-adverb[2].

Also, the transformationalist position, in which it is a fundamental assumption that the nouns are derived from the verbs which
appear in the source sentences, makes it necessary to postulate
hypothetical lexical items (cf. Lakoff, 1970a, 56ff.). Consider
such pairs as

(9)   verbs   nouns

        transgress   -   transgression

        progress   -   progression

      ✶ aggress   -   agression

        criticize   -   criticism

      ✶ critique   -   critique

----

1. For discussion of 'by + NP' in such sentences, see also Fraser,
   1970 (in Jacobs and Rosenbaum, 1970) 87f. Fraser's proposal is
   very similar to that made by Chomsky, to which we return in the
   next section.

2. As indicated in note 2 on p. 401, (8) raises an important question. More specifically, the problem is to explain the source
   of 'certain' and 'cruel' in the following grammatical NPs:

   The enemy's $\left\{ \begin{array}{l} \text{cruel} \\ \text{certain} \end{array} \right\}$ destruction of the regiment

The two nonexistent verbs must appear in the deep structure of such
sentences as

> (10) The enemey's aggression was stopped
> (11) The reviewer's critique of the book was penetrating

in order for the analysis to attain the maximum degree of generalization. Hypothetical lexical items must be marked as <u>positive
absolute exceptions</u>: they must meet the SI of the nominalization
rule and they must undergo the rule (cf. above, p. 210, note 2)[1].

So far we have been concerned with abstract nouns[2]. Another
type of noun derived by transformations is <u>agent nouns</u>. Usually,
the derivational affix is -er or -or, as in

> | (12) | verbs | | nouns |
> |------|-------|---|-------|
> | | transgress | - | transgressor |
> | | paint | - | painter |
> | | rob | - | robber |

The deep structure of a sentence like

> (13) Peter is a singer of songs

also involves an embedded sentence containing the verb from which
the agent noun is derived[3].

----

1. In a generative semantics framework, hypothetical lexical items
   would be accounted for in terms of derivational constraints on
   lexical insertion (cf. Lakoff, 1970a, Preface, McCawley, 1968d
   (in Darden et al., 1968) 75f., and below, p. 486).

2. Frequently, such nouns denote a 'completed activity'. Compare
   the following two sentences:

   > (a) The girl's destroying of the sandcastle took only a
   >   few minutes
   > (b) The enemy's destruction of our tanks was a severe blow

   In (a) (an example of <u>action nominalization</u> (cf. Lees, 1960a
   and below, section IV.<u>G.17.4</u>)), 'destroying' focuses on the
   action in progress, as it were. By contrast, in (b) 'destruction'
   denotes that the act of destroying is completed. In other cases,
   an abstract noun denotes the result of the action, as in

   > (c) The boy stood admiring his new invention

   It is possible that these semantic peculiarities could be accounted for by generating a set of generalized features on the
   host nominal in the way proposed by Fraser, 1970. Observe that,
   given the KP-hypothesis, these semantic facts <u>should</u> be predictable from the deep structures.

3. The details of the deep structure are far from clear. It would
   presumably be something like this (see next page):

Observe that in some cases the object in the deep structure
VP may be moved to the front of the nominalized verb to form a compound noun[1]:

(14) John is a $\left\{ \begin{array}{l} \text{manufacturer of cars} \\ \text{car-manufacturer} \end{array} \right\}$

The analysis of agent nouns also requires hypothetical verbs in a
number of cases. An obvious example is[2]

(15) transgress - transgression - transgressor
     ✳ aggress   - aggression   - aggressor

Consider further

(16) We must be hospitable to the benefactors of the college

in which 'the college' is the object of 'benefactor'. In order
to generalize the transformational analysis to (16), a hypothetical
verb '✳ benefact' must be posited. It is arguable that something
similar would be true of a paradigm like[3]

(17) A Dane was once the ruler of England
(18) A Dane once ruled England
(19) A Dane was once the king of England
(20) ✳ A Dane once kinged England

A third kind of nominalization is <u>objective</u> nominalization.
An example would be

(21) I love Dickens's tales

Again, the transformational analysis requires an underlying sentence containing the VP 'tell things', from which the noun can be

----

(Peter be someone (someone sing songs))   (perhaps with 'some-
$_{S_1}$ $_{S_2}$ $_{S_2}$ $_{S_1}$
one' in the matrix marked by a feature like, say, (+ Agentive)).

1. The syntactic structure of compound nouns has been studied in
   detail by Lees, 1960a. We may note in passing that Lees
   (1970a) has discussed his original findings in the light of
   the further development of linguistic theory - in particular
   case grammar.

2. It seems quite likely that many of the lexical items which
   are now hypothetical may materialize in the language some day.

3. Such derivations are proposed by Lakoff, 1970a. It is clear
   that they are mainly semantically motivated and thus take a
   step away from the standard theory towards generative semantics -
   meaning-based syntax.

derived[1,2]. Further examples are

   (22) I loathe your perspiration

   (23) I stand by my beliefs

   (24) Goneril and Regan's foul deeds are the cause of Lear's madness

Consider next such sentences as

   (25) John thinks that you are a fool

   (26) It is John's opinion that you are a fool

   (27) John's remark that this was above him infuriated us all

   (28) John's idea that he is a superman is intolerable

In (25) and (27) the 'that'-clauses are clearly objects: in (25) of the transitive verb 'think' and in (27) of the nominalized transitive verb 'remark'. The same would seem to be the case in (26) and (28). In other words, to be consistent, we must assume that the nouns 'opinion' and 'idea' are nominalizations of hypothetical verbs like '* opinionate' (cf. 'opinionated') and '* ideate'. If this is true, the derivation of sentences like (29) and (30)

   (29) I disagree with your ideas

   (30) I would like to hear your opinions

involves one and two embedded sentences respectively.

IV.G.17.3. The lexicalist hypothesis

    In his important paper on nominalization (1970), Chomsky argues that nominalized structures are not derived by transformations at all, but generated directly in the base. In this section we will try to isolate briefly, and relatively informally, the core of Chomsky's arguments, which have caused a good deal of debate in the literature[3].

----

1. There are semantic objections to deriving 'tales' from something like 'tell things'. A tale is not just a story of things, but a story of exciting, romantic things. See next section.

2. By this analysis, then, the derivation provided for sentence (60) of section IV.C.1 is wrong: 'author' would have to be derived from '* someone auths something'.

3. The reader who wishes to familiarize himself with the details of the lexicalist hypothesis and its implications for linguistic theory should consult Jackendoff, 1975a. Jackendoff elaborates on Chomsky's proposals viewing them also in the light of Emonds' theory of structure preserving transformations.

Before we proceed to exemplify the lexicalist hypothesis,
some general points must be made.

We turn first to the structure of lexical items. We have seen
that in the transformational approach to nominalization, a noun like
'criticism' is derived from the verb 'criticize'; only the verb is
entered in the lexicon. In contrast to this, Chomsky proposes that
items like 'criticize'/'criticism' are entered as one <u>neutral</u> lexical item specified as $(+ N) \vee (+ V)$ (the form 'criticism' would be
formed by a low-level morphological rule)[1]. This item has a fixed
set of selectional and strict subcategorization features, such that
a dependency relation may hold between one subset of the features
and $(+ N)$, and between another subset of the features and $(+ V)$.
Much the same would hold for semantic features.

The second point we need to make is that nominalized structures
generated by the base rules are subject to a number of different
transformational rules. In this connection, the passive rule is of
special interest. It consists of three elementary operations: (a)
<u>agent postposing</u>, which substitutes the subject NP for Passive in
the substring 'by + Passive' (in the manner-adverb analysis of the
passive); (b) <u>NP preposing</u>, which shifts the object NP to subject
position; (c) the insertion of 'be + en', which we will ignore in
this section. Suppose now that (a) and (b) are viewed as being - in
principle - independent operations. In that case, the passive (or
rather what remains of it) can be generalized to NP structures and
such sentences as (4) and (5) of the preceding section generated
by agent postposing[2].

The third point relates to syntactic features. Recall that at
the end of section IV.C.2.4, we emphasized that syntactic-feature
analysis could be extended to prelexical category symbols (cf. also

----

1. In this approach, then, the similarities between verbs, adjectives, and nouns noted in section IV.C.1 would be accounted for
   in the lexicon rather than in terms of abstract deep-structure
   categories such as VERB or 'Contentive'. Very roughly, lexical
   entries would take the form illustrated on p. 262. Note that in
   the lexicalist hypothesis the derivation of sentence (60) of
   section IV.C.1 would be essentially correct: there would be a
   PS-rule defining certain PPs as complements of nouns.

2. Observe that in this analysis the argument from the cycle considered in the preceding section collapses: whereas, in the traditional formulation, the passive rule is cyclic, there is no
   evidence that agent postposing - as an independent operation -
   must be cyclic (for further discussion, see Newmeyer, 1971).

above, p. 367f. and notes). This is precisely what Chomsky proposes
to do. Specifically, he adds to the grammar rules of the following
kind (cf. also McCawley, 1968a (in Bach and Harms, 1968) 147):

Det $\longrightarrow$ ($\pm$ Def (NP))

thus associating definiteness with a full noun phrase. A further rule
may assign the feature (+ Poss) to the NP in certain circumstances.

Consider now the following sentence (adapted from Chomsky):

(1) I admired John's picture

Generally, this is assumed to be derived from something like (cf.
also above, p. 128, note 1):

(2) I admired the picture that John has

A rule, which we may refer to as <u>possessive preposing</u>, fronts and
possessivizes 'John', which now takes the place of the definite determiner. If the deep-structure determiner is specified (+ Demonstrative), the derived possessive NP must be shifted to the right
by a rule which we will call <u>possessive movement</u>:

(3) I admired that picture of John's

The rule is also obligatory if the determiner is specified (- Def):

(4) I admired a picture of John's

and blocks if the determiner is specified (+ Def, - Demonstrative):

(5) * I admired the picture of John's

unless the head noun is followed by a restrictive relative clause,
in which case the rule is obligatory:

(6) * John's picture which she kept talking about has been
stolen

(7) The picture of John's which she kept talking about has
been stolen

Observe now that (1) may also mean 'a picture representing
John'; that is, 'John's' is the object of 'picture'. Chomsky proposes that (1) in this reading should be derived from

(8) I admired the picture of John

by NP preposing, which, then, has the same output as possessive
preposing. But this does not exhaust the description of (1); it has
one further reading: 'the picture that John made'. How to derive

that? Before we try to answer this question, we must introduce the
concepts of <u>alienable</u> and <u>inalienable possession</u>. Consider the
following sentences:

(9) John's car is red
(10) The car that John has is red
(11) John's tooth hurts
(12) * The tooth that John has hurts
(13) John's car is missing
(14) John's arm is missing
(15) John has a missing arm
(16) * John has a missing car

The pattern of (un)grammaticality of these sentences suggests that
there are two different ways in which one may 'possess' things. Inalienable possession, as exemplified by (11) and (14), implies that
"the 'possessed' item is contingently associated with the possessor"
(Lyons, 1968, 301). By contrast, in a relationship of alienable possession, exemplified by (9) and (13), the possessed item is one
which is not <u>necessarily</u> associated with the possessor, but one
which, for example, may be given away to someone else. According
to the general <u>rationale</u> of the standard theory, the difference
between alienable and inalienable possession should be made explicit
in the deep structure, which forms the input to the rules of semantic
interpretation. Chomsky proposes that the possessive noun phrase
in an inalienable possessive structure should be generated directly
in the base. By this analysis, the NP of (1) in the inalienable
reading (i.e. 'John made the picture') would have roughly the following deep structure:

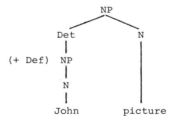

If the determiner NP is not moved by any T-rule, it is assigned
the feature (+ Poss) by a later rule.

   Assuming that a deep structure possessive (or perhaps rather
potentially possessive) determiner NP is well motivated, we may now
proceed to consider

(17) The picture by John was stolen

as derived from

(18) John's picture

in the inalienable interpretation by the rule of agent postposing.
But, as we have noted, (18) is three-ways ambiguous. In other words,
we must prevent the rule of agent postposing from operating on the
underlying structure of (18) as derived by possessive preposing or
NP preposing. The solution to this problem, of course, is rule-
ordering:

    1. Inalienable possession (deep structure)

    2. Agent postposing

    3. Alienable possession (derived by possessive preposing)

    4. Possessive movement

    5. NP preposing

In the light of the discussion so far, let us now examine a
couple of examples which involve neutral lexical entries with a
Boolean condition on category features (i.e. (+ V) $\lor$ (+ N)). Consider the following sentences:

(19) Falstaff's rejection is painful

(20) The President's denial of the facts is painful

According to the lexicalist hypothesis, they would have the following rough deep structures:

(19a)

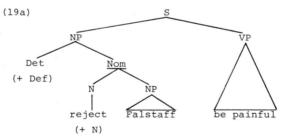

which, by the insertion of 'of' and the application of a low-level
morphological rule, may be converted into

(21) The rejection of Falstaff is painful

or - by NP preposing and possessivization - into (19), and

(20a)

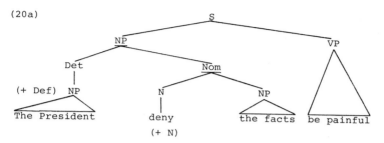

which may surface as (20) or be converted by agent postposing into

(21) The denial of the facts by the President is painful

Observe now that the underscored nodes in the two trees strongly resemble (parts of) sentence structure. In particular, Nom in
(19a) and (20a) corresponds to VP, and NP in (20a) to S. Given this
similarity, it is immediately obvious that the statement of selectional and strict subcategorization features can be generalized to
cover nominalized structures[1].

Chomsky musters a number of arguments in support of the lexicalist hypothesis. Of these, we will briefly consider two.

(a) <u>Restricted productivity</u>. By this is meant the limitations
on underlying structures with respect to nominalization. For example, the structures underlying

(22) Jane is $\left\{ \begin{array}{l} \text{(a) difficult} \\ \text{(b) reluctant} \\ \text{(c) certain} \\ \text{(d) willing} \end{array} \right\}$ to leave

may not all nominalize:

(23) Jane's $\left\{ \begin{array}{l} \text{(a) * difficulty} \\ \text{(b) reluctance} \\ \text{(c) * certainty} \\ \text{(d) willingness} \end{array} \right\}$ to leave

It is true that the four sentences of (22) have undergone different
T-rules (equi NP deletion ((b) and (d)) and it replacement (object-

----

1. Chomsky develops a sophisticated rule schema known as the <u>X-bar</u>
<u>convention</u> (or the X̄-convention) to capture this similarity, which
is of fundamental importance to the lexicalist hypothesis. We
will not go into the details of this. The interested reader is
referred to the paper by Jackendoff mentioned in note 3 on p.
406. For discussion of the X-bar convention within the framework
of case grammar, see Stockwell at al., 1968, Vol. I, Chapter 1.

to-subject raising in (a) and subject-to-subject raising in (c)).
However, given a base P-marker like (1a) of the preceding section,
these rules all apply on a lower cycle than the nominalization
transformation (we are assuming here, for the sake of argument, that
extraposition, which, as we have seen, operates prior to object-
to-subject raising, is a cyclic rule[1]). In other words, by the time
the cycle on which nominalization operates is reached, the embedded
sentences all qualify for nominalization. It is quite difficult to
see, then, how the rule could be constrained so as to generate
(23b) and (23d), but not (23a) and (23c): T-rules operating on
higher cycles do not keep track of which rules have applied on lower cycles (there are no transformation-markers, let alone global
constraints in the theory)[2]. In the lexicalist hypothesis, the pattern of (23) would be accounted for in the lexicon. For example,
'certain' would be entered with the specification $(+ N) \lor (+ Adj)$
and with the information that if it is predicated of a (+ Human)
subject (recall the similarity between nominalized structures and
sentences), it can be followed by a sentential complement, whereas,
if it is predicated of a (+ Abstract) subject, it cannot. This entry,
then, would predict the grammaticality of (22c) (the deep-structure
subject being 'Jane to leave' and hence (+ Abstract) (cf. in this
connection (2a) of section IV.D.2)), the ungrammaticality of (23c)
(in which the strict subcategorization feature has been violated
('certainty' is followed by a sentential complement despite the
fact that it is not predicated of 'Jane')), and the grammaticality
of (24) and (25):

(24) John is certain that he will be there on time

(25) John's certainty that he will be there on time

(b) <u>The idiosyncratic semantic relationship between verbs and
nouns</u>. Consider (26) and (27) (and compare (21) of section IV.G.17.2):

----

1. Object-to-subject raising is a cyclic rule (cf. 'John appears
   to be difficult to please'). Therefore, if object-to-subject
   raising is contingent on the prior application of extraposition,
   extraposition must be in the cycle. This constitutes counterevidence to the analysis of extraposition as a last-cyclic rule.
   Consequently, if this analysis is to be upheld, it must be shown
   that object-to-subject raising is independent of extraposition.

2. This argument would collapse if it could be shown that nominalization must operate before all cyclic rules (i.e. be a precyclic
   rule) (cf. Newmeyer, 1970, 1971, and above, p. 407, note 2). In
   that case, the SIs of the raising rules could not be met after
   the application of nominalization. Hence the ungrammaticality of
   (23a) and (23c). By contrast, the SI of equi NP deletion would
   still be met. Hence the grammaticality of (23b) and (23d).

(26) I read about the things he had done

(27) I read about his deeds

(26) and (27) are not synonymous. In particular, 'deeds' in (27)
means something like 'very important things done'. This fact can be
stated quite easily in the lexicalist approach in terms of semantic
features associated with ' do (+ N)', but not with 'do (+ V)'. If
such semantic relationships between lexical items are to be accounted
for in the syntactic rather than in the semantic component, it can
obviously lead to a great proliferation of syntactic structures[1].

   With this, we leave the lexicalist hypothesis proper. It is
clear that the issue between lexicalists and transformationalists
involves some very fundamental aspects of linguistic theory, such
as the nature of the passive rule, the status of rules with respect
to the cycle, the structure of lexical entries, the place of derivational morphology in the grammar, semantic relationships, etc.
The reader who turns to the literature on this subject will soon
find himself involved in a maze of arguments and counterarguments.
All of them are weighty. Perhaps, after studying these arguments,
he would come to the conclusion that the battle is at a draw. As
will appear from the discussion in the next section, this conclusion would not be entirely unwarranted.

IV.G.17.4. The "ing-form"

   The term 'ing-form' is traditionally employed to describe a
number of different phenomena in English which have in common the
fact that the suffix 'ing' is added to a verb stem. Consider the
following sentences:

A (1) There is now a big red building on the site

   (2) We saw eighteen famous buildings in London

   (3) I bought three paintings by Picasso

   (4) He studied Sir Christopher Wren's buildings

B (5) He is familiar with the writings by Iris Murdoch

   (6) * I admire a writing by Picasso

C (7) He was worried about Tessie's smoking so many cigarettes

----

   For extensive discussion of the interaction of raising and
   nominalization, see Postal, 1974, Chapter 10. Postal's chief
   argument is that some nominalized structures involve raising.
   It would follow from this (a) that nominalization must be a
   transformation and (b) that the rule cannot be precyclic.

1. For some discussion of this point, see Newmeyer, 1971, 791f.
   Cf. also below, section V.C.4.

   (8) He likes swallowing his drinks quickly

   (9) * He likes quick swallowing his drinks

D (10) Her tearing up of the letter had a certain dramatic effect

  (11) Their cruel slaughtering of the lions went on for the whole day

  (12) * Their slaughtering cruelly of the lions went on for the whole day

E (13) I am reading

  (14) I have been washing my car, which you have not

  (15) I saw them fighting each other

  (16) The police were seen by some of those present beating up the prisoners

A. The forms here have a number of the characteristics of nouns proper: they are (+ Countable) and may, accordingly, be preceded by the indefinite article and quantifiers[1]. Furthermore, they may be preceded by adjectives which have no corresponding adverbial forms. Yet, they show some verbal characteristics: a word like 'painting' may be construed with a postposed agent ((3)). (4) is ambiguous: the possessive noun may express an alienable[2] as well as an inalienable relationship. Presumably, in most dialects, (4) may also undergo agent postposing:

  (17) The buildings by Sir Christopher Wren

It would seem that such forms could be accounted for quite naturally in the lexicalist hypothesis. Thus 'build' could be entered as a neutral lexical item specified $(+ N) \bigvee (+ V)$ with disjunctive sets of semantic and contextual features to account for such sentences as (1) on the one hand and (18) and (19) on the other:

  (18) They built the house in three weeks

  (19) Their building of the house took three weeks

Furthermore, if (17) is ungrammatical in some dialects, this could be accounted for in terms of a rule feature: (- agent postposing)[3].

----

1. Other 'ing-forms' are (- Countable). This is true of 'writing' in 'I admire his beautiful writing' (cf. Lees, 1960a, 64f.).

2. Admittedly, the name Sir Christopher Wren makes the alienable interpretation somewhat unlikely.

3. In the same way as the generation of ungrammatical 'objective genitives' could be blocked by a rule feature (- NP preposing) associated with the category feature (+ N).

The only alternative would be to have two separate entries: one
for the noun 'building' in (1) and (2), and one for (18) and (19).
This would be redundant; besides, it would miss the generalization
that 'ing-forms' which can occur in the full set of noun environments always contain a verb stem. On the other hand, the transformationalist approach could, in many cases, capture the same generalization. Thus, it is quite possible to claim that 'building' in
(1) and (2), and 'paintings' in (3) are derived by objective nominalization (in the same way as, say, 'tales').

   B. From the transformational point of view, (5) is clearly
a case of objective nominalization (the things which Iris Murdoch
writes). (6) reveals an idiosyncratic constraint in comparison with,
say,

   (20) I bought a painting by Picasso

Again, it would seem that this can be quite easily accounted for
in the lexicalist framework in terms of a feature (+ Plur) associated with 'write (+ N)' in this sense (but not in the sense of
'hand-writing'). By contrast, the nominalization rule would have
to be constrained accordingly.

   C. The examples in C are gerundial noun phrase complement sentences: they are generated as complements of 'it' and are thus immediately dominated by NP. If it should turn out that verb phrase
complementation is not sufficiently motivated (cf. notes to section IV.G.16), we can make the generalization that all gerunds of
this type are instances of nominalized sentences[1].

   D. The type of 'ing-form' represented by the sentences in D
has only been touched upon marginally (cf. above, p. 404, note 2).
They are instances of action nominalization. Note that an essential
difference between C and D is the behaviour of adverbs: in C -ly-
adverbs may be generated in the embedded sentence, whereas the corresponding adjectives may not occur. In D the opposite holds. The
sentences in D can be generated both lexically and transformationally. Let us proceed to show how, without committing ourselves to any
solution. Consider for example

   (21) * Her tearing of the letter up had a certain dramatic
        effect

----

1. The generation of such sentences is not at issue in the lexi-
   calist-transformationalist controversy.

as against (10) and

 (22) She was worried about her having torn the letter up

Assuming now a transformational analysis of nominalization, what
has happened in (21) is that particle movement has applied to the
embedded sentence prior to nominalization (on the next cycle). One
way of preventing the generation of (21) is to make particle-move-
ment a last-cyclic rule, following nominalization (as proposed by
Ross, 1967, 151ff.)[1]. In the lexicalist hypothesis, 'tear up' would
be inserted under N and the nonapplication of particle movement
would follow automatically (the SI of the rule could not be met).
Other differences between D and C relate to aspect (cf. also sentences (28) of section IV.G.16.5 and (6) of section IV.G.17.2):

 (23) He was proud of having swum the Channel in less than
    fourteen hours
 (24) * His having slaughtered of the lions was revolting

to negation[2] (cf. (7) of section IV.G.17.2):

 (25) I noticed his not drinking anything at all last night
 (26) * I observed his not lighting of your cigarette at
    the table

and to dative movement

 (27) The renting of the house to the newcomers took only
    a couple of minutes
 (28) * The renting (of) the newcomers (of) the house took
    only a couple of minutes

----

1. Of course, once again, if nominalization can be shown to be
precyclic, this condition on particle movement would not be
required. However, in the light of Postal's arguments (referred
to in the note on p. 412), this is not likely. For discussion
of last-cyclic rules and the principles involved, see also
Jackendoff, 1972, Chapter 9 and notes to section IV.G.16.

2. Nemeyer, 1970 (in Campbell et al., 1970) 409f. points out that
these restrictions follow naturally from the semantic structure of the underlying sentence. Thus, on the assumption that
the nominalization trigger (N in S_1 of (la) in section IV.G.
17.2) is associated with a feature (+ Act) (cf. also above,
p. 404, note 2) it is simply logically inconsistent to assert
that an act took place and then proceed to negate that act.
In the same way, perfective aspect in the embedded sentence
would "violate presuppositions relating act to its complement".

In order to rule out (28), dative movement must apply after nominalization - must, in effect, be a last-cyclic rule[1]. The ungrammaticality of (24), (26), and (28) follows automatically from the
lexicalist hypothesis: categories like 'aspect' and 'negation' are
incompatible with the feature (+ N); in the same way, the SI of
dative movement simply cannot be met.

Finally, we may note that agent postposing also applies to
action nominalizations. This, of course, is true in either approach:

> (29) For a moment I was taken in by my sister's shedding of
>   tears
> (30) For a moment I was taken in by the shedding of tears by
>   my sister
> (31) The climber's conquering of Mount Everest took three
>   weeks
> (32) The conquering of Mount Everest by the climber took three
>   weeks

Agent postposing also applies to intransitive verbs ('by' being
frequently replaced by 'of'):

> (33) The baby's weeping distressed the mother
> (34) The weeping of the baby distressed the mother

The sentences in E illustrate progressive aspect. At first
sight, this seems to be quite unrelated to the other phenomena discussed in this section. However, the problem is how to account consistently for such sentences as (14), (15), and (16). Let us look
first at (14). The question that may be asked is this: what does
'which' pronominalize (cf. above, p. 346)? The answer is: 'which'
replaces 'wash my car' + progressive aspect. Of these, the former
is dominated by VP, the latter by Aux. Since 'have' is also dominated by Aux, 'which' does not replace a constituent, and this
would seem to be the minimum requirement on pronominalization. Suppose now that we agree that 'be' and 'have' should not be generated
by PS-rule 12, but should be analysed as main verbs. In that case,
the underlying structure of the matrix sentence (more correctly,

----

1. For discussion, see Jackendoff, 1972, Chapter 9. Jackendoff
   points out that defining dative movement as a last-cyclic
   rule is incompatible with other arguments which show dative
   movement to be a cyclic rule (as it is normally assumed to be).
   Once again, this paradox could be resolved only if nominalization were a precyclic rule.

the first conjunct, since the relative clause is nonrestrictive)
would be

(14a)

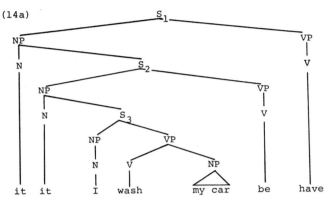

To this structure complementizer insertion applies, inserting the
progressive complementizer in S_3 ('ing') and the perfective complementizer in S_2 ('en'). Successive application of it replacement
would yield a surface structure like

(14b)

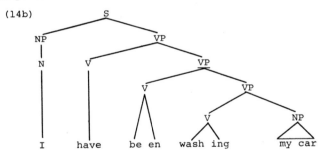

It is the underlined constituent which is pronominalized. Note
that such an analysis is based on a purely syntactic argument.
Once it becomes reinforced by semantic arguments, it leads directly
to generative semantics (cf. McCawley, 1971a).

Given such an analysis, we can account for (13), (15), and (16)
along the lines suggested above, p. 399: they are all instances of
noun phrase complementation.

It would appear, then, that we can make the generalization
that all the 'ing-forms' considered in this section are bound up
with nominalization in some way or other.

IV.G.18. Pronominalization

IV.G.18.1. Introductory remarks

In this section we shall be concerned with matters pertaining to the syntax of anaphoric pronouns, in particular, the pronoun one, the personal pronouns, and the reflexive pronouns. We may define a pronoun as anaphoric if it has an antecedent within the same sentence. Reflexive and personal pronouns differ in that the antecedent of the former must be within the same simplex sentence (at least in the typical cases), whereas the antecedent of the latter cannot, in general, be in the same simplex sentence.

In this exposition pronominalization is viewed as a transformational process involving two NP nodes. We will, following Langacker, 1969, refer to the antecedent as NP_a and the NP undergoing pronominalization as NP_p.

In the case of 'one', which replaces an NP contained within another NP (cf. above, section IV.G.14.5)[1], there must be weak identity between NP_a and NP_p. In the case of personal and reflexive pronouns, which replace entire NPs, NP_a and NP_p must be coreferential.

Consider now the following sentences:

(1) The professor says that $\left\{ \begin{array}{c} \text{he} \\ \text{she} \end{array} \right\}$ is happy

(2) The professor who is pregnant says that $\left\{ \begin{array}{c} \text{* he} \\ \text{she} \end{array} \right\}$ is happy

(3) I have heard of the celebrated senator from South Dakota, but I have never met him

(4) The senator from South Dakota met the one from California

(5) The big boy hit the little one

(6) One little boy hit another one

In (1) the NP 'the professor' is (0 Masculine). Consequently, both 'he' and 'she' are grammatical. In (2) 'he' is ungrammatical. This shows that the personal pronoun replaces the entire NP 'the professor who is pregnant'. In the same way, 'him' replaces 'the celebrated senator from South Dakota' in (3). In (4), however, 'one'

----

1. In the sentence 'he wanted a new hat, and so I gave him one', 'one' seemingly replaces the entire NP 'a new hat'. However, a case could be made that 'one' in this sentence is a suppletive form of the indefinite article 'a', the pronoun having been deleted. That is, an intermediate stage in the derivation of the sentence would be ' ... I gave him a one'.

replaces only 'senator', and clearly the two NPs are only weakly
identical, not coreferential. By the same token, 'one' replaces
'boy' in (5), and 'little boy' in (6)[1].

It should be noted that personal pronouns are not necessarily
anaphoric. In

(7) He liked Jane

'he' has no sentence-internal antecedent. Of course, it refers to
some person assumed by the speaker to be known to the addressee,
but this is not syntactically relevant in a sentence grammar.

(8) John told me that he liked Jane

is ambiguous: 'he' may or may not be coreferential with 'John'[2].
To account for this ambiguity in syntactic terms, it seems to be
necessary to assume that noncoreferential personal pronouns are not
transformationally derived, but inserted directly in deep structures.

IV.G.18.2. On the genesis of pronouns

Although we shall continue to make the assumption that pronominalization is a substitution operation, mention should be made
of a different approach, which has been the subject of much discussion in the literature.

In 1966 Postal, in his well-known paper "On So-called Pronouns
in English", challenged the substitution theory and argued that
personal and reflexive pronouns are suppletive forms of the definite article. For example, Postal would derive

(1) The boy$_1$ said that he$_1$ was ill

from

(1a) boy$_1$ said it boy$_1$ be ill

essentially by the following steps:

    (a) Pronominalization of NP$_p$; roughly 'boy' $\Longrightarrow$ 'one'.

    (b) Segmentalization of features from NP$_p$ to article position

----

1. 'Senator' and 'boy' are NPs only under the assumption that the
   determiners have been Chomsky-adjoined to the deep structure
   NP (cf. above, p. 356, note).

2. The same is true of 'she' in (2), and of 'he' and 'she' in (1).
   By the same token, 'he' in (2) is not ungrammatical if it is
   not coreferential with the subject NP.

(roughly in the way sketched in section IV.C.2.4). Since NP_p has
the features (among others) (+ Human, + Masculine, + III Person,
+ Sing), the article will be realized as 'he' (the phonological
matrix being inserted in the second lexical pass).

    (c) <u>Pronoun deletion</u>: 'he one' $\Longrightarrow$ 'he'[1].

    What syntactic evidence can be invoked in support of such a
proposal? Note first of all that the pronoun deletion rule comes
late in the derivation. Postal maintains that the personal pronouns
might well have had the forms '⁕ Ione', '⁕ usones', '⁕ itone',
'⁕ sheone', etc. True, these forms look rather monstrous, but in
fact they do occur dialectically[2]. Note further such NPs as

    (2) <u>Us</u> better <u>ones</u>/<u>you</u> quieter <u>ones</u>

in which a modifier separates the pronoun article and the undeleted
pronoun.

    Apart from such examples as (2), the most important arguments
advanced by Postal are: (a) pronouns occur in much the same environments as definite NPs:

    (3) Big as the man was

    (4) Big as $\left\{ \begin{array}{l} \text{I was} \\ \text{you were} \end{array} \right\}$

    (5) ⁕ Big as a woman was[3]

    (6) ⁕ Big as sŏme cars were

(b) the analysis underscores the similarity between personal pronouns and reflexive pronouns. The main difference is that the pro-
form in the reflexives is the noun stem 'self'/'selves'. The feature (+ Pro) is segmented from the noun in the usual way[4], but the
pronoun deletion rule does not apply; (c) the forms 'you' and 'we'
function overtly as articles in a number of cases:

    (7) You guys over there

    (8) We Danes like to travel

----

1. This account is drastically oversimplified. Several steps in the
   derivation have been left out (e.g. <u>definitization</u> and <u>article
   attachment</u>).

2. Cf. Jespersen, 1909-49, Vol. II, 261-62 (as quoted by Postal,
   <u>op. cit</u>. (in Jacobs and Rosenbaum, 1970) 81, note 23).

3. Note (as remarked by Postal, <u>op. cit</u>., 77, note 9) that this
   does not apply to a generic 'a(n)': 'big as an elephant is'.

4. A further feature (+ Genitive) is attached to the article except
   in the forms 'themselves', 'himself', and 'itself'.

(d) paradigms like

    (9) I saw the film you recommended

    (10) I saw the one you recommended

    (11) I saw the film

    (12) * I saw the one

(9) contains an NP dominating the string Det + N + restrictive relative clause. So does (10), but here the head noun is a pronoun. (11) is identical with (9), except for the relative clause. (12) is related to (10) as (11) is to (9), but (12) is ungrammatical. Postal proposes that the gap in the system is filled by the third person personal pronouns. The proper version of (12), then, is

    (13) I saw it

This is corroborated by the fact that these pronouns cannot be followed by a restrictive relative clause:

    (14) * I saw it you recommended

In other words, pronoun deletion and suppletion can operate only if there is no restrictive modifier.

    In this analysis, it is possible to make some significant generalizations with respect to pronominalization. The pivotal point of the generalizations is the assumption that at some stage of the derivation, all pronominalization (with the exception of reflexivization) involves the reduction of a lexical noun to 'one'[1]. From this, features are segmented and shifted to article position.

IV.G.18.3. Forwards and backwards pronominalization

    It is an important feature of English grammar that NP_a need not precede NP_p[2]: pronominalization (we are restricting our attention now to personal pronouns) may operate right to left as well as left to right. Consider such sentences as

----

1. This is true only of anaphoric pronouns. The ambiguity of sentence (8) in the preceding section would be explained in the following way: In the noncoreferential reading, the feature (+ Pro) is present in the deep structure; in the coreferential reading, (+ Pro) is transformationally inserted. In other words, in the noncoreferential reading, 'one' does not originate in a lexical noun. Apart from this, however, the two readings have identical derivations.

2. The term 'antecedent', therefore, is somewhat misleading in this context.

(1) That Jane teased him$_1$ didn't worry Jim$_1$

(2) That Jane teased Jim$_1$ didn't worry him$_1$

(3) John$_1$ said that he$_1$ would come

(4) * He$_1$ said that John$_1$ would come

(5) The car which hit her$_1$ has been pointed out to the police by the little girl$_1$

(6) The car which hit the little girl$_1$ has been pointed out to the police by her$_1$

(7) While he$_1$ wasn't looking the dog bit John$_1$ in the leg

(8) While John$_1$ wasn't looking the dog bit him$_1$ in the leg

(9) The dog bit John$_1$ in the leg while he$_1$ wasn't looking

(10) * The dog bit him$_1$ in the leg while John$_1$ wasn't looking

These sentences demonstrate that the relationship between backwards and forwards pronominalization is a complex one. The question is whether there is a general principle which will correctly predict which of the sentences are grammatical and which are ungrammatical. Before we tackle this problem, let us state the rule of pronominalization in its general form (cf. Ross, 1969e (in Reibel and Schane, 1969) 192):

(11) SI   X - NP - Y - NP - Z
         1   2   3   4   5 $\Longrightarrow$

    SC (a) 1   2   3   4   5
                      (+ Pro)

       (b) 1   2   3   4   5
              (+ Pro)

         Conditions: 2 = 4; obligatory; (a) is unconstrained;
                     (b) is restricted.

In order to illustrate the restrictions on (b), we must now introduce Langacker's important notion of command. He defines this as follows (1969 (in Reibel and Schane, 1969) 167)[1]:

> ... a node A "commands" another node B if (1) neither A nor B dominates the other; and (2) the S-node that most immediately dominates A also dominates B.

We can illustrate the relation of command in terms of the following P-markers:

----

1. Ross, loc. cit. states a similar constraint and in an interesting note discusses the criteria by which the notion 'subordinate

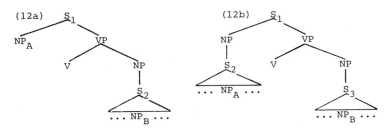

It will be seen that only (12a) meets the definition of the command-relation: in (12b) S_2 most immediately dominates NP_A, but it does not dominate NP_B; hence no relation of command.

With respect to this relation, NP_p may be pronominalized unless NP_p both precedes and commands NP_a. Let us now try to apply this constraint on backwards pronominalization to (1)-(10). Clearly, (4) is ruled out by the constraint: NP_p precedes and commands NP_a:

(4a)

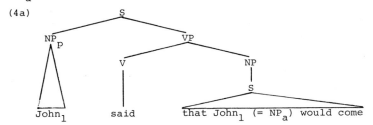

As against this, 'him' in (1) precedes, but does <u>not</u> command 'Jim'.

To account for (5)-(10), recourse must be had to rule-ordering in addition to the command-precedence constraint. In (5) and (6) two rules are involved, namely passivization and pronominalization. The underlying bracketed string of the two sentences is, roughly

(13) $($ $($ the little girl$_1$ $)$ has pointed out to the police
S_1 NP_1 NP_1

$($ the car $($ the car hit the little girl$_1$ $)$ $)$ $)$
NP_2 S_2 S_2 NP_2 S_1

Forwards pronominalization will obligatorily pronominalize 'the little girl' in S_2, deriving

----

clause' may possibly be defined. It is clear that this notion is of crucial importance to pronominalization, since, as we have noted, NP_a and NP_p can never be in the same simplex sentence.

(14) The little girl$_1$ has pointed out to the police the car
     which hit her$_1$

Backwards pronominalization is blocked by the constraint (NP$_p$ both
precedes and commands NP$_a$):

(15) * She$_1$ has pointed out to the police the car which hit
     the little girl$_1$

But (15) would seem to be a necessary intermediate structure to
derive the correct (6). This problem is avoided by ordering passivization before pronominalization. The passive rule, then, will
derive from (13) (reordering NP$_1$ and NP$_2$):

(16) The car which hit the little girl$_1$ has been pointed out
     to the police by the little girl$_1$

To this forwards pronominalization can apply (according to our
rule, it always can). Backwards pronominalization can also apply:
the first occurrence of 'the little girl' no longer commands the
second occurrence.

In (8)-(10) pronominalization interacts with adverb preposing
(which, in this case, has preposed an adverbial clause). This, too,
must precede pronominalization. Otherwise (8) could not be generated (because backwards pronominalization in (10) is blocked by
the constraint (NP$_p$ precedes and commands NP$_a$)).

IV.G.18.4. Some problems

There are numerous difficulties involved in the account of
pronominalization. Here we will look briefly at some problems having
to do (a) with the ordering of rules, (b) the transformational cycle,
and (c) the finiteness of deep structures.

Consider first the following sentences (cf. Lakoff, 1968a, 2)[1]:

(1) John$_1$ heard a whizzing snake near him$_1$
(2) * He$_1$ heard a whizzing snake near John$_1$
(3) Near him$_1$ John$_1$ heard a whizzing snake
(4) * Near John$_1$ he$_1$ heard a whizzing snake

----

1. Observe that these sentences contradict the principle that NP$_a$
and NP$_p$ cannot occur in the same simplex sentence. They also,
furthermore, contradict the principle that reflexivization is
obligatory when the two coreferential NPs occur in the same simplex sentence. In fact, they constitute quite recalcitrant cases.
For further discussion, see below, section IV.G.18.6.

Suppose now that we insist on the ordering adverb preposing - pronominalization, which we have already established. Then we would
expect (4) to be grammatical: it seems to be an ordinary case of
forward pronominalization. Furthermore, we would expect (3) to be
ungrammatical: it should be ruled out by the command constraint
(NP_p both precedes and commands NP_a). If we reverse the ordering,
there is no problem; but that invariably leads to a paradox relative
to (7)-(10) of the preceding section.

   There are even cases in which neither way of ordering the two
rules predicts the correct result. Lakoff, op. cit., 3f. gives the
following example:

   (5) In his apartment where Mary stays John gives her pot to
       smoke

(5) has the following rough underlying structure:

(5a)

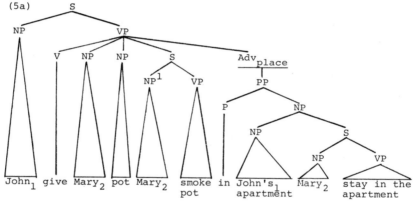

How can (5) be derived? Suppose the order is pronominalization -
adverb preposing. Then the first occurrence of 'Mary' must undergo
backwards pronominalization prior to adverb preposing, but this
is impossible (NP_p precedes and commands NP_a). On the other hand,
'John's' must undergo forwards pronominalization, and this is always possible. If, however, we adopt the reverse ordering, then
indeed forwards pronominalization may apply to the first occurrence
of 'Mary', but now 'John's' must undergo backwards pronominalization, and this is ruled out by the constraint (NP_p now both precedes

----

1. This NP will be deleted by equi NP deletion and is not relevant
   to the discussion of pronominalization.

and commands NP$_a$, i.e. the S node which most immediately dominates NP$_p$ also dominates NP$_a$. Let us leave it at that for the moment.

So far, we have made the tacit assumption that pronominaliza-tion is a cyclic rule. Ross, 1969e argues elegantly that it must be on the basis of evidence provided by such a sentence as

(6) * Knowing that Peter$_1$ had failed annoyed him$_1$

Why is (6) ungrammatical? It seems to be an ordinary case of for-wards pronominalization. To answer this question, we need to con-sider the underlying structure of (6):

(6a)

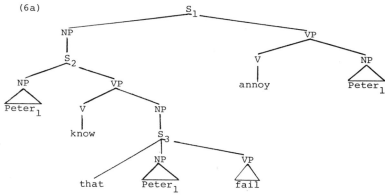

On the first cycle (S$_3$), nothing of interest happens. On the second cycle (S$_2$), forwards pronominalization will operate, converting 'Peter' in S$_3$ into 'he'. Backwards pronominalization cannot apply on this cycle because NP$_p$ ('Peter' in S$_2$) both precedes and commands NP$_a$. Hence, when we reach the last cycle the structure is (assuming that the complementizer 'Poss - ing' is inserted in S$_2$):

(7) Peter's$_1$ knowing that he$_1$ had failed annoyed Peter$_1$

The next step is the deletion of 'Peter's' in the embedded subject sentence by equi NP deletion:

(8) Knowing that he$_1$ had failed annoyed Peter$_1$

The crucial point, then, is that backwards pronominalization is blocked on the second cycle. If it had not been blocked, the input to the last cycle would have been

(9) * His$_1$ knowing that Peter$_1$ had failed annoyed Peter$_1$

If 'his' is deleted from this, there is nothing to prevent the application of forwards pronominalization, the result being the ungrammatical (6). The command constraint in conjunction with the
cyclic principle, then, can account neatly for the ungrammaticality
of (6) and the grammaticality of (8).

On the other hand, there is strong counterevidence to the hypothesis that pronominalization is in the cycle. Lakoff, op. cit.,
26ff. shows, convincingly it seems to me, that there are cases
similar to (6)-(9) which simply cannot be accounted for by pronominalization as a cyclic rule. Furthermore, the following set
of assumptions and concomitant conclusions leads to the same result:

(a) Nominalization is a transformation.

(b) Given (a), particle movement must be a last-cyclic rule
(cf. above, p. 416).

(c) It can be shown on independent grounds that extraposition
follows particle movement.

(d) Given (b) and (c), extraposition must be a last-cyclic
rule.

(e) Extraposition (in all versions, i.e. 'ordinary' extraposition, extraposition from NP, and cleft extraposition) produce structures which have a bearing on pronominalization.

(f) Given (e), pronominalization must be a last-cyclic rule,
following extraposition.

Consider now the following sentences:

(10) That John$_1$ failed a second time rather worries him$_1$
(11) That he$_1$ failed a second time rather worries John$_1$
(12) * It rather worries him$_1$ that John$_1$ failed a second time
(13) It rather worries John$_1$ that he$_1$ failed a second time
(14) A lecturer who loved Mary$_1$ eloped with her$_1$
(15) * A lecturer eloped with her$_1$ who loved Mary$_1$
(16) What disturbed John$_1$ was my disregarding him$_1$
(17) * What disturbed him$_1$ was my disregarding John$_1$
.(18) It was my disregarding John$_1$ that disturbed him$_1$
(19) It was my disregarding him$_1$ that disturbed John$_1$
(20) That Jane likes John$_1$ is one of the things which he$_1$
     doesn't understand
(21) That Jane likes him$_1$ is one of the things which John$_1$
     doesn't understand

Under the assumption that extraposition precedes pronominalization,
(12) and (15) are blocked by the constraint (NP_p precedes and commands NP_a). (17) is interesting. It is a pseudo-cleft sentence. In
its deep structure there is nothing to prevent backwards pronominalization (NP_p precedes but does not command NP_a). The question is,
then, why it is ungrammatical. The answer would seem to hinge on
the nature of 'be': it is equative. It may be the case, then, that
backwards pronominalization blocks across equative 'be' (cf. also
Postal, 1971, 23). Now, (18) and (19) are cleft sentences. As we
have seen, part of their derivation involves cleft extraposition.
Therefore, if this rule precedes pronominalization on the last
cycle, the relative clauses are shifted to the 'safe' side of equative 'be', and pronominalization works backwards (as well as forwards) as it should. The derivation of (20) and (21) is straightforward because 'be' is not equative, but attributive.

Recall now that Wh-fronting, when it applies to nonembedded
interrogative sentences, operates on the last cycle (cf. above,
section IV.G.11.3 and note). Since Wh-fronting creates environments which are relevant to pronominalization, this rule must follow it and hence be last-cyclic. Consider the following sentences,
which are both grammatical (cf. Postal, 1970b, 1971, 84f.):

(22) Who that $John_1$ saw do you thing that he_1 is thinking of
(23) Who that he_1 saw do you think that $John_1$ is thinking of

The underlying structure of these two sentences looks something
like this:

(24) (Q you think it ($John_1$ think of (Wh-someone ($John_1$
    S_1 S_2 NP S_3

    see   Wh - someone))))
    (+ Rel) S_3 NP S_2 S_1

Now, if pronominalization applied cyclically, forwards pronominalization would operate obligatorily on the second cycle (S_2), whereas
backwards pronominalization would block. In other words, it would
be possible to derive only (22). If, however, the NP (i.e. Wh-someone + the relative clause) is moved on the final cycle by the
Wh-fronting rule, the proper environment for backwards pronominalization is created: NP_p precedes but no longer commands NP_a.
Thus both (22) and (23) are generated.

It seems, then, that the analysis of pronominalization invariably leads to paradoxes, both with respect to rule-ordering
and with respect to the cycle. Noting this, Lakoff, op. cit., concludes that there is something wrong with the formulation of the
rule as given in the preceding section. Thus, to account for the
fully grammatical (5), pronominalization, which follows adverb
preposing, must - contrary to what the precedence-command constraint asserts - be allowed to go backwards from a subordinate
clause and affect a nonsubject NP in the main clause. Forwards pronominalization must also be constrained (here too the subject-non-
subject distinction is crucial). Lakoff further argues that not
only is the rule last-cyclic, but that it <u>cannot</u> be followed by
any other rule; this (p. 10) "is a necessary fact, a fact about
the nature of anaphoric processes in language, not a fact about
one rule of English". The strongest piece of evidence in support of
this hypothesis is that anaphoric relationships interact with low-
level phonetic stress assignment rules (rules, that is, which operate after the normal phonological rules). For example, a direct object, which is normally stressed, cannot both be stressed and serve
as the antecedent of an anaphoric pronoun:

(25) When he_1 entered the room Mary kissed $\left\{ \begin{array}{c} * \; \underline{John}_1 \\ John_1 \end{array} \right\}$

This being the case, Lakoff argues that to the highest possible degree the constraints on pronominalization should be stated as output conditions. However, for reasons which we cannot go into here,
neither output conditions nor conditions on the pronominalization
rule itself can account for (6)-(9) and related phenomena. Consequently, there must be some kind of transformational constraint in
the grammar which is not associated with the pronominalization rule.
We will not pursue this matter any further. Suffice it to have indicated that the conditions on pronominalization which we discussed
in the preceding section are doubtless incapable of handling all
the facts.

The last problem to be discussed relates to the question of
finiteness in length of deep structures. Bach and Peters (see
Bach, 1970) have pointed out that the following three assumptions:

(a) Deep structures are finite in lenth
(b) Pronominalization is a transformation as stated in rule
     (11) of the preceding section, and as such

(c) operates on full NPs (including relative clauses)

are incompatible. This becomes apparent in those cases where pronouns have replaced NPs containing relative clauses. Consider the
following sentence (cf. Bach, op. cit., 121):

(26) The man who shows he$_1$ deserves it$_2$ will get the prize$_2$
he$_1$ desires

The deep structure of (1) is

(1a) The man who shows that the man deserves the prize that
the man who shows that the man deserves the prize that
the man ... (ad infinitum) will get the prize that the
man who shows that the man deserves the prize that the
man who shows ... (ad infinitum)

To avoid this dilemma, it is clear that one of the three assumptions must be given up. Furthermore, it will have to be either (b)
or (c) (since there is universal agreement that deep structures
should be finite in length). Suppose now that (b) is given up. In
that case, pronouns must be generated directly in deep structure
and there must be semantic rules to account for coreference. This
is essentially the approach taken by adherents of the extended
standard theory. The most thorough-going exposition of the interpretivist analysis of pronouns is Jackendoff, 1972. Alternatively,
assumption (c) might go. We would then need to set up more abstract deep structures than those envisaged by adherents of the
(extended) standard theory. We return to this in section V.C.

Meanwhile, we will consider some other examples of deeper
deep structures which seem to be required, given the validity of
assumptions (c) and (d) and the KP-hypothesis.

IV.G.18.5. Deeper deep structures

Consider the following sentence (cf. McCawley, 1967 (in
Rosenberg and Travis, 1971) 518ff. and Lakoff, 1970a, Chapter 5):

(1) I must strengthen this argument, but I don't know yet
how to set about it

(1) is ambiguous: it may mean (a) 'my argument is not exactly weak,
but it can be made stronger', or (b) 'my argument is weak, I must
make it strong'. In other words, the verb 'strengthen' reflects
both the positive and the comparative form of the adjective. The

KP-hypothesis, of course, requires that this ambiguity should be
made explicit in the deep structure. Consequently, the underlying
lexical item must be the adjective 'strong' and not the verb
'strengthen'. The verb 'strengthen' denotes <u>change</u>. What we need,
then, is an abstract element which can combine with the adjective
'strong' to form a verb of change. Before we turn to a possible
deep structure for (1), we must consider the pronoun 'it': which
NP does 'it' replace? It cannot be 'this argument'; it must be the
phrase 'strengthen this argument', but that is a VP, and as we have
formulated the rule, it should be an NP. This would seem to point
to an underlying structure which is abstract enough to define
'strengthen this argument' as an NP. Observe now that (1) is transformationally related to

(2) I must cause this argument to become strong(er)

From (2) three things appear: (a) 'this argument' and 'strong' are
now related in a subject-predicate relationship, (b) the verb 'become' is an explicit semantic representation of the notion of
'change', and (c) 'this argument to become strong(er)' is the object of the verb 'cause' and hence an NP. Both (a), (b), and (c)
must be specified in the deep structure of (1), which must therefore be something like this (in the noncomparative reading and
omitting 'must'):

(1a)

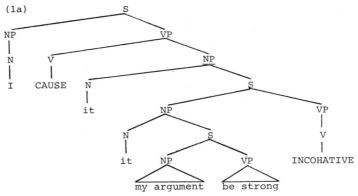

CAUSE and INCOHATIVE should be interpreted as abstract predicates.
INCOHATIVE is transformationally incorporated into the adjective
'strong' to form a verb of change, and this verb in turn combines

with CAUSE to form a <u>causative verb</u>[1]. The underscored NP is that
which is pronominalized by 'it'.

The pronoun 'it' in (1), then, is an example of a syntactic
fact which can force the analyst to posit more abstract deep structures than originally countenanced in the theory.

Locative adverbs present similar problems. The question is
what 'it' pronominalizes in (3) (cf. Lakoff, 1970c; for discussion,
see also Chomsky, 1972, 90f. and Jackendoff, 1972, 272ff.):

> (3) The workers went on strike in Copenhagen, but <u>it</u> hap-
> pened only sporadically in the province

It seems clear that the locative adverb 'in Copenhagen' cannot be
included in the pronominalized constituent. Our PS-rules would assign the following rough deep structure to the first conjunct of (3):

(3a)

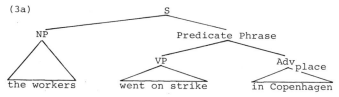

In (3a) 'in Copenhagen' is dominated by the same S as 'the workers
went on strike'. Hence it cannot be the S which is pronominalized.
It must be 'the workers went on strike'. But this is not even a
constituent. One possible solution is to set up the locative adverbial as a deep structure VP in a higher clause (cf. also above,
p. 305):

(3b)

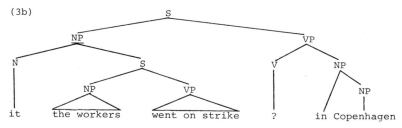

In (3b) ? stands for an abstract underlying verb with a reading

----

1. There is no need to go into the nature of the T-rules here. In
   a generative semantics framework, there would be a rule of <u>pred-
   icate raising</u>. See further below, section V.C.4.

something like 'take place'. In English, but not in all languages,
this verb is deleted in surface structure. Given the validity of
(3b), 'it' in (3) pronominalizes the underscored NP in (3b).

IV.G.18.6. Reflexivization

The rule of reflexivization has been discussed at various
points of the exposition. It was formulated on p. 201. The two
main constraints are, as we have seen, (a) the two NPs involved
must be coreferential, and (b) they must occur in the same simplex
sentence. The rule always operates left to right (for a qualification, see below). Clearly, this fact follows directly from the command constraint: the first coreferential NP always precedes and
commands the second coreferential NP.

There are a number of phenomena which are difficult to bring
to heel. The difficulties are caused by the simplex S constraint.
We have already encountered some of them, viz. in the attempt to
state the interrelationship between reflexivization on the one
hand and pseudo-clefting and S pruning on the other (above, pp.
373f., 389ff.). Let us now examine the following sentences[1]:

(1) The men$_1$ threw a smokescreen around themselves$_1$

(2) The men$_1$ found a smokescreen around them$_1$

(3) He$_1$ saw an aeroplane circling above him$_1$

(4) She$_1$ married beneath her$_1$

(5) He$_1$ pushed the girl behind $\left\{\begin{array}{l} \text{him}_1 \\ \text{him(self)}_1 \end{array}\right\}$

(6) He$_1$ found the blanket over him$_1$

(7) He$_1$ has control over himself$_1$

(8) He$_1$ drew the blanket over him$_1$

(9) He$_1$ kept it near him$_1$

(10) He$_1$ drew it toward him$_1$

(11) John$_1$ told Bill a story about $\left\{\begin{array}{l} \text{himself}_1 \\ \text{* him}_1 \end{array}\right\}$

(12) Tom$_1$ told Dick$_1$ Harry's story about $\left\{\begin{array}{l} \text{him}_1 \\ \text{* himself}_1 \end{array}\right\}$

Given condition (b), it is immediately obvious that the chief prob-

----

1. (1), (2), (6), and (7) are taken from Lees and Klima, 1963,
   18f., (9) and (10) from Chomsky, 1965, 146f., and (11) and (12)
   from Jackendoff, 1972, 133. Note that 'him' in (12) may be coreferential with either 'Tom' or 'Dick'.

lem confronting us is whether or not it is possible to postulate
a two-sentence source for those of the sentences in which the rule
has failed to apply. (1) is straightforward ('around themselves'
being defined as a sentence-internal adverbial by our rules). (2)
may perhaps be analysed as containing a complement sentence:

(2a) (the men found a smokescreen (the smokescreen be
     S_1 S_2

     around them))
            S_2 S_1

Reflexivization does not apply on the first cycle (S_2). On the
last cycle (S_1), reflexivization does not apply either, but equi
NP deletion (which, we assume, must be ordered after reflexivization
(cf. above, p. 395)) does apply, removing 'the smokescreen' from S_2.
The S node is pruned, and 'to be' optionally deleted. (6) and (9)
may presumably be analysed in the same way as (2). (7) differs
from (6) in that 'over' is an integral part of the complex transitive verb 'have control over' (the semantic equivalent of the
verb 'control'). (7) therefore is one sentence in deep structure
and reflexivization is correctly predicted. In (3) it is clear
that relative reduction has applied. As this results in the
pruning of the S node, it is difficult to explain why reflexivization has not applied on the top cycle (cf. also section IV.G.16.6).
The only way to resolve this difficulty would be to place an ad-
hoc and completely arbitrary condition on the pruning convention
that would ensure that the S is retained over the truncated clause
in order to prevent reflexivization from applying[1,2]. Suppose, however,
that we do accept such a condition. In that case, we might consider
deriving (4) from something like 'she married someone who was beneath her' by relative reduction. In addition, object deletion would
have to delete 'someone'. However, deletion would operate on the
following structure: ((someone)   (beneath her)   )   , and
                    NP NP   NP Adv   Adv NP
this is clearly a violation of the A-over-A principle. (5) is ambiguous. On one reading, it means 'the girl who was behind him';
on another, the prepositional phrase is an adverb of direction.
On the former reading, reflexivization does not apply (because of

----

1. This might also account for sentences (7) and (32) of section
   IV.G.16.6).

2. It is possible, of course, that (2) might also be derived by
   relative reduction. However, it seems to have more in common
   with (6), which could clearly not be so derived.

the ad-hoc condition on pruning); on the latter, it seems to be optional (though 'him' seems more natural than 'himself'). This presents a new difficulty, since normally the rule is obligatory. (8)
and (10) are recalcitrant and can perhaps not be given a systematic
explanation (cf. Chomsky, 1965, 146f.).

(11) and (12) lead into new difficulties. Both contain what
is generally referred to as <u>picture nouns</u>. Suppose that (11) had
not contained a reflexive pronoun, but a proper noun like, say,
'Eric'. It would then be tempting to analyse 'about Eric' as the
remnants of a relative clause. With the reflexive pronoun this
does not work. For in that case, pruning would necessarily have
to apply before reflexivization on the last cycle, and we would be
saddled with a paradox relative to (3), (4), and (5) (on the first
reading). In other words, the relative reduction analysis encounters
all sorts of difficulties. We might assume instead that (11) <u>is</u> a
simplex sentence. However, (12) immediately thwarts that assumption:
why is the reflexive pronoun in (12) ungrammatical? It has been suggested that picture nouns should be derived from underlying abstract
verbs in the way discussed in section IV.G.17.2. One motivation for
this is that phrases like 'about him(self)' in (11) and (12) are
intuitively felt to be related to 'story' as objects. In that analysis, then, both (11) and (12) have a two-sentence source. They are
the result of nominalization. The underlying structure would be
something like this (cf. McCawley, 1968d) (we ignore the problem
relating to dative movement (cf. above, p. 417 and note))[1]:

$$(13) \quad (\ \begin{Bmatrix} \text{John}_1 \\ \text{Tom}_1 \end{Bmatrix}_{S_1} \quad \text{told} \ \begin{Bmatrix} \text{Bill} \\ \text{Dick} \end{Bmatrix} \quad \text{Det - N} \ (\ \begin{Bmatrix} \text{someone} \\ \text{Harry} \end{Bmatrix}_{S_2}$$

$$\text{✱ story} \ \begin{Bmatrix} \text{John}_1 \\ \text{Tom}_1 \end{Bmatrix} \ )\ )_{S_2\ S_1}$$

The derivation might be roughly as follows: In (11) the generic subject 'someone' is deleted. This causes S_2 to be pruned. Reflexivization, which we will assume precedes nominalization, may now apply
on the top cycle. In (12) reflexivization cannot apply on the S_1
cycle, because nominalization, which also causes pruning, has not yet
applied. After nominalization, 'Tom' undergoes forwards pronominal-

----

1. Note that 'himself' in (12) is grammatical if it is coreferential with 'Harry's'. In that case 'Harry' would be the object
   of the embedded sentence instead of 'Tom' and reflexivization
   would apply obligatorily on the lower cycle.

ization.

It has been noted by Jackendoff (e.g. 1972, 131ff.) that postulating abstract underlying 'picture verbs' cannot preserve the
simplex S constraint in every case[1]. Thus in the following sentence
NP_p and NP_a are obviously not in the same simplex sentence[2]:

(14) $John_1$ took comfort in the thought that what his friends
     expected to hear from the witnesses in the box would be

     a pack of lies about his wife and $\left\{ \begin{array}{l} * \ him_1 \\ himself_1 \end{array} \right\}$

Jackendoff has further noted that in some cases picture nouns allow backwards reflexivization (i.e. the rule operates right to
left). An example is

(15) The fact that there is a painting of $\left\{ \begin{array}{l} himself_1 \\ him \end{array} \right\}$

     hanging in the National Gallery rather pleases $John_1$

It seems to be a condition on backwards reflexivization that the
antecedent of the reflexive pronoun should be in the main clause
relative to the cycle on which reflexivization takes place. This is
the case in (15), but not in

(16) The fact that there was a picture of $\left\{ \begin{array}{l} * \ himself_1 \\ him_1 \end{array} \right\}$ in the

     victim's wallet caused the police to suspect that Tom_1
     was the killer

On the whole, however, many of the phenomena discussed in this
section are somewhat marginal. In the vast majority of cases, the
simplex S constraint makes the correct predictions. Consequently,
as we have seen time and again, the rule of reflexivization is of
great importance to the construction of syntactic arguments.

Notes and some further references

IV.G.2. For the agreement rule stated in terms of features, see also
Jacobs and Rosenbaum, 1968, 130ff.

----

1. Such facts are invoked by Jackendoff as substantive evidence in
   support of the interpretivist approach to pronouns (cf. above,
   p. 431).

2. See in this connection also Ross, 1970a. Ross points out that
   'like' phrases do not obey the constraint. An example is 'he
   seemed to be trying to convince us that a guy like himself could
   never have done a thing like that'. Cf. also sentences (1), (2),
   and (3) in the notes to section IV.D.17.

IV.G.3,4. The formulation of affix hopping in the text is a fairly
conservative one. For discussion of the auxiliary in terms of features and segmentalization transformations, see Jacobs and Rosenbaum,
1968, 110ff. In section IV.C.1 we were at pains to demonstrate
the special status of 'be' (as a main verb). Therefore we distinguished 'be' from V in PS-rule 6. However, it is clear that this
formulation prevents a satisfactory statement of affix hopping in
terms of Chomsky-adjunction (which always involves adjunction of
some element to a node, not to a terminal symbol) One way out of
this dilemma would be to revise PS-rule 6 as follows:

$$VP \longrightarrow \begin{Bmatrix} Cop \\ V \end{Bmatrix}$$

and have 'be' entered in the lexicon with the category feature
(+ Cop). Cf. also Chomsky, 1965, 107. The 'be + en' of passive
sentences presents a similar problem. In particular, for 'be + en'
to be encompassed by the rule as formulated here, it would be necessary to have it immediately dominated by a node other than Aux.
This difficulty reflects the more general problem of providing an
adequate account of 'be' in passive sentences. The reader may wonder why 'do' should be generated by a T-rule rather than be generated by a PS-rule and then be deleted in certain contexts by a do
deletion rule. Such an analysis would be quite possible and has
been proposed by many linguists. For some discussion, see Borkin
et al. (eds.), 1972, 12ff., Postal, 1974, 387ff., and Akmajian and
Heny, 1975, 131ff. In a wider context the status of 'do' raises a
number of questions. We return to some of these questions in sections IV.G.14.4 and 15.1 below.

IV.G.5. We have taken dative movement involving 'for' and 'to' to
be one rule. See in this connection Fillmore, 1965, Kuroda, 1968b,
and Postal, 1971, 125ff. Consult further Jackendoff and Culicover,
1971 and Borkin et al. (eds.), 1972, 18ff. The rule of topicalization (so named by Ross, 1967, 115f. (identical to Postal's Y-move-
ment (1971, 142)) is a last-cyclic, unbounded left movement rule
(cf. p. 286 and note). In other words, it may front a constituent
over any number of embedded sentences. Consider now (1)-(8):

(1) To my mother he said he had promised to give the book
(2) The book he said he had promised to give to my mother
(3) ? The book he said he had promised to give my mother
(4) ? My mother he said he had promised to give the book
(5) For my mother he said he had promised to buy the old house
(6) The old house he said he had promised to buy for my mother
(7) * The old house he said he had promised to buy my mother
(8) * My mother he said he had promised to buy the old house

These sentences seem to confirm the statement made in the text with
respect to the interaction of topicalization and dative movement.
It would follow from this that topicalization must be formulated in
such a way that it cannot move an NP which occurs in the immediate
proximity of another NP (this could be done by stating conditions
on the variables surrounding the NP to be moved (alternatively,
the fact could be accounted for in terms of a global constraint on
topicalization)). We have assumed that dative movement is a cyclic
rule. However, there is some evidence that it is last-cyclic (cf. p.
416f.). If it is, we could block the derivation of sentences like (7)
and (8) by ordering topicalization before dative movement on the
last cycle (after the application of the former, the SI of the latter could not be met). As indicated in the text, the general effect
of topicalization is thematic emphasis. Other rules have the same
effect. Adverb preposing is one of them (see also notes to section
IV.G.14).

IV.G.6. On particles and particle movement, consult Fraser, 1966
and Legum, 1968. Ross, 1967, 27ff. discusses the interaction of
particle movement and complex NP shift. Postal, 1974, 412ff. is
concerned with the relationship between particle movement and the
raising rule. On particles and prepositions in such sentences as
(32)-(37), see also Jackendoff, 1973. Emonds, 1972b has considered
the interaction of particles with dative movement and reformulated
dative movement within his theory of structure preserving transformations (Emonds would consider such sentences as (22) in the text
as grammatical). For discussion of Emonds' proposal, see Jackendoff,
1975a, 19ff. Langendoen, 1970a discusses the functional implications
of particle movement. The following sentences are considered:

   (1) The assailant knocked the man who put the rebellion which
       caused the banks to close down down down
   (2) The assailant knocked down the man who put down the
       rebellion which caused the banks to close down

(1) is derived from (2) by particle movement. Langendoen argues
that (1) is a grammatical, but unacceptable sentence. He views the
relationship between such sentences as an explanation of the optionality of particle movement: the rule will not apply if it
reduces intellegibility (i.e. if it renders deep structures inac-
cessible). This seems a plausible enough hypothesis. However, it
is language-specific. As noted in the text, particle movement is
obligatory in Danish. Consider the following examples (translational
equivalents):

   (3a) * Han slog <u>ned</u> den mand som have skrevet <u>ned</u> ordene
   (3b) He knocked <u>down</u> the man who had written <u>down</u> the words
   (4a) Han slog den mand som havde skrevet ordene <u>ned</u> <u>ned</u>
   (4b) He knocked the man who had written the words <u>down</u> <u>down</u>
   (5a) Han slog den mand <u>ned</u> som have skrevet ordene <u>ned</u>
   (5b) He knocked the man <u>down</u> who had written the words <u>down</u>

Of these, (5a) is the most natural Danish sentence (obviously). It
is derived from (4a) by extraposition from NP. It follows from this
that a functional explanation of the Danish facts in such cases
must focus on the rule of extraposition from NP. In other words,
English has two ways of preventing mind-bogglers from coming to the
surface where Danish has only one.

IV.G.7. Most accounts of transformational grammar still assume
that the passive rule is optional and state it in its classic
Syntactic Structures form. Special mention should be made of an
analysis proposed by Hasegawa, 1968. Hasegawa would derive a sentence like 'the man was killed by the car' from a deep structure
of the following kind (see overleaf):
In other words, a passive sentence is a two-sentence structure in
which 'be' is a transitive verb in the highest sentence. Passivization applies on the top cycle. The two NPs in the embedded sentence
are reordered; after this equi NP deletion deletes 'the man' in the
embedded sentence. This analysis has certain advantages. Above all,
it explains the presence of 'be' in passive sentences (although not
the presence of 'by'). However, it encounters difficulties in some
cases. Perhaps the most serious trouble arises with fixed idiomatic
phrases (cf. above, p. 89f.). Thus the derivation of the sentence
'recourse was had to semantic criteria by traditional grammarians'
would require that 'recourse' be posited as the subject of 'be'
in the topmost sentence. But 'recourse' cannot occur independently
as a subject in deep structure. For discussion of Hasegawa's pro-

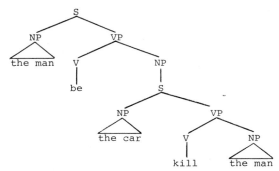

posal, see Stockwell et al., 1968, Vol. II, 841ff., McCawley, 1970b
(especially note 6), Chomsky, 1970 (in Jacobs and Rosenbaum, 1970)
219, note 29, Perlmutter, 1970b (in Jacobs and Rosenbaum, 1970)
109ff., and R. Lakoff, 1971a. R. Lakoff's paper provides a critical
discussion of the different approaches to the passive construction. A standard work on passive sentences is Svartvik, 1966.

IV.G.8. On 'there', see Long, 1968, Borkin et al. (eds.), 1972,
24ff., and Huddleston, 1971, 321ff. Akmajian and Heny, 1975 discuss
the rule in great detail and provide arguments for the NP status
of 'there' (cf. also p. 367f.). In this connection, see also Chomsky,
1970 (in Jacobs and Rosenbaum, 1970) 220, note 32. On existential
sentences, see further Lyons, 1968, 388ff.

IV.G.9. Stockwell et al., 1968, Vol. I, 255ff. present a critical
summary of approaches to negation up through 1968. The analysis
of 'some' and 'any' proposed by Fillmore, 1967 and adopted by
Stockwell et al. has been subjected to a good deal of criticism.
See for example R. Lakoff, 1969b and Jackendoff, 1972. For an analysis of negation involving the generation of 'not' in its surface
structure positions with a concomitant set of semantic interpretation rules,see Jackendoff, 1969. The question of the interrelationship between quantifiers and negation (and also other rules such
as passive and interrogation) has played a central role in the
debate about the nature of deep structure. We return to this in
section V.C.1. The reader who wishes to familiarize himself with
some of the problems and the arguments which have been brought
to bear on them should consult such works as Carden, 1968, Baker,
1970a, Partee, 1970, Lakoff, 1970d, Lakoff, 1970a, 173ff., and
Jackendoff, 1971, 1972, Chapter Eight. On double negatives, which
we have not discussed, but which are an essential feature of English grammar, see Baker, 1970b. Not transportation (alternatively
negative raising) was first discussed by Fillmore, 1963. It has
received a good deal of attention and there is no general agreement
as to whether the rule exists or not. See for example Klima, 1964,
Jackendoff, 1969, Lindholm, 1969, Lakoff, 1970a, 30ff., 1970c,
Carden, 1971, Chapin, 1973, Cattell, 1973, and Seuren, 1974a.

IV.G.10. On the traditional account of imperative sentences, see
Postal, 1964c. For an overview, see Stockwell et al., 1968, Vol.
II, 659ff. The many facets of the imperative construction are in-
vestigated in Bolinger, 1967a. For example, Bolinger notes that a
sentence like

(1) Take a shot of LSD every day and be a happier person

seems to be more related to an 'if-then'-construction than to the imperative (the same is true of sentence (8) in section IV.G.10.2: a housewife who sees this sentence in a store knows that she can only win a dishwasher if she buys something) (cf. also Jespersen, 1924, 314f.). For discussion of the imperative, consult further such works as Thorne, 1966, Arbini, 1969, and Borkin et al. (eds.), 1972. For an attempted explanation of the difference between 'Let us go' and 'Let's go', see Huddleston, 1971, 52ff. For discussion of the interrelationship between questions and imperative sentences in terms of speech act theory, see Sadock, 1970 and Green, 1975.

IV.G.11. On questions, see Katz and Postal, 1964, 79ff., Stockwell et al., 1968, Vol. II, 625ff., and Huddleston, 1971, 9ff. The analysis of 'Wh+either-or' as an adverb does not seem to be very well motivated. For example, as noted by Huddleston, op. cit., 15, it is difficult to find environments in which 'yes' or 'no' and 'either-or' are mutually substitutable. Furthermore, the tree on p. 320 makes it virtually impossible to provide a natural deep structure for negative questions. It might be descriptively more adequate to derive yes-no questions from an underlying structure containing two disjunctively coordinated sentences, the second of which is negated. Thus, 'did Peter come' would be derived from (Q whether (Peter came) or (Neg Peter came)), (part of) the second conjunct being optionally deleted. Given that this hypothesis is correct, it is natural to assume that in the underlying structure of a negative question, Neg is contained in the first rather than in the second conjunct (cf. Stockwell et al., 1968, Vol. II, 640 and Langendoen, 1970b, 168ff.). Katz, 1972, Chapter V adopts the double-sentence source of yes-no questions but continues to analyse 'whether' as an adverb. On the question of 'wh-words' in English (interrogative and relative pronouns), see Chomsky, 1962, Koutsoudas, 1968, and Kuroda, 1968a. Bach, 1971 discusses the universal aspects of question formation. For a reply to the universalist assumption, see Wachowicz, 1974. The problems relating to the precise formulation of a tag-question rule are discussed in some detail in Akmajian and Heny, 1975, 202ff. On tag-questions, see also Arbini, 1969 and Huddleston, 1970a. We are concerned in the text only with non-embedded sentences. As we noted, the rule of Wh-fronting operates on the last cycle in such cases. Consider now the following sentences:

(1) He asked me to tell him <u>who</u> we thought <u>NP</u> would come

(2) He asked me whether she would come

In (1) the underscored NP has been questioned and fronted as indicated; (2) contains an embedded yes-no question. We could account for such questions by positing Q also in embedded sentences. In other words, in the deep structures of (1) and (2), there would be a Q preceding 'we' and 'whether' respectively. In (1) the SI of the fronting rule would only be met on the cycle in which Q occurs (i.e. it would not be met on the lowest cycle). This mode of rule application has been referred to as higher trigger cyclic (Postal, 1972b, 212). In other words, Wh-fronting is 'last-cyclic' only where nonembedded sentences are concerned. However, there is one serious difficulty about this proposal: embedded questions have no independent illocutionary force. Consequently, Q in an embedded sentence is reduced into a mere syntactic device in much the same way as in tag-questions. We merely note this problem and offer no solutions. For further discussion of problems relating to the generation of questions, consult such works as Baker, 1970c, Bresnan, 1970, Kuno and Robinson, 1973, and Langacker, 1974b.

IV.G.12. The sketchy account of comparative sentences given here is based mainly on Lees, 1961. Comparative sentences present a number of intricate problems. Consult such papers as Smith, 1961, Pilch, 1965, Doherty and Schwarz, 1967, Huddleston, 1967 (see also idem, 1971, Chapter 6), Stanley, 1969, Hale, 1970, and Bresnan, 1973. The rules of deletion under identity are difficult to formulate. In particular, a number of problems relating to constituency are involved. For discussion, see Ross, 1969c and 1970b. Consult also Maling, 1972 and Hankamer, 1973.

IV.G.13. A pioneering paper on conjunction is Gleitman, 1965. Gleitman adopts the view that the grammar should provide for only conjunction reduction, as does also Schane, 1966. The opposite view is taken by Wierzbicka, 1972 (written in 1967) and Dougherty, 1970a, 1971. Arguments that the grammar should provide for both phrasal conjunction and conjunction reduction may be found in Smith, 1969 (written in 1965), and Lakoff and Peters, 1969 (first published in 1966). Stockwell et al., 1968, Vol. I, 319ff. provide an overview of approaches. Transformational rule schemata are given in some detail. Dik, 1968, 94ff. discusses the theoretical implications of incorporating rule schemata in the grammar and also provides a critique of transformational analysis of conjunction in general. R. Lakoff, 1971b explores the semantic constraints on conjunction. McCawley, 1968a rejects conjunction reduction and analyses conjunction in terms of symbolic logic. For some discussion of McCawley's proposal, see Chomsky, 1972, 76ff. Finally: the ordering paradox noted in the text can be resolved under Hasegawa's analysis of passive sentences (cf. notes to IV.G.7). The reader is invited to work this out.

IV.G.14. The most important works on relative clauses were cited in the text. As is well known, relative pronouns in restrictive clauses alternate between what may be called wh-forms and that. Since 'that' is more restricted in use than the wh-forms, it is reasonable to consider the former marked, the latter unmarked. A third possibility is, as we have seen, zero. This in turn is more restricted than 'that' and is therefore marked relative to 'that'. Since it is the case that wherever we have zero we can also have 'that', it is natural to assume that the deletion of the relative pronoun proceeds via a stage of 'that-replace-wh':

$$\text{wh-forms} \Longrightarrow \underset{\text{stage 1}}{\text{that}} \Longrightarrow \underset{\text{stage 2}}{\emptyset}$$

Stage 1 must be constrained. In particular, the wh-form must occupy the initial position in the relative clause. Thus we may have

(1) The book from which he read was interesting
(2) The book which he read from was interesting
(3) ∎ The book from that he read was interesting
(4) The book that he read from was interesting

The most important constraint on stage 2 is that the relative pronoun must not be the subject (with the exceptions noted in the text). Consult Huddleston, 1971, 229 and Stockwell et al., 1968, Vol. II, rules 31 and 34 in the rule chart. Consider now the following sentence:

    (5) Tigers, which are carnivores, are dangerous animals
(5), in which the relative clause is nonrestrictive, entails
    (6) Tigers are carnivores
which in turn makes a generic statement. Recall now the constraint
on relativization mentioned in note 2 on p. 347. Under the assumption that the same relative rule generates restrictive as well as
nonrestrictive relative clauses, this constraint must be global
in nature: the rule must 'know about' the origin of the clause
on which it is operating. The only alternative would seem to be
for the grammar to contain two distinct relative clause rules (as
suggested by Ross, 1967, 115). The derivation of attributive adjectives from underlying relative clauses facilitates the statement
of selectional restrictions: these now have to be stated only with
respect to predicative adjectives, whereas, otherwise, they would
have to be duplicated in order to account for the same adjectives
in attributive position. Not all attributive adjectives can be derived from underlying relative clauses. Thus 'heavy' in 'a heavy
smoker' is the surface reflex of an underlying adverb. The selectional properties shared by adjectives and adverbs could be stated
in terms of redundancy rules. The statement made in the text that
PPs cannot be preposed stands in need of qualification. Consider
a sentence like 'I expect my New York friend to take care of this'.
In this, 'New York' is most naturally seen as being derived from
an underlying structure like 'my friend who is from New York'. In
other words, 'New York' in attributive position is a surface reflex
of an underlying PP in a relative clause. There are a number of
constraints on modifier preposing which we have not discussed. One
relates to negation and leads back to the problem of how a sentence
like 'a not (un)happy person entered the room' should be characterized (cf. above, p. 43). The trees on p. 356 raise an important
question concerning pruning. It seems counterintuitive to claim
that in the NP 'an English cottage', 'English' is an adjective
which is an adjective phrase which is a verb phrase which is a
predicate phrase. What seems to be required is "a principle for
deleting single-branching non-terminal nodes which carry no relevant
information" (Robinson, 1970, 283). We may note here that this
specific aspect of the derived constituent structure problem (in
conjunction with the desirability of formalizing the notion 'head
of' (i.e. the notion of endocentricity)) has led to a reformulation
of the base by some scholars in terms of dependency relations - so-
called dependency grammars. We will not go into this. The interested
reader is referred to such papers as Hays, 1964 and Robinson, 1969,
1970. Pied Piping is discussed extensively in Postal, 1971. Observe
that if PPs are defined as NPs in deep structure, the definition
of 'indirect object' in configurational terms will no longer hold.
It will now have to be defined in terms of the relative order of
the NPs under the immediate domination of VP (cf. p. 282). Note also
that this analysis of PPs seems to make it possible to collapse
the rules of topicalization and adverb preposing where adverbial
PPs are concerned (cf. Postal, 1971, 196f.).

IV.G.15. An overall introduction to the approaches to sentence
clefting may be found in Stockwell et al., 1968, Vol. II, 799ff.
The analysis of 'what' as derived from 'the thing which' makes it
impossible to state any relationship between pseudo-cleft and cleft
sentences. Akmajian, 1970 (following some suggestions made by
Chomsky) proposes that pseudo-cleft sentences be derived from head-
less clauses, i.e. clauses having 'it' as their head). Thus a sentence like

(1) What I bought yesterday was a new car

has the following underlying structure:

(1a) ((it (I bought something yesterday)   )
   S_1 NP S_2 S_2 NP
     was a new car)
                  S_1

To (1a) relativization may apply deriving (1). Alternatively, relativization and cleft extraposition may derive

(2) It was a new car that I bought yesterday

In this analysis, then, cleft extraposition is an optional rule. Furthermore, pseudo-clefting is not restricted to sentences beginning with 'what'. Thus

(3) Who I met yesterday was my best friend

is possible in some dialects. Akmajian points out that such dialect variations can be explained naturally in terms of the optional-obligatory parameter with respect to cleft extraposition. Consider further such sentences as

(4) Why I haven't written to you before is because I haven't
    had the time
(5) It is because I haven't had the time that I haven't
    written to you before
(6) Where he met her was in Cambridge
(7) It was in Cambridge that he met her

Presumably, (4) as well as (6) are substandard. Again, this is explained naturally if it is assumed that cleft extraposition is optional in such cases in some dialects. For a different approach to 'do' in pseudo-cleft (and other) sentences, see Ross, 1972. Ross generates 'do' in remote structure (the paper is written in the generative semantics framework - hence the term 'remote' (for which, see Postal, 1970c) rather than 'deep') and concludes, convincingly, that this has advantages over the insertion analysis.

IV.G.16. A controversial issue in the literature is the distinction between noun phrase and verb phrase complementation. It is likely that this distinction should not be maintained. The main reason for making use of it in the text was that it provides a clear illustration in configurational terms of the crucial structural difference between such sentences as (1) and (2):

(1) I wanted John to go
(2) I persuaded John to go

For discussion of verb phrase complementation, see Stockwell et al., 1968, Vol. II, 536ff., Bowers, 1968, Huddleston, 1969, Borkin et al. (eds.), 1972, 30ff., and, last but not least, Rosenbaum's Preface to his own work (1967). If the distinction can be eliminated from the grammar, all the sentence types discussed in this section are immediately dominated by NP (cf. also p. 415). This generalization could easily be stated under a verb-initial analysis of English (for which, see below, section V.A): structures would be differentiated in terms of the number of NPs cooccurring with the verb (or predicate (including adjectives)):

```
                 S
         _____/|____
        Pred  (NP)  (NP)  NP
                            |
                            S
```

The analysis of 'it' is beset with a number of problems. For some
discussion, see Langendoen, 1966, Morgan, 1968, and - within the
framework of generative semantics - McCawley, 1970a. We discussed
the question of 'it' provisionally in section IV.A.8. We there
invoked some Danish sentences which seemed to support the deep structure analysis. However, in the light of the factive-nonfactive
distinction, this argument crumbles. In particular, there seems to
be the same correlation between the optional 'det' preceding subject and object clauses and factivity in Danish sentences as there
is between the optional 'it' preceding object clauses and factivity
in English sentences. Thus (restricting the attention to 'that'-
clauses) we get such translational equivalents as

(1a) I regret (it) that he left
(1b) Jeg beklager (det) at han rejste
(2a) I suppose (* it) that he will come
(2b) Jeg formoder (* det) at han vil komme
(3a) That he has admitted this much is significant
(3b) (Det) at han har indrømmet så meget er betydningsfuldt
(4a) That it will rain tomorrow is possible
(4b) (* Det) at det regner i morgen er muligt
(5a) That he will die within a month is probable
(5b) (* Det) at han dør inden for en måned er sandsynligt

The Kiparskys propose that 'it' in a sentence like (1a) should be
analysed as a pronominal substitute for 'the fact' (i.e. 'the fact'
may either be deleted or pronominalized). One difficulty about this
proposal is that the pronoun would not replace a full NP, indeed not
even a constituent. Pronominalization would apply to a structure like

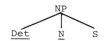

in which 'it' would replace the two underscored nodes. For the
full range of counterarguments, see Stockwell et al., 1968, Vol. II,
577ff. The authors note, however, that the idea of pronominalization
is "appealing". The idea, despite the formal difficulties involved,
is no less appealing in view of the Danish facts. The difference
between the two languages, then, would be that Danish allows pronominalization of 'den kendsgerning' (Danish for 'the fact') in
subject clauses. Furthermore, Danish optional 'det' in subject
clauses is not the equivalent of the semantically empty expletive
'it'/'det' (as we assumed in section IV.A.8). Thus (5b) undergoes
extraposition:

(5c) Det er sandsynligt at han dør inden for en måned

So of course does, say, (3b):

(3c) Det er betydningsfuldt at han har indrømmet så meget

However, 'det' in (3b), unlike 'det' in (3c) and (5c), has a semantic value which matches the meaning of 'fact'. It would seem,
then, that a natural explanation of the facts pertaining to Danish
subject clauses would be that 'the fact' may optionally be pronominalized. If it is not pronominalized, the sentence may undergo
extraposition, the semantically empty 'det' being substituted for
the extraposed clause. We will not go into further detail over this
question. Suffice it to have indicated the nature of the data. We
can conclude that, contrary to the assumption made in section IV.A.8,
these data do not seem to lend support to the deep structure ana-

lysis of 'it'. The raising of 'there' from embedded sentences to
subject position in a higher clause has been invoked as an argument
in support of global derivational constraints. For example, in

(6) There were believed to be some surprises in store for us
(7) There was believed to have been a burglar in the house

the agreement rule, operating on the top cycle, must 'know' about
the number of the subject in the embedded sentence. It should be
noted that this would have no effect on the argument given on p.
58: under the new formulation, there would simply be some speakers
who do not have this constraint in their grammar. On global constraints, see references cited on p. 224. See further Cole, 1974 and
Hurford, 1975. In connection with (32)-(34) of section IV.G.16.6,
mention should be made of the principle of strict cyclicity. This
has been formulated by Jackendoff, 1972, 374 in the following way:
"For a transformation to be applied correctly, the main clause (relative to the present cycle) must play an essential part in its application". Given the validity of this principle, the problem discussed in the text would not arise: reflexivization operates on S_2 and
is completely independent of S_1. The strict cyclicity principle
would have important theoretical consequences, not least for the
notion of last-cyclic rules. For example, it would no longer be possible to formulate extraposition and particle movement as last-cyclic.
The principle - as a formal universal - would greatly delimit the
class of possible grammars (for discussion, see also Chomsky, 1973
and Bach, 1974, 242ff.). Chapter 5 of Jackendoff, 1972 expounds the
interpretivist approach to complementation. In this there is no rule
of equi NP deletion. Coreferentiality is determined in the semantic
component. As remarked before, the most thorough-going study of
raising is Postal, 1974. See also Bresnan, 1976.

IV.G.17. Lees, 1960a is the classic work on nominalization. For
further discussion of the lexicalist hypothesis, see Stockwell et
al., 1968, Vol. I, 1ff., Vol. II, 699ff., and Chomsky, 1972, 162ff.
The lexicalist hypothesis plays an important role in the interpretivist theory developed in Jackendoff, 1972. It should be noted that
the possible generalization with respect to 'ing-forms' is perhaps
rather weak within the lexicalist hypothesis. Consider

(1) John's teasing of the cat upset her
(2) John's teasing the cat upset her

(1) is an example of action nominalization; (2) contains a gerundial
complement clause. Now, according to the lexicalist hypothesis,
'ing' in (1) is an affix on a par with, say, 'ism' in 'criticism',
whereas in (2) it is a complementizer inserted in a sentence under
the immediate domination of NP. In other words, the two occurrences
of 'ing' are, in the last analysis, totally unrelated. On the 'ing-
form', see also Grady, 1967. For the relationship between such sentences as 'he polished the car'/'he gave the car a polish', see
Nickel, 1968.

IV.G.18. An overview of problems relating to pronominalization is
provided by Stockwell et al., 1968, Vol. I, 185ff. With respect
to the sentences discussed on p. 356f., it should be noted that when
'one' pronominalizes part of the antecedent NP and has its own
modifiers, it can often be difficult to determine precisely what
'one' replaces. For some discussion, see Stockwell et al., op. cit.,
Vol. I, 206ff. For a critique of Postal's analysis of the personal
pronouns, see Sommerstein, 1972. It is noteworthy that the two
scholars are at least in agreement that there is a connection between pronouns and articles. On picture reflexives, see also
Postal, 1971, 185ff.

CHAPTER V

TRANSFORMATIONAL-GENERATIVE GRAMMAR -
DEEP STRUCTURE

V.A. INTRODUCTORY

Let us begin by quoting the following comment on the development of transformational-generative grammar made by Lees, one of
the pioneers of the theory (1970b (in Jacobs and Rosenbaum, 1970)
138):

> ... what we have been calling "deep structure" may well
> actually be some intermediate level of representation, in fact
> perhaps not even a definable level of linguistic structure at
> all - something like what is represented in a traditional pho-
> nemic transcription as compared with a systematic mophopho-
> nemic representation or a frankly phonetic transcription.
>   Secondly, there is strong implication that the deepest syn-
> tactic level of representation which functions in a linguistic
> description is so close to what we might call the meaning of
> a sentence that there might be no validity to maintaining the
> distinction between these.

In this final chapter, we shall be concerned with some of the
implications of Lees' statement - with what has aptly been termed
'the battle of deep structure' (Langacker, 1967, VI). It will be
convenient to divide the subject into two parts: case grammar and
generative semantics. It should be stressed, however, that these
two approaches have many similarities: they can be (and have been
by some scholars (e.g. Langendoen, 1970b and Frantz, 1974)) collapsed into one.

Before we turn to case grammar and generative semantics, some
general points should be made.

Recall the relational definitions of the functional notions

447

'subject of' and 'object of' given in section IV.A.6. These definitions, which are assumed to be of universal validity, do not, of
course, imply that all languages are subject-initial in their deep
structure. For example, they would accommodate languages with deep
structures like (1) or (2):

(1)

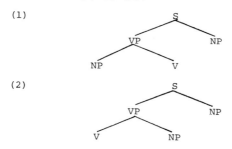

(2)

that is OVS-languages (where O = object and S = subject) or VOS-
languages. Now, as we recall, the initial PS-rules for English are
(omitting categories not pertinent to the argument here):

(3) S ———→ NP + VP
     VP ———→ V + NP

(3) defines English as a deep structure SVO-language. We know that
in unmarked declarative sentences this is also the order found in
surface structure. (3), then, is a necessary precondition for a
grammar of English to meet what we have called the 'similarity
constraint' on grammars (cf. above, p. 218). Observe next that the
relational definitions do not allow for languages having the order
VSO in their deep structure. This means that if there are languages
which have this order in their surface structure (and there are),
the universal validity of the definitions is falsified unless it can
be shown that the surface VSO-order is transformationally derived
from some deep structure order which satisfies the definitions. On
the other hand, if this can be shown to be the case, the similarity
constraint will no longer stand up. So, as pointed out by Bach,
1974, 275f., one of the assumptions will simply have to be given up
(possibly both).

    Now, given the dichotomy between deep and surface structure,
there is no a priori reason to assume that English is a deep structure SVO-language as envisaged in the standard theory. In fact, a
substantial body of evidence has been accumulated by McCawley, 1970b

in support of an underlying VSO-order for English. There is no reason to reiterate McCawley's arguments here. The main point, however, is that, given this underlying order, it becomes a good deal simpler to state a number of transformational rules, such as passive and raising[1,2].

The VSO-hypothesis makes it possible to align deep structures with the predicate-initial formulae of symbolic logic. It should be stressed, however, that this alignment of underlying structures with logic is motivated primarily by syntactic considerations. It is not a case of logic being superimposed on language, as it were. Henceforth, we will make the assumption that English is predicate-initial in deep structure. We remain uncommitted for the moment with respect to the order of the arguments.

The next point we must make is that, given the fact that there may be a quite radical difference between deep structures on the one hand and the order in which constituents show up in surface structure on the other, speculations naturally arise whether there might be a <u>universal base</u> for all languages (as distinct from universal formal constraints on the rules which generate base structures). In other words, if it is the case that the deep structure of an English sentence is a predicate followed by a number of arguments (ordered or unordered), the question that can be raised is whether all languages show the same property in their deep structure. Generative semanticists have been prone to accept the universal base hypothesis (see also Fillmore, 1968 (in Bach and Harms, 1968) 1f.).

----

1. The raising rule would now look like this:

$$\text{SI} \quad X - V - (NP) \quad \underset{NP}{[} \; \underset{S}{[} \; V - NP - Y \; \underset{S}{]} \; \underset{NP}{]} - Z$$

	1	2	3	4	5	6	7
SC	1	2	3+5	4	Ø	6	7

$\Longrightarrow$

If the third term is present, the raised NP becomes the object (as in 'John wants Jim to go'). If it is not present, the raised NP eventually becomes the subject (by the rule of subject formation - the new version of the old Aux inversion rule) as in 'John is likely to be there'.

2. Note that, logically, there are other possibilities. For example, it has been argued by Ross, 1973 that English is an underlying SOV-language. A further possibility would be that the arguments (in the sense of section IV.D.18) are unordered. This is the claim made in case grammar. For some counterarguments to the VSO-hypothesis, see Berman, 1974.

In passing from autonomous syntax to semantically oriented grammars, we do not leave the domain of transformational grammar. In
particular, there are still two rule-related levels of structure:
deep, or rather <u>remote</u>, and surface structure. However, increasingly
abstract underlying structures require increasingly powerful transformational rules. For example, we have hinted at the existence of
a rule of predicate raising which can derive surface structure
verbs (cf. above, p. 432f.). Furthermore, if transformations are
to preserve meaning (i.e. if the KP-hypothesis is to be upheld
(and generative semantics is the KP-hypothesis taken to its logical
terminus)), global rules, i.e. global derivational constraints in
the now familiar sense, are required in the grammar on purely semantic grounds.

We indicated in section IV.D.20 that in generative semantics
remote structures are identical to semantic representations. Does
this mean, then, that there is no longer a semantic component in
the grammar? The answer to this question must be no. For if there
were no semantic component, this would mean that everything relevant
to the semantic interpretation should be represented explicitly in
the underlying structure. This would be impossible. For example,
it has been shown that a sentence S may entail an infinite set of
sentences (cf. Bach, 1974, 227 - see also Seuren, 1974b, 16). Since
remote structures must be finite in length (cf. also above, p. 431),
some entailment relations must be stated by means of a rule which
has as its input a semantic representation. Consider in this connection also the following statement by McCawley, 1973, 238: " ...
generative semanticists do not require the "deep structure" of a
contradictory sentence to (in effect) bear a sign saying "I'm
self-contradictory"". In other words, if contradictoriness is to be
incorporated in the theory, it must be accounted for by rules of
inference in the semantic component. Furthermore, the precise status of presuppositions relative to semantic representations is by
no means clear. Fillmore, who was one of the pioneers in the study
of the linguistic relevance of the notion of presupposition, has
often discussed this question in terms of what we may call "computa-
tional imagery" (cf. Fillmore, 1971a (in Fillmore and Langendoen,
1971) 277 and 1972 (in Davidson and Harman, 1972) 21f. The idea is
that the grammar contains a component which can compute the set of
presuppositions determining the utterance of the sentence from its
syntactico-semantic structure.

It follows from the discussion in the preceding paragraph that
the characterization of the opposed parties in the battle of deep
structure in terms of the labels 'interpretivists' and 'generativ-
ists' may turn out to be slightly misleading. In a certain sense,
remote structures still undergo interpretation: they form the input
to a set of rules of inference. However, interpretivism, so defined, is nevertheless radically different from 'traditional'
interpretivism. In particular, there are no projection rules and
selectional restrictions are defined as presuppositions about intended referents in the way illustrated earlier. Putative semantic
anomalies are explicated in terms of possible messages in possible
worlds or possible situations.

Generative semanticists take the position that the illocutionary force of a sentence is represented in remote structure in
the form of a governing performative sentence (cf. also Fillmore,
op. cit., 20).

In the following sections, we shall be concerned with the
underlying structure 'proper' in case grammar and generative semantics. Nothing further will be said about illocutionary force
and only little about presuppositions.

V.B. CASE GRAMMAR

V.B.1. <u>'Subject' and 'object'</u>

In section III.1 we sketched briefly the genesis of the notions
'subject' and 'object'. We saw that 'subject' was originally defined as 'that about which a statement is made by the predicate'
(a definition which is still current (see for example Zandvoort,
1957, 196)); let us agree to call this the <u>thematic</u> definition of
'subject'. Furthermore, the subject of a sentence is traditionally
defined as the 'actor' or 'agent'. By the same token, in transitive
sentences the object is that noun phrase which is being acted upon -
the 'patient'.

Consider now the following configuration:

(1)

This, as we know, forms the input to the semantic rules of interpretation in the standard theory. The question that can be asked,
then, is this: what semantic constants, if any, are associated with
the relations (a) $[NP,S]$ and (b) $[NP,VP,S]$? Let us first consider
(a). A possible answer would be that the subject constitutes the
theme of the sentence. This would certainly be true of a sentence
like

(2) John opened the door

in which 'John' is the theme and also the deep-structure subject.
But consider now (3):

(3) The door was opened

derived by passive and agent deletion from

(3a) Someone opened the door

If we maintained the definition of $[NP,S]$ as the theme of the sentence, we would assert, in effect, that (3) makes a statement about
'someone'. This is clearly inadequate (cf. also Huddleston, 1970b,
502f.). Something similar obtains in sentences which have undergone
topicalization. Compare for example (4) and (5):

(4) My teacher hasn't read this book
(5) This book my teacher hasn't read

In (5) the object is the theme of the sentence. We must conclude,
then, that the first of the two traditional definitions of the notion 'subject' is not a viable semantic constant for $[NP,S]$. There
remains the second. Consider such sentences as

(6) <u>John</u> killed the monster
(7) <u>John</u> died
(8) <u>John</u> received a letter from Margaret
(9) <u>The leaden casket</u> contained Portia's portrait
(10) <u>John</u> likes soldiering
(11) <u>John</u> shouted
(12) <u>John</u> heard someone shouting

It is intuitively obvious that the semantic status of the underlined
subjects cannot be yoked together under the general heading of
'agency'. In other words, neither of the traditional definitions of

'subject' will work as a semantic constant for $[NP,S]$.

    Consider next (b). It has long been recognized in traditional grammar that 'patient' is not an adequate semantic definition of all objects. In particular, a distinction should be made between <u>ef</u>fected and <u>af</u>fected objects. The difference between the two kinds of objects appears from the following sentences:

    (13) John made the chair
    (14) John repaired the chair

In (13) the chair comes into being through John's activity, whereas in (14) John's exercises his skills on something which is already in existence. Furthermore, both kinds of objects may occur with the same verb (cf. Jespersen, 1924, 160):

    (15) John is digging the garden
    (16) John has just started digging a grave

'Patient', therefore, is not a possible semantic constant for $[NP,VP,S]$.

    The question that can then be asked is this: why should the notions 'subject of' and 'object of' be defined in terms of semantically undefinable configurations at all? Why should they not rather be interpreted as purely superficial phenomena? It is this question which most fundamentally underlies the theory of case grammar.

    Consider now further such sentences as

    (17) The ball moved
    (18) John moved the ball
    (19) John moved

'Move' is a member of a class of verbs which may optionally be construed with one or two NPs, such that the object NP in the transitive sentence becomes the subject in the corresponding intransitive sentence. Let us look first at (18). In this 'John' is clearly the agent and 'the ball' the patient (the affected object). In (17) 'the ball' is the "grammatical" subject, but it is not the agent: the semantic relationship between 'the ball' and 'move' remains constant; that is, in (17) 'the ball' is as much the patient as it is in (18). (19) is ambiguous: 'John' may be the agent - he moves voluntarily, or 'John' may be the patient - someone pushes him. The relationship between such sentences as (17) and (18) is known as <u>erga</u>-

<u>tivity</u>.

Recall now once again the KP-hypothesis: meaning should be determinable from deep structures. How can this be brought to bear on (6)-(12) (assuming the framework of the standard theory)? The answer to this question seems to be clear: the relevant semantic information must be coded into the lexicon, in particular into verbs; only thus can the projection rules assign the correct reading to the subject NP (cf. Katz, 1972, 111ff.). This is certainly possible. However, this approach takes for granted the validity of the configurational definitions of 'subject' and 'object'. It does not explain them. Furthermore, it involves the assignment of totally different underlying structures to such pairs of sentences as

(20a) John received a letter from Margaret
(20b) Margaret sent a letter to John
(21a) The leaden casket contained Portia's portrait
(21b) Portia's portrait was in the leaden casket
(22a) John likes soldiering
(22b) Soldiering pleases John

etc. This seems to be counterintuitive and motivated ultimately by the desire to preserve maximum distributional similarity between deep and surface structure.

How about (17)-(19)? One way of accounting for them would be to specify two[1] lexical items of the phonological form <u>move</u>, one transitive, the other intransitive, and build into their structure the requisite information concerning the semantic interpretation of the surrounding noun phrases. This would lead to a great proliferation of lexical items. A different approach is the <u>causative analysis</u>[2] (cf. also above, p. 432f.). According to this the deep structures of (17) and (18) would be respectively (17a) and (18a):

(17a)

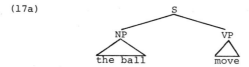

----

1. Perhaps three: the ambiguity of (19) is contingent on the subject being + ANIMATE. That is, the roles assigned by predicates to NPs are interrelated with selectional features.

2. Etymologically, the term 'ergative' derives from a Greek verb meaning 'cause, make, bring about'.

(18a)

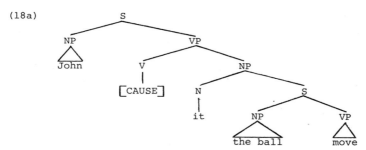

This approach is not particularly commendable from the point of
view of the standard theory. As we have noted before, it results
in more abstract deep structures than originally envisaged. This
becomes even more pronounced if the ambiguity of (19) is to be
made explicit in terms of configurational representations. Thus,
in one reading, it would have a deep structure like (17a), whereas
in the other reading, the deep structure would have to contain a
subjectless causative sentence[1].

On the whole, then, the account of the notions 'subject' and
'object' poses a number of intricate problems.

V.B.2. Underlying structure in a Fillmorean case grammar

The base rules in a case grammar of the type proposed by
Fillmore, 1968 look something like this:

1. S $\longrightarrow$ M + Prop
2. Prop $\longrightarrow$ Predicate + C_1 ... C_n
3. Pred $\longrightarrow$ $\left\{ \begin{matrix} V \\ Adj \end{matrix} \right\}$
4. C $\longrightarrow$ K + NP
5. NP $\longrightarrow$ Det + N

They should be interpreted in the following way: M = modality; this
should be understood in a wide sense: it includes tense, aspect,
etc.[2]; Prop = proposition; a sentence, then, always consists of a

----

1. For further discussion of the causative analysis from different
   points of view, see Lakoff, 1970a, 41ff., Hall Partee, 1971
   (in Fillmore and Langendoen, 1971) 7f., Fillmore, 1972 (in
   Davidson and Harman, 1972) 3ff., and Jackendoff, 1972, 26ff.

2. M would also accommodate sentence adverbs, negation, questions,
   etc. It should be noted that modality in this sense precludes
   the analysis of modal verbs and auxiliary verbs as main verbs.
   This is one point, then, where case grammar and generative
   semantics do not converge.

modal category plus a proposition; the proposition is expanded
into a predicate plus a number of <u>cases</u> (C); the cases are given
such labels as <u>Agent</u> (A), <u>Dative</u> (D), <u>Objective</u> (O), <u>Locative</u> (L),
and <u>Instrumental</u> (I)[1]; C is expanded into K + NP; K is a <u>case
marker</u>, i.e. a preposition.

　　Given this base component, it is clear that underlying structures must undergo T-rules which place NPs in surface subject and
object positions. In other words, surface order is entirely a result of mapping between remote and surface structure.

　　Consider now the following classic examples (cf. Fillmore,
1966a (in Reibel and Schane, 1969) 369f.):

　　(1) The janitor opened the door with the key
　　(2) The janitor opened the door
　　(3) The key opened the door
　　(4) The door opened
　　(5) The door was opened by the janitor

(1) would have the following underlying structure:

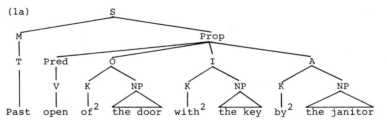

(1a)

In the derivation of (1) from (1a), A is adjoined as left daughter
of S, the preposition and the case label being deleted. After the
deletion of O and 'of', 'the door' becomes the direct object. In
(2) the same has happened; only, there is no I in the sentence. In
(3) the I has become the subject, and in (4) the O. This suggests
that the subject rule is sensitive to a <u>hierarchy of cases</u>. Fillmore
(1968 (in Bach and Harms, 1968) 33) postulates for English the fol-

----

1. Of these O, which is not to be confused with the surface structure notion 'direct object', is the semantically most neutral
case. I shall assume that the semantic implications of the rest
of the cases can, to some degree, be inferred from the labels.
The definitions may be found in Fillmore, <u>op. cit.</u>, 24f. It
should be noted that some of the cases have subsequently been
redefined. Thus D has been replaced by <u>Experiencer</u>, and L by
<u>Source</u> and <u>Goal</u>. For discussion, see Fillmore, 1971c.

2. We return to the question of prepositions in section V.B.4.

lowing rule: "If there is an A, it becomes the subject; otherwise,
if there is an I, it becomes the subject; otherwise, the subject
is the O". This principle would apply to a verb like 'open'. It is
clear that the notion of a hierarchy with respect to subject formation is of crucial importance in case grammar (cf. also Langendoen,
1970b, 70).

Consider now (5). Apparently, the subject hierarchy just noted
has been overruled: the O has been moved into subject position in
spite of the fact that there is an A in the sentence. This, however,
is precisely what happens in passive sentences. In other words, the
subject hierarchy is unmarked. When it is overruled by the passive,
the choice of subject is marked.

We turn now to a slightly different problem. The sentences

   (6) The table has five books on it
   (7) Five books are on the table
   (8) There are five books on the table

are synonymous in a significant way. In (6) 'books' is clearly O,
in (7) and (8) 'table' is L. Suppose now that we want to account
for the synonymy between (6), (7), and (8) in terms of cases. We
would then have to posit a common underlying structure something
like this:

(9)

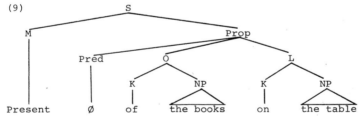

There are three possibilities of subject formation: (a) O becomes
the subject, in which case 'be' (defined as a dummy tense-carrier)
is adjoined to Present under the domination of M; (b) L is copied
in subject position, the original NP being pronominalized by 'it,
and 'have' filling the hitherto empty Predicate; (c) L is copied
and pronominalized by 'there' in subject position, 'be' being inserted under M.

In conclusion, then, subject placement, under specifiable
conditions, obeys the following principle:

(a) Unmarked: case hierarchy

(b) Marked: passive

(c) Copying + pronominalization

In the light of this, the reader may wish to account for the semantic roles played by the subjects in sentences (6)-(12) and (20)-(22) of the preceding section.

V.B.3. The structure of verbs

Observe that the prelexical category VP is now eliminated from the grammar (something which case grammar has in common with generative semantics). Given such underlying structures, it is possible to collapse selectional and strict subcategorization features. In particular, each predicate has a case frame specifying with which cases it can (or must) cooccur; consequently, it is possible to state the selectional restrictions on the nouns to be inserted under the domination of the different cases[1].

Let us look at some examples. The verbs 'die' and 'kill' would perhaps be entered in the lexicon with the following case frames (in addition to which, of course, they would have a semantic specification):

die (+ ___ D) - kill (+ ___ D + A)

With 'die' there is only one case. Since the subject formation rule is obligatory, this must become the subject:

(1) John died

With 'kill' the case hierarchy operates. There is an A: it must become the subject:

(2) The hunters killed the dinosaur

However, 'kill' should not be related only to 'die', but also to verbs like 'murder' and 'assassinate'. Consider for example the following sentences:

----

1. In fact this differentiates case grammar only from the subcategorization model of the standard theory. In the dummy-symbol model, selectional features and strict subcategorization features are not necessarily separated (even if selectional features are defined as syntactic rather than semantic features) (cf. above, pp. 119, note, 180). Furthermore, the whole machinery of selectional features would no longer form part of a case grammar (see for example Fillmore, 1971a and 1972).

(3) The English killed a large number of enemies with dumdum
    bullets
(4) Dumdum bullets killed a large number of enemies
(5) Fred murdered the woman with an old Indian sword
(6) * An old Indian sword murdered the woman
(7) He assassinated the President
(8) ? He assassinated the President with a Winchester
(9) * A Winchester assassinated the President

(3) shows that 'kill' may also be construed with I. In (4) there
is no A; consequently, I has become the subject, as predicted by
the case hierarchy. It follows from this that 'kill' can take
either two or three arguments. If it takes two, one is D, and the
other either I or A. Therefore, we must revise the entry for 'kill'
accordingly (the notation (X∤Y) meaning 'at least one, optionally
both'):

    kill (+ ___ D (I∤A))

Turning now to (5) and (6), we observe that 'murder' and 'kill',
which are frequently synonymous[1], have different case frames:
'murder' obligatorily requires an A, which, in accordance with
the case hierarchy, must become the surface subject. The case
frame for 'murder' must be

    murder (+ ___ D (I) A)

'Assassinate' seems to be different from the other two. Informants
tell me that it is unnatural with an I[2]. If this is correct, the
case frame would be

    assassinate (+ ___ D + A)

    This type of lexical analysis can provide a natural explana-
tion of the relationship between converses like 'buy' and 'sell'.
It was suggested in section IV.D.8 that sentences like (10) and (11):
----

1. The difference between them has to do with presuppositions:
   'murder' asserts 'cause to become dead' and presupposes 'with
   malice aforethought'. 'Kill' does not have this presupposition.
   Note that since sentences containing 'kill' and 'murder' do not
   necessarily have the same truth value, the presupposition of
   'murder' must form an integral part of its semantic structure.

2. This may have to do with the presupposition of 'assassinate':
   the victim is an important person. Perhaps, therefore, information about the instrument used in perpetrating the act is
   judged to be unimportant. If I am mistaken, 'assassinate' has
   the same case frame as 'murder'.

(10) Jim sold the car to John

(11) John bought the car from Jim

are synonymous. In terms of truth value, there is little doubt that
this is correct: if (10) is true, so is (11), and vice versa. Yet,
there are subtle semantic distinctions. In particular, it seems
that in both sentences the subject has agency superimposed on its
purely locative function (in both sentences 'Jim' is the source
and 'John' is the goal). A telling piece of evidence in support of
this analysis is provided by Fillmore, 1969b (in Kiefer, 1969) 117f.
He cites the following sentences:

(12) He sells eggs very skilfully

(13) He buys eggs very skilfully

and argues that 'skilfully' is not a manner adverb, but rather
a 'subject-oriented' adverb, that is, one which predicates something of the agent of the sentence. At a deeper level of analysis,
therefore, (10) and (11) are not synonymous (on converses, see also
Anderson, 1971, 128ff.).

Let us conclude this section by returning to sentences (17)-
(19) of section V.B.1. They could perhaps be explained in terms
of the following case frame for 'move':

move (+ ___ (O﹛A))

V.B.4. Some further issues

The main problem confronting the case grammarian is to isolate
a reasonably small set of semantically well defined cases or roles
and provide adequate syntactic criteria by which they can be defined in a given language.

A number of tests are available for the isolation of cases.
Consider for example the following sentences (cf. Fillmore, 1968):

(1) John smashed the window

(2) A stone smashed the window

(3) John smashed the window with a stone

(4) * John and a stone smashed the window

The ungrammaticality of (4) is clearly not due to a violation of
selectional restrictions (alternatively, a presupposition failure);
if it had been, (2) would have been ungrammatical (or anomalous).
Rather, it is ascribable to the fact that two NPs which contract

different case relations with the predicate cannot be conjoined.
By contrast, if they are in the same case, they can:

    (5) The tanker and the freighter collided

Digressing a little from the main theme, we may note that the peculiarities of sentences (10) and (11) of section IV.G.13.3 may now
perhaps be accounted for:

    (6) The passenger liner collided with the Swedish rock
    (7) * The passenger liner and the Swedish rock collided

(6) cannot be derived by phrasal conjunction for the reasons noted
earlier. In the standard theory, the only way of accounting for (6)
would be to define 'with the Swedish rock' as some kind of adverbial. Case grammar provides a more natural explanation. Suppose
that 'collide' is entered in the lexicon with the following case
frame:

    collide (+ __ O(I))

with the stipulation that if there is an O, but no I, the O must
dominate two conjoined NPs. Given this entry, the case hierarchy
predicts that the conjoined NPs must become the subject in (5)
(after which conjunct movement may of course apply) and that I
must become the subject in (6). The ungrammaticality of (7) is due
to a selectional violation: the noun inserted under I in a sentence
like (6) (and the nouns inserted under O in a sentence like (5))
must satisfy a selectional requirement like, say, + MOTION[1].

    It is also generally assumed that there cannot be two occur-
rences of the same case within the same simplex sentence[2,3]. This
appears from such sentences as

----

1. By this analysis, 'the tanker collided with the freighter' is
   ambiguous: 'the tanker' may be either I or O. If it is O, the
   sentence is derived by conjunct movement; if it is I, I has
   become the subject in accordance with the case hierarchy.

2. We have restricted the attention to simplex sentences. Relative
   clauses are generated in much the same way as in traditional
   transformational grammar. Complement sentences are embedded under
   O. Thus the adjective 'certain' might have a case frame like
   (+ __ (D)S), in which S should be interpreted as being dominated
   by $\overline{O}$. The optionality of D would account for such sentences as
   'John is certain that he will be there on time' and 'John is
   certain to be there on time'. In the latter, there is no D.

3. In some cases, particularly with Os, this test is not too reliable.
   Thus in 'the guy on the corner over there is my boss', there seem
   to be two Os. Cf. Huddleston, 1970b. See in this connection also
   Fillmore's discussion of the verb 'resemble' (1971c, 7f.).

(8) John smashed the window with a $\left\{ \begin{matrix} \text{hammer} \\ \text{stone} \end{matrix} \right\}$

(9) A $\left\{ \begin{matrix} \text{hammer} \\ \text{stone} \end{matrix} \right\}$ smashed the window

(10) * A hammer smashed the window with a stone

(10) is ungrammatical because there are two Is.

   A further test is the preposition test. The basic assumption
is that each case is associated with one unmarked preposition
(hence the prepositions in (1a) of section V.B.2). Thus 'by' typically occurs with A: it appears on the surface in passive sentences. However, in some instances, 'by' must be transformationally inserted. Consider the following sentence:

(11) Mary received a letter this morning

In this 'Mary' is D, 'a letter' O. There is no A. Yet, from (11)
may be derived

(12) A letter was received by Mary this morning

Since the unmarked Dative preposition is 'to', (12) can only be
accounted for in terms of a preposition replacement rule. By contrast, the derivation of

(13) The new Ambassador was received by the Queen this morning

in which 'the Queen' is A and 'the new Ambassador' D, is straightforward: 'by' is present in the underlying structure[1].

   I is accompanied by 'by' or 'with'. 'With' occurs in sentences which have an A (in (15) A has been deleted by agent deletion)[2]:

(14) John killed the bear $\left\{ \begin{matrix} \text{* by} \\ \text{with} \end{matrix} \right\}$ a gun

(15) The safe was opened $\left\{ \begin{matrix} \text{with} \\ \text{* by} \end{matrix} \right\}$ a crowbar

   In the majority of cases, O becomes the surface object (or
subject) and therefore occurs with no overt preposition. If O does
not undergo object (or subject) placement, the preposition occurs
in surface structure. Since, in many cases, it is 'of', we can
perhaps regard this as the unmarked Objective case marker. Compare such pairs of sentences as

----

1. Presumably, the lexicon must contain two homonymous items
   'receive' with different case frames.
2. See, however, sentence (9) of section IV.E.5.

    (16) He stole the money from the woman

    (17) He robbed the woman of the money

    (18) This arrangement ruined my life

    (19) This arrangement deprived me of my independence

In (16) 'money' is O, 'woman' L. O becomes the surface object. In
(17) it is the other way round: L becomes the object; consequently,
O retains its preposition. Similarly in (19). In (18) there are only
two arguments, I and O. The case hierarchy predicts that I becomes
the subject. O becomes the object and loses its preposition. O may
also be signalled by 'with' in surface structure. Compare the following pairs of sentences:

    (20) She gave a ring to the king

    (21) She presented the king with a ring

    (22) They smeared paint on the wall

    (23) They smeared the wall with paint[1]

In many cases, the preposition is idiosyncratically dependent on
the predicate and may not undergo deletion after object placement:

    (24) Talk about it to her

    (25) They decided on the boat despite its price[2]

    The prepositions we have discussed so far are semantically
empty, their sole function being to signal the case relation which
the noun phrase contracts with the predicate.

    The prepositions associated with L are more recalcitrant. They
all add semantic information, and there is no single unmarked locativ
preposition. The problems involved in giving a systematic account of
the semantics of place are extremely complex and not something we
can go into here (for some comments, see Fillmore, 1971c; consult
also Leech, 1969a, Chapter 8).

    Case grammar, then, makes a serious attempt to provide an ex-
planation of the distribution of English prepositions. An immensely
complicated task, but one which must be countenanced by any adequate linguistic theory. When Postal first suggested that prepositions should be transformationally inserted by Chomsky-adjunction to NPs (cf. above, p. 362f.)[2], he commented on the difficulties

----

1. For further discussion of this sentence and others like it, see
   notes to this section.

2. Cf. above, p. 293 and note. The case grammar analysis avoids the
   arbitrary definition of some objects as PPs (as would of course
   also the insertion analysis (and the alternative analysis proposed by Lakoff, 1970a, 162)).

involved in providing a proper account for the actual "shape" of
the prepositions, concluding that "the lexical head of the NP, its
logical relation to verbal elements, lexical properties of the
verbal head, and other factors play a role" (1971, 206). It is to
the study of these relations and properties that the case grammarian addresses himself.

So far we have concentrated on differentiating criteria. For
example, the one-case-per-simplex-sentence hypothesis may serve
to distinguish <u>different</u> cases without actually identifying them.
Further syntactic criteria may be brought to bear on the definition
on each <u>individual</u> case (the preposition test can be said to fall
somewhere in between these two sets of criteria). We will briefly
consider A.

Most of the criteria invoked in defining A syntactically are
bound up with the stative-nonstative distinction (cf. Lakoff, 1966
and Fillmore, 1968 (in Bach and Harms, 1968) 31). In general, it
seems to be the case that A can be correlated with nonstativity.
This would predict that sentences which contain an A have the following characteristics: (a) They can take the progressive aspect:

  (26) John drove the car
  (27) John was driving the car
  (28) John knew the answer
  (29) * John was knowing the answer

However, there are counterexamples to this. Thus, as we have seen,
'die' has one argument which is D. But

  (30) My father is dying

is grammatical nevertheless. (b) They respond positively to a do
test (cf. also above, p. 373f.):

  (31) John killed the monster with a hammer
  (32) What John did was kill the monster with a hammer
  (33) John died yesterday
  (34) * What John did yesterday was die
  (35) What did John do? $\left\{ \begin{array}{l} \text{* He experienced a lot} \\ \text{He read a lot} \end{array} \right\}$

(c) They can contain manner adverbs (which, on this interpretation,
state something about the way in which the agent performs the action
denoted by the verb (cf. above, p. 460)):

  (36) John read the book thoroughly

(37) ⁎ John owned the house carefully

(d) They can undergo imperativization[1]:

(38) Drive carefully
(39) Walk home
(40) ⁎ Undergo a development
(41) ⁎ Owe me some money

V.B.5. Concluding remarks

Case theory grew out of the study of the _uses_ to which cases
are put in languages with morphologically differentiated case systems. It is essential to note that morphological signalling is to
be interpreted as a surface structure phenomenon: a way of representing deep cases conceived of as syntactic primitives which make
an essential contribution to semantic interpretation. For example,
we know that there is a class of verbs in Latin which 'take two
accusatives':

(1) Consul senatorem sententiam rogavit
(2) Magister puerum Latinam docuit

The theory predicts that these two accusatives are surface reflexes
of _different_ deep cases and derived from these by grammatical rules.
The two sentences do not contradict the principle that there is
only one occurrence of each case in a simplex sentence: this is a
(tentative) formal universal constraint on deep grammar.

Notes and some further references

The discussion in the text is based mainly on Fillmore, 1966a and
1968. The 1968-monograph is basic and also places the model in
relation to traditional case theory (standard works here are
Hjelmslev, 1935 and Jakobson, 1936 - see also Jespersen, 1924).
Fillmore, 1971c, 34ff. points out that it is unsatisfactory to assign categorial status to cases and that this merely duplicates
the notational shortcomings of the standard theory with respect to
adverbs (cf. above, p. 103). For discussion of case grammar and
constituent structure, see also Anderson, 1971, 27ff. Anderson's
model should be compared with the proposals made in Fillmore, 1971c.
Stockwell et al., 1968 adopt the case grammar framework. See especially Vol. I, Chapter III. Langendoen, 1970b provides a reasonably

----

1. Imperativization is a somewhat unreliable test. Thus in sentences
   like 'don't break down' and 'don't believe a word of it', the
   deleted 'you' is not A, but D. However, it is arguable that the
   subject has a certain measure of control over the situation
   expressed in the verb. For further discussion, see Huddleston,
   1970b. Cf. also above, p. 313, note 2.

elementary introduction to case grammar. Cook, 1973 has formulated
a set of postulates for case grammar. Nilsen, 1972 is a study of
the semantic structure of deep cases in terms of features. Mention
should be made of the treatment of inalienable possession in a
case grammar. Fillmore proposes to derive a sentence like

(1) John hit my arm

from an underlying structure with a predicate and two arguments,
one of which is A, the other L. The grammar contains a rule which
generates an adnominal Dative. The (relevant) underlying structure
of (1) would be, accordingly:

(1a)

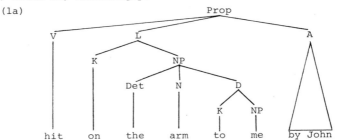

What has happened in (1) is that the A has become the subject and
D has been possessivized. Alternatively, the L might become the
subject (marked subject choice), D being possessivized:

(2) My arm was hit by John

A third possibility is that D may become the object - the preposition being deleted; A becomes the subject:

(3) John hit me on the arm

Finally, D may become the subject:

(5) I was hit on the arm by John

Alienable possessives are derived in the same way as in the standard theory. Fillmore's grammar, then, like Chomsky's (1970), provides two sources for possessive NPs. The case analysis receives
its strongest support from the fact that in many languages inalienable possessive relationships may be expressed overtly by
means of a dative and/or a genitive. For examples and references,
consult Fillmore, 1968 (in Bach and Harms, 1968) 61ff. Stockwell
et al., 1968, Vol. II, 702ff. discuss this matter at some length.
In view of the arguments adduced there, it seems that the distinction for English becomes somewhat blurred, or at least so vague
that no syntactic arguments can be built upon it. On inalienable
possession, see also Anderson, 1971, 114f. A number of counterarguments to case grammar have been advanced by adherents of the
standard theory. One of them relates to such sentences as

(6) They smeared the wall with paint
(7) They smeared paint on the wall

In (6) we have taken 'with paint' to be O; 'the wall' is L. It is
natural to assume that (6) and (7) are transformationally related.
However, in that case, the rule has changed meaning: when one
smears a wall with paint, one smears paint all over the wall,

whereas when one smears paint on a wall, this is not the case.
The 'all-over' reading has been referred to as the <u>holistic</u> interpretation (in contradistinction to the <u>partitive</u> interpretation
of (7)) (cf. Anderson, S., 1971b). The same phenomenon is manifest
in

    (8) The garden is swarming with bees
    (9) Bees are swarming in the garden

only, this time the holistic interpretation is assigned to the subject in (8). The argument then is that in a number of well-defined cases the holistic interpretation of L correlates precisely
with 'subject' and 'object' as defined in the standard theory.
There is little doubt that this argument has great force. It can
be countered only by a case theory which allows the systematic assignment of more than one case to each NP (cf. Anderson, 1971,
95ff.)[1]. For further discussion of such sentences, see Fillmore,
1966a (in Reibel and Schane, 1969) 370, 1968 (in Bach and Harms,
1968) 48, Hall Partee, 1971 (in Fillmore and Langendoen, 1971)
21ff., Anderson, S., 1971b, Chomsky, 1972, 173ff., Vestergaard,
1973, and Mellema, 1974. Mellema's paper provides an overall
critique of case grammar. See further Dougherty, 1970b. On prepositions and cases, consult also Starosta, 1973. Agentivity
is discussed by Cruse, 1973 and stativity by Lee, 1973. It should
be noted that there are many points of similarity between case
grammar and systemic grammar as developed by Halliday and others.
See Halliday, 1967, 1968, 1970, 1973 and Hudson, 1972.

V.C. GENERATIVE SEMANTICS

V.C.1. <u>Generative semantics versus the extended standard theory</u>

    Let us begin by reconsidering such sentences as (cf. above,
sections IV.G.9.2,4):

    (1) I didn't meet some people I knew
    (2) I didn't meet any people I knew
    (3) Many students didn't come to the lecture
    (4) Not many students came to the lecture

We have seen that the difference between them can be accounted for
in terms of the ($\pm$ Specific) distinction. Thus in (1) 'some' is
(+ Specific). Hence it has not been converted into 'any'. In (3)
'many students' is (+ Specific), and this has affected the Neg

----

1. In the <u>Case for Case</u> only one case function is associated with
   each NP. Elsewhere (e.g. 1969b) Fillmore allows more than one
   case to be assigned to one NP. For discusssion, see also
   Jackendoff, 1972, 34ff.

placement rule.

Many linguists have questioned the validity of the some any
rule. For example, it has been proposed that the use of 'some' and
'any' should be accounted for in terms of presuppositions and that
hence 'some' and 'any' are distinct lexical items (for arguments,
see R. Lakoff, 1969b (cf. also above, p. 327)). Suppose now that
we adopt this approach to 'some' and 'any' and eliminate the
(± Specific) distinction as a transformation-trigger from the
grammar. We are then left with the problem of how to account for
the semantic difference between (3) and (4). There are two ways
in which this problem is currently tackled.

(a) Under the extended standard theory (equivalently the
interpretivist approach) the semantic readings are obtained by
rules of interpretation which operate on surface structures. In
particular, there is a rule which determines the scope of negation
of quantifiers by a left-to-right order principle: if a quantifier
occurs to the right of 'not' in surface structure, it falls within
the scope of the negation. Conversely, if 'not' occurs to the
right of a quantifier, it falls within the scope of the quantifier
(cf. Jackendoff, 1972, Chapter Eight)[1].

The extended standard theory involves the abandonment of the
KP-hypothesis. In particular, transformations are allowed to
change meaning. Consider for example the operation of topicalization in such sentences as

(5) He didn't see many girls
(6) Many girls he didn't see

They differ in meaning, and the difference is predicted by the
above left-to-right order principle. The same is true of quantifiers which cross each other in the derivation of a passive sentence:

(7) Many students admire few lecturers
(8) Few lecturers are admired by many students

In (7) 'few' falls within the scope of 'many' in surface structure,
in (8) it is the other way round.

(b) In generative semantics the KP-hypothesis is retained in

----

1. There are some exceptions to this. Thus in 'all that glitters
   is not gold', 'all' is clearly within the scope of 'not', i.e.
   the sentence is synonymous with 'not all that glitters is gold'.
   For discussion of such sentences, see Katz, 1972, 168ff.

its strongest possible form. Consequently, the semantic difference
between such sentences as (3) and (4), and (7) and (8) should be
explicated in terms of remote structure. Note that (3) and (4) can
be paraphrased as

> (3a) The students who didn't come to the lecture were many
> (4a) The students who came to the lecture were not many

This suggests that quantifiers like 'many' may be analysed as predicates of higher sentences in remote structure. Assuming that
'not' is also an underlying predicate, (3) and (4) would have the
following remote structures (omitting details):

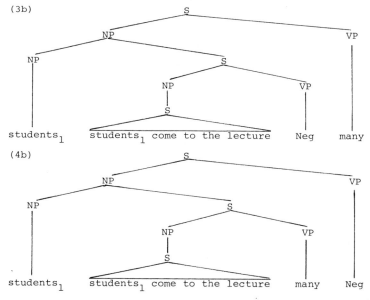

The crucial point about these structures (which would look rather
different if the trees were adapted to the formulae of symbolic
logic rather than to the requirements of the standard theory (cf.
below, section V.C.3)) is the relative height of Neg and 'many':
it reflects surface structure order (the highest predicate is that
which occurs first in surface structure). The relevant transformations (Neg placement and <u>quantifier lowering</u> (to be discussed pres-

ently)) operate cyclically, converting (3b) and (4b) into (3) and
(4), or - if quantifier lowering does not apply - into (3a) and
(4a).

Consider next the underlying structures of (7) and (8) which
would be required by the hierarchical principle (cf. Lakoff, 1971b
(in Steinberg and Jakobovits, 1971)):

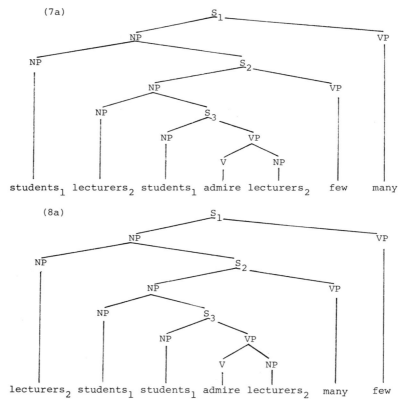

For (7) to be derived from (7a), a cyclic rule of quantifier
lowering must operate. In (7a) this would take 'few' (on the second
cycle (S_2)) and adjoin it to 'lecturers' in S_3. It would, furthermore, delete the occurrence of the coreferential 'lecturers' in
S_2 (whose only function is to identify the noun in S_3 to which the
quantifier is to be adjoined). On the last cycle (S_1), 'many' would

be lowered and adjoined to 'students' in S_3 ('students' in S_1 being deleted). After the application of the passive rule to S_3 in (8a), the same operations would derive (8) from (8a).

Quantifier lowering, however, is not sufficient to maintain semantic constancy through the derivation of (7) and (8). The trouble is that the passive rule may apply on the lowest cycle in (7a), deriving

(9) Lecturers are admired by students

When quantifier lowering applies on the higher cycles, the result will be

(10) Few lecturers are admired by many students

which is, then, falsely predicted to be synonymous with (7). Conversely, the passive rule may not apply on the lowest cycle in (8a). If it does not, quantifier lowering results in

(11) Many students admire few lecturers

which is not synonymous with (8). In other words, depending on whether or not the passive rule applies on the lowest cycle of (7a) and (8a), both of these structures may underlie (7) and (8). To prevent this, Lakoff proposes a derivational constraint of roughly the following kind: If an underlying structure contains two quantifiers Q_1 and Q_2, and if it is the case that Q_1 commands Q_2, then, in the derived surface structure, one of two conditions must be met: (a) either Q_1 still commands Q_2, or (b) if Q_1 and Q_2 command each other, Q_1 precedes Q_2. In other words, "if an underlying asymmetric command-relationship breaks down in surface structure, a precede-relationship takes over" (the latter being necessarily asymmetric).

If we apply this derivational constraint to (7a) and (8a) in conjunction with the rule of quantifier lowering, it will be seen that it blocks the derivation of (7) from (8a), and of (8) from (7a). For example, in (8a) 'few' commands 'many', whereas in (7) 'many' and 'few' command each other, but 'many' also precedes 'few'.

Lakoff applies this constraint to a number of other phenomena. We will not go into further detail. The main point is to note the nature of a derivational constraint: it can keep track of the derivation, so to speak (hence the term 'global'). In this particular case, the constraint specifies a well-formedness condition holding between remote and surface structure and prevents trans-

formations ('local' derivational constraints) from changing the
meaning of the sentence[1].

With respect to such sentences as we have considered so far,
then, the issue between interpretivists and generative semanticists
is fairly clear-cut. Interpretivists posit relatively "shallow"
deep structures and provide the grammar with a powerful semantic
component: semantic rules can operate on deep structures, surface
structures, and even intermediate structures. By contrast, generative semanticists set up highly abstract underlying structures
and postulate powerful transformational rules and constraints on
rules.

We turn now to the nature of semantic representations. Generative semanticists argue that the output of the rules of the semantic component in the (extended) standard theory are formal objects
of a different nature from the input: the input is a P-marker, the
output is not. From the point of view of generative semanticists,
then, the goal must be to prove that they <u>should</u> be P-markers[2].
A number of arguments have been presented that they should be.
One argument takes the following form (Lakoff, 1970e):

----

1. For critical discussion of quantifier lowering and its implications, see for example Hall Partee, 1970, 1971, Chomsky, 1972,
   180ff., and Jackendoff, 1972, 339ff. Katz, 1972, 439ff. discusses the problem from the point of view of the standard theory
   (i.e. the deep structure interpretivist position). In essence,
   Katz proposes that - if necessary - a reading which specifies
   the relative scope of quantifiers and negation may be assigned
   to 'by + Passive'. Hall Partee, 1971 provides a general overview
   of the KP-hypothesis and its consequences. On derivational constraints, see also section IV.E.8 and references cited in the
   notes on p. 224.

2. It is important to underscore 'should'. The question is not
   whether they <u>can</u> be. Virtually anything can be represented in
   terms of a P-marker. Furthermore, over the years, the output
   of the semantic component of the standard theory has come to
   be increasingly <u>structured</u> formal objects. Thus, in Jackendoff's
   grammar (1972, 91), the projection rules operating on the following sentence:

       (1) Probably Max was carefully climbing the walls

   have as their output

       (2) PROBABLE (CAREFUL (MAX, CLIMB (MAX, THE WALLS)))

   Clearly, (2) is easily converted into a P-marker. Compare in
   this connection also the entry for 'chase' given by Katz, 1972,
   165ff. and the semantic representations formulated by Bierwisch,
   1970a (in Lyons, 1970b) 178ff. See further Katz, 1971b, Chomsky,
   1972, 136ff., and Bach, 1974, 227ff.

1. Assume that the grammar contains semantic interpretation rules operating on surface structures (which are of course P-markers).

2. Assume that the grammar does not contain any rules which delete under identity[1].

3. Assume that the relative scope of negation and quantifiers is defined by the left-to-right order principle.

Given these three assumptions, it can be shown that rules of interpretation must apply sequentially. In other words, the output of some rule may form the input to some rule. It follows from this that the output of semantic rules <u>must</u> be P-markers.

Given that semantic representations must be P-markers, then, in effect, the rules of the semantic component map one syntactic structure into another syntactic structure. The question that is then asked is why there should be anything but syntactic rules in the grammar, syntactic rules which map underlying semantic representations into surface structures.

A further argument against the (extended) standard theory relates to the structure of lexical items. We return to this in section V.C.4.

V.C.2. <u>Noun phrases</u>

In the standard theory each noun phrase is arbitrarily assigned a referential index corresponding to the intended referent (cf. above, section IV.D.15). It has been argued by generative semanticists (notably Bach, 1968 and McCawley 1970a) that this way of representing the meaning of noun phrases is inadequate. Specifically, Bach offers a number of arguments in support of the hypothesis that all nouns originate as predicates: they should be derived from relative clauses whose head is a referential index by the familiar rule of relative reduction and a further rule of index replacement. Thus a noun phrase like 'the bachelor' in

(1) The bachelor won

would have roughly the following derivation (ignoring the question

----

1. This is a further characteristic of the interpretivist position (cf. also above, p. 446). For example, there is no rule of VP deletion. Thus the proper semantic interpretation of the anaphoric expression in a sentence like 'I want a new car, and Peter does too' must be effected by an interpretive rule.

of the source of the definite article):

```
( x ( x be bachelor )  )  ═══════⟹
NP    S              S  NP
  ( x bachelor )  ══════⟹
NP              NP
  ( the bachelor )
NP                NP
```

Let us cite a few of Bach's arguments. Consider the following sentence:

(2) The man has known his wife since she was two weeks old

The crucial point about this sentence is that a girl who is two
weeks old cannot be anybody's <u>wife</u>. The logical meaning of 'wife'
in the sentence is 'the person who is <u>now</u> the man's wife'; that
is, 'wife' contains a tense element which is part of the meaning
of the sentence (cf. also Lakoff, 1972a (in Davidson and Harman,
1972) 599f.). This can be captured under the analysis proposed by
Bach in the following way:

(3) The man has known x who <u>is</u> his wife since x was two
    weeks old

In the same way, noun phrases may contain a future element[1]:

(4) Hopefully, John will finish the book

derived from

(5) Hopefully John will finish x which <u>will be</u> a book

This account of noun phrases would also provide a solution
to the problem of the scope of Neg in the sentence discussed in
section IV.G.9.3:

(6) The stone didn't hit the boy

Under the present analysis, (6) would have three different underlying structures, in each of which the scope of Neg would be a
sentence:

(6a) Neg (x (x be a stone) hit y (y be a boy))

(6b) x (Neg x be a stone) hit y (y be a boy)

(6c) x (x be a stone) hit y (Neg y be a boy)

----

1. It is worth noting that in some languages nouns are morphologically marked for tense. For comments on this, see Hockett, 1958, 238.
   Consult also Whorf (in Carroll, ed., 1956, 207ff.). In Bach's
   analysis, then, nouns, verbs, and adjectives all belong to the
   same remote structure category: they are all predicates (cf.
   above, p. 123).

The analysis is further corroborated by the ambiguity of such sentences as

(7) Peter said that he saw the professor

In this, the speaker reports a statement made by Peter. Peter himself may have said, say

(8) I saw the tall fellow living next door to John

without knowing what the man's profession is. This information is supplied by the speaker of (7). Alternatively, he may have said

(9) I saw the professor

Under the present analysis of noun phrases, the two meanings of (7) can be rendered in roughly the following way (a more explicit representation will be given in the next section[1]):

(7a) Peter said that he saw x who, according to me, is the professor

(7b) Peter said that he saw x who, according to him, is the professor

The basic assumption underlying the approach to noun phrases sketched in this section is that referential indices constitute

----

1. The ambiguity manifested by (7) is due to the fact that the NP 'the professor' occurs in a position that may be either referentially <u>transparent</u> or referentially <u>opaque</u>. Referential transparency/opacity can be defined in terms of truth value in the following way: If a noun phrase occurs in a referentially transparent context, substitution of coreferential terms for that noun phrase preserves truth value, whereas this may not be the case in referentially opaque contexts. Thus in the (transparent) reading of (7) represented by (7a), it is the speaker who identifies x as 'the professor'; he knows that x and 'the professor' are coreferential. In other words, in this reading, substitution of the object NP of (8) for 'the professor' in (7) would preserve truth value. In the (opaque) reading of (7) represented by (7b), substitution of the object NP of (8) for 'the professor' in (7) would not preserve truth value unless Peter happens to believe that the two NPs are coreferential. The distinction between referential transparency and opacity has received much attention in the philosophical literature. We will not pursue the matter any further. The main point is that the grammar must explicitate the ambiguity of sentences like (7). Generative semanticists argue that this explicitation should be made in terms of remote logical structure, whereas adherents of the (extended) standard theory would postulate rules of semantic interpretation (see for example Katz, 1972, 261ff. and Jackendoff, 1975b).

the speaker's mental picture of the universe. When he speaks, he
selects a small subset of these indices and identifies them in
terms of noun phrases. In the words of McCawley, 1970a (in Jacobs
and Rosenbaum, 1970) 173): "noun phrases ... fulfill a function
roughly comparable to that of postulates and definitions in mathematics: they state properties which the speaker assumes to be
possessed by the conceptual entities involved in what he is saying and are used chiefly to identify the things that the speaker is
talking about" (cf. also McCawley, 1968a (in Bach and Harms, 1968)
138ff.).

V.C.3. Some examples of remote semantic structures

We will make the assumption in this section (and the next)
that English is a VSO-language in remote structure. In other words,
we will assume that the underlying structure of a sentence like

(1) John loves Mary

is (ignoring Tense[1]):

(1a)

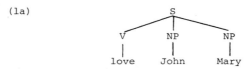

In (1a), which clearly bears much resemblance to the formulae of
the predicate calculus provisionally discussed in section IV.D.18.,
the first argument following the predicate is the subject, and the
second the direct object. These two functions, then, are defined
in terms of order[2].

(1a), however, is not deep enough to meet the definition of
noun phrases given in the preceding section. We must revise it[3]:

----

1. As has been said before, Tense, like the auxiliaries and the
   modal verbs, are analysed as main verbs in generative semantics.
   We will not go into the details of this question.

2. If we wanted to combine generative semantics with case grammar,
   we could have the NPs dominated by (categorially interpreted)
   case labels. Furthermore, we would have to abandon the special
   modality constituent of case grammar.

3. For the structure of the relative clauses, in particular, the
   predicate 'called', see Bach, 1968 (in Bach and Harms, 1968) 121
   and note.

(1b)

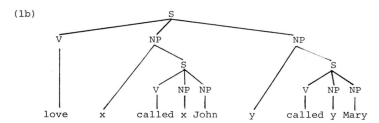

We assume, then, that the relative reduction rule can also delete the predicate 'called'.

There is evidence, especially from facts pertaining to pro-nominalization, that (1b) is an intermediate rather than a remote structure: the index-identifying propositions (i.e. the relative clauses) should originate outside the proposition that contains the index. (1b) should presumably be revised once again as follows[1]:

(1c)

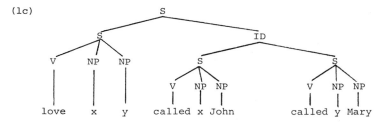

Let us now return to sentence (7) of the preceding section. The two readings of that can be represented as follows (cf. also McCawley, 1973, 223f.):

(2) = (7a)

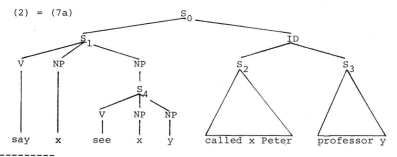

----

1. I borrow the node ID in the sense 'identificatory constituent' from Frantz, 1974.

(3) = (7b)

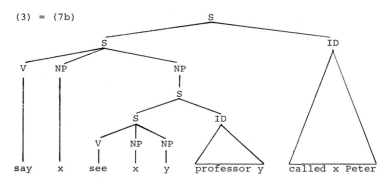

In (2) the proposition 'professor y' is not attributed to (i.e. does not fall within the scope of) what x said: he merely said that he saw some y; the specific identification of y is made by the speaker. In (3) the opposite is true. In either case, the ID constituents are adjoined to the indices which they match. Thus in (2) the S_2 of ID is adjoined to the NP dominating x in S_1, and S_3 to the NP dominating y in S_4. This leaves us with one 'floating' index, namely the x of S_4. This is pronominalized. In this way, (2) and (3) both end up as (7) in surface structure.

Observe that in this analysis, pronominalization is a kind of reverse process from what it is in the standard theory: any referential index which does not have an ID constituent adjoined to it ends up as a pronoun in surface structure. Precisely which indices are pronominalized is a matter of general constraints on pronominalization of the type which we have already discussed.

This account of pronominalization has the advantage of obviating the difficulties caused by the Bach-Peters paradox. It thus provides a remote-structure alternative to the interpretivist position mentioned in section IV.G.18.4. In particular, pronominalization no longer operates on full NPs containing relative clauses[1].

Returning now to the sentences discussed in section IV.D.18 (in particular (13), (14), (17), and (18)), they would have underlying structures of roughly the following kind[2]:

----

1. For some discussion, see Karttunen, 1969 and Hall Partee, 1972.

2. There would be other ways of representing their logical structure. Compare Lakoff, 1972a (in Davidson and Harman, 1972) 556, McCawley, 1972 (in Davidson and Harman, 1972) 531ff. and McCawley, 1970a (in Jacobs and Rosenbaum, 1970) 181f.

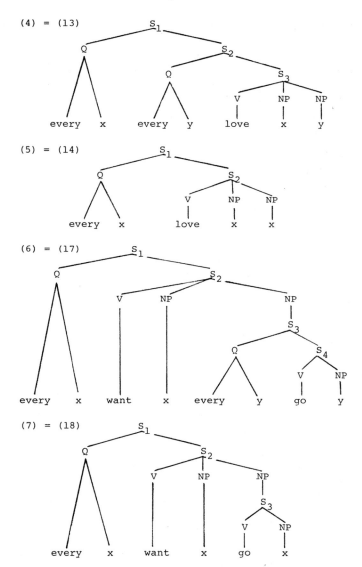

where x and y range over the set of all human beings. Quantifier
lowering applies cyclically in all four structures. In (5) the

reflexive rule applies on the S_2 cycle. In (7) equi NP deletion applies on the S_2 cycle.

In the standard theory, deep structures are generated by PS-rules in the now familiar way. In the generative semantics model, there are no PS-rules. Instead, there is an unordered set of <u>node admissibility conditions</u> which define well-formedness of semantic representations (cf. McCawley, 1968c). For example, one condition might take the following form:

$$S: \left[P\ NP^n \right] n \geqslant 1$$

It asserts that an S node immediately dominating a predicate (henceforth we will use the symbol P in the sense 'predicate') and one or more NP(s) is a well-formed structure. Another condition would be

$$NP: \left\{ x\ S \right\}$$

which states that an NP immediately dominates an index or a sentence. An essential difference between PS-rules and node admissibility conditions is that the former generate <u>strings</u> from which P-markers are derived by the algorithm described on p. 68, whereas the latter generate trees directly. It is also important to note that remote structures of this kind are conspicuously simpler and less language-specific than the deep structures of the standard theory. In particular, there is no Aux node, no VP node, no Det node, no Adv nodes, etc.

A further difference between generative semantics and the standard theory is that the notion of a possible message in a possible world or a possible situation implies that generation is restricted only by the limitations on human thought. The qualification 'and only' in 'all and only the sentences of L' now merely means that sentences which violate certain 'low-level' constraints should be ruled out. For example, a generative semanticist would agree that a sentence like

(8) * Gave a ring John Mary

is ungrammatical, whereas he would claim that

(9) The car owns John

is perfectly well-formed if uttered by someone who wonders that John can be bothered spending every evening and every Sunday on the car[1].

----

1. In other words, the grammar would not contain any machinery for generating (9) derivatively (cf. above, p. 150).

V.C.4. Lexical items

In the standard theory it is a basic assumption that lexical items are inserted <u>en bloc</u> prior to the operation of the properly syntactic (i.e. cyclic) rules. In fact, deep structure, P_i, is defined as that point of a derivation when lexical insertion is completed (with the exception of those lexical items which are inserted in the second lexical pass). It is further assumed that lexical items constitute the entities in which the ingredients of meaning - the semantic features - are clustered. These entities form the input to the projection rules, which, given the grammatical relations defined by the base P-marker, derive the semantic representation of the entire sentence.

Against this it has been argued by generative semanticists that the claim that deep <u>structures</u> play a crucial role in semantic interpretation is without content in a number of cases. Consider the following sentences:

(1) Everybody talks about John's deeds
(2) Everybody talks about the important things that John has done

(1) and (2) are roughly synonymous. They would have deep structures of the following kinds (assuming the lexicalist hypothesis and omitting details not pertinent to the point):

(1a)

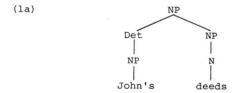

(2a) (see overleaf)

The meaning of (2), then, would be derived by the projection rules from a very complex underlying structure which contains no less than two embedded sentences. By contrast, the meaning of 'deeds' would be internal to the item itself. The projection rules would not come into play at all, since there is no relevant structure in (1a) upon which they could operate. On the other hand, the semantic representation which defines the meaning of 'deeds' must be something like (2a). Consequently, the semantic component

(2a)

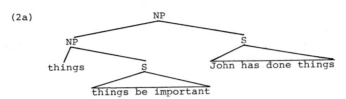

must be powerful enough to derive complex syntactico-semantic structures from single lexical items[1]. On the basis of such evidence,
the generative semanticist concludes that the meaning of lexical
items should be stated in syntactic terms, i.e. be an integral
part of the P-marker which constitutes the semantic representation
of the sentence.

Such arguments in themselves, however, are not sufficient to
invalidate the hypothesis that the lexical item is the basic unit
in the semantic component. They only point to the syntactic or-
ganization of the meaning of some lexical items. If, in addition
to this, however, it can be shown that the meaning ingredients of
some items must occur in nonadjacent positions in remote structure,
then the lexical item principle breaks down and the projection
rules are deprived of their input. Furthermore, if semantic primes
occur scattered over P-markers in remote structure, they must be
brought together by the operation of transformational rules prior
to lexical insertion. Consequently, there can be no level of deep
structure defined as P_i (i.e. the P-marker as it looks after lexical
insertion and before the application of the cyclic rules).

A number of cases have been adduced in support of the hypothesis that the meaning ingredients of verbs must occur in nonadjacent positions in remote structure. One such case concerns the
verb 'remind'. Postal, 1970c has argued persuasively that a sentence like

(3) John reminds me of Peter

must have an underlying structure of roughly the following kind:

----

1. In this sense, therefore, the lexicalist hypothesis represents
   a step away from the standard theory, although, in principle,
   it is not incompatible with the deep structure interpretivist
   hypothesis. For a similar example, not involving the lexicalist-
   transformationalist issue, see Postal, 1970c, 106ff.

(3a)

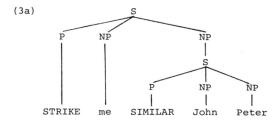

STRIKE and SIMILAR are (potential[1]) semantic primes or <u>atomic pred-icates</u> which define the meaning of 'remind'. For the details of the argument, the reader is referred to Postal's paper (which, in general, provides a clear statement of the rationale of generative semantics). The main point to be noted here is that the meaning of 'remind' is interspersed, as it were, among the constituents which define the semantic representation of the sentence and that hence lexical insertion cannot take place at the point of the derivation defined by (3a) (there is no single node under which 'remind' could be inserted). A number of transformations, including the well-established cyclic rule of subject-to-object raising and the (not so well-established) rule of predicate raising (which will be il-lustrated presently) must operate before 'remind' can be inserted. In other words, (3a), provided it is valid (and it has been sub-jected to a good deal of criticism (see for example, Kimball, 1970 and Bolinger 1971)), undermines the conception of a level of deep structure defined as P_i.

Another celebrated example is McCawley's treatment of the verb 'kill' (1968d). Let us illustrate this in some detail. The meaning of 'kill' can be represented in terms of the following atomic predicates CAUSE BECOME NOT ALIVE[2]. In a theory in which meaning is given a syntactic representation, the lexical item 'kill' would replace the following structure (see overleaf): The predicates are independently motivated. In particular, the language has a two-place predicate 'cause', a one-place predicate 'not', a one-place predicate 'alive', and a one-place predicate 'come about'.

----

1. They may be susceptible of further analysis.
2. For critical discussion, see for example Fodor, 1970 and Wierzbicka, 1975. Fodor's arguments are discussed by Seuren, 1974b, 10ff.

(4)

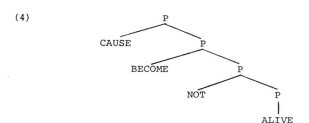

Observe that there are various subtrees:

(5)

(6)

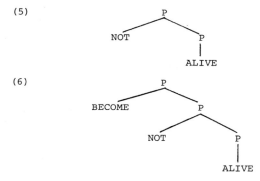

(5) defines the meaning of 'dead', and (6) the meaning of 'die'.
By this analysis, the remote structure of a sentence like

   (7) Poison killed the girl

would be (omitting details with respect to the NPs - see next page):
The rule of predicate raising, which is cyclic and optional,
has the effect of adjoining the P of an S as the right daughter of
the P in the sentence next above (as appears from (4)-(6)). If
it applies on all cycles, the outcome, after subject formation,
will be (7). But there are various other possibilities. For example,
the combined operation of predicate raising, subject-to-object
raising and subject formation would derive

   (8) Poison caused the girl to die

   If predicate raising applies to (3a), it will derive

(3b)

(7a)[1]

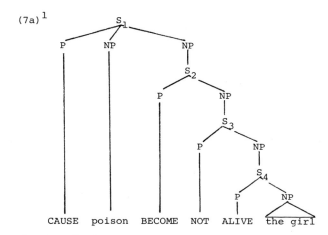

CAUSE   poison   BECOME   NOT   ALIVE   the girl

The phonological form _remind_ is sensitive to this structure and hence can replace it. If, on the other hand, predicate raising does not apply to (3a), the ultimate output of the T-rules will be (after the appropriate lexical items have been inserted):

(3c) John strikes me as being similar to Peter

or

(3d) John strikes me as resembling Peter

This type of semantic analysis can be brought to bear on nouns as well. Thus in the remote semantic structure of a sentence like 'the woman died', the noun 'woman' would occur in a sentence under the domination of the ID constituent, that is, outside the main proposition. This identificatory sentence might have roughly the following structure (note that 'and' is analysed as a multiplace predicate):

----

1. One of the arguments in support of a semantic structure like (7a) relates to the scope-ambiguity of 'almost' in a sentence like 'Peter almost killed the cat'. This has several readings. In one reading, it means that Peter did something that brought the cat close to death (in the sense that it had perhaps only one life left). In that reading the scope of 'almost' (which is also analysed as a predicate) would be the subtree NOT (ALIVE (the cat)). Cf. McCawley, op. cit., 79. For some further evidence, see also Green, 1972 (in Peranteau et al., 1972) 91f.

(8)

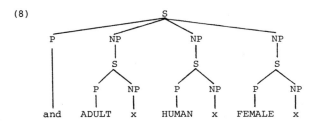

After the application of conjunction reduction (which would be another instance of a syntactic rule operating prior to lexical insertion) and adjunction to a referential index, the structure would
look something like this:

(9)

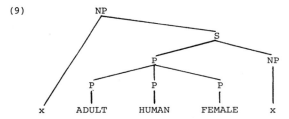

For this predicate, the phonological matrix <u>woman</u> would be substituted.

   Recall the concept of hypothetical lexical items discussed
in section IV.G.17.2. Under the present analysis, these would be
redefined in terms of atomic predicates. For example, the lexicon
would contain the noun 'aggression', but not the verb '* aggress'.
The remote semantic structure of a sentence into which 'aggression'
is ultimately to be inserted would contain the relevant atomic
predicate. It would then be stated as a derivational constraint
on the insertion of 'aggression' that the semantic representation
has undergone the appropriate transformations at the point when
the insertion takes place. In the same way, entries for verbs like
'shout' (cf. above, section IV.E.8) would contain information about
the derivational history of sentences into which they may be inserted[1].

----

1. For discussion of derivational constraints on lexical insertion,
   see Lakoff, 1970a, X and 1970b, 633f.

Lexical items do not contain the information stated in the
standard theory in terms of syntactic features. This information
is obtained directly from the semantic representations. For example, if the predicate CALLED is absent from the constituent
identidying a referential index, the noun is a common noun. Number
is defined in terms of presuppositions about intended referents.
The distribution of determiners is bound up in complex ways with
the referential status of NPs; and so on. We will not go into the
details of these highly complicated questions. It can be said in
general, however, that pragmatic assumptions about the world we
live in and the things we talk about play an integral part in
the structure of a grammar as conceived of by the generative semanticists. Indeed, the term 'generative pragmatics' is in use
(Færch, 1975).

Notes and some further references

Generative semantics took its beginning with Lakoff's 1965-dis-
sertation (1970a). Consider for example again the tree on p. 432.
Clearly this is, in principle, a remote semantic structure. Likewise, the formalism developed by Lakoff to handle exceptions is
a direct precursor of the concept of global derivational constraints
on lexical insertion. Important is also a short unpublished paper
by Lakoff and Ross with the revealing title "Is Deep Structure
Necessary?" (1967). Seuren, 1972 is a succinct discussion of the
central issues in the battle of deep structure. On logic and remote structure, consult such works as Lakoff, 1972a, McCawley,
1967, 1968a, 1970a, 1972, and Harman, 1972. The important point
about Postal's analysis of the semantic structure of 'remind' is
that the properly syntactic rule subject-to-object raising must
apply prior to lexical insertion. Other purely syntactic arguments
have been brought to bear on this matter. Consider again the case
of picture nouns (cf. above, p. 436). In the generative semantics
framework, the insertion of these would be subject to derivational
constraints. In particular, as we have seen, reflexivization must
apply to the object noun of the underlying atomic predicate before the predicate undergoes nominalization. Likewise, Ross's complex NP constraint has been invoked in evidence (cf. McCawley,
1971c). At this point, mention must be made of the concept of
shallow structure (a term coined by Postal). It is defined as the
level of structure which results from the application of all cyclic
rules. Shallow structures form the input to post-cyclic rules (such
as subject formation, topicalization, Wh-fronting, and extraposition). Now, given a level of shallow structure, there are two possibilities with respect to lexical insertion: (1) lexical items
are inserted en bloc at the level of shallow structure, or (2)
lexical insertion rules are 'anywhere rules' interspersed with
syntactic transformations from remote to shallow structure (cf.
McCawley, 1968d and Lakoff, 1971b). For further discussion of the
syntactic structure of lexical items ('lexical decomposition'),
see such works as Lakoff, 1972a, Green, 1972, and de Rijk, 1974

(first written in 1968). Frantz, 1974 is a reasonably manageable introduction to the main tenets of generative semantics; provides a good bibliography. Seuren (ed.), 1974b contains some of the most important papers on generative semantics. For critical discussion of generative semantics from the point of view of the standard theory, see Katz, 1971b, 1972, Chapter 8, 1973c, and from the point of view of the extended standard theory, Chomsky, 1972, Hasegawa, 1972 (cf. McCawley, 1973) and Jackendoff, 1972. A recent discussion of semantic representations as conceived of in the extended standard theory is Jackendoff, 1976. Langendoen and Bever, 1973 is particularly instructive in that it deals with one specific problem from the point of view of the standard theory, the extended standard theory , and generative semantics. In the text, we have dealt only with the extended standard theory, according to which semantic interpretation is in part determined by surface structure. It should be noted, however, that Chomsky has recently proposed that semantic interpretation - including functional structure (i.e., in particular, the notions 'subject-of' and 'object-of') - is determined entirely by surface structure (see especially Chomsky 1973 and 1975, Chapter 3). This proposal entails a considerably richer interpretation of the notion 'surface structure' than that envisaged in the (extended) standard theory. In particular, surface structures must contain traces indicating the effect of movement rules. By way of illustration, we may turn once again to sentence (2) of section IV.D.2 (cf. also p. 390f.). In Chomsky's analysis, this would have roughly the following derivation:

$$(\underset{S_1}{Y_2} \text{ seems } (\underset{S_2}{Y_1} \text{ be certain } (\text{ Peter be there })_{S_3})_{S_2})_{S_1} \implies$$

$$(\underset{S_1}{Y_2} \text{ seems } (\underset{S_2}{\text{ Peter be certain }} (\text{ t be there })_{S_3})_{S_2})_{S_3} \implies$$

$$(\underset{S_1}{\text{ Peter seems be certain }} (\text{ t be there })_{S_3})_{S_1}$$

In this derivation, subject-to-subject raising has applied cyclically. In the surface structure, a trace ('t'), which is bound by the raised NP according to the principles of precedence and command, has been left in S_3, indicating the position of 'Peter' in the base P-marker. This trace is available to the semantic rules, now operating on surface structures. 'Peter', then, correctly, will be defined as the 'logical' subject of 'be there'. The trace theory of movement rules has been the subject of much debate in the recent literature (consult for example recent issues of Linguistic Inquiry). Recent research has shown that the universal base hypothesis, given the power of transformational rules inherent in the Aspects model, is a nonempirical issue; that is, the universal base hypothesis, attractive as it is, cannot be falsified. For the mathematical proof, see Peters and Ritchie, 1969. It is clear that, in the face of such evidence, the main task confronting the theoretician is that of constraining the power of transformations as much as possible. The principle of strict cyclicity referred to on p. 446 is an illustration of such attempts. On the other hand, there is perhaps reason to take note of the following statement by Bach (1974, 265): " ... there is a gross mismatch between what is explicitly given by the theory of transformational grammar (in any of its variants) and the implicit working hypotheses that linguists in fact use. For example, no linguist would ever seriously propose a transformation like the ones used by Peters and Ritchie for their proofs".

EPILOGUE

"In syntax meaning is everything". To the structuralists, the
philosophy underlying this statement, once made by Jespersen, was
anathema. Meaning, they argued, was something that was not amenable
to empirical investigation and hence could not serve as a valid
scientific heuristic. Instead, the linguist should turn to the observationally accessible data: language was sounds in the air, and
so sounds in the air should be the starting point of linguistic
analysis. This attitude, as we have seen, had two conspicuous consequences. First, the preoccupation with sound meant that syntax
came last in the descriptive hierarchy, and often enough was never
really reached. Secondly, semantics was relegated from the purview
of linguistics (except in the somewhat impoverished form called
'sameness or difference in meaning').

The advent of transformational-generative grammar with the
publication of Syntactic Structures gave pride of place to syntax:
the new model began where many structuralists had been prone to
leave off. Although, from the beginning, the new theory did not incorporate semantics in any systematic way, yet meaning was not entirely disregarded. Thus arguments built on syntactic ambiguity
(as witness the famous sentence 'flying planes can be dangerous')
are essentially semantic in nature.

In 1963 and 1964 the first serious attempt was made to in-
tegrate the new theory of syntax with a theory of semantics. This
may be seen as the second, and perhaps the most important, of two
stages in the overthrow of structuralism.

489

The incorporation of semantics in the theory soon spelt trouble. In numerous cases it became apparent that the hypothesis that deep structures uniquely determine the meaning of sentences would require much deeper deep structures than those envisaged in the standard theory. These in turn came to resemble, more and more, abstract syntactic representations of the meaning of sentences. The development of generative semantics, therefore, was an inevitable consequence of the standard theory. It could be countered only by giving up the KP-hypothesis in its strongest form and enriching the theory by interpretive rules operating on surface structures.

The reader must now turn to the literature and form his own judgments. Should he come to the conclusion that generative semantics gains an ascendancy over the extended standard theory, then, with Jespersen's statement in mind, he may well say: "the development has come full circle".

BIBLIOGRAPHY

Aarsleff, H. (1970). "The History of Linguistics and Professor
    Chomsky". Language, 46: 570-85.
Adams, D., Campbell, M.A., Cohen, V., Lovins, J., Maxwell, E.,
    Nygren, C., and Reighard, J. (eds.) (1971). Papers from the
    Seventh Regional Meeting of the Chicago Linguistic Society.
    Chicago: Department of Linguistics, University of Chicago.
Akmajian, A. (1970). "On Deriving Cleft Sentences from Pseudo-
    Cleft Sentences". Linguistic Inquiry, 1: 149-68.
  - and Heny, F. (1975). An Introduction to the Principles of
    Transformational Syntax. Cambridge, Mass.: MIT Press.
Allen, H.B. (ed.) (1964). Readings in Applied English Linguistics.
    New York: Appleton-Century-Crofts.
Anderson, J.M. (1971). The Grammar of Case. Towards a Localistic
    Theory. London: Cambridge University Press.
Anderson, S.R. (1971a). "On the Linguistic Status of the Performa-
    tive/Constative Distinction". Bloomington, Indiana: Indiana
    University Linguistics Club.
  - (1971b). "On the Role of Deep Structure in Semantic Interpreta-
    tion". Foundations of Language, 7: 387-96.
  - and Kiparsky, P. (eds.) (1973). A Festschrift for Morris Halle.
    New York: Holt, Rinehart and Winston.
Antley, K. (1974). "McCawley's Theory of Selectional Restrictions".
    Foundations of Language, 11: 257-74.
Arbini, R. (1969). "Tag-questions and Tag-imperatives in English".
    Journal of Linguistics, 5: 205-14.
Arens, H. (1955). Sprachwissenschaft, der Gang ihrer Entwicklung
    von der Antike bis zur Gegenwart. Munich: Karl Alber.
Austin, J.L. (1962). How to Do Things with Words. Cambridge, Mass.:
    Harvard University Press.
Bach, E. (1964). An Introduction to Transformational Grammars.
    New York: Holt, Rinehart and Winston.
  - (1965a). "Structural Linguistics and the Philosophy of Science".
    Diogenes, 51: 111-28.
  - (1965b). "On Some Recurrent Types of Transformations". In
    Kreidler, C.W. (ed.) Monograph Series on Languages and Lin-
    guistics No. 18. Washington: Georgetown University Press.
  - (1967). "HAVE and BE in English Syntax". Language, 43: 462-85.
  - (1968). "Nouns and Noun Phrases". In Bach and Harms (1968).
  - (1970). "Problominalization". Linguistic Inquiry, 1: 121-22.

491

Bach, E. (1971). "Questions". Linguistic Inquiry, 2: 153-66.
-   (1974). Syntactic Theory. New York: Holt, Rinehart and Winston.
-   and Harms, R.T. (eds.) (1968). Universals in Linguistic Theory.
    New York: Holt, Rinehart and Winston.
Baker, C.L. (1970a). "A Note on Scope of Quantifiers and Negation".
    Linguistic Inquiry, 1: 136-38.
-   (1970b). "Double Negatives". Linguistic Inquiry, 1: 169-86.
-   (1970c). "Notes on the Description of English Questions: The
    Role of an Abstract Question Morpheme". Foundations of Lan-
    guage 6: 197-219. Reprinted in Seuren (1974b).
-   and Brame, M.K. (1972). "'Global Rules': A Rejoinder". Lan-
    guage. 48: 51-75.
Baugh, A.C. (1959). A History of the English Language. Second rev.
    ed. New York: Appleton-Century-Crofts. (First published 1935).
Bazell, C.E. (1962). "Meaning and the Morpheme". Word, 18: 132-42.
Becker, A.L. and Arms, D.G. (1969). "Prepositions as Predicates".
    In Binnick et al. (1969).
Bendix, E.H. (1966). Componential Analysis of General Vocabulary.
    (Part 2 of International Journal of American Linguistics, 32).
    Bloomington, Indiana: Indiana University Press. The Hague:
    Mouton.
Berlin, B. and Kay, P. (1969). Basic Color Terms. Berkeley and Los
    Angeles: University of California Press.
Berman, A. (1974). "On the VSO Hypothesis". Linguistic Inquiry,
    5: 1-36.
Bever, T.G. (1970). "The Cognitive Basis for Linguistic Structures".
    In Hayes, R.J. (ed.) (1970) Cognition and the Development of
    Language. New York: Wiley.
Bierwisch, M. (1969). "On Certain Problems of Semantic Representa-
    tions". Foundations of Language, 5: 153-84.
-   (1970a). "Semantics". In Lyons (1970b).
-   (1970b). "On Classifying Semantic Features". In Bierwisch and
    Heidolph (1970). Also in Steinberg and Jakobovits (1971).
-   (1972). "Generative Grammar and European Linguistics". In
    Sebeok, T.A. (ed.) Current Trends in Linguistics, Vol. 9.
    The Hague: Mouton.
-   and Heidolph, K.E. (eds.) (1970). Progress in Linguistics.
    The Hague: Mouton.
Binnick, R.I., Davison, A., Green, G.M., and Morgan, J.L. (eds.)
    (1969). Papers from the Fifth Regional Meeting of the Chicago
    Linguistic Society. Chicago: Department of Linguistics: Uni-
    versity of Chicago.
Bloch, B. (1948). "A Set of Postulates for Phonemic Analysis".
    Language, 24: 3-46.
Bloomfield, L. (1926). "A Set of Postulates for the Science of Lan-
    guage". Language, 2: 153-64.
-   (1933). Language. New York: Holt, Rinehart and Winston.
Bolinger, D.L. (1965). "The Atomization of Meaning". Language, 41:
    555-73.
-   (1967a). "The Imperative in English". In To Honor Roman
    Jakobson. The Hague: Mouton.
-   (1967b). "Adjectives in English: Attribution and Predication".
    Lingua, 18: 1-34.
-   (1968). Aspects of Language. New York: Harcourt, Brace and
    World.
-   (1971). "Semantic Overloading: A Study of the Verb Remind".
    Language, 47: 522-47.
Borkin, A. et al. (eds.) (1972). Where the Rules Fail: A Student's
    Guide. An Unauthorized Appendix to M.K. Burt's FROM DEEP TO
    SURFACE STRUCTURE. Bloomington, Indiana: Indiana University
    Linguistics Club.

Bowers, F. (1968). "English Complex Sentence Formation". Journal
of Linguistics, 4: 83-88.
Bresnan, J.W. (1970). "On Complementizers: Toward a Syntactic
Theory of Complement Types". Foundations of Language, 6:
297-321.
- (1973). "Syntax of the Comparative Clause Construction in
English". Linguistic Inquiry, 4: 275-345. ·
- (1976). "Nonarguments for Raising". Linguistic Inquiry, 7:
485-501.
Brown, R. and Gilman, A. (1960). "The Pronouns of Power and
Solidarity". In Sebeok, T.A. (ed.) (1960) Style in Language.
Cambridge, Mass.: MIT Press.
Bursill-Hall, G. (1963). "Medieval Grammatical Theories". Canadian
Journal of Linguistics, 9: 39-54.
Burt, M.K. (1971). From Deep to Surface Structure. An Introduction
to Transformational Syntax. New York: Harper and Row.
Campbell, M.A., Lindholm, J., Davison, A., Fisher, W., Furbee, L.,
Lovins, J., Maxwell, E., Reighard, J., and Straight, S. (eds.)
(1970). Papers from the Sixth Regional Meeting of the Chicago
Linguistic Society. Chicago: Department of Linguistics, Univer-
sity of Chicago.
Carden, G. (1968). "English Quantifiers". In Kuno, S. (ed.)
Mathematical Linguistics and Automatic Translation. Report
NSF-20. Harvard Computation Laboratory.
- (1971). "A Dialect Argument for NOT-Transportation". Linguistic
Inquiry, 2: 423-26.
Carnap, R. (1956). Meaning and Necessity. Second ed. Chicago:
Chicago University Press.
Carroll, J.B. (1953). The Study of Language. A Survey of Linguistics
and Related Disciplines in America. Cambridge, Mass.: Harvard
University Press.   ·
- (ed.) (1956). Language, Thought, and Reality. Selected Writings
of Benjamin Lee Whorf. Cambridge, Mass.: MIT Press.
Cattell, R. (1973). "Negative Transportation and Tag Questions".
Language, 49: 366-78.
- (1976). "Constraints on Movement Rules". Language, 52: 18-50.
Chapin, P.G. (1973). "Quasi-modals". Journal of Linguistics, 9: 1-10.
Chomsky, N.A. (1956). "Three Models for the Description of Language".
I.R.E. Transactions on Information Theory, IT-2: 113-24.
- (1957). Syntactic Structures. The Hague: Mouton.
- (1959a). Review of B.F. Skinner, Verbal Behavior. Language, 35:
26-58. Reprinted in Fodor and Katz (1964).
- (1959b). "On Certain Formal Properties of Grammars". Information and Control, 2, 137-67.
- (1961a). "On the Notion "Rule of Grammar"". In Jakobson, R.
(ed.) Structure of Language and its Mathematical Aspects
(Proceedings of the Twelfth Symposium on Applied Mathematics).
Providence, R.I.: American Mathematical Society. Reprinted in
Fodor and Katz (1964).
- (1961b). "Some Methodological Remarks on Generative Grammar".
Word, 17: 219-39. Reprinted in Allen, (1964).
- (1962). "A Transformational Approach to Syntax". In Hill, A.A.
(ed.) Proceedings of the Third Texas Conference on Problems
of Linguistic Analysis in English: 124-58. Austin, Texas: The
University of Texas. Reprinted in Fodor and Katz (1964).
- (1963). "Formal Properties of Grammar". In Luce, R.D., Bush,
R.B., and Galanter, E. (eds.) Handbook of Mathematical
Psychology, II. New York: Wiley.
- (1964a). Current Issues in Linguistic Theory. The Hague:
Mouton. Also in Fodor and Katz (1964).

- (1964b). "The Logical Basis of Linguistic Theory". In Lunt, H.G. (ed.) Proceedings of the Ninth International Congress of Linguistics. The Hague: Mouton.
- (1965). Aspects of the Theory of Syntax. Cambridge, Mass.: MIT Press.
- (1966a). Cartesian Linguistics: A Chapter in the History of Rationalist Thought. New York: Harper and Row.
- (1966b). Topics in the Theory of Generative Grammar. The Hague: Mouton.
- (1967a). "The Formal Nature of Language". In Lenneberg (1967).
- (1967b). "Some General Properties of Phonological Rules". Language, 43: 102-28.
- (1968). Language and Mind. New York: Harcourt, Brace and World.
- (1970). "Remarks on Nominalization". In Jacobs and Rosenbaum (1970). Also in Chomsky (1972).
- (1972). Studies in Semantics in Generative Grammar. The Hague: Mouton.
- (1973). "Conditions on Transformations". In Anderson and Kiparsky (1973).
- (1975). Reflections on Language. New York: Pantheon Books.
- and Halle, M. (1965). "Some Controversial Questions in Phonological Theory". Journal of Linguistics, 1: 97-138.
- (1968). The Sound Pattern of English. New York: Harper and Row.
- and Miller, G.A. (1963). "Introduction to the Formal Analysis of Natural Languages". In Luce, R.D., Bush, R., and Galanter, E. (eds.) Handbook of Mathematical Psychology, II. New York: Wiley.
Coates, W.A. (1964). "Meaning in Morphemes and Compound Lexical Units". In Lunt, H.G. (ed.) Proceedings of the Ninth International Congress of Linguistics. The Hague: Mouton.
Cole, P. (1974). "On the Relative Power of Global and Index Grammar: The Lakoff-Baker-Brame Controversy". Foundations of Language, 11: 543-50.
- and Morgan, J.L. (eds.) (1975). Syntax and Semantics, III. Speech Acts. New York: Academic Press.
Cook, W.A. (1969). Introduction to Tagmemic Analysis. New York: Holt, Rinehart and Winston.
- (1973). "A Set of Postulates for Case Grammar Analysis". Languages and Linguistics. Working Papers, 4: 35-49.
Cruse, D.A. (1973). "Some Thoughts on Agentivity". Journal of Linguistics, 9: 11-23.
Darden, B.J., Bailey, C.-J.N., and Davison, A. (eds.) (1968). Papers from the Fourth Regional Meeting of the Chicago Linguistic Society. Chicago: Department of Linguistics, University of Chicago.
Davidson, D. and Harman, G. (eds.) (1972). Semantics of Natural Language. Dordrecht: Reidel.
Derwing, B.L. (1973). Transformational Grammar as a Theory of Language Acquisition. London: Cambridge University Press.
Dik, S.C. (1967). "Some Critical Remarks on the Treatment of Morphological Structure in Transformational Generative Grammar". Lingua, 18: 352-83.
- (1968). Coordination. Its Implications for the Theory of General Linguistics. Amsterdam: North-Holland.
- (1973). "Crossing Coreference Again". Foundations of Language, 9: 306-26.
Dingwall, W.O. (1963). "Transformational Grammar: Form and Theory". Lingua, 12: 233-75.
- (1966). "Recent Developments in Transformational Generative Grammar". Lingua, 16: 292-316.
Dinneen, F.P. (1967). An Introduction to General Linguistics. New York: Holt, Rinehart and Winston.

Doherty, P.C. and Schwartz, A. (1967). "The Syntax of the Compared
    Adjective in English". Language, 43: 903-36.
Dougherty, R.C. (1970a, 1971). "A Grammar of Coordinate Conjoined
    Structures". I Language, 46: 850-98. II Language, 47: 298-
    339.
-   (1970b). Review of Bach and Harms (1968). Foundations of Lan-
    guage, 6: 505-61.
Dykema, K.W. (1961). "Where Our Grammar Came From". College English,
    22: 455-65. Reprinted in Allen (1964).
Emonds, J. (1970). Root and Structure Preserving Transformations.
    Bloomington, Indiana: Indiana University Linguistics Club.
-   (1972a). "A Reformulation of Certain Syntactic Transforma-
    tions". In Peters, S. (ed.) Goals of Linguistic Theory.
    Englewood Cliffs, N.J.: Prentice-Hall.
-   (1972b). "Evidence that Indirect Object Movement is a Struc-
    ture Preserving Rule". Foundations of Language, 8: 546-61.
Færch, C. (1975). "Deictic NPs and Generative Pragmatics".
    Foundations of Language, 13: 319-48.
Fillmore, C.J. (1963). "The Position of Embedding Transformations"
    in a Grammar". Word, 19: 208-31.
-   (1965). Indirect Object Constructions in English and the
    Ordering of Transformations. The Hague: Mouton.
-   (1966a). "Toward a Modern Theory of Case". Project on Linguis-
    tic Analysis, Report No. 13. Columbus, Ohio: The Ohio State
    University Research Foundation. Reprinted in Reibel and Schane
    (1969).
-   (1966b). "A Proposal Concerning English Prepositions". In
    Dinneen, F.P. (ed.) Monograph Series on Languages and Lin-
    guistics No. 19. Washington: Georgetown University Press.
-   (1967). "On the Syntax of Preverbs". Glossa, 1: 91-125.
-   (1968) "The Case for Case". In Bach and Harms (1968).
-   (1969a). Review of Bendix (1966). General Linguistics, 9: 41-65.
-   (1969b). "Types of Lexical Information". In Kiefer (1969) and
    Steinberg and Jakobovits (1971).
-   (1971a). "Verbs of Judging: An Exercise in Semantic Descrip-
    tion". In Fillmore and Langendoen (1971).
-   (1971b). "Entailment Rules in a Semantic Theory". In Rosenberg
    and Travis (1971). (First published 1965).
-   (1971c). "Some Problems for Case Grammar". The Ohio State
    University. Center for Advanced Studies in the Behavioral
    Sciences.
-   (1972). "Subjects, Speakers, and Roles". In Davidson and
    Harman (1972).
-   and Langendoen, D.T. (eds.) (1971). Studies in Linguistic
    Semantics. New York: Holt, Rinehart and Winston.
Firth, J.R. (1964). Papers in Linguistics 1934-1954. London: Oxford
    University Press.
Fodor, J.A. (1970). "Three Reasons for Not Deriving "Kill" from
    "Cause to Die"". Linguistic Inquiry, 1: 429-38.
-   and Katz, J.J. (eds.) (1964). The Structure of Language.
    Readings in the Philosophy of Language. Englewood Cliffs. N.J.:
    Prentice-Hall.
Fowler, R. (1963). "Meaning and the Theory of the Morpheme".
    Lingua, 12: 165-76.
-   (1971). An Introduction to Transformational Syntax. London:
    Routledge and Kegan Paul.
Frantz, G.D. (1974). "Generative Semantics. An Introduction with
    Bibliography". Bloomington, Indiana: Indiana University Lin-
    guistics Club.

Fraser, B. (1966). "Some Remarks on the Verb-Particle Construction
    in English". In Dinneen, F.P. (ed.) Monograph Series on Lan-
    guages and Linguistics No. 19. Washington: Georgetown Uni-
    versity Press.
  - (1970). "Some Remarks on the Action Nominalization in Eng-
    lish". In Jacobs and Rosenbaum (1970).
  - (1971). "An Examination of the Performative Analysis".
    Bloomington, Indiana: Indiana University Linguistics Club.
  - (1973). "On Accounting for Illocutionary Forces". In Anderson
    and Kiparsky (1973).
Fries, C.C. (1940). American English Grammar. New York: Appleton-
    Century-Crofts.
  - (1952). The Structure of English. An Introduction to the Con-
    struction of English Sentences. New York: Harcourt, Brace and
    World
Fry, D.B. (1970). "Speech Reception and Perception". In Lyons (1970b).
Fudge, E.C. (1970). "Phonology". In Lyons (1970b).
Gardner, R.A. and Gardner, B.T. (1969). "Teaching Sign Language
    to a Chimpanzee". Science, 16: 664-72.
Garner, R. (1971). ""Presupposition" in Philosophy and Linguistics".
    In Fillmore and Langendoen (1971).
Gefen, R. (1968). "Linguistic Theory and Language Description in·
    Jespersen". Lingua, 19: 386-404.
Gimson, A.C. (1962). An Introduction to the Pronunciation of English.
    London: Edward Arnold.
Gleason, H.A., Jr. (1961). An Introduction to Descriptive Linguistics.
    Second rev. ed. New York: Holt, Rinehart and Winston.
  _ (1965). Linguistics and English Grammar. New York: Holt,
    Rinehart and Winston.
Gleitman, L.R. (1965). "Coordinating Conjunctions in English".
    Language, 41: 260-93. Reprinted in Reibel and Schane (1969).
Goodenough, W.H. (1956). "Componential Analysis and the Study of
    Meaning". Language, 32: 195-216.
Gordon, D. and Lakoff, G. (1975). "Conversational Postulates".
    In Cole and Morgan (1975). (First published 1971).
Grady, M. (1967). "On the Essential Nominalizing Function of
    English ING". Linguistics, 34: 5-11.
Green, G.M. (1972). "Some Observations on the Syntax and Semantics
    of Instrumental Verbs". In Peranteau et al. (1972).
  - (1975). "How to Get People to Do Things with Words". In
    Cole and Morgan (1975).
Greenberg, J.H. (ed.) (1963). Universals in Language. Cambridge,
    Mass.: MIT Press.
Grice, H.P. (1975). "Logic and Conversation". In Cole and Morgan
    (1975).
Grinder, J.T. (1970). "Super Equi-NP Deletion". In Campbell et al.
    (1970).
  - (1972). "On the Cycle in Syntax". In Kimball (1972).
Gross, M. (1972). Mathematical Models in Linguistics. Englewood
    Cliffs, N.J.: Prentice-Hall.
Haas, W. (1973). Review of Lyons, 1968. Journal of Linguistics, 9:
    71-113.
Hale, A. (1970). "Conditions on English Comparative Clause
    Pairings". In Jacobs and Rosenbaum (1970).
Hall, R.A. (1960). Linguistics and Your Language. New York:
    Doubleday Anchor Books. (Second rev. ed. of Leave Your Lan-
    guage Alone (1950). Ithaca: Linguistica).
Halle, M. (1958). "Questions of Linguistics". Supplement to Il
    Nuovo-Cimento, 13, Series X: 494-517. Republished in a revised
    version under the title "On the Bases of Phonology" in Fodor
    and Katz (1964).

Halle, M. (1959). The Sound Pattern of Russian. The Hague: Mouton.
-    (1962). "Phonology in Generative Grammar". Word, 18: 54-72.
     Reprinted in Fodor and Katz (1964).
-    (1973). "Prolegomena to a Theory of Word Formation". Lin-
     guistic Inquiry, 4: 1-16.
Halliday, M.A.K. (1961). "Categories of the Theory of Grammar".
     Word, 17: 241-92.
-    (1967-1968). "Notes on Transitivity and Theme in English".
     Journal of Linguistics, a and b 3: 37-81, 199-244, c 4: 179-215.
-    (1970). "Language Structure and Language Function". In Lyons
     (1970b).
-    (1973). Explorations in the Functions of Language. London:
     Edward Arnold.
Hankamer, J. (1973). "Unacceptable Ambiguity". Linguistic Inquiry,
     4: 17-68.
Harman, G. (1967). "Psychological Aspects of the Theory of Syntax".
     Journal of Philosophy, 64: 75-87. Reprinted in Rosenberg and
     Travis (1971).
-    (1972). "Deep Structure as Logical Form". In Davidson and
     Harman (1972).
Harms, R.T. (1968). Introduction to Phonological Theory. Englewood
     Cliffs, N.J.: Prentice-Hall.
Harris, Z.S. (1942). "Morpheme Alternants in Linguistic Analysis".
     Language, 18: 169-80.
-    (1955). "From Phoneme to Morpheme". Language, 31: 190-222.
-    (1957). "Co-occurrence and Transformation in Linguistic
     Structure". Language, 33: 283-340. Reprinted in Fodor and Katz
     (1964).
-    (1960). Structural Linguistics. Chicago: Chicago University
     Press. (First published 1951 as Methods in Structural Lin-
     guistics).
Hartung, C.V. (1962). "The Persistence of Tradition in Grammar".
     Quarterly Journal of Speech, 48: 174-86. Reprinted in Allen
     (1964).
Hasegawa, K. (1968). "The Passive Construction in English". Lan-
     guage, 44: 230-44.
-    (1972). "Transformations and Semantic Interpretation". Lin-
     guistic Inquiry, 3: 141-59.
Hays, D.G. (1964). "Dependency Theory: A Formalism and Some Ob-
     servations". Language, 40: 511-25.
Hill. A.A. (1958). Introduction to Linguistic Structures. From
     Sound to Sentence in English. New York: Harcourt, Brace and
     World.
Hjelmslev, L. (1935). La Catégorie des Cas. Étude de Grammaire
     Générale. Acta Jutlandica. Aarsskrift for Aarhus universitet:
     Universitetsforlaget.
-    (1953). Prolegomena to a Theory of Language. Bloomington,
     Indiana: Indiana University Press. (Translated from Omkring
     Sprogteoriens Grundlæggelse (1943) by F.J. Whitfield).
Hockett, C.F. (1947). "Problems of Morphemic Analysis". Language,
     23: 321-43.
-    (1954). "Two Models of Grammatical Description". Word, 10:
     210-34.
-    (1955). A Manuel of Phonology. Bloomington, Indiana: Indiana
     University Press.
-    (1958). A Course in Modern Linguistics. New York: Macmillan.
-    (1961). "Linguistic Elements and Their Relations". Language,
     37: 29-53.
-    (1968). The State of the Art. The Hague: Mouton.

Householder, F.W. (1965). "On Some Recent Claims in Phonological
     Theory". Journal of Linguistics, 1: 13-34.
   - "Phonological Theory: A Brief Comment". Journal of
     Linguistics, 2: 99-100.
Huddleston, R.D. (1967). "More on the English Comparative".
     Journal of Linguistics, 3: 91-102.
   - (1969). Review of Rosenbaum (1967). Lingua, 23: 241-73.
   - (1970a). "Two Approaches to the Analysis of Tags".
     Journal of Linguistics, 6: 215-22.
   - (1970b). "Some Remarks on Case Grammar", Linguistic Inquiry,
     1: 501-11.
   - (1971). The Sentence in Written English. London: Cambridge
     University Press.
   - (1974). "Further Remarks on the Analysis of Auxiliaries as
     Main Verbs". Foundations of Language, 11: 215-29.
Hudson, R.A. (1972). English Complex Sentences. An Introduction to
     Systemic Grammar. Amsterdam: North-Holland.
Hurford, J.R. (1975). "Global Grammar and Index Grammar". Foundations
     of Language, 13: 585-89.
Hymes, D. (1970). "On Communicative Competence". In Gumperz, J.J.
     and Hymes D. (eds.) (1970) Directions in Sociolinguistics.
     New York: Holt, Rinehart and Winston.
Ikegami, Y. (1967). "Structural Semantics. A Survey and Problems".
     Linguistics, 33: 49-67.
Itkonen, E. (1975). "Concerning the Relationship between Linguistics
     and Logic". Bloomington, Indiana: Indiana University
     Linguistics Club.
Ivić, P. (1965). "Roman Jakobson and the Growth of Phonology".
     Linguistics, 18: 35-78.
Jackendoff, R.S. (1968). "Speculations on Presentences and
     Determiners". Bloomington, Indiana: Indiana University Lin-
     guistics Club.
   - (1969). "An Interpretive Theory of Negation". Foundations of
     Language, 5: 218-41.
   - (1971). "On Some Questionable Arguments about Quantifiers
     and Negation". Language, 47: 282-97.
   - (1972). Semantic Interpretation in Generative Grammar. Cam-
     bridge, Mass.: MIT Press.
   - (1973). "The Base Rules for Prepositional Phrases". In Anderson
     and Kiparsky (1973).
   - (1975a). "Introduction to the $\bar{X}$ Convention". Bloomington,
     Indiana: Indiana University Linguistics Club.
   - (1975b). "On Belief-Contexts". Linguistic Inquiry, 6: 53-93.
   - (1976). "Toward an Explanatory Semantic Representation".
     Linguistic Inquiry, 7: 89-150.
   - and Culicover, W.P. (1971). "A Reconsideration of Dative
     Movement". Foundations of Language, 7: 397-412.
Jacobs, R.A. and Rosenbaum, P.S. (1968). English Transformational
     Grammar. Waltham, Mass.: Ginn.
   - (eds.) (1970). Readings in English Transformational Grammar.
     Waltham, Mass.: Ginn.
Jacobson, S. (1964). Adverbial Positions in English. Stockholm:
     AB Studentbok.
   - (1971). Studies in English Transformational Grammar. Stockholm:
     Almqvist and Wiksell.
Jakobson, R. (1936). "Beitrag zur allgemeinen Kasuslehre".
     Travaux du Cercle Linguistique de Prague, 6: 240-88.
   - Fant, G.M., and Halle, M. (1963). Preliminaries to Speech
     Analysis. Second ed. Cambridge Mass.: MIT Press.

Jacobson, R. and Halle, M. (1956). Fundamentals of Language.
    The Hague: Mouton.
Jespersen, O. (1909-49). A Modern English Grammar on Historical
    Principles. London: Allen and Unwin.
  - (1922). Language, Its Nature, Origin and Development. London:
    Allen and Unwin.
  - (1924). The Philosophy of Grammar. London: Allen and Unwin.
  - (1933). Essentials of English Grammar. London: Allen and Unwin.
Jones, D. (1950). The Phoneme; Its Nature and Use. Cambridge: Heffer.
  - (1964). An Outline of English Phonetics. Ninth ed. Cambridge:
    Heffer.
Joos, M. (ed.) (1957). Readings in Linguistics. Washington, D.C.:
    American Council of Learned Societies. (Republished as
    Readings in Linguistics, I (1966). Chicago: Chicago University
    Press).
Karttunen, L. (1969). "Pronouns and Variables". In Binnick et al.
    (1969).
  - (1973). "Presuppositions of Compound Sentences". Linguistic
    Inquiry, 4: 169-93.
Katz, J.J. (1964a). "Mentalism in Linguistics". Language, 40:
    124-37. Reprinted in Rosenberg and Travis (1971).
  - (1964b). "Semi-sentences". In Fodor and Katz (1964).
  - (1964c). "Analyticity and Contradiction in Natural Language".
    In Fodor and Katz (1964).
  - (1966). The Philosophy of Language. New York: Harper and Row.
  - (1971a). Linguistic Philosophy. London: Allen and Unwin.
  - (1971b). "Generative Semantics is Interpretive Semantics".
    Linguistic Inquiry, 2: 313-331.
  - (1972). Semantic Theory. New York: Harper and Row.
  - (1973a). "On Defining "Presupposition"". Linguistic Inquiry,
    4: 256-60.
  - (1973b). "Compositionality, Idiomaticity, and Lexical Substi-
    tion". In Anderson and Kiparsky (1973).
  - (1973c). "Interpretive Semantics Meets the Zombies".
    Foundations of Language, 9: 549-96.
  - and Fodor, J.A. (1963). "The Structure of a Semantic Theory".
    Language, 39: 170-210. Reprinted in Fodor and Katz (1964).
  - and Langendoen, D.T. (1976). "Pragmatics and Presuppositions".
    Language, 52: 1-17.
  - and Postal, P.M. (1964). An Integrated Theory of Linguistic
    Descriptions. Cambridge, Mass.: MIT Press.
Keenan, E.L. (1971). "Two Kinds of Presupposition in Natural Lan-
    guage". In Fillmore and Langendoen, (1971).
Kiefer, F. (ed.). (1969). Studies in Syntax and Semantics. Dordrecht:
    Reidel.
  - and Ruwet, N. (eds.) (1971). Generative Grammar in Europe.
    Dordrecht: Reidel.
Kimball, J.P. (1970). "'Remind' Remains". Linguistic Inquiry, 1:
    511-23.
  - (1972). "Cyclic and Linear Grammars". In Kimball (1972).
  - (ed.) (1972). Syntax and Semantics, I. New York and London:
    Seminar Press.
King, R.D. (1969). Historical Linguistics and Generative Grammar.
    Englewood Cliffs, N.J: Prentice-Hall.
Kiparsky, P. (1968). "Linguistic Universals and Linguistic Change".
    In Bach and Harms (1968).
  - (1970). "Historical Linguistics". In Lyons (1970b).
  - and Kiparsky, C. (1970). "Fact". In Bierwisch and Heidolph
    (1970).
Klima, E.S. (1964). "Negation in English". In Fodor and Katz (1964).

Kooij, J.G. (1971). Ambiguity in Natural Languages. Amsterdam: North-Holland.

Koutsoudas, A. (1966). Writing Transformational Grammars: An Introduction. New York: McGraw-Hill.

- (1968). "On Wh-words in English". Journal of Linguistics, 4: 267-73.

- (1972). "The Strict Order Fallacy". Language, 48: 88-96

- (1973). "Extrinsic Order and the Complex NP Constraint". Linguistic Inquiry, 4: 69-81.

Kronasser, H. (1952). Handbuch der Semasiologie. Kurze Einführung in die Geschichte, Problematik und Terminologie der Bedeutungslehre. Heidelberg: Carl Winter Universitätsverlag.

Kruisinga, E. (1925). A Handbook of Present-Day English. Fourth ed. Utrecht: Kemink and Zoon.

Kuhn, T. (1962). The Structure of Scientific Revolutions. Chicago: Chicago University Press.

Kuno, S. (1973). "Constraints on Internal Clauses and Sentential Subjects". Linguistic Inquiry, 4: 363-87.

- and Robinson, J.J. (1972). "Multiple Wh Questions". Linguistic Inquiry, 3: 463-89.

Kuroda, S.Y. (1968a). "English Relativization and Certain Related Problems". Language, 44: 244-66. Reprinted in Reibel and Schane (1969).

- (1968b). Review of Fillmore (1965). Language, 44: 374-78.

- (1969). "Remarks on Selectional Restrictions and Presuppositions". In Kiefer (1969).

Lakoff, G. (1966). "Stative Adjectives and Verbs in English". In Mathematical Linguistics and Automatic Translation, Report NSF-17. Cambridge, Mass: The Computation Laboratory of Harvard University.

- (1968a). "Pronouns and Reference". Bloomington, Indiana: Indiana University Linguistics Club.

- (1968b). "Counterparts, or the Problem of Reference in Transformational Grammar". Bloomington, Indiana: Indiana University Linguistics Club.

- (1968c). Deep and Surface Grammar. Bloomington, Indiana: Indiana University Linguistics Club.

- (1970a). Irregularity in Syntax. New York: Holt, Rinehart and Winston.

- (1970b). "Global Rules". Language, 46: 627-39. Reprinted in Seuren (1974b).

- (1970c). "Pronominalization, Negation, and the Analysis of Adverbs". In Jacobs and Rosenbaum (1970).

- (1970d). "Repartee, or a Reply to "Negation, Conjunction, and Quantifiers"". Foundations of Language, 6: 389-422.

- (1970e). "An Example of a Descriptively Inadequate Interpretive Theory". Linguistic Inquiry, 1: 539-42.

- (1971a). "Presupposition and Relative Well-formedness". In Steinberg and Jakobovits (1971).

- (1971b). "On Generative Semantics". In Steinberg and Jakobovits (1971).

- (1971c). "The Role of Deduction in Grammar". In Fillmore and Langendoen (1971).

- (1972a). "Linguistics and Natural Logic". In Davidson and Harman (1972).

- (1972b). "Hedges: A Study in Meaning Criteria and the Logic of Fuzzy Concepts". In Peranteau et al. (1972).

- (1972c). "The Arbitrary Basis of Transformational Grammar". Language, 48: 76-87.

- (1973). "Observations on Transderivational Constraints". In Kachru, B. et al. (eds.) Issues in Linguistics. Urbana: University of Illinois Press.

Lakoff, G. and Peters, S. (1969). "Phrasal Conjunction and Sym-
    metric Predicates". In Reibel and Schane (1969). (First writ-
    ten in 1966).
-   and Ross, J.R. (1967). "Is Deep Structure Necessary?".
    Bloomington, Indiana: Indiana University Linguistics Club
    (1973).
Lakoff, R. (1969a). "A Syntactic Argument for Negative Transporta-
    tion". In Binnick et al. (1969). Reprinted in Seuren (1974b).
-   (1969b). "Some Reasons Why There Can't Be Any Some-Any Rule".
    Language, 45: 608-15.
-   (1971a). "Passive Resistance". In Adams et al. (1971).
-   (1971b). "If's, And's, and But's about Conjunction". In
    Fillmore and Langendoen (1971).
Lancelot, C. and Arnould, A. (1660). Grammaire générale et
    raisonnée. Paris.
Langacker, R.W. (1967). Language and Its Structure. Some Fundamen-
    tal Linguistic Concepts. New York: Harcourt, Brace and World.
-   (1969). "On Pronominalization and the Chain of Command". In
    Reibel and Schane (1969).
-   (1974a). "Movement Rules in Functional Perspective". Language,
    50: 630-64.
-   (1974b). "The Question of Q". Foundations of Language, 11:
    1-37.
Langendoen, D.T. (1966). "The Syntax of the English Expletive "It"".
    In Dinneen, F.P. (ed.) Monograph Series on Languages
    and Linguistics, No. 19. Washington. Georgetown University
    Press.
-   (1969). The Study of Syntax. The Generative-Transformational
    Approach to American English. New York: Holt, Rinehart and
    Winston.
-   (1970a). "The Accessibility of Deep Structures". In Jacobs
    and Rosenbaum (1970).
-   (1970b). Essentials of English Grammar. New York: Holt,
    Rinehart and Winston.
-   and Bever, T.G. (1973). "Can a Not Unhappy Person be Called
    a Not Sad One?". In Anderson and Kiparsky (1973).
-   and Savin, H.B. (1971). "The Projection Problem for Presup-
    positions". In Fillmore and Langendoen (1971).
Laver, J. (1970). "The Production of Speech". In Lyons (1970b).
Lee, D.A. (1971). "Quantifiers and Identity in Relativization".
    Lingua, 27: 1-19.
-   (1973). "Stative and Case Grammar". Foundations of Language,
    10: 545-68.
Leech, G.N. (1969a). Towards a Semantic Description of English.
    London: Longmans.
-   (1969b). A Linguistic Guide to English Poetry. London: Longmans.
-   (1974). Semantics. London: Penguin Books.
Lees, R.B. (1960a). The Grammar of English Nominalizations.
    Bloomington, Indiana: Indiana University Press. The Hague:
    Mouton.
-   (1960b). "A Multiply Ambiguous Adjectival Construction in
    English". Language, 36: 207-21.
-   (1961). "Grammatical Analysis of the English Comparative Con-
    struction". Word, 17: 171-85. Reprinted in Reibel and Schane
    (1969).
-   (1962). "Transformation Grammars and the Fries Framework".
    In Allen (1964).
-   (1963). "Analysis of the "Cleft Sentence" in English".
    Zeitschrift für Phonetik, 16: 371-88.

Lees, R.B. (1970a). "Problems in the Grammatical Analysis of
    English Nominal Compounds". In Bierwisch and Heidolph (1970).
  - (1970b). "On Very Deep Grammatical Structure". In Jacobs and
    Rosenbaum (1970).
  - and Klima, E.S. (1963). "Rules for English Pronominalization".
    Language, 39: 17-28. Reprinted in Reibel and Schane (1969).
Legum, S.E. (1968). "The Verb-Particle Construction in English,
    Basic or Derived?". In Darden et al. (1968).
Lehmann, T. (1972). "Some Arguments against Ordered Rules". Lan-
    guage, 48: 541-50.
Lehmann, W.P. (1962). Historical Linguistics. An Introduction.
    New York: Holt, Rinehart and Winston.
Lehrer, A. (1970). "Verbs and Deletable Objects". Lingua, 25:
    227-53.
Lenneberg, E.H. (1967). Biological Foundations of Language. New
    York: Wiley.
Leonard, S.A. (1962). The Doctrine of Correctness in English Usage
    1700-1800. New York: Russell and Russell. (First published
    1929).
Lester, M. (1971). Introductory Transformational Grammar of English.
    New York: Holt, Rinehart and Winston.
Levin, S.R. (1960). "Comparing Traditional and Structural Grammar".
    College English, 21: 260-65. Reprinted in Allen (1964).
Liles, B.L. (1971). An Introductory Transformational Grammar.
    Englewood Cliffs, N.J.: Prentice-Hall.
Lindholm, J.M. (1969). "Negative Raising and Sentence Pronominaliza-
    tion". In Binnick et al. (1969).
Long, R.B. (1961). The Sentence and Its Parts. A Grammar of Con-
    temporary English. Chicago: Chicago University Press.
  - (1968). "Expletive There and the There Transformation".
    Journal of English Linguistics, 2: 12-22.
Lounsbury, F.G. (1964). "The Structural Analysis of Kinship Se-
    mantics". In Lunt, H.G. (ed.) Proceedings of the Ninth
    International Congress of Linguistics. The Hague: Mouton.
Lowth, R. (1762). A Short Introduction to English Grammar. London.
    (Reference to the 1775-edition).
Lyons, J. (1963). Structural Semantics. An Analysis of Part of the
    Vocabulary of Plato. Publications of the Philological Society,
    XX. Oxford: Blackwell.
  - (1966a). "Towards a "Notional" Theory of the "Parts of Speech"".
    Journal of Linguistics, 2: 119-26.
  - (1966b). Review of Chomsky (1965). Philosophical Quarterly,
    16: 393-95.
  - (1966c). Review of Katz and Postal (1964). Journal of Lin-
    guistics, 2: 119-26.
  - (1968). Introduction to Theoretical Linguistics. London:
    Cambridge University Press.
  - (1970a). Chomsky. London: Fontana/Collins.
  - (ed.) (1970b). New Horizons in Linguistics. London: Penguin
    Books.
  - (1970c). "Generative Syntax". In Lyons (1970b).
Maclay, H. (1971). "Overview". In Steinberg and Jakobovits (1971).
Macnamara, J. (1972). "Parsimony and the Lexicon". Language, 47:
    359-74.
Maling, J.M. (1972). "On 'Gapping and the Order of Constituents'".
    Linguistic Inquiry, 3: 101-108.
Marchand, H. (1969). The Categories and Types of Present-Day
    English Word-Formation. Second ed. Munich: C.H. Beck.
    (First published 1960).

Martinet, A. (1960). Éléments de Linguistique Générale. Paris:
    Armand Colin. (English translation by E. Palmer. London:
    Faber and Faber).
Matthews, P.H. (1961). "Transformational Grammar". Archivum
    Linguisticum, 13: 196-209.
    - (1965). "Problems of Selection in Transformational Grammar".
    Journal of Linguistics, 1: 35-47.
    - (1967). Review of Chomsky (1965). Journal of Linguistics, 3:
    119-52.
    - (1968). "Some Remarks on the Householder-Halle Controversy".
    Journal of Linguistics, 4: 275-83.
    - (1970). "Recent Developments in Morphology". In Lyons (1970b).
Matthews, R.I. (1971). "Concerning a "Linguistic Theory" of
    Metaphor". Foundations of Language, 7: 413-25.
McCawley, J.D. (1967). "Meaning and the Description of Language".
    Kotoba no uchū, 9: 10-18, 10: 38-48, 11: 51-57. Reprinted
    in Rosenberg and Travis (1971).
    - (1968a). "The Role of Semantics in a Grammar". In Bach and
    Harms (1968).
    - (1968b). "How to Find Semantic Universals in the Event There
    Are Any". Linguistic Institute Packet of Papers. University
    of Illinois.
    - (1968c). "Concerning the Base Component in a Transformational
    Grammar". Foundations of Language, 4: 243-69.
    - (1968d). "Lexical Insertion in a Transformational Grammar
    without Deep Structure". In Darden et al. (1968).
    - (1970a). "Where Do Noun Phrases Come From?". In Jacobs and
    Rosenbaum (1970). Reprinted in a revised edition in Steinberg
    and Jakobovits (1971).
    - (1970b). "English as a VSO Language". Language, 46: 286-99.
    Reprinted in Seuren (1974b).
    - (1971a). "Tense and Time Reference in English". In Fillmore
    and Langendoen (1971).
    - (1971b). "Interpretive Semantics Meets Frankenstein". Founda-
    tions of Language, 7: 285-95.
    - (1971c). "Prelexical Syntax". In O'Brien, R.J. (ed.) Mono-
    graph Series on Languages and Linguistics No. 24. Washington:
    Georgetown University Press. Reprinted in Seuren (1974b).
    - (1972). "A Program for Logic". In Davidson and Harman (1972).
    - (1973). "External NPs Versus Annotated Deep Structures".
    Linguistic Inquiry, 4: 221-38.
McLaughlin, J.C. (1969). Aspects of the History of English.
    New York: Holt, Rinehart and Winston.
McNeill, D. (1970). The Acquisition of Language. New York: Harper
    and Row.
Mellema, P. (1974). "A Brief against Case Grammar". Foundations of
    Language, 11: 39-76.
Morgan, J.L. (1968). "Some Strange Aspects of It". In Darden et al.
    (1968).
Newmeyer, F.J. (1970). "The Derivation of the English Action
    Nominalization". In Campbell et al. (1970).
    - (1971). "The Source of Derived Nominals in English". Lan-
    guage, 47: 786-96.
Nickel, G. (1968). "Complex Verbal Structures in English". Inter-
    national Review of Applied Linguistics, 6: 2-21.
Nida, E.A. (1949). Morphology: A Descriptive Analysis of Words.
    Second ed. Ann Arbor, Mich.: University of Michigan Press.
    - (1966). A Synopsis of English Syntax. The Hague: Mouton.
    (First published 1960).

Nilsen, D.L.F. (1972). Toward a Semantic Specification of Deep
    Case. The Hague: Mouton.
Noll, C.A. (1975). Review of Fowler (1971). Lingua, 34: 343-64.
Ogden, C.K. (1932). Opposition. London: Kegan Paul.
Palmer, F.R. (1964). "Grammatical Categories and Their Phonetic
    Exponents". In Lunt, H.G. (ed.) Proceedings of the Ninth
    International Congress of Linguistics. The Hague: Mouton.
  - (ed.) (1970). Prosodic Analysis. Oxford University Press.
Partee, B.H. (1970). "Negation, Conjunction, and Quantifiers:
    Syntax versus Semantics". Foundations of Language, 6:
    153-65.
  - (1971). "On the Requirement that Transformations Preserve
    Meaning". In Fillmore and Langendoen (1971).
  - (1972). "Opacity, Coreference, and Pronouns". In Davidson
    and Harman (1972).
Pedersen, H. (1931). Linguistic Science in the Nineteenth Century.
    (Translated by J.W. Spargo). Cambridge, Mass: Harvard Uni-
    versity Press. (Republished in 1959 as The Discovery of
    Language. Bloomington, Indiana: Indiana University Press).
Peranteau, P.M., Levi, J.N., and Phares, G.C. (eds.) (1972).
    Papers from the Eighth Regional Meeting of the Chicago Lin-
    guistic Society. Chicago: Department of Linguistics, Chicago
    University Press.
Perlmutter, D.M. (1970a). "On the Article in English". In Bierwisch
    and Heidolph (1970).
  - (1970b). "The Two Verbs Begin". In Jacobs and Rosenbaum (1970).
  - (1971). Deep and Surface Structure Constraints. New York:
    Holt, Rinehart and Winston.
Peters, S. and Ritchie, R.W. (1969). "A Note on the Universal
    Base Hypothesis". Journal of Linguistics, 5: 150-52.
Pike, K.L. (1947). Phonemics. Ann Arbor, Mich.: University of
    Michigan Press.
Pilch, H. (1965). "Comparative Constructions in English". Language,
    41: 37-58.
Postal, P.M. (1964a). Constituent Structure. A Study of Contemporary
    Models of Syntactic Description. Bloomington - The Hague:
    Mouton.
  - (1964b). "The Limitations of Phrase Structure Grammars".
    In Fodor and Katz (1964).
  - (1964c). "Underlying and Superficial Linguistic Structure".
    Harvard Educational Review, 34: 246-66.
  - (1968). Aspects of Phonological Theory. New York: Harper and
    Row.
  - (1970a). "On so-called Pronouns in English". In Jacobs and
    Rosenbaum (1970). Also in Reibel and Schane (1969).
  - (1970b). "On Coreferential Complement Subject Deletion".
    Linguistic Inquiry, 1: 439-500.
  - (1970c). "On the Surface Verb 'Remind'". Linguistic Inquiry, 1:
    37-120. Reprinted in Fillmore and Langendoen (1971).
  - (1971). Cross-over Phenomena. New York: Holt, Rinehart and
    Winston.
  - (1972a). "A Global Constraint on Pronominalization". Lin-
    guistic Inquiry, 3: 35-59.
  - (1972b). "On Some Rules That Are Not Successive Cyclic".
    Linguistic Inquiry, 3: 211-22.
  - (1974). On Raising. One Rule of English Grammar and Its
    Theoretical Implications. Cambridge, Mass.: MIT Press.
  - and Ross, J.R. (1971). "Tough Movement Si, Tough Deletion
    No". Linguistic Inquiry, 2: 544-46.

Poutsma, H. (1914-29). A Grammar of Late Modern English. Second
    ed. Groningen: P. Noordhoff.
Price, J.T. (1974). "Linguistic Competence and Metaphorical Use".
    Foundations of Language, 11: 253-56.
Pride, J.B. (1970). "Sociolinguistics". In Lyons (1970b).
Quirk, R. (1955). "Colloquial English and Communication". In
    Studies in Communication, Communications Research Centre,
    University College, London: 169-182. London: Secker and
    Warburg.
  - Greenbaum, S., Leech, G.N., and Svartvik, J. (1972). A Gram-
    mar of Contemporary English. London: Longmans.
Reibel, D.A. and Schane, S.A. (eds.) (1969). Modern Studies in
    English. Readings in Transformational Grammar. Englewood
    Cliffs. N.J.: Prentice-Hall.
Reichenbach. H. (1947). Elements of Symbolic Logic. New York:
    The Free Press.
Rijk de, R.P.G. (1974). "A Note on Prelexical Predicate Raising".
    In Seuren (1974b).
Ringen, C. (1972). "On Arguments for Rule Ordering". Foundations
    of Language, 8: 266-73.
Robbin, J.W. (1969). Mathematical Logic. A First Course. New York:
    W.A. Benjamin.
Roberts, P. (1962). English Sentences. New York: Harcourt, Brace
    and World.
Robins, R.H. (1951). Ancient and Medieval Grammatical Theory in
    Europe. London: Bell.
  - (1957). "Aspects of Prosodic Analysis". Proceedings of the
    University of Durham Philosophical Society, Vol. I, series
    B, 1: 1-12. Reprinted in Palmer (1970).
  - (1964). General Linguistics. An Introductory Survey. London:
    Longmans.
  - (1966). "The Development of the Word Class System of the
    European Grammatical Tradition". Foundations of Language, 2:
    3-19.
  - (1967). A Short History of Linguistics. London: Longmans.
Robinson, J.J. (1969). "Case, Category, and Configuration".
    Journal of Linguistics, 6: 57-80.
  - (1970). "Dependency Structures and Transformational Rules".
    Language, 46: 25-85.
Rosenbaum, P.S. (1967). The Grammar of English Predicate Complement
    Constructions. Cambridge, Mass.: MIT Press.
Rosenberg, J.F. and Travis, C. (eds.) (1971). Readings in the
    Philosophy of Language. Englewood Cliffs, N.J.: Prentice-
    Hall.
Ross, J.R. (1967). Constraints on Variables in Syntax. Bloomington,
    Indiana: Indiana University Linguistics Club.
  - (1969a). "Auxiliaries as Main Verbs". In Todd, W. (ed.)
    (1969) Studies in Philosophical Linguistics, Series One.
    Evanston, Ill.: Great Expectations.
  - (1969b). "Adjectives as Noun Phrases". In Reibel and Schane
    (1969).
  - (1969c). "Guess Who?" In Binnick et al. (1969).
  - (1969d). "A Proposed Rule of Tree-pruning". In Reibel and
    Schane (1969).
  - (1969e). "On the Cyclic Nature of English Pronominalization".
    In Reibel and Schane (1969).
  - (1970a). "On Declarative Sentences". In Jacobs and Rosenbaum
    (1970).
  - (1970b). "Gapping and the Order of Constituents". In Bierwisch
    and Heidolph (1970).

Ross, J.R. (1972). "Act". In Davidson and Harman (1972).
 - (1973). "The Penthouse Principle and the Order of Constitu-
    ents". In Corum, C., Smith-Stark, T. and Weiser, A. (eds.)
    You Take the High Node and I'll Take the Low Node, Papers
    from the Comparative Syntax Festival. Chicago: Department
    of Linguistics, Chicago University Press.
Ruwet, N. (1973). An Introduction to Generative Grammar. Amsterdam:
    North-Holland.
Sadock, J.M. (1970). "Whimperatives". In Sadock, J.M. and Vanek, A.
    (eds.) Studies Presented to Robert B. Lees by his Students.
    Edmonton, Ill.: Linguistic Research Inc.
 - (1975). Toward a Linguistic Theory of Speech Acts. New York:
    Academic Press.
Sampson, G. (1969). Noun-phrase Indexing, Pronouns and the 'Definite
    Article'. New Haven, Conn.: Yale University Linguistic
    Automation Project.
Sandmann, G. (1954). Subject and Predicate. Edinburgh: Edinburgh
    University Publications, Language and Literature, 5.
Sapir, E. (1949). Selected Writings (ed. Mandelbaum, D.G.).
    Berkeley, Calif.: University of California Press.
Saussure, F. de (1955). Cours de Linguistique Générale. Fifth ed.
    Paris: Payot. (First published posthumously 1916). English
    translation by W. Baskin: Course in General Linguistics
    (1959). New York: Philosophical Library.
Schachter, P. (1973a). "On Syntactic Categories". Bloomington,
    Indiana: Indiana University Linguistics Club.
 - (1973b). "Focus and Relativization". Language, 49: 19-46.
Schane, S.A. (1966). "A Schema for Sentence Coordination".
    Information System Language Studies 10, MTP-10. The MITRE
    Corporation, Bedford.
 - (1973). Generative Phonology. Englewood Cliffs, N.J.:
    Prentice-Hall.
Schibsbye, K, (1965). A Modern English Grammar. London: Oxford
    University Press.
Searle, J.R. (1969). Speech Acts. An Essay in the Philosophy of
    Language. London: Cambridge University Press.
Seuren, P.A.M. (1969). Operators and Nucleus. London: Cambridge
    University Press.
 - (1972). "Autonomous versus Semantic Syntax". Foundations of
    Language, 8: 237-65. Reprinted in Seuren (1974b).
 - (1974a). "Negative's Travels". In Seuren (1974b).
 - (ed.) (1974b). Semantic Syntax. London: Oxford University
    Press.
Skinner, B.F. (1957). Verbal Behavior. New York: Appleton-
    Century-Crofts.
Smith, C.S. (1961). "A Class of Complex Modifiers in English".
    Language, 37: 247-63.
 - (1964). "Determiners and Relative Clauses in Generative Gram-
    mar". Language, 40: 37-52. Reprinted in Reibel and Schane
    (1969).
 - (1969). "Ambiguous Sentences with and". In Reibel and Schane
    (1969).
Sommerstein, A. (1972). "On the So-called Definite Article in
    English". Linguistic Inquiry, 3: 197-209.
Stalnaker, R.C. (1970). "Pragmatics". Synthese, 22: 272-89.
Stanley, R. (1967). "Redundancy Rules in Phonology". Language,
    43: 393-436.
 - (1969). "The English Comparative Adjective Construction".
    In Binnick et al. (1969).

Starosta, S. (1973). "The Faces of Case". In Language Sciences, 25: 1-14. Indiana University.
Steinberg, D.D. and Jakobovits, L.A. (eds.) (1971). Semantics. An Interdisciplinary Reader in Philosophy, Linguistics and Psychology. London: Cambridge University Press.
Stockwell, R.P., Schachter, P., and Partee, B.H. (1968). Integration of Transformational Theories on English Syntax. Government Document ESD-TR-68-419, Los Angeles (UESP 1968).
Strang, B.M.H. (1962). Modern English Structure. London: Edward Arnold.
 - (1964). "Theory and Practice in Morpheme Identification". In Lunt, H.G. (ed.) Proceedings of the Ninth International Congress of Linguistics. The Hague: Mouton.
Svartvik, J. (1966). On Voice in the English Verb. The Hague: Mouton.
Sweet, H. (1891). A New English Grammar. Oxford.
Swadesh, M. and Voegelin, C.F. (1939). "A Problem in Phonological Alternation". Language, 15: 1-10.
Thomas, O. (1965). Transformational Grammar and the Teacher of English. New York: Holt, Rinehart and Winston.
Thompson, S.A. (1968). "Relative Clauses and Conjunctions". Working Papers in Linguistics, 1: 80-99. Ohio State University.
 - (1971). "The Deep Structure of Relative Clauses". In Fillmore and Langendoen (1971).
Thorne, J.P. (1966). "English Imperative Sentences". Journal of Linguistics, 2: 69-78.
Trager G.L. and Smith, H.L. (1951). An Outline of English Structure. Studies in Linguistics. Occasional Paper 3.
Trubetzkoy, N.S. (1939). Grundzüge der Phonologie. Prague: Cercle linguistique de Prague.
Ullmann, S. (1957). The Principles of Semantics. Second ed. Glasgow: Jackson. Oxford: Blackwell.
 - (1962). Semantics. An Introduction to the Science of Meaning. Oxford: Blackwell.
 - (1963). "Semantic Universals". In Greenberg (1963).
 - (1972). "Semantics". In Sebeok, T.A. (ed.) Current Trends in Linguistics, Vol. 9. The Hague: Mouton.
Vachek, J. (1966). The Linguistic School of Prague. Bloomington, Indiana: Indiana University Press.
Van Fraassen, B.C. (1968). "Presupposition, Implication, and Self-reference". Journal of Philosophy, 65: 132-52.
Vestergaard, T. (1973). "A Note on Objective, Instrumental, and Affected in English". Studia Linguistica, 27: 85-89.
Wachowicz , K.A. (1974). "Against the Universality of a Single Wh-question Movement". Foundations of Language, 11: 155-66.
Wall, R. (1972). Introduction to Mathematical Linguistics. Englewood Cliffs, N.J.: Prentice-Hall
Weinreich, U. (1972). Explorations in Semantic Theory. The Hague: Mouton. First published 1966 in Sebeok, T.A. (ed.) Current Trends in Linguistics, Vol. 3. The Hague: Mouton.
Wells, R.S. (1947). "Immediate Constituents". Language, 21: 27-39.
Wierzbicka, A. (1972). Semantic Primitives. New York: Athenaeum.
 - (1975). "Why "Kill" Does Not Mean "Cause to Die": The Semantics of Action Sentences". Foundations of Language, 13: 491-528.
Wilson, D. (1975). "Presupposition, Assertion, and Lexical Items". Linguistic Inquiry, 6: 95-114.

Zandvoort, R.W. (1957). A Handbook of English Grammar. London:
    Longmans.
Ziff, P. (1974). "The Number of English Sentences". Foundations
    of Language, 11: 519-32.
Öhman, S. (1953). "Theories of the "Linguistic Field"". Word, 9:
    123-34.

ADDITIONAL BIBLIOGRAPHICAL NOTES

P. 80. The statement made here stands in need of qualification.
Currently, an alternative approach to grammatical functions - so-
called relational grammar - is being developed. In this, grammatical
relations are hierarchically organized theoretical primitives. Syntactic rules have access to these relations and can change them in
specific ways. On relational grammar, see the papers in Peter Cole
and Jerrold M. Sadock (eds.), Grammatical Relations. Syntax and
Semantics, Vol. 8, New York etc., 1977.

P. 126. For an attempt to extend the generative approach to problems of text grammar, see Teun A. van Dijk, Some Aspects of Text
Grammars, The Hague, 1972.

P. 411. A recent study of the $\overline{X}$ convention and its implications for
phrase structure is Ray Jackendoff, $\overline{X}$ Syntax. A Study of Phrase
Structure, Cambridge, Mass. and London, 1977.

Section V.B. Torben Vestergaard, Prepositional Phrases and Prepositional Verbs, The Hague, 1977 is a contribution to the study of
the grammatical function of prepositional phrases in terms of case
grammar.

General. The reader's attention should be drawn to Rodney Huddleston,
An Introduction to English Transformational Syntax, London, 1976.
Unfortunately, this excellent study was published too late for me
to be able to incorporate specific references to it. Reference
must also be made to John Lyons' recently published monumental
work Semantics I-II, Cambridge etc. 1977. Peter W. Culicover,
Thomas Wasow and Adrian Akmajian (eds.), Formal Syntax, New York
etc., 1977 is a collection of papers illustrative of the present
state of autonomous syntax. In the Preface there is an interesting
discussion of the schism between autonomous syntax and generative
semantics. The latter is moving more and more towards a pragmatically oriented theory of language. For a tabulation of the main differences between the 'formal' and 'functional' paradigms of linguistic science, see Simon C. Dik, Functional Grammar, Amsterdam,
1978.

SUBJECT INDEX

A